Churchill/Ford/Walker's

Sales Force Management

McGraw-Hill/Irwin Series in Marketing

Churchill/Ford/Walker's

Sales Force Management

Ninth Edition

Mark W. Johnston
*Crummer Graduate School
of Business
Rollins College*

Greg W. Marshall
*Crummer Graduate School
of Business
Rollins College*

Boston   Burr Ridge, IL   Dubuque, IA   New York   San Francisco   St. Louis
Bangkok   Bogotá   Caracas   Kuala Lumpur   Lisbon   London   Madrid   Mexico City
Milan   Montreal   New Delhi   Santiago   Seoul   Singapore   Sydney   Taipei   Toronto

McGraw-Hill
Irwin

CHURCHILL/FORD/WALKER'S SALES FORCE MANAGEMENT
Published by McGraw-Hill/Irwin, a business unit of The McGraw-Hill Companies, Inc., 1221 Avenue of the
Americas, New York, NY, 10020. Copyright © 2009, 2006, 2003, 2000, 1997, 1993, 1990, 1985, 1981 by The
McGraw-Hill Companies, Inc. All rights reserved. No part of this publication may be reproduced or distributed
in any form or by any means, or stored in a database or retrieval system, without the prior written consent of
The McGraw-Hill Companies, Inc., including, but not limited to, in any network or other electronic storage or
transmission, or broadcast for distance learning.

Some ancillaries, including electronic and print components, may not be available to customers outside the
United States.

This book is printed on acid-free paper.

1 2 3 4 5 6 7 8 9 0 WCK/WCK 0 9 8

ISBN 978-0-07-352987-5
MHID 0-07-352987-7

Publisher: *Paul Ducham*
Sponsoring editor: *Dana L. Woo*
Editorial assistant: *Devon Raemisch*
Associate marketing manager: *Dean Karampelas*
Project manager: *Kathryn D. Mikulic*
Lead production supervisor: *Michael R. McCormick*
Design coordinator: *Joanne Mennemeier*
Senior photo research coordinator: *Jeremy Cheshareck*
Media project manager: *Srikanth Potluri, Hurix Systems Pvt. Ltd.*
Cover design: *JoAnne Schopler*
Typeface: *10/12 Times New Roman*
Compositor: *Laserwords Private Limited*
Printer: *Quebecor World Versailles Inc.*

*To order copies or request permission to reproduce Ivey materials, contact Ivey Publishing, Ivey Management
Services, c/o Richard Ivey School of Business, The University of Western Ontario, London, Ontario, Canada,
N6A 3K7; phone (519) 661-3208, fax (519) 661-3882, e-mail cases@ivey.uwo.ca. One time permission to
reproduce granted by Ivey Management Services on November 1, 2007.*

Library of Congress Cataloging-in-Publication Data

Johnston, Mark W.
    Churchill/Ford/Walker's sales force management / Mark W. Johnston,
Greg W. Marshall.—9th ed.
        p. cm.—(McGraw-Hill/Irwin series in marketing)
    Includes index.
    ISBN-13: 978-0-07-352987-5 (alk. paper)
    ISBN-10: 0-07-352987-7 (alk. paper)
    1. Sales management. I. Marshall, Greg W. II. Title.
HF5438.4.C48 2009
658.8'1—dc22
                                                        2008002851

To Susan and Grace

—Mark

To Patti and Justin

—Greg

About the Authors

Mark W. Johnston, Ph.D.

Mark W. Johnston is the Alan and Sandra Gerry Professor of Marketing and Ethics at the Roy E. Crummer Graduate School of Business, Rollins College in Winter Park, Florida. He earned his Ph.D. in marketing in 1986 from Texas A&M University. Prior to receiving his doctorate, he worked in industry as a sales and marketing representative for a leading distributor of photographic equipment. His research has resulted in published articles in a number of professional journals such as *Journal of Marketing Research, Journal of Applied Psychology, Journal of Personal Selling & Sales Management,* and many others.

Mark has been retained as a consultant for firms in the personal health care, chemical, transportation, service, and telecommunications industries. He has consulted on a wide range of issues involving strategic sales force structure, sales force performance, sales force technology implementation, market analysis, sales training, and international market decisions. Finally, Mark has conducted a number of seminars around the world on a variety of topics, including motivation, managing turnover in the organization, sales training issues, ethical issues in marketing, and improving overall sales performance.

Greg W. Marshall, Ph.D.

Greg W. Marshall is the Charles Harwood Professor of Marketing and Strategy in the Crummer Graduate School of Business at Rollins College, Winter Park, Florida. He earned his Ph.D. in marketing from Oklahoma State University. Greg's industry experience includes 13 years in selling and sales management, product management, and retailing with companies such as Warner Lambert, Mennen, and Target Stores. When he left Warner Lambert in 1986 to enter academe, he was the manager of the top-performing sales district in the United States. In addition, he has served as a consultant and trainer for a variety of organizations in both the private and public sectors, primarily in the areas of marketing planning, strategy development, and service quality.

Greg is an active researcher in sales management, having published more than 40 refereed articles in a variety of marketing journals, and he serves on the editorial review board of the *Journal of the Academy of Marketing Science, Journal of Business Research, and Industrial Marketing Management.* He is editor of the *Journal of Marketing Theory and Practice* and is past editor of the *Journal of Personal Selling & Sales Management*

Greg is on the board of directors of the Direct Selling Education Foundation, is past president of the Academic Division of the American Marketing Association, and is a fellow and past president of the Society for Marketing Advances.

In addition to working together on Churchill/Ford/Walker's *Sales Force Management,* Mark and Greg are the co-authors of two other McGraw-Hill/Irwin titles: *Relationship Selling,* 2e and *Marketing Management* (forthcoming).

Preface

INTRODUCTION

This ninth edition carries on the tradition from previous editions, incorporating the latest research and management practices into an easy-to-read yet comprehensive learning tool. You will notice many changes, particularly in the amount and format of application-oriented, student-focused learning exercises. This edition integrates new, innovative learning tools and the latest in sales management theory and practice. At the same time, we have taken great care to preserve the excellent framework and principles from editions one through seven. In short, we have taken the best from earlier editions and added relevant, real-world student learning tools and up-to-date sales management theory and practice to create this ninth edition of *Sales Force Management.*

Still without peer, *Sales Force Management* remains the definitive text in the field. Building on the tradition of excellence established by Gil Churchill, Neil Ford, and Orv Walker, in this ninth edition Mark Johnston and Greg Marshall again team up to maintain the quality and integrity of earlier editions while breaking new ground.

WHY WRITE THIS BOOK?

For most of the twentieth century, the practice of sales management was an unfortunate combination of tradition, folklore, personal experiences, and intuition. Sales managers had very little in the way of research or management theory to help better understand the motives and behaviors of their own salespeople. As a result, there was practically no support for the sales manager in the field.

Fortunately, during the 1970s sales academicians and researchers began to conduct empirical studies and develop theoretical models to explain salesperson behavior and motivation. Sales managers found the information invaluable and added their own insights, further refining and enhancing the sales management knowledge base. Today, sales research appears in all the leading marketing journals, and one journal is singularly dedicated to the field of sales management (*Journal of Personal Selling & Sales Management*).

It is not surprising that, as changes were occurring in sales management, the rest of the organization also was experiencing significant transformation. Concepts like strategic alliances, customer relationship management, and value creation brought revolution to every part of the organization, including the sales force. Today, salespeople are expected to have new skills, more information, and instant answers. This makes managing the sales force an even more formidable challenge. Old ways will no longer work—sales force management is undergoing change at an increasing rate, and success in the future will be defined, in part, by how well sales managers learn to manage in this new world.

From the beginning, *Sales Force Management* filled the need for a single, detailed summary of sales management theory, analysis of sales force research, and review of its implications for the organization. Other books provide a cursory appraisal of relevant research or fail to keep pace with current knowledge and trends. Our primary goal in the ninth edition is the same as it was in the first: offer students a thorough, up-to-date, and integrated overview of accumulated theory and research relevant to sales management.

In writing such a book, however, we know that simply presenting a summary of theories and research would be incredibly dull (we were students, too) and, even worse, provide little real insight for students interested in learning how a sales manager can *apply* this information in the real world. Put simply, our second goal is to highlight how real managers apply these theories and principles in their own organizations. By identifying recent practices, applications, and the use of state-of-the-art technology, we combine real-world sales management *best practices* with cutting-edge theory and empirical research—all in a single source.

STRUCTURE OF THE BOOK

Over the book's history, a framework has been developed that portrays sales managers' activities as three interrelated, sequential processes, each of which influences the various determinants of salesperson performance. The ninth edition continues to use this time-tested and insightful structure.

1. *Formulation* **of a sales program.**   This process involves organizing and planning the company's overall personal selling efforts and ensuring that the selling initiative is integrated with the other elements of the firm's marketing strategy.

2. *Implementation* **of the sales program.**   This involves selecting appropriate sales personnel, providing effective training and development, as well as compensation.

3. *Evaluation and control* **of the sales program.**   This involves employing proper metrics to monitor and evaluate sales force performance so adjustments can be made to either the sales program or its implementation as needed.

Chapter 1 introduces the subject of sales management with an overview of the field, including key aspects of the external and internal environment of selling. The remainder of the book is divided into three sections corresponding to the three processes described above.

- **Part One: Formulation of a Sales Program (Chapters 2 through 5)**   This section examines the process of buying and selling, including a strong emphasis on selling as a career and the role of organizational buyers; linkages of sales management to business- and marketing-level strategies; organizing for success in sales management; and the strategic role of information in forecasting, setting quotas, designing sales territories, and conducting sales analysis. A continuing feature of this edition is emphasis on customer relationship management (CRM) and its link to sales management.

- **Part Two: Implementation of the Sales Program (Chapters 6 through 11)**   This section provides an overview of the determinants of sales performance with the special focus on a salesperson's role perceptions and motivation. It then proceeds to examine decisions involving the recruitment and selection of sales personnel, sales training, and the design of compensation and incentive programs.

- **Part Three: Evaluation and Control of the Sales Program (Chapters 12 and 13)**   This section discusses techniques for monitoring and controlling sales force behavior and performance. It examines various approaches for conducting behavioral and other performance analyses.

THE APPROACH OF THE BOOK

Sales Force Management is designed for use in a course on sales management at either the undergraduate or graduate level. It also complements a variety of teaching approaches. Instructors who focus primarily on either a lecture/discussion format or case format will find plenty of material for any teaching calendar in the chapters, enhanced by the end-of-chapter Breakout Questions and discussion-centered Leadership Challenges. For those adopting a more case-oriented approach, we have included a number of new and updated cases in both a long and short format. These cases may be found at the end of each chapter as well as the end of the three major parts of the book. These end-of-part cases emphasize issues discussed within the chapters that comprise that part. And, for the first time, a sales management role play is provided for each chapter.

FEATURES OF THE NINTH EDITION

We subscribe to the old adage, "if it isn't broke, don't fix it." The philosophy in creating the ninth edition was to begin by updating and enhancing the best parts of *Sales Force Management.* As a result, those who have used previous editions will be comfortable with the eighth edition. However, there are a number of significant changes—most notably in the structure, format and number of cases, the addition of Role Plays, and the coverage of new concepts, ideas, and practices. Feature boxes in the chapters, as well as company examples, have been aggressively updated.

Our first task was to review the literature (both the business press and academic journals) for new ideas, concepts, and practices. From this, a thorough revision of each chapter was undertaken, incorporating new material and updating examples. Discussions in some chapters were expanded to reflect new areas of emphasis in the field. In every case, our goal is to provide a readable, comprehensive discussion.

A signature feature in earlier editions was the cases that allowed students to apply what they were learning. Our goal in this edition is to maintain this important and valuable learning methodology while updating the format, structure, and length of the cases. Feedback from colleagues as well as our own analysis suggested that in addition to the long cases at the end of each section, shorter cases in each chapter allow for greater, more focused classroom discussion as well as the opportunity for individual assignments, offering great value-added learning for students. The ninth edition features a sales management minicase written especially for each chapter.

Strategic Partnership with HR Chally Group—New

HR Chally Group joins the ninth edition of *Sales Force Management* as a strategic partner. Based in Dayton, Ohio, HR Chally is a leading global consultancy focused on enterprise-wide talent management. Their work forms the basis for a completely new set of chapter openers in this new edition of *Sales Force Management*. Students and their instructors will enjoy and appreciate reading how the Chally findings are applied to real-world topics facing sales managers today. No other sales management textbook offers this feature of combining cutting-edge research with sales management practice.

Learning Objectives—Updated

Each chapter has succinct learning objectives based on chapter material. Using active language to emphasize the expected student learning outcomes, these objectives enable professors to guide discussions and develop tests so that students get the most out of the book.

Key Terms—Updated

The key terms have been moved to the end of each chapter and updated to reflect changes to the material. They are highlighted in bold within the body of the chapter to help students focus on key ideas and concepts. Professors find these terms can create the basis for assessing students' understanding of the chapter.

Feature Boxes: Innovation, Technology, and Leadership—New and Updated

These three themes drive much of sales management theory and practice today and form the basis for the feature boxes throughout the ninth edition. Many boxes have been revised and new ones have been added to highlight the latest trends in sales management. As with the opening vignettes, the feature boxes are designed to illustrate material presented in the chapters in an applied context. Professors will benefit from incorporating these features into class discussion and exercises, and students will find it easier to apply the concepts they are learning in the chapter.

Breakout Questions—New and Updated

Timely discussion questions, called Breakout Questions, can be found at the end of each chapter. These make for great discussion starters as well good review questions for exams.

Leadership Challenge—Updated

Leadership is an essential characteristic of successful sales managers. While we include it as a feature box in the text, our goal is to engage the student more directly in learning and applying leadership issues. As a result (and not found in any other sales management text), a unique set of short end-of-chapter leadership cases will test the student's ability to make leadership decisions. Short and focused on issues from that chapter, the Leadership Challenges ask students to assess a real situation from a manager's perspective, make decisions, and often develop an implementation strategy.

Role Plays—Updated

Both in the field and classroom, it is widely accepted that role-playing is a valuable tool for helping salespeople and students apply what they are learning. For the ninth edition we have updated the complete set of Role Plays, one for each chapter. Each Role Play enables students to work together to employ important sales management concepts they have learned in that particular chapter.

Minicases—Updated

Each chapter contains a Minicase enabling students to apply directly what they are learning in the chapter. These Minicases, written specifically for *Sales Force Management,* are short and designed to be used in a variety of ways. For example, they are great for discussion starters in class or as individual assignments. Additionally, student teams can be assigned to analyze the case and make a presentation to the class. Feedback from colleagues was a key driver in creating these shorter, more focused cases that will certainly enhance student learning. Key issues from the chapter will be brought out for the students as they analyze the case. Each minicase ends with a set of directed, action-oriented questions that force the student to integrate the chapter material.

Cases—New and Updated

A major revision of the end-of-part cases took place in preparing the ninth edition. Three new sales management cases from the Ivey School of Business at the University of Western Ontario have been included—one at the end of each major part of the book. Also, two major cases have been written specifically for *Sales Force Management* and we have updated four other favorites. These end-of-part cases bring in new technologies and managerial concepts. In addition, spreadsheet analyses have also been updated and included on the book's website—www.mhhe.com/sfm9e.

Suggested Readings—New and Updated

At the end of each chapter is a list of suggested readings for students and professors. These readings have been completely updated for the ninth edition and include many new references that represent cutting-edge ideas and state-of-the-art knowledge on the subjects within the chapter.

Video—Updated

The video offerings for *Sales Force Management* have been updated and expanded. Careful attention was given to providing effective video packages that enhance and expand on the material covered in the book.

PowerPoint Slides—New and Updated

Many instructors like using PowerPoint to support their in-class presentations, and students have come to find these slide presentations a valuable learning tool. The PowerPoint package for this edition has been greatly enhanced with an updated, new look. The material is presented in an effective and interesting graphic design that complements the graphic elements of the book. The slides are flexible enough for instructors to include their own material yet comprehensive enough to stand alone.

Instructor's Manual—Updated

The Instructor's Manual provides an overview of each chapter, answers to discussion questions, as well as a discussion guide for Leadership Challenges, Minicases, and Role Plays. A comprehensive test bank is also included.

Web Site—Updated

Instructors will appreciate the book's Web site (*www.mhhe.com/sfm9e*), which has been built specifically for the ninth edition. Here you can communicate with the authors, share teaching ideas and resources, and stay up to date on companies and issues discussed in the text.

ACKNOWLEDGMENTS

Books are the result of hard work by many people, and we very much appreciate the efforts of numerous individuals associated with this new edition. First, as this book is built on the research and hard work of sales management academicians and practitioners, we would like to thank the many scholars and colleagues who have contributed to the body of sales force research over the past 40+ years. We reference their work and honor their contributions to the field.

Kevin Ness created the value-adding Minicases in this edition. Susan Johnston worked diligently on the Instructor's Manual and did a great job creating the new PowerPoint slides under tight deadlines. We would also like to offer a sincere thanks to the great people at McGraw-Hill/Irwin, and especially Devon Raemisch and Dean Karampelas, for their hard work and support during the revision process. Several people at HR Chally Group deserve thanks for making the strategic partnership to develop the chapter openers great. In particular, Howard and Sally Stevens, Jeanne Frawley, Megan Leasher, Corey Miller, and Sue Pearson have our utmost appreciation.

To our friends and academic colleagues we offer a simple but heartfelt thank-you. Creating this ninth edition of *Sales Force Management* was a labor of love, and your insights were essential to the project's success. Finally, to our families who endured countless hours spent working into the night during the writing process, we appreciate your love, support, and encouragement. You are our heroes—thank you.

Mark W. Johnston, Rollins College

Greg W. Marshall, Rollins College

January 2008

Brief Contents

Contents

Chapter Eleven
Salesperson Compensation and Incentives   343

Comprehensive Cases for Part Two   377

PART THREE
EVALUATION AND CONTROL OF THE SALES PROGRAM   406

Chapter Twelve
Cost Analysis   408

Chapter Thirteen
Evaluating Salesperson Performance   439

Chapter **One**

Introduction to Sales Management in the Twenty-First Century

Change is the Central Theme in Sales Management Today

Changing dynamics between buyers and sellers are being driven by larger societal trends affecting us all. The proliferation of information, mobility of the workforce, ease of communication, globalization of markets . . . these and other trends have altered the way we work and live. The guiding philosophy of the best sales organizations today is to add value to the customer's business and ultimately become *the* vendor of preference.

To be the vendor of preference means sales organizations must change their corporate culture. The whole firm must be customer driven, with people and processes aligned for the central purpose of adding value to customers. The focus has to change from price and delivery to ease of use—not only of the product itself but also in every aspect of doing business with the seller. The sales role is changing from product developers to relationship managers and from solution sellers to true client consultants and partners. Order taking, service, technical support, and product expertise are often supplied by other members of a cross-functional client team, not the salesperson him-/herself.

Changing Customer Needs Drive Changes in Salespeople

From the customer's perspective, expectations and needs from sales forces are dramatically different from a decade ago. From the 2007 Chally report in the customers' own words:

- Need #1: *Be personally accountable for our desired results.* Clients want to work with a real partner who takes as much ownership of the outcomes as they do.

- Need #2: *Understand our business.* Deep knowledge of a customer's competencies, strategies, challenges, opportunities, and culture is required.

- Need #3: *Be on our side.* Customers expect a salesperson to advocate for them inside the vendor firm, navigating through internal processes and bureaucracy to solve customer problems and meet customer needs.

- Need #4: *Design the right applications.* Today's salesperson must think well beyond product features to understand and affect customized product applications.

- Need #5: *Be easily accessible.* Like most other aspects of global society today, salespeople are expected to be connected and available whenever the customer reaches out.

- Need #6: *Solve our problems.* Despite the overuse of the word "solutions" in reference to client offerings (goods or services), the metaphor of salesperson as physician who diagnoses, prescribes, and resolves client issues—not just sells them products—is a valid one.

- Need #7: *Be creative in responding to our needs.* Innovation and creativity in working with clients toward business improvements is central to the modern sales role.

Changing Sales Management Agendas

Changes in customer needs and the resulting recasting of the sales role have created a concurrent shift in emphasis among benchmark agenda items of sales managers in world-class sales organizations. The 2007 Chally report identifies the following areas of sales management focus:

1. *Creating a customer-driven culture.* Sales managers must facilitate the sales role by knocking down organizational impediments to salesperson–client partnerships.

2. *Recruiting and selecting the right sales talent.* Because the sales role has dramatically changed, different skills and abilities are sought after today from sales job candidates. Sales managers have to recalibrate their approaches to securing the best sales talent.

3. *Training and developing for the right set of skills.* Because of the accelerating pace of change in today's business milieu, ongoing training and professional development of the sales force has never been a higher priority.

4. *Segmenting markets in meaningful ways.* Nowadays, a number of tasks that were traditionally performed by "marketers" are now squarely a part of the sales role. Salespeople have to be given the knowledge and tools to intelligently manage the customer relationship and customize product applications to individual customer requirements.

5. *Implementing formal sales processes.* Sales managers must get smarter about setting objectives and concurrently developing and executing the right metrics to measure success. Best practices benchmarking and continuous process improvement are now concepts that must be understood and mastered.

6. *Developing enabling information technology.* Given the real-time nature of managing today's customer relationships, sales managers have to ensure the sales

force is capable of leveraging the right technology at the right time in the process.

7. *Integrating other business functions with sales.* Traditionally, the sales force has among the least understood organizational functions by others in the firm and mostly resided in its own silo. Changing customer needs and the resulting changes in the sales role require sales managers to operate more broadly and strategically within an organization to enable client relationship success.

With Changes Come Opportunities

The changes in customers, sales roles, and sales management agendas are profound and represent critical knowledge for anyone pursuing a business career. The changes bring unprecedented opportunities for sales organizations to rethink their business models to better add value to clients in ways never before possible. This chapter continues the dialogue about change and introduces you to many important aspects of successful sales management in the twenty-first century.

Source: HR Chally Group (2007), *The Chally World Class Excellence Research Report: The Route to the Summit.* Dayton, OH: HR Chally Group.

LEARNING OBJECTIVES

Sales management is one of the most important elements in the success of modern organizations. When major trends emerge, such as the shift of the economy more toward small to medium-sized businesses, it is encumbent upon sales managers to react with new selling approaches. And not only is personal selling the most expensive component of the marketing mix for most companies, but it is the firm's most direct link to the customer. While Thoreau may have believed that the world will beat a path to the door of the company with the best mousetrap, the world needs someone to show how that mousetrap is better—and that role usually belongs to the salesperson. Otherwise, that sale may never occur. Therefore, management of the sales force is one of the most important executive responsibilities.

This chapter introduces you to the field of sales management. After reading it, you should be able to

- Identify and discuss key trends affecting sales organizations and sales managers today.
- Present a general overview of the sales management process.
- Identify and illustrate the key external and internal environmental factors that influence the development of marketing strategies and sales programs.

SALES MANAGEMENT IN THE TWENTY-FIRST CENTURY

As reflected in the chapter opener, personal selling and, consequently, sales management are undergoing dramatic changes. These changes are being driven by several behavioral, technological, and managerial forces that are dramatically and irrevocably altering the way salespeople understand, prepare for, and accomplish their jobs. Among the behavioral forces are rising customer expectations, globalization of markets, and demassification of domestic markets; technological forces include sales force automation, virtual sales offices, and electronic sales channels; and managerial forces consist of a shift to direct marketing alternatives, outsourcing of sales functions, and a blending of the sales and marketing functions.[1]

Salespeople and those who manage them realize these changes affect every aspect of sales management from the way the sales department is structured to the selection, training, motivation, and compensation of individual salespeople. Sales organizations are being reinvented to better address the needs of the changing marketplace. A number of critical issues have been identified in reinventing the sales organization, including the following: (1) building long-term relationships with customers, which involves assessing customer value and prioritizing customers; (2) creating sales organizational structures that are more nimble and adaptable to the needs of different customer groups; (3) gaining greater job ownership and commitment from salespeople by removing functional barriers within the organization and leveraging the team experience; (4) shifting sales management style from commanding to coaching; (5) leveraging available technology for sales success; and (6) better integrating salesperson performance evaluation to incorporate the full range of activities and outcomes relevant within sales jobs today.[2]

In the broadest perspective, these new-age issues in sales management represent three key themes: (1) innovation—willingness to think outside the box, do things differently, and embrace change; (2) technology—the broad spectrum of technological tools now available to sales managers and sales organizations; and (3) leadership—the capability to make things happen for the benefit of the sales organization and its customers. The chapter opener provides vivid examples of each of these issues at play as firms modify the way they do business to accommodate the twenty-first century marketplace. Throughout the chapters in this book, you will find highlighted feature boxes calling attention to industry examples of innovation, technology, and leadership among sales organizations. Now we introduce the themes and briefly address their impact on personal selling and sales management. In addition, we will also introduce the issues of globalization and ethics in sales management.

Innovation Fuels Success in Selling Today

For many years the dominant sales approach was **transactional selling**—a series of transactions, each one involving separate organizations entering into an independent transaction involving the delivery of a product or service in return for compensation. In today's highly competitive environment, however, customers realize there are benefits in building relationships between themselves and their suppliers and have thus turned to **relationship selling** approaches. For example, Xerox has identified fewer than 500 vendors with which it wants to do business. In contrast, in 1989 more than 5,000 vendors were supplying Xerox. As a result of buyers narrowing their vendor pool, salespeople are being asked to do more, working with customers to solve their problems, improve efficiencies, and, in general, add value to their customers' business. More and more companies have salespeople with offices at or near their customers' facilities. FedEx-Kinko's, for example, has offices for all key vendors at its corporate headquarters in California, and Procter & Gamble stations key salespeople at Wal-Mart's headquarters city of Bentonville, Arkansas.

Providing this level of service is expensive, however, and it cannot be provided equally to all customers across the board. As a result, sales managers must prioritize their customers, creating partnerships with some while seeking to maximize efficiencies with others. In essence, organizations are creating a multilayered sales strategy that seeks to create

Innovation What Smaller Prospects Want 1.1

As we move further into the twenty-first century, small to medium-sized businesses will continue to become more and more important to sales organizations. But what does this trend mean to sales managers who desire to keep their sales force on top of the trend? Below are five key takeaways from discussions with small business executives that can help sales managers with this opportunity. Smaller prospects want

1. *The opportunity to buy online.* Because many rely heavily on the Internet for research, purchasing, and selling, small business owners are perfectly content to establish relationships with sellers—at least initially—via Web sites and e-mail. "Small business owners don't mind electronic communications," says Elliott Ettenberg, CEO of marketing consultancy Ettenberg and Company.

2. *Partners, not entertainers.* Executives at small and midsize businesses don't have the time or inclination to be courted with three-martini lunches and tickets to ball games, common ploys in traditional buyer–seller courtship. "The old model was, 'We'll bring along the senior vice president of sales and take them to a football game,'" Ettenberg says. "But owners of smaller companies don't care about that. They are looking for support from the large companies that supply them."

3. *Simplicity.* Once you do get in front of small and midsize business executives and owners, keep sales pitches straightforward and direct. And show how your product or service can really help them run their businesses more efficiently.

4. *No cold calls.* "Just putting reps in cars and cold-calling on these small accounts doesn't make financial sense," says Ray Boggs, vice president of small and midsize business research at technology consultancy IDC. Jennifer Velarde, owner of Chicago handbag designer and retailer 1154 Lill, agrees. "I find a cold-call drop-in from a salesperson to be very frustrating," she says. "Ninety-nine percent of the time, I don't have time to listen to their spiel."

5. *A single point of contact.* Fully integrate services on the back end so that when small and midsize business owners seek guidance with a suite of products or services, they can phone into a call center and deal with only one representative. Otherwise, you run the risk of frustrating and alienating them.

Source: Jennifer Gilbert, "Small but Mighty," *Sales & Marketing Management*, January 2004, pp. 30–35.

 unique and even more strategic relationships with the best customers while streamlining a transaction-based relationship with others who demand less service.[3] Shell Oil, for example, found that some smaller buyers did not want or have time for personal visits by salespeople. When the company reallocated personal sales efforts to larger accounts and began using only telemarketing to call on smaller accounts, it found that all customers, even those assigned to telemarketing, were more satisfied. Selling costs were reduced, sales increased, and profits soared.

The innovations in selling and sales management described in the chapter opener were necessitated by the major changes in the customer marketplace. One major trend is toward more small business customers. Much of the success selling firms achieve with smaller, entrepreneurial customers is due to simply listening to what these customers want from a vendor. Innovation 1.1 provides insights on the kinds of things smaller customers want.

Sales Effectiveness Is Enhanced through Technology

Broadly speaking, technology has had a profound effect on almost every facet of personal selling. Laptop computers make it easy to have huge databases or complete customer records at the fingertips of the salesperson, cellular phones make it possible to communicate with the salesperson almost continuously, and DVDs and other video innovations enhance training and provide excellent tools for conveying information. Of course, the

Internet has taken the interaction between customer and company to a new level, creating the ability to remain in touch with the customer (update information, handle questions, deal with complaints) in ways that have not been possible in the past. Companies are still learning how to best incorporate new technology into the business of selling.

The Internet's ability to inform, persuade, and enhance the personal selling component makes it a critical part of sales management in the twenty-first century. For today's young salespeople and buyers, the Internet is simply a given—they can't imagine what business was like before it! Nearly every company of any size has created an extensive, integrative, and interactive Web site to sell and service customers. Both Dell Computer and HP are great examples. Although Dell's primary strategy began as direct selling and HP's began by selling through retailers, both now experience strength in sales, customer satisfaction, and loyalty that are greatly enhanced by their Web presence. The Web site has become an important sales tool as account managers work with customers to help them see the benefits of ordering online.

Because the Internet is such a significant tool for the twenty-first century salesperson, we have integrated the Internet throughout the text. Specifically, we have included Web sites for companies discussed in introductory scenarios, cases, and example boxes throughout. In addition, we have created a Web site for you to browse with up-to-date information about personal selling and sales management and additional exercises you can do to test your knowledge (*www.mhhe.com/sfm9e*).

But don't think technology is just about the Internet alone. Electronic data interchange (EDI) systems in manufacturing and efficient consumer response (ECR) systems in retailing enable companies to tie their computers directly to their customers. When a customer's computer recognizes a low inventory, it can generate an order directly to the vendor's computer, which then schedules the product for delivery (and in some cases even schedules the product for manufacturing). Thus, order and delivery systems have become just-in-time delivery systems. In addition, customer relationship management (CRM) systems are driving the overall customer capturing and retention enterprise in many firms.

Chapter 3 provides a more extensive discussion of CRM and how it fits into various elements of sales management. For now, take a look at Technology 1.2 for some insights on the status of CRM.

Leadership Is a Key Component in Sales Management Success

In the sales environment of the twenty-first century, traditional work relationships are being questioned and often replaced with new ones. Nowhere is this more prevalent than in the relationship between salesperson and sales manager. In the traditional top-down bureaucratic style, managers were the supervisors responsible for administering the sales force. Conversely, they were held directly accountable for the actions of their salespeople. Words like *control* and *manage* were used to describe their activities.

The highly dynamic and competitive environment of the twenty-first century demands a more responsive, flexible approach to sales management. Sales forces are becoming less hierarchical with fewer layers of management while more responsibility is being given to the salesperson. Leading versus managing is an important distinction for today's successful sales manager. Effective sales management is now more often defined by how good a leader you are than how good a manager. Effective leadership of salespeople includes (1) communicating with salespeople rather than controlling them, (2) becoming a cheerleader and coach instead of a supervisor or boss, and (3) empowering salespeople to make decisions rather than directing them. Common across these items is an approach of mentoring, rather than directing, salespeople.[4] Being an effective leader requires new

Technology — Impact of CRM on Selling is Underivable — 1.2

In Chapter 3 you will learn the basics of customer relationship management (CRM) and how it fits into the world of selling and sales management. At its essence, CRM provides an organization the opportunity to better manage customer relationships through comprehensive, integrated technology capabilities. CRM systems are in use by a large number of firms today and offer great promise for aiding sales performance, but unfortunately they have not always provided the desired return on the investment required to implement and operate them.

For now, let's introduce three key recent impacts of CRM on the sales process inside firms and on the way CRM systems are purchased, sold, installed, and used. These impacts were identified by a group of leading CRM experts during an interview by *Selling Power* who were asked to focus on key trends in CRM.

1. *Management is largely responsible for the success or failure of CRM.* In the earlier days of CRM, many firms jumped on the "let's buy a CRM system" bandwagon with little thought about how to make it work. This resulted in a number of highly publicized failures. However, the poor results nearly universally are traceable not to the system but rather to the management of them by the organization. No organization can throw up its proverbial hands and say "that's it for us—no more CRM for this firm!" Talk about giving the competition an advantage. The fact is that the core CRM premise of building business strategies enabled with

technology to increase customer loyalty and satisfaction remains a powerful strategic driver of revenue.

2. *Sales managers, in particular, are under the gun to make CRM work effectively.* Because of the key role played by salespeople in managing customer relationships, sales managers are beginning to build in more and more incentives to get their salespeople to take advantage of CRM for such activities as prospecting, cross-selling of multiple products or lines, developing customized offerings to customers, and the general process of account management. Metrics used by sales managers to assess how well their salespeople use CRM include customer loyalty and retention rates, amount of cross-selling done, and the number of prospects who become customers.

3. *CRM simply **must** fulfill return on investment ROI expectations.* One way to approach this is to reduce the level of investment in CRM—but of course, nobody wants an inferior program. In answer to this dilemma, today it is possible to literally rent high-quality CRM systems that are Web-based. These vendors are capitalizing of companies' desire for more customization, less cash out, ease of access and use, and flexibility in terms of capabilities. Online CRM is definitely the wave of the future.

Source: Geoffrey James, "Six Changes in CRM," *Selling Power Source Book,* 2003, pp. 26–29.

and different skills from the traditional manager role. One way to begin the journey toward being a good leader is summarized in the concept of servant leadership, which is discussed in Leadership 1.3.

Sales Management Is a Global Endeavor

Innovation, technology, and leadership are pervasive themes in sales management today. Because companies now operate in a global marketplace, these themes play out on a global stage. Products are designed in one country, manufactured in another, and marketed around the world. In some cases, competitors in one part of the world are partners in another. IBM and EDS are a classic example, with each simultaneously competing with and partnering with the other. Global suppliers have increased the importance of vendor relationships not only around the country but around the world. The internationalization of business was, for many years, considered a process of big multinational corporations. However, in today's global society even small domestic companies are doing business in international markets as a result of independent distributor relationships, trade shows, and the ability of the Internet to generate awareness and interest literally anywhere in the world.

Leadership Servant Leadership   1.3

In recent years, approaches to leadership have taken nearly mystic qualities. One new-age approach is *servant leadership*. Robert Greenleaf, who retired in 1964 from an executive position with AT&T, spent the rest of his life writing and studying about leadership and the characteristics of leaders. Today, the Robert K. Greenleaf Center is located in Indianapolis.

Greenleaf's servant leadership is based on 10 key characteristics that he viewed as central to the development of servant leaders: (1) listening, (2) empathy, (3) healing, (4) awareness, (5) persuasion, (6) conceptualization, (7) foresight, (8) stewardship, (9) commitment to the growth of people, and (10) building community. The power of the concept of servant leadership can be stated in five points:

• The servant leader takes his or her people and their work very seriously. The leader believes that the work exists for the people as much as the people exist for the work.

• The servant leader listens to his or her people and takes his or her lead from them. The leader believes that he or she will not have all the answers but that the people who are working with the customers will have the answers.

• The servant leader heals and builds trust. The leader is open with his or her people and lets them vent.

• The servant leader is self-effacing. The leader allocates the rewards and glory to his or her people.

• The servant leader sees him- or herself as a steward. The leader must have a long-term perspective and must be a visionary. The leader leads the conversations, the visions are shared, and a stronger shared vision emerges from the dialogue.

Given the complexities of modern sales organizations and their environment, sales managers can gain substantial insight from learning how to create an environment for success among their salespeople through servant leadership.

Source: Ideas derived from the Web site of the Robert K. Greenleaf Center for Servant Leadership, *www.greenleaf.org*.

This global focus is driven by a number of factors. As noted earlier, the ability to communicate anywhere in the world with relative ease has opened new markets. Potential customers worldwide can call, fax, or e-mail questions or orders easily. Even more significant is the realization that, for many companies, significant growth opportunities lie outside domestic markets. This is especially true in the United States as companies as diverse as DuPont, Microsoft, and Coca-Cola acknowledge that most of their growth, and consequently much of their investment over the next few years, will be outside the United States. Finally, many companies have become more international because their customers are global. For example, Acadia Corporation, a supplier of equipment to the automobile industry, moved into international markets at the request of its largest customers, the Big 3 automakers in the United States.

All of these changes have led to dramatic transformations in the focus of personal selling and the way the sales force is managed. Diversity in the sales force has created new challenges for sales managers. In addition, managers need to understand a wide range of environmental differences (cultural, legal, behavioral) in the selling process. Indeed, a number of companies require managers to spend time overseas because they believe it is important for the individual to learn an international perspective. Innovation 1.4 provides a nice illustration of the innovations needed for a successful global selling strategy, especially from a cultural perspective.

Ethics Underlies All Selling and Sales Management Activities

Characterizing sales as trending toward more ethical behavior may be unfair to the many ethical salespeople of the past. But it is true that ethical selling practices, just like ethics

Innovation   Bridging the Culture Gap in Global Selling   1.4

To achieve sales success on a global scale, you have to begin by bridging the culture gap.

As technology and transportation make the world smaller and smaller, today's business environment calls for a multicultural selling strategy. Even if your territory is limited to the United States, you may sell to customers with cultural backgrounds very different from yours. With these customers, strong relationships come from understanding and honoring those differences, not denying them.

These five tips will help you learn to speak your customer's language, whatever it might be.

1. *View your customers in terms of their ethnic core values.* We are all the product of our unique cultural experience, and your prospects and customers are no exception. Learn to understand them from their cultural perspective, not yours. Without actually imitating them, try to match your style to your customers. Are they reserved and solemn or chatty and cheerful? What's their speaking style? What qualities do they look for in a business partner? Honesty? Good work ethic? Creativity? Ambition?

   Also, find out how your customers want to be sold. In some cultures, for example, you must establish a strong relationship with your customer before you can expect a sale. Whether your customers are from Main Street, U.S.A., or Bangkok, Thailand, find out their wants, needs, problems, and challenges and sell them the way they want to be sold.

2. *Get in sync.* You can also help bridge the culture gap with your customers by being willing to do business their way. For example, while much of the United States and the United Kingdom adopts a task-oriented approach to business, much of China, Japan, and the Middle East is more relationship oriented. Research the role of salespeople from your customer's culture, and make any changes you feel would make your customer more comfortable with you or more satisfied with your performance. Find out what constitutes a day in your customer's business life. For example, if standard business practice in your buyer's country is to take a two- or three-hour break in the afternoon, you need to know so you can schedule your calls accordingly. Just as a car's clutch allows for smooth and easy acceleration, you must mesh your sales gears with your customer's buying gears to establish a harmonious relationship.

3. *Follow your customer's lead.* Once you get synchronized with your customers' business practices, you have to make the changes carry over to your actual sales and presentation techniques. Before you start preparing your presentation, ask open-ended questions to find out your customer's core values and hot buttons.

   Consider how your customer's perception of your product and its benefits might change with different cultures. Show your customers that you've taken the time to identify their special needs and that you have their best interests in mind. By incorporating their unique cultural perspective in the selling relationship, you'll help earn their trust and respect.

4. *See others honestly.* Smart salespeople know you can't judge a book by its cover if you expect to make a sale. Your customers may be able to read your true perceptions of them more accurately than you think, so put away your prejudices or biases before you make your first call. You can help evaluate your prospects fairly by recognizing that we all have different perceptions, by identifying the source of our perceptions, then listing them, comparing them to reality, and being able to discard those that are inaccurate. Remember that you can be tolerant and respectful of another person's culture without being comfortable with or condoning every aspect of it. For every viewpoint or custom of your buyer's that seems strange to you, you may have an opinion or habit that seems odd to your customer.

5. *Adopt the perspective of other cultures.* Learning a lot about your customers' cultures is helpful, but to reap the full benefits of your knowledge you must use it to view the world through your customers' eyes. Imagine what it's like to face the challenges your customers face with their background. Hearing your Japanese customer say he feels tremendous pressure to succeed may help you understand him, but the information may be even more helpful if you try to understand it from the Japanese perspective. Find out all you can about the values and beliefs of the entire culture, their outlook on life and on you, and your value to their business. You know what you and your product can do for your customers, but what does that mean to them?

Customers are more likely to trust, and buy, from people who are like them. While you obviously can't adopt a whole new way of life to make a sale, you can show knowledge of and respect for cultural differences to build trust with your customers. As long as you're willing to meet your customers halfway across the culture gap, you might find some common ground on which to stand, and sell.

Source: Frank Beeman, "Selling around the World," *Selling Power*, www.sellingpower.com.

in all aspects of business, is more prominent due to the seemingly endless business ethics debacles in the news like Halliburton, Enron, and the subprime mortgage meltdown. For example, the U.S. government has developed Federal Sentencing Guidelines that are designed to punish firms that allow salespeople (and other employees) to engage in unethical behavior. Penalties are reduced for firms that have required ethics training and have adopted other policies that encourage ethical behavior.

Even without encouragement from the government, the increasingly long-term nature of business relationships requires higher ethical standards than did earlier transactional selling approaches. A sucker may be born every minute, but if your business depends on repeat purchase and word-of-mouth advertising you can't sucker customers and hope to stay in business. Put another way, long-term relationships and customer loyalty are impossible to maintain in an atmosphere of distrust brought on by unethical sales approaches. Throughout this book you will notice a strong theme of highly ethical practice in selling and sales management. We encourage all sales organizations to develop a formal code of ethical conduct to attempt to engrain ethical behaviors in their organizational culture.[5]

WHAT IS INVOLVED IN SALES MANAGEMENT

Two key points should be made at the outset about sales management in the twenty-first century. First, modern companies realize that selling is an indispensable component of an effective marketing strategy. In fact, it has become popular to discuss selling as a "boardroom topic." That is, top management acknowledges the critical role of personal selling in building customer relationships, and customers have come to rely on the problem-solving capabilities of a well-trained sales force. As a result, the management of these seller–customer aspects of the firm—sales management—has become a more exciting and challenging career opportunity than ever before.

Second, managing a sales force is a *dynamic* process. Sales management programs must be formulated to respond effectively to a firm's environmental circumstances (both external and internal, or organizational, environment), and they must be consistent with the organization's marketing strategies. At the same time, good sales management practices are essential for the successful implementation of a firm's competitive and marketing strategies. To help understand the scope of the sales management task, we define **sales management** as all activities, processes, and decisions involved in managing the sales function in an organization.

Managing a sales force well involves understanding the complexity of selling activities as well as the decisions involved in managing those activities. The purpose of this book is to provide you with an understanding of the role of the sales management function in marketing and the entire organization, as well as in the marketplace. In addition, the book carefully examines the activities and decisions that comprise an effective sales management program.

Selling Process

Many people have misconceptions about the selling process, the activities carried out by salespeople, and the personal characteristics necessary for a successful sales career. To complicate matters even more, various selling jobs can involve very different tasks and require different skills and abilities. Just imagine the differences involved in selling across the many divisions of a diversified company such as General Electric, which sells an amazingly wide array of products and services from light bulbs to jet engines to home appliances to financial services. Each has its own sales force and its own markets. Selling skills and requirements can vary greatly among the different businesses due to the different buying processes and needs in the various markets, as well as different levels of product complexity.

To reduce misconceptions about personal selling, and to establish a solid foundation of knowledge for our subsequent discussion of sales force management, Chapter 2 examines buying processes and selling processes in detail. Then, Chapter 3 broadens the sales role to a more strategic level, emphasizing key aspects of customer relationship strategies.

Sales Management Process

The **sales management process,** or process of effective management of a company's sales force, involves three interrelated sets of decisions or processes.

1. *The **formulation** of a sales program.* The sales program should consider the environmental factors faced by the firm. Sales executives organize and plan the company's overall personal selling efforts and integrate these with the other elements of the firm's marketing strategy. The formulation process is represented by Part One of this book.

2. *The **implementation** of the sales program.* The implementation phase involves selecting appropriate sales personnel and designing and implementing approaches that will direct their efforts toward the desired objectives. The implementation process is represented by Part Two of this book.

3. *The **evaluation and control** of the sales program.* The evaluation phase involves developing methods for monitoring and evaluating sales force performance through appropriate metrics. Evaluation and control allows for adjustment of the sales program or the way it is implemented when performance is unsatisfactory. The evaluation and control process is represented by Part Three of this book.

The specific activities involved in these three processes, along with the variables that influence those activities, are summarized in the model of sales management in Exhibit 1.1. This model serves as a road map for the overall sales management process: formulation, implementation, and evaluation and control of the sales program for the organization. You will be introduced to each of these three major aspects of sales management at the beginning of each of the three major parts of the book.

For now, peruse the model and get a feel for the flow. You will note that the external and internal (also known as organizational) environments flow into the other aspects of the model. Before we can begin to learn about formulation, implementation, and evaluation and control of a sales program, we first need to gain a clear understanding of the key external and internal (organizational) factors in the environment that may affect the sales manager's ability to execute the remaining aspects of the model. On the external side, the demands of potential customers and the actions of competitors are two obvious environmental factors. Other external environmental factors such as energy prices, technological advances, government regulations, and social concerns can affect a company's selling initiatives. For instance, when gasoline prices spike, you'd better believe sales managers caution their salespeople about making unnecessary trips in company cars.

On the organizational side, environmental factors such as human and financial resources, the firm's production capacity, and its expertise in research and development can either help or hinder the sales force's ability to pursue customers or expand its market share.

EXHIBIT 1.1   An overview of sales management

ENVIRONMENTAL FACTORS IMPACT SUCCESS IN SELLING

External and internal (organizational) environmental factors influence sales managers in four basic ways.

1. *Environmental forces can constrain the organization's ability to pursue certain marketing strategies or activities.* An example is when the government declares the sale of a product to be illegal or when a well-entrenched competitor makes it unattractive for the firm to enter a new market.

2. *Environmental variables, and changes in those variables over time, help determine the ultimate success or failure of marketing strategies.* The rapid growth in the number of women in the labor force in recent years, for instance, helped ensure the success of Stouffer's Lean Cuisine, ConAgra's Healthy Choice, and other quality brands of convenient frozen entrées.

3. *Changes in the environment can create new marketing opportunities for an organization,* as when a new technology allows development of new products. The emergence of electronic commerce software, for instance, enabled HP to develop solutions to problems such as security, design, and flow of data over the Internet, some of the more important challenges that customers face. As one customer said, "There is a lot of value in companies like HP offering to help customers put up electronic commerce sites."

4. *Environmental variables are affected and changed by marketing activities,* as when new products and promotional programs help to change lifestyles and social values. In

view of the increased activity by consumer groups, environmentalists, and other public interest groups and agencies, marketers today must consider how proposed programs will affect the environment as well as how the environment will affect the programs.

Consequently, one of the most important—but increasingly difficult—parts of any sales manager's job is to monitor the environment, predict how it might change, and develop strategies and plans for the sales function that are suited to the environmental conditions. Because selling is but one part of the overall marketing initiatives of the firm, the sales program must be adapted to the environmental circumstances faced by the firm as a whole. Chapter 3 ties the sales manager's role to overall marketing and business planning.

EXTERNAL ENVIRONMENT

By definition, factors in the **external environment** are beyond the control of the individual manager; however, companies do try to influence external conditions to the extent they can through political lobbying, public relations campaigns, and the like. But for the most part, the sales manager must take the environment as it exists and adapt strategies to fit it.

Markets consist of people. As the demographic, educational, and other characteristics of the population change, market opportunities change. This also affects opportunities in business markets, since an organization's demand for goods and services is derived from the demand for its own products. Further, economic systems are becoming more open, meaning that there is ever-increasing competition from global companies. External environmental factors can affect the way a company competes globally, which will then influence how the company competes locally.

As indicated in Exhibit 1.2, variables in the external environment that affect sales and marketing may be grouped into five broad categories: (1) **economic,** which includes

EXHIBIT 1.2
Components of the external environment

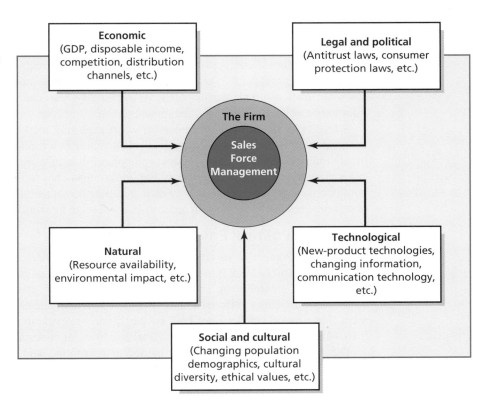

competition; (2) **legal and political;** (3) **technological;** (4) **social and cultural,** focused on ethics; and (5) **natural.**

Economic Environment

People and organizations cannot buy goods and services unless they have the money. The total potential demand for a product within a given country depends on that country's economic conditions—the amount of growth, the unemployment rate, and the level of inflation. These factors must be considered when analyzing market opportunities and developing sales forecasts. Keep in mind, though, that global economic conditions also influence many firms' ability to earn a profit. Companies as diverse as Intel, Caterpillar, and DuPont have been adversely impacted at the bottom line in their European operations due to the unfavorable exchange rate between the U.S. dollar and the Euro.

A second aspect of the economic environment is the existing distribution structure in an industry. This includes the number, types, and availability of wholesalers, retailers, and other intermediaries a firm might use to distribute its product. Much of a firm's personal selling effort may be directed to trying to persuade such intermediaries to stock and provide marketing support for the company's products.

Understanding Competitors

Another critical economic variable is the amount of competition in the firm's industry—both the number of competing firms and their relative strengths in the marketplace. Ideally, a company's marketing and sales programs should be designed to gain a differential advantage over competitors. For example, rather than trying to compete with the low prices of foreign competitors such as Komatsu, Caterpillar has been successful in the heavy construction equipment business by providing superior product quality and excellent service, while charging prices as much as 10 to 20 percent higher than its competitors. Salespeople go head to head with competitors on a daily basis; as a result, the sales force is often the first to observe changes in competitive strategy and activity. One of the critical issues is getting information from the sales force to strategic planners so that the company can act on those observations. Reports that detail competitive activity, such as analyses of lost sales, can summarize competitive activity for sales and marketing management. Sophisticated customer relationship management (CRM) software systems can greatly aid in facilitating information collection, analysis, and dissemination.

Salespeople are particularly important when exploring market opportunities in other countries. Given the added risks involved when selling in a foreign country, accurate and timely market information may be more important than in domestic marketing. In many cases, foreign salespeople are the only link the company has to the customer. Companies with international sales forces survey their salespeople, with either formal written surveys or informal telephone surveys, in order to assess foreign markets.[6]

Legal and Political Environment

Many of the changes in society's values are eventually reflected in new laws and government regulations—that is, where the social–cultural–ethical environment intersects the legal–political environment. In recent years, the number of laws regulating the conduct of business, including personal selling, has increased dramatically at all levels of government. Three broad categories of laws are particularly relevant to sales programs: (1) antitrust, (2) consumer protection, and (3) equal employment opportunity.

The antitrust laws are aimed primarily at preserving and enhancing competition among firms in an industry. They restrict marketing practices that would tend to reduce

EXHIBIT 1.3
Selected antitrust and consumer protection laws

Antitrust Provisions

Conspiracies among competing firms to *control their prices,* or to *allocate markets* among themselves, are per se illegal under the Sherman Act.

The Robinson-Patman Act prohibits a firm and its representatives from *discriminating in the prices or services* offered to competing customers. The major purpose of this law is to protect smaller customers from being placed at a competitive disadvantage by "key account" programs or price promotions that offer special incentives to larger buyers. However, the law does allow a marketer to grant discounts to larger buyers based on savings in the costs of manufacturing or distributing the product. Thus, some quantity discounts are legal.

Tying agreements, where a seller forces a buyer to purchase one product to gain the right to purchase another, are illegal under the Clayton and Sherman Acts. A personal computer manufacturer, for example, cannot force a customer to agree to buy extra drives, a scanner, a printer, and so forth as a precondition for buying the computer itself.

Reciprocal dealing arrangements, the "I'll buy from you if you buy from me" type of agreements, are illegal where the effect is to injure competition. Such arrangements do tend to be anticompetitive because large companies—which are large buyers as well as large suppliers—tend to have an advantage over smaller firms.

The Federal Trade Commission Act prohibits *unfair methods of competition* in general. Thus, deceptive product claims, interfering with the actions of a competitor's sales representative, and other unfair acts are illegal.

Consumer Protection Provisions

The Fair Packaging and Labeling Act makes *unfair or deceptive packaging* or labeling of certain consumer commodities illegal.

The Truth-in-Lending Act requires *full disclosure of all finance charges* on consumer credit agreements.

State *cooling-off* laws allow consumers to cancel contracts signed with door-to-door sellers within a limited number of days after agreeing to such contracts.

The Federal Trade Commission requires that door-to-door salespeople who work for companies engaged in interstate commerce clearly announce their purpose when making calls on potential customers.

Many cities and towns have so-called Green River Ordinances, which require all door-to-door salespeople to obtain a license.

competition and give one firm a monopoly through unfair competition. Several antitrust and consumer protection law provisions of particular relevance to sales management are outlined in Exhibit 1.3.

The restrictions on anticompetitive behavior spelled out in the antitrust laws apply to firms selling goods or services to intermediaries, business users, or ultimate consumers. When a firm sells to consumer markets, however, it faces additional restrictions imposed by federal, state, and local consumer protection laws. These laws are aimed more directly at protecting consumer welfare by setting standards of quality and safety. They also require that consumers be provided with accurate information to use in making purchase decisions. Since personal selling is one means of providing consumers with information, many laws requiring full disclosure and prohibiting deceptive or misleading information have a direct impact on selling activities.

Misrepresentation of a company's product by a salesperson can have both ethical and legal consequences, whether the salesperson is dealing with end-user consumers or organizational customers. Many salespeople are unaware that they assume legal obligations every time they approach a customer. By making certain statements, they can embroil their companies in a lawsuit and ruin the very business relationship they are trying to establish. But recent court cases around the United States have held firms liable for multimillion-dollar judgments for misrepresentation or breach of warranty due to statements made by their salespeople, particularly when the sale involved big-ticket, high-tech products or services.

Over the past few years, at both the federal and state level "no-call" lists have become prevalent, blocking the ability for firms to do telemarketing to customers who choose to be listed. Severe fines are imposed on sales organizations that violate these no-call lists. While this legal development may not directly affect salespeople in business settings through personal contact, because telemarketing and teleselling are often used to support in-person selling approaches, many companies have had to adjust their overall sales programs to comply with these regulations.

One other type of legislation has a direct effect on sales managers as they attempt to implement their sales programs: the equal employment opportunity laws. It is unlawful to discriminate against a person in either hiring or promotion because of race, religion, nationality, sex, or age. For this reason, certain types of aptitude tests are illegal if they are culturally or sexually biased or if they are not valid predictors of a person's job performance. The legal aspects of recruiting and selecting sales representatives, as well as other issues related to the increasing cultural diversity of the labor force, are examined in Chapter 9.

Technological Environment

As mentioned earlier, technology not only influences sales strategies; it often drives the firm's capability to effectively sell. Of course, the impact of technology is obvious with companies like IBM and HP. But in the generally low-tech world of propane sales, Blue Rhino is one company that has used technology to capture significant market share. By improving the processes of filling and storing tanks, the company has begun to dominate a market that was largely populated by small, independent dealers. In one *King of the Hill* episode, Hank Hill's propane company has to reduce its workforce due to the loss in sales to the local MegaLo Mart. While the *King of the Hill* plot may seem made-up, that is exactly what Blue Rhino has done. Blue Rhino dominates by distributing through the country's largest and fastest-growing retailers (Wal-Mart, Home Depot, and Lowe's), a distribution strategy made possible by better technology.

The most obvious impact of the technological environment on marketing is in providing opportunities for product development. Technology advances have been occurring at a rapidly increasing rate, and new products are accounting for an increasing percentage of total sales in many industries. For example, historically at 3M more than half of the current sales volume is generated by products that were not in existence five years ago. Most analysts believe the importance of new products and services to the marketing success of many firms will continue to accelerate. Rapid development of new products requires adjusting a firm's sales programs. New sales plans must be formulated, the sales representatives must be retrained, and, in some cases, new reps must be hired.

Advancing technology also affects sales management in more direct ways. Improvements in transportation, communications, and data processing are changing the way sales territories are defined, sales reps are deployed, and sales performance is evaluated and controlled in many companies. New communication technologies—together with the escalating costs of a traditional field sales call—are changing how the personal selling function is carried out.

Technology   Enterprise E-mail System   1.5

Applied Industrial Technologies is a $2 billion company with no CRM package. According to their CIO, Jim Hopper, "We never implemented any packaged systems, because they weren't architected the way we do business. We never pushed anything on our salespeople, we just responded to their requests for additional functionality. Really, what started out as a series of 'quick fixes' ended up being full-blown systems."

In fact, their primary form of customer information sharing is a highly evolved enterprise e-mail system that has been customized with functionality to support their particular business model. According to Ted Carl, VP of Strategic Accounts, "We do not have a CRM system. We have talked about it many, many times. We have a very effective e-mail system. If any salesperson or manager at any level touches a particular customer, we can send e-mail directly to that group of individuals through our e-mail system. We communicate very effectively, and it is done with the push of a button. It is all connected through account numbers and so on, and it gives us the ability to roll up the process, to share that across the sales force, and to view what other people are doing."

Source: HR Chally Group (2007), *The Chally World Class Excellence Research Report: The Route to the Summit.* Dayton, OH: HR Chally Group.

The satchel full of samples has given way to the laptop computer; and telemarketing, teleconferencing, and computerized reordering have replaced the face-to-face sales call in a growing number of situations. Consequently, the nature of many sales jobs—and the role of the sales manager in supervising the sales force—has changed dramatically in recent years. We will explore the impact of these new technologies in highlighted feature boxes throughout this book. An interesting example of a firm's technological adaptation is provided in Technology 1.5.

Social and Cultural Environment: Ethics

The values of a society affect marketing and sales programs in a variety of ways. Firms develop new products in response to trends in consumer tastes and preferences. In the United States, the well-documented demographic trends of aging society, greater influx of minorities as a percentage of total population, two-income households, greater mobility, and ever increasing desire for more leisure time and more convenience-oriented products all have greatly affected selling.

In twenty-first century sales management, nowhere is the impact of societal values more important than in the way social values set the standards for ethical behavior. **Ethics** is more than simply a matter of complying with the laws and regulations we will discuss later in this section. That is, a particular action may be legal but not ethical. For instance, when a salesperson makes extreme, unsubstantiated statements such as "Our product runs rings around Brand X," the rep may be engaging in legal puffery to make a sale, but many salespeople (and their customers) view such little white lies as unethical.

Ethics is concerned with the development of moral standards by which actions and situations can be judged. It focuses on those actions that may result in actual or potential harm of some kind (e.g., economic, mental, physical) to an individual, group, or organization. Thus, ethics is more proactive than the law. Ethical standards attempt to anticipate and avoid social problems, whereas most laws and regulations emerge only after the negative consequences of an action become apparent.[7]

Two sets of ethical dilemmas are of particular concern to sales managers. The first set is embedded in the manager's dealings with the salespeople. Ethical issues involved in relationships between a sales manager and the sales force include such things as fairness and equal treatment of all social groups in hiring and promotion, respect for the individual in supervisory practices and training programs, and fairness and integrity in the design of sales territories, assignment of quotas, and determination of compensation and incentive rewards. Ethical issues pervade nearly all aspects of sales force management.

The second set of ethical issues arises from the interactions between salespeople and their customers. These issues only indirectly involve the sales manager because the manager cannot always directly observe or control the actions of every member of the sales force. But managers have a responsibility to establish standards of ethical behavior for their subordinates, communicate them clearly, and enforce them vigorously.

One might ask why a manager should be responsible for providing moral guidance to subordinates. One might even question whether setting and enforcing standards of ethical conduct for the sales force infringes on the freedom of its individual members and their right to make their own moral choices. While such questions may be legitimate topics for philosophical debate, there is a compelling and practical organizational reason for a firm to impose ethical standards to guide employees' dealings with customers: Unethical selling practices make buyers reluctant to deal with a supplier and are likely to result in the loss of sales and profits over time.

Not all customers or competing suppliers adhere to the same ethical standards. As a result, salespeople sometimes feel pressure to engage in actions that are inconsistent with what they believe to be right—in terms of either personal values or formal company standards. Such pressures arise because the sales reps, or sometimes their managers, believe a questionable action is necessary to close a sale or maintain parity with the competition. This point was illustrated by a survey of 59 top sales executives concerning commercial bribery—attempts to influence a potential customer by giving gifts or kickbacks. While nearly two-thirds of the executives considered bribes unethical and did not want to pay them, 88 percent also felt that not paying bribes might put their firms at a competitive disadvantage.

Uncertainty about what to do in such situations—often due to a lack of direction from management—may lead to job stress, poor sales performance, and unhappy customers. Many selling situations involving ethical issues are not addressed by management directives, and many sales personnel want more explicit guidelines to help them resolve such issues. Management can help salespeople avoid the stress and inconsistent performance associated with ethical dilemmas by developing written policies that address problem situations.

The important thing, however, is not just to have a formal policy but to have one that is helpful to the sales force. Such policies should provide clear guidelines for decision making and action so that employees facing similar situations will handle them in a way consistent with the organization's goals. To further reduce uncertainty, policies must be clearly communicated to both sales personnel and customers. The most effective way for management to influence the ethical performance of their salespeople, however, is to lead by example. Formal policies do not have much impact when top management gives lip service to one set of standards while practicing another. Sales managers who expect ethical behavior from their employees should apply high ethical standards to their own actions and decisions.

The level of ethical standards in the sales force ultimately is a reflection of the integrity of the firm, as manifest in its culture and value system. Leadership 1.6 discusses the issue of integrity as an organizational value.

Natural Environment

Nature influences demand for many products. Of course, natural disasters such as tornados and floods can influence demand for building products and the like. But unseasonable

Leadership   Valuing Integrity in Organizations   1.6

Many organizations include *integrity* in their values and in their marketing communications to prospects and customers. *Integrity* has many meanings: living one's word, delivering on promises, alignment of beliefs and actions, wholeness, honesty, sincerity, and authenticity, to name a few.

Opportunities abound in the daily world of selling and sales management for breaks in integrity to occur. Breaks in integrity by leaders have a particularly high negative impact. People develop trust in others on the basis of observed actions more than spoken or written words. Furthermore, salespeople tend to emulate their managers' behavior or that of others who appear to be valued. Trust is such an important factor, both to the salesperson–sales manager relationship and to the overall sales organization–client relationship, that integrity must be protected at all cost in order to preserve a high level of trust.

Don't assume everyone understands the meaning of integrity. Your organization's interpretation of integrity, aligned with its values and mission, needs to be made explicit. Stephen Covey talks about "emotional bank accounts" wherein our actions make either deposits or withdrawals to our own or others' accounts. "If you make and keep promises, you build a reserve of trust," he reasons.

In a high-trust environment, employees, customers, and suppliers genuinely want to be part of the organization and eagerly refer others as potential employees and customers. Warren Bennis notes, "Integrity is the basis of trust, which is not as much an ingredient of leadership as it is a product. It is the one quality that cannot be acquired, but must be earned. It is given by co-workers and followers; without it, the leader can't function."

Organizational pursuit of integrity satisfies a basic human need for trust in relationships and breeds higher employee and customer loyalty, which leads to improved performance and profitability. A company can measure its "integrity quotient" by delineating all promises or agreements and measuring the degree to which they are kept with customers, employees, and suppliers. Steps should be taken to assure products and services fulfill their promises. One approach is to regularly audit product and service performance relative to the promises made in marketing materials and sales presentations and to use the assessment to focus improvement efforts to achieve closer alignment.

Sources: Muel Kaptein, "An Integrity Injection for Business," *BusinessWeek,* December 29, 2006, *www.businessweek.com;* Karen Trisko, "Power of Integrity," *Executive Excellence,* May 2001, p. 16.

weather can damage or enhance sales, depending on the type of product. La Niña (the opposite effect of El Niño) may cause an increase in snow for the Northwest, leading cities to boost their orders for road salt. Even one snowy Friday after Thanksgiving can negatively impact sales for those retailers that rely on the date's usual high customer traffic.

The natural environment is an important consideration in the development of marketing and sales plans. The natural environment is the source of all the raw materials and energy resources needed to make, package, promote, and distribute a product. Over the past 15 years, firms in many industries—such as steel, aluminum, plastics, and synthetic fibers—have encountered resource or energy shortages that have forced them to limit sales of their products. One might assume that sales representatives could take life easy under such circumstances, letting customers come to them for badly needed goods. But the sales force often has to work harder during product shortages, and well-formulated account management policies become even more crucial for the firm's success.

During such periods, the sales organization may be engaged in **demarketing** of part or all of its product line. The sales force is often required to help administer rationing programs, which allocate scarce supplies according to each customer's purchase history. Since shortages are usually temporary, though, sellers have to be sensitive to their customers' problems so they will not lose customers when the shortage is over. Consequently, account management policies must treat all customers fairly, minimize conflict, and maintain the firm's competitive position for the future.

Growing social concern about the possible negative impacts of products and production processes on the natural environment also has important implications for marketing and sales programs. This is increasingly true for firms that sell to organizations as well as for manufacturers of consumer goods. For instance, countries in the European Economic Community have passed legislation requiring manufacturers to take back, and either reuse or recycle, materials used in packaging and shipping their products.

Summary: Impact of the External Environment

Keeping a close watch on, and attempting to forecast changes in, the external environment as a basis for formulating marketing and sales plans is easier said than done. Many examples exist of well-executed sales and marketing programs that came to grief because one or more elements of the environment changed unexpectedly.

A classic example is the *Encyclopaedia Britannica*. First published 225 years ago in Edinburgh, Scotland, Britannica's sales peaked at $650 million, with profits of $40 million, in 1990. During the early 1990s, competitors entered the market with CD-ROM encyclopedia packages at prices ranging from $99 to $395. Britannica's management failed to foresee or to respond to this threat by either adopting the new technology or altering the firm's traditional direct selling strategy. Instead, the company continued to sell only hardbound sets of encyclopedias priced at $1,500 through its 2,300-person direct sales force. By 1994, seven million U.S. households had purchased CD-ROM encyclopedias, Britannica had reduced its sales force by more than half, its sales had declined drastically, and the firm was in financial trouble. Its business is now focused on the Internet and the delivery of information online.[8]

Newspapers now find themselves in a similar situation, as Generation Y clearly prefers receiving their news online instead of the old fashioned print way over morning coffee. In 2006, online media outlets topped newspapers in classified advertising dollars for the first time. Major newspapers such as *The Wall Street Journal, New York Times,* and *USA Today* are all responding by revamping their Web sites, filling them with exclusive content and adding more blogs and multimedia features.[9]

Part of the reason for such failures to predict changes in the environment is that many companies do not use sophisticated techniques for environmental scanning and forecasting. Environmental scanning and forecasting within business firms occur primarily in response to current crises rather than in an attempt to identify future threats and opportunities, and their use of these techniques likely varies depending on the level of volitility in their environment.

INTERNAL (ORGANIZATIONAL) ENVIRONMENT

The policies, resources, and talents of the organization also make up a very important part of the marketer's environment. Sales managers may have some influence over higher level organizational factors due to their participation in planning processes, but in the short run, sales programs must be designed to fit within organizational situations and limitations. The variables in the **internal (organizational) environment** can be grouped into six broad categories: (1) goals, objectives, and culture; (2) human resources; (3) financial resources; (4) production and supply chain capabilities; (5) service capabilities; and (6) research and development and technological capabilities. These variables are portrayed in Exhibit 1.4.

Goals, Objectives, and Culture

Successful management of customer relationships begins with top management's specification of a company mission and objectives that create a customer-centric organization. As

EXHIBIT 1.4
**Components of the
internal environment**

the company mission and objectives change, customer management approaches must be adjusted accordingly. A well-defined mission together with a successful corporate history and top management's values and beliefs leads to development of a strong **corporate culture.** Such cultures shape the attitudes and actions of employees and help determine the kinds of plans, policies, and procedures salespeople and their managers can implement.

Periodically, *Sales & Marketing Management* magazine, a major trade publication covering the selling industry, publishes a special report on America's 25 best sales forces. Firms that have appeared regularly on the list include Baxter International (health care), Cisco Systems (information technology), Charles Schwab (financial services), and General Mills (consumer products). The common thread among these and other top-performing sales organizations is a culture, embraced from top management to all facets of the firm, that focuses on getting close, and staying close, to the customer. The customer-centric culture of these firms is manifest through the mission, goals, and objectives they work to achieve. In 2007, the HR Chally Group issued its report on best practices of sales organizations, "The Chally World Class Sales Excellence Research Report." This report cites "establishing a customer-driven culture" as the first and foremost priority for high-performance selling firms in the twenty-first century.[10]

We have already mentioned the central role of ethics and legal considerations in selling today. Much of what drives ethical behavior in sales organizations is the tone set by upper management, as well as the overall culture of the firm.

Human Resources

Modern sales organizations are highly complex and dynamic enterprises, as are their customers' firms. The sheer number of people in many sales organizations, together with the widely varying needs in terms of key success factors in relationship selling creates challenges. In view of the difficulties involved in recruiting highly qualified people for sales positions and the often-lengthy training programs needed to bring new salespeople up to speed on knowledge and skills, it is often difficult to expand a sales force rapidly to take advantage of new products or growing markets. In some cases, however, it may be possible for a firm to compensate for a lack of knowledgeable employees by utilizing outside agencies or specialists on a fee-for-service or commission basis. For example, many companies use distributors when entering new markets, particularly foreign markets, because entering the market can be accomplished so much more quickly by utilizing preexisting sales forces.

Financial Resources

An organization's financial strength influences many aspects of its customer relationship initiatives. It can constrain the firm's ability to develop new value-adding products as well as the size of its promotional budget and sales force. Companies sometimes must take drastic measures, such as merging with a larger firm, to obtain the financial resources necessary to realize their full potential in the marketplace. For example, Procter & Gamble and Gillette's merger in the highly competitive consumer health products sector provided the latter's product line the benefits of the more extensive global supply chain expertise of the former. Often selling firms and buying firms will form their own partnerships and alliances that create financial benefits for both.

Production and Supply Chain Capabilities

The organization's production capacity, the technology and equipment available in its plants, and even the location of its production facilities can influence the relationship selling initiative. A company may be prevented from expanding its product line or moving into new geographic areas because it does not have the capacity to serve increased demand or because transportation costs make the product's price uncompetitive. Vendors doing business with Wal-Mart are expected to fulfill orders within 24 hours and to deliver the goods to the Wal-Mart warehouses within a two-hour assigned appointment window. Suppliers that don't meet this requirement pay Wal-Mart for every dollar of lost margin. It is no wonder Wal-Mart's vendors are willing to invest the necessary capital to tie their information systems directly in with Wal-Mart's systems so the whole ordering and fullfillment process can be handled seamlessly and at maximum speed. As another example of supply chain efficiency but on the e-commerce side, CEO Jeff Bezos at amazon.com developed a network of distribution centers nationwide long before Amazon's sales volume was sufficient to financially support the warehouse capacity, principally because he wanted to ensure seamless distribution and service after the sale and avoid inventory stockouts.

Service Capabilities

Delivering a high level of service quality is an important organizational capability. Firms that provide great service typically enjoy a strong competitive advantage in the marketplace and make it difficult both for (1) other firms to compete for the same customers and (2) customers to switch to competitor sales organizations, often despite price advantages competitors may have.[11]

Research and Development and Technological Capabilities

An organization's technological and engineering expertise is a major factor in determining whether it will be an industry leader or follower in both the development of value-adding products and high-quality service delivery. Excellence in engineering and design can also serve as a major promotional appeal in a firm's marketing and sales programs, as customers are attracted to innovators and industry leaders. Some companies are investing heavily in technology, particularly technology that can help meet relationship selling objectives. In such cases, the firm's salespeople can communicate the R&D and technological sophistication to customers as important value-adding aspects of the company and its products. This capability helps avoid the trap of overrelying on price to get the sale.

IMPACT OF THE ENVIRONMENT: THE HP EXPERIENCE

In recent years HP (Hewlett-Packard) has embarked on a reinvention of its culture, structure, and processes. This has resulted in HP overtaking Dell as the number one seller of personal computers. HP's initiative was in recognition of the number and magnitude of **discontinuous changes** in the computer industry—environmental changes so different from what has been experienced before that firms competing in that space must take drastic strategic action in order to be successful. Their experiences illustrate several important points about how factors in the environment influence marketing and sales management decisions and programs.

1. To be successful, a firm's marketing plans must be adapted to the influences and constraints imposed by both the external and internal corporate environments. As those environments change, appropriate adjustments must be made in the firm's marketing strategy.

    Rapid technological and competitive changes in HP's external environment forced the firm to respond with a corporate reinvention. HP has restructured itself in order to give more autonomy and flexibility to its various divisions or strategic business units (SBUs). Internal organizational changes within HP—including the creation of sales teams that gave the account manager full product line responsibility—facilitated the company's ability to effectively implement its new strategy without having to endure a lengthy review and approval process.

2. A firm's sales program is only one part of an integrated marketing communication strategy. As changes are made in other parts of the marketing strategy, the sales program must be adjusted if it is to remain effective.

    HP's new marketing strategy would have been difficult to implement effectively within the confines of its old geographical sales force structure. In order to sell open system solutions to customers' problems, sales reps had to develop a more in-depth understanding of individual customers and the specific problems they face. Thus, major changes in sales policies and programs—such as the switch to an industry-focused organization structure where each sales rep specializes in a single industry, as well as increased sales training to improve the reps' knowledge of target industries—were crucial prerequisites for the ultimate success of HP's new marketing approach. But customers' needs for all of HP's product lines led to another shift, from single-line salespeople to a sales team managed by an account manager.

3. Regardless of how well conceived a sales program is or how well it is integrated into a firm's overall marketing strategy, its implementation depends on the willingness and ability of individual members of the sales force to carry out its policies and procedures. Factors in the external and corporate environments can directly influence a salesperson's actions in the field and the rep's ability to achieve the desired level of performance. HP's sales force largely embraced the change that gave them single-industry territories, for they were able to leverage knowledge about one customer when calling on another. When the company reorganized and gave each rep full product-line responsibility, the move worked in part because most salespeople wanted to serve each customer with a full line of products.

Summary

Sales organizations and their managers have been affected by a number of important changes in recent years. It is critical for students of selling and sales management to fully understand these trends and how they affect the success of the sales effort. In this book, we identify and develop three key themes throughout: innovation, technology, and leadership. Along with these themes, we identify important global and ethical issues for twenty-first century sales managers.

Effective management requires a solid understanding of the activities one is trying to manage. Unfortunately, many people have misconceptions about the selling process, the activities carried out by salespeople, and the personal characteristics necessary for a successful career in professional sales. In part, these misconceptions arise because different types of selling jobs involve different kinds of tasks and require different skills and abilities from the people who do them.

Sales management involves three interrelated processes: (1) formulation of a sales program, (2) implementation of the sales program, and (3) evaluation and control of the sales program. An overarching model of sales management was presented for students' initial perusal in this introductory chapter. Each major section of the book elaborates one process. The remaining parts of this book describe the variables and sales management activities involved in each of these processes: Part One is focused on formulation, Part Two on implementation, and Part Three on evaluation and control.

Environmental factors that can impact sales management are grouped into the two broad categories of external and internal (organizational) environments. The external environment includes the following elements: (1) economic, which includes competition; (2) legal and political; (3) technological; (4) social and cultural, focused on ethics; and (5) natural. The internal environment includes these elements related to the organization itself: (1) goals, objectives, and culture; (2) human resources; (3) financial resources; (4) production and supply chain capabilities; (5) service capabilities; and (6) research and development and technological capabilities. Gaining a thorough and accurate picture of these environmental influencers is essential to successful sales management in the twenty-first century.

Key Terms

transactional selling	external environment	internal (organizational)
relationship selling	*economic*	environment
leading versus managing	*legal and political*	corporate culture
sales management	*technological*	discontinuous change
sales management process	*social and cultural*	
formulation	*natural*	
implementation	ethics	
evaluation and control	demarketing	

Breakout Questions

1. Does the Internet replace the need for salespeople? In what situations is the Internet most likely to replace salespeople? What characteristics of a situation would make the Internet least likely to replace salespeople?

2. A number of organizations that did not consider marketing part of their business activities in the past have found the need to begin to market their services. Nowhere is this more prevalent than in the nonprofit community. While not "selling" a product or service, public service organizations such as the Red Cross have developmental

officers who market the organization in the community. How might you "sell" a public service organization in the community? What is different about this versus selling for a for-profit enterprise? What would be your goals and how would you accomplish them?

3. Salespeople are also called *sales representatives*. Define the term *representative*. Whom does the salesperson represent? Why is it important to recognize the different groups that salespeople represent? How does this recognition of who is represented influence sales management?

4. What do you think the differences would be in the selling process for the following products and services? How would managing the sales process differ for each?

- Selling Planter's Peanuts to your grocer.
- Selling Planter's Peanuts to Southwest Airlines to be given to their customers.
- Selling telecommunications equipment costing $1 to $2 million to the U.S. government.
- Selling telecommunications equipment costing $1 to $2 million to General Electric.
- Selling five-year leases on prime retail space in Beverly Hills.

5. Describe the typical salesperson as illustrated in movies, books, and television shows. Why does that image exist as the stereotypical salesperson (be specific)? What role does ethics play in perpetuating the stereotype? Whose responsibility is it to see that a company's code of ethics is carried out?

6. Changes in the technological environment have the potential to significantly affect the activities of the sales force. Automation can offer the sales force a competitive advantage—if the sales force is motivated to use computers and other technological methods that are part of automation. What steps should management adopt to ensure that the sales force buys into the company's automation system? Especially, what can the sales organization do to promote technology use by more senior salespeople (senior in age, that is)?

Leadership Challenge: The New Kid on the Block

Grace Hart had established herself as an exceptional salesperson at Digital Medical Instruments (DMI). Only seven years out of college, she had become a sales manager at DMI; then Medical Imaging Technologies (MIT) sought her out to become one of five regional sales managers. MIT was a much larger company than DMI, and Grace knew this was a great opportunity. After several weeks of considering all the options, she took the job at MIT.

She faced several challenges as she arrived for her first day at MIT. Although she had experience in medical imaging equipment, she was not familiar with the specifics of MIT's product line or customers. More significant, Grace did not know many of MIT's sales force, including the 60 salespeople or the three district sales managers in her region. Sales in this region had not been keeping pace with the growth in other parts of the country, and senior management at MIT believed it was time for major changes. They had passed over the district sales managers and gone outside the company to hire Grace.

Grace is considering her first moves at MIT. She knows there is much to learn, and she also knows senior management is expecting sales to increase in her region. As "the new kid on the block," she knows that everyone will be evaluating her. People will be watching to assess her strengths and weaknesses. Salespeople and managers want to know what kind of boss Grace will be. Senior management expects things to improve in the region quickly and have given Grace a great deal of latitude to make whatever changes she feels are necessary. Much is riding on how Grace handles this new job. Her ability to manage the sales force effectively is critical to her success.

Questions

1. You are Grace Hart. What are the first three things you would want to learn about the sales environment at MIT?

2. Consider the elements of sales force management talked about in Chapter 1. What area of sales management do you think would be *most difficult* for Grace to learn about as "the new kid on the block"?

3. What advice would you give to Grace on her first day at MIT?

Role Play: Inventron Pharmaceuticals

Situation

Karen Tedesco just returned from a three-day trip and picked up a voice mail in her home office from Cindy Cherry, regional sales manager for Inventron Pharmaceuticals. Karen is the district sales manager for the states of Oklahoma, Arkansas, Texas, and Louisiana. Cindy is in charge of all of Inventron's operations west of the Mississippi River. Inventron is a relatively small, specialty pharmaceutical manufacturer with production facilities in Morristown, New Jersey. Its products focus on an array of medicines for the dog and cat market, and its primary customers are veterinarians. Throughout the United States, Inventron has two sales regions, 12 sales districts, and 124 salespeople.

Cindy's message presents a nice opportunity for Karen to help Inventron with some planning for next year's business. Inventron's VP of sales, Hugh Butts, has delegated the task of developing an external environmental analysis to Cindy but with the caveat that she bring one of her best district managers into the process. Cindy has selected Karen for this role. The instructions are for Cindy and Karen to individually prepare a list of the external environmental factors they believe will impact the small animal pharmaceutical business next year and explain why each factor is important and how it might affect business. Then Cindy will travel from the regional office in Denver to Karen's office in Dallas to meet, compare their lists, and come to concensus about what to send to Hugh as input on the plan.

Characters in the Role Play

Karen Tedesco, district manager for Inventron Pharmaceuticals

Cindy Cherry, regional manager for Inventron Pharmaceuticals (Karen's boss)

Assignment

Break into pairs, with one student playing each character. It doesn't matter what the actual gender mix of your pair is. First, work separately to come up with a list of external environmental factors likely to impact Inventron and its industry over the next year, why each factor is important, and how it might affect business. Then get together and role-play the meeting between Karen and Cindy. Share your lists, being certain you discuss each of the proposed factors. After discussing each factor, come to a concensus on a final list of factors that you would be comfortable forwarding to the VP of sales.

Minicase: iTeam, Inc.

iTeam, Inc., is a high-tech company based in Walnut Creek, California (26 miles northeast of San Francisco) that produces, markets, and sells computer systems, computer peripherals, and other consumer electronic products to corporate customers and electronics retailers.

iTeam, formed as an entrepreneurial start-up by CEO Andrew Taylor along with several of his classmates from business school, has had a charmed life so far. With aggressive pricing and a tremendous internal Research and Development group, iTeam has grown exponentially in its first five years of existence and has customers throughout the United States. However, a more challenging reality has begun to set in.

At first, iTeam sold its products only locally and on a relatively small scale. But now that it has expanded to selling nationally, it is in direct competition with larger, global firms. Because of manufacturing and supply chain efficiencies, these competitors offer equal or lower prices than iTeam with greater product diversity and more value-added services. Although iTeam's past success has been based on lower-than-market prices, it now finds that its costs have increased and that profit margins have shrunk to the point that it cannot price its products any lower.

In addition, sales have been difficult to predict because the high-tech market has fluctuated and corporate high-tech spending has been erratic. Although the high-tech economy has been forecast to increase in the coming two years, Andrew Taylor is skeptical.

iTeam has attempted to keep costs low by establishing call centers in India and Ireland and obtaining most of its supply components from China. Although this overseas outsourcing has reduced costs, unfortunately it has also reduced product quality. The firm has also come under fire in the media for laying off U.S. employees in favor of outsourcing the work to foreign workers, and iTeam's board of directors is pressuring Andrew to be more socially responsible in this area.

To further complicate matters, it has come to Andrew's attention that the Environmental Protection Agency has proposed regulations that will greatly restrict levels of lead and mercury levels in electronics products and that will impose disposal obligations on producers of electronic goods.

Andrew thinks the answer to iTeam's growing pains is to expand sales by selling to customers in Europe and Asia. However, such an expansion will require an investment in an expanded supply chain, including new distribution channels and the development of relationships with new customers and suppliers. It will also require changes in iTeam's manufacturing system in order to increase the firm's production capacity.

Most important, iTeam's sales force may need to be developed as well. iTeam grew so quickly that it never established a formal sales program. Consistent with Andrew's personal philosophy of "Who says there is no 'I' in 'team'?", iTeam has been pretty informal in managing its sales force, deferring mostly to aggressive individual salesperson effort and commission-based pay. Also, because of iTeam's former price advantage, the sales reps have never really had to develop relationships with customers or retail partners to generate sales—price seemed to be enough to keep customers satisfied.

Andrew Taylor and iTeam have much to consider as they determine how to move into the future.

Questions

1. What aspects of the external environment are most likely to affect iTeam, Inc.'s future planning, and what impact might each factor have?

2. What aspects of the internal (organizational) environment at iTeam are most likely to affect its future planning, and what impact might each factor have?

3. What advice can you give to Andrew Taylor with respect to iTeam's future sales program? In your opinion, what steps should he take, given the external environment and the company's current circumstances?

Suggested Readings

Bosworth, Michael T., and John R. Holland. *Customer Centric Selling.* New York: McGraw-Hill, 2004.

Jones, Eli, Steven P. Brown, Andris A. Zoltners, and Barton A. Weitz. "The Changing Environment of Selling and Sales Management." *Journal of Personal Selling & Sales Management* 25 (Spring 2005), pp. 105–11.

Kashyap, Vishal, Aurea Helena Puga Riberiro, Anthony Asare, and Thomas G. Brashear. "Developing Sales Force Relationalism: The Role of Distributive and Procedural Justice." *Journal of Personal Selling & Sales Management* 27 (Summer 2007) pp. 235–45.

Menguc, Bulent, Sang-Lin Han, and Seigyoung Auh. "A Test of a Model of New Salespeople's Socialization and Adjustment in a Collectivist Culture." *Journal of Personal Selling & Sales Management* 27 (Spring 2007) pp. 149–67.

Robertson, Bruce, Andrea L. Dixon, and David Curry. "An Agenda for Selling and Sales Management Research: Using the Financial Industry's Forward Thinkers for Insight." *Journal of Personal Selling & Sales Management* 26 (Summer 2006) pp. 293–303.

Part **One**

Formulation of a Sales Program

The environment	Marketing strategy	Sales management activities

External environment
- Economic
- Legal and political
- Technological
- Social and cultural
- Natural

Internal (organizational) environment
- Goals, objectives, and culture
- Human resources
- Financial resources
- Production and supply chain capabilities
- Service capabilities
- R&D and technological capabilities

- Target markets
- Products
- Pricing policies
- Distribution channels
- Promotion policies
- Personal selling
- Advertising
- Sales promotion

Account management policies

Sales force organization

Sales planning
- Demand forecasts
- Quotas and budgets

Deployment
- Territory design
- Routing

The formulation of a sales program requires five major sets of decisions:

1. How can the personal selling effort be best adapted to the company's environment and integrated with the other elements of the firm's marketing strategy? In addition, how does personal selling fit into a strategy of adding value to the relationship between the company and the customer?

2. How can various types of potential customers best be approached, persuaded, and serviced? In other words, what account management practices should be adopted?

3. How should the sales function be organized to call on and manage various types of customers as efficiently and effectively as possible? How are teams created to handle specific customer issues? Who should be on those teams?

4. What level of performance can each member of the sales force realistically be expected to attain during the next planning period? Sales managers are involved in forecasting demand and setting quotas and budgets.

5. In view of the firm's account management practices and demand forecasts, how should the sales force be deployed? How should sales territories be defined? What is the best way for each salesperson's time to be allocated within a territory?

In Part One, we examine the decisions and activities involved in formulating a sales program. First, sales managers must gain a thorough understanding about sellers and buyers in business-to-business markets, the topical focus of Chapter 2. In Chapter 3, we explore issues of selling and the sales function in the context of marketing management and strategy, and discuss customer relationship management (CRM), market orientation, and relationship selling. Chapter 4 examines alternative ways of organizing the sales force for success. Finally, Chapter 5 covers several key uses of information in sales force management including demand estimation and sales quotas, designing sales territories, and sales analysis.

Chapter Two

The Process of Selling and Buying

The Case for a Focus on the Sales Process

In the old world of selling, a salesperson departed the office in the morning and hopefully returned in the afternoon with newly signed contracts in his or her brief-case. As long as the contracts kept coming in, what happened between the salesperson's departure and return was of little consequence to sales management. Although this mode of selling was once an acceptable way of life, it has fallen out of favor with sales management for at least two good reasons:

1. This is not a teachable, repeatable way to sell. Consequently, it cannot be lever-aged across a sales force or used to train new salespeople when they come on board. If sales management has no definition of how they want their salespeople to sell, then their only means of improvement is to fire the least productive sales-people and roll the dice on the next. Formal sales processes allow a company to scale its sales force by teaching its salespeople how to succeed.

2. With no process steps or milestones, it is impossible to measure and manage the improvement of the sales force. If all a sales manager knows is the number of people who departed in the morning and the number of contracts that returned in the afternoon, there is no way to identify opportunities for improvement. For-mal sales processes are required to measure and manage a sales force.

World-class sales organizations understand this and strive to develop standard oper-ating procedures for their people to follow.

Sell How Your Customers Buy

Ultimately, it is the customer who decides whether or not a salesperson gets the sale. They usually award the prize to the salesperson that has been there with them dur-ing every step of their buying cycle, meeting customer need after customer need by presenting the right information at the right time. To win a sale then, a salesperson's sales process must match perfectly with the customer's buying process. The two should be mirror images.

All too often, though, sales forces define their sales processes from their own per-spective, not the customer's. This puts them at risk of calling on the wrong people, at the wrong time, with the wrong message. Inappropriate sales processes probably kill more sales than sales managers will ever know.

When formalizing sales processes, world-class sales forces view their actions from the customer's perspective. They design a way of selling that is reflective of the way their customer buys, not just the way they want to sell. The deck is therefore stacked in their favor when they compete with other salespeople who are making it up as they go along.

Clearly Define Your Selling Roles

The tasks of selling are becoming more complicated. Particularly in a business-to-business environment, any given sale may involve interactions with several different buyer types, such as an end-user, chief financial officer, business unit leader, etc. To address this reality, sales forces have been required to bring several corresponding seller types into these pursuits, such as an account manager, technical specialist, financial analyst, and others. This team approach to selling is very powerful, but it presents formidable challenges in coordinating the participants to avoid overlapping tasks or leaving tasks unattended.

World-class sales forces that engage in complex, team sales are careful to have clearly defined the roles and responsibilities for each and every team member. This helps to ensure that the customer's buying needs are being met by the proper type of seller, so they can proceed through their buying process without delay or frustration. It also avoids internal friction among the sellers, which lets sales executives manage instead of playing the role of arbitrator.

Source: HR Chally Group (2007), *The Chally World Class Excellence Research Report: The Route to the Summit.* Dayton, OH: HR Chally Group.

LEARNING OBJECTIVES

This chapter focuses on the process of selling and buying in the organizational marketplace. Many factors are driving the world of professional selling toward a relationship-based approach. This transformation has created a challenging, invigorating, and rewarding environment in which to pursue a career in selling.

Knowledge of the drivers of change in selling, the key success factors required in selling, the activities salespeople perform on the job, and the different kinds of selling jobs available go a long way toward helping a person make a decision if he or she might like to pursue selling as a career path. Successful salespeople always understand the roles that different individuals within the client company play in moving the relationship along, the buying decision process used by their clients, and how their clients go about making different types of purchases and how those differences impact the salesperson's approach to the client.

After reading this chapter you should be able to

- Recognize the key drivers of change in selling and sales management.

- Understand the best practices in selling that lead to exceeding customer expectations.

- Explain the historical basis for stereotypical views of selling in society.

- Point out a variety of reasons why sales jobs can be highly satisfying.

- Identify and explain key success factors for salesperson performance.
- Discuss and give examples of different types of selling jobs.
- List and explain the role of various participants in an organizational buying center.
- Describe the relationship between buying centers and selling centers and the nature of team selling.
- Outline the stages in organizational buyer decision making.
- Point out the nature of different organizational buying situations.

DRIVERS OF CHANGE IN SELLING AND SALES MANAGEMENT

The nature of selling has changed. Sales organizations are being reinvented to better address the needs of the changing marketplace. Six critical **drivers of change** have been identified in reinventing sales organizations so they can compete successfully in today's selling environment:

1. *Building long-term relationships with customers.* This includes assessing customer value and focusing on high-priority customers.

2. *Creating sales organizational structures that are more nimble and adaptable to the needs of different customer groups.* Leadership 2.1 shows how, by providing clarity of vision and process, the "new IBM" is freeing up its worldwide sales organization to become more flexible.

3. *Gaining greater job ownership and commitment from salespeople.* This can be accomplished by removing functional barriers within the organization and by leveraging the team experience.

4. *Shifting sales management style from commanding to coaching.* Or, put another way, today's sales managers must create an environment that allows salespeople to use their talents and abilities to successfully secure, build, and maintain relationships with profitable customers. While item 3 above implies that in the past, organizational structure was a common stumbling block to salesperson success, item 4 recognizes that sales managers themselves also are often guilty of blocking successful relationship selling. For selling to change, management of salespeople must also change accordingly.

5. *Leveraging available technology for sales success.* Clearly, salespeople today have more types of technological tools at their disposal than ever before. The sales organizations that make the best use of technology will have a strong competitive edge over others.

6. *Better integrating salesperson performance evaluation.* A real weakness of many sales organizations in the past was in how they evaluated and ultimately rewarded their salespeople. The move from transactional selling to relationship selling, coupled with the use of selling teams and a more coaching style of management, necessitates rethinking the performance evaluation and reward process for sales organizations. In Chapters 12 and 13, this critical topic will be discussed in the context of developing a more seamless performance management system that incorporates the full range of activities and outcomes relevant within sales jobs today.[1]

Leadership   IBM Is Becoming Nimble by Gaining Clarity   2.1

A key element of IBM CEO Sam Palmisano's remaking of their sales organization is to make the company more nimble. Nimble firms (1) constantly monitor and communicate with customers, (2) are proactive instead of reactive in meeting customer needs, (3) practice adaptive selling by carefully sensing customer needs in each interaction and adapting the form and message of the communication to those needs, and (4) are flexible at all times and open to creative and out-of-the-box solutions.

Palmisano has opened the door for IBM's sales organization to be more nimble by providing clarity of vision and direction via four major strategies:

- Salespeople don't work as individuals anymore. New tactics group them into teams to serve selected large customers, clusters of customers, or small and medium-sized customers. The system decreases confusion for the customer and allows salespeople to drive sales through the pipeline faster.

- Every salesperson follows the same seven-step selling method to ensure consistency. The strategy keeps everybody—from field reps to Palmisano—on the same page regarding sales leads.

- One universal reporting system takes the guesswork out of numbers. Instead of wasting valuable meeting time debating whose calculations are correct, the system makes sure all numbers are consistent. Meetings are devoted to coaching, coming up with solutions to problems, and discussing leads.

- The sales organization strictly adheres to a cadence of meetings, which allows sellers to be in the field more because they are expected to attend only one 30-minute meeting with their direct managers each week. The meeting structure ensures the flow of information, decisions, and coaching among sellers, managers, and executives.

Palmisano, his senior executive team, and in fact IBM's sales organization as a whole are committed to being the best sales organization in the world. They aim to do this by focusing on understanding and serving their customers through value-added selling. Big Blue is going to be a great sales force to watch over the next several years as they execute these new strategies.

Source: Erin Strout, "Blue Skies Ahead?" *Sales & Marketing Management,* March 2003, pp. 25–29. Reprinted with permission.

OVERVIEW OF SELLING AS A CAREER

Recruiting and keeping excellent salespeople can be difficult. One reason is that many college students hold somewhat negative attitudes toward selling as a potential career as a result of stereotypes based on old styles of selling where salespeople used "hard sell" techniques to get buyers to purchase products they didn't really need.

The old style of selling is embodied in several icons of American media—one from a classic play, one from a classic television show, and two from classic movies. In his Pulitzer Prize–winning play *Death of a Salesman,* Arthur Miller immortalized old-style selling through the play's principal character Willie Loman (as in "low man" on the totem pole of life). Poor Willie left for long sales trips on the road at the beginning of every week, returned a tired and disheartened peddler at the end of every week, and worked his customers based "on a smile and a shoeshine." His family was collapsing in his absence, his own self-esteem was at rock bottom, his customers were defecting to other vendors at an alarming rate, and there seemed to be no hope of improvement for Willie on any front. This sad, demoralizing image of selling, while certainly fine in the context of dramatic license, has been emblazoned on every kid who ever read or acted in the play in junior high or high school.

Then in the late 1970s along came the television show *WKRP in Cincinnati* about a lovable cast of characters employed in a third-rate rock-and-roll FM radio station. One character who was arguably not so lovable was Herb Tarleck, sales manager for WKRP.

Throughout the series, Herb was played as a back-slapping, white-shoe-and-polyester-suit-wearing buffoon who exhibited questionable ethics and made sales only through pure luck. The show was a top draw during much of its four-year run from 1978–1982, and Herb's image has never fully vanished from view because of reruns on cable channels.

Two classic movies also provide negative portrayals of selling practices. An image of high-power real estate selling was emblazoned on the public psyche in David Mamet's Pulitzer Prize–winning play *Glengarry Glen Ross,* which came out on the screen in 1992 featuring a stellar cast including Al Pacino and Jack Lemmon. The film has become a cult favorite as a movie and DVD rental. In it, times are tough at Premier Properties, a boiler-room-style real estate sales company. Shelly "the machine" Levene and Dave Moss are veteran salesmen, but only Ricky Roma is on a hot sales streak. Sales leads for the new Glengarry property development could turn everything around, but the "front office" is holding the leads back until the "losers" prove themselves on the street. Then someone decides to take matters into his own hands, stealing the Glengarry leads and leaving everyone else wondering who did it. The verbal exchange among these men desperate to make sales is riveting.

A second classic movie portraying sales stereotypes is 2000's *Boiler Room.* In it, an overly ambitious group of schemers operate an illegal stock brokerage firm. Much of the action revolves around cold-calling prospects from the telephone book, trying to get "pigeons" to invest in mostly bogus stocks. Their success-at-any-price mentality and lifestyle redefines the notion of ill-gained wealth and disregard for ethics.

Images of salespeople personified by Willie Loman, Herb Tarleck, and the other characters have become embedded in the American culture. Even in countries outside the United States, people harbor similar stereotypical images of American salespeople. It's not an image that is entirely undeserved, as some unprofessional and unethical salespeople always have and always will exist (just as unprofessional people exist in any profession). In the profession of selling, we seem to consistently have to prove our value to society just a little more than other professions. But the effort is worth it to those who love the profession, because there's no doubt about it: Sales jobs are important to society, they're challenging to those who occupy them, and they are also potentially one of the most rewarding career tracks one can take.

Why Sales Jobs Are So Rewarding

For most professional salespeople, it is precisely the complexity and challenge of their jobs that motivate them to perform at a high level and provide a sense of satisfaction with their choice of careers. A number of satisfaction surveys over the years have found generally high levels of job satisfaction among professional salespeople across a broad cross section of firms and industries. Although these surveys did find some areas of dissatisfaction, that unhappiness tended to focus on the policies and actions of the salesperson's firm or sales manager, not on the nature of the sales job itself.[2]

Why are so many professional salespeople generally quite satisfied with their jobs? Some attractive aspects of selling careers include the following:

1. **Autonomy,** or the freedom of action and opportunities for personal initiative.

2. Multifaceted and challenging activities as part of the job, **sales activities** that will be addressed later in this chapter.

3. Financial rewards—salespeople hired right out of college, for example, tend to start at higher salaries than most other professions and also tend to keep up well during their careers with the compensation of their peers outside of sales (due to the nature of sales compensation being linked directly to performance).

4. Favorable working conditions, often via telecommuting with a virtual office, and with less minute-to-minute direct supervision than most other careers.

5. Excellent opportunities for career development and advancement.

High Job Autonomy

A common complaint among workers in many professions is that they are too closely supervised. They complain about the micromanagement of bosses and about rules and standard operating procedures that constrain their freedom to do their jobs as they see fit. Salespeople, on the other hand, spend most of their time working directly with customers with no one around to supervise their every move. They are relatively free to organize their own time and to get the job done in their own way as long as they show good results.

The freedom of a selling career appeals to people who value their independence, who are confident they can cope with most situations they will encounter, and who like to show personal initiative in deciding how to get their job done. However, with this freedom comes responsibilities and potential pressures. Salespeople are responsible for managing their existing customer relationships and developing new ones. Although no one closely supervises the salesperson's behavior, management usually keeps close tabs on the *results* of that behavior: sales volume, quota attainment, expenses, and the like. As reflected in Leadership 2.1, Big Blue is watching closely the results from its salespeople! To be successful, then, salespeople must be able to manage themselves, to organize time wisely, and to make the right decisions about how to do the job.

High Job Variety

If variety in a job is the spice of life, sales jobs are hot peppers. Most people soon become bored doing routine tasks. Fortunately, boredom is seldom a problem among professional salespeople, as sales positions tend to be high in **job variety.** Each customer has different needs and problems for which the salesperson can work to develop unique solutions. Those problems are often anything but trivial, and a salesperson must display insight, creativity, and analytical skill to close a sale. Many sales consultants expect creative problem solving to become even more important to sales success in the future. Innovation 2.2 provides ideas on developing a more creative approach to selling.

Opportunities for Rewards

To make the sales job even more interesting, as we learned in Chapter 1 the internal and external environment is constantly changing. Salespeople must frequently adjust their sales presentations and other activities to shifts in economic and competitive conditions. At IBM under Sam Palmisano, salespeople have had to shift their emphasis from selling *products* to selling *integrated business solutions.* In fact, IBM has recast its focus from that of a product manufacturer to a broad-based information technology consultancy. For many people in the selling profession, variety and challenge are the most rewarding aspects of their jobs. Sales jobs offer great opportunity for developing a sense of accomplishment and opportunities for personal growth. As we will see in Chapter 6, these are important sources of **intrinsic rewards** and satisfaction—that is, rewards inherent to satisfaction derived from elements of the job or role itself, as opposed to **extrinsic rewards,** which are rewards bestowed on the salesperson by the company.

Make no mistake, though, selling can be a very lucrative profession in terms of extrinsic rewards as well. More important, the growth of a salesperson's earnings—particularly, the earnings of someone receiving a large proportion of incentive pay—is determined largely by performance, and often no arbitrary limits are placed on the maximum amount a salesperson can earn. Consequently, a salesperson's compensation can grow faster and

Innovation   How to Create Your Own Creativity   2.2

The ability to be creative when prospecting, working with customers, and developing solutions has always been an important aspect of salesperson success. Being creative will allow you to provide your customers with new and innovative ways to solve their problems or improve their situation. Creativity does not come easily to many salespeople. Barriers to creativity arise every day, and your ability to identify and conquer these ever-present obstacles will help you increase your sales success. Potential barriers include the following:

- *Routine* can be one of the most common barriers to your personal creativity. Following the same routine every day will certainly not stimulate you, potentially leading to a serious lack of creativity and innovation in both your career and personal life. Some routine is definitely necessary, even inevitable and desirable, but too much of it will certainly not help your creative juices flow. Try varying the ways and times you do things in your every day schedule.

- *Fatigue* is another highly common barrier to creativity in salespeople. Giving your all every day to meet and exceed customer expectations is admirable. However, you need to take some serious downtime if you want to avoid burnout. Burnout is not conducive to stimulating your creativity. Take time to play. During this playtime you will find your creative juices will flow. You are likely to find an elusive answer to a customer's problem when you're not at work, and when you least expect it.

- Negative thoughts—*pessimism*—can also present barriers to your creative thinking ability. Thinking pessimistically is obviously destructive to anything, and your creative ability is no different. The optimist sees an opportunity in every problem, but the pessimist sees a problem in every opportunity. You undoubtedly know this, but knowing something and doing it are two different things. By approaching any sales problem with an open and positive mind, you are sure to stimulate your creativity exponentially. It will allow you to try new and inventive ways to solve your customers' problems and fulfill your customers' needs and wants.

- *Fear* is a concept that fits into the category of negative thinking. If you fear trying anything new in your sales activity, then you will most certainly fail to tap into your creative juices. Conquering your fear of using new ways to approach, help, or service your customers will help you conquer a serious and common barrier to creativity. It's up to you how you choose to face your fear, and if you face it with courage your ability to use your creativity will surely increase.

- Any *crisis* presents an interesting scenario for testing your creative ability. If you view a crisis as a phenomenal opportunity to tap into your creative abilities, then you are on the right track. Salespeople who fear crisis situations and fail to see them as chances to prevent the same problems from arising in the future are thwarting their own creativity. Creatively solving any crisis situation can also provide you with the possibility that new and creative ways of doing things may emerge from the current crisis.

- Unfortunately, *making excuses* is often a common practice among average or poor salespeople. Blaming your own failures on outside factors is just too easy. You must avoid doing this if you intend to maximize your sales performance and stimulate your creativity. Blaming your own shortcomings on factors such as a bad territory or your competition will do nothing for you, your sales performance, or your income. Take responsibility for your mistakes and your lost sales, and use what you've learned to creatively approach your customers' problems, needs, and wants.

An excellent way to stimulate your own creativity is to read and study the creativity of others. Biographies, success stories, articles, and examples can help inspire you to reach the higher levels of creativity other innovators have reached themselves.

You should not feel limited by just the above ideas. Develop and use your own personal methods that will allow you to cultivate your creativity. The key is simply to realize what exactly is harming your creativity and then conquer it. This will help improve your sales performance, as well as your own self-image, and this is priceless in creating your own creativity and your own successful future.

Source: Bill Brooks, "How to Create Your Own Creativity," *American Salesman*, October 2002, pp. 3–6.

reach higher levels than that of personnel in other departments at comparable levels in an organization.

Exhibit 2.1 shows compensation information gleaned from a survey of 2,644 sales and marketing executives in a variety of industries. It also illustrates how compensation varies among top-level, mid-level, and low-level sales performers. Of course, new college

EXHIBIT 2.1 Compensation trends in selling

Average salary for salespeople in 2006

	Total compensation	Base salary	Bonus plus commission
Executive	$147,824	$99,800	$48,440
Top performer	161,501	91,452	74,539
Mid-level performer	99,501	62,625	36,772
Low-level performer	70,994	47,702	20,835
Average	119,637	75,905	44,888

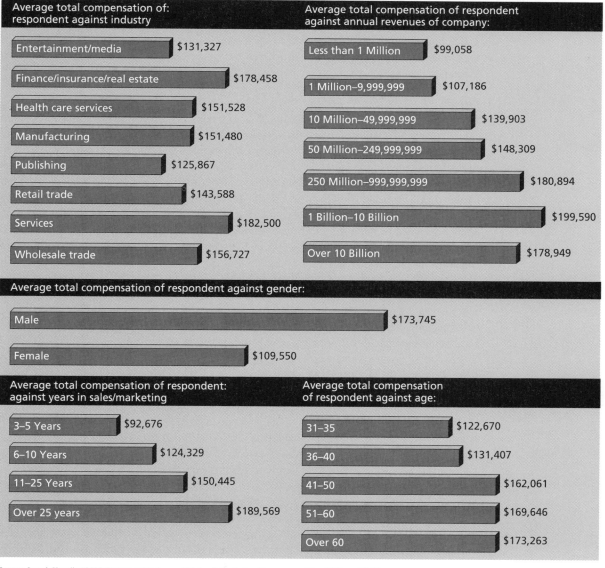

Average total compensation of: respondent against industry

- Entertainment/media — $131,327
- Finance/insurance/real estate — $178,458
- Health care services — $151,528
- Manufacturing — $151,480
- Publishing — $125,867
- Retail trade — $143,588
- Services — $182,500
- Wholesale trade — $156,727

Average total compensation of respondent against annual revenues of company:

- Less than 1 Million — $99,058
- 1 Million–9,999,999 — $107,186
- 10 Million–49,999,999 — $139,903
- 50 Million–249,999,999 — $148,309
- 250 Million–999,999,999 — $180,894
- 1 Billion–10 Billion — $199,590
- Over 10 Billion — $178,949

Average total compensation of respondent against gender:

- Male — $173,745
- Female — $109,550

Average total compensation of respondent: against years in sales/marketing

- 3–5 Years — $92,676
- 6–10 Years — $124,329
- 11–25 Years — $150,445
- Over 25 years — $189,569

Average total compensation of respondent against age:

- 31–35 — $122,670
- 36–40 — $131,407
- 41–50 — $162,061
- 51–60 — $169,646
- Over 60 — $173,263

Source: Joseph Kornik, "2007 Compensation Survey." *Sales & Marketing Management,* May 2007, pp. 27–39.

graduates will start out significantly below the top, but as one can see from Exhibit 2.1, the opportunity exists for considerable compensation growth based on performance.

Favorable Working Conditions

If the stereotypes of sales jobs addressed earlier were true, salespeople would be expected to travel extensively, live on big expense accounts, spend much of their time entertaining potential clients, and consequently have little time for home and family life. Such a situation represents a lack of balance between one's work life and family life such that work is encroaching on family—**work-family conflict.** Again, this is not an accurate description of the working conditions encountered by most salespeople. Some selling jobs require extensive travel, but the majority of salespeople can secure rewarding positions that allow them to be at home most every night. Indeed, with the increasing use of computer networks, e-mail, video conferencing, and the like, the trend for more than a decade has been for more and more salespeople to **telecommute.** That is, they work from a remote or **virtual office** such as out of the home and seldom even travel to their companies' offices.[3]

For all the advantages and attractiveness of telecommuting to the salesperson, as well as the efficiencies and cost-saving aspects to the sales organization, operating out of a virtual office does create a challenge for keeping the sales force fully socialized to the culture of the organization. Leadership 2.3 illustrates the benefits and organizational challenges a virtual office environment can create.

Moving up in the Organization

Given the wealth of knowledge about a firm's customers, competitors, and products—and the experience at building effective relationships—that a sales job can provide, it is not surprising that often CEOs such as Sam Palmisano at IBM come up through the sales ranks into the executive suite. Likewise, Jeff Immelt spent more than 20 years in various sales and marketing positions at General Electric before being named the successor to Jack Welch as CEO. Anne Mulcahy, president and CEO of Xerox, spent most of her 25 years at the company in sales. She advises that those who climb the corporate ladder from the sales rung need to be willing to take on non-sales-oriented assignments along the way to broaden their experience. Exhibit 2.2 provides advice for aspiring salespeople on how to improve the odds of one day becoming CEO.

Although salespeople are sometimes reluctant to give up their high-paying jobs to move into managerial positions, most firms recognize the importance of good managerial talent and reward it appropriately, particularly as a person reaches the top executive levels of the sales organization. Total compensation of more than $250,000 a year is not unheard of for national sales managers or vice presidents of sales in large firms.

Of course, many managerial opportunities are available to successful salespeople at lower levels of the corporate hierarchy as well, most obviously in sales management, product or brand management, and general marketing management. Several possible career tracks salespeople might follow are illustrated in Exhibit 2.3.

Promoting top salespeople into management can sometimes cause problems. Successful selling often requires different personal skills and abilities than does successful management. No guarantee exists that a good salesperson will also be a good sales manager. Also, successful salespeople have been known to refuse promotion to managerial positions—because they enjoy selling, or they can make more money in sales than in management, or both. Finally, recent trends toward corporate downsizing, flatter organizational structures, and cross-functional selling teams have changed the number and nature of managerial opportunities available for successful salespeople. As noted earlier in the chapter, the sales manager of the future is more likely to be a coach or team leader rather than an authority figure isolated in the upper reaches of a corporate hierarchy.

Leadership   Working from Home has Benefits, Challenges   2.3

Traffic surrounding Microsoft headquarters in Redmond, Wash., has become so congested that Washington State Governor Chris Gregoire nearly missed a 9 a.m. speech at the company's main campus one recent morning. Roads leading to the software maker simply weren't designed to handle the 35,000 commuters who report for work there each day. The gridlock that greeted Gregoire was just the latest reminder that Microsoft needs to tackle its commuter crisis—and quick.

So Microsoft has embarked on a program aimed at getting more employees to work from home and other off-site locales, joining the growing ranks of companies to catch the virtual-workplace wave. About 14 percent of the U.S. workforce gets its job done at a home office more than two days per week, says Charlie Grantham, executive producer of consulting firm Work Design Collaborative. That's up from 11 percent in 2004, and is set to grow to 17 percent by 2009.

Benefits of letting employees work from outside the office include keeping cars off the road, helping a company to bolster its green bona fides. But the practice can also foster employee retention, boost worker productivity, and slash real estate costs. At IBM, about 42 percent of the company's 330,000 employees work on the road, from home, or at a client location, saving the computer company about $100 million in real estate-related expenses a year. And virtual workers are about 16 percent more productive than office workers, according to Grantham's research.

For all the benefits of freeing workers from the office, drawbacks abound. First, not everyone wants to leave. Some fear they will step off the corporate ladder, while others need a busy environment to stay productive. Some managers are reluctant to scatter direct reports because keeping tabs on a virtual workforce can be harder than managing those close at hand. Some virtual workers can feel lonely, isolated, or deprived of vital training and mentoring. And communication breakdowns can impede innovation, trust, job satisfaction, and performance.

While many relish the chance to strike a better work-life balance by working from home, some are surprisingly resistant to being stationed outside the office. Of the approximately 25 percent of workers who could feasibly telecommute, less than half would do so more than two days a week, and 14 percent wouldn't telecommute at all, according to a survey conducted by research firm Rockbridge Associates and the Center for Excellence in Service at the University of Maryland's Robert H. Smith School of Business.

This reluctance may be fueled by fear that if they're out of sight, they will be out of mind, too. About 61 percent of global executives say they think telecommuters are less likely to advance in their careers, compared with employees in a traditional office setting, according to a survey conducted by Futurestep, a subsidiary of Korn/Ferry International.

Even workers who are eager to telecommute encounter hurdles. Many managers simply don't know how to manage a virtual workforce. "Projects fail, and companies assume that the workers can't do the work," says Colleen Garton, author of *Managing without Walls.* "But a high percentage of time, it's the manager." Over time, some employees begin to feel isolated, and virtual teams suffer from communication breakdown.

For virtual workers, there are plenty of ways to stay in touch, be it through e-mail, phone, or instant messaging. The trick, say experienced virtual workers, is helping managers know how employees like to communicate. IBM discovered that workers who spend three or more days without talking to a manager or colleagues start to feel disconnected. "Employees used to feel that IBM meant 'I'm By Myself,'" says Dan Pelino, general manager for health care and life sciences at IBM. "We learned that it was important for managers to understand that people feel that way and to create new collaborative environments and to ask what they're doing." IBM teams use tools that provide customizable online team spaces, or portals that can be tailored to a specific project—complete with calendars, task lists, discussion forums, and document libraries. IBM also provides a universal messaging service that lets executives give a single phone number to clients and colleagues. The service then forwards calls to wherever that executive might be located, be it at home, on cell phone, or in a so-called eMobility Center, one of the temporary offices set up by IBM in locations around the world.

Sometimes virtual workers simply miss that informal advice that colleagues give in an office setting. At IBM, the company has tried to make sure virtual workers receive needed coaching and mentoring. That can range from a sales exec getting advice from a colleague before an important sales call to more formal events at the office, where senior executives run roundtables.

As Microsoft establishes a formal virtual-work program, the company will likely have no trouble with the technology part of the equation. "Nearly 100 percent of our people have at some time worked virtually," says Lisa Brummel, senior vice-president of human resources at Microsoft. Indeed, the company makes many of the tools that virtual workers need. Yet, figuring out how to use that technology wisely in a virtual environment requires a bit more thought. Microsoft can just ask IBM's Pelino, who cautions, "We learned from trial and error." Until then, beware traffic jams in Redmond.

Source: Rachael King, "Working from Home: It's in the Details," *BusinessWeek,* February 12, 2007, *www.businessweek.com.*

EXHIBIT 2.2   From salesperson to CEO

With companies increasingly focusing on customer satisfaction and building long-term relationships with customers, they are tapping the sales and marketing ranks to fill CEO positions. Here are five steps you can take to place yourself in that swanky corner office:

- *Understand the whole business.* Sales and marketing people can become quite focused on just sales and marketing. Customer relationships are vital, but make sure to gain knowledge of how the rest of a company works. No executive can be CEO without being able to talk the talk about every aspect of a company.

- *Take on extra responsibilities.* In an effort to understand other parts of your business, spend time with other departments. Learn what it's like to be a factory worker or a researcher. Not only will this give you overall insight, but it will undoubtedly get you respect throughout the organization.

- *Show you want it.* Knowledge and experience are important for attaining the top spot, but proving your desire is vital. Let the people above you know your aspirations and constantly prove to them why you're qualified.

- *Gain self-awareness.* No CEO can be good at leading without fully understanding his or her strengths and weaknesses. Ask for honest assessments from your employees, your bosses, and your customers. Process that knowledge and improve on it.

- *Network, network, network.* You have to know the top people to become one of them. It may feel like a game at some point, but no executive can get the head job unless he or she continuously has meaningful conversations with top brass.

Source: Eilene Zimmerman, "So You Wanna Be a CEO," *Sales & Marketing Management,* January 2000, p. 33.

Key Success Factors in Selling

Although certainly many career advancement opportunities are available to the successful salesperson, not all sales recruits turn out to be successful. Some are fired, others quit and seek different careers, and some simply languish on the lower rungs of the sales hierarchy for a long time. Not everyone possesses the key success factors necessary to make it in selling, which raises the question, What personal characteristics and abilities are related to successful sales performance? This is somewhat difficult to answer because different types of sales jobs require different key success factors. Nevertheless, in this section we tackle the issue by presenting a sales managers' perspective on what factors are most important to successful selling today.

Given the shift in selling from transactional to more relationship-oriented approaches, it is reasonable to presume that the factors considered by sales managers to be critical to success in managing customer relationships would be different from those required in former

EXHIBIT 2.3   Possible career tracks for salespeople

EXHIBIT 2.4
**Sales managers'
importance ratings
of success factors
for professional
salespeople**

Source: Greg W. Marshall,
Daniel J. Goebel, and
William C. Moncrief, "Hiring
for Success at the Buyer–Seller
Interface," *Journal of Business
Research* 56 (2003), pp. 247–
55. Copyright 2003, reprinted
with permission from Elsevier.

Success Factors in Selling	Mean	S.D.
Highest level of importance		
Listening skills	6.502	0.683
Follow-up skills	6.358	0.772
Ability to adapt sales style from situation to situation	6.321	0.687
Tenacity-sticking with a task	6.107	0.924
Well organized	6.084	0.889
Verbal communication skills	6.047	0.808
Proficiency in interacting with people at all levels of a customer's organization	6.000	0.991
Demonstrated ability to overcome objections	5.981	1.085
Closing skills	5.944	1.109
Personal planning and time management skills	5.944	0.946
Proficiency in interacting with people at all levels of your organization	5.912	0.994
Negotiation skills	5.827	0.975
Dresses in appropriate attire	5.791	1.063
Empathy with the customer	5.723	1.074
Planning skills	5.685	0.966
Prospecting skills	5.673	1.209
Creativity	5.670	0.936
Ability to empathize with others	5.549	1.105
Skills in preparing for a sales call	5.526	1.219
Decision-making ability	5.502	1.023

Note: All items were scaled as follows: 1 = of no importance at all in hiring decisions, 7 = of the utmost importance in hiring decisions.
S.D. = standard deviation.

approaches to selling. These success factors take the form of skills, content knowledge, and other attributes sales managers look for when hiring a salesperson. Knowing what sales managers consider important to the success in a sales job is very useful information for anyone thinking of selling as a career choice.

A recent study asked 215 sales managers from a variety of industries to rate the importance of 60 key success factors developed from interviews with salespeople and sales managers.[4] The top 20 factors are presented in Exhibit 2.4.

Perusal of Exhibit 2.4 reveals some interesting trends in the key success factors in selling today. Let's examine the top 10 in more detail.

Listening Skills

The top-rated item is listening skills. Others have found through their own research that buyer–seller relationships are significantly strengthened when salespeople consistently employ effective listening skills, especially using *active* listening.[5] Ironically, selling courses and in sales training seminars almost always focus more on teaching salespeople to speak and write, but not to listen. Leadership 2.4 provides tips on how salespeople can develop successful active listening.

Follow-up Skills

A key difference between transactional and relationship selling approaches is the effort devoted by the salesperson to the ongoing maintenance and management of the relationship, especially between actually face-to-face encounters with the customer. Remember from Chapter 1 that relationship selling has three components: securing, building, and

Leadership   The Power of Active Listening   2.4

It is a commonly known fact that when you are listening intently to what someone is telling you, you are going to have a much more positive reaction when it is your turn to be heard. Unfortunately, salespeople seem to forget this all-important fact when they are attempting to convey the value of their product to their customer.

Actively listening to customers not only increases the effectiveness of the interaction between you and your customer, it also greatly increases your chance of making the sale. When you actively listen to the customer, you are better able to understand that customer's needs, and in turn, you are even better able to express the ways in which your product of service can benefit the customer.

Below are several tips that can help you to be a better active listener. If you pay attention and actively internalize these tips, you are already on your way to improving your selling skills.

1. *Open your mind and ears.* Switch off all negative thoughts and feelings about the person and be receptive to the messages he or she is giving. Don't allow your opinion of that person to interfere with your chances of eventually closing the sale. Perhaps you find the manner in which the person dresses or speaks to be distasteful. Don't let your disdain show itself, because you may not get past the first few minutes of your conversation.

2. *The importance of the first sentence.* Listen from the first sentence. You need to temporarily put aside or forget whatever it is that you're preoccupied with at the time of your interaction. If you do appear preoccupied, then your customer will know it and will surely feel unimportant. Any customer who feels unimportant to a salesperson will likely take his or her business elsewhere.

3. *Analyze.* Analyze what is being said. Don't ever try to figure out what the customer is going to say. You should pay attention to exactly what the customer is saying at that given moment. Even the slowest listeners can think faster than the fastest talkers. Again, think only about what is being said at the given time.

4. *Really listen.* Don't just "not talk." This means that you should not only appear to be listening—you should actively assist the customer in conveying his or her message. While your silence may cause you to appear to be listening, the customer may begin to feel as if you are not truly listening if you do not give some sort of feedback to what they are saying.

5. *Avoid interruptions.* Never interrupt, but always be interruptible. Interrupting your customer is not only rude, but is also very damaging to your chances of making the sale. Another extremely positive aspect of this tip involves the fact that your allowing the customer to feel that he or she is able to interrupt you is quite conducing to a feeling resembling a bond between the two of you. You appear to truly care about what he or she is saying, which can build a very positive relationship.

6. *Always ask questions.* A tip that goes hand-in-hand with the previous tip is to ask questions. To stimulate people to talk and help you clarify your understanding of what they mean, let them know you take them seriously by drawing them out. When you ask questions, you reinforce the idea that you are truly listening, not simply standing there, waiting for your turn to speak.

7. *Remember what is said.* This involves logging important points into your mental computer. You should take notes if you feel that such action is necessary. Also, try to make connections between apparently isolated remarks.

8. *Pay attention.* Blocking out interruptions and distractions are essential steps in becoming an effective active listener. You should concentrate so fully on what is being said that you don't even notice visual and audible distractions. When you allow these outside factors to steal your attention, your customer may possibly assume that your original attention was forced, thereby causing your chances of completing a sale to dramatically decrease.

9. *Respond to what is said.* An obvious aspect of actively listening to your customer is to be responsive. However, this tip is not so obvious to some salespeople because many never seem to follow this advice. For those who don't know what this means, you should get your whole body into listening and showing that you are paying attention. Look the person squarely in the eyes and use facial expressions.

10. *Relax.* The final and most important tip in the process of active listening is to stay cool. You should emanate complete relaxation through your entire conversation with the customer. Don't overreact to highly charged words and tones, because quite often people calm down after being allowed to vent their anger and frustration. Furthermore, your calm is likely to rub off on your customer, creating a conversation environment that is far less stressful.

Active listening is an important aspect of successful selling. If you are unable to convey your heartfelt interest in what your customer is saying, your chances of actually closing the sale and ultimately building a customer relationship are greatly decreased.

Source: Bill Brooks, "The Power of Active Listening," *Agency Sales,* December 2003, p. 47.

maintaining the relationship. EMC Corporation, a computer storage company, has a reputation for being obsessed with follow-up. Its sales and service teams work hard to anticipate and fix trouble before it's even recognized as a problem by the client. Anything from a toppled storage system to a change in the storage room's temperature causes the boxes to beam home warning messages and activate a response system from EMC reps, often before clients are even aware of the problem. Twenty-three remote locations around the globe position field reps to quickly follow up in person if necessary. In fact, CEO Mike Ruettgers even commits to responding in person within eight hours in the case of a severe service failure.

Ability to Adapt Sales Style from Situation to Situation

The practice of **adaptive selling** is the altering of sales behaviors during a customer interaction or across customer interactions based on perceived information about the nature of the selling situation.[6] This is analogous to the idea discussed earlier of being a nimble firm. Being adaptive allows the salesperson to better practice relationship selling by understanding customer needs and problems and by providing solutions.

Tenacity—Sticking with a Task

Nurturing customer relationships is a long-term proposition. Unlike forms of selling where the objective is to simply close a sale on one client and then move on to the next, managing relationships is a process that requires patience and the willingness to work with a client, often over long periods, before the potential benefits of the relationship to both parties are realized. Great salespeople always keep the big picture while also working on the details. This perspective facilitates tenacity and yields results that are worth the wait.

Well Organized

As the content and responsibilities of sales jobs have increased in complexity and buying organizations have become more complicated to navigate, the ability of a salesperson to skillfully prioritize and arrange the work has increased as a key success factor. Being well organized is a component of effective time and territory management.

Verbal Communication Skills

It is of value to note a second time that this factor, while obviously critical to sales success, *is* rated lower in importance by sales managers than listening skills. Salespeople must be great communicators.

Proficiency in Interacting with People at All Levels of a Customer's Organization

Selling today often involves communication and interaction with many people within the client firm besides the purchasing agent. Later in this chapter we will identify individuals in other roles within firms that may be just as, or even more, important to developing the relationship with the client firm than the buyer or purchasing agent.

Demonstrated Ability to Overcome Objections

A customer may have a number of concerns about any given purchase that the salesperson must work to overcome to the satisfaction of the customer. Objections are a natural and expected part of any sales process. By developing a trusting relationship over the long run with the client, and by working to negotiate win-win solutions, objections can be minimized.

Closing Skills

Obviously, in order for a salesperson to be successful, he or she has to generate business from clients.

Personal Planning and Time Management Skills

As with being well organized, being good at personal planning and managing your time will serve you well in a sales career. Nowadays, both these success factors have been augmented substantially through technology including PDAs, laptop computers, and e-mail.

SELLING ACTIVITIES

Given what we have learned so far about today's world of selling, including the key success factors sales managers believe are important, it should not be too surprising to learn that salespeople who work for IBM in developing client solutions spend a large portion of their time collecting information about potential customers, planning, coordinating the activities of other functional departments, and servicing existing customers, in addition to making sales calls. It is difficult to specify the full range of activities in which salespeople engage because they can vary greatly across companies and types of sales jobs. However, in one extensive study, a sample of 1,393 salespeople from 51 firms rated 121 possible activities on a seven-point scale according to how frequently they performed each activity during a typical month. These responses were examined statistically to identify the underlying categories of various activities. Ten different dimensions, or job factors, were identified.[7] These factors are shown in Exhibit 2.5, along with examples of the specific activities involved in each dimension.

One obvious conclusion from the study is that a salesperson's job often involves a wide variety of activities beyond simply calling on customers, making sales presentations, and taking orders. While the first two factors in Exhibit 2.5 are directly related to selling and order taking, factors 3 and 5 focus on activities involved in servicing customers after a sale is made (follow-up). Similarly, factors 4, 6, and 7 incorporate a variety of administrative duties, including such things as collecting and communicating information about customers to sales and marketing executives in the company, attending periodic training sessions, and helping to recruit and develop new salespeople. Finally, some salespeople also expend a good deal of effort helping to build distribution channels and maintain reseller support (factor 10).

Another study was conducted to update this original list of selling activities based on changes in the field of selling. Six activities dropped off and 49 new activities entered. The 49 new activities are organized in a matrix in Exhibit 2.6. The activities are grouped by either technology or nontechnology activities, and by five key content categories of communication, sales process, relationship-oriented, team-related, and database. The majority of new activities centered on the use of technology in communication (14 new activities, including e-mail, Internet, laptops, voice mail, fax, cellular phone, pager, and virtual office) and nontechnology-driven activities in the sales process (14 new activities, including adaptive selling, avoidance of litigation, sell value-added services, target key accounts, consultative selling, and sell unique competencies).[8]

Several important conclusions can be drawn from this research. First, salespeople have experienced rather substantial **job enlargement** over the past decade. That is, the sales role today is broader than in the past and contains substantially more activities. One hopes that the efficiencies gained from the technological advances help offset the sheer number of additional activities salespeople perform today. Second, on the technology side of new

EXHIBIT 2.5
Sales job factors and selected associated activities

Source: Adapted from William C. Moncrief III, "Selling Activity and Sales Position Taxonomies for Industrial Salesforces," *Journal of Marketing Research* 23 (August 1986), pp. 266–71.

1. **Selling function**
   Plan selling activities
   Search out leads
   Call potential accounts
   Identify decision makers
   Prepare sales presentation
   Make sales presentation
   Overcome objections
   Introduce new products
   Call new accounts
2. **Working with others**
   Write up orders
   Expedite orders
   Handle back orders
   Handle shipping problems
   Find lost orders
3. **Servicing the product**
   Learn about the product
   Test equipment
   Supervise installation
   Train customers
   Supervise repairs
   Perform maintenance
4. **Managing information**
   Provide technical information
   Receive feedback
   Provide feedback
   Check with superiors
5. **Servicing the account**
   Stock shelves

   Set up displays
   Take inventory for client
   Handle local advertising
6. **Attending conferences and meetings**
   Attend sales conferences
   Attend regional sales meetings
   Work at client conferences
   Set up product exhibitions
   Attend periodic training sessions
7. **Training and recruiting**
   Recruit new sales reps
   Train new salespeople
   Travel with trainees
8. **Entertaining**
   Entertain clients with golf and so forth
   Take clients to dinner
   Take clients out for drink
   Take clients out to lunch
   Throw parties for clients
9. **Traveling**
   Travel out of town
   Spend nights on the road
   Travel in town
10. **Distribution**
    Establish good relations with distributors
    Sell to distributors
    Handle credit
    Collect past due accounts

activities, sales organizations need to work to ensure that all salespeople receive proper training and support on the acceptance and use of the available technology. Finally, it is essential that performance management systems (appraisals, rewards) be updated to properly reflect the dimensions and activities of sales positions today. Otherwise, salespeople will be evaluated and rewarded based on an out-of-date model of their jobs.

The increasing number of nonselling and administrative activities means that many salespeople spend only a small portion of their time actually selling. In firms that sell complicated or customized products or service systems to large customers, the proportion of selling time may be even lower. The increasing involvement of salespeople in nonselling activities is one major reason why the average **cost of a sales call** has risen consistently in recent years. It takes the performance of many nonselling activities over a long period of time to successfully practice relationship selling. Depending on the industry, the average cost of a sales call today is likely over $300.

High selling costs explain why the search for new ways to improve sales force efficiency has become increasingly urgent in recent years. Using new technologies, reallocating sales effort to customer retention, and purifying the sales job by eliminating nonessential tasks are some of the strategies companies have used to reduce selling costs and increase sales force efficiency.

EXHIBIT 2.6   Matrix of updated selling activities

	Communication	Sales	Relationship	Team	Database
Technology	E-mail Dictaphone Internet Laptop (CD- ROM) Voice mail Fax Cellular phone Pager Web page* Newsletters Audiovideo conference Provide technical info Overnight services Maintain virtual office	Set up appointments Script sales pitch from database Use software for customer background Laptop for presentation* VCR for presentation Provide technol- ogy ability to customers	Web page*	Conference calls	Collect new information from database Enter informa- tion/data on laptop* Update customer files
Nontechnology	Practice language skills	Adaptive selling Conduct research at customers' business Avoid potential litigation Plan for multiple calls to close deal Sell value- added services Respond to referrals Write thank-yous* Target key accounts Pick up sales supplies Consultative sales Listen Ask questions Read body language Sell unique competencies	Bring in vendor/ alliance Develop relationship Hand- hold customer Write thank-yous* Purchase dealers Call on CEOs Build rapport with buying center Network Build trust Train brokers	Mentor Make sale and turn it over to someone else Coordinate with sales support	

Source: Greg W. Marshall, William C. Moncrief, and Felicia G. Lassk, "The Current State of Sales Force Activities," *Industrial Marketing Management* 28 (January 1999),
pp. 87–98.
*Appears in more than one cell.

TYPES OF SELLING JOBS

Not every salesperson engages in all of the activities listed in Exhibits 2.5 and 2.6. Nor does every salesperson devote the same amount of time and effort to the same kinds of activities. The many different types of selling jobs involve widely different tasks and responsibilities, require different types of training and skills, and offer varying levels of compensation and opportunities for personal satisfaction and advancement. And, perhaps most important, different kinds of selling jobs bring different levels and types of opportunities for managing customer relationships. Two broad categories of selling are selling in business-to-consumer markets and selling in business-to-business markets.

Selling in Business-to-Consumer versus Business-to-Business Markets

In terms of sheer numbers, most salespeople are employed in various kinds of **retail selling.** These jobs involve selling goods and services to **end-user consumers** for their own personal use. Thus salespeople here are referred to as selling in the **business-to-consumer (B2C) market.** Examples are direct sellers (Avon, Mary Kay, etc.), residential real estate brokers, and retail store salespeople. However, a much greater amount of relationship selling is accounted for by the **business-to-business (B2B) market,** which used to be called **industrial selling**—the sale of goods and services to non-end-user consumers. Selling in business-to-business markets involves three types of customers:

1. *Sales to resellers,* as when a salesperson for Hanes sells underwear to a retail store, which in turn resells the goods to its customers.

2. *Sales to business users,* as when a salesperson for General Electric sells materials or parts to Boeing, which uses them to produce another product; or when a Xerox salesperson sells a law firm a copier to be used in conducting the firm's business.

3. *Sales to institutions,* as when Dell sells a computer to a not-for-profit hospital or a government agency.

In some instances, the key success factors and sales activities relevant to both B2C and B2B markets, and in managing the two types of sales forces, are very similar. Success in either type of selling requires interpersonal and communications skills, solid knowledge of the products being sold, an ability to discover the customer's needs and solve his or her problems, and the creativity necessary to show the customer how a particular product or service can help satisfy those needs and problems. Similarly, managers must recruit and train appropriate people for both types of sales jobs, provide them with objectives consistent with the firm's overall marketing or merchandising program, supervise them, motivate them, and evaluate their performance.

But B2C and B2B selling also differ in some important ways. Many of the goods and services sold by B2B salespeople are more expensive and technically complex than those in B2C. Similarly, B2B customers tend to be larger and to engage in extensive decision-making processes involving many people. Consequently, the key success factors and activities involved in selling to business buyers are often quite different from those in retail selling. Furthermore, the decisions made in effectively managing a B2B sales force are broader than those required for a B2C sales force. Although some topics in this book apply reasonably well to both types of selling situations, most apply more directly to the B2B. Overall, throughout this book we focus more on the B2B side of sales force management.

Classifying Types of B2B Sales Jobs

Even within the area of B2B selling, many different types of jobs exist requiring different skills. One of the most commonly used, and useful, classification systems for selling jobs is provided below.[9] It identifies four types of B2B selling found across a variety of industries:

1. **Trade servicer.** The sales force's primary responsibility is to increase business from current and potential customers by providing them with merchandising and promotional assistance. The "trade" referred to in the label is the group of resellers such as retailers or distributors with whom this sales force does business. A Procter & Gamble salesperson selling soap and laundry products to chain-store personnel is an example of trade selling.

2. **Missionary seller.** The sales force's primary job is to increase business from current and potential customers by providing them with product information and other personal selling assistance. Missionary salespeople often do not take orders from customers directly but persuade customers to buy their firm's product from distributors or other wholesale suppliers. Anheuser-Busch does missionary selling when its salespeople call on bar owners and encourage them to order a particular brand of beer from the local Budweiser distributor. Similarly, pharmaceutical reps, or **detailers,** call on doctors as representatives of pharmaceutical manufacturers. When Pfizer first introduced Zyrtec, a top-selling allergy drug, its salespeople communicated with the physicians in their area to alert them to the efficacy of the product, to explain its advantages over other allergy medication such as Allegra and Clarinex, and to influence them to prescribe it to their patients. Note that the Pfizer salesperson normally doesn't "sell" any product directly to the physicians.

3. **Technical seller.** The sales force's primary responsibility is to increase business from current customers and potential customers by providing them with technical and engineering information and assistance. A sales engineer from the General Electric jet engine company calling on Boeing is engaged in technical selling. The trend nowadays is for most technical selling to be accomplished through cross-functional selling teams. This is because the complexity of many of the products and associated services involved in technical selling make it difficult for any one salesperson to master all aspects of this sale.

4. **New business seller.** The sales force's primary responsibility is to identify and obtain business from new customers. In relationship selling, this is analogous to a focus on securing and building the customer relationship.

Each type of sales job involves somewhat different activities. The differing nature of each also implies differences in key success factors. In the next section, we see how the sales process often operates in practice.

STAGES IN THE SELLING PROCESS

A popular approach to understanding the stages of the selling process consists of the six steps diagrammed in Exhibit 2.7: (1) prospecting for customers, (2) opening the relationship, (3) qualifying the prospect, (4) presenting the sales message, (5) closing the sale, and (6) servicing the account.

EXHIBIT 2.7   **Stages of the selling process**

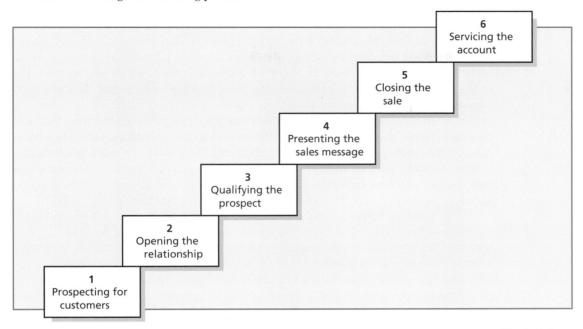

Source: F. Robert Dwyer and John F. Tanner, *Business Marketing: Connecting Strategy, Relationships, and Learning* (New York: McGrawHill/Irwin, 2008).

Although the selling process involves only a few distinct steps, the specific activities involved at each step—and the way those activities are carried out—can vary greatly depending on the type of sales position, such as missionary versus trade salesperson, and on the firm's overall selling and customer relationship strategy. Consequently, a firm's sales program should incorporate account management policies to guide each salesperson and ensure that all selling efforts are consistent with the firm's marketing and relationship strategy. We will examine the rationale and content of account management policies in more detail in Chapter 4. The following discussion of the stages in the selling process also mentions some of the more common account management policies used to direct sales representatives.

Prospecting for Customers

In many types of selling, prospecting for new customers is critical. It can also be one of the most disheartening aspects of selling, especially for beginning salespeople. Prospecting efforts are often met with rejection, and immediate payoffs are usually minimal. Nevertheless, the ability to uncover potential new customers often separates the successful from the unsuccessful salesperson.

In some consumer goods businesses, prospecting for new customers simply involves cold canvassing—going from house to house knocking on doors. In most cases, though, the target market is more narrowly defined, and the salesperson must identify prospects within that target segment. Salespeople use a variety of information sources to identify relevant prospects, including trade association and industry directories, telephone directories, other salespeople, other customers, suppliers, nonsales employees of the firm, and social and professional contacts.

Telemarketing is used by many firms to find prospects. Outbound telemarketing involves calling potential customers at their home or office, either to make a sale or to make an appointment for a field representative. Inbound telemarketing, where prospective customers call a toll-free number for more information, is also used to identify and qualify prospects. When prospects call for more information about a product or service, a representative attempts to determine the extent of interest and whether the prospect meets the company's qualifications for new customers. If so, information about the caller is passed on to the appropriate salesperson or regional office.

The Internet is also proving a useful technology for generating leads to potential new customers. While an increasing number of firms are soliciting orders directly via a home page on the Internet, many—particularly those selling relatively complex goods or services—use their Internet sites primarily to provide technical product information to customers or potential customers. These firms can have their salespeople follow up on technical inquiries from potential new accounts with a more traditional sales call.[10]

A firm's account management policies should address how much emphasis salespeople should give to prospecting for new customers versus prospecting and servicing existing accounts. The appropriate policy depends on the selling and customer relationship strategy selected, the nature of its product, and the firm's customers. If the firm's strategy is transactional, if the product is in the introductory stage of its life cycle, if it is an infrequently purchased durable good, or if the typical customer does not require much service after the sale, sales reps should devote substantial time to prospecting for new customers. This is the case in industries such as insurance and residential construction. Such firms may design their compensation systems to reward their salespeople more heavily for making sales to new customers than for servicing old ones, as we shall see in Chapter 11.

A company that desires strategic partnerships will assign a specific salesperson to each account. Firms with large market shares or those that sell frequently purchased nondurable products or products that require substantial service after the sale to guarantee customer satisfaction should adopt a policy that encourages sales reps to devote most of their efforts to servicing existing customers. Food manufacturers that sell products to retail supermarkets and firms that produce component parts and supplies for other manufacturers fall into this category. Some very large customers may require so much servicing that a sales rep is assigned to do nothing but cater to that customer's needs. In such circumstances, firms have specialized their sales positions so that some representatives service only existing accounts, while others spend all their time prospecting for and opening relationships with new customers.

Opening the Relationship

In the initial approach to a prospective customer, the sales representative should try to open the relationship by accomplishing two things: (1) determine who within the organization is likely to have the greatest influence or authority to initiate the purchase process and who will ultimately purchase the product, and (2) generate enough interest within the firm to obtain the information needed to qualify the prospect as a worthwhile potential customer. An organizational buying center often consists of individuals who play different roles in making the purchase decision. Thus, it is important for the salesperson to identify the key decision makers, their desires, and their relative influence.

Selling organizations can formulate policies to guide sales reps in approaching prospective customers. When the firm's product is inexpensive and routinely purchased, salespeople might be instructed to deal entirely with the purchasing department. For more technically complex and expensive products, the sales representative might be urged to identify and seek appointments with influencers and decision makers in various functional departments and at several managerial levels. When the purchase decision is likely to be very complex, involving many people within the customer's organization, the seller might adopt a policy of multilevel or team selling.

Qualifying the Prospect

Before salespeople attempt to set up an appointment for a major sales presentation or spend much time trying to establish a relationship with a prospective account, they should first qualify the prospect to determine if he or she qualifies as a worthwhile potential customer. If the account does not qualify, the sales rep can spend the time better elsewhere.

Qualification is difficult for some salespeople. It requires them to put aside their eternal optimism and make an objective, realistic judgment about the probability of making a profitable sale. The qualification process involves finding the answers to three important questions:

1. Does the prospect have a need for my product or service?

2. Can I make the people responsible for buying so aware of that need that I can make a sale?

3. Will the sale be profitable to my company?[11]

To answer such questions, the sales rep must learn about the prospect's operations, the types of products it makes, its customers, its competitors, and the likely future demand for its products. Information also must be obtained concerning who the customer's present suppliers are and whether any special relationships exist with those firms that would make it difficult for the prospect to change suppliers. Finally, the financial health and the credit rating of the prospect should be checked.

Because so many different types of information are needed, nonselling departments within the company—such as the credit and collections department—often are involved in the qualification process when large purchases are made. Frequently, however, credit departments do not get involved until after the prospect has agreed to buy and filled out a credit application. In these situations, company policies should be formulated to guide the salesperson's judgment concerning whether a specific prospect qualifies as a customer. These policies might spell out minimum acceptable standards for such things as the prospect's annual dollar value of purchases in the product category or credit rating. Similarly, some firms specify a minimum order size to avoid dealing with very small customers and to improve the efficiency of their order-processing and shipping operations. Issues related to prioritizing customers are discussed in Chapter 3.

Presenting the Sales Message

The sales presentation is the core of the selling process. The salesperson transmits information about a product or service and attempts to persuade the prospect to become a customer. Making good presentations is a critical aspect of the sales job. Unfortunately, many salespeople do not perform this activity very well. Past studies have discovered that 40 percent of purchasing agents perceive the presentations they witness as less than good. In a recent survey of purchasing executives, the following five presentation-related complaints were among the top 10 complaints the managers had about the salespeople with whom they deal:

• Running down competitors.

• Being too aggressive or abrasive.

• Having inadequate knowledge of competitors' products or services.

- Having inadequate knowledge of the client's business or organization.
- Delivering poor presentations.[12]

One decision that must be made in preparing for an effective sales presentation concerns how many members of the buying firm should attend. Since more than one person is typically involved in making a purchase decision, should a sales presentation be given to all of them as a group? The answer depends on whether the members of the buying center have divergent attitudes and concerns, and whether those concerns can all be addressed effectively in a single presentation. If not, scheduling a series of one-to-one presentations with different members of the buying group might be more effective.

In many cases, the best way to convince prospects of a product's advantage is to demonstrate it, particularly if the product is technically complex. Two rules should be followed in preparing an effective product demonstration. First, the demonstration should be carefully rehearsed to reduce the possibility of even a minor malfunction. Second, the demonstration should be designed to give members of the buying center hands-on experience with the product. For example, Xerox's salespeople learn about their clients' office operations so they can demonstrate their products actually doing the tasks they would do after they are purchased.

Different firms have widely varying policies concerning how sales presentations should be organized, what selling points should be stressed, and how forcefully the presentation should be made. Door-to-door salespeople and telephone salespeople are often trained to deliver the same memorized, forceful presentation to every prospect. A person selling computer systems may be trained in low-key selling, in which the salesperson primarily acts as a source of technical information and advice and does little pushing of the company's particular computers. The section later in this chapter on alternative selling approaches provides additional insight on presentational approaches.

Today, the proliferation of relationship selling has resulted in salespeople being called on to give more formal presentations to multiple members of a client organization. For example, often selling firms may give quarterly or annual account review presentations to clients. These presentations typically involve the buying team and selling team as well as members of management from both sides. A firm's policy on sales presentations should be consistent with its other policies for managing accounts. To formulate intelligent sales presentation policies, a sales manager must know about alternative presentation methods and their relative advantages and limitations. Space limitations of this chapter make it difficult to present a lengthy discussion of such issues. The interested student is urged to examine a personal selling textbook where a variety of sales presentation methods are discussed and evaluated in more detail.

Closing the Sale

Closing the sale refers to obtaining a final agreement to purchase. All the salesperson's efforts are wasted unless the client "signs on the dotted line"; yet this is where many salespeople fail. It is natural for buyers to try to delay making purchase decisions. But as the time it takes the salesperson to close the sale increases, the profit to be made from the sale may go down, and the risk of losing the sale increases. Consequently, the salesperson's task is to facilitate the client making a timely final decision. Often, this may best be accomplished by simply asking for an order. "May I write that order up for you?" and "When do you want it delivered?" are common closings. Another closing tactic is to ask the client to choose between two alternative decisions, such as, "Will that be cash or charge?" or "Did you want the blue one or the red one?" In B2B buying and selling, organizational buyers and other decision makers have had extensive training in buying and selling techniques and can identify manipulative closing techniques, so care should be used in selecting a natural way to ask for the sale.

Servicing the Account

The salesperson's job is not finished when the sale is made. Many types of service and assistance must be provided to customers after a sale to ensure their satisfaction and repeat business. Excellent service after the sale bolsters customer loyalty and fosters long-term relationships with customers. But this is another area in which some salespeople do not perform well. When a customer stops buying from a company, much of the time it's because the customer thinks the selling firm's salespeople developed an indifferent attitude after the product was delivered. The salesperson should follow up each sale to make sure no problems exist with delivery schedules, quality of goods, or customer billing. In addition, often the salesperson or members of a sales team supervise the installation of equipment, train the customer's employees in its use, and ensure proper maintenance in order to reduce problems that may lead to customer dissatisfaction.

This kind of postsale service can pay great dividends for both the salesperson and the selling firm, leading to the sale of other, related products and services.[13] For instance, in many capital equipment lines, service contracts, along with supplies and replacement parts, account for greater dollar sales revenue and higher profit margins than the original equipment. A firm's selling and customer relationship strategy should dictate what type of postsale or ongoing service should occur.

To truly understand the selling process, why successful salespeople do what they do, and how to most effectively manage their efforts, it is important to also understand how B2B customers make purchase decisions. After all, in relationship selling, the focus by the salesperson and his or her entire organization is aimed at fulfilling customer needs and solving customer problems. Therefore, the next sections shift the focus of our discussion from the selling side to the buying side to examine the participants in the B2B buying process, the stages of this buying process exhibited by many organizations, and finally the nature of organizational buying situations.

PARTICIPANTS IN THE ORGANIZATIONAL BUYING PROCESS—THE BUYING CENTER

In order to make a decision on a technologically sophisticated IT solution from IBM, a wide variety of individuals in a client firm may participate in the decision process, including computer analysts, customer service representatives, procurement personnel, users, and others. The various participants in a buying process may be grouped into seven categories: initiators, users, influencers, gatekeepers, buyers, deciders, and controllers.[14] Together, the individuals assuming these roles form the **buying center,** which represents all the people who participate in buying or influencing the purchase of a particular product. American Airlines operates the largest aviation maintenance and equipment base in the world at its Tulsa, Oklahoma, facility. Mechanics there use a wide variety of products purchased by American from hundreds of vendors. A variety of people at American participate in the purchase of these products in one way or another. Participants in that buying process include the following:

- **Initiators** are the people who perceive a problem or opportunity that may require the purchase of a new product or service and thereby start the buying process. The initiator

Entire Team

can be almost anyone at any level in the firm. Complaints from maintenance workers at American Airlines about outmoded and inefficient equipment, for instance, might trigger the purchase of new machinery. Alternatively, the decision to replace the equipment might be initiated through top management's strategic planning deliberations on how to make the airline more cost efficient and effective.

- **Users,** the people in the organization who must use or work with the product or service, often influence the purchase decision. For example, drill-press operators at American Airlines might request that the purchasing agent buy drill bits from a particular supplier because they stay sharp longer and reduce downtime in the plant. Users often volunteer to initiate a purchase, so it is possible that the same people may play more than one role.

- **Influencers** provide information for evaluating alternative products and suppliers, and often play a major role in determining the specifications and criteria to use in making the purchase decision. Influencers are usually technical experts from various departments and can include users. At American Airlines, for example, flight engineers or pilots often influence purchase decisions on the basis of their experience with the performance of various vendor options.

- **Gatekeepers** control the flow of information to other people involved in the purchasing process. A gatekeeper may control information going to the organization's purchasing agents, the suppliers' salespeople, and others on the selling and buying teams. Gatekeepers influence a purchase by controlling the kind and amount of information that reaches the decision makers. Information technology people are frequent gatekeepers because they often hold the *information* that is key to decision making in a firm. There are two types of gatekeepers: screens (like secretaries at American Airlines who can decide whose telephone call is put through to the executive or purchasing agent) and filters (such as the American Airlines purchasing agent who gathers proposals from three different companies and decides what to tell others in the buying center about each company). The purchasing agent filters information, choosing to pass along some, but not all, of the information in order to influence the decision.

- The **buyer** is the person who actually contacts the selling organization and places the order. In most organizations, buyers have the authority to negotiate purchases. In some cases, they are given wide discretion. In other instances, they are constrained by technical specifications and other contract requirements determined by technical experts and top administrators. At American Airlines, the level of authority to buy is determined by the size and type of purchase involved. As in many organizations, sometimes the decision is referred to a buying committee who may either vote or work to reach a consensus decision on which vendor to buy from or which product to buy.

- The **decider** is the person with the final authority to make a purchase decision. Sometimes buyers have this authority, but often it is retained by higher executives in the organization. When American Airlines buys a complete, systemwide computer installation and upgrade, for instance, the final decision is likely to be made by the chief executive or a top management committee.

- The **controller** is the person who determines the budget for the purchase. Sometimes the budget is set independently of the purchase—for example, the administrative office at American Airlines' Tulsa facility may receive a budget for office equipment set by corporate headquarters in Fort Worth at the start of the fiscal year. Then if the copier needs to be replaced or some other unexpected high-dollar expense looms, the cost would have to somehow fit in that budget. At other times, the controller may be an engineer or a line manager who is trying to keep the cost of the new maintenance procedure within a certain budget.

Estimates of the number of people in the buying center for a typical purchase range from 3 to 12. Different members of the buying center may participate, and exert different amounts of influence, at different stages in the decision process.[15] For example, at American Airlines people from engineering, quality control, and R&D often exert the greatest influence on the development of specifications and criteria that a new maintenance product must meet, whereas the purchasing manager often has more influence when it comes time to choose among alternative suppliers.

The makeup and size of the buying center varies with the amount of risk perceived by the firm when buying a particular product. The buying center tends to be smaller, and the relative influence of the purchasing manager greater, when reordering products the firm has purchased in the past than when buying something for the first time or buying something that is seen as risky.[16] **Perceived risk** is a function of the complexity of the product and situation, the relative importance of the purchase, time pressure to make a decision, and the degree of uncertainty about the product's efficacy. Similarly, customers' buying centers are more likely to involve a wider variety of participants when they are considering the purchase of a technically complex, expensive product, such as a computer system, than when the purchase involves a simpler or less costly product.[17]

Selling Centers and Buying Centers

Given that major customers' buying centers often consist of people from different functional areas with different viewpoints and concerns, those concerns can often be most effectively addressed by a team of experts from equivalent functional departments in the selling firm, or even from different divisions within the company. Recently, companies have begun to look at the existence of a **selling center** that brings together individuals from around the organization (marketing, customer service, sales, engineering, and others) to help the salesperson do his or her job more effectively. As in a customer's buying center, the selling organization needs to work together to present a unified, well-coordinated effort to the customer.[18] Since different members of the buying center may be active at different stages of the purchase process, an important part of sales planning involves trying to determine who the sales organization should contact, when each contact should be made, who should make each contact, and what kinds of information and communication each buying center member is likely to find most useful and persuasive.

The key is establishing a **team selling** structure within the sales organization that best meets customer needs. For example, a common structure would make the salesperson (i.e., account manager) responsible for working with the entire selling team in order to manage the customer relationship. Often, such customer relationship teams include representatives from a number of functional departments within the sales organization such as R&D, operations, and finance. In an increasing number of situations, customer relationship teams maintain offices in or very near to the customer's facilities and one or more members of the customer relationship team are located in close geographic proximity to the customer.

At Oracle, the world's largest producer of CRM software, the team for a major account such as General Motors is led by an Oracle account executive. The account executive has a global team of salespeople as direct reports but can also draw from the full functional resources of Oracle to provide solutions for GM at any location in the world. Such an approach creates a **matrix organization** of direct reports and supporting internal consultants at Siebel who bring their collective expertise to bear for this major client.

Team selling can also present some coordination, motivation, and compensation problems. Sam Palmisano's predecessor at IBM, Lou Gerstner, has frequently spoken out publicly on the difficulties of performance management in team selling environments; it is a key theme in the book he released after his retirement.[19] Team selling is expensive and involves a substantial commitment of human resources, including management. Thus, team-based approaches tend to be most appropriate for the very largest customers, especially those with buying centers, where the potential business over time represents enough dollars and entails enough cross-functional interaction between various areas of both firms to justify the high costs of the team approach. Such a customer is often referred to as a **key account.** Key accounts generally have a senior salesperson assigned as a key account manager who works with a team that is dedicated to serving that large and very important customer.

ORGANIZATIONAL BUYING DECISION STAGES

We have seen that different members of a buying center may exert influence at different stages in the decision process. This raises the question of what stages are involved. One widely recognized framework identifies seven steps that organizational buyers take in making purchase decisions: (1) anticipation or recognition of a problem or need, (2) determination and description of the characteristics and the quantity of the needed item, (3) search for and qualification of potential suppliers, (4) acquisition and analysis of proposals or bids, (5) evaluation of proposals and selection of suppliers, (6) selection of an order routine, and (7) performance evaluation and feedback.[20] These **organizational buying decision stages** are portrayed graphically in Exhibit 2.8.

Stage One: Anticipation or Recognition of a Problem or Need

Many organizational purchases are motivated by the requirements of the firm's production processes, merchandise inventory, or day-to-day operations. In such a case, the firm's demand for goods and services is **derived demand.** Its needs are derived from its customers' demand for the goods or services it produces or markets. For example, the demand for luggage is derived in part from the demand for air travel. The luggage department at Macy's Department Store loses customers, and Samsonite (a leading luggage manufacturer) loses customers, when people don't travel. This characteristic of derived demand can make organizational markets quite volatile, because a small change in the market can result in a relatively large change in the organization's sales.

Many different situations can lead someone to recognize a need for a particular product or service. In some cases, need recognition may be almost automatic, as when the computerized inventory control system at Wal-Mart reports that the stock of an item has fallen below the reorder level. In other cases, a need may arise when someone identifies a better way of operating, such at the American Airlines Maintenance and Equipment Base when an engineer or mechanic suggests a better procedure than what is currently in practice. New needs might also evolve when the focus of the firm's operations changes, as when top management decides to make a new product line. Procter & Gamble introduced Crest Whitestrips which sell for considerably more on the grocer's shelf than any other Crest product, because P&G wanted to get into the business of more professional products that will raise its average sale and profit per item. In all these situations, needs may be recognized, and the purchasing process may be initiated, by a variety of people in the organization, including users, technical personnel, top management, and purchasing managers.

EXHIBIT 2.8
Organizational buying decision stages

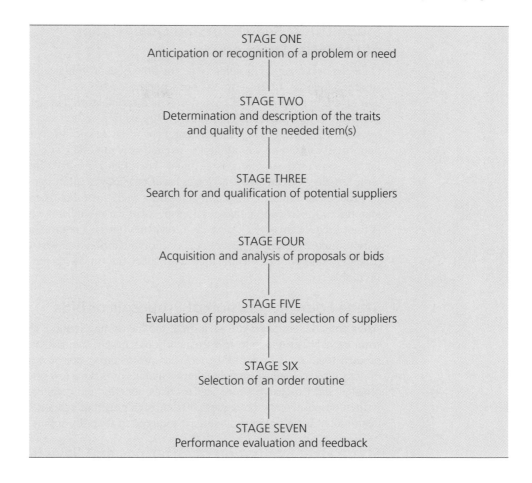

STAGE ONE
Anticipation or recognition of a problem or need

STAGE TWO
Determination and description of the traits
and quality of the needed item(s)

STAGE THREE
Search for and qualification of potential suppliers

STAGE FOUR
Acquisition and analysis of proposals or bids

STAGE FIVE
Evaluation of proposals and selection of suppliers

STAGE SIX
Selection of an order routine

STAGE SEVEN
Performance evaluation and feedback

Stage Two: Determination and Description of the Characteristics and Quantity of the Needed Item(s)

In organizational buying settings, the types and quantities of goods and services to be purchased are usually dictated by the demand for the firm's outputs and the requirements of its production process and operations. Consequently, the criteria used in specifying the needed materials and equipment must usually be technically precise. Similarly, the quantities needed must be carefully considered to avoid excessive inventories or downtime caused by lack of needed materials. For these reasons, a variety of technical experts, as well as the people who will use the materials or equipment, are commonly involved in this stage.

It is not enough for the using department and the technical experts to develop a detailed set of specifications for the needed item, however. They must also communicate a clear and precise description of *what* is needed, *how much* is needed, and *when* it is needed to other members of the buying center and to potential suppliers. Say Ford Motor Company's design and marketing groups make a decision to change the specifications of a car's interior and electronic systems. This must be communicated effectively to purchasing so that the vendor, often Lear Corporation, can begin the process of changing the parts Ford relies on purchasing from it to satisfy picky customers in this market.

Stage Three: Search for and Qualification of Potential Suppliers

Once the organization has clearly defined the type of item needed, a search for potential suppliers begins. If the item has been purchased before, this search may be limited to one or a few suppliers that have performed satisfactorily in the past. From the seller's perspective, one advantage of relationship selling is that the level of familiarity and trust between the buying and selling firm often results in that seller getting the first opportunity to bid on supplying the needed new products, and often this step of searching for potential suppliers is skipped. Historically, Ford Motor Company has gone with **single-source suppliers** wherever possible to minimize the variation in quality of production inputs. This approach bodes well for Lear Corporation whenever Ford announces specification changes on aspects of car models on which Lear supplies parts. If the purchase involves a new item, or if the item is complex and expensive (again, if the product represents a risky decision), organizational buyers often search for several potential suppliers to ensure they can select the one with the best product and most favorable terms.

Stage Four: Acquisition of Proposals or Bids

After potential suppliers are identified, the buyer may request specific proposals or bids from each. When the item is a frequently purchased, standardized, or technically simple product (e.g., nails or copier paper), this process may not be very extensive. The buyer might simply consult several suppliers' catalogs or make a few phone calls. For more complicated and expensive goods and services, lengthy and detailed sales presentations and written proposals may be requested from each potential vendor. Governmental and other institutional buyers almost always are required to formally solicit bids.

Stage Five: Evaluation of Offerings and Selection of Suppliers

During this stage of the purchasing process, members of the buying center examine the acceptability of the various proposals and potential suppliers. Also, the buying organization and one or more potential vendors may engage in negotiation about various aspects of the deal. Ultimately, one or more suppliers are selected, and purchase agreements are signed.

The people in the buying organization's purchasing department (i.e., the buyers) usually evaluate offerings and select the supplier. However, others in the buying center, such as technical and administrative personnel, may also play a role in supplier selection, especially when the purchase is complex and costly.

What criteria do members of the buying center use in selecting a supplier? Because organizational buying is largely a rational decision-making process, we would expect "rational" criteria to be considered most important—such as the value-added aspects of the product, the service offered by the supplier, and the like. However, social and emotional factors can also influence this decision. Organizational buyers and other buying center members are, after all, human just like buyers in the B2C marketplace. A number of aspects of difference can be contrasted between consumer versus organizational buyer behavior, as summarized in Exhibit 2.9.

The relative importance of different supplier selection criteria varies across organizations and the types of products or services being purchased. For example, product quality tends to be more important in the purchase of technically complex products, whereas price and customer service are relatively more important for more standardized, nontechnical items, that is, **commodity products.** Fortunately, firms engaged in relationship selling

EXHIBIT 2.9
Consumer versus
organizational buyer
behavior

Aspect of the Purchase	Consumer Buyer	Organizational Buyer
Use	Personal, family, or household	Production, operations, or resale
Buyer motivation	Personal	Organizational and personal
Buyer knowledge of product or service	Lower	Higher
Likelihood of group decision making	Lower	Higher
Dollar amount of purchases	Lower	Higher
Quantity of purchase or order size	Smaller	Larger
Frequency of purchase	More	Less
Number of cyclical purchases	Lower	Higher
Amount of negotiation and competitive bidding	Little	Much

greatly increase the likelihood that buying firms will look past price as a sole determinant of vendor selection. Instead, because the buyer will have much more complete knowledge about you and your products, they will have a better understanding of the overall value to their organization of buying from you versus one of your competitors with whom they do not have a long-standing relationship.

Stage Six: Selection of an Order Routine

Until the purchased item is delivered, it is of no use to the organization. Consequently, after an order has been placed with a supplier, the purchasing department often tries to match the delivery of the goods with the company's need for the product. Other internal activities also must occur when the order is delivered. The goods must be received, inspected, paid for, and entered in the firm's inventory records. These activities represent some of the additional costs that may not be readily apparent to the buying firm. Retailers have become very aggressive in asking vendors to cover these types of costs by charging sales organizations **slotting allowances.** Slotting allowances are fees charged by a retailer for the privilege of having them set up a new item in their IT system, program it into inventory, and ultimately make distribution of the item to the stores. Slotting allowances can be costly to manufacturers, and it is not unusual for major retailers to charge slotting fees in the thousands of dollars per new item stocked.

Stage Seven: Performance Evaluation and Feedback

When the goods have been delivered, evaluation by the customer begins. This evaluation focuses on both the product and the supplier's service performance. This is a stage where follow-up by the salesperson is critically important. The goods are inspected to determine whether they meet the specifications described in the purchase agreement. Later, users judge whether the purchased item performs according to expectations. Similarly, the supplier's performance can be evaluated on such criteria as promptness of delivery, quality of the product, and service after the sale. In many organizations, this evaluation is a formal process, involving written reports from the user department and other persons involved in the purchase. The purchasing department keeps the information for use in evaluating proposals and selecting suppliers the next time a similar purchase is made.

THE NATURE OF ORGANIZATIONAL BUYING SITUATIONS

The steps just described apply largely to **new-task purchases,** where a customer is buying a relatively complex and expensive product or service for the first time (e.g., a new piece of production equipment or a new computer system), or **modified rebuy** purchase decisions, where a customer is interested in modifying the product specifications, prices, or other terms it has been receiving from existing suppliers and is willing to consider dealing with new suppliers to make these things happen.

At the other extreme is the **straight rebuy,** where a customer is reordering an item it has purchased many times (e.g., office supplies, bulk chemicals). Such **repeat purchases** tend to be much more routine than the new-task situation or the modified rebuy. Straight rebuys are often carried out by members of the purchasing department (buyers) with little influence from other members of the buying center, and many of the steps just described (involved with searching for and evaluating alternative suppliers) are dropped. Instead, the buyer may choose from among the suppliers on a "pre-approved" list, giving weight to the company's past satisfaction with those suppliers and their products.

Purchasing departments are often organized hierarchically on the basis of these different buying situations. For example, at Wal-Mart's buying office new buyers begin as analysts and assistants, primarily monitoring straight rebuys. New-task purchases and modified rebuys that require more direct vendor contact are handled by more seasoned veterans in the buying office.

From the seller's viewpoint, being an "in" or approved supplier can provide a significant competitive advantage, and the process of relationship selling certainly enhances such favored positions with current customers. For potential suppliers not on a buyer's approved list, the strategic selling problem is more difficult. The objective of an **out supplier** must be to move the customer away from the automatic reordering procedures of a straight rebuy toward the more extensive evaluation processes of a modified rebuy. Since, as we've already seen, the need to consider a change in suppliers can be identified and communicated by a variety of members of a firm's buying center, an out supplier might urge its salespeople to bypass the customer's purchasing department and call directly on users or technical personnel. The goal is for the salesperson to try to convince users, influencers, and others that his or her products offer advantages on some important dimension—such as technical design, quality, performance, or financial criteria—over the products the client is currently purchasing. Finding someone to play the role of initiator can be difficult, but it is possible if latent dissatisfaction exists.

Kamen Wiping Materials Co., Inc. in Wichita, Kansas, sells high-quality recycled cloth wiping rags to manufacturers. The business essentially consists of banks of huge industrial-sized washing machines. Kamen buys soiled wiping cloths, cleans them, and then resells them to manufacturers in a variety of industries at prices much lower than paper or new cloth rags. President Len Goldstein is famous for getting companies such as Cessna, Beechcraft, and other heavy users of wiping materials to change wiping cloth vendors (and even change from paper to cloth, which is a big switch) by scouting out who in the company can benefit the most from the change. This person then becomes the initiator. Here, with most organizational buying decisions, what benefits the company ultimately benefits the members of the buying center, especially the purchasing agent. If buying from Kamen makes various members of the buying center look like heroes for saving money, being environmentally friendly, and so forth, Len Goldstein knows he has a great chance of getting the sale—and keeping the customer.

Summary

Selling is a great career path that can also lead to significant upward mobility professionally, especially into sales management. The drivers of change we talked about in this chapter all translate into opportunities for salespeople to contribute a high level of value to their customers and their own organizations. Salespeople and their managers can and should benchmark their own approaches to managing customer relationships against the best practices of world-class sales organizations.

Selling today is so far removed from the stereotypical societal view of old-style selling as to bear no resemblance whatsoever. The key success factors needed in relationship selling all point to professionalism, strong skills, and broad and deep content knowledge that allow the salesperson to maximize his or her performance and thus rewards. It is especially interesting to examine the sales activities performed by salespeople today. Quite a few new activities have been added in recent years, driven largely by technology and the move from transactional to relationship selling approaches. Then too, understanding the categories of selling jobs available aids in decision making about whether or how to enter the selling profession. It is valuable to understand the process of selling through identification of its six stages.

Because customers are the primary focus of relationship sellers, gaining knowledge about the world of organizational buying greatly enhances the effectiveness of a salesperson in his or her role as a customer relationship manager. Many people in a client firm may influence the buyer–seller relationship and the decision of what to buy, and salespeople must carefully study each of their customers to learn what dynamics are at play within each buying center situation. Often, selling firms form selling centers and initiate team-selling approaches to better serve buying centers, especially with large and complex customers (key accounts). Of course, salespeople need to fully understand and appreciate the stages of the organizational buying decision process that each of their customers goes through so the salesperson can work to add value throughout the purchasing process. Different organizational buying decision situations require different communication between buyer and seller, and the seller must be knowledgeable enough about the nature of each purchase to properly manage the process on his or her end.

Overall, the more expertise a salesperson has about how his or her own organization operates and how the customer's firm operates, the more likely the salesperson will be able to sell solutions for the customer and add value to both organizations.

Key Terms

drivers of change
autonomy
sales activities
job variety
intrinsic rewards
extrinsic rewards
work-family conflict
telecommute
virtual office
adaptive selling
job enlargement
cost of a sales call

retail selling
end-user consumer
business-to-consumer
  (B2C) market
business-to-business (B2B)
  market
industrial selling
trade servicer
missionary seller
detailer
technical seller
new business seller

buying center
initiator
user
influencer
gatekeeper
buyers
decider
controller
perceived risk
selling center
team selling
matrix organization

key account	single-source suppliers	modified rebuy
organizational buying	commodity products	straight rebuy
decision stages	slotting allowances	repeat purchases
derived demand	new-task purchases	out supplier

Breakout Questions

1. What does it mean to be "nimble" as a salesperson and as a sales organization? How is IBM becoming more nimble?

2. Take a piece of paper and draw a line down the middle. Write "Pros" on the top left and "Cons" on the top right. Now, from your own perspective, come up with as many issues as you can on both sides regarding relationship selling as a career choice for you. Be sure to note *why* you list each item as you do.

3. Creativity is important to sales success. What is creativity? Give a specific example of something or several things you have done that you think is especially creative. How might creativity be taught or trained to salespeople?

4. Telecommuting and using a virtual office are major aspects of many professional sales positions. How to you feel about telecommuting and virtual office in a job? What aspects of telecommuting and virtual office are you most and least attracted to?

5. What aspects of sales jobs do you believe provide a strong foundation for moving up in an organization?

6. Review the top 20 key success factors for relationship selling as listed in Exhibit 2.4. Which of these factors are currently *your* strongest points? Which need the most work? How do you plan to capitalize on the strengths and improve on the weaknesses?

7. Pick any three of the selling activities presented in Exhibits 2.5 and 2.6 that you would *most* like to perform and then pick any three you would *least* like to perform. Explain your rationale for listing each as you did.

8. The chapter outlines the roles different members of a buying center play within an organizational buying context. Think of an example of a purchase process you were involved in as an end-user consumer (i.e., not an organizational buyer). Can you come up with examples of people who played these same buying center roles in the context of your example? Try to connect as many specific people to specific buying center roles as you can within the context of your particular purchase.

9. The organizational buying center varies as a function of size of the company and product or service being purchased. How does size of the company influence the composition of the buying center? How might the composition of the buying center differ for each of the following products?

    a. Purchasing a new computer for personal use.
    b. Purchasing a new copy machine for the office.
    c. Selecting a different public accounting firm.
    d. Selecting a new textbook for a sales management course.
    e. Choosing a different source for industrial oils and lubricants.
    f. Purchasing a new machine.
    g. Choosing a marketing research firm.

10. Explain the differences among a new-task purchase, modified rebuy, and straight rebuy. How is each situation likely to alter the way a salesperson approaches a client?

11. In the past, salespeople tended to have the edge over most buyers in terms of information. However, over the past 15 years access to timely and accurate information related

to their business has changed how purchasing agents view their jobs. For one thing, they have been able to get a better handle on their costs and better determine which items to buy and from whom. How has this proliferation of information affected the relationship, both interpersonally and professionally, between purchasing agents and the sales reps calling on them?

Leadership Challenge: B2C versus B2B

Charles Renner has been considering the implications of senior management's new growth strategy. As head of sales for Integrity Building Supplies, he had been responsible for a national sales force of more than 300 salespeople that sold building supplies to contractors and large developers around the country. He, and more important, his sales force, knew how to sell the company's products and services in a business-to-business setting. They had a great reputation in the home building business nationally, and for many contractors Integrity had become their supplier of first choice for many basic building supplies.

Senior management at Integrity, however, had determined there was a real opportunity for company growth by creating a retail (business-to-consumer) channel to target the homeowner wanting to take on home repair projects. They believed that they could not compete directly with Home Depot and Lowe's on price or selection but they could compete successfully on service. Charles agreed that the home do-it-yourself market was huge and Home Depot and Lowe's often did not provide adequate after-sale service or guidance to individuals wanting to take on these kinds of projects.

The company's board of directors had approved Integrity's move into retail operations and targeted two cities, Atlanta and Dallas, as test markets for the concept. They were both large cities with a significant number of homeowners who enjoyed do-it-yourself projects; in addition, Dallas was the headquarters for Integrity.

Among the many challenges facing Charles as he pondered the future was the sales culture at Integrity. The company had been a B2B organization for its entire 60-year history. Everyone in the organization, including him, knew how to sell to other businesses (contractors, developers) but had no experience selling to consumers who had much less understanding of the products or how to use them. He knew that becoming a B2C company would require a number of changes to the sales culture.

Questions

1. What are the major differences Charles will encounter between a B2B selling environment and a B2C environment?
2. As head of sales for Integrity, what are the two most significant challenges Charles will encounter in putting together a retail sales force?

Role Play: Emblem Foods

Situation

Emblem Foods manufactures and sells a wide variety of "healthier" snack products that are typically merchandised in the diet section of supermarkets. Emblem's product line includes salty snacks (such as crackers), sweet snacks (such as cookies and some pastries), and some packaged power bar products. All of Emblem's products are lower sugar and fat than standard fare.

Bridgette Face has been on the job as a salesperson at Emblem Foods for four weeks. She was hired right out of undergraduate business school at Mercury College, where she majored in marketing. During this first month, she spent the first and fourth weeks in a formal training program at the home office, the second week making sales calls on some of her accounts with her sales manager Geoff Knard, and the third week making sales calls alone. Bridgette really likes her job and the company so far, and she has already impressed Geoff and the trainers at the home office with her enthusiasm and professionalism.

Geoff and a recruiter from the home office are planning to make a recruiting trip to Mercury College next month. Mercury is only 90 miles from Bridgette's home base with Emblem, and Geoff has asked her to join them to help tell the next crop of graduates why careers in selling can be great. The goal is of course to attract good students to interview for careers with Emblem. Bridgette and Geoff are meeting for breakfast in a few minutes to discuss the upcoming trip.

Bonnie has never done any recruiting before, and at age 24 she is only a year older than many of the students she will visit with during the campus visit. She needs to find out what to tell them to convince them that the old stereotypes of selling are not true in today's professional selling situations. She wants to use this meeting to get Geoff to give her ideas on how to "sell" top students on considering a career with Emblem. Geoff comes prepared to help Bonnie overcome resistance she may hear to sales careers from top potential candidates.

Characters in the Role Play

Bridgette Face, territory manager for Emblem Foods

Geoff Knard, district sales manager for Emblem Foods

Assignment

Break into pairs, with one student playing each character. It doesn't matter what the actual gender mix of your pair is. Before you stage the meeting between Bridgette and Geoff, work separately to come up with a set of the stereotypical bad and the good of sales careers. At the meeting, each person should share ideas and the two should work together to prepare for the recruiting trip. Be sure Bridgette is prepared to convey the many rewarding aspects of selling to the students and to deal with questions about the stereotypes.

Minicase: Rising Action Bakery and Power Flour, LLC

Joe Reeka is a senior sales representative for Power Flour, LLC, a supplier of flour to private-label brands in supermarkets as well as to bakeries. Power Flour has developed a new white flour with a nontraditional bleaching agent, which will allow for the baking of bread products with lower carbohydrates but without a change in taste. Joe feels this new flour product would be ideal to sell to Rising Action Bakery and has sent information on the new flour to its purchasing department.

Rising Action Bakery is a small but growing chain of bakeries in Colorado, specializing in "home-baked" premium bread products. Its products are baked at a central bakery and shipped to its retail stores. The CEO is Ana Paula Gutierrez, and she has a small senior management team consisting of a production and operations manager, Dawn Chiles; a sales and marketing manager, Nimesh Patel; a purchasing manager, Joan Wells; a finance and accounting manager, Matt Simon; and a store coordination manager, Dan Levy. Each manager leads an assistant manager/coordinator and an executive assistant. Rising Action also has a store manager and staff for each of its 24 retail stores.

Ana Paula and her five managers are meeting to discuss the results of the sales and marketing department's recent market research study on the future of low-carbohydrate diets. The results indicated that the trend may not continue, but that low-carb bread products would be in high demand for at least the next two to three years. Sales numbers have been down since the rise in popularity of low-carbohydrate diets, and Nimesh is concerned with maintaining, or hopefully increasing, Rising Action's market share by adding low-carb products to the marketing mix. Dawn's main concern is to produce the low-carb bread efficiently and without having to purchase new equipment. Dawn's assistant manager handles determination of quantities for ordering and would be involved with developing the new bread product and determining the type and amount of flour to be used. Matt is concerned that this will be a large investment in a possibly short-lived product and that the forecasted budgets did not anticipate such an outlay for inventory expense.

Joan is worried about purchasing the right amount of flour for the production needs but also keeping within the budgets determined by finance. Further, Joan is bound by Rising Action's policy of getting three bids on supply purchases. Dan is excited at the prospect of new low-carb products for the retail stores but must make the store managers aware of the changes. The stores would be instrumental in collecting feedback from their customers to determine the success of the new products. Ana Paula trusts the decision making of her management team, but ultimately she is responsible for the new products and especially has a hand in developing recipes that are up to Rising Action's taste standards.

Joan's purchasing assistant, Janice, received the written sales information from Joe Reeka of Flour Power about the new low-carb flour and has called him back for further information.

Questions

1. What participants in the organizational buying process can you identify at Rising Action?

2. Who should Joe contact and get to know at Rising Action Bakery in order to develop the relationship with the company and achieve a sale and why? What types of information would appeal to each participant in the buying process?

3. Why would a relationship selling approach be more effective than a transactional selling approach for Joe and Flour Power?

4. What stages of the buying process can you identify in this case? Explain.

Suggested Readings

Belonax, Joseph J., Jr., Stephen J. Newell, and Richard E. Plank. "The Role of Purchase Importance on Buyer Perceptions of the Trust and Expertise Components of Supplier and Salesperson Credibility in Business-to-Business Relationships." *Journal of Personal Selling & Sales Management* 27 (Summer 2007) pp. 247–58.

Moncrief, William C., Greg W. Marshall, and Felicia G. Lassk. "A Contemporary Taxonomy of Sales Positions." *Journal of Personal Selling & Sales Management* 26 (Winter 2006) pp. 55–65.

Rodriguez Cano, Cynthia, James S. Boyles, and Cynthia J. Bean. "Communication Media Preferences in Business-to-Business Transactions: An Examination of the Purchase Process." *Journal of Personal Selling & Sales Management* 25 (Summer 2005) pp. 283–94.

Rutherford, Brian N., James S. Boles, Hiram C. Barksdale Jr., and Julie T. Johnson. "Single Source Supply versus Multiple Source Supply: A Study into the Relationship between Satisfaction and Propensity to Stay within a Service Setting." *Journal of Personal Selling & Sales Management* 26 (Fall 2006) pp. 371–79.

Sydow Campbell, Kim, Lenita Davis, and Lauren Skinner. "Rapport Management During the Exploration Phase of the Salesperson-Customer Relationship." *Journal of Personal Selling & Sales Management* 26 (Fall 2006) pp. 359–70.

Wagner, Judy A., and Noreen M. Klein. "Who Wants to Go First? Order Effects within a Series of Competitive Sales Presentations." *Journal of Personal Selling & Sales Management* 27 (Summer 2007) pp. 259–76.

Chapter **Three**

Linking Strategies and the Sales Role in the Era of Customer Relationship Management

The Importance of Integrating Sales with Other Business Functions

Looking back in time, it is fair to say that the sales function operated as a stand-alone entity for many years. In truth, the sales force has been something of a mystery to the rest of the organization. Whether because of the widely dispersed footprint of most sales forces or perhaps the renegade image of salespeople as individualists, sales has stood alone and frankly never seemed to mind.

The most classic example of the sales force being at odds with other business functions is the tenuous relationship that has existed over time between sales and marketing. These two functions that are so aligned in their ultimate objectives (i.e., to acquire and retain profitable customers) seemed to have bickered back and forth since the beginning of time. Marketing accuses sales of failing to execute on their elegantly designed marketing strategies, while sales accuses marketing of sitting in an ivory tower unaware of the real-world challenges they face in the field. It has appeared for decades as though the siblings would never move beyond their distrust of one another.

The icy relationship between sales and marketing has now warmed in most top organizations. In part, this improved relationship has been driven by sales' adoption of concepts like customer segmentation and value propositions, which were traditionally in marketing's realm. Similarly, marketing has come under pressure from executives to demonstrate their ability to drive revenue growth, traditionally a metric directly attributable to sales. These trends, along with the implementation of CRM to improve the sharing of information, have contributed to sales' and marketing's decision to join forces.

Marketing is not the only corporate function that has begun to integrate itself with sales, though. With the introduction of technology like sales force automation (SFA) in the 1990s, sales has come to depend heavily on the information technology (IT) department for its mission-critical tools. And as the demand for talented professional salespeople has come to outstrip supply, sales has also developed an intimate relationship with human resources to help them identify, hire, retain, and develop world class sellers and managers.

The willingness of various departments within world class sales companies to link with the sales leaders specifically to work on common initiatives seems to be a direct outcome of progress in building a customer-driven culture. Managers and individual contributors throughout the organization start to judge the value of their contribution by its impact on both internal and external customers. When a common external objective becomes the focus, intra-political positioning begins to diminish in favor of the "bonding" impetus from all parties facing a common "enemy," such as customer dissatisfaction or the competition. The constant refocus of attention on the external goal of delighting customers and surpassing competitors creates an enthusiasm and project momentum that usually dwarfs all but the most imbedded turf issues. In addition, recognition and even key compensation elements that are geared to broader company goals tend to melt the functional silos that occur in most "traditional" organizations.

The incidence of cross-functional meetings increases. Operations meetings routinely include customer service reps and have salespeople participating by teleconference. Human resources and training departments regularly meet with sales to review the tracking associated with the efficiency and effectiveness of the selection, development, and retention processes for customer-interfacing personnel. IT professionals design and develop tools through extensive field study and user input so that the resulting automated processes reduce workload and come across as intuitive and user friendly.

The boundaries between functions blur as more initiatives are collaborative from onset to completion rather than a series of sequential outcomes managed separately within each function. "Team" becomes an adjective attached to the core values of the total organization, and it is not just politically correct corporate speak. In short, leading sales forces no longer view themselves as self-contained entities with all of their required support functions within. Their sales executives have purposefully narrowed their scope so they can concentrate on what they do best—adding value through personal interactions with customers. Marketing, IT, HR, and other corporate peers are more capable in their areas of expertise, and they are being called on to support sales in meaningful ways. The more tightly sales can integrate itself with other parts of the organization, the more leverage they will have to ratchet up their own performance.

Source: HR Chally Group (2007), *The Chally World Class Excellence Research Report: The Route to the Summit.* Dayton, OH: HR Chally Group.

LEARNING OBJECTIVES

Successful organizations today place the customer at the center of firm strategies and processes. Such customer-centric business models place the sales force in a crucial role, as salespeople are the first line of customer contact in most firms. Thus, salespeople and the selling function are key success factors in modern organizations.

An important comprehensive customer-centric business model is called customer relationship management, or CRM. This chapter provides an overview of CRM and then proceeds to illustrate how the sales force and selling function interface with strategies and processes in market-oriented, customer-centric firms. The process of strategy development and implementation is outlined, and specific guidance is provided on how personal selling can contribute to marketing strategy and what salespeople can do to maximize the success of long-term customer relationships.

After reading this chapter you should be able to

- Understand and outline the key components and goals of CRM.

- Explain the importance of a market orientation and how a market orientation is fostered within a firm.

- Identify the key steps in developing and implementing strategies.

- Describe the role of personal selling in marketing strategy.

- Outline the stages in developing strategic partnership relationships between organizations.

- Discuss the actions salespeople can take to ensure successful long-term buyer–seller relationships.

WHAT IS CUSTOMER RELATIONSHIP MANAGEMENT?

For many years, introductory marketing textbooks have talked about the **marketing concept** as an overarching business philosophy. At its essence, companies practicing the marketing concept turn to consumers themselves for input in making strategic decisions about what products to market, where to market the products and how to get them to market, at what price, and how to communicate with consumers about the products. These four elements (product, distribution, price, and promotion) are referred to as the **marketing mix.** The elements of the marketing mix represent the "tool kit" marketers use to develop marketing strategy. Personal selling fits into the marketing mix as part of a firm's **marketing communication mix,** or **promotion mix,** along with the other elements of the promotional message used by a firm to communicate with customers: advertising, sales promotion, direct marketing, and public relation/publicity.

Recently, the operationalization or implementation of the marketing concept has become known as a **market orientation.** That is, the actions taken by a firm that is market-oriented would be focused on aligning all the various organizational processes and functions toward maximizing the firm's success in the competitive marketplace.[1] Not surprisingly, a successful market orientation requires that the firm place the customer in the center of all strategic decisions and firm activities. Thus, a key component of market orientation is exhibiting a **customer orientation** in all levels and units of an organization. Considerable research indicates that firms with a higher level of customer orientation are usually more successful than less customer-oriented firms. Firms high in customer orientation are often referred to as **customer-centric,** because they have the customer at the center of their business model.

From a selling function perspective, a customer-centric culture includes, but is not limited to, the following major components:[2]

1. Adopting of a relationship or partnership business model, with mutually shared rewards and risk management.

2. Defining the selling role in terms of the provision of customer business consultation and solutions.

3. Increasing formalization of customer analysis processes and agreements.

4. Taking a proactive leadership role in educating customers about value chain and cost reduction opportunities.

5. Focusing on continuous improvement principles stressing customer satisfaction.

The efforts a firm makes toward cultivating a culture that is market-oriented and customer-centric require a high degree of **formalization** within the firm. Formalization means that structure, processes and tools, and managerial knowledge and commitment are formally established in support of the culture. With these things in place, strategies and programs may be successfully developed and executed toward the goals related to customer centricity. In general, these goals revolve around establishing and maintaining long-term customer relationships. Today, the most prevalent formalization of a customer-centric culture is **customer relationship management (CRM).**

CRM is a comprehensive business model for increasing revenues and profits by focusing on customers. More specifically, CRM refers to "any application or initiative designed to help your company optimize interactions with customers, suppliers, or prospects via one or more touchpoints—such as a call center, salesperson, distributor, store, branch office, Web, or e-mail—for the purpose of acquiring, retaining, or cross-selling customers."[3]

PriceWaterhouseCoopers Consulting has defined CRM as "a journey of strategic, process, organizational, and technical change whereby a company seeks to better manage its enterprise around customer behaviors. This entails acquiring knowledge about customers and deploying this information at each touchpoint to attain increased revenue and operational efficiencies."[4] **Touchpoints** are viewed as the intersection of a business event that takes place via a channel using a medium (e.g., online inquiry from a prospect, telephone follow-up with a purchaser on a service issue, face-to-face encounter with a salesperson, etc.). At their essence, touchpoints are where the selling firm touches the customer in some way, thus allowing for information about customers to be collected.

The above definitions of CRM lead one to conclude that it is both an overarching philosophy of business that puts the customer at the center of strategic decision making (i.e., a customer-centric enterprise) and a programmatic, integrated implementation system (i.e., software-driven) involving a variety of channels and providers, all of which interact to contribute to the delivery of customer value. Many companies are now adopting CRM as a mission-critical business strategy. These companies are redesigning internal and external business processes and associated information systems to make it easier for customers to do business with them. Because the focus of CRM is aligning the organization's internal and external systems to be customer-centric, marketing as a discipline becomes a core contributor to the success of CRM by virtue of its disciplinary expertise on customers. Specifically, the sales force is a group within most firms that can add substantial value to the success of this process. And as we saw in the chapter opener from HR Chally Group, integrating sales with other organizational functions is critical to firm success.

Many of the concepts underlying CRM are not at all new. One might open a Principles of Marketing textbook from 20 years ago and find a discussion of many of the tenets of what we now refer to as CRM, albeit not particularly integrated or cross-functional in scope. What has changed in the environment to allow for the more integrated approach to customers represented by modern CRM is *technology.* More sophisticated approaches to data management are a key enabler of CRM. Yet, it is a serious mistake to consider CRM as mere software. In fact, many firms are struggling with their CRM initiatives precisely because they have bought the sophisticated software but do not have the culture, structure, leadership, or internal technical expertise to make the initiative successful.

The next section provides a foundation for understanding the concept of CRM. Then, in the remainder of the chapter we expand our discussion of the role of personal selling and the sales force in market-oriented firms and in developing and executing marketing strategies.

From Mass Marketing to One-to-One Marketing

CRM has its evolutionary roots in the progression of marketing, as enabled by advancing technology. Exhibit 3.1 illustrates this evolution from mass marketing, through target marketing, to customer marketing, to one-to-one marketing.

Mass marketing evolved in the early 1900s and dominated marketing management and strategy for decades. In the 1960s, many firms began to apply principles of segmentation, **target marketing,** and positioning to create different strategies and marketing programs for different consumer groups. A major change in mind-set precipitates a shift from targeted consumer marketing (i.e., marketing to big groups of like-minded buyers) to **customer marketing,** or a focus on developing relationships with individuals. This approach first gained widespread attention in the 1980s. Many of the issues on relationship selling and strategic partnering presented later in this chapter relate to customer marketing.

EXHIBIT 3.1   **Marketing evolution with characteristics and technology attributes**

Source: Ronald S. Swift, *Accelerating Customer Relationships: Using CRM and Relationship Technologies* (Upper Saddle River, NJ: Prentice Hall PTR, 2001), p. 38.

Ultimately, the sophistication and multiplicity of available technology today enable true **one-to-one marketing,** as some firms are now able to truly customize offerings for individual users. This concept has been introduced and expanded upon in several books by Don Peppers and Martha Rogers.[5]

As mentioned earlier, CRM enters the picture as a process that provides internal formalization for enabling successful customer marketing and one-to-one marketing. CRM has three major objectives:

1. *Customer retention.* The ability to retain loyal and profitable customers and channels to grow the business profitably.

2. *Customer acquisition.* Acquisition of the right customers, based on known or learned characteristics, which drive growth and increased margins.

3. *Customer profitability.* Increased individual customer margins, while offering the right products at the right time.[6]

Thus, a key realization is that CRM involves the process of acquiring, retaining, and growing profitable customers. It requires a clear focus on the service attributes that represent value to the customer and that create loyalty. Simply put, **customer value** means that when the customer weighs the costs (monetary and otherwise) of a relationship with a seller, the benefits realized from that relationship outweigh the costs. Building **customer loyalty** is an important goal of CRM processes because loyal customers are typically highly satisfied with the relationship and the product offering and are very unlikely to switch to another company and its products or brands.

CRM has several advantages over traditional mass media marketing, as has been typically used in support of mass marketing and target marketing. The advantages are that CRM

- Reduces advertising costs.

- Makes it easier to target specific customers by focusing on their needs.

- Makes it easier to track the effectiveness of a given promotional (marketing communications) campaign.

- Allows organizations to compete for customers based on service, not prices.

- Prevents overspending on low-value clients or underspending on high-value ones.

- Speeds the time it takes to develop and market a product (the marketing cycle).

- Improves use of the customer channel, thus making the most of each contact with a customer.[7]

One of the most important concepts in CRM is that of the **lifetime value of a customer.** In his books on customer loyalty, Fredrick Reichheld has demonstrated time and again that investment in CRM yields more successful long-term relationships with customers and that these relationships pay off handsomely in terms of cost savings, revenue growth, profits, referrals, and other important business success factors. It is possible to actually calculate an estimate of the projected financial returns from a customer, providing a very useful strategic tool for deciding which customers deserve what levels of investment of various resources (money, people, time, information, etc.). Such analysis has raised the prospects of **firing a customer** who exhibits a low predicted lifetime value and investing resources elsewhere. Of course, such action assumes other, more attractive customers exist for one's investment.[8]

CRM Process Cycle

The process cycle for CRM may be broken down into the following four elements: (1) knowledge discovery, (2) market planning, (3) customer interaction, and (4) analysis and refinement[9] (see Exhibit 3.2).

Knowledge Discovery

This is the process of analyzing the customer information acquired through the touchpoints mentioned earlier. These might include point-of-sale systems, call center files, Internet accesses, records from direct sales, and any other customer contact experiences. A customer-centric **data warehouse** environment is the optimal approach to handling the data and transforming it into useful information for customer strategy development. A data warehouse environment affords the opportunity to combine large amounts of information and then use **data mining** techniques to learn more about current and potential customers.

A variety of software products are available to help manage the knowledge discovery phase. Some of these are discussed in Technology 3.1.

Market Planning

This is a key use of the output of the knowledge and discovery phase, in that marketing and customer strategies and programs are now developed. These involve the use of the marketing mix and especially the promotion mix in integrated ways. This process will be discussed in detail later in the chapter.

Customer Interaction

This phase represents the actual implementation of the strategies and programs. This includes the personal selling effort, as well as all other customer-directed interactions. These must be aimed at all the customer touchpoints, or channels of customer contact, both in person and electronically.

EXHIBIT 3.2
The CRM process cycle

Source: Ronald S. Swift, *Accelerating Customer Relationships: Using CRM and Relationship Technologies* (Upper Saddle River, NJ: Prentice Hall PTR, 2001), p. 40.

Technology   Making Sense of Sales Process Software   3.1

Giles Barton knows the frustration of tossing good money after bad. Barton, president of 50-employee Expeditor Systems in Alpharetta, Ga., has poured more than $200,000 into customer relationship management (CRM) software in the past decade. But early CRM products were too rudimentary for his $5 million company, which makes custom lighting panels—almost like mini-stop lights posted outside examining room doors—that tell doctors which patients need immediate attention. None of the software ever offered enough customization. "We never really had what we wanted," says Barton, no matter what he spent.

Plenty of small business owners know exactly what he means. CRM products began to appear about a decade ago with the seemingly simple aim of helping companies coordinate their sales processes and improve the bottom line. But the software had glitches and often couldn't be integrated with other systems. In 2001 more than 55 percent of CRM projects failed to meet corporate expectations, according to Gartner, a consulting firm in Stamford, Conn.

The good news is that CRM software keeps getting better, particularly for small businesses. These days, about one-third of CRM projects miss the mark, says Bob Thompson, founder of CustomerThink.com (formerly CRMguru.com), a Web portal for the industry in Burlingame, Calif. That's still pretty scary, but Thompson says many flameouts aren't the result of problems with the technology. Much of what CRM software does is automate processes, so it's only as good as the procedures you've already established. "What drives success and failure is your strategy, how you deal with customers as an organization," says Thompson. Also important: whether a company has clear goals for the implementation from the get-go.

There are about 10 CRM products geared to small business on the market, ranging from basic contact management for sales pros to multifunction packages that include marketing-campaign management, customer support, and accounting. Most allow you to handle customer contacts and communications in a central location, forecast sales, track leads, and evaluate employee performance. Pipeline management features, for example, show execs which opportunities each salesperson is pursuing. And frequent reports make it easy to determine which salespeople are performing well and to get sales forecasts without wading through reams of paper.

You can buy CRM software either as a desktop application, loaded onto a server, or as a hosted service. Nearly all CRM software makers are now integrating their products with Microsoft Outlook. Some vendors offer easy integration with QuickBooks and other back-office systems. Many provide access through wireless PDAs.

By carefully picking the right package for your company, you can raise the odds of success—both for your future sales and for the software itself. Your choice depends on the size of your company, your needs, and your budget. Then it's a matter of finding products that sport the features you want.

Companies with only a handful of employees can get started with standard packages from GoldMine or ACT! for about $200 a user. These let you centralize contact information, schedule appointments, and forecast and track sales opportunities. If you want to share information among more than five employees, you'll need to upgrade to ACT! Premium for Workgroups 2006 or Gold-Mine Corporate Edition, which require a server and cost about $400 to $600 per person. Keith Lewandoski, senior financial consultant for Barrell Investment Group, a $1 million, eight-employee financial planning firm in Quechee, Vt., began using the basic version of GoldMine last year after outgrowing Outlook. Lewandoski uses the software to store client contact information, make follow-up notes, schedule meetings, automate mailings—even send out birthday cards. He spent about $180 but so far he's the only user. Because GoldMine can be used either on the desktop or networked using a server, Lewandoski is thinking about giving the entire office access to help his staff work together better as a team.

Companies whose needs go beyond sales force automation might consider products that offer marketing, customer service, and support features, as well as some customization, running about $750 to $850 annually for each user. Customer service and support capabilities range from case management and automated routing of calls to service scheduling and service contracts. Marketing features may include e-mail marketing, tracking budgets on campaigns, and lead management. So if a computer company has extra inventory of laptop battery packs, it can dice its customer list and e-mail promotional coupons to target only laptop customers, and then track the response.

Products with these broader capabilities include server-based software, such as Microsoft Dynamics CRM 3.0, and hosted services, such as Salesforce.com and NetSuite Small Business. Salesforce.com is a good bet for growing companies. That's because it has offerings for very small companies as well as those with more than 100 employees, saving you the trouble of converting to a new product as your company grows. NetSuite Small Business is

(continued)

Technology   *concluded*   3.1

the only product that offers accounting features and Web site management. Two others—Sage CRM and Sugar Professional—are available as either a hosted service or as server software.

While the previous version of Microsoft Dynamics CRM 1.2 was plagued by problems, including limited functionality and difficulty installing the software on servers, the company and its resellers claim those kinks are gone from Microsoft CRM 3.0, released in December, 2005. "I can take a customer who is using Outlook and very easily transition their business to Microsoft CRM without a lot of pain," says Anne Stanton, president of the Norwich Group in Norwich, Vt., a technical consultant who is a registered Microsoft partner but also recommends other brands.

For many months, the five employees of TonerZone.com had to manually reenter customer information into their ordering, shipping, and customer service systems because those products couldn't integrate with ACT! In 2003, Ilan Douek, president of the Los Angeles company, began using NetSuite Small Business instead. "Now when an order comes in we don't have to manually enter information again, all the way to printing the UPS label," says Douek. His salespeople segment the customer database using transaction history to create targeted marketing campaigns for such products as Hewlett-Packard inkjet cartridges. They can also determine whether the customer owns products such as a Brother fax machine or a Canon copier and try to cross-sell or up-sell.

Douek says revenues have soared from $1 million in 2003 to more than $5 million in 2005. Without NetSuite, he estimates he'd need four more employees in customer service, five more in fulfillment, and one additional IT person. That, he says, would cost about $16,000 in salaries each month, easily justifying the service's monthly fee of $1,800.

Other fast-growth entrepreneurs may eventually need a more advanced CRM system that can be heavily customized. In August 2003, Barton's Expeditor Systems began using such a package—Sage CRM SalesLogix. As with other high-end packages, SalesLogix requires a full-time administrator on staff as well as someone to customize the software. But Barton says, "it runs so well that we have one administrative person responsible for it, and she's not a computer person." He's even more pleased that his employees can parse Expeditor's customer list to track down the status of an order. "We want to manage the customers by who is in line for installation, and now the installation and service department can work from that point of view," he says.

SalesLogix sells for a one-time fee of $995 a user. For a company with 50 employees, that's a significant chunk of change. But Barton says his company is running more efficiently. "We got a return on investment almost instantly," says Barton. It was a long time coming.

Source: "Making Sense of Sales," *BusinessWeek,* Spring 2006, *www.businessweek.com.*

Analysis and Refinement

Finally, the analysis and refinement phase of the CRM process is where learning takes place based on customer response to the implemented strategies and programs. This is a continuous dialogue with customers that is facilitated by all of the inputs for customer feedback. Over time, adjustments made to the firm's overall customer initiatives should yield more and more efficient investment of resources in the endeavor such that **return on customer investment** is maximized.

Toward a Relationship-Based Enterprise

As stated at the beginning of this section, CRM represents both an overarching business philosophy and a process or tool to facilitate a truly customer-driven enterprise. Facilitating long-term, win-win relationships between buyer and seller firms is a central tenet of CRM. In order to move toward being a relationship-based enterprise, and to improve the effectiveness of CRM initiatives, 10 critical questions must be answered.[10] These questions may be grouped by the following categories: customers, the relationship, and managerial decision making.

Customers

1. Who are our customers?

2. What do our customers want and expect?

3. What is the value potential of our customers?

The Relationship

4. What kind of relationship do we want to build with our customers?

5. How do we foster exchange?

6. How do we work together and share control?

Managerial Decision Making

7. Who are we?

8. How do we organize to move value closer to our customers?

9. How do we measure and manage our performance?

10. How do we increase our capacity for change?

Gaining satisfactory answers to these questions is fundamental to the success of CRM and to becoming a relationship-based firm. The answers guide (1) the evolution of the firm's relationships with customers, (2) the creation of a companywide relationship management game plan, and (3) the selection of solutions with the most appropriate combination and application of supporting technology.[11]

Given the promise of CRM, it is unfortunate that we must report a high failure and abandonment rate for CRM initiatives. Leadership 3.2 provides insight into reasons why CRM fails.

The remainder of this chapter builds on our knowledge of the importance of customer relationships by (1) introducing the concept of market orientation, (2) outlining the process of developing strategies, (3) explaining the role of personal selling in marketing strategy, and (4) providing insights into key issues of personal selling in the relationship era.

THE IMPORTANCE OF MARKET ORIENTATION

If asked to describe marketing, many people may list activities that describe only selling. And even though some companies call salespeople *marketing representatives,* selling and marketing are not synonymous. As students of marketing know, marketing involves creating products and services that satisfy customer needs, pricing those products and services to meet the customer's budget and make a profit for the firm, placing those products and services so that the customer can access them, and promoting the products and services so that the customer is aware of where they are and what they do. To some degree, the trend toward calling salespeople *marketing representatives* is an accurate portrayal because salespeople often identify customer needs, tailor products and services to meet those needs, negotiate price, and so forth. As mentioned earlier, personal selling is a part of the promotional mix of a firm, which of course represents part of a firm's marketing mix.

The marketing concept states that the key to business success is to identify and satisfy customer needs. Recall that companies that have adopted the marketing concept as a philosophy or way of doing business are considered market-oriented companies. In a market-oriented company, salespeople play a very important role because they not only

Leadership   CRM Failures Are Often Management's Fault   3.2

Here's a mantra worth repeating: CRM software isn't stupid. People are stupid (or they can be)—especially the "management" kind of people. Problems leading to CRM failure often are traced to organizational, not software, issues. Below are some key reasons for CRM system flops in sales organizations, along with critical fixes to the problems.

1. *Lack of focus.* **Problem:** Purchasing one CRM software package after another, usually through upgrading, under the auspices of finding a system that fits our needs. **Critical fix:** Reverse the process. Involve everyone in determining in advance what the key desired deliverables are, then purchase the system that meets these goals.

2. *No change management initiative in place.* **Problem:** Successful CRM installation is not a "technology first, change follows" process. **Fix:** Heavy-duty discussions and formal plans for organizational change must be in place before the CRM switch is thrown. This includes change in culture, structure, and process. Technology is an enabler of sales success, not a change agent for a sales organization.

3. *Minimal buy-in.* **Problem:** Salespeople can be fiercely independent. Particularly, very successful salespeople may balk at changing their customer approach substantively. **Fix:** Salespeople must be involved in the CRM planning process from day one to ensure their interests are fully integrated into the system. Alignment of internal organizational performance management issues, such as incentives and rewards, is key.

4. *Business units are silos.* **Problem:** CRM needs cross-functional integration of information gathering, analysis, and dissemination inside a firm to work. A recent report from the Meta Group indicates that half of companies surveyed say lack of cross-functional planning and communication among departments within their own firms is the leading difficulty in CRM. The biggest mistake is thinking CRM is "owned" by the IT people simply because the process is software-driven. **Fix:** Cross-disciplinary teams should be established from the initiation of the planning stages for CRM that require IT and sales managers to work together (as well as other functional players like marketing, accounting, and sales support). If anyone should "own" CRM, it should be the customer contact team within a firm, which usually means the sales force.

5. *Complicated procedures.* **Problem:** Firms often end up using CRM to automate processes that are already inefficient. **Fix:** Reengineer first; implement CRM second. Eliminate or change processes that don't funnel into whatever your defined outcome goals are for the CRM initiative.

6. *Poor training.* **Problem:** CRM doesn't work on autopilot. A great CRM system in the hands of a poorly trained (or untrained) customer contact person spells disaster. **Fix:** Make initial and ongoing training priority one in implementing CRM. Formalize a system for employee feedback to management on system successes and failures, and especially foster a climate for employee input on ideas for system improvements. The best firms institutionalize this through reward systems with payoffs to employees who help increase the effectiveness of the CRM program.

Despite the fact that these potential pitfalls of CRM implementation, if not properly addressed, can be devastating to a firm financially, operationally, and culturally, the good news is that each of these issues can be proactively dealt with by the firm. As stated in the beginning: If the CRM system fails, the first place to look is not within the software but within the ranks of management.

Source: Kathleen Cholewka, "CRM: The Failures Are Your Fault," *Sales & Marketing Management* 154 (January 2002), pp. 23–24.

identify customer needs and satisfy those needs through the sale of a product or service but must also represent the customer to various areas within the sales company. Companies that can adapt quickly to meet changing customer requirements will be successful—it is the responsibility of the sales force to see that those changing requirements are communicated to the right people so that the company can change. Customer centricity, or being customer-centric, is a key element of a market orientation.

So selling is important, not only because of the company's immediate need to generate revenue through the sale of products and services, or only because selling often is the largest marketing expense, but also because the future of the company depends on salespeople who can carry the voice of the customer throughout the firm. Managing the selling function is one of the most important management functions in any organization, not just because selling is so important (as we saw in Chapter 2) but also because managing selling is unique. Were it not unique, a separate course in sales management would not be necessary!

How Market Orientation Affects Performance

Market-driven companies, or those with a strong market orientation, are superior in two important ways. First, market-driven companies do a better job of market sensing, or anticipating market requirements ahead of the competition. Market sensing is the gathering of information from the market. The sales force should be one important avenue of market sensing, but other avenues include observing competitors' and customers' actions at trade shows, market research, and monitoring customer complaints.

Similarly, the second important difference is that market-driven companies are able to develop stronger relationships with their customers and their channels of distribution. Stronger relationships include more direct lines of communication. Instead of all communication going between a purchasing agent and a salesperson, interaction among engineers, for example, in all three firms (customer, manufacturer, and supplier) can occur. Stronger relationships can result in greater attention to the customer throughout the firm.

Neither important skill (market sensing and relationship building) can develop, however, without the presence of adequate spanning processes, or processes that link internal processes with the customer. Sales management is an important link in the spanning process, as sales managers must represent the sales force and customers to others in the company. For example, salespeople are often the first in the company to run into a new competitor. It takes the sales manager, however, to make sure that those responsible for pricing or product development are aware of the method by which the new competitor is attacking the market. Exhibit 3.3 illustrates the relationship of internal processes with

EXHIBIT 3.3 **Classifying capabilities of market-oriented firms**

Source: George S. Day, "Capabilities of Market-Driven Organizations," *Journal of Marketing* 58 (October 1994), pp. 37–52. Reprinted by permission of the American Marketing Association.

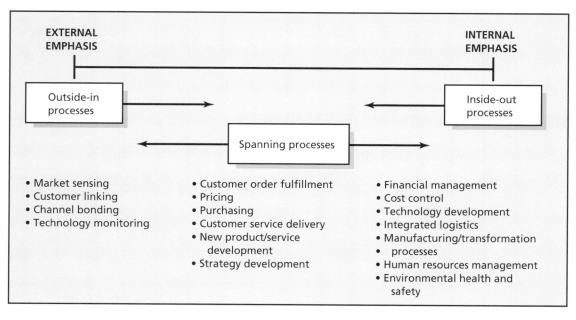

spanning processes to link with customer requirements in market-oriented firms. In this exhibit, internal processes such as financial management are shown to link with spanning processes, such as order fulfillment, which then impact customer-linking processes or other external processes. For internal processes to contribute to the value delivered by the value chain, adequate spanning processes must exist.

Internal Partnering to Create a Market Orientation

Internal and external processes are often in conflict, as different sets of objectives are sought. Sales management wants every potential customer to buy, for example, while the credit department wants only creditworthy accounts. Internal partnering is one spanning process that, when done well, can result in managing such conflict so that it has a positive effect on the firm. Internal partnering, or creating partnering relationships with other functional areas (customers and suppliers within the firm), can also serve to carry market requirements to those managers in charge of internal processes, such as credit approval. Internal partnering is a spanning process that creates a framework or environment for other spanning processes, such as postsale service, new product development, or market penetration and development processes. The result is a market orientation throughout the firm and not just in the sales force.

The customer's voice must be carried to many parts of the firm—internal partnering is one mechanism for carrying that voice. Recognize, though, that it is the sales manager's responsibility to build these internal partnerships. Although a customer focus should pervade the firm, rarely do information systems, employment selection systems, personnel evaluation systems, or other systems encourage departments, other than sales, to take the initiative. In fact, it is more likely that just the opposite is true, that incentives abound to not listen to the customer. For example, it costs manufacturing managers to change production from one product to another, yet a sales manager may need to be able to offer different products in order to meet the customer's objectives.

Being market-oriented and customer-centric requires that a firm have a solid foundation of identity. A solid foundation of identity is a clear understanding of what the company is and is striving to be. Too much information is available to try to learn it all, just as too many potential opportunities exist in the marketplace to try to serve them all. A company creates an identity that helps focus learning and market orientation by first creating a sound mission and appropriate goals. Clarity in mission and goals provides the focus, or **strategic direction,** on which a firm's marketing strategy may be built and implemented. The next section provides a primer on this process.

THE PROCESS OF STRATEGY DEVELOPMENT

Company Mission and Goals

An organization's **mission statement** attempts to answer the most basic questions about its reason for being. What is our business? What should it be? These seem like simple questions, but they are often difficult for management to answer. Too many mission statements are full of platitudes and attributes that everyone has, rather than focusing on elements that truly define the organization. To illustrate the problem, a group of managers from more than 20 companies identified the same mission statement as being that of their own company![12]

Many organizations define their missions too narrowly by focusing on the production of a particular product or service. As technology and customer needs change, specific products and services become obsolete, and firms that define their mission in narrow terms can become obsolete as well. Few streetcar companies are in business today, for instance, but many organizations are attempting to satisfy the need for urban mass transit through a variety of other means.

The most appropriate way for a firm to define its mission is in terms of the broad human needs it will try to satisfy. Many people are familiar with Dell's customer-focused direct business model, and the company's success in creating leading value for customers and investors. Less well known is the unique environment forged by Michael Dell and the people of Dell since the company's founding in 1984.

Dell characterizes that environment in a statement of corporate philosophy on its Web site called the "Soul of Dell." It defines the kind of company we are and aspire to become, serves as a guide for our actions around the world, and ultimately forms the basis of our "winning culture."

Below are the core elements of the Soul of Dell:

Customers: We believe in creating loyal customers by providing a superior experience at a great value. We are committed to direct relationships, providing the best products and services based on standards-based technology, and outperforming the competition with value and a superior customer experience.

The Dell Team: We believe our continued success lies in teamwork and the opportunity each team member has to learn, develop and grow. We are committed to being a meritocracy, and to developing, retaining and attracting the best people, reflective of our worldwide marketplace.

Direct Relationships: We believe in being direct in all we do. We are committed to behaving ethically; responding to customer needs in a timely and reasonable manner; fostering open communications and building effective relationships with customers, partners, suppliers and each other; and operating without inefficient hierarchy and bureaucracy.

Global Citizenship: We believe in participating responsibly in the global marketplace. We are committed to understanding and respecting the laws, values and cultures wherever we do business; profitably growing in all markets; promoting a healthy business climate globally; and contributing positively in every community we call home, both personally and organizationally.

Winning: We have a passion for winning in everything we do. We are committed to operational excellence, superior customer experience, leading in the global markets we serve, being known as a great company and great place to work, and providing superior shareholder value over time.[13]

When an organization's mission is defined in terms of satisfying a need, it becomes easier to identify attractive market opportunities. When an oil company defines its mission as satisfying people's energy needs, it is then clear that the company should be exploring a variety of energy sources, such as solar power, in addition to locating new sources of petroleum. Similarly, a clearly defined mission helps management evaluate available opportunities and avoid those that are inconsistent with the firm's purpose.

Goals, or objectives, flow from the company's mission and represent more specific targets the firm wishes to meet. Example areas for goal-setting are a firm's financial position, how well it is doing in the marketplace, the quality of its products, and the level of satisfaction of its customers. **Objectives** are simply more specific than goals. So, for example, Procter & Gamble might have a goal to maintain its position as number one in market share in the toothpaste category, but flowing from this might be quite a few specific objectives such as increasing sales on Crest pump by 5 percent in 2006. Generally, good objectives should always be (1) specific, (2) measurable, (3) and realistically attainable.

SBU Strategy

In organizations with multiple divisions or **strategic business units** (SBUs), each SBU is likely to have its own objectives and a distinct strategy for accomplishing them. For example, General Electric has many strategic business units competing in quite distinct markets—appliances, aircraft, plastics, and power systems, to name a few. The keystone of a business-level strategy is a decision about how the business will compete in its industry to achieve a **sustainable competitive advantage** (SCA). An SCA is based on the set of **distinctive competencies** exhibited by the firm. That is, what quality or attribute of the organization sets it aside from its competitors? How is it, or how will it be, different from the rest of the pack?[14] Dell, for example, has as one of its distinctive competencies the capability of offering customers a wide variety of features they can build into a computer in various combinations. An SBU may contain a number of different products or brands, and its competitive strategy will influence and constrain the marketing goals/objectives, strategies, and functional programs—including the activities of the sales force—appropriate for each of those products.

Several authors have developed classification systems that identify a few common or **generic strategies** pursued by business units across a variety of industries. The best known of these was developed by Michael Porter. He defined three basic competitive strategies: low cost, differentiation, and niche (or focus).[15] Another popular typology of competitive strategies was developed by Miles and Snow. They classified strategies according to the emphasis placed on growth through new product and market development, and they labeled the resulting categories prospector, defender, and analyzer strategies.[16] Brief definitions of these six generic business strategies are provided in Exhibit 3.4.

For an SBU to effectively implement its competitive strategy, the marketing strategies and functional marketing programs for each of its products or product lines should be tailored to the requirements of that strategy. For example, when Hewlett-Packard acquired Compaq, it shifted Compaq from a differentiation strategy focused on offering technically superior products to a more price-oriented, low-cost competitive strategy. Innovation 3.3 provides insight into how HP is currently positioning Compaq in the marketplace. Some specific implications of different competitive strategies for a business's selling programs and activities are also summarized in Exhibit 3.4.[17]

The strategy process represents a series of steps. These steps are portrayed in Exhibit 3.5. Once a business has decided how it will compete in order to gain a sustainable advantage over other firms, it must then decide where to compete: what specific product markets or market segments it will target. This decision involves assessing the available market opportunities.

Step One: Analyze Market Opportunities

In the broadest sense, a **market opportunity** exists whenever some human need is unsatisfied. However, an unsatisfied need represents a viable and attractive opportunity for a firm only if:

1. The opportunity is consistent with the mission and objectives of the firm.

2. Enough potential customers exist for the needed product or service so the total potential sales volume is, or will be, substantial.

3. The firm has the necessary resources and expertise to capture an adequate share of the total market.

EXHIBIT 3.4 Generic business strategies and their implications for the sales force

Source: Adapted from William L. Cron and Michael Levy, "Sales Management Performance Evaluation: A Residual Income Perspective," *Journal of Personal Selling & Sales Management* 7 (August 1987), pp. 57–66.

Porter's typology	Sales force implications
Low-cost supplier	
Aggressive construction of efficient-scale facilities, vigorous pursuit of cost reductions from experience, tight cost and overhead control, usually associated with high relative market share.	Servicing large current customers, pursuing large prospects, minimizing costs, selling on the basis of price, and usually assuming significant order-taking responsibilities.
Differentiation	
Creation of something perceived industrywide as being unique. Provides insulation against competitive rivalry because of brand loyalty and resulting lower sensitivity to price.	Selling nonprice benefits, generating orders, providing high quality of customer service and responsiveness, possibly significant amount of prospecting if high growth industry, selecting customers based on low price sensitivity. Usually requires a high-quality sales force.
Niche (or focus)	
Service of a particular target market, with each functional policy developed with this target market in mind. Although market share in the industry might be low, the firm dominates a segment within the industry.	Becoming experts in the operations and opportunities associated with the target market. Focusing customer attention on nonprice benefits and allocating selling time to the target market.

Miles and Snow's typology	Sales force implications
Prospector	
Attempt to pioneer in product market development. Offer a frequently changing product line and be willing to sacrifice short-term profits to gain a long-term stronghold in their markets.	Primary focus is on sales volume growth. Territory management emphasizes customer penetration and prospecting.
Defender	
Offer a limited, stable product line to a predictable market. Markets are generally in the late growth or early maturity phase of the product life cycle. Emphasis is on being the low-cost producer through high volume.	Maintain the current customer base. Very little prospecting for new customers is involved. Customer service is emphasized along with greater account penetration.
Analyzer	
Choose high-growth markets while holding onto substantial mature markets. Analyzers are an intermediate type of firm. They make fewer and slower product market changes than prospectors, but are less committed to stability and efficiency than defenders.	Must balance multiple roles—servicing existing customers, prospecting for new customers, uncovering new applications, holding onto distribution of mature products, and supporting campaigns for new products.

Evaluating market opportunities involves first evaluating the environmental factors affecting the market and estimating the total market potential for a good or service. Next, the firm must evaluate its capabilities and strengths compared with those of competitors to estimate the share of the total market potential it can reasonably hope to secure. Later, after a specific marketing strategy has been determined, the firm can develop sales forecasts of the actual sales volume it expects to attain over a specified time period.

Innovation   Hewlett-Packard's New, Simple Compaq   3.3

From the start, the Compaq personal-computer brand posed a dilemma when Hewlett-Packard acquired it five years ago. Compaq was struggling in the consumer market, as was HP's own brand. Dell, with its low prices and direct sales over the phone and the Web, was eating HP's lunch. "Some people suggested we drop Compaq," recalls Satjiv Chahil, HP's senior vice-president of marketing for the PC business. "But we said, 'No, it's a valuable brand. We'll position it for the future.'"

That recasting has been a long time coming, as the Compaq brand has been losing market share in the key U.S. consumer market. But now that HP has managed to turn around its core namesake line, the company is rethinking how it defines Compaq. Long marketed as a PC that is merely a good value for the money, HP wants to convey the notion that Compaq also offers, as executives say, "simplicity."

Any company juggling multiple consumer brands must figure out how to position them so that buyers understand they are distinct and appreciate the differences. HP has experienced that problem. As recently as a few years ago, there wasn't much difference between the HP and Compaq product lines. "They both tended to play in the middle market," says Chahil. "Over the years, HP and Compaq had blurred."

EVERYDAY IMAGE

But with an intense design and marketing effort begun in 2005, the company has elevated the HP brand to a premium level. That move has helped drive the company's financial turnaround and propel it to the top spot in market-share rankings, zipping past rival Dell. Now, the challenge is to jump-start Compaq with a brand message that doesn't tread on HP's upscale image.

HP, through celebrity-laden marketing and souped-up products, presents its namesake line as an "aspirational" brand that offers high-end entertainment and multimedia. It markets the bulk of its notebooks, for instance, as "entertainment" products, ranging in price from $580 to $1,050. A step higher is its "extreme multimedia" notebook priced at $3,000. By contrast, HP wants Compaq to project the image of being "approachable and tangible," says Stacy Wolff, a PC design director at HP. "It's simple, affordable, and meant to appeal to someone who just wants a PC." The company currently markets Compaq products as appropriate for "everyday computing."

KEEP THE CUSTOMER SATISFIED

Who is the typical Compaq customer? Among the potential segments are students, women who are ambivalent about having loads of multimedia features, and small businesses. Using a second brand to target slices of the consumer market can be wise, analysts say. "The market demands segmentation," says David Daoud, analyst at industry researcher IDC. "If you have just one brand and can't serve different segments, you could be in trouble. HP recognizes that when you're dealing with a mature and saturated market, you need to go for niche customers and their needs."

And Compaq's market share has been declining for years. In 2006, Compaq held about a 7 percent share of U.S. desktop sales, down from 12 percent the prior year. In laptops, its share was 11 percent, down from 11.6 percent in 2005 and 12.5 percent in 2004. While a new marketing message could shore up Compaq's own share, it could also help HP hang on to price-sensitive customers who might otherwise defect to Dell, Toshiba, or other competitors. "HP wants to protect itself from competitors nipping away at the low end," says John Allen, a principal of Highbridge Consulting. A revamped Compaq "could protect the company's total market share without degrading the upper-end HP image."

A MINIMALIST APPROACH

Design teams are already working on the next generation of Compaq machines, expected to reach the market next year and geared toward the notion of simple and minimal. For example, current Compaq laptops use multiple shades of gray and black, and the keyboard and monitor areas have many surfaces of varying heights. In the future, internal surfaces will appear monochromatic, smoother, and "less broken up," says HP's Wolff. Even though other PC makers are selling machines in a range of colors, the Compaq brand is likely to stick with shades of gray. By contrast, the HP-brand PCs feature fancy black-lacquer finishes, some decorated with extra touches including a wave-like pattern inspired by a Zen rock garden.

Despite the growing popularity of add-on multimedia features, ranging from cameras to fancy speakers and microphones, Compaq designers will make a conscious effort to hold back. The overriding message: Compaq machines just get the job done. With a Compaq PC, "the

(continued)

Innovation   *concluded*   3.3

audio components are meant to be purposeful, vs. having a testosterone-charged speaker," says Wolff. "HP PCs have gaming features like speakers and lights. You won't see that in Compaq. We'll strive to not put in a lot of extra components and pieces."

Although customers won't see the new minimalist Compaq products for months, the company has already redesigned the most visible element of its marketing: the logo. The old logo spelled out the entire brand name. The new logo, which was introduced a few months ago, is almost square and is a cross between a C and a Q. "It's a line that traces a simple shape," says HP's Chahil, adding that the company drew inspiration from the king of minimalist design: Calvin Klein.

Source: Louise Lee, "Hewlett-Packard's New, Simple Compaq," *BusinessWeek* (August 16, 2007), *www.businessweek.com*.

These estimates of total market potential, company sales potential, and sales forecasts are critical to the firm's sales plans. They provide the basis for defining sales territories, deploying salespeople, and setting sales quotas. Methods for analyzing market opportunities and generating sales forecasts are examined in more detail in Chapter 5.

Market opportunities usually do not involve every consumer or organizational buyer in the marketplace. Market opportunities should be defined, and marketing strategies developed, for specific target markets, which usually consist of only one or a few customer segments with relatively homogeneous preferences and characteristics.

EXHIBIT 3.5

Steps in developing and implementing strategies

Step Two: Generate Strategies

Strategy generation is a creative task. Typically, several strategies will achieve the same objective. For example, a computer firm interested in increasing its market share might (1) attempt to leapfrog its competitors by introducing a technically superior new generation of computers, (2) attempt to become the low-cost producer and compete aggressively on price, or (3) appeal to customers by developing more convenient distribution channels, such as Dell Computers, which sells its products online and by phone but also offers customers the opportunity to order from manned kiosks in shopping malls and airports.

The key at this stage is to be as creative as possible. The idea is not to evaluate strategies but to generate them. Not only is listing some "far-out" strategies acceptable at this stage, but it is desirable. Later stages in the process will reduce this original list to a more reasonable set. However, generating as many ideas as possible to begin with will ensure that the better strategies are entertained when evaluating alternatives. Even the most sophisticated evaluation procedure cannot select the optimal strategy if no one has thought of it.

Step Three: Select the Strategy

The criteria used to select the most promising marketing strategy should be directly related to the objectives to be accomplished. For example, if the major marketing objective is to increase market share, then those strategies likely to yield high share increases should be scrutinized. Typically, however, a business will have several marketing objectives, and the strategy that is best for one might be detrimental in achieving another. Thus, the best overall strategy may not be the best for any single objective.

Step Four: Program the Marketing Mix

A **marketing program** combines elements of the marketing mix to implement the strategy. It reflects a particular allocation of financial and human resources. The decision involves three questions: (1) How much is going to be spent on the total marketing effort? (2) How is that expenditure going to be allocated among the elements of the marketing mix? (3) How are the dollars and effort allocated to an element going to be divided among the possible activities? The program level is where the formulation of the firm's sales program often enters the planning picture—it is one part of the firm's overall marketing communications program.

Step Five: Review and Revise the Strategy

Those in charge of the functional areas of the business are typically charged with generating plans for the functions they supervise. This raises the possibility that the marketing plan prepared by a product manager may be incompatible with the business unit's financial or production plans. For example, the cash flows generated by projected product sales might be insufficient or provide too low a return on capital to produce the product. The various functional plans, therefore, must be reviewed and integrated into a cohesive whole at the business-unit and corporate level.

Step Six: Audit and Adjust the Strategy

Today's volatile environment makes planning crucial and also necessitates periodic evaluations of these plans. As competitors adjust their strategies and other environmental conditions change, it may be necessary to revise the firm's plans and programs.

When goals and objectives have been spelled out in specific and measurable terms during the planning process, controlling the marketing plan is rather straightforward.

It involves periodic comparisons of actual results with the sales volume, market share, expense budgets, and other objectives specified in the plan. When the results deviate from planned levels, management can attempt to find out why and, if necessary, take corrective action. This could involve adjusting specific elements of the marketing mix, adopting a new marketing strategy, or possibly reevaluating market opportunities.

The sales manager plays a major role in this evaluation and control process since he or she is responsible for evaluating the results of the sales program. Part Three of this book is devoted to a discussion of this control and adjustment process.

PERSONAL SELLING'S ROLE IN MARKETING STRATEGY

As mentioned earlier, a number of choices face strategic planners, choices that include the type of strategy la Porter or Miles and Snow. Another choice facing strategic marketing planners is the type of relationship desired with the market or segments of the market. The nature of the sales force and its role in carrying out a firm's marketing strategy depend on the type of relationship with the market desired by the organization. Other factors, such as the cost to serve a market, also affect the role of the sales force, as we will discuss.

Role of the Relationship

Most people think of relationships as the bonds that exist between people, and that definition works in many social instances. In business, though, it is more helpful to recognize that relationships occur along a continuum that can be defined by the types of transactions between a buyer and seller. Three basic relationship types exist along this continuum: market exchanges, functional relationships, and strategic partnerships. Exhibit 3.6 summarizes the characteristics of each of these relationship types.

Market Exchanges

At one end of the continuum are **market exchanges,** or one-shot transactions that occur between a buyer and seller without much thought of future interaction. For example, consider a gasoline purchase. Most people purchase gasoline where it is convenient when they are low on gas. They don't buy gasoline at the same place time after time because they like the clerk and want to do business with that store. Yet, over time, it is possible that a large percentage of purchases are made at the same gas station. These purchases still represent market exchanges because it is the location of the station that drives the purchase—it is on the way to work or closest to the house and so on.

EXHIBIT 3.6
Types of relationships between buyers and sellers

Source: Barton Weitz, Stephen Castleberry, and John Tanner, *Selling: Building Partnerships,* 6th ed. (New York: Irwin/ McGraw-Hill, 2005).

Characteristics of the relationship	Type of Relationship		
	Market exchange	Functional relationship	Strategic partnership
Time horizon	Short term	Long term	Long term
Concern for other party	Low	Medium	High
Trust	Low	High	High
Investment in relationship	Low/medium	High	High
Nature of relationship	Conflict, bargaining	Cooperation	Collaboration
Risk in relationship	Low	Medium	High
Potential benefits	Low	Medium	High

Do salespeople have a role in market exchanges? Yes, but that role may be different or even uncomfortable for traditional sales forces. Neil Rackham described four different roles for salespeople operating in a market exchange (transactional) selling environment:[18]

1. *Create new value.* Find a way to create a truly distinctive offering, either by product innovation or by developing truly distinctive services that are of real and measurable value to customers and, in so doing, escape a transactional role.

2. *Adapt.* Reengineer your sales approach to succeed in transactional selling by relentlessly stripping out sales and related costs.

3. *Make the market.* Find ways to profit from the transaction itself, either in addition to or in place of the profit you make from the products you sell. A great example of this is the SABRE airline reservation system originally operated by American Airlines parent AMR Corporation. While air travel has become increasingly a commodity, SABRE has positioned itself to make money from the transactions a commodity-driven system generates.

4. *Exit.* If you can't figure out a way to succeed in this type of sale, then seriously consider disengaging from the transactional segment of the market, this transactional product or product line, or this transactional customer type.

From the above, it may be obvious that several characteristics of a market can influence the use of a market exchange relationship strategy. Characteristics such as lack of product differentiation (i.e., commodity products), competition primarily on price, and similar factors can necessitate a market exchange strategy.

Functional Relationships

As we move along the continuum portrayed in Exhibit 3.6, **functional relationships** reflect the middle area. Functional relationships are long-term relationships between buyer and seller based on close personal friendships. These personal relationships create a climate of cooperation, with open and honest communication.

When functional relationships are appropriate, the salesperson's relationship with the buyer is critical. Examples include financial planning (where the broker becomes a trusted confidant of the client) and contract manufacturing, an industry where salespeople develop strong relationships with product designers so that the sellers' components are included in new products.

Functional relationships can be appropriate when a high level of personal trust is required to manage the business relationship and when the salesperson has special expertise that provides competitive advantage. In these situations, it is in the buyer's best interest to seek a functional relationship. Functional relationships can grow for other reasons that are not strategic.

One danger of functional relationships for the selling organization becomes reality when one party leaves. If the buyer changes jobs, even within the buying organization, a new functional relationship must be created. Similarly, if the salesperson leaves, the relationship is at risk, particularly if the salesperson goes to a competing company. In some industries, it is quite common for salespeople to take their accounts with them—these are industries characterized by functional relationships.

Strategic Partnerships

At the far end of the continuum from market exchanges are **strategic partnerships.** Strategic partnerships are long-term relationships in which the partners make significant investments to improve profitability of both companies and jointly achieve strategic objectives. In a true strategic partnership, the relationship is between two organizations and reflects a wide range of personal relationships between members of the two organizations. Thus, the relationship is no longer solely salesperson-centered.

The salesperson still plays an important role, however. This relationship requires direct communication with production, product designers, and others, but the salesperson is responsible for ensuring that the relationship remains strong. Salespeople are both relationship managers and general managers, because they are responsible for ensuring the mutual profitability that arises out of the relationship. As relationship managers, they work directly with the buyer to codevelop joint strategic programs and to strengthen the relationship. As general managers, they work within their own organization to see that the strategic programs are carried out.

Strategic partnerships cannot be created with every customer, nor should they be. Strategic partnerships should only be created with customers that are large and can make the investments needed worthwhile, with customers that are innovative and can provide technology that other customers cannot, or with customers that provide access to markets better than any other customer. For example, Procter & Gamble and Wal-Mart share a well-publicized strategic partnership. Wal-Mart teaches P&G supply chain management methods that enable P&G to be more profitable with all customers. Wal-Mart benefits from P&G's market knowledge and marketing technology. Through this knowledge and technology, Wal-Mart is able to codevelop new markets and new products with P&G so that both companies can capitalize on market opportunities.

PERSONAL SELLING IN THE RELATIONSHIP ERA

The name of the game today for sales organizations is the development of long-term relationships with customers. As we have seen, a CRM model provides internal organizational formalization to support this goal and promote customer loyalty. As we have also learned, often the end result may be a strategic partnership between the seller and buyer firms. What is the role of the salesperson in the era of CRM and customer-centric firms? Some have tried to claim that, given advanced technology, electronic channels, and increased tendency for categories of goods and services to be viewed as commodities by customers, the role of personal selling in the twenty-first century will be greatly diminished. However, in our view quite the opposite is true. Certainly, the sales role has changed in modern organizations. But rather than it being diminished, we contend that salespeople have a stronger role than ever before in the success of a firm's customer-centric strategy. The key is, what specifically should salespeople do to maximize the success of long-term-relationship-driven organizations? This section examines some of these sales role issues.

Salespeople have a key role to play in fostering successful relationships. Relationships between organizations that result in strategic partnerships generally go through four stages: awareness, exploration, expansion, and commitment. The focus in our discussion below is on the last three of these stages because these distinguish transactional market exchanges from strategic partnerships vis-à-vis Exhibit 3.6. Remember that a key goal in today's organizations is gaining customer loyalty.

Stage One: Exploration

In the exploration stage, each side tries to determine the potential value of the relationship. As time goes on, the relationship becomes defined through the development of expectations for each party and the results of individual transactions or interactions. For example, the buyer begins by evaluating the timeliness of follow-ups to requests for information or makes a purchase and tests the seller's product and service. At the same time, trust and personal relationships develop. Building **trust** is a very important part of developing long-term relationships and represents confidence that a salesperson's word or promise can be believed and that the salesperson has the long-term interests of the customer at the core of his or her approach to doing business.

A strong exploration stage is important for the relationship to flourish over time. When the buyer tries the product for the first time, that customer is excited about receiving the benefits of the product as promised by the salesperson. A poor initial experience is extremely difficult to overcome. Beginning the relationship well requires the salesperson to set the proper expectations, monitor order processing and delivery, ensure proper use of the product, and assist in servicing the customer.

Set Proper Expectations

Many businesspeople try "to underpromise and overdeliver," a catchphrase to encourage salespeople not to promise more than they can deliver, but also to remind salespeople to try to deliver more than was promised in order to pleasantly surprise the buyer. **Customer delight,** or exceeding customer expectations to a surprising degree, is a powerful way to gain customer loyalty. Overpromising can get the initial sale, but a dissatisfied customer not only will not buy again but also will tell many others to avoid that salesperson and his or her company.

Monitor Order Processing and Delivery

The first expectation the buyer has is that the product will be delivered on time and ready to use. A common temptation is to quote a short delivery time in order to win the sale, even when the rep knows that delivery time can't be met. Giving in to such temptation causes trouble with the customer and with those responsible for the shipping function. Neither will be happy with the salesperson who makes such promises. On the other hand, the salesperson should monitor the order processing and delivery processes to make sure that nothing goes wrong.

Ensure Proper Use

Some buyers may know how to operate the basic features of a product, but if the product is not operating at maximum efficiency, the customer is losing value. Many firms have staffed a customer service department or tasked their technical support group with training customers, but it is still the salesperson's responsibility to make sure that the customer is getting full value of use.

Assist in Servicing

Not all quiet customers are happy. Recent research indicates that users may be dissatisfied long before decision makers are aware of it.[19] Salespeople can learn of such problems by working closely with their company's technical or customer support personnel. Then they can address similar situations in other accounts before the problems grow into complaints.

Complaints may arise at any stage of the relationship, but when complaints arise during the exploration stage, the salesperson has the opportunity to prove commitment to the account. When customers sense that commitment, either through the handling of a complaint or through other forms of special attention, they may be ready to move into the expansion stage.

Stage Two: Expansion

The expansion stage of the relationship process is marked by the opportunity to sell new products or increase the share of the account's business. Trust is developing, allowing the salesperson to focus on identifying additional needs and recommending solutions. Several strategies, including generating repeat sales, cross-selling, and full-line selling, may be used to expand business with current accounts and move them toward loyalty and long-term commitment to the relationship.

Generating Repeat Sales and Upgrading

In some situations, the most appropriate strategy is to generate repeat orders, particularly for supply items and other operating needs. Generating repeat sales requires recognizing buying cycles and being present at buying time. **Upgrading** is convincing the buyer to use a higher-quality product or newer product and is similar to generating repeat sales. The buyer selects the upgrade because it meets needs better or more efficiently than did the old product.

Full-Line Selling

Selling the entire line of associated products is called **full-line selling.** Many companies try to get their foot in the door with any sale in order to prove their company's worth as a supplier. The hope is that the buyer will want to purchase the full line after trying out the company. Full-line selling is not the same as full-line forcing, a practice used when a company has one top-selling product that it sells through distributors. Full-line forcing occurs when the company forces distributors to carry the full line in order to be able to sell the top seller. Full-line selling is a sales strategy that involves leveraging the relationship in order to sell the entire line of products. Full-line forcing is a questionable sales tactic, one that got Microsoft a great deal of negative publicity when it bundled its Web browser with its operating system. In contrast, full-line selling is a legitimate method of strengthening the relationship.

Cross-Selling

Cross-selling is similar to full-line selling but reflects selling products that may not be related. Cross-selling works best when the salesperson can leverage the existing relationship with the buyer. Trust in the salesperson and the selling organization already exists; therefore, the sale should not be as difficult if the proper needs exist. If the buying center for the second product line changes greatly, cross-selling becomes more like the initial sale.

Stage Three: Commitment

The basis of expanding a relationship is a solid foundation of customer loyalty. Loyal customers not only exhibit repeat purchase behavior; they also are very reluctant to switch suppliers because of their high level of trust and satisfaction with the salesperson, the selling firm, and its products. As such, customers who are truly loyal are committed to the relationship.

When the buyer–seller relationship has reached the commitment stage, a stated or implied pledge to continue the relationship is in place. Formally, this pledge may begin with the seller being designated a **preferred supplier.** Although preferred supplier status may mean different things in different companies, in general it means that the supplier is assured a large percentage of the buyer's business and will get the first opportunity to earn any new business.[20] In firms with **total quality management (TQM)** initiatives in place, all members of the organization are focused on continually working to eliminate errors and defects in all aspects of their products and processes. Sophisticated quality measurement systems and empowerment of employees to take action to fix quality problems are hallmarks of TQM. In such firms, suppliers are typically required to meet rigorous standards in order to be on a preferred supplier list. These standards typically center on making sure the supplier consistently meets the same quality standards as the selling firm. Boeing, Motorola, and Harley-Davidson, for example, all are longtime TQM proponents. Each of these firms closely monitors the quality standards of their parts suppliers and will quickly take a supplier off the preferred list if a pattern of quality problems develops. In the retail field, both Wal-Mart and Target aggressively require that their merchandise suppliers adhere to rigorous quality and product safety standards, and both have active in-house and product testing programs to ensure compliance.

Securing Commitment

Commitment in a relationship should permeate both organizations, supported by a market-oriented and customer-centric culture. Commitment comes from both organizations, and the salesperson must secure commitment not only from the customer but also from the rest of his or her own company. Senior management must be convinced of the benefits of developing a long-term relationship with the account so that the appropriate investments will be made. Additionally, the salesperson has to see that others in the organization are empowered to serve the needs of this customer. For example, if Wal-Mart has a problem with Procter & Gamble's billing process, P&G's corporate billing department should work directly with Wal-Mart's accounts payable group to resolve the issue and design a more appropriate process. Alignment of billing, shipping, and other key systems is a hallmark of a strong business partnership.

As discussed in Chapter 2, selling activities vary depending on the type of sales job, the firm's relationship strategy, and the stage of the relationship. One element, though, that is common is that a competitive advantage may be gained by matching the selling process to how customers want to buy. Few people exclaim to their friends, "Look at the car I was sold!" Rather they say, "Look at the car I bought!" As we learned in Chapter 2, recognizing how buyers want to buy and creating a selling process that enhances that decision process is an important method of gaining competitive advantage.

PERSONAL SELLING'S ROLE IN THE MARKETING COMMUNICATION MIX

As we have seen, the sales force plays a key role in accomplishing a relationship strategy. A sales force, as we discussed earlier, is just one element in the marketing communication mix. Other elements, such as advertising, sales promotion, direct marketing, and public relation/publicity, are also used to communicate a relationship strategy. Taken as a whole, the various ways the firm strategically communicates its message about its products to the marketplace are referred to as its **integrated marketing communication (IMC)** strategy. The choice of such elements can influence the role of the sales force, and concurrently the role of the sales force affects other marketing communication choices. This is why effective marketing communication must truly be integrated in the way it uses personal selling, advertising, and the other communication options. The factors that affect the actual role of the sales force include the cost to serve a market segment at the desired service level for the realized market value.

Each customer has a desired service level. In recent years, Xerox has altered its selling options away from just the standard company sales force and into more independent distributors in order to cut costs and increase market coverage. This is possible because a small account for Xerox would not need a Xerox representative assigned to them so long as other sales channels can satisfy the account's needs. Nor would it make sense for Xerox because the realized market value, or profit, of that account would be too low. The challenge for sales managers is balancing the customer's desired service level with the appropriate cost to serve so that a profit is made. In Chapter 5 we address how information may be used to develop and assign sales territories and perform sales analysis.

Advantages and Disadvantages of Selling in Marketing Communication

The advantages of personal selling as a marketing communication tool stem largely from its face-to-face communication with a potential customer. Personal sales messages are often more persuasive than advertising or publicity in the mass media. Another advantage of face-to-face contact in personal selling is that the sales representative can communicate a larger amount of complex information than can be transmitted with other promotional tools. The salesperson can demonstrate the product or use visual aids. And since the salesperson is likely to call on the same client many times, the rep can devote a great deal of time to learning about that client's problems and needs and to educating the client about the advantages of appropriate products or services. The long-term contact in personal selling is particularly important when the product or service can be customized to fit the needs of an individual customer—as is often the case in functional and strategic relationships—or when the terms of sale are open to negotiation.

The primary disadvantage of personal selling as a marketing communication tool is that a sales rep can communicate with only a small number of potential customers. Consequently, personal selling is much more costly per person reached than the other promotional tools. An advertisement in a publication such as *Newsweek* or *Time* costs only pennies per reader, but as we saw in Chapter 2, the cost of a single sales call often costs hundreds of dollars.

Bottom line, personal selling should play a substantial role in a firm's marketing communication mix only when the tasks involved are performed better by face-to-face selling than any other method. Such communication tasks include the following:

1. Transmitting large amounts of complex information about the firm's products or policies.

2. Adapting product offerings or promotional appeals to the unique needs and interests of specific customers.

3. Convincing customers that the firm's products or services are better on at least some dimensions than similar offerings of competitors.

As Exhibit 3.7 indicates, the communication tasks actually faced by a business—and the appropriate amount of personal selling effort to be used in the IMC strategy—depend on the business's objectives, marketing strategy, and resources; the number and type of customers in its target market; and the nature of the other elements of its marketing mix: (1) product characteristics, (2) distribution practices, and (3) pricing policies.

Company Resources, Goals, and Marketing Strategy

Although the costs per person reached are high for personal selling, a successful personal selling effort may require a smaller total financial outlay than either an advertising or a sales promotion campaign. One major advertising agency refuses to represent consumer goods manufacturers unless they are willing to spend at least $5 million annually on their advertising campaigns. The agency believes an effective national advertising campaign cannot be undertaken for less. The high costs involved in extensive advertising and sales promotion efforts limit their use by smaller firms. Such firms must often rely on personal selling—perhaps supplemented with less expensive advertising or other forms of communication such as the Internet or trade shows—as their primary promotional tool.

EXHIBIT 3.7   Factors influencing the role of personal selling in a firm's IMC strategy

If the firm's goal is to expand distribution by persuading more wholesalers or retailers to carry the product, then a strong personal selling effort and perhaps a trade promotion program are indicated. The highly persuasive nature of personal selling also makes it an appropriate tool when the objective is to take market share away from established competitors, especially if the product is a relatively complex industrial or consumer durable good. Finally, if the objective is simply to maintain the market share of a well-established product, "reminder" advertising should play the primary role in the marketing communication mix.

Characteristics of the Target Market

Because various marketing communications tools differ greatly in their costs per person reached, the number of potential customers in the firm's target market, their size, and their geographic distribution influence the communications mix. For example, in order to justify the higher costs, personal selling is most often emphasized when the target market contains relatively few customers, the average customer is likely to place a relatively large order, and customers are clustered close together. Firms that sell to industrial markets with few potential customers, and those that distribute their products through a small number of wholesale intermediaries, commonly rely on personal selling as their primary marketing communication mix element. Firms that sell to large, geographically dispersed, consumer markets place primary emphasis on the more cost-efficient advertising and sales promotion methods.

Product Characteristics

Most marketing textbooks suggest that the marketing communication mixes for industrial products concentrate heavily on personal selling; those for consumer durable goods utilize a combination of personal selling and advertising; and producers of consumer nondurable goods rely most heavily on advertising and sales promotion. The reason is that industrial goods and consumer durables tend to be more complex than consumer nondurable goods, so potential buyers need more information to make a purchase decision. Also, industrial goods can often be designed or modified to meet the needs of individual customers, and consumer durables (as well as complex services, such as financial or insurance services) often present the buyer with a range of options.

These generalizations should be viewed with some caution. Industrial goods producers usually stress personal selling, but they might also do extensive advertising and public relations to build awareness of the company and its products so the sales force can gain access to potential customers more easily.[21] Similarly, although a consumer goods producer such as Nabisco might spend large sums on media advertising and sales promotion, it is also likely to field a sales force to call on retailers and build reseller support in its distribution channels.

To make matters even more complicated, the Internet and the whole field of electronic commerce are blurring the distinctions among the various promotional tools. A company's Web site can (1) communicate large amounts of product information, (2) generate leads for the firm's field sales force to follow up, or (3) allow interested customers to bypass face-to-face contact with a salesperson and order the firm's products electronically.

Distribution Practices

As mentioned, personal selling is often necessary to build reseller support and develop adequate distribution for a product, regardless of whether it is a consumer good or industrial good. The importance of the sales force's role in building a distribution channel is affected by the firm's strategy for influencing resellers to buy its product. When a firm follows a **pull strategy,** it attempts to build strong customer demand for its brand. The focus is on a strong advertising program aimed at end users. This encourages wholesalers and retailers to carry the product to satisfy their customers and reap the resulting sales and profits.

The manufacturer's sales force often plays a support role in implementing a pull strategy. Because demand is primarily created through advertising to end users, salespeople must ensure that sufficient product is on the shelf, proper shelf signing is up, off-shelf displays are built, and store personnel are familiar with the products.

When a firm uses a **push strategy** to build reseller support, it offers direct incentives to potential wholesalers and retailers to encourage them to stock the product. When consumers see the product in the store, it is hoped that they will like it and buy it. A wide range of incentives may be offered to resellers, including the following: (1) development of **just-in-time reorder and delivery** programs that help resellers reduce their investments in inventory and improve inventory turnover, (2) **category management** programs in which manufacturers work with resellers to maximize sales volumes and margins in the product categories in which the selling firm's products are represented, (3) price promotions, (4) volume discounts, (5) contests for the reseller's salespeople, (6) training programs for resellers, (7) cooperative advertising programs, and (8) point-of-purchase promotional materials.

The manufacturer's sales force plays a principal role in implementing a push strategy. The sales force must explain the advantages of carrying and promoting the supplier's products to prospective channel members, persuade them to stock and aggressively merchandise those products, and maintain cooperative relationships with the firm's channel partners over time.[22]

Pricing Policies

A firm's pricing policies can also influence the composition of its marketing communication mix. Big-ticket items, both industrial goods and consumer durables, typically require substantial amounts of personal selling. Such expensive products are often technically or aesthetically sophisticated, and customers perceive substantial risk in purchasing them. Therefore, potential buyers usually want the kind of detailed information and advice they can get only from a salesperson before making their decisions.

Also, personal selling is essential in marketing products or services where the ultimate selling price is open to negotiation. Although negotiated pricing policies are most commonly found among marketers of industrial goods and services, they are also followed in the sale of some consumer durables, such as automobiles.

Within the marketing communication mix, the importance of personal selling relative to advertising depends on various characteristics of the firm's marketing strategy, including the size and nature of the target market, the complexity and service requirements of the product, and the other elements of the marketing mix. The impact of these factors on the design of IMC strategy is summarized in Exhibit 3.8.

Computerized Ordering and Customer Alliances

To further strengthen relationships with major customers, firms are forming **supply chain alliances** with those customers involving the development of joint information and reorder systems. For instance, Procter & Gamble has formed alliances with major supermarket chains, such as Kroger, Publix, and Safeway, to develop a restocking system called **efficient consumer response (ECR).** Sales information from the stores' checkout scanners is sent directly to P&G's computers, which figure out automatically when to replenish each product and schedule deliveries direct to each store. This paperless exchange minimizes mistakes and billbacks, minimizes inventory, decreases out-of-stocks, and improves cash flow.[23]

EXHIBIT 3.8
Illustrative factors that influence the design of IMC strategy

Source: Adapted from David W. Cravens and Nigel F. Piercy, *Strategic Marketing*, 8th ed. (New York: Irwin/McGraw-Hill, 2005), p. 348.

IMPROVING CUSTOMER SATISFACTION AND LOYALTY THROUGH FEEDBACK

As discussed in the earlier section on CRM, maintaining the loyalty of major current customers can be crucial for improving a business's profitability as its markets mature and is therefore an important element of any sales strategy. Recall, though, that this chapter also earlier discussed the importance of a market orientation and the role of customer requirements in determining firm success. Maintaining customer loyalty is one outcome of a market orientation. Customer-focused companies, those that cultivate loyal customers with whom a functional or strategic relationship is shared, have substantial advantages across several key performance dimensions versus other companies. Such firms not only avoid the high costs associated with acquiring a new customer but typically benefit because loyal customers (1) tend to concentrate their purchases, thus leading to larger volumes and lower selling and distribution costs, (2) provide positive word-of-mouth and customer referrals, and (3) may be willing to pay premium prices for the value they receive.[24]

Periodic measurement of customer satisfaction is important, then, because a dissatisfied customer is unlikely to remain loyal to a company over time. Importantly, however, the corollary is not always true: Customers who describe themselves as satisfied are not necessarily loyal. Indeed, one author estimates that 60 to 80 percent of customer defectors in most businesses said they were "satisfied" or "very satisfied" on the last customer survey before their defection.[25] In the interim, perhaps, competitors improved their offerings, the customer's requirements changed, or other environmental factors shifted. The point is that businesses that measure customer satisfaction should be commended—but urged not to stop there. Satisfaction measures need to be supplemented with examinations of customer behavior, such as measures of the annual retention rate, frequency of purchases, and the percentage of a customer's total purchases captured by the firm.

Most important, defecting customers should be studied in detail to discover why the selling firm failed to provide sufficient value to retain their loyalty. Analyzing such failures often provides more useful information than satisfaction measures because they stand out as a clear, understandable message telling the organization exactly where improvements are needed. In fact, gaining feedback from customers on the performance of a selling firm has been institutionalized in many organizations. IBM, for example, includes such feedback as a formal part of its performance evaluation process for everyone who interacts directly with a client. This idea of 360-degree performance feedback is discussed further in Chapter 13. Innovation 3.4 provides insights on the importance of salespeople leveraging value to gain customer loyalty.

Major Account Teams

In Chapter 2, the concept of the buying center was introduced. Sometimes, customers who are strategic partners of a selling organization become so large and complex that a parallel concept to the buying center is implemented on the seller side of the relationship. In such cases, a firm may assign a **selling team** of representatives from various functional departments of the company to a single customer. The selling team may include representatives from different levels in the company's management hierarchy, too. In fact, it has become increasingly common for executives at the very top of firms, even CEOs, to get directly involved in selling to major strategic partner customers. Such an approach is called **top-to-top selling.** Legend has it that when Lou Gerstner took over the reins as CEO of IBM, he was shocked by how little the executives in the company actually knew about IBM's customers. Many had apparently not called on a customer in many years.

Innovation Leveraging Value in the New Era of Selling 3.4

Are some salespeople stuck in the wrong era? It sounds like a strange question. But if salespeople find themselves forced to compete on price to sell value-added products or services—or even if they're trying to sell solutions to problems that customers know they have—the answer is probably yes. Business and the sales profession at large have evolved tremendously during the past 50 years. The problem is, some salespeople (and the companies that hire them) haven't kept pace with the evolution.

Many people who sell for a living are relying on methods that worked just fine in, say, the 80s, and even the 90s. But the world has advanced substantially. Products and services have grown increasingly complex, as have the business issues and problems they address. Customers have many problems to solve, many options available to solve them, and are having great difficulty sorting it all out.

John Sullivan, a principal with Learning Partners, divides professional selling into three eras when teaching his clients how their sales organizations should serve their customers:

- *Era 1 (1950–1975).* The early 50s saw the first appearance of literature devoted to professional selling. The role of the salesperson was characterized as a "persuader." The economy was experiencing unlimited demand and a somewhat limited range of products and services. Customers were open to ideas and willing to spend. The job of the salesperson was to present a compelling story and convince the customer to buy their product. The training was based on the psychology of stimulus and response, and the skills being taught focused on presenting, persuading, and closing. This era fell out of favor to mainstream business as the customer "wised up" to the manipulative techniques. Nevertheless, the Era 1 approach is alive and well today in all too many salespeople and businesses.

- *Era 2 (1975–1995).* The economy saw more and more suppliers, globalization was emerging, and customers began to have choices, not to mention an increasing level of sophistication. The role of the salesperson evolved to that of a problem solver/consultant. The consultative, strategic, and solutions approaches to selling were embraced, and the skills of questioning and listening were emphasized. Establishing trust and building relationships were key objectives. The problems were well understood, the solutions were fairly straightforward, and the salesperson's success was tied to his or her ability to understand the customer's view of the problem, align the solution to match this view, and convince the customer that the solution is the best choice. The common form of the "needs analysis" involved these questions of the customer: What issues are you experiencing? What do you want to happen? and What do you need to be successful? In short, What do you need? The key distinction of Era 2 is customers were assumed to have a clear understanding of the answers to these three questions, and for the most part they did.

- *Era 3 (1995–?)* The distinguishing characteristic of Era 3 is the increasing complexity of business problems and the solutions that address them. Coupled with an economy that is in a state of overcapacity, customers are overwhelmed with choices and options and are looking for guidance from salespeople—unfortunately, that guidance frequently is not forthcoming. With the abundance of alternatives, the solutions not only look the same, in many cases they are the same. To help customers thoroughly understand the problems they face and sort through the available alternatives, the role of the salesperson in Era 3 is that of a business adviser and a source of competitive advantage. The skills that are required are more attributed to that of a process analyst and project manager and were certainly not looked for in the selling profession during Eras 1 and 2. The objective of the Era 3 salesperson is to create solutions that customers would have been able to think of or put together on their own. The sales professional and his or her team do a deep analysis of the customer's business, look at the issues beyond the expertise of the customer, and collaborate with the customer to tailor a solution. The salesperson brings a capability and process knowledge the customer does not possess.

So how do salespeople begin to operate successfully in Era 3? The answer begins and ends with the V-word: *value.* Obviously, products themselves must have inherent value, but that's not enough. The value provided must be leveraged across a full spectrum of the customer's business—it must enable your customer to have a unique competitive advantage, and your salespeople must be able to measure the financial impact of that value.

In Era 3, a sales organization must serve as a secret weapon for its customer. Salespeople must think for their customers, creating revenue-building solutions that they don't have the time or the wherewithal to come up with or implement for themselves. This brave new world is a challenge for the professional salesperson, sure, but it's also a treasure trove of opportunity.

Source: Jeff Thull, "Selling in Era 3: How to Leverage Value to Win—and Keep—Profitable Customers," *The American Salesman,* January 2004, p. 12.

Gerstner immediately instituted a policy that all top-level executives would spend a substantial amount of time in the executive suites of IBM's biggest strategic partners, doing top-to-top selling. This approach has been credited as a major factor in IBM's turnaround in the mid-1990s, as executives received a clear and direct message about what changes needed to be made to win customers back to IBM.[26]

Implementing a major account management program that includes team selling or top-to-top selling can have important implications for the way a firm organizes its sales force. These issues are discussed in Chapter 4.

Summary

This chapter has highlighted the importance of long-term relationships to organizational success. Firms today strive to create a market-oriented, customer-centric culture. Within such a culture, the role of personal selling is vital to the successful development and implementation of marketing strategies.

CRM provides the firm with necessary formalization for success. That is, a well-implemented CRM business model offers structure, processes and tools, and managerial knowledge and commitment in support of the customer-centric culture. With these things in place, marketing strategies and programs may be successfully developed and executed toward the goals related to customer centricity. In general, these goals revolve around establishing and maintaining long-term customer relationships.

Key Terms

marketing concept
marketing mix
marketing communication
  mix (promotion mix)
market orientation
customer orientation
customer-centric
formalization
customer relationship
  management (CRM)
touchpoints
mass marketing
target marketing
customer marketing
one-to-one marketing
customer value
customer loyalty
lifetime value of a customer
firing a customer

data warehouse
data mining
return on customer
  investment
strategic direction
mission statement
goals
objectives
strategic business units
sustainable competitive
  advantage
distinctive competencies
generic strategies
market opportunity
marketing program
market exchanges
functional relationships
strategic partnerships
trust

customer delight
upgrading
full-line selling
cross-selling
preferred supplier
total quality management
  (TQM)
integrated marketing
  communication (IMC)
pull strategy
push strategy
just-in-time reorder and
  delivery
category management
supply chain alliances
efficient consumer
  response (ECR)
selling team
top-to-top selling

Breakout Questions

1. One of the great debates in CRM is who should have ownership of the process. In many firms, IT people seem to be the guardians of CRM's secrets. This is because, as we have learned, a key facet of CRM is its information management capabilities. Who do you think should have ownership of CRM in a firm? Is it really necessary that CRM have an owner? What does ownership of the process imply in terms of actions and behaviors? What is the role of upper management in all this?

2. Is it possible for a firm to be successful without a market orientation? Can you come up with examples of firms that are not very market-oriented but still are leaders in their competitive marketplace?

3. The promotion mix (also known as the integrated marketing communications mix) consists of the various ways the firm communicates with its customers about its product offerings. These include personal selling, advertising, public relations and publicity, sales promotion (sales support of the advertising effort through signage, displays, etc.), direct response, electronic media, and the like. Find an example of a company that you believe does a really good job of actually integrating these approaches to communications. What are the things that make this company's approach so successful?

4. Consider the three basic relationship types described in the chapter: market exchanges (transactional), functional relationships, and strategic partnerships. For each, provide an example of a different sales organization that you believe does a good job with that particular relationship type. What evidence do you have that each is successful?

5. Based on what you have learned about strategic partnerships, what two organizations (either supplier-customer or supplier-supplier) can you identify that are not currently in a partnership but you believe would benefit from one? List the benefits to both parties of forging such an alliance. List any potential problems you believe might emanate from the alliance. What can the firms do to reduce the chances for these potential problems?

6. Strategic partnerships often require direct peer-to-peer communication at the senior executive level between buying firm and selling firm. What are the advantages of having top corporate officers, CEOs in some cases, become directly involved in the selling process? What are the disadvantages? What types of challenges does such direct involvement present to the salesperson and sales manager responsible for the client?

7. Refer to Exhibit 3.4. Using the Miles and Snow typology, how might the marketing strategies and programs of a prospector SBU vary from those adopted by a defender SBU within the same company? Which of these options do you believe would be best: (*a*) a sales force that sells only for the prospector SBU, or (*b*) a sales force that is shared between the two SBUs and sells for both the prospector and defender SBU? What are the relevant issues that led to your response?

Leadership Challenge: Whose CRM Is It Anyway?

Alice Klein wondered what she should do next as she hung up the phone. As vice president of sales for New World Manufacturing, she was responsible for more than 200 salespeople around the country. New World was a manufacturer of precision components for bicycles (gear shift mechanisms). Among the company's clients were Cannondale and Giant Bicycles as well as other leading bicycle companies around the world. In addition to the original equipment manufacturer (OEM) market, New World did a great deal of business selling after-market accessories to bicycle retailers.

Alice had pushed hard for a CRM system to be implemented at New World. Finally, as part of an overall upgrade of the IT system at the company, senior management had purchased a CRM package that included state-of-the-art software and hardware to help

New World do a better job of managing its customer relationships. It was expensive to get the package Alice and other executives knew was the best solution. The final cost ran into several million dollars plus additional training time.

It is now six months since the purchase of the system and Elliot Whitney, vice president of information technology, just called Alice to say he still had not received a detailed summary of the information needed by the sales force. He told Alice that senior management was asking about the status of the CRM system. They wanted the entire company to benefit from the system and were looking forward to its implementation.

The company had a lot of information about its customers as well as other data that could be incorporated into its CRM system (internal billing, price, and production schedules). Alice was well aware of the system's potential and had spent a great deal of time thinking about how the sales force could use it most effectively. After hanging up with Elliot she knew it was time to decide how the new CRM system would be implemented with the sales force.

Questions

1. You are Alice Klein. What critical information do you think would be most helpful for the sales force to be able to access about the relationship between New World and its customers?

2. What technology would you use to deliver this information from the CRM system to the sales person (PDA, laptop, cell phone, or something else), and why would you choose that technology?

3. What kinds of issues do you think might come up for New World as it implements the CRM system with the sales force? (For example, possible salesperson resistance to collecting information for the CRM system.)

Role Play: Serendipity Wireless

Situation

Ellie Rodriguez was puzzled. Sales were just not coming in year-to-date for her area at the forecast rate, despite an improving economy and a solid marketing plan. Ellie had been hired 15 months ago as B2B sales manager for the Boston market for Serendipity Wireless, an up-and-coming player in the overall cell phone market. While many cellular providers focused primarily on the B2C market through retail outlets, Serendipity's focal business was in supplying product and service to small-to medium-sized businesses. Ellie has six years of progressively broader sales and sales management experience with a B2C provider in the wireless industry and saw the opportunity at Serendipity as a way to gain experience in B2B.

Over the past few weeks she has spent a lot of time digging into the sales data for the seven salespeople working for her in the Boston district. Also, she has been increasing the amount of time riding with her reps to see how they are handling their territories. As a result, she has become more and more concerned that a couple of the reps are not effectively utilizing Serendipity's in-house CRM system to its fullest potential. For reps Leo Leone and Carla Cadwallader, it seems that they are neither effectively converting leads into customers nor cross-selling the full line of Serendipity products and services to the customers they do sign up. This evidence is a sure sign they are not using the CRM system advantageously. If these two reps could improve their sales by just 8 percent year-to-date, Ellie's whole district would be on plan. Interestingly, these two are Ellie's most senior reps both in age and in length of service with Serendipity.

Ellie calls a meeting with Leo and Carla for tomorrow to discuss the situation and provide ideas on how they can better use Serendipity's CRM system.

Characters in the Role Play

Ellie Rodriguez, Boston district sales manager for Serendipity

Leo Leone, salesperson for Serendipity

Carla Cadwallader, salesperson for Serendipity

Assignment

Break into groups of three, with one student playing each character. It doesn't matter what the actual gender mix of your group is. Before you stage the meeting, the student playing Ellie should work to prepare a list of benefits of utilizing a CRM system such as Serendipity's. Be mindful that Leo and Carla are senior reps who have been successful in the past; however, you *must* convince them of the ways CRM can help them be successful in the future.

Also before the meeting, the students playing Leo and Carla should work to prepare a list of reasons they don't want to use the CRM system. Think about both (1) why especially a senior salesperson might be reluctant to utilize such a system and (2) what might be some drawbacks or impediments to CRM in general. Then get together and role-play the meeting. Ellie should lead the discussion, and Leo and Carla should stand firm in their resistance, at least for a while. Ultimately, it will be important for the three to come to agreement about how Leo and Carla will begin to utilize the CRM system. Finish the meeting with a list of specific actions they can take to make this happen, along with what Ellie can do to help.

Minicase: TransSprech, A.G.

You are a consultant for an international management strategy consulting firm. Your firm has been approached by Herr (Mr.) Hans Wursching, CEO of TransSprech, A.G., a newly formed cellular phone service and phone provider, based in Stuttgart, Germany. TransSprech has a satellite GSM network with complete coverage in Europe and the United States, as well as throughout most countries in the world. The company has established some semblance of a marketing and management strategy, and you have been asked to review the current strategy and help the company go to the next level by growing its sales.

You recently conducted the initial information gathering meeting with Herr Wursching, and received the following mass of information:

- TransSprech maintains corporate offices in numerous cities around the world. However, its customer service outlets and retail sales are conducted through the company Web site, as well as though licensed electronics retailers. It does not maintain its own customer service or retail locations.

- Its target markets are both companies and individuals wanting cellular phone service with worldwide coverage and who are willing to pay a premium to get it. It already has about 3,000 customers worldwide and is hoping to grow to 10,000 by year-end.

- Corporate customers are more valuable customers because they are buying in larger volumes. Establishing a customer base is very important as this company attempts to establish itself.

- There is not a sales force established. So far the company has received many customers in response to its advertising.

- It offers individual customers four different cost plans with respect to the cellular service, as well as five different phone options. However, corporate customers can negotiate variations within the established options.

- The phones themselves are similar to those used by TransSprech's competitors, but the satellite network providing the coverage is far more advanced.

- The company has retained a Berlin-based advertising and public relations agency to develop a worldwide advertising campaign. Print and television ads have recently saturated the European market and will soon be shown in the U.S. market. The company is currently running several promotions to get its product and name known; however, its long-term goal is to offer a premium, nondiscounted product that is desired because of its value and quality, not low price.

- Because the company and its product are in the early stages of development, there have been technical problems, and the company has had to provide a great deal of service to its customers.

- Herr Wursching understands that it costs more to acquire new customers than to retain existing ones, so he would like to establish a CRM plan at some point to improve customer loyalty and retention. He has a well-trained customer service operator staff in place. However, he does not want to invest in a complicated software system right away. His current technology is giving him enough problems, he says.

Questions

1. What is the company's strategy with respect to each of the 4 Ps of the marketing mix?
2. Based on the current marketing strategy, should the company's promotion mix focus be on personal selling or on advertising?
3. What further questions might you ask Herr Wursching to help his company move toward a more relationship-based business and establish CRM initiatives? What other recommendations might you make for him with respect to CRM?

Suggested Readings

Arnett, Dennis B., and Vishag Badrinarayanan. "Enhancing Customer-Needs-Driven CRM Strategies: Core Selling Teams, Knowledge Management Competence, and Relationship Marketing Competence." *Journal of Personal Selling & Sales Management* 25 (Fall 2005) pp. 329–43.

Baldauf, Artur, David W. Cravens, and Nigel F. Piercy. "Sales Management Control Research—Synthesis and an Agenda for Future Research." *Journal of Personal Selling & Sales Management* 25 (Winter 2005) pp. 7–26.

Landry, Timothy D., Todd J. Arnold, and Aaron Arndt. "A Compendium of Sales-Related Literature in Customer Relationship Management: Processes and Technologies with Managerial Implications." *Journal of Personal Selling & Sales Management* 25 (Summer 2005) pp. 231–51.

Le Meunier-FitzHugh, Ken, and Nigel F. Piercy. "Does Collaboration Between Sales and Marketing Affect Business Performance?" *The Journal of Personal Selling & Sales Management* 27 (Summer 2007) pp. 207–20.

Raman, Pushkala, C. Michael Wittmann, and Nancy A. Rauseo. "Leveraging CRM for Sales: The Role of Organizational Capabilities in Successful CRM Implementation." *Journal of Personal Selling & Sales Management* 26 (Winter 2006) pp. 39–53.

Rouziès, Dominique, Erin Anderson, Ajay K. Kohli, and Ronald E. Michaels. "Sales and Marketing Integration: A Proposed Framework." *Journal of Personal Selling & Sales Management* 25 (Spring 2005) pp. 113–22.

Tanner Jr., John F., Michael Ahearne, Thomas W. Leigh, Charolette H. Mason, and William C. Moncrief. "CRM in Sales-Intensive Organizations: A Review and Future Directions." *Journal of Personal Selling & Sales Management* 25 (Spring 2005) pp. 169–80.

Chapter **Four**

Organizing the Sales Effort

Organize the Sales Force around Customers, Not Products

Companies used to exist in a product-centric world. Manufacturing and marketing were aligned by products, so it made sense from the company's perspective to align salespeople that way too. Product line salespeople were trained intensely in product features and functions, and they went forth into the world to douse their customers in their product expertise. And then the world shifted.

Customers now demand that sales forces exist in *their* world. Their world is business issue-centric, not product-centric, and salespeople need a thorough understanding of the customers' business issues to add any value. This requires sales forces to organize themselves in such a fashion that they can work intimately with certain segments of customers. Customer-driven companies must now organize their sales forces around markets, not around product lines.

Having said this, it is worth mentioning that in certain cases, product lines and market segments do align on a one-to-one basis. An example would be a single-line manufacturer of large industry-specific equipment. If the product is highly tailored to a particular type of customer, then a product-centric sales force is appropriate. But this is becoming the exception rather than the rule.

Deploy Sales Resources Wisely across Market Segments

Not all customers are created equal. As the saying goes, "If you're treating your best customers the same as your worst, then you're doing a disservice to your best customers." Most executives would agree that the best customers are the ones that produce the most profits for their company, but their sales forces do not always behave in that way. Left to their own devices, salespeople choose their "best" customers based on a number of criteria: size, ease of access, friendliness, geographic convenience, product mix, familiarity, etc. In reality, salespeople do not always spend their precious time with their most profitable customers.

World class sales forces take control of this issue by directing their salespeople toward the right customers. Through account planning processes, managerial oversight, or other similar means, companies can guide their sales force to the customers they desire, and then collect information to measure their compliance. By simply managing their salespeople's effort, a company can make a lot of headway toward better allocating their resources.

Sales managers may also attack these issues structurally by installing separate sales forces to pursue different market segments. A common strategy is to use lower cost channels such as telesales to serve lower profit market segments, while maintaining an outside sales force for high profit customers. By building the coverage model into an organizational framework, management avoids the inherent messiness of trying to make a single sales force serve multiple segments in completely different ways.

Source: HR Chally Group (2007), *The Chally World Class Excellence Research Report: The Route to the Summit.* Dayton, OH: HR Chally Group.

LEARNING OBJECTIVES

Organizing the sales force is one of the most important decisions made by sales management. It has a significant impact on every aspect of the salesperson's performance. Changes in the way selling is done, the increasing importance of effectively managing customer relationships, and the need to assimilate new technologies in the selling function have led to fundamental changes in the organization of today's sales forces.

After reading this chapter, you should be able to

- Identify the purposes of sales organization.

- Understand the different horizontal organizational structures of a sales force.

- Outline the major issues in key account and team selling.

- Discuss key vertical structure issues in sales organizations.

- Identify important issues in starting a new sales force from the ground up.

THE INCREASING IMPORTANCE OF SALES ORGANIZATION DECISIONS

Organizing the activities and management of the sales force is a major part of strategic sales planning. Until recently, however, significant cultural and organizational restructuring was not common among either industrial or consumer goods marketers. Once a firm had an organizational structure in place, its managers tended to take it for granted—at least until performance problems became apparent. But in recent years, increasing rates of change in markets, technology, and competition have forced managers to pay closer attention to their sales organizations and to be more proactive in restructuring those organizations when necessary.[1]

A strong corporate vision and effective strategic market planning are closely linked with how the organization is structured and how it interacts with its customers. This chapter stresses the importance of designing an appropriate organizational framework for the sales force as an integral part of a firm's sales program and examines issues involved in developing such a framework. It begins with a discussion of the purposes of organization—the things a good organizational plan should accomplish. Next, issues related to the horizontal organization of the sales effort are explored. Horizontal organization is concerned with how specific selling activities are divided among various members of the sales force. Finally, the vertical structuring of the sales organization is discussed. Vertical structuring refers to organizing a firm's sales managers and their activities rather than the personnel in the sales force. An understanding of these issues should provide greater appreciation for the crucial role organizational decisions play in developing an effective sales program.

PURPOSES OF SALES ORGANIZATION

An organizational structure is simply an arrangement of activities involving a group of people. The goal in designing an organization is to divide and coordinate activities so the group can accomplish its common objectives better by acting as a group than by acting as individuals. The starting point in organizing a sales force is determining the goals or objectives to be accomplished. These are specified in the firm's overall marketing plan. The selling activities necessary to accomplish the firm's marketing objectives must then be divided and allocated to members of the sales force so the objectives can be achieved with as little duplication of effort as possible. An organizational structure should serve the following purposes:

1. Activities should be divided and arranged in such a way that the firm can benefit from the specialization of labor.

2. The organizational structures should provide for stability and continuity in the firm's selling efforts.

3. The structure should provide for the coordination of the various activities assigned to different persons in the sales force and different departments in the firm.

Division and Specialization of Labor

Two centuries ago, Adam Smith pointed out that dividing any function into its component activities and assigning each activity to a specialist can increase the efficiency with which almost anything is performed. **Division and specialization of labor** increase productivity because each specialist can concentrate efforts and become more proficient at the assigned task. Also, management can assign individuals only to those activities for which they have aptitude.

In some cases, the personal selling function is so simple and straightforward a firm could gain few if any benefits by applying the principles of division and specialization of labor to its sales force. Salespeople in such companies are expected to carry out all the activities necessary to sell all the products in the company's line to all types of customers within their territories. But in many firms, the selling function is sufficiently complicated that dividing the necessary selling activities can increase efficiency and effectiveness. Different activities are assigned to various specialists, creating two or more specialized sales forces. Today, many firms find that partnering with specialists such as resellers and distributors can enhance the effectiveness of its own sales force.

Management must decide the best way to divide the required selling activities to gain the maximum benefits of specialization within the sales force. Should independent agent intermediaries be used to perform some or all of the firm's selling efforts? Should selling activities be organized by product, by customer type, or by selling function (for example, prospecting for new accounts versus servicing old customers)? As discussed later in this chapter, each basis for horizontally structuring the sales organization has its own advantages and disadvantages. Which one is best depends on the firm's objectives, target market, product line, and other internal and external factors. And a key issue today is the impact of e-commerce and online selling and sales support on organizing the overall sales initiative.

Division and specialization of labor can benefit managerial functions as well as selling functions. Some firms use a simple **line organization,** a type of vertical organization in which the chain of command runs from the chief sales executive down through levels of subordinates. Each subordinate is responsible to only one person on the next higher level, and each is expected to perform all the necessary sales management activities relevant to his or her own level.

The most common form of vertical organization structure, especially in medium- and large-size firms, is the **line and staff organization.** In this form, several sales management activities, such as personnel selection, training, and distributor relations, are assigned to separate staff specialists. This type of specialization, however, raises some questions concerning organizational design, such as

1. What specific functions should be assigned to staff executives?

2. How can staff activities be integrated with those of line sales managers, and should those activities be performed in-house or outsourced to independent contractors, such as personnel agencies and training firms?

These questions are examined further later in this chapter.

Stability and Continuity of Organizational Performance

Although many companies use division and specialization of labor in designing their sales organizations, they sometimes ignore a related caveat concerning good organizational design: Organize activities, not people. In other words, activities should be assigned to positions within the sales organization without regard to the talents or preferences of current employees.

Once an ideal organizational structure has been designed, people can be trained or, if need be, recruited to fill positions within the structure. Over time, those in lower positions should be given the experience and training necessary to enable them to move into higher positions. In athletic terms, the organization should "build depth at all positions." This provides stability and continuity of performance for the organization. The same activities are carried out at the same positions within the firm even if specific individuals are promoted or leave.

Coordination and Integration

The advantages of the division and specialization of labor are clear, but specialization also causes a problem for managers. When activities are divided and performed by different individuals, those activities must be coordinated and integrated so all efforts are directed at accomplishing the same objective. The more an organization's tasks are divided among specialists, the more difficult integrating those tasks becomes. The problem is even worse when outside agents, such as manufacturers' representatives, are used, because the manager has no formal authority over them and cannot always control their actions.

Sales managers must be concerned about the coordination and integration of the efforts of their salespeople in three ways. First, the activities of the sales force must be integrated with the needs and concerns of customers. Second, the firm's selling activities must be coordinated with those of other departments, such as production, product development, logistics, and finance. Finally, if the firm divides its selling tasks among specialized units within the sales force, all those tasks must be integrated.

Consequently, the primary function of the vertical structure of a firm's sales organization is to ensure these three kinds of integration. Questions of vertical organization—such as how many levels of sales management the firm should have, the appropriate span of control for each sales executive, and the most effective use of staff specialists—should be examined with an eye toward effective integration of the firm's overall selling efforts.

HORIZONTAL STRUCTURE OF THE SALES FORCE

There is no best way to divide selling activities among members of the sales force. The best sales organization varies with the objectives, strategies, and tasks of the firm. Furthermore, as the firm's environment, objectives, or marketing strategy changes, its sales force may have to be reorganized. Several key questions are central to this discussion:

1. Should the company employ its own salespeople, or should some or all of its selling efforts be contracted to outside agents, such as manufacturers' representatives?

2. How many different sales forces should the company have, and how should they be arranged?

3. Should separate sales representatives be assigned to different products, types of customers, or sales functions?

4. Who should be responsible for selling to major national accounts?

5. How should firms organize their sales and marketing efforts when they enter foreign markets and become global competitors?

Four common bases are used for structuring the sales effort, and each has unique advantages that make it appropriate for a firm under certain circumstances. The first issue to be decided is whether the firm should hire its own salespeople or use outside agents. When the decision is to use a company sales force, alternative approaches include (1) geographic organization, (2) organization by type of product, (3) organization by type of customer, and (4) organization by selling function.

Deciding on a Company Sales Force or Independent Agents

This book focuses primarily on issues associated with managing an internal company sales force, where all of the salespeople and their managers are employees of the firm. In many cases, though, the use of independent agents instead of company salespeople is an important option. IBM, Xerox, and other firms employ both a highly trained sales force and a network of business partners around the world to help market their products and services. In such cases, firms usually rely on agents to cover geographic areas with relatively few customers or low sales potential—territories that may not justify the cost of a full-time company salesperson. It is not unusual for a firm to use both company salespeople and independent agents. Today, the term **outsourcing the sales force** is popularly used to indicate the use of agents.

Types of Agents

The two most common types of intermediaries a manufacturer might use to perform the selling function are manufacturers' representatives and selling (or sales) agents. **Manufacturers' representatives** (or reps) are intermediaries who sell part of the output of their principals—the manufacturers they represent—on an extended contract basis. They take neither ownership nor physical possession of the goods they sell but concentrate instead on the selling function. They are compensated solely by commissions.

Reps have no authority to modify their principals' instructions concerning the prices, terms of sale, and so forth to be offered to potential buyers. Manufacturers' reps cover a specific and limited territory and specialize in a limited range of products, although they commonly represent several related but noncompeting product lines from different manufacturers.

These characteristics give reps the advantages of having (1) many established contacts with potential customers in their territories, (2) familiarity with the technical nature and applications of the types of products in which they specialize, (3) the ability to keep expenses low by spreading fixed costs over the products of several different manufacturers, and (4) the appearance as a totally variable cost item on their principals' income statements, since the reps' commissions vary directly with the amount of goods sold.[2] Finding the right rep is a critical business decision for the sales organization. Exhibit 4.1 provides useful guidelines for selecting a rep.

Selling agents are also intermediaries who do not take title or possession of the goods they sell and are compensated solely by commissions from their principals. They differ from reps, however, in that they usually handle the entire output of a principal (operating as the entire sales force for the manufacturer rather than as a representative in a single, specified territory). Selling agents are usually granted broader authority by their principals to modify prices and terms of sale, and they actively shape the manufacturer's promotional and sales programs.

Deciding When Outside Agents Are Appropriate

The decision about whether to use independent agents or a company sales force to cover a particular product or market involves a variety of considerations and trade-offs. Four important sets of factors for a manager to consider are (1) economic criteria, (2) control, (3) transaction costs, and (4) strategic flexibility.[3]

EXHIBIT 4.1

Six C's of finding the right rep

Source: Dan Hanover, "Independents Day," *Sales & Marketing Management,* April 2000, pp. 65–68.

Compatible lines	Find a rep with a complementary porfolio, one your product fits into seamlessly. An electrical wiring manufacturer, for example, benefits from having its merchandise sold right alongside conductors and converters.
Compatible territories	Don't hire a rep who sells in barren markets. Look for a seller who moves merchandise in regions saturated with current or potential customers. Find a seller who knows his or her region and knows who to sell your products to in that area.
Compatible customers	Ultimately you want to hire an independent rep who is already selling in your industry and knows about your company and your customers. But regardless, find a rep who knows the types of customers you're looking to target.
Credibility of the rep	The independent sales rep is not only a revenue generator, but he or she is a company ambassador (for you!). Often your rep is the only person associated with your company that certain customers ever meet or talk with. Make sure you send the right ambassador into the field.
Capabilities	Are your products the rep's primary account or a secondary account? Find out how much attention you can expect from the rep. Then you can decide if the right person will be selling your products.
Credits	Check references and do a background check. How long has the rep been selling? For whom? With what success?

EXHIBIT 4.2

Cost comparison between a company sales force and independent agents

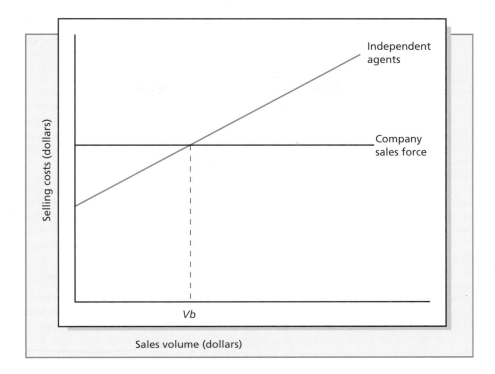

Economic Criteria   In a given selling situation, a company sales force and independent agents are likely to produce different levels of costs and sales volume. A first step in deciding which form of sales organization to use is to estimate and compare the costs of the two alternatives. A simplified example of such a cost comparison is illustrated in Exhibit 4.2.

The fixed costs of using external agents are lower than those of using a company sales force because of less administrative overhead and because agents do not receive a salary or reimbursement for field selling expenses. But costs of using agents tend to rise faster as sales volume increases because agents usually receive larger commissions than company salespeople. Consequently, a break-even level of sales volume exists (*Vb* in Exhibit 4.2) below which the costs of external agents are lower but above which a company sales force becomes more efficient. This helps explain why agents tend to be used by smaller firms or by larger firms in their smaller territories where sales volume is too low to warrant a company sales force.

Low fixed costs also make agents attractive when a firm is moving into new territories or product lines where success is uncertain. Since the agent does not get paid unless sales are made, the costs of failure are minimized.

The other side of the economic equation is sales volume. The critical question is whether company salespeople are likely to produce a higher volume of total sales than agents in a given situation. Most sales and marketing managers believe they will because company salespeople concentrate entirely on the firm's products, they may be better trained, they may be more aggressive since their future depends on the company's success, and customers often prefer to deal directly with a supplier. On the other hand, agents' contacts and experience in an industry can make them more effective than company salespeople, particularly when the company is new or is moving into a new geographic area or product line.

Control and Strategic Criteria   Regardless of which organizational form produces the greatest sales in the short run, many managers argue that an internal sales force is preferable to agents in the long run due to the difficulty of controlling agents and getting them to conform to their principals' strategic objectives. Agents are seen as independent actors who can be expected to pursue their own short-run objectives. This makes them reluctant to engage in activities with a long-run strategic payoff to their principal, such as cultivating new accounts or small customers with growth potential, performing service and support activities, or promoting new products. Some research supports this argument, suggesting manufacturers' representatives are more dissatisfied with close supervision and attempts to control their behavior than are company salespeople.[4]

Managers can control a company sales force in many different ways—through the selection, training, and supervision of personnel; establishment of operating procedures and policies; formal evaluation and reward mechanisms; and ultimately transferring or firing salespeople whose performance is not satisfactory.

Independent agents can also be replaced if their performance falls below the manufacturer's expectations. But in many cases, it is difficult for the manufacturer to tell whether an agent's poor performance is due to lack of effort or to factors beyond the agent's control, such as difficult competitive or market conditions. While company salespeople can be monitored on a regular basis, it is usually more difficult and costly—and sometimes impossible—to monitor the behavior of independent agents.[5] Finally, switching costs (such as contractual restrictions on termination) or customer loyalty to the agent may make it difficult for a manufacturer to replace an agent with its own salespeople.[6]

Transaction Costs   Even when a manufacturer decides a poor-performing agent should be replaced, it may be difficult to find an acceptable replacement. This is particularly likely when an intermediary must invest in specialized (or transaction-specific) assets, such as extensive product training or specialized capital equipment, to sell the manufacturer's product or service effectively. It might take a new manufacturer's rep months to learn enough about a technically complex product and its applications to do an effective selling job. The difficulty of finding acceptable replacements for poor-performing agents under such circumstances makes it even harder for the manufacturer to control those agents.

The theory of **transaction cost analysis (TCA)** states that when substantial transaction-specific assets are necessary to sell a manufacturer's product, the costs of using and administering independent agents (i.e., the manufacturer's transaction costs) are likely to be higher than the costs of hiring and managing a company sales force. This is because TCA assumes independent agents will pursue their own self-interests—even at the expense of the manufacturer they represent—when they think they can get away with it. For instance, they might provide only cursory postsale service or expend too little effort calling on smaller accounts because they are unlikely to earn big commissions from such activities. Because agents are most likely to be able to get away with such behaviors when it is difficult for the manufacturer to monitor or replace them, the transaction cost of using agents under such circumstances is likely to be high.[7]

Recently, however, analysts have questioned TCA's assumption that independent agents will always put their own short-term interests ahead of those of the manufacturer when they can avoid getting caught and replaced. These analysts argue that when both manufacturer and agent believe their relationship can be mutually beneficial for years, norms of trust and cooperation can develop.[8]

Strategic Flexibility   Another important strategic issue to consider when deciding whether to use agents or company salespeople is flexibility. Generally, a vertically

Innovation   Missionary Selling Trends toward Outsourcing in Retail Stores

4.1

Traditionally, consumer products sales organizations prided themselves on their service in retail stores. Not long ago, it would not have been unusual for a salesperson for a major packaged goods firm to have a call list with several hundred supermarkets, drugstores, and discount stores on it. Each would be dutifully contacted on a regularly established route, and the salesperson would perform "missionary" duties such as merchandising the shelves and displays, informing clerks and managers of promotions and new products, and putting up sales promotion materials.

For many manufacturers whose primary market is the retail industry, such missionary selling has gone the way of the dinosaur. Narrowing margins, increased demands by retailers for lower costs, and downsizing and flattening of sales organizations have put an end to such activities by most company sales forces. And concurrently, retail organizations that in the past ran their own rotating merchandising crews have largely abandoned the practice as a cost-cutting move.

These trends have opened the door to a new cottage industry—the outsourced missionary sales force. These organizations tend to be regional entrepreneurs, focused on specific retail industry sectors. They do no direct selling, and the salespeople employed by such firms are not highly paid. However, many such firms provide plenty of opportunity to reps for flexibile schedules and job sharing, and as such the positions generally have attracted quite good personnel.

A key question is, who do these outsourced reps work for: the manufacturer or the retailer (or to make it more complicated, we could throw in the manufacturer's direct selling agent organization)? The answer is: It depends. Most such entrepreneurial firms are perfectly willing to contract with any member of the channel to provide their missionary services. Training, bonding of employees, and all management of their activities, including reporting, are provided by the rep firm.

As with many changes in today's selling environment, this trend shows that change breeds opportunity to those who are quick to respond to market needs.

Source: Dan Ailooni-Charas, "Outsourcing Merchandising," *MMR: The Newspaper for Drug, Discount, and Supermarket Chains* 17, no. 22 (December 18, 2000), p. 22.

integrated distribution system incorporating a company sales force is the most difficult to alter quickly. Specialized agent intermediaries can often be added or dismissed at short notice, especially if no specialized assets are needed to sell the manufacturer's product and the firm does not have to sign long-term contracts to gain agents' support.

Firms facing uncertain and rapidly changing competitive or market environments or those in industries characterized by shifting technology and short product life cycles are often best advised to rely on independent agents to preserve the flexibility of their distribution channels.[9] An example of the use of outsourced missionary sellers is presented in Innovation 4.1.

Most marketing executives argue it is best to use agents in volatile environments, to represent a small company, or for territories with low sales potential where the benefits from scale economies outweigh the difficulties of motivating and controlling the agent's behavior. It is usually preferable to switch to direct salespeople as soon as a company or territory can support the higher fixed costs or when specialized knowledge or other assets are required to do an effective selling job.

Geographic Organization

The simplest and most common method of organizing a company sales force is by **geographic organization.** Here, individual salespeople are assigned to separate geographic territories. In this type of organization, each salesperson is responsible for

EXHIBIT 4.3   Geographic sales organization

performing all the activities necessary to sell all the products in the company's line to all potential customers in the territory. A geographic sales organization is illustrated in Exhibit 4.3.

The geographic sales organization has several strengths. Most important, it tends to have the lowest cost. Because there is only one salesperson in each territory and territories tend to be smaller than they are under other forms of organization, travel time and expenses are minimized. Also, fewer managerial levels are required for coordination. Thus, sales administration and overhead expenses are kept relatively low.

The simplicity of a geographic organizational structure leads to another advantage involving the firm's relationships with its customers. Because only one salesperson calls on each customer, confusion seldom exists about (1) who is responsible for what or (2) to whom the customer should talk when problems arise.

The major disadvantage of a geographic sales organization is that it does not provide any benefits of the division and specialization of labor. Each salesperson is expected to be a jack-of-all-trades. Each must sell all the firm's products to all types of customers and perform all the selling functions.

Also, this organizational structure provides the individual salesperson with freedom to make decisions concerning which selling functions to perform, what products to empha-size, and on which customers to concentrate. Unfortunately, salespeople are likely to expend most of this effort on the functions they perform best and on the products and customers they perceive to be most rewarding, whether or not such effort is consistent with management's objectives and account management policies.

Management can try to direct the efforts of salespeople through close supervision, well-designed compensation and evaluation plans, and clearly defined statements of policy, but the basic problem remains. Since each salesperson is expected to perform a full range of selling functions, the sales rep, rather than management, can control the way the selling effort is allocated across products, customers, and selling tasks.

Although a geographic approach to sales organization has its limitations, its basic sim-plicity and low cost make it very popular among smaller firms, particularly those with limited uncomplicated product lines. Also, while it is unusual for larger organizations to rely exclusively on geographic organization, they do commonly use it in conjunction with other organizational forms. For example, a firm may have two separate sales forces for different products in its line, but each sales force is likely to be organized geographically.

Product Organization

Some companies have separate sales forces for each product or product category in their line, as shown in Exhibit 4.4. A classic example of a **product organization** is the 3M Company. 3M has more than 50 divisions manufacturing a diverse assortment of products ranging from Scotch tape to abrasives to medical equipment, and many of those divisions have their own separate sales force.

The primary advantage of organizing the sales force by product is that individual salespeople can develop familiarity with the technical attributes, applications, and the most effective selling methods associated with a single product or related products. Also, when the firm's manufacturing facilities are organized by product type—as when separate factories produce each product—a product-oriented organization can lead to closer cooperation between sales and production. This can be very beneficial when the product is tailored to fit the specifications of different customers or when production and delivery schedules are critical in gaining and keeping a customer.

Finally, a product-oriented sales organization enables sales management to control the allocation of selling effort across the various products in the company's line. If management decides more effort should be devoted to a particular product, it can simply assign more salespeople to that product.

EXHIBIT 4.4   Sales force organized by product type

The major disadvantage of a sales force organized by product type is duplication of effort. Salespeople from different product divisions are assigned to the same geographic areas and may call on the same customers. Procter & Gamble, historically a product organization, has consolidated product lines under fewer separate selling divisions that employ a team selling approach. This change was precipitated in part because organizational buyers had to deal with too many P&G salespeople. Consumer product marketing folklore is rife with tales about waiting rooms in which every chair was occupied by a P&G rep waiting to see the same buyer.

Such duplication leads to higher selling expenses than would be the case with a simple geographic organization. It also creates a need for greater coordination across the various product divisions, which, in turn, requires more sales management personnel and higher administrative costs. Finally, such duplication can cause confusion and frustration among the firm's customers when they must deal with two or more representatives from the same supplier.

Since the major advantage of a product-oriented organization is that it allows salespeople to develop specialized knowledge of one or a few products, this form of organization is most commonly used by firms with large and diverse product lines. It is also used by manufacturers of highly technical products that require different kinds of technical expertise or different selling methods. That is the primary reason some firms such as 3M, with many different product lines based on widely differing technologies, continue to organize their sales force by product despite the cost disadvantages.

Organization by Customer Type or Markets

As reflected in the chapter opener, it has become increasingly popular for sales forces to use an approach of **organization by customer type.** This type of customer-oriented sales organization is shown in Exhibit 4.5.

Organizing a sales force by customer type is a natural extension of the marketing concept and reflects a strategy of market segmentation. When salespeople specialize in calling on a particular type of customer, they gain a better understanding of such customers' needs

EXHIBIT 4.5   Sales force organized by customer type

and requirements. They can also be trained to use different selling approaches for different markets and to implement specialized marketing and promotional programs.

A related advantage of customer specialization is that as salespeople become familiar with their customers' specific businesses and needs, they are more likely to discover ideas for new products and marketing approaches that will appeal to those customers. This can be a definite advantage in rapidly changing, highly competitive markets. Finally, this organizational structure allows marketing managers to control the allocation of selling effort to different markets by varying the sizes of the specialized sales forces.

The disadvantages of a customer-oriented sales organization are much the same as those of a product-oriented structure. Having different salespeople calling on different types of customers in the same territory can lead to higher selling expenses and administrative costs. Also, when customer firms have different departments or divisions operating in different industries, two or more salespeople may call on the same customer. This can cause confusion and frustration among customers.

Many firms must believe the advantages of a customer-oriented sales organization outweigh its limitations because it is growing in popularity as an organizational approach. This is particularly true for firms with products that have widely different applications in different markets or firms that must use different approaches when selling to different types of customers, as when a company sells to the government as well as to private industry. Also, specialization by customer type is a useful form of organization when a firm's marketing objectives include the penetration of previously untapped markets.

Organization by Selling Function

Different types of selling tasks often require different abilities and skills on the part of the salesperson. Thus, it may be logical under some circumstances to use an approach of **organization by selling function** so different salespeople specialize in performing different selling functions. One such functional organization is to have one sales force specialize in prospecting for and developing new accounts, while a second force maintains and services old customers.

Such functional specialization can be difficult to implement, however. Since a firm is likely to assign its most competent, experienced, and professionally impressive salespeople to the new-accounts sales force, new customers might object to being turned over from the salesperson who won their patronage to someone else who serves as a maintenance salesperson. It also can be difficult for management to coordinate the development and maintenance functions because feelings of rivalry and jealousy are likely to exist between the two sales forces.

Another form of functional specialization, however, is commonly and successfully used by many industrial product firms: *developmental salespeople* who are responsible for assisting in the development and early sales of new products. Developmental salespeople usually conduct market research, assist the firm's research and development and engineering departments, and sell new products as they are developed. These specialists are often part of a firm's research and development department rather than the regular sales force. Such specialists can help ensure development of successful new products, particularly when they are experienced and knowledgeable about customers' operations and needs as well as about their own firm's technical and production capabilities.

The Role of Telemarketing

One form of specialization by selling function that has gained great popularity in recent years is the use of inside telephone salespeople and outside field salespeople to accomplish separate selling objectives. Obviously, not all selling functions can be performed over the phone, but **telemarketing** has proven useful for carrying out selected activities, including the following:

- Prospecting for and qualifying potential new accounts, which can then be turned over to field salespeople for personal contact. This function often can be facilitated by including a toll-free phone number in all of the firm's promotional materials so interested potential customers can call to obtain more information about advertised products or services.

- Servicing existing accounts quickly when unexpected problems arise, such as through the use of technical-assistance hotlines.

- Seeking repeat purchases from existing accounts that cannot be covered efficiently in person, such as small or marginal customers and those in remote geographic locations.

- Gaining quicker communication of newsworthy developments, such as the introduction of new or improved products or special sales programs.[10]

It is important at this juncture to again make the distinction that we are focusing on selling in business-to-business settings. Telemarketing in business-to-consumer settings has been under considerable fire in recent years, resulting in legislation against unethical and nuisance practices. "Do not call" lists at both the state and federal level now include millions of consumers. Telemarketing in the business-to-business space is a different story.

The popularity of telemarketing to supplement the activities of the field sales force is growing for two reasons: (1) many customers like it and (2) it can increase the productivity of a firm's sales efforts. From the customers' view, the increased centralization of purchasing together with growing numbers of product alternatives and potential suppliers in many industries has increased demands on the time of purchasing agents and other members of organizations' buying centers. Consequently, they like sales contacts over the phone—particularly for routine purposes, such as soliciting reorders or relaying information about special sales programs and price promotions—because telephone sales calls take less time than personal sales calls.

From the seller's viewpoint, a combination of inside and outside salespeople—together with an appropriate mix of other media, such as targeted advertising, direct mail, toll-free phone lines, and a home page on the Internet—offers a way of improving the overall efficiency of the sales force.[11] Moving some salespeople inside and using them in conjunction with other promotional efforts allows the firm to lower the cost of routine sales activities substantially. At the same time, it enables the more expensive outside sales force to concentrate on activities with the highest potential long-term payout, such as new-account generation and the servicing of major customers. The efficiency of telemarketing makes it particularly useful for implementing an account management policy that directs different amounts of effort toward classifications of customers based on differences in size or potential. In the past, some firms prohibited sales forces from calling on very small customers—or told them to visit such accounts infrequently—because their purchase volume was not large enough to cover the cost of a sales call and still contribute to profit. But today, small businesses account for an increasingly large portion of the overall sales volume in many industries—revenue that firms can not afford to turn away. An inside sales force can call on such customers regularly and with much lower costs than is possible with an outside sales force.

Today, the issue of inside versus outside selling is inextricably linked to a firm's overall customer relationship strategy (see Chapter 3) and technological capabilities. Technology 4.2 on Centex Home Equity Corp. provides a vivid example of this integration.

Technology   Centex Home Equity Corp. Integrates Database Capabilities and Telemarketing Strategy   4.2

Dallas-based Centex Home Equity Corp. is a leader in second mortgages and home equity loans. It is also a leader in utilizing effective database marketing to link to telemarketing capabilities for its products. "What our research has found is that you can't just target homeowners," says Steve Scruton, senior vice president for Marketing Information and Technology Inc., a leading provider of databases and database analysis software to formulate prospecting solutions. "You have to match homeowners against other data in order to predict, or model, both a homeowner's willingness to borrow and willingness and ability to repay."

Scruton and his firm have been working with Centex for four years to help it achieve a competitive advantage by creating a strong functional prospect database. "A strong database has meant a fivefold advantage in our ability to market successfully," says Rob Greenbaum, Centex's vice president of marketing. "When we solicit business from a prospect universe, there's a five times greater probability we will originate a successful response to a loan offer."

Once Centex identifies a particular prospect universe, telemarketing provides a key strategic thrust. Telemarketing is the company's medium of choice because a prospect may be transferred seamlessly to a loan officer if they are ready to discuss a financial product. Centex outsources its telemarketing efforts to mid-sized vendors that specialize in the mortgage industry. "It's not a complex script (provided to the vendors), because it's just to prequalify that there is interest (from the prospect)," Greenbaum says.

Centex augments the primary prospecting via telemarketing with follow-up information by direct mail, if the prospect is not ready to buy now. The direct mail efforts used are an envelope package that includes a letter featuring copy that gives an example of the type of loan the person might qualify for and several response vehicles, including a toll-free number and a Web address. The company's Web site provides prospects with user-friendly information about home equity loans, including a chart that allows them to calculate how much they can borrow.

Centex was recently ranked #1 in customer satisfaction by J.D. Powers in 10 major markets and in the top three in 12 other markets. Chairman and CEO Andrew J. Hannigan attributed the strong performance on the firm's effective communication with customers through all stages of the construction process.

Sources: Ken Smalling, "Centex Homes Ranks Highest in Customer Satisfaction in 10 major U.S. Markets, According to Independent Study," *www.investors.com,* September 14, 2005; Alicia Orr, "Predicting a Need," *Target Marketing,* February 2001, pp. 62–64.

As we discuss later in this book, however, implementing two or more specialized sales forces, as in the case of inside and outside salespeople, can create interesting challenges for sales managers. Since each specialized sales force focuses on different types of selling activities, separate policies and procedures are often required. For example, some authorities suggest that an effective telemarketing program requires the development of standardized scripts for the salesperson to follow, even though their counterparts in the field might have much more flexibility to tailor their presentations to the needs of individual customers. Such differences in policies and procedures may require recruitment of different types of salespeople for the two sales forces and development of different training and compensation programs for each.[12]

ORGANIZING TO SERVICE NATIONAL AND KEY ACCOUNTS

Regardless of how their sales forces are organized, many firms are developing new organizational approaches to deliver the customer service necessary to attract and maintain large and important customers—their **national** or **key accounts.** Robert J. Hershock, former corporate vice president, marketing, 3M, said this about 3M's sales approach:

"Today, the sales representative needs to be a business manager who is responsible for key accounts. He or she must be able to customize products and services, knowledgeable about key account strategies and objectives, and capable of building and implementing key account business plans."[13] As discussed in Chapter 1, the increasing technical complexity of products, industrial concentration, and the trend toward centralized purchasing make a few major accounts critical to the marketing success of many firms in both industrial and consumer goods industries. Moreover, in the ever-increasing global marketplace, national accounts often become global accounts demanding a high degree of coordination with their suppliers. At IBM, 75 percent of revenues are generated from "industry solutions accounts," which represent its largest customers. It's those Fortune 500 accounts in which IBM is providing consulting to corporate America's top executives—a strategy of "targeting boardrooms." According to a survey by Management Consultant International, IBM is now the world's largest consultancy, with revenues surpassing Accenture, CapGemini, Ernst & Young, PricewaterhouseCoopers, and Deloitte Consulting.[14] On the customer side, Xerox announced in the late 1990s that it was cutting its list of suppliers by 90 percent. Such trends suggest that companies are looking at developing fewer but more substantial relationships with a limited set of suppliers.[15]

To provide the level of service demanded by key accounts, firms such as IBM adopt an overall selling philosophy of major account management and partnering. This approach stresses the dual goals of making sales and developing long-term relationships with major customers. Firms believe national account management policies will improve coordination of selling activities and communications with key customers. This should enable the seller to capture a larger share of the purchases made by those customers and to improve profitability.[16] Benefits accrue inside the firm as well. Everyone in the organization works a little harder when they know the customer is significant and has a long-term relationship with the firm.

When a firm decides to implement a national account program, it must address the issue of who in the organization should be responsible for the functions of managing the business of the national accounts. Some firms have no special organizational arrangements for handling their major customers; they rely on members of their regular sales force, supported by other members of their company, to manage national and key accounts. This requires no additional administrative or selling expense.

The disadvantage is that major accounts often require more detailed and sophisticated treatment than smaller customers. Consequently, servicing major accounts may require more experience, expertise, and organizational authority than many salespeople possess. Also, if the sales force is compensated largely by commission, difficult questions may arise about which salesperson should get the commissions for sales to national accounts when one person calls on a customer's headquarters while others service its stores or plants in various territories.

In view of these difficulties, many firms have adopted special organizational arrangements for the major account management function. These arrangements include (1) assigning key accounts to top sales executives, (2) creating a separate corporate division, and (3) creating a separate sales force to handle major accounts.[17]

Assigning Key Accounts to Sales Executives

The use of sales or marketing executives to call on the firm's national or key accounts is a common practice, especially among smaller firms that do not have the resources to support a separate division or sales force. It is also common when the firm has relatively few major accounts to be serviced. In addition to the relatively low cost of the approach, it has the advantage of having important customers serviced by people who are high enough in the organizational hierarchy to make, or at least to influence, decisions concerning the allocation of production capacity, inventory levels, and prices. Consequently, they can provide flexible and responsive service.

One problem with this approach is that the managers who are given key account responsibilities sometimes develop a warped view of their firm's marketing objectives. They sometimes allocate too much of the firm's resources to their own accounts to the detriment of smaller, but still profitable, customers. In other words, such managers sometimes become obsessed with getting all the business they can from their large customers without paying sufficient attention to the overall impact on sales, operations, or profits.

Another problem is that assigning important selling tasks to managers takes time away from their management activities. This can hinder the coordination and effectiveness of the firm's overall selling and marketing efforts.

A Separate Key Account Division

Some firms create a separate corporate division for dealing with major accounts. For example, some apparel companies have separate divisions for making and selling private-label clothing to large general-merchandise chains, such as Target, Sears, and JCPenney. This approach allows for close integration of manufacturing, logistics, marketing, and sales activities. This can be important when one or a few major customers account for such a large proportion of a firm's total sales volume that variations in their purchases have a major impact on the firm's production schedules, inventories, and allocation of resources.

The major disadvantages of this approach are the duplication of effort and the additional expense involved in creating an entire manufacturing and marketing organization for only one or a few customers. It is also risky because the success or failure of the entire division is dependent on the whims of one or a few customers.

A Separate Sales Force for Key Accounts

Rather than creating an entire separate division to deal with major customers, a company may create a separate national or key account sales force. A separate sales force has several advantages in dealing with key accounts. By concentrating on only one or a few major customers, the account manager can become very familiar with each customer's problems and needs and can devote the time necessary to provide a high level of service to each customer. Also, the firm can select its most competent and experienced salespeople to become members of the national account sales force, thus ensuring that important customers receive expert sales attention.

Finally, a separate national account sales force provides an internal benefit to the selling company. Because only the most competent salespeople are typically assigned to national accounts, such an assignment is often viewed as a desirable promotion. Thus, promotion to the national account sales force can be used to motivate and reward top salespeople who are either not suited for or not interested in moving into sales management.

In addition to the problem of allocating national account sales to individual members of the field sales force, using a separate sales force for major accounts suffers from many of the other disadvantages associated with organizing sales efforts by customer type. The most troubling problems concern the duplication of effort within the sales organization and the resulting higher selling and administrative expenses.

Team Selling

As we learned in Chapters 2 and 3, today the relationship between customers and sales organizations is complex. Nowadays, salespeople are asked to demonstrate a stronger knowledge of the customer's businesses than ever before as well as provide a more consistent and beneficial interface with the customer—in other words, better service. As we learned in Chapter 3, one way companies deal with these demands is to assign specialists inside the firm to individual customers—**team selling.** A number of benefits are achieved by allocating more individuals, each with a unique talent, to each customer. First, questions can be answered faster, which reduces the need for the "I will get back to you on that" response to customer inquiries. Second, people with similar interests can speak directly with one another. A technical question from the customer's engineering department can be answered by another engineer in the supplier's support sales team.

The key is identifying a team selling structure that meets the needs of customers. For example, a common structure would make the account manager responsible for working with the entire team selling to and servicing major customers. Often, such major account teams include representatives from a number of functional departments within the firm, such as R&D, operations, and finance. Given that major customers' buying centers often consist of people from different functional areas with different viewpoints and concerns, those concerns can often be most effectively addressed by a team of experts from equivalent functional departments in the selling firm, or even from different divisions within the company. Recently, companies have begun to look at the existence of a **selling center** that brings together individuals from around the organization (marketing, customer service, sales, engineering, and others) to help the salesperson do his or her job more effectively. These selling centers are analogous to the concept of selling teams discussed in Chapter 3. Just as customers have buying centers, the selling organization needs to work together to present a unified, well-coordinated effort to the customer.[18] In an increasing number of companies, sales organizations maintain offices in the customer's facilities. Lear Corporation, a leading global supplier of automotive interior systems, maintains sales offices on the premises of each of its major customers, who are many of the major automotive firms around the world.[19]

At IBM, the team for a major account such as EDS is led by an IBM account executive. The account executive has a global team of salespeople as direct reports, but can also draw from the full functional resources of IBM to provide solutions for EDS at any location in the world. Such an approach creates a **matrix organization** of direct reports and supporting internal consultants who bring their collective expertise to bear for the client.

Team selling can also present some coordination, motivation, and compensation problems. Lou Gerstner, former CEO of IBM, has frequently spoken out on the difficulties of performance management in team selling environments.[20] Team selling is most appropriate for the very largest customers, where the potential purchase represents enough dollars and involves enough functions to justify the high costs. Although team selling is usually used to win new accounts, it is sometimes also used with lower-level personnel for maintenance selling. Production schedulers, expeditors, and shipping personnel may join the sales team to keep an existing account satisfied.[21]

A number of important recent trends in team selling are presented in Leadership 4.3.

Multilevel Selling

Multilevel selling is a variation of team selling. In multilevel selling, the sales team consists of personnel from various managerial levels who call on their counterparts in the buying organization. Thus, the account manager might call on the customer's purchasing department while the selling firm's vice president of finance calls on the buyer's financial vice president. Sometimes this involves setting up a permanent team to coordinate activities with the customer. Often, however, this is an ad hoc arrangement where individuals

Leadership   Breakthroughs in Team Selling   4.3

Team selling with everyone working toward a common goal sounds like a great idea: Together, everyone achieves more—and all that. Many sales organizations alter compensation plans and add incentives designed to spur a more team-oriented approach to selling. Yet, says Linda Kuritzkes, a Haddonfield, NJ–based compensation consultant, many of these efforts fail to produce the desired team cohesion and sometimes even generate resentment and dissention in the ranks. She suggests a variety of reasons for this outcome, including

- Company salespeople hired for their killer sales skills tend to be motivated by personal achievement, not team goals.

- Organizations are structured in silos that encourage districts to compete against one another.

- Sales managers are compensated on the basis of their reported performance and are not encouraged to collaborate with other offices.

- Different team members report to different managers so the entire team doesn't get a unified message.

Despite these formidable obstacles, all is not lost, Kuritzkes says. It is still possible to motivate your sales staff to work more in unison. The first issue, she says, is to make sure your team focus will deliver genuine benefits to the bottom line. Ask yourself: Are there true synergies to be achieved by the team that can't be met by salespeople focused on individual achievement? If so, what are they? Once you've identified the tangible benefits to a team-selling approach, Kuritzkes suggests you make changes in the following areas to ensure the new approach will work.

1. *Hiring.* Rather than going after lone wolves, modify hiring practices to recruit individuals who are inclined toward achieving group goals.

2. *Management.* Create a management structure that's aligned with the new team orientation. If individual salespeople have more than one boss, make sure the managers are all working from the same strategic playbook.

3. *Compensation.* Add a team component to the compensation and incentive plan. Rather than applying a one-size-fits-all approach, base metrics on the expectations and functions of each team member. Try to keep things simple, however, so everyone readily understands the measurements and can track results. If possible, pilot the program to iron out the kinks before implementing a wider rollout.

4. *Communication.* Discuss the new plan ahead of time with each district. If you've piloted the program, share the results, even if they were not all positive. By getting ahead of the new changes you will build credibility among your salespeople and have a greater chance of developing early buy-in.

In closing, Kuritzkes notes that aligning these elements is not merely helpful for promoting team selling—they're absolutely essential. "Team-based incentives do work," she says, "provided there is a compelling business need for teamwork, the appropriate individuals are selected and trained, and the compensation plan reinforces the business goals and motivates the team members."

Source: Malcolm Fleschner, "Breakthroughs in Group Selling," *SellingPower.com.*

at different levels are responsible for maintaining a relationship with the key customer but not as part of an established team.

This approach represents proper organizational etiquette—each member of the selling team calls on a person with corresponding status and authority. Also, it is useful for higher-level executives to participate in opening a relationship with a major new prospect, since they have the authority to make concessions and establish policies necessary to win and maintain that prospect as a customer. When the interaction takes place at the highest levels of both firms, the process is called *top-to-top selling,* as discussed in Chapter 3.

Co-Marketing Alliances

In some high-tech industries, such as computers and telecommunications, customers buy systems made up of components manufactured by two or more different suppliers. In some cases, suppliers rely on independent intermediaries, such as value-added resellers (VARs), to combine their components with those from other suppliers to create a system to meet the needs of a particular end user. Increasingly, however, individual suppliers are forming **co-marketing alliances** and developing joint marketing and sales programs to sell integrated systems directly to the ultimate customer.

In some cases, even competitors develop marketing alliances to maximize their resources. When Warner-Lambert's Parke-Davis pharmaceutical division created the lipid-regulating drug Lipitor, the product offered significant advantages over anything else in the market. However, the firm lacked the sales force necessary to market the drug effectively. Warner-Lambert partnered with Pfizer, a company with a powerful sales force, to create a joint effort managed by a team of individuals from both companies. Salespeople from both firms worked together to maximize the sales of Lipitor in a given territory.[22] Interestingly, a few years later Pfizer acquired Warner-Lambert.

Logistical Alliances and Computerized Ordering

Another recent technological change under way in many industries is the formation of **logistical alliances** involving the development of computerized information and ordering systems. Such systems enable customers to place an order directly, and often automatically, via a dedicated telephone or satellite link to a supplier's computer. Firms such as Procter & Gamble and 3M have formed alliances with major supermarket chains and mass merchandisers, such as Publix and Wal-Mart, to develop automatic restocking systems. Sales information from the retailer's checkout scanners is sent directly to the supplier's computers, which figure out automatically when to replenish each product and schedule deliveries directly to each of the retailer's stores. Such paperless exchanges reduce mistakes and billbacks, minimize inventory levels, decrease out-of-stocks, and improve cash flow.

Although to date such systems have been most widely adopted by manufacturers of relatively standardized consumer products, many industrial goods manufacturers are also developing computerized reordering systems. This is particularly true for firms that customize their products to a customer's order. By having orders sent directly to its computer, the supplier can quickly organize production schedules, speed up the production process, and minimize finished goods inventories.[23]

From the customer's point of view, computerized ordering is more convenient, more flexible, and less time consuming than placing orders through a salesperson. From the supplier's perspective, linking major customers to a dedicated reorder system can help tie those customers to the firm and increase the proportion of purchases they make from a single source.[24] Cisco Systems, a leading producer of Internet working equipment, created a Web site so customers could track their orders more efficiently as well as reorder commonly replaced items. The results have been dramatic, as sales from the site were in excess of $75 million in the first year.

One question that is yet to be answered is, How might computerized reorder systems change the role of the sales force? Will salespeople become largely redundant, or will being freed from the more routine order-taking activities enable firms to refocus personal selling efforts on more complex communications, problem solving, and customer servicing tasks? When Cisco introduced its Web site so customers could track and order more efficiently, salespeople were concerned it would have a negative effect on their interaction with customers. The reality was much different. Cisco salespeople are able to devote more time to actually selling products rather than reordering or tracking existing orders.

VERTICAL STRUCTURE OF THE SALES ORGANIZATION

The beginning of this chapter stressed that the sales organization must be structured vertically as well as horizontally. The vertical organizational structure clearly defines what managerial positions have the authority for carrying out specific sales management activities. This vertical structure also provides for the effective integration and coordination of selling efforts throughout the firm.

Two key questions that must be answered in designing an effective vertical structure for a sales organization are (1) how many levels of sales managers should there be? and (2) how many people should each manager supervise or **span of control?** These questions are related. For a given number of salespeople, the greater the span of control, the fewer the levels of management, and the fewer managers needed.

Major differences of opinion exist about the best policy concerning span of control and the number of vertical levels for a sales organization. Some managers think they have greater control and attain greater responsiveness when the sales force has a "flat" organization with few management levels. They argue that few levels between the top sales executive and the field salespeople facilitate communication and more direct control. But some managers argue that such flat organizations actually limit communication and control because they necessitate large spans of control.

The flat organization with large spans of control has lower administrative costs because of the relatively small number of managers involved. Some argue, however, that such cost savings are an illusion because the lower quantity and quality of management can lead to less effectiveness and productivity.

In view of these disagreements, it is difficult to generalize about the most appropriate number of management levels and span of control for a specific organization. However, managers have a few guidelines to follow. The span of control should be smaller and the number of levels of management should be larger when (1) the sales task is complex, (2) the profit impact of each salesperson's performance is high, and (3) the salespeople in the organization are well paid and professional. In other words, the more difficult and important the sales job, the greater the management support and supervision that should be provided to the members of the sales force.

Another general rule is that the span of control should usually be smaller at higher levels in the sales organization because top-level managers should have more time for analysis and decision making. Also, the people who report to them typically have more complicated jobs and require more organizational support and communication than persons in lower-level jobs.

In addition to deciding how many subordinates sales managers should supervise, another question addresses how much authority each manager should be given in managing subordinates. Where should the authority to hire, fire, and evaluate field salespeople be located within the organization? In some sales organizations, first-level field or district sales managers have the authority to hire their own salespeople. In other organizations, the authority to hire and fire is located at higher management levels.

As a general rule of organization, the more important a decision to the success of a firm, the higher the level of management that should make that decision. In firms that hire many low-paid salespeople who perform relatively routine selling tasks and have only a small impact on the firm's overall profit performance, hiring and evaluation authority is usually given to first-level sales managers. Firms that have professional salespeople who perform complex selling tasks and have a major profit impact usually place the authority to hire and fire at higher levels. This is particularly true when the sales force is viewed as a training ground for future sales or marketing managers.

Selling Responsibilities

In addition to their supervisory and policy-making roles, many sales managers, particularly those at the field or district level, continue to be actively involved in selling activities. Since many sales managers are promoted to their positions only after proving to be competent and effective salespeople, their employers are often reluctant to lose the benefit of their selling skills. Consequently, sales managers are often allowed to continue servicing at least a few of their largest customers after they join the ranks of management.

Some firms rely on their sales managers for selling and servicing key accounts. Sales managers often prefer this kind of arrangement. They are reluctant to give up the opportunities for commissions and direct contact with the marketplace that they gain by being actively involved in selling. The danger is that sales managers sometimes spend too much time selling and not enough time managing their subordinates. Consequently, some firms limit the amount of actual selling in which managers can engage. This is particularly true in large firms where coordinating and supervising a vast sales force require a great deal of attention by management personnel.

Sales-Related Functions

Many firms face markets that demand high levels of service. Firms that sell capital equipment, for instance, must provide their customers with installation and maintenance service; fashion manufacturers must provide rapid order processing and delivery; and firms that sell electronic components must offer special product design and engineering services. These services must be integrated with the rest of the firm's marketing and selling activities for the company to compete effectively.[25]

The question from an organizational viewpoint, though, is whether sales managers should be given the authority to control such sales-related functions. The answer depends on the function and the characteristics and needs of the firm's customers. Order processing and expediting are low visibility but quite important sales-related functions. In some firms, persons responsible for order processing report to top-level sales management, whereas in other firms they report to operations management, perhaps as part of an inventory control or data processing department. Usually, the more important rapid order processing and delivery are for keeping customers satisfied, the more appropriate it is for sales management to have authority over this function.

Repair and engineering services tend to be responsible to the sales organization in some firms and to the manufacturing or operations department in others. Again, such functions are most likely to be attached to the sales organization when they play a critical role in winning and maintaining customers. This is particularly true when the product must be designed or modified to meet customer specifications before a sale can be made.

The credit function is almost always the responsibility of the firm's controller or treasurer, and it seldom reports to the sales organization because salespeople and their managers may be tempted to be too generous with credit terms to close a sale.

In firms where sales-related functions do not report directly to the sales organization, team selling is often a useful means of coordinating such functions, at least when dealing with major customers where the cost of such an approach is justified. Although the account manager has no formal authority to control the actions of team members from other departments, he or she can coordinate the team's activities at the field level.

The Impact of New Technologies

Many of the preceding conclusions about appropriate spans of control and managerial responsibilities for sales managers must be taken with the caveat that the vertical structure of sales organizations is subject to change in the future due to the impact of new communications and information processing technologies. Companies realize that maximizing the sales effort requires that each salesperson be equipped with an array of technologies. The use of technologies has evolved from productivity enhancers (time management and contact management software; proposal generators) to CRM systems as discussed in Chapter 3, with the capability to drive the entire customer acquisition and retention management process.

Staff Support and Outsourcing

Many large sales organizations utilize some staff personnel in addition to their line sales managers. Staff executives are responsible for a limited range of specific activities, but they do not have the broad operating responsibility or authority of line managers. Staff executives commonly perform tasks requiring specialized knowledge or abilities that the average sales manager does not have the time to develop. They may also help collect and analyze information that line managers need for decision making. Thus, the most common functions performed by staff specialists in a sales organization are recruitment, training, and sales analysis. A typical line and staff sales organization is diagrammed in Exhibit 4.6.

EXHIBIT 4.6   Line and staff sales organization

The creative use of staff specialists can enable a sales force to function with fewer managers because of the benefits of specialization and division of labor. It can also improve the effectiveness of the sales organization while cutting costs. In addition, staff positions can be used as a training ground for future top-level sales managers.

On the other hand, staff positions are justified only when the sales organization is large enough so staff specialists have enough work to keep them busy. Increasingly, however, even the largest firms are questioning whether in-house staff specialists are really justified. A growing number of firms are outsourcing some staff functions through the use of specialized suppliers, such as recruiting and personnel testing services and training firms. The rationale for this trend is similar to the argument discussed earlier concerning the use of company salespeople versus independent agents. Activities that do not rely directly on a firm's core competencies (i.e., that do not require specialized or transaction-specific assets) often can be performed more effectively and efficiently by outside specialists on a contractual basis.[26]

ADDITIONAL SALES ORGANIZATIONAL ISSUES

Sometimes, the opportunity arises to start from scratch to build a new sales force. Such an opportunity should allow the sales manager to avoid pitfalls and create an initial organizational structure and cultural environment that maximizes the potential for success. The following are six key building blocks to starting a sales force:

- *Start with a strategy.* Define the sales force's mission, skill sets, and customer benefits.

- *Appoint an expansion team.* Get hiring input from human resource executives and the executives who will manage the new sales force.

- *Leverage existing strengths.* Look for new hires within your own ranks, your personal business network, as well as your clients and suppliers.

- *Go to the press.* Articles touting your business model and management team can attract both customers and salespeople.

- *Avoid compensation snafus.* If the new team must work hand-in-hand with the existing sales force, consider paying them both for the sale. Don't kill a million dollar investment by pinching pennies.

- *Provide support.* Get out in the field with your salespeople and show them how to pitch the product. Share best practices in conference calls.[27]

Sales managers assigned to lead the effort of creating a new sales force can employ best practices to create an organization designed for high performance.

Although many issues concerning the strategic organization of the sales force have been examined in this chapter, some related questions have yet to be explored. How many salespeople should a firm hire? How should these people be deployed? How should sales territories be defined? What quota, if any, should be assigned to each sales territory?

The answers to these questions depend on the markets to be served, the potential sales volume in those markets, and the selling effort necessary to capture a desired share of the potential volume. These issues are addressed in Chapter 5.

Summary

This chapter examined important issues regarding the organization of the sales force. It looked at the benefits a good organizational plan can provide the major issues involved in deciding on the horizontal and vertical organization of the sales effort.

A good organizational plan should satisfy three criteria. First, it should allow the firm to realize the benefits that can be derived from the division and specialization of labor. Second, it should provide for stability and continuity in the firm's selling efforts. This can best be accomplished by organizing activities and not people. Third, it should produce effective coordination of the various activities assigned to different persons in the sales force and different departments in the firm.

Questions of horizontal organization focus on how specific selling activities are to be divided among members of the sales force. The first issue to be resolved is whether to use company employees to perform the sales function or to rely on outside manufacturers' representatives or sales agents. The cost of using outside agents is usually lower than that of a company sales force at relatively low sales volumes. However, most executives believe company employees will generate greater levels of sales and are easier to control than agents.

When a firm employs its own sales force, four types of horizontal organization are commonly found, structured according to (1) geography, (2) type of product, (3) type of customer, and (4) selling function. Geographic organization is the simplest and most common. It possesses the advantages of low cost and clear identification of which salesperson is responsible for each customer. Its primary disadvantage is that it does not provide the firm with any benefits from division and specialization of labor.

Specializing the sales force along product lines allows salespeople to develop great familiarity with the technical attributes, applications, and most effective methods of selling those products. This can be advantageous when products are technically complex or when the firm's manufacturing facilities are also organized by product type. The major disadvantage associated with organization by product type is duplication of effort.

Organizing a sales force by type of customer or market served allows salespeople to better understand the needs and requirements of the various types of customers. Salespeople are more likely to discover ideas for new products and marketing approaches that will appeal to those customers. However, this scheme also produces duplication of effort, which tends to increase selling and administrative expenses.

A selling function organizational philosophy holds that people should be allowed to do what they do best. Thus, it makes sense to have, say, one sales force specializing in prospecting for and developing new accounts while another maintains and services existing customers. These arrangements are often difficult to implement because of coordination problems.

In addition to deciding on a basic structure, a firm needs to specify how it intends to service national and key accounts in its horizontal organizational plans. Three arrangements are most commonly found: (1) assigning key accounts to top sales executives, (2) creating a separate corporate division, and (3) creating a separate major account sales force.

Two key questions must be addressed in deciding on an effective vertical structure of the sales organization: (1) How many levels of sales managers should there be? (2) How many people should each manager supervise? The answers are related: For a given number of salespeople, a greater span of control produces fewer levels of management. Although it is difficult to unequivocally state the optimal span of control for a firm, it is generally true that the span of control should be smaller in those firms where (1) the sales task is complex, (2) the profit impact of each salesperson's performance is high, and (3) the salespeople in the organization are well paid and professional.

Another question that must be addressed in designing the vertical structure of a sales organization is, How much authority should be given each manager in the sales management hierarchy, particularly with respect to hiring, firing, and evaluating subordinates? As a general rule, the more important such decisions are to the firm, the higher the level of management that should make such decisions.

Starting up a sales force from scratch requires strong leadership skills and a high degree of experience and preparation on the part of the sales manager. It can be one of the most rewarding assignments in one's career, and it provides the opportunity to take advantage of knowledge of best practices to avoid pitfalls and create a high-performance organization.

Key Terms

division and specialization of labor
line organization
line and staff organization
outsourcing the sales force
manufacturers' representatives
selling agents

transaction cost analysis (TCA)
geographic organization
product organization
organization by customer type
organization by selling function
telemarketing

national or key accounts
team selling
selling center
matrix organization
multilevel selling
co-marketing alliances
logistical alliances
span of control

Breakout Questions

1. Intronics Corporation, a manufacturer of electronic circuit boards, reaches the market through the services of 75 manufacturers' agencies. Most of the agencies average two sales agents who call on Intronics customers. The agents also represent seven to eight other manufacturers that produce noncompetitive products. Intronics wants to eliminate the agents and develop its own company sales force. How many salespeople do you think Intronics will have to hire? What issues affect your assessment of how many salespeople are needed?

2. IBM, Xerox, P&G, and many other companies have reorganized to better serve their largest customers. How might a global company reorganize itself to maximize effectiveness with its most important customers? As senior sales management, how would you define "most important" customer (by current sales, future potential sales, or some other criteria)?

3. The chapter mentions the theory of transaction cost analysis. What role does transaction cost analysis play in the decision to use a company sales force rather than independent manufacturers' agents?

4. Telemarketing has resulted in the development of inside sales forces. Some companies assign sales trainees to the inside or telephone sales force as part of the training program in preparation for an outside sales position. Other companies view the two positions as separate. What functions would an inside (telephone) sales force perform? How would these functions differ from those performed by the external sales force? How would compensation plans differ if they differ at all?

5. LaMarche's Enterprise manufactures both technical and nontechnical products. Its sales forces are organized in the same manner. The technical sales force has 175 people, and

the nontechnical group numbers 128. To what extent would such a division affect the following?

a. Recruiting.

b. Sales training.

c. Compensation.

d. Supervision.

e. Span of control.

6. Many firms, such as Centex Home Equity Corp., are augmenting their telemarketing efforts with strong database marketing initiatives. What would be an effective role of a Web site in further supporting the success of a firm's telemarketing initiative?

Leadership Challenge: Inside or Outside

Susan Jones was thinking about the future as she drove home from an important day at her company, Satin Organic Products. In a little over nine years, she had taken a small organic milk company and become a major supplier to large health food grocery chains like Whole Foods and Trader Joe's. During that time, Susan and her vice president of marketing, Sal Clermont, had handled all the sales responsibilities. Working directly with the buyers, Susan and Sal had built an outstanding reputation as people who cared about the quality of their products and their relationship with customers.

Now Susan was faced with a challenge. Susan and Sal would no longer be able to handle the sales responsibilities by themselves. The company had grown too big and needed sales representation in the field. At present, an analysis of the company's current and near-term future plans had determined a need for seven individuals. Four people were required to handle the company's key accounts (Whole Foods and Trader Joe's) and three were needed to call on potential new customers in areas close to the company's expanding operations in the Midwest.

In talking with Sal and others in the food business, Susan realized there were two basic choices and unlimited combinations of those two choices. First, she could hire seven sales-people as employees of the Satin Organic Products. This had certain advantages but was also the most expensive. The second alternative was to hire outside sales agents who knew the food business and the customers. This alternative also had advantages and disadvantages.

Susan knew that she and Sal would have to make a decision soon. Their large customers were demanding more service, and there were a number of new business opportunities that they had not been able to go after because of other responsibilities.

Questions

1. Using the information in Chapter 4, discuss the advantages and disadvantages of having your own sales force versus hiring outside sales agents.

2. How should Susan set up the sales force for Satin Organic Products and why?

Role Play: Blue Tern Mills-A

Situation

Agnes Klondyke is excited. As national sales manager for Blue Tern Mills, a major manufacturer of traditional salty snacks (nuts, chips, and crackers), she knows that new product development is the lifeblood of the business. But wow . . . the e-mail she got this morning from Blue Tern's CEO Max Pugh really takes the cake (no pun intended of course). Max reports that Blue Tern's acquisition of the Hello brand of healthy grain cereals and packaged healthy snacks has been completed. Beginning in about six months, Blue Tern's sales force will begin selling the new line, which has previously been sold by manufacturer's agents.

Later that afternoon, Agnes got a call from Max to discuss gearing up for selling the new line. Blue Tern's sales force has been organized geographically, with each salesperson selling the entire line of 211 Blue Tern snack products. The problem is that the Hello line adds 117 new products to the mix, and many of these products are sold in different kinds of outlets from Blue Tern items—for example, while some supermarkets, drugstores, and discount stores might sell both Blue Tern and Hello products, the Hello line is also sold in health food stores, in some gyms, and over the Internet. Agnes is quickly realizing that she has a major reorganization task ahead for the company's sales force.

Max has asked for a new organization plan for selling both lines, and he wants the plan on his desk in two weeks. Agnes calls Alan Knorr, West Coast regional manager for Blue Tern, and Penny Pugsley, director of sales for Hello, to a meeting to discuss ideas for the transition and development of a new organizational scheme for Blue Tern's sales force. Penny is cooperative, as in the acquisition she has been promised the vacant East Coast regional manager slot at Blue Tern. Vital facts about Blue Tern's current sales organization: (1) it is organized geographically, with 212 salespeople, 20 district managers, and two regional managers; (2) all the salespeople sell the full Blue Tern product line to all types of retailers; and (3) there are no major account salespeople.

Max has made it clear that he will financially support whatever changes this decision team recommends, including adding some salespeople where needed to support the additional anticipated sales volume from the Hello line. The key question of course is, Is their current simple geographic approach optimal for the new situation?

Characters in the Role Play

Agnes Klondyke, national sales manager for Blue Tern Mills

Alan Knorr, West Coast sales manager for Blue Tern Mills

Penny Pugsley, currently the director of sales for Hello Healthy Grain Foods and soon to be East Coast sales manager for Blue Tern Mills; note that Penny's job at Hello has been to supervise its network of manufacturer's reprepresentatives (Hello does not have its own sales force).

Assignment

Break into groups of three, with one student playing each character. It doesn't matter what the actual gender mix of your group is. Before you stage the meeting among Agnes, Alan, and Penny, work separately to come up with a proposed new organization plan for Blue Tern's sales force and a transition plan for making the change happen. Remember, Blue Tern must be ready to start selling both lines in six months. Then get together and role-play the meeting. Share your ideas, especially discussing the pros and cons of different new organization schemes for the sales force. After the discussion, come to agreement among yourselves on what will be the best type of sales organization for the firm and list key aspects of implementing the change so that the transition with customers is as smoothe as possible.

Minicase: Fondren Publishing, Inc.

Fondren Publishing, Inc., based in Cambridge, Massachusetts, is one of the leading worldwide publishers of academic journals in the area of science and technology. It has more than 2,000 titles in its stable of products and publishes them in both print and electronic formats. Its primary customers are trade customers, who collect academic journal content from several different publisher sources and then package the content and resell it to retail customers. To a lesser extent, Fondren also sells directly to retail customers such as universities, libraries, societies/associations (e.g., Society of Environmental Engineers), and individuals (e.g., professors, scientists).

Fondren's sales force is known for being dynamic and knowledgeable, and some members of its sales team have been with the company for as many as 17 years. It traditionally has had a geographically structured sales force, divided into 14 regions: 6 in the United States, 4 in Europe, 4 in Asia-Pacific. Fondren's largest trade customer, by far, is New York–based AcademCo., which has a 35 percent share in its market and is responsible for 20 percent of Fondren's sales revenues. Therefore, the regional sales team covering the Northeastern United States is extralarge to accommodate this customer.

Just last week, a deal was reached for Fondren to merge with another journal publisher, Bronson & Sons. Bronson specializes in health science titles, which will add more than 750 new titles to those of Fondren. Bronson has fewer trade customers than Fondren and focuses on its direct customers such as societies, universities, and individuals. Bronson, like Fondren, used a geographic sales structure, but was limited to the United States, which was divided into four regions.

Although the arrangement is a "merger," Fondren has a controlling interest and will blend Bronson's products with its existing products under the Fondren name. Fondren's executives are meeting to decide on how the new merged company will be structured, including how the sales force will be structured.

The executives also want to use this merger and restructuring opportunity to enhance the company's customer service activities. Currently, the customer service department handles the fulfillment and maintenance of new and existing subscriptions (renewals, change of address, and so forth) through telephone operators. Fondren's IT department has plans to implement a new customer service and fulfillment system, which will be able to record and track particular customer information, as well as offer the customer service functions through an online Web interface.

To this point, the sales representatives would make the initial sale, and then turn the customer over to the customer service function for maintenance. Joe Elliott, director of customer service and fulfillment, has a vision in which customer service representatives would be able to contribute to sales by up-selling or cross-selling Fondren products when the reps are in contact with customers.

Questions

1. How should Fondren structure its sales force after the merger with Bronson? Why? What are the potential advantages and disadvantages of the structure you chose?
2. How should Fondren treat its key account(s)? Why?
3. What selling approach could Fondren take to coordinate its selling endeavors with its customer service and fulfillment operations?

Suggested Readings

Arnett, Dennis B., Barry A. Macy, and James B. Wilcox. "The Role of Core Selling Teams in Supplier-Buyer Relationships." *Journal of Personal Selling & Sales Management* 25 (Winter 2005), pp. 27–42.

Bantham, John H., Kevin G. Celuch, and Chickery J. Kasouf. "A Perspective on Partnerships Based on Interdependence and Dialectical Theory." *Journal of Business Research* 56 (April 2003), pp. 265–74.

Blyth, Jim. "Using Trade Fairs in Key Account Management." *Industrial Marketing Management* 31 (October 2002), pp. 627–35.

Dixon, Andrea L., Jule B. Gassenheimer, and Terri Feldman Barr. "Bridging the Distance between Us: How Initial Responses to Sales Team Conflict Help Shape Core Selling

Team Outcomes." *Journal of Personal Selling & Sales Management* 22 (Fall 2002), pp. 247–57.

Dixon, Andrea L., Jule B. Gassenheimer, and Terri Feldman Barr. "Identifying the Lone Wolf: A Team Perspective." *Journal of Personal Selling & Sales Management* 23 (Summer 2003), pp. 205–19.

Georges, Laurent, and Andreas Eggert. "Key Account Managers' Role within the Value Creation Process of Collaborative Relationships." *Journal of Business-to-Business Marketing* 10, no. 4 (2003), pp. 1–4.

Jones, Eli, Andrea L. Dixon, Lawrence B. Chonko, and Joseph P. Cannon. "Key Accounts and Team Selling: A Review, Framework, and Research Agenda." *Journal of Personal Selling & Sales Management* 25 (Spring 2005), pp. 181–89.

Lewin, Jeffrey E. "An Empirical Investigation of the Effects of Downsizing on Buyer–Seller Relationships." *Journal of Business Research* 56 (April 2003), pp. 283–93.

Schulz, Roberta J., and Kenneth R. Evans. "Strategic Collaborative Communication by Key Account Representatives." *Journal of Personal Selling & Sales Management* 22 (Winter 2002), pp. 23–31.

Sengupta, Sangit, Robert E. Krapfel, and Michael A. Pusateri. "An Empirical Investigation of Key Account Salesperson Effectiveness." *Journal of Personal Selling & Sales Management* 20 (Fall 2000), pp. 253–61.

Sparks, John R., and Joseph A. Schenk. "Socialization Communication, Organizational Citizenship Behaviors, and Sales in a Multilevel Marketing Organization." *Journal of Personal Selling & Sales Management* 26 (Spring 2006), pp. 161–80.

Weeks, William A., James Roberts, Lawrence B. Chonko, and Eli Jones. "Organizational Readiness for Change, Individual Fear of Change, and Sales Manager Performance: An Empirical Investigation." *Journal of Personal Selling & Sales Management* 24 (Winter 2004), pp. 7–17.

Chapter **Five**

The Strategic Role of Information in Sales Management

Putting Information Technology into Perspective

Information Technology (IT) has been the most notable addition to the business landscape in the last 30 years. From the vexing "dumb terminals" of the 1970s to the "PC on every desktop" of Bill Gates's dreams, computers and their supporting infrastructure have come to permeate every aspect of twenty-first century business.

Businesses, though, have struggled to keep the role of information technology in perspective. Like others before it, computers are simply another (albeit dramatically more powerful) tool to improve the operations of a company. When the cash register entered the market in the late nineteenth century, store owners understood its role in adding accuracy and control to an existing business process—calculating and collecting store receipts. When the plain paper copier was introduced in the mid-Twentieth century, businesses quickly grasped its role in facilitating another existing business process—reproducing printed materials.

But the IT revolution of the late twentieth century put "tools" in a completely different light. Companies often want information to not just improve the way they do business; they expect it to transform the way they do business. Perhaps because of the large financial investment involved, sales executives want technology to be the "silver bullet" that will eliminate all the problems of the sales force. No doubt, these high expectations are one reason that legions of CRM systems have failed to deliver their anticipated results. In the end, it is better to view IT as an enabler of business rather than a transformer of it.

Leading sales forces tend to agree. They understand that, with rare exception, sellers cannot alter the way their customers want to buy. Successful selling is determined by the salespeople's ability to satisfy their buyers' needs at every step of the buying process, regardless of what tools support them. They focus first on determining how they need to do business and then purchase information technology to play a supporting role.

That is not to say, though, that world-class sales forces shun technology in favor of manual processes. To the contrary, these sales forces invest heavily in software and infrastructure to improve their salespeople's efficiency and effectiveness. They do spend millions on CRM systems, and they do depend on information systems to connect and align the far-flung resources of their organization. Without superior technology, these sales forces would not be able to provide the levels of personalization, attentiveness, and consistency that make them world-class in the eyes of their customers.

In sum, information and information technology are among the most valuable assets that sales forces and their managers possess. Designed and implemented properly, IT can dramatically improve the sales forces' productivity and substantially influence their customers' buying experience. It is incumbent on managers of both Sales and IT to be diligent in how they use position information and related technologies within the organization to ensure they add, not detract, from salesperson effectiveness and efficiency.

Source: HR Chally Group (2007), *The Chally World Class Excellence Research Report: The Route to the Summit.* Dayton, OH: HR Chally Group.

LEARNING OBJECTIVES

Sales managers are both users and generators of information. The sales manager's role with regard to generating, analyzing, and disseminating information is vital to the success of both the firm's marketing strategy and the success of its individual salespeople. Important decisions at all levels of the organization are affected by how well sales managers use information.

This chapter presents a look at several of the key ways sales managers perform this vital information management role including forecasting sales, setting quotas, establishing the size and territory design of the sales force, and performing sales analysis for managerial decision making. Specifically, after reading this chapter, you should be able to

- Discuss the differences between market potential, sales potential, sales forecast, and sales quota.

- Understand the various methods by which sales managers develop sales forecasts.

- Outline the process of setting a sales quota.

- Explain the various types of quotas used in sales management.

- Discuss key approaches to determining sales force size.

- Describe the sales territory design process.

- Understand the importance of sales analysis for managerial decision making.

- Conduct a sales analysis.

USING INFORMATION IN MANAGERIAL DECISION MAKING AND PLANNING

It has been said that information is the fuel that drives the engine in managerial decision making. This is no different in sales management from any other managerial endeavor. Sales managers are charged with making decisions and developing plans that impact multifaceted areas of a company. One of these areas, sales forecasting, is directly linked with the overall market opportunity analysis of the firm.

Developing sales forecasts is one of the most important uses of information by sales managers. And concurrently, the sales forecasts they develop become an integral part of an organization's overall planning and strategy development efforts. Without good sales forecasts, it is impossible for companies to properly invest against their market opportunities. Sales managers must understand the various approaches to forecasting and appreciate the value of utilizing multiple methods of sales forecasting before making a decision on the final forecast to present to the firm.

For the sales manager, the forecast allows for the development of estimates of demand for individual sales territories and subsequently for the establishment of specific sales quotas by territory and by salesperson. Quotas are very important both to the firm and to its individual salespeople. For the firm, the aggregate of sales quotas during a particular performance period represents an operationalization of the sales forecast, and thus progress by the sales organization toward quota achievement is closely monitored by top management. For the individual salesperson, quotas provide specific goals to work toward that are tailored to his or her sales territory. Ordinarily, important elements of compensation and other rewards are linked to quota achievement. Because of the importance of quotas, sales managers must make certain they use the information available to select the proper type of quotas for the situation and to ensure that the level of the quotas is established in a fair and accurate manner.

Another important use of information by sales managers is in determining the optimal size of the sales force. A variety of quantitative analytical approaches are available for making this determination, all of which are driven by information. Once the size of the sales force is set, sales managers turn their analysis toward designing the sales territories. Finally, information is vital to the capability of sales managers to perform sales analyses.

In this chapter, we discuss each of these major strategic uses of information by sales managers and provide a context for sales managers to make better use of the information available to them for decision making.

INTRODUCTION TO MARKET OPPORTUNITY ANALYSIS

Market opportunity analysis requires an understanding of the differences in the notions of market potential, sales potential, sales forecast, and sales quota.

Market potential is an estimate of the possible sales of a commodity, a group of commodities, or a service for an entire industry in a market during a stated period under ideal conditions. A market is a customer group in a specific geographic area.

Sales potential refers to the portion of the market potential that a particular firm can reasonably expect to achieve. Market potential represents the maximum possible sales for all sellers of the good or service under ideal conditions, while sales potential reflects the maximum possible sales for an individual firm.

The **sales forecast** is an estimate of the dollar or unit sales for a specified future period. The forecast may be for a specified item of merchandise or for an entire line. It may be for a market as a whole or for any portion of it. Importantly, a sales forecast specifies the commodity, customer group, geographic area, and time period and includes a specific marketing plan and accompanying marketing program as essential elements. If the proposed plan is changed, predicted sales are also expected to change.

Naturally, forecast sales are typically less than the company's sales potential for a number of reasons. The firm may not have sufficient production capacity to realize its full potential, or its distribution network may not be sufficiently developed, or its financial resources may be limited. Likewise, forecast sales for an industry are typically less than the industry's market potential.

Sales quotas are sales goals assigned to a marketing unit for use in managing sales efforts. The marketing unit in question might be an individual salesperson, a sales territory, a branch office, a region, a dealer or distributor, or a district, just to name a few possibilities. Each salesperson in each sales territory might be assigned a sales volume goal for the next year. Sales quotas are typically a key measurement used to evaluate the personal selling effort. They apply to specific periods and can be specified in great detail, for example, sales of a particular item to a specified customer by sales rep J. Jones in June.

Exhibit 5.1 shows the relationship between potentials, forecasts, and quotas. Typically the process begins with an assessment of the economic environment. Sometimes this is simply an implicit assessment of the immediate future. Then, given an initial estimate of industry potential and the company's competitive position, the firm's sales potential can be estimated. This in turn leads to an initial sales forecast, often based on the presumption that the marketing effort will be similar to what it was last year. The initial forecast is then compared with objectives established for the proposed marketing effort. If the marketing program is expected to achieve the objectives, both the program and the sales forecast are adopted. That is rare, however. Usually it is necessary to redesign the marketing program and then revise the sales forecast, often several times.

The objectives may also need revising, but eventually the process should produce agreement between the forecast or expected sales and the objectives. The sales forecast is then used as a key input in setting individual sales quotas (goals). In addition, it also serves as a basic piece of information in establishing budgets for the various functional areas.

METHODS OF SALES FORECASTING

The sales forecast is one of the most important information tools used by management and lies at the heart of most companies' planning efforts. Top management uses the sales forecast to allocate resources among functional areas and to control the operations of the firm. Finance uses it to project cash flows, to decide on capital appropriations, and to establish operating budgets. Production uses it to determine quantities and schedules and to control inventories. Human resources uses it to plan personnel requirements and also as an input in collective bargaining. Purchasing uses it to plan the company's overall materials requirements and also to schedule their arrival. Marketing uses it to plan marketing and sales programs and to allocate resources among the various marketing activities. The importance of accurate sales forecasts is exacerbated as companies coordinate their efforts on a global scale.

The sales forecast is also of fundamental importance in planning and evaluating the personal selling effort. Sales managers use it for setting sales quotas, as input to the compensation plan, and in evaluating the field sales force, among other things. Because sales managers rely so heavily on sales forecasts for decision making, and also are integral to the

EXHIBIT 5.1
Market potential, sales potential, and sales forecasting process

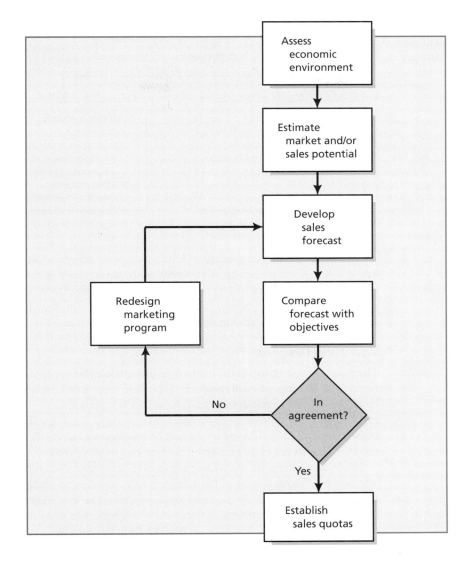

formulation of sales forecasts, it is important that they be familiar with the techniques used in forecast development. The subjective and objective methods discussed in this chapter are listed in Exhibit 5.2.[1]

Each method has advantages and disadvantages, which are summarized in Exhibit 5.3, and the decision of which method to use will not always be clear.[2] In a typical company, the decision will likely depend on its level of technical sophistication, the existence of historic sales data, and the proposed use of the forecast.

Subjective Methods of Forecasting

Subjective forecasting methods do not rely primarily on sophisticated quantitative (empirical) analytical approaches in developing the forecast.

User Expectations

The **user expectations method** of forecasting sales is also known as the *buyers' intentions method* because it relies on answers from customers regarding their expected consumption or purchases of the product.

The user expectations method of forecasting sales may provide estimates closer to market or sales potential than to sales forecasts. In reality, user groups would have difficulty anticipating the industry's or a particular firm's marketing efforts. Rather, the user estimates reflect their anticipated needs. From the sellers' standpoint, they provide a measure of the opportunities available among a particular segment of users.

Sales Force Composite

The **sales force composite** method of forecasting sales is so named because the initial input is the opinion of each member of the field sales staff. Each person states how much he or she expects to sell during the forecast period. Subsequently, these estimates are typically adjusted at various levels of sales management. They are likely to be checked, discussed, and possibly changed by the branch manager and on up the sales organization chart until the figures are finally accepted at corporate headquarters.

When forecasting via sales force composite, organizations typically use historical information about the accuracy of the salespeople's estimates to make adjustments to the raw forecast data provided by the field sales organization. For various reasons, salespeople may be motivated to either underestimate or overestimate what they expect to sell during a period. For example, if quotas are derived from the forecast, salespeople may underestimate their sales volume in order to "sandbag" business and get assigned a smaller quota. Thus, when their sales results come in they give the appearance of a stronger performance. Alternatively, if certain of the company's products are in short supply (such as in a materials shortage or rapid growth market) or are available to customers in limited quantities (such as a short-term promotion), salespeople may overestimate their sales volume in hopes of securing a greater allocation of scarce products.

Jury of Executive Opinion

The **jury of executive opinion** (or jury of expert opinion) method is a formal or informal internal poll of key executives within the selling company in order to gain their assessment of sales possibilities. The separate assessments are combined into a sales forecast for the company. Sometimes this is done by simply averaging the individual judgments; but other times disparate views are resolved through group discussion toward consensus. The initial views may reflect no more than the executive's hunch about what is going to happen, or the opinion may be based on considerable factual material, sometimes even an initial forecast prepared by other means.

EXHIBIT 5.3   **Summary of advantages and disadvantages of various sales forecasting techniques**

Sales Forecasting Method	Advantages	Disadvantages
Subjective methods		
User expectations	1. Forecast estimates obtained directly from buyers 2. Projected product usage information can be greatly detailed 3. Insights gathered aid in the planning of marketing strategy 4. Useful for new-product forecasting	1. Potential customers must be few and well defined 2. Does not work well for consumer goods 3. Depends on the accuracy of user's estimates 4. Expensive, time-consuming, labor intensive
Sales force composite	1. Involves the people (sales personnel) who will be held responsible for the results 2. Is fairly accurate 3. Aids in controlling and directing the sales effort 4. Forecast is available for individual sales territories	1. Estimators (sales personnel) have a vested interest and therefore may be biased 2. Elaborate schemes sometimes necessary to counteract bias 3. If estimates are biased, process to correct the data can be expensive
Jury of executive opinion	1. Easily done, very quick 2. Does not require elaborate statistics 3. Utilizes collective wisdom of the top people 4. Useful for new or innovative products	1. Produces aggregate forecasts 2. Expensive 3. Disperses responsibility for the forecast 4. Group dynamics operate
Delphi technique	1. Minimizes effects of group dynamics 2. Can utilize statistical information	1. Can be expensive and time-consuming
Objective methods		
Market test	1. Provides ultimate test of consumers' reactions to the product 2. Allows the assessment of the effectiveness of the total marketing program 3. Useful for new and innovative products	1. Lets competitors know what firm is doing 2. Invites competitive reaction 3. Expensive and time-consuming to set up 4. Often takes a long time to accurately assess level of initial and repeat demand
Time-series analysis	1. Utilizes historical data 2. Objective, inexpensive	1. Not useful for new or innovative products 2. Factors for trend, cyclical, seasonal, or product life-cycle phase must be accurately assessed and included 3. Technical skill and good judgment required 4. Final forecast difficult to break down into individual territory estimates 5. Ignores planned marketing effort
Statistical demand analysis	1. Great intuitive appeal 2. Requires quantification of assumptions underlying the estimates 3. Allows management to check results 4. Uncovers hidden factors affecting sales 5. Method is objective	1. Factors affecting sales must remain constant and be accurately identified to produce an accurate estimate 2. Requires technical skill and expertise 3. Some managers reluctant to use method due to its sophistication

Delphi Technique

In gaining expert opinion, one method for controlling group dynamics to produce a more accurate forecast is the **Delphi technique.** Delphi uses an iterative approach with repeated measurement and controlled anonymous feedback, instead of direct confrontation and debate among the experts preparing the forecast.[3] Each individual involved prepares a forecast using whatever facts, figures, and general knowledge of the environment he or she has available. Then the forecasts are collected, and an anonymous summary is prepared by the person supervising the process. The summary is distributed to each person who participated in the initial phase. Typically, the summary lists each forecast figure, the average (median), and some summary measure of the spread of the estimates. Often, those whose initial estimates fell outside the midrange of responses are asked to express their reasons for these extreme positions. These explanations are then incorporated into the summary. The participants study the summary and submit a revised forecast. The process is then repeated. Typically, several rounds of these iterations take place. The method is based on the premise that, with repeated measurements (1) the range of responses will decrease and the estimates will converge; and (2) the total group response or median will move successively toward the "correct" or "true" answer.

Objective Methods of Forecasting

Objective forecasting methods rely primarily on more sophisticated quantitative (empirical) analytical approaches in developing the forecast.

Market Test

The typical **market test** (or test market) involves placing a product in several representative geographic areas to see how well it performs and then projecting that experience to the market as a whole. Often this is done for a new product or an improved version of an old product.

Many firms consider the market test to be the final gauge of consumer acceptance of a new product and ultimate measure of market potential. A. C. Nielsen data, for example, indicate roughly three out of four products that have been test marketed succeed, whereas four out of five that have not been test marketed fail. Despite this fact, market tests have several drawbacks:

- Market tests are costly to administer and are more conducive to testing of consumer products than industrial products.

- The time involved in conducting a market test can be considerable.

- Because a product is being test marketed, it receives more attention in the market test than it can ever receive on a national scale, giving an unrealistic picture of the product's potential.

- A market test, because it is so visible to competitors, can reveal a firm's hand on its new-product launch strategy, thus allowing competitors time to formulate a market response before full market introduction.

All in all, a market test can be a highly successful sales forecasting technique but one that should not be used unless and until all the positives and negatives have been evaluated by management.

Time-Series Analysis

Approaches to sales forecasting using **time-series analysis** rely on the analysis of historical data to develop a prediction for the future. The sophistication of these analyses can vary widely. At the most simplistic extreme, the forecaster might simply forecast next year's sales to be equal to this year's sales. Such a forecast might be reasonably accurate for a mature industry that is experiencing little growth or market turbulence. However, barring these conditions, more sophisticated time-series approaches must be considered. Three of these methods, moving averages, exponential smoothing, and decomposition, are discussed here.[4]

Moving Average   The **moving average** method is conceptually quite simple. Consider the forecast that next year's sales will be equal to this year's sales. Such a forecast might be subject to large error if there is much fluctuation in sales from one year to the next. To allow for such randomness, we might consider using some kind of average of recent values. For example, we might average the last two years' sales, the last three years' sales, the last five years' sales, or any number of other periods. The forecast would simply be the average that resulted. The number of observations included in the average is typically determined by trial and error. Differing numbers of periods are tried, and the number of periods that produces the most accurate forecasts of the trial data is used to develop the forecast model. Once determined, it remains constant. The term *moving average* is used because a new average is computed and used as a forecast as each new observation becomes available.

Exhibit 5.4 presents a moving average forecast example with 16 years of historical sales data and also the resulting forecasts for a number of years using two- and four-year moving averages. Exhibit 5.5 displays the results graphically. The entry 4,305 for 1995, under the two-year moving average method, for example, is the average of the sales of 4,200 units in 1993 and 4,410 units in 1994. Similarly, the forecast of 5,520 units in 2008 represents the average of the number of units sold in 2006 and 2007. The forecast of 5,772 units in 2008 under the four-year moving average method, on the other hand, represents the average number of units sold during the four-year period 2004–2007. Obviously, it takes more data to begin forecasting with four-year than with two-year moving averages. This is an important consideration when starting to forecast sales for a new product.

EXHIBIT 5.4

Example of a moving average forecast

Year	Actual sales	Forecast sales	
		Two-year moving average	**Four-year moving average**
1993	4,200		
1994	4,410		
1995	4,322	4,305	
1996	4,106	4,366	
1997	4,311	4,214	4,260
1998	4,742	4,209	4,287
1999	4,837	4,527	4,370
2000	5,030	4,790	4,499
2001	4,779	4,934	4,730
2002	4,970	4,905	4,847
2003	5,716	4,875	4,904
2004	6,116	5,343	5,128
2005	5,932	5,916	5,395
2006	5,576	6,024	5,684
2007	5,465	5,754	5,835
2008		5,520	5,772

EXHIBIT 5.5

Graph of actual and forecast sales using moving averages

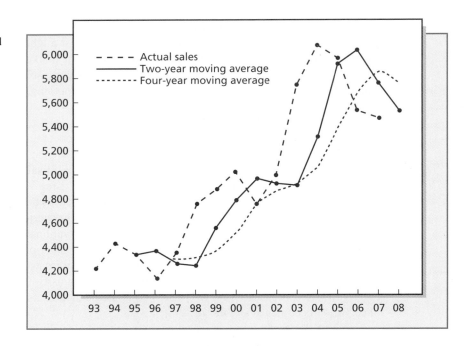

Exponential Smoothing   The method of moving averages gives equal weight to each of the last *n* values in forecasting the next value, where *n* represents the number of years used. Thus, when *n* = 4 (the four-year moving average is being used), equal weight is given to each of the last four years' sales in predicting the sales for next year. In a four-year moving average, no weight is given to any sales five or more years previous.

Exponential smoothing is a type of moving average. However, instead of weighting all observations equally in generating the forecast, exponential smoothing weights the most recent observations heaviest, for good reason. The most recent observations contain the most information about what is likely to happen in the future, and they should logically be given more weight.

The key decision affecting the use of exponential smoothing is the choice of the *smoothing constant,* referred to as α in the algorithm for calculating exponential smoothing, which is constrained to be between 0 and 1. High values of α give great weight to recent observations and little weight to distant sales; low values of α, on the other hand, give more weight to older observations. If sales change slowly, low values of α work fine. When sales experience rapid changes and fluctuations, however, high values of a should be used so that the forecast series responds to these changes quickly. The value of α is normally determined empirically; various values of α are tried, and the one that produces the smallest forecast error when applied to the historical series is adopted.

Decomposition   The **decomposition** method of sales forecasting is typically applied to monthly or quarterly data where a seasonal pattern is evident and the manager wishes to forecast sales not only for the year but also for each period in the year. It is important to determine what portion of sales changes represents an overall, fundamental change in demand and what portion is due to seasonality in demand. For example, Hawaiian Tropic would like to separate out how much of its sales increase in suntan lotion is attributable to the general trend toward increased skin protection from the sun and how much is due to peak seasonal demand in May–September. The decomposition method attempts to isolate four separate portions of a time series: the trend, cyclical, seasonal, and random factors.

- The *trend* reflects the long-run changes experienced in the series when the cyclical, seasonal, and irregular components are removed. It is typically assumed to be a straight line.

- The *cyclical factor* is not always present because it reflects the waves in a series when the seasonal and irregular components are removed. These ups and downs typically occur over a long period, perhaps two to five years. Some products experience little cyclical fluctuation (canned peas), whereas others experience a great deal (housing starts).

- *Seasonality* reflects the annual fluctuation in the series due to the natural seasons. The seasonal factor normally repeats itself each year, although the exact pattern of sales may be different from year to year.

- The *random factor* is what is left after the influence of the trend, cyclical, and seasonal factors is removed.

Exhibit 5.6 shows the calculation of a simple seasonal index based on five years of sales history. The data suggest definite seasonal and trend components in the series. The fourth quarter of every year is always the best quarter; the first quarter is the worst. At the same time, sales each year are higher than they were the year previous. One could calculate a seasonal index for each year by simply dividing quarterly sales by the yearly average per quarter. It is much more typical, though, to base the calculation of the seasonal index on several years of data to smooth out the random fluctuations that occur by quarter.

In using the decomposition method, the analyst typically first determines the seasonal pattern and removes its impact to identify the trend. Then the cyclical factor is estimated. After the three components are isolated, the forecast is developed by applying each factor in turn to the historical data.

Statistical Demand Analysis

Time-series methods attempt to determine the relationship between sales and time as the basis of the forecast for the future. **Statistical demand analysis** attempts to determine the relationship between sales and the important factors affecting sales to forecast the future. Typically, regression analysis is used to estimate the relationship. The emphasis is not to isolate all factors that affect sales but simply to identify those that have the most

EXHIBIT 5.6
Calculation of a
seasonal index

Year	Quarter				Total	Quarter average
	1	**2**	**3**	**4**	**Total**	**average**
2004	82.8	105.8	119.6	151.8	460.0	115.0
2005	93.1	117.6	122.5	156.9	490.1	122.5
2006	92.0	122.4	132.6	163.2	510.2	127.6
2007	95.3	129.0	151.3	185.0	560.6	140.2
2008	120.1	138.1	162.2	180.2	600.6	150.2
Five-year average	96.7	122.6	137.6	167.4	524.3	131.1
Seasonal index*	73.8	93.5	105.0	127.7		

*The seasonal index equals the quarterly average divided by the overall quarterly average times 100; for the first quarter, for example, the seasonal index equals $(96.7 \div 131.1) \times 100 = 73.8$.

dramatic impact on sales and then to estimate the magnitude of the impact. The predictor variables in statistical demand analysis often are historical indexes such as leading economic indicators and other similar measures. For example, a lumber products company might use housing starts, interest rates, and a seasonal shift in demand during summer months to forecast its sales.

CHOOSING A FORECASTING METHOD

The sales manager faced with a forecasting problem has a dilemma: Which forecasting method should be used and how accurate is the forecast likely to be? The dilemma is particularly acute when several methods are tried and the forecasts don't agree, which is more often the norm rather than the exception.

A number of studies have attempted to assess forecast accuracy using the various techniques. Some studies have been conducted within individual companies; others have used selected data series to which the various forecasting techniques have been systematically applied. One of the most extensive comparisons involved 1,001 time series from a variety of sources in which each series was forecast with each of 24 extrapolation methods. The general conclusion was that the method used made little difference with respect to forecast accuracy.[5] Similarly, comparisons of forecast accuracy of objective versus subjective methods gave no clear conclusion as to which method is superior. Some of the comparisons seem to favor the quantitative methods,[6] but others found that the subjective methods produce more accurate forecasts.[7]

In general, the various forecast comparisons suggest that no method is likely to be superior under all conditions. Rather, a number of factors are likely to affect the superiority of any particular technique, including the stability of the data series, the time horizon, the degree of structure imposed on the process, the degree to which computers were used, and deseasonalization of the data. Overall, the best approach seems to be the utilization of multiple methods of forecasting, including a combination of subjective and objective methods, comparing the results, and then employing managerial judgment to make a decision on the final forecast.

Increasingly, firms are turning to **scenario planning** when developing sales forecasts. Scenario planning involves asking those preparing the forecast a series of "what-if" questions, where the what-ifs reflect different environmental changes that could occur. Some very unlikely changes are considered along with more probable events. The key idea is not so much to have one scenario that gets it right but rather to have a set of scenarios that illuminate the major forces driving the system, their interrelationships, and the critical uncertainties.[8]

DEVELOPING TERRITORY ESTIMATES

Not only must firms develop global estimates of demand, but most also develop territory-by-territory estimates. Territory estimates recognize the condition that the potential for any product may not be uniform by area. Territory demand estimates allow for effective planning, directing, and controlling of salespeople in that the estimates affect the following:

1. The design of sales territories.

2. The procedures used to identify potential customers.

3. The establishment of sales quotas.

4. Compensation levels and the mix of components in the firm's sales compensation scheme.

5. The evaluation of salespeople's performance.

The development of territory demand estimates is typically different for industrial versus consumer goods. Territory demand estimates for industrial goods are often developed by relating sales to some common denominator. The common denominator or market factor might be the number of total employees, number of production employees, value added by manufacturing process, value of materials consumed, value of products shipped, or expenditures for new plant and equipment. Say the ratio of sales per employee is developed for each of several identifiable markets. By then looking at the number of employees in a particular geographic area within each of those identifiable markets, one can estimate the total demand for the product within the area.

The identifiable markets are usually defined using the **North American Industry Classification System (NAICS).** The NAICS replaced the former system of Standard Industrial Classification (SIC) codes. These systems were developed by the U.S. Bureau of the Census for organizing the reporting of business information such as employment, value added in manufacturing, capital expenditures, and total sales. Each major industry in the United States is assigned a two-digit number, indicating the group to which it belongs. The types of businesses making up each industry are further identified by additional digits.

While firms selling to industrial consumers rely most heavily on identifiable market segments using NAICS codes when estimating territory demand, sellers of consumer goods are more apt to rely on aggregate conditions in each territory. Sometimes this will be a single variable or market factor like the number of households, population, or perhaps the level of income in the area. In other instances, the firm attempts to relate demand to several variables combined in a systematic way. The demand for washing machines, for example, has been shown through statistical demand regression analysis to be a function of the following predictor variables: (1) the level of consumers' stock of washing machines, (2) the number of wired dwelling units, (3) disposable personal income, (4) net credit, and (5) the price index for house furnishings. Since these statistics are published by area, a firm can use the regression equation to estimate demand by area.

Many firms are willing to expend the effort necessary to develop an expression for the relationship between total demand for the product and several variables that are logically related to its sales. Many other firms, however, are content to base their estimates of territory demand on one of the standard multiple-factor indexes that have been developed.

One of the most popular standard indexes is the Buying Power Index (BPI), which is generated and published by *Sales & Marketing Management* magazine. The index considers income, population, and retail sales. These are weighted by the factors 5, 2, and 3, respectively, to generate a single number for a geographic region. This number is used to estimate the share of total market demand in the area.[9]

As one might expect, the BPI is not especially useful for estimating territory potentials for industrial products. Nor is it especially useful for infrequently purchased, high-priced consumer goods. It is very popular, though, when estimating territory potential for frequently purchased, low-priced convenience goods. One strategy for a firm selling consumer goods is to determine empirically if the BPI correlates with industry sales by area. A firm is fortunate when it does because the BPI is convenient—it is updated annually and is available by small geographic area. If the index does not correlate well with sales of the product, then the firm is probably better off (1) using a single market factor or (2) developing its own index using factors logically related to sales and some a priori or empirically determined weights regarding their relative importance.

PURPOSES AND CHARACTERISTICS OF SALES QUOTAS

As discussed earlier in the chapter, goals assigned to salespeople are called *quotas*. Quotas are one of the most valuable devices sales managers have for planning the field selling effort, and they are indispensable for evaluating the effectiveness of that effort. They help managers plan the amount of sales and profit that will be available at the end of the planning period and anticipate the activities of the sales team. Quotas are also often used to motivate salespeople and as such must be reasonable. Volume quotas are typically set to a level that is less than the sales potential in the territory and equal to or slightly above the sales forecast for the territory, although they also may be set less than the sales forecast if conditions warrant.

Sales quotas apply to specific periods and may be expressed in dollars or physical units. Thus, management can specify quarterly, annual, and longer-term quotas for each of the company's field representatives in both dollars and physical units. It might even specify these goals for individual products and customers. The product quotas can be varied systematically to reflect the profitability of different items in the line, and customer quotas can be varied to reflect the relative desirability of serving particular accounts.

Purposes of Quotas

Quotas facilitate the planning and control of the field selling effort in a number of ways. Two important contributions of sales quotas are in (1) providing incentives for sales representatives and (2) evaluating salespeople's performance.

Quotas serve as incentives for sales in several ways. In essence, they are an objective to be secured and a challenge to be met. For example, the definite objective of selling $200,000 worth of product X this year, particularly with the opportunity to achieve some desired reward if the quota is met or exceeded, is more motivation to most salespeople than the indefinite charge to go out and do better. It seems one can always do better. Quotas also influence salespeople's incentive through sales contests. A key notion underlying such contests is that those who perform "best" will receive the contest prizes. Quotas can also create incentive via their key role in the compensation systems of most firms. More will be said about these reward and compensation issues in later chapters, but it should be noted here that many firms use a commission or bonus plan, sometimes in conjunction with their base salary plan. In such schemes, salespeople are paid in direct proportion to what they sell (commission plan), or they receive some percentage increment for sales in excess of target sales (bonus plan). Typically, such plans are tied directly to sales quotas. Even when salespeople are compensated with salary only, quotas can provide incentive when salary raises are tied to quota attainment in the previous year.

Quotas also provide a quantitative (objective) standard against which the performance of individual sales representatives or other marketing units can be evaluated. They allow management to recognize salespeople who are performing particularly well and those who may be experiencing difficulty in performance. They provide a basis for developmental actions by the manager and salesperson to ensure a greater level of performance in the future. Issues of performance evaluation of salespeople are discussed in detail in Chapter 13.

Characteristics of a Good Quota

For a quota to be effective, it must be (1) attainable, (2) easy to understand, (3) complete, and (4) timely. Some argue that quotas should be set high so they can be achieved only with extraordinary effort. Although most salespeople may not reach their quotas, the argument is that they are spurred to greater effort than they would have expended in the absence of such a "carrot." Although perhaps intuitively appealing, high quotas can cause problems. They can create ill will among salespeople. They can also cause salespeople to engage in unethical and other undesirable behaviors to make their quotas. One of the main reasons cited for Sears's public relations nightmare with its auto centers several years ago was its unrealistic sales quotas, which influenced employees to sell auto services to customers that they didn't need. Unrealistic sales quotas also caused its major-appliance and Allstate Insurance (Allstate used to be part of Sears) salespeople to engage in similar undesirable behaviors.[10]

The use of very high "carrot" quotas seems to be the exception rather than the rule and is generally not recommended. The prevailing philosophy is that quotas should be realistic. They should represent attainable goals that can be achieved with normal or reasonable, not Herculean, efforts. That seems to motivate most salespeople best.

Quotas should be not only realistic but also easy to understand. Complex quota plans may cause suspicion and mistrust among sales representatives and thereby discourage rather than motivate them. It helps when salespeople can be shown exactly how their quotas were derived. They are much more likely to accept quotas that are related to market potential when they can see the assumptions used in translating the potential estimate into sales goals.

Another desirable feature of a quota plan is that it is complete. It should cover the many criteria on which sales reps are to be judged. Thus, if all sales representatives are supposed to engage in new-account development, it is important to specify how much. Otherwise that activity will likely be neglected while the salesperson pursues volume and profit goals. Similarly, volume and profit goals should be adjusted to allow for the time the representative has to spend identifying and soliciting new accounts.

Finally, the quota system should allow for timely feedback of results to salespeople. Quotas for a sales period should be calculated and announced right away. Delays in providing this information not only dilute the advantages of using quotas but also create ambiguity, as the salesperson gets well into another performance period without knowing how he or she fared in the prior period.

SETTING QUOTAS

In setting quotas, the sales manager must first decide on the types of quotas the firm will use. Then, specific quota levels must be established.

Types of Quotas

There are three basic types of quotas: (1) those emphasizing sales or some aspect of sales volume, (2) those that focus on the activities in which sales representatives are supposed to engage, and (3) those that examine financial criteria such as gross margin or contribution to overhead. Sales volume quotas are the most popular.[11]

Sales Volume Quotas

The popularity of **sales volume quotas,** those that emphasize dollar sales or some other aspect of sales volume, is understandable. They can be related directly to market potential and thereby be made more credible, are easily understood by the salespeople who must achieve them, and are consistent with what most salespeople envision their jobs to be—that is, to sell. Sales volume quotas may be expressed in dollars, physical units, or points.

The concept of point quotas deserves explanation. A certain number of points are given for each dollar or unit sale of particular products. For example, each $100 of sales of product X might be worth three points; of product Y, two points; and of product Z, one point. Alternatively, each ton of steel tubing sold might be worth five points, while each ton of bar stock might be worth only two points. The total sales quota for the salesperson is expressed as the total number of points he or she is expected to achieve. The point system is typically used when a firm wants to emphasize certain products in the line. Those that are more profitable, for example, might be assigned more points.

Point quotas can also be used to promote selective emphases. New products might receive more points than old ones to encourage sales representatives to push them. A given dollar of sales to new accounts might be worth more points than the same level of sales to more established accounts. Point quota systems allow sales managers to design quota systems that promote certain desired goals, and at the same time point quotas can be easily understood by salespeople.

Activity Quotas

Activity quotas attempt to recognize the investment nature of a salesperson's efforts. For example, the letter to a prospect, the product demonstration, and the arrangement of a display may not produce an immediate sale. On the other hand, they may influence a future sale. If the quota system emphasizes only sales volume, salespeople may be inclined to neglect these activities. Today, many activities are necessary to support long-term client relationships. It is appropriate that these activities be considered for quota development. Some common types of activity quotas are listed in Exhibit 5.7.

Financial Quotas

Financial quotas help focus salespeople on the cost and profit implications of what they sell. All else being equal, it is easy to understand that salespeople might emphasize products in their line that are relatively easy to sell or concentrate on customers with whom they feel most comfortable interacting. Unfortunately, these products may be costly to produce and have a lower-than-average return, and these customers may not purchase much and may be less profitable than other potential accounts. Financial quotas attempt to direct salespeople's efforts to more profitable products and customers. Common bases for developing financial quotas are gross margin, net profit, and selling expenses, although most any financial measure could be used.

Administering financial quotas can present difficulties. Their calculation is not straightforward. And the profit a salesperson produces is affected by many factors beyond his or her control—competitive reaction, economic conditions, and the firm's willingness to negotiate on price, for example. Many would argue that in most cases it is unreasonable to hold an individual salesperson responsible for such external influences.

Quota Level

Next, the sales manager must decide the level for each type of quota. In establishing these levels, the sales manager must balance a number of factors, including the potential available

EXHIBIT 5.7
Common types of activity quotas

Number of
1. Calls on new accounts.
2. Letters to potential customers.
3. Proposals submitted.
4. Field demonstrations arranged.
5. Service calls made.
6. Equipment installations supervised.
7. Displays arranged.
8. Dealer sales meetings held.
9. Meetings and conventions attended.
10. Past-due accounts collected.

in the territory, the impact of the quota level on the salesperson's motivation, the long-term objectives of the company, and the impact on short-term profitability. When discussing quota levels, it is useful to separate sales volume, activity, and financial quotas.

Sales Volume Quotas

Some firms simply set sales volume quotas on the basis of past sales. Each marketing unit is exhorted to "beat last year's sales." Sometimes the standard is the average of sales in the territory over some past time period—five years, for example. The most attractive feature of this quota-setting scheme is that it is easy to administer. One does not have to engage in an extensive analysis to determine what the quotas should be. This makes it inexpensive to use. Also, salespeople readily understand it.

Unfortunately, such quotas ignore current conditions. A territory may be rapidly growing, and the influx of new potential customers could justify a much larger increase than the 7 percent established by the overall company's sales forecast. Alternatively, the territory might be so intensely competitive or the business climate may be so poor that any increase in the assigned sales quota is not justified.

A quota based solely on past sales ignores territory potentials and provides a poor yardstick for evaluating individual sales reps. Two salespeople, for example, might each have generated $300,000 in sales last year. It clearly makes a difference in what one can expect from each of them this year if the market potential in one territory is $500,000 while that in the other is $1 million. The firm may be forgoing tremendous market opportunities simply because it is unaware of them.

A quota based solely on past years' sales can also demoralize salespeople and cause undesirable behaviors. For example, a salesperson who has realized quota for one year may be tempted to delay placing orders secured at the end of the year until the new accounting cycle begins. This accomplishes two things: It makes his or her quota for the next year lower, and it gives him or her a start on satisfying that quota.

Territory potential provides a useful start for establishing quotas for territory sales volume. However, the firm should not adhere strictly to a formula that relates quota to potential, but it should attempt to reflect the special situations within each territory.

Determining how to set territory quotas that reflect the special situations within each territory is often difficult. On one hand, the sales representative who serves the territory should be involved in setting the territory quota, because he or she should have the most intimate knowledge of the conditions in the territory. On the other hand, since the rep will be affected by the quota established, he or she may not be impartial. One might expect sales representatives to understate potential to generate lower, easier-to-reach quotas.

Activity Quotas

The levels for activity quotas are most likely to be set according to the territory conditions. They require a detailed analysis of the work needed to cover the territory effectively. Activity quotas are affected by the size of the territory and by the number of accounts and prospects the salesperson is expected to call on. The size of the representative's customers can also make a difference, as can their purchasing patterns. These factors affect the number of times the salesperson needs to call on them in the period, the number of service calls or calls to demonstrate the use of the firm's equipment he or she must make, and so on.

The inputs for activity quotas can come from at least three sources: (1) discussions between the sales representative serving the territory and the sales manager, (2) the salesperson's reports, and (3) research on the market and its potential.

Financial Quotas

The levels of financial quotas are typically set to reflect the financial goals of the firm. For example, a firm may want a particular net profit or gross margin on all sales in a territory. Suppose the potential for a representative is basically concentrated on two products—one with a gross margin of 30 percent and one with a gross margin of 40 percent. The sales manager could shift the relative attention given to one versus the other by assigning a gross margin goal of 37 percent. The salesperson would then have to sell a greater proportion of the products with 40 percent margin to achieve that goal than if the goal were 34 percent.

DETERMINING SALES FORCE SIZE

Another critical use of information by sales managers is in determining the size of the sales force. Salespeople are among the most productive assets of a company, and they are also among the most expensive. Determining the optimal number to employ presents several fundamental dilemmas. On the one hand, increasing the number of salespeople will increase sales volume. On the other hand, it will also increase costs. Achieving the optimal balance between these considerations, although difficult, is vitally important to a firm's success.

The optimal number of territories depends on the design of the individual territories. Different assignments to salespeople and even different call patterns can produce different sales levels. Of course, the number of calls the sales force must make directly affects the number of salespeople the firm needs. In sum, the number of sales territories and the design of individual territories must be looked at as interrelated decisions whose outcomes affect each other.

The decisions need to be made jointly and not sequentially. **Sales force deployment** refers to the three interrelated decisions of (1) sales force size or the number of territories, (2) design of the individual territories, and (3) allocation of the total selling effort to accounts. Such simultaneous decisions are implemented through software-driven sales force deployment models. At the same time, it is useful for discussion purposes to separate these issues so as to call attention to the underlying considerations of each. Consequently, the subsequent discussion first addresses the issue of sales force size and then the issue of sales territory design. However, the size of the sales force may need to be revised as a result of the sales territory design.[12]

Several techniques are available for determining the size of the field sales force. Three of the more popular are the (1) breakdown, (2) workload, and (3) incremental methods.

Breakdown Method

The **breakdown method** is conceptually one of the simplest. An average salesperson is treated as a salesperson unit, and each salesperson unit is assumed to possess the same productivity potential. To determine the size of the sales force needed, divide total forecast sales for the company by the sales likely to be produced by each individual. Mathematically,

$$N = S/P$$

where

N = number of sales personnel needed

S = forecasted sales volume

P = estimated productivity of one salesperson unit

Thus, a firm that had forecast sales of $5 million and in which each salesperson unit could be expected to sell $250,000 would need 20 salespeople. Although conceptually simple and easy to use, the breakdown method is not without its problems. For one thing, it uses reverse logic. It treats sales force size as a consequence of sales volume; instead, determining the number of salespeople needed should be a proactive element of the overall strategic marketing plan. Also, the estimate of productivity per salesperson can be problematic in that it fails to account for differences in (1) ability levels of salespeople, (2) potential in the markets they service, and (3) level of competition across sales territories. Then too, the breakdown method does not take into account turnover in the sales force. New salespeople are usually not as productive as those who have been on the job for several years. The formula can be modified to allow for sales force turnover, but it loses some of its simplicity and conceptual appeal.

Finally, a key shortcoming of the breakdown method is that it does not allow for profitability. It treats sales as the end in itself rather than as the means to an end. The number of salespeople is determined as a function of the level of forecast sales, not as a determinant of targeted profit.

Workload Method

The basic premise underlying the **workload method** of determining sales force size (or, as it is sometimes called, the *buildup method*) is that all sales personnel should shoulder an equal amount of work. Management estimates the work required to serve the entire market. The total work calculation is treated as a function of the number of accounts, how often each should be called on, and for how long. This estimate is then divided by the amount of work an individual salesperson should be able to handle, and the result is the total number of salespeople required.[13] Specifically, the method consists of six steps, as illustrated in Exhibit 5.8 and discussed below.

1. *Classify all the firm's customers into categories.* Often the classification is based on the level of sales to each customer. A popular approach is to identify and prioritize accounts as A, B, or C based on sales volume. Classification could be based on other criteria also, such as customer's type of business, credit rating, product line, and potential for future purchases.

   Any classification system should reflect the different amounts of selling effort required to service the different classes of accounts and consequently the attractiveness of each class of accounts to the firm. Suppose, for example, the firm had 1,030 accounts that could be classified into three basic types or classes, as follows:

   Type A: Large or very attractive—200

   Type B: Medium or moderately attractive—350

   Type C: Small, but still attractive—480

2. *Determine the frequency with which each type of account should be called upon and the desired length of each call.* These inputs can be generated in several ways. They can be based directly on the judgments of management, or they might be based on more formal analysis of historical information. Suppose the firm estimates that class A accounts should be called on every two weeks, class B accounts once a month, and class C accounts every other month. It also estimates that the length of the typical call should be 60 minutes, 30 minutes, and 20 minutes, respectively. The number of contact hours per year for each type of account is thus calculated as

   Class A: 26 times/year × 60 minutes/call = 1,560 minutes, or 26 hours

   Class B: 12 times/year × 30 minutes/call = 360 minutes, or 6 hours

   Class C: 6 times/year × 20 minutes/call = 120 minutes, or 2 hours

EXHIBIT 5.8

Steps to determine sales force size by the workload method

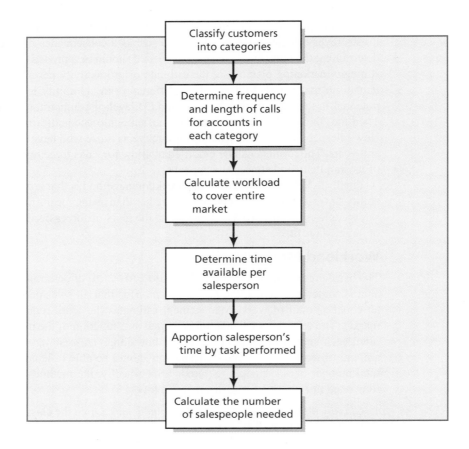

Classify customers into categories

Determine frequency and length of calls for accounts in each category

Calculate workload to cover entire market

Determine time available per salesperson

Apportion salesperson's time by task performed

Calculate the number of salespeople needed

3. *Calculate the workload involved in covering the entire market.* The total work involved in covering each class of account is given by multiplying the number of such accounts by the number of contact hours per year. These products are summed to estimate the work entailed in covering all the various types of accounts:

Class A: 200 accounts × 26 hours/account = 5,200 hours

Class B: 350 accounts × 6 hours/account = 2,100 hours

Class C: 480 accounts × 2 hours/account =   960 hours

Total   = 8,260 hours

4. *Determine the time available per salesperson.* For this calculation, one must estimate the number of hours the typical salesperson works per week and then multiply that by the number of weeks the representative will work during the year. Suppose the typical workweek is 40 hours and the average salesperson can be expected to work 48 weeks during the year, after allowing for vacation time, sickness, and other emergencies. This suggests the average representative has 1,920 hours available per year. That is,

$$40 \text{ hours/week} \times 48 \text{ weeks/year} = 1{,}920 \text{ hours/year}$$

5. *Apportion the salesperson's time by task performed.* Unfortunately, not all the salesperson's time is consumed in face-to-face customer contact. Much of it is devoted to nonselling activities such as making reports, attending meetings, and making service calls.

Another major portion may be spent traveling. Suppose a time study of salespeople's effort suggested the following division:

Selling   40 percent =   768 hours/year

Nonselling   30 percent =   576 hours/year

Traveling   30 percent =   576 hours/year

                    100 percent = 1,920 hours/year

6. *Calculate the number of salespeople needed.* The number of salespeople the firm will need can now be readily determined by dividing the total number of hours needed to serve the entire market by the number of hours available per salesperson for selling. That is, by the calculation

$$\frac{8{,}260 \text{ hours}}{768 \text{ hours/salesperson}} = 10.75, \text{ or } 11 \text{ salespeople}$$

The workload, or buildup, method is a very common way to determine sales force size. It has several attractive features. It is easy to understand, and it explicitly recognizes that different types of accounts should be called on with different frequencies. The inputs are readily available or can be secured without much trouble.

Unfortunately, it also possesses some weaknesses. It does not allow for differences in sales response among accounts that receive the same sales effort. Two class A accounts might respond differently to sales effort. One may be content with the products and services of the firm and continue to order even if the salesperson does not call every two weeks. Another, which does most of its business with a competitor, may willingly switch some of its orders if it receives more frequent contact. Also, the method does not explicitly consider the profitability of the call frequencies. It does not take into account such factors as the cost of servicing and the gross margins on the product mix purchased by the account.[14]

Finally, the method assumes that all salespeople use their time with equal efficiency— for example, that each will have 768 hours available for face-to-face selling. This is simply not true. Some are better able to plan their calls to generate more direct selling time. Those in smaller geographic territories can spend less time traveling and more time selling. Some more than others simply make good use of the selling time they have available, as the quality of time invested in a sales call is at least as important as the quantity of time spent. The buildup method does not explicitly consider these dimensions.

Incremental Method

The basic premise underlying the **incremental method** of determining sales force size is that sales representatives should be added as long as the incremental profit produced by their addition exceeds the incremental costs.[15] The method recognizes that decreasing returns will likely be associated with the addition of salespeople. Thus, while one more salesperson might produce $300,000, two more might produce only $550,000 in new sales. The incremental sales produced by the first salesperson is $300,000 but for the second salesperson is $250,000. Suppose the addition of a third salesperson could be expected to produce $225,000 in new sales and a fourth, $200,000. Adding all four would increase sales by $975,000. Suppose further that the company's profit margin was 20 percent, and placing another salesperson in the field cost $50,000 on average. This situation is summarized in Exhibit 5.9.

The analysis in Exhibit 5.9 suggests that two salespeople should be added. At that point, the incremental profit from the additional salespeople equals the incremental cost. Adding

EXHIBIT 5.9   **Illustration of the incremental approach to determining sales force size**

Number of additional salespeople (1)	Total additional revenue (2)	Incremental revenue due to additional salesperson (3)	Total additional profit* (4)	Incremental profit due to additional salesperson (5)	Total additional cost (6)	Incremental cost due to additional salesperson (7)
1	$300,000	$300,000	$ 60,000	$60,000	$ 50,000	$50,000
2	550,000	250,000	110,000	50,000	100,000	50,000
3	775,000	225,000	155,000	44,500	150,000	50,000
4	975,000	200,000	195,000	40,000	200,000	50,000

*Based on assumption of 20 percent profit margin.

more than two salespeople would cause profits to go down, as is seen by subtracting column (6) "total additional cost" from column (4) "total additional profit."

The incremental approach to determining sales force size is conceptually sound. Also, it is consistent with the empirical evidence that decreasing returns can be expected with additional salespeople. Decreasing returns can also be expected with other territory design features such as the number of buyers per salesperson, the number of calls the salesperson makes on an account, and the actual time the representative spends in face-to-face contact.[16]

A key disadvantage of the incremental approach is that it is the most difficult to implement of the three approaches we have reviewed. Although the cost of an additional salesperson can be estimated with reasonable accuracy, estimating the likely profit is difficult. It depends on the additional revenue the salesperson is expected to produce, and that depends on how the territories are restructured, who is assigned to each territory, and how effective they might be. To compound things further, the profitability of the new arrangement also depends on the mix of products generating the sales increase and how profitable each is to the company.

DESIGNING SALES TERRITORIES

After the number of sales territories has been determined, the sales manager can address the issue of territory design. The stages involved in territory design are shown in Exhibit 5.10. The sales manager strives for the ideal of making all territories equal with respect to the amount of sales potential they contain and the amount of work it takes a salesperson to cover them effectively. When territories are basically equal in potential, it is easier to evaluate each representative's performance and to compare salespeople. (A discussion of the potential problems in integrating territory difficulty differences into performance evaluations of salespeople is presented in Chapter 13.) Equal workloads tend to improve sales force morale and diminish disputes between management and the sales force. While considering these questions, the sales manager should take into account the impact on market response of particular territory structures and call frequencies. Obviously, it is difficult, if not impossible, to achieve an optimal balance with respect to all these factors. The sales manager should do his or her best to ensure the highest degree of fairness and equity in territory design.

Stages in Sales Territory Design

Step 1: Select Basic Control Unit

The basic control unit is the most elemental geographic area used to form sales territories— county or city, for example. As a general rule, small geographic control units are preferable

EXHIBIT 5.10
Stages in territory design

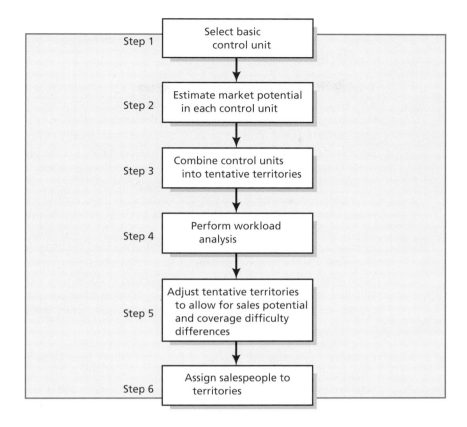

Step 1 — Select basic control unit

Step 2 — Estimate market potential in each control unit

Step 3 — Combine control units into tentative territories

Step 4 — Perform workload analysis

Step 5 — Adjust tentative territories to allow for sales potential and coverage difficulty differences

Step 6 — Assign salespeople to territories

to large ones. With large units, areas with low potential may be hidden by their inclusion in areas with high potential, and vice versa. This makes it difficult to pinpoint true geographic potential, which is a primary reason for forming geographically defined sales territories in the first place. Also, small control units make it easier to adjust sales territories when conditions warrant. It is much easier to reassign the accounts in a particular county from one salesperson to another, for example, than it is to reassign all the accounts in a state. Some commonly used basic control units are states, trading areas, counties, cities or metropolitan statistical areas (MSAs), and ZIP code areas.

States   Although it has become less popular, some companies still use states as basic control because of inherent advantages. State boundaries are clearly defined and thus are simple and inexpensive to use. A good deal of statistical data are accumulated by state, which makes it easy to analyze territory potential.

One primary weakness of using states as control units is that buying habits, or consumption patterns, do not reflect state boundaries because a state represents a political rather than an economic division of the national market. Consumption patterns in Gary, Indiana, for example, may have more in common with those in Chicago than with those in other parts of Indiana. Also, the size of states makes it difficult to pinpoint problem areas. A problem in Ohio may be localized in Cincinnati, but it is hard to determine that if the only figures available are for Ohio as a whole. States also contain great variations in market potential; the potential in New York City alone, for example, might be greater than the combined potential of all the Rocky Mountain states.

State units are sometimes used by firms that do not have the sophistication or staff to use counties or smaller geographic units—for example, firms at the early stages of territory design. States are also used by firms that cover a national market with only a few sales representatives, particularly when they can specify potential accounts by name (e.g., a firm selling dryers to paper mills).

Trading Areas   Trading areas are made up of a principal city and the surrounding dependent area. A trading area is an economic unit that ignores political and other noneconomic boundaries. Trading areas recognize that consumers who live in New Jersey, for example, may prefer to shop in New York City rather than locally. The trading area for a food processor in western Iowa might be wholesalers located in the upper Midwest rather than those in nearby Kansas. As such, trading areas reflect economic factors and are based on consumer buying habits and normal trading patterns.

A major disadvantage of using trading areas as basic control units is that they vary from product to product and must be referred to in terms of specific products. Thus, a company whose salespeople sell multiple product lines may have difficulty defining sales territories by trade areas. Another difficulty is that it is often hard to obtain detailed statistics for trading areas. This in turn makes them expensive to use as geographic control units, although some firms adjust the boundaries of the trading areas so they coincide with county lines. Whether or not a firm formally uses trading areas as basic control units, it should consider the logical trading areas for the products it produces when specifying the boundaries of each sales territory.

Counties   Counties are probably the most widely used basic geographic control unit. They permit a more fine-tuned analysis of the market than do states or trading areas, given that more than 3,000 counties exist and only 50 states and a varying number of trading areas depending on the product. One dramatic advantage of using counties as control units is the wealth of statistical data available by county. For example, the *County and City Data Book,* published biennially by the Bureau of the Census, provides statistics by county on such things as population, education, employment, income, housing, banking, manufacturing output, capital expenditures, retail and wholesale sales, and mineral and agricultural output. This county data is also readily available at the Bureau of Census Web site. Another advantage of counties is that their size permits easy reassignment from one sales territory to another. Thus, sales territories can be altered to reflect changing economic conditions without major upheaval in basic service. Furthermore, potentials do not have to be recalculated before doing so.

The most serious drawback to using counties as basic control units is that in some cases they are still too large. Los Angeles County, Cook County (Chicago), Dade County (Miami), and Harris County (Houston), for example, may require several sales representatives. In such cases, it is necessary to divide these counties into even smaller basic control units.

Metropolitan Statistical Areas (MSAs)   Historically, when most of the market potential was within city boundaries, the city was a good basic control unit. Cities are rarely satisfactory anymore, however. For many products, the area surrounding a city now contains as much or more potential than the central city. Consequently, many firms that formerly used cities now employ broader classification systems to help them identify and organize their territories. Developed by the Census Bureau, the control unit is called a metropolitan statistical area, or MSA.

MSAs are integrated economic and social units with a large population nucleus. Exhibit 5.11 ranks the 10 largest population centers in the United States in order of size based on U.S. census data.

EXHIBIT 5.11 Ten largest MSAs in decreasing order of size

Rank	Area	2006 Population (in 000s)
1	New York–Northern New Jersey–Long Island, NY–NJ–PA	18,818.5
2	Los Angeles–Long Beach–Santa Ana, CA	12,950.1
3	Chicago–Naperville–Joliet, IL–IN–WI	9,505.7
4	Dallas–Fort Worth–Arlington, TX	6,004.0
5	Philadelphia–Camden–Wilmington, PA–NJ–DE–MD	5,826.7
6	Houston–Sugar Land–Baytown, TX	5,539.9
7	Miami–Fort Lauderdale–Miami Beach, FL	5,463.9
8	Washington–Arlington–Alexandria, DC–VA–MD–WV	5,290.4
9	Atlanta–Sandy Springs–Marietta, GA	5,138.2
10	Detroit–Warren–Livonia, MI	4,469.0

Source: U.S. Bureau of the Census, *www.census.gov.*

The heavy concentration of population, income, and retail sales in the MSAs explains why many firms are content to concentrate their field selling efforts on them. Some assign all their field representatives to such large areas. Such a strategy minimizes travel time and expense because of the geographic concentration of MSAs.

ZIP Code and Other Areas Some firms, for which city or MSA boundaries are too large, use ZIP code areas as basic control units. The U.S. Postal Service has defined more than 36,000 five-digit ZIP code areas. An advantage of ZIP code areas is that they are often relatively homogeneous with respect to basic socioeconomic data. Whereas residents within an MSA might display great heterogeneity, those within a ZIP code area are more likely to be relatively similar in age, income, education, and so forth and to even display similar consumption patterns. Although the Bureau of the Census typically does not publish data by ZIP code area, an industry has developed to tabulate such data by arbitrary geographic boundaries. The *geodemographers,* as they are typically called, combine census data with their own survey data or data they gather from administrative records such as motor vehicle registrations or credit transactions to produce customized products for their clients.

A typical product involves the cluster analysis of census-produced data to produce homogeneous groups that describe the American population. For example, Claritas (the first firm to do this and still one of the leaders in the industry) used more than 500 demographic variables in its PRIZM NE (Potential Ratings in Zip Markets—New Edition) system when classifying residential neighborhoods. This system breaks the 25,000 + neighborhood areas in the United States into 66 types based on consumer behavior and lifestyle. Each of the types has a name that endeavors to describe the people living there, such as Urban Achievers, Shotguns and Pickups, Pools and Patios, and so on. Claritas and the other suppliers will do a customized analysis for whatever geographic boundaries a client specifies. Alternatively, a client can send a tape listing the ZIP code addresses of some customer database, and the geodemographer will attach the cluster codes.

One disadvantage of using ZIP code areas as basic control units is that the boundaries change over time. However, with the new technology for computerized geographic information systems (GIS), that is less of a problem than it used to be in that the boundaries can easily be reconfigured with the aid of specialized software.

Step 2: Estimate Market Potential

Step 2 in territory design involves estimating market potential in each basic control unit. This is done using one of the schemes suggested earlier in this chapter. If a relationship can be established between sales of the product in question and some other variable or variables, for example, this relationship can be applied to each basic control unit. Data must be available for each of the variables for the small geographic area, though. Sometimes the potential within each basic control unit is estimated by considering the likely demand from each customer and prospect in the control unit. This works much better for industrial goods manufacturers than it does for consumer goods producers. The consumers of industrial goods are typically fewer in number and more easily identified. Furthermore, each typically buys much more product than is true with consumer goods buyers. This makes it worthwhile to identify at least the larger ones by name, to estimate the likely demand from each, and to add up these individual estimates to produce an estimate for the territory as a whole.

Step 3: Form Tentative Territories

Step 3 in territory design involves combining contiguous basic control units into larger geographic aggregates. Adjoining units are combined to prevent salespeople from having to crisscross paths while skipping over geographic areas covered by another representative. The basic emphasis at this stage is to make the tentative territories as equal as possible in market potential. Differences in workload or sales potential (the share of total market potential a company expects to achieve) because of different levels of competitive activity are not taken into account at this stage. It is also presumed that all sales representatives have relatively equal abilities. Importantly, all these assumptions are relaxed at subsequent stages of the territory planning process. The attempt at this stage is simply to develop an approximation of the final territory alignment. The total number of territories defined equals the number of territories the firm has previously determined it needs. If the firm has not yet made such a calculation, it needs to do so now.

Step 4: Perform Workload Analysis

Once tentative initial boundaries have been established for all sales territories, it is necessary to determine how much work is required to cover each territory. Ideally, firms like to form sales territories that are equal in both potential and workload. Although step 3 should produce territories roughly equal in potential, the territories will probably be decidedly unequal with respect to the amount of work necessary to cover them adequately. In step 4, the analyst tries to estimate the amount of work involved in covering each.

Account Analysis   Typically, the workload analysis considers each customer in the territory, with emphasis on the larger ones. The analysis is often conducted in two stages. First, the sales potential for each customer and prospect in the territory is estimated. This step is often called an **account analysis.** The sales potential estimate derived from the account analysis is then used to decide how often each account should be called on and for how long. The total effort required to cover the territory can be determined by considering the number of accounts, the number of calls to be made on each, the duration of each call, and the estimated amount of nonselling and travel time.

Criteria for Classifying Accounts   Total sales potential is one criterion used to classify accounts into categories dictating the frequency and length of sales calls. A number of other criteria have been suggested as well for determining the attractiveness of an individual account to the firm. The key is to identify those factors likely to affect the productivity of the sales call. Some of these other factors include competitive pressures for the account, the prestige of the account, how many products the firm produces that the account buys, and the number and level of buying influences within the account.[17] The factors that affect the productivity of an individual sales call are likely to change from firm to firm.

Determining Account Call Rates   Once the specific factors affecting the productivity of a sales call have been isolated, they can be treated in various ways. One way is to use the ABC account classification approach discussed earlier in the chapter (see "Workload Method"). Another way is to employ a variation of the matrix concept of strategic planning, which suggests that accounts, like strategic business units or markets, can be divided along two dimensions reflecting the overall opportunity they represent and the firm's abilities to capitalize on those opportunities. In the case of accounts, the division should reflect (1) the attractiveness of the account to the firm and (2) the likely difficulties to be encountered in managing the account.[18] The accounts are then sorted into either a four- or nine-cell strategic planning matrix. For example, Exhibit 5.12 uses the criteria of account potential and the firm's competitive advantage or disadvantage with the account to classify accounts into four cells. It would use different call frequencies in each cell. The heaviest call rates in the

EXHIBIT 5.12
Account planning matrix

	Strong ← Competitive strength → **Weak**	
High Account potential **Low**	**Opportunity** Account offers good opportunity. It has high potential and sales organization has a differential advantage in serving it. **Strategy** Commit high levels of sales resources to take advantage of the opportunity. 1	**Opportunity** Account may represent a good opportunity. Sales organization needs to overcome its competitive disadvantage and strengthen its position to capitalize on the opportunity. **Strategy** Either direct a high level of sales resources to improve position and to take advantage of the opportunity or shift resources to other accounts. 2
	Opportunity Account offers stable opportunity since sales organization has differential advantage in serving it. **Strategy** Allocate moderate level of sales resources to maintain current advantage. 3	**Opportunity** Account offers little opportunity. Its potential is small and the sales organization is at a competitive disadvantage in serving it. **Strategy** Devote minimal level of resources to the account or consider abandoning the account altogether. 4

sample matrix depicted in Exhibit 5.12 would be on accounts in cells 1, 2, and possibly 3, depending on the firm's abilities to overcome its competitive disadvantages. The lowest planned call rates would be on accounts in cell 4.

Determining Call Frequencies Account by Account   Accounts do not have to be divided into classes and call frequencies set at the same level for all accounts in the class. Rather, the firm might want to determine the workload in each tentative territory on an account-by-account basis. Several approaches may be used to accomplish this. The firm can rate each account on each factor deemed critical to the success of the sales call effort and then develop a sales effort allocation index for each account. The sales effort allocation index is formed by multiplying each rating score by its factor importance weight, summing over all factors, and then dividing by the sum of the importance weights. The resulting sales effort allocation index reflects the relative amount of sales call effort that should be allocated to the account in comparison to other accounts—the larger the index, the greater the number of planned calls on the account.

Another approach is to estimate the likely sales to be realized from each account as a function of the number of calls on the account. Two popular ways exist for estimating the function relating sales to the number of calls on an account: empirical-based methods and judgment-based methods.[19] Empirical-based approaches use regression analysis to estimate the function relating historical sales in each territory to an a priori set of predictors likely to affect sales, including the number of calls. The function so determined represents the line of average sales relationship across all planning and control units.[20]

The judgment-based approaches require that someone in the sales organization, typically the salesperson serving the account but sometimes the sales manager, estimate the sales-per-sales-call function so that the optimal number of calls to be made on each account can be determined. CRM systems provide a wealth of opportunity for data collection toward estimating future sales based on calls on particular customers.

Determine Total Workload   When the account analysis is complete, a workload analysis can be performed for each territory. The procedure parallels that discussed earlier in the chapter for determining the size of the sales force using the workload method. The total amount of face-to-face contact is computed by multiplying the frequency with which each type of account should be called on by the number of such accounts. The products are then summed. This figure is combined with estimates of the nonselling and travel time necessary to cover the territory to determine the total amount of work involved in covering that territory. A similar set of calculations is made for each tentative territory.

Step 5: Adjust Tentative Territories

Step 5 in territory planning adjusts the boundaries of the tentative territories established in step 3 to compensate for the differences in workload found in step 4. It is possible, for example, that Washington, Oregon, Montana, Idaho, Wyoming, and Utah together might contain the same sales potential as Ohio. Since considerably less travel time would be necessary to cover the Ohio territory, the workload in the two territories would be far from equal and adjustments will need to be made.

While attempting to balance potentials and workloads across territories, the analyst must keep in mind that the sales volume potential per account is not fixed. It is likely to vary with the number of calls made. Although computer call allocation models consider this, it is not taken into account when, for example, the firm uses the ABC account classification approach and relies exclusively on historical sales when making account classifications. Clearly, reciprocal causation exists between account attractiveness and account effort.

Account attractiveness affects how hard the account should be worked. At the same time, the number of calls and length of the calls affect the sales likely to be realized from the account. Yet this reciprocal causation is only implicitly recognized in some schemes used to determine workloads for territories. The firm needs a mechanism for balancing potentials and workloads when adjusting the initial territories if it is not using a computer model.

Step 6: Assign Salespeople to Territories

After territory boundaries are established, the analyst can determine which salesperson should be assigned to which territory. Up to now, it has generally been assumed that no differences in abilities exist among salespersons or in the effectiveness of different salespeople with different accounts or products. Of course, in reality such differences do arise. All salespeople do not have the same ability nor are they equally effective with the same customers or products. At this stage in territory planning, the analyst should consider such differences and attempt to assign each salesperson to the territory where his or her relative contribution to the company's success will be the greatest.

Unfortunately, the ideal match cannot always be accomplished. It would be too disruptive to an established sales force with established sales territories to change practically all account coverage. Changing territory assignments can upset salespeople. If the firm is operating without assigned sales territories, then the realignment might be closer to the ideal. However, the reality is that a firm with established territories typically must be content to change assignments incrementally and on a more limited basis.

The actual assignment of salespeople to sales territories also incorporates personal considerations. The firm may not want to change salesperson call assignments for particular accounts because of the potential for lost business. It may not want to reduce sales force size even if the analysis suggests it should because of morale problems associated with downsizing. Even increasing sales force size can be disruptive. More salespeople mean more sales territories, which means redrawing existing boundaries, changing quotas, and disrupting potential for incentive pay. In sum, sales managers will want to reflect people considerations when they redraw territory boundaries. They will want to minimize disruptions to existing personal relationships between salespeople and customers.

SALES ANALYSIS FOR MANAGERIAL DECISION MAKING

The process of **sales analysis** represents another heavy use of information in that it involves gathering, classifying, comparing, and studying company sales data. It may "simply involve the comparison of total company sales in two different time periods. Or it may entail subjecting thousands of component sales (or sales-related) figures to a variety of comparisons—among themselves, with external data, and with like figures for earlier periods of time."[21]

A major benefit of even the most elementary sales analysis is in highlighting those products, customers, orders, or territories in which the firm's sales are concentrated. A heavy concentration is very common and the phenomenon is often called the **80:20 principle,** or the concentration ratio. This means it is not at all unusual to find 80 percent of the customers or products accounting for only 20 percent of total sales. Conversely, the remaining 20 percent of the customers or products account for 80 percent of the total sales volume. The same phenomenon applies to orders and territories in that only a small percentage of the total number of orders or a few of the firm's many territories account for the great percentage of its sales. The 80:20 principle describes the general situation, although, of course, the exact concentration ratio varies by company.

EXHIBIT 5.13 Key decisions when conducting a sales analysis

Managers wishing to undertake a sales analysis must decide (1) the type of evaluation system, (2) the sources of information, and (3) the type of aggregation of information that will be used. Exhibit 5.13 provides an overview of the nature of these decisions.

Type of Evaluation System

The first major decision related to sales analysis is the type of evaluation system to use. The type of evaluation system determines how the sales analysis will be conducted. Will it be a simple sales analysis, or a comparative analysis? When it is to be a comparative analysis, two additional questions arise: (1) What is to be the base for the comparison? (2) What type of reporting and control system is to be used?

In a simple sales analysis, the facts are listed and not measured against any standard. In a comparative analysis or, as it is sometimes called, a performance analysis, comparisons are made. Consider, for example, the data in Exhibit 5.14. A simple sales analysis would be restricted to the facts in column 1. These figures suggest Dawson sold the most and Barrington the least. A performance analysis would attempt to go beyond the mere listing of sales to determine where they are greatest and poorest—that is, it would try to make comparisons against some "standard." In Exhibit 5.14, the standard is the quota for each

EXHIBIT 5.14
Differences between
simple sales analysis
and comparative
analysis

Sales representative	(1) 2008 sales ($000)	(2) 2008 quota ($000)	(3) Performance index
Diane Barrington	$760.9	$700	108.7
John Bendt	793.5	690	115.0
James Dawson	859.2	895	96.0
Gloria Richardson	837.0	775	108.0
Walter Keyes	780.3	765	102.0

salesperson, and column 3 provides a performance index for each. This performance index is calculated as the ratio of actual sales to sales quota ($PI = S/Q \times 100$). It suggests Dawson was not the "best" in 2008, but rather Bendt was. In fact, Dawson realized the smallest percentage of total potential as judged by quota.

Bases for Comparison

The comparison with quota is only one type of comparison that can be made. Quota is one of the most common standards because it is very useful, particularly when quotas have been specified well. However, some firms resort to other bases of comparison for a sales analysis, and management must decide which bases of comparison are best for their particular situation. Options might include (1) this year's sales versus last year's sales or the average of a number of prior years' sales; (2) this year's sales versus forecasted sales; (3) sales in one territory versus sales in another, either absolutely or in relation to the ratios in prior years; and (4) the percentage change in sales from one territory to another, as compared with last year.

Such comparisons are certainly better than simply viewing raw sales figures, but they are not generally as productive as a "true" performance analysis. In the latter, variations from planned performance are highlighted, and the reasons for such exceptions are isolated.

Type of Reporting System

The other major issue that arises in a comparative sales analysis is the type of reporting and control system to be used. For example, if one relevant comparison is to be sales as a percentage of quota, this statistic would be provided for each salesperson, branch, district, region, customer, product, and every other unit by which sales are to be analyzed. The problem with this is that it can inundate the sales manager with information. To aid the sales manager, the reports can focus on exceptions, or significant deviations from the norm or from budget. Sales managers can then concentrate on the exceptions while having the full profile of comparisons for assessing the significance of what happened.

Sources of Information for Sales Analysis

A second class of major decisions that must be made with respect to sales analysis is what information is to serve as input to the system and how the basic source documents are to be processed. To address this question, the firm first needs to determine the types of comparisons to be made. A comparison with sales in other territories will require fewer documents than a comparison against market potential or quota or against the average sales in the territory for the last five years. The firm also needs to decide the extent to which preparing the sales report should be integrated with preparing other types of reports. These may include inventory or production reports or sales reports for other company units such as other divisions.

Generally, one of the most productive source documents is the sales invoice. From this, the following information can usually be extracted:

- Customer name and location.

- Product(s) or service(s) sold.

- Volume and dollar amount of the transaction.

- Salesperson (or agent) responsible for the sale.

- End use of product sold.

- Location of customer facility where product is to be shipped or used.

- Customer's industry, class of trade, or channel of distribution.

- Terms of sale and applicable discount.

- Freight paid or to be collected.

- Shipment point for the order.

- Transportation used in shipment.

Other documents provide more specialized output. Some of the more important of these are listed in Exhibit 5.15. As we learned in Chapter 3, CRM systems facilitate the capturing of the customer information referred to in Exhibit 5.15. This customer information can be analyzed and applied to particular sales analysis questions.

Software that links processes such as bid estimation, order entry, shipping, billing systems, and other work processes is called an **enterprise resource planning** system, or **ERP.** Boeing uses an ERP system to price out airplanes. Each airline and private customer who buys a jet will fit out each jet differently. As a result, the salesperson's proposal has to account for each different item in order to derive a price. Plus, commission has to be paid on the sale, parts have to be ordered for manufacturing, delivery has to be scheduled—and the ERP helps manage all of these functions. As with CRM, the information generated through enterprise software is an invaluable resource in sales analysis. Technology 5.1 provides several tips to ensure an ERP system delivers value.

Type of Aggregation of Information to Be Used in Sales Analysis

The third major decision management must confront when designing a sales analysis is which variables will serve as points of aggregation. Without such categories, the firm would be forced to analyze every transaction in isolation or would need to look at sales in the total aggregate. The latter is not particularly informative, and the former is almost impossible. The most common and instructive procedure is to assemble and tabulate sales by some appropriate groupings, such as these:

- Geographic regions such as states, counties, regions, or salespeople's territories.

- Product, package size, grade, or color.

- Customer or customer size.

- Market, including class of customer, end use, or channel of distribution.

- Method of sale, including mail, telephone, or direct salespeople.

- Size of order.

- Financial arrangement such as cash or charge.

EXHIBIT 5.15
**Other sources
of information
for sales analysis**

Cash register receipts
Type (cash or credit) and dollar amount of transaction by department
  by salesperson

Salesperson's call reports
Customers and prospects called on (company and individual seen;
  planned or unplanned calls)
Products discussed
Orders obtained
Customers' product needs and usage
Other significant information about customers
Distribution of salespeople's time among customer calls, travel, and
  office work
Sales-related activities: meetings, conventions, etc.

Salespeople's expense accounts
Expenses by day by item (hotel, meals, travel, etc.)

Individual customer (and prospect) records
Name and location and customer number
Number of calls by company salesperson (agents)
Sales by company (in dollars or units by product or service by location
  of customer facility)
Customer's industry, class of trade, or trade channel
Estimated total annual usage of each product or service sold by
  the company
Estimated annual purchases from the company of each such product
  or service
Location (in terms of company sales territory)

Financial records
Sales revenue (by products, geographic markets, customers, class
  of trade, unit of sales organization, etc.)
Direct sales expenses (similarly classified)
Overhead sales costs (similarly classified)
Profits (similarly classified)

Credit memos
Returns and allowances

Warranty cards
Indirect measures of dealer sales
Customer service

The classes of information a company may use depend on such things as its size, the
diversity of its product line, the geographic extent of its sales area, the number of markets
and customers it serves, and the level and type of management for which the information
is to be supplied. The firms with a product management form of organization, for example,
would be interested in sales by product groups. Product managers might focus on territory-
by-territory sales of their products. On the other hand, sales managers will likely be much

Technology   Six Ways to Ensure an Enterprise Resource   5.1
Planning (ERP) System Implementation
Delivers Value

Robbins-Gioia, an Alexandria, Va.–based program management consulting firm, recently reported that 51 percent of Enterprise Resource Planning (ERP) projects are considered failures, while a full 30 percent far exceed budget and miss their completion dates by a wide margin. These numbers can be attributed to inherent problems in what are generally considered best practices for enterprise systems implementations.

Consider the idea of executive sponsorship of the ERP initiative: What are the chances of an executive admitting to being less than fully committed to an ongoing ERP project, even if the implementation team doesn't feel completely supported? What can a company do to improve the chances that its next implementation effort won't flop? Here are some suggestions:

1. FOCUS ON REAPING MEASURABLE BUSINESS BENEFITS

Projects are much more likely to succeed when a company views the adoption of a new enterprise system as an opportunity to improve the way it does business, rather than an interruption of the status quo. This means tackling change-management issues head-on by giving people all the information they need about the new system, and how it will impact their jobs.

One manufacturer with a track record for successful implementations rarely green lights a project that isn't expected to boost productivity or cut costs by at least 25 percent—and 50 percent or more is the actual goal. To ensure these levels of performance, the projects are formally managed, monitored, and controlled. To achieve breakthrough improvements, both users and IT staff members must have the same definition of project success.

Great projects target the achievement of specific business performance, and assess potential, define business metrics that matter, report progress, and continue to do so until targeted benchmarks are reached. Key metrics include cycle times, employee productivity, and margins.

2. ESTABLISH A PROGRAM MANAGEMENT OFFICE (PMO)

Every growing company has a distinctive competitive advantage. It's the primary thing that attracts customers—and their dollars. Companies that make the most of this advantage learn to embed the processes that make them stand above the competition into their IT infrastructures. This requires making a leap beyond basic project management, which focuses on tasks and completion dates. Basic project management does not concern itself with strategic alignment or achieving tangible business improvement.

A disciplined PMO is the evolution of project work into business value creation within IT. The PMO seeks delivery of business benefits that can be gained through IT investment. This group becomes the soul of IT. Tuned into the business and the company's future strategies, it routinely performs IT needs assessment and portfolio management, and assists line-of-business executives with business case development.

PMO gives projects context within the overarching goals of business value, but its role also subsumes projects—and many of the silos of IT. A strong PMO can handle a range of tasks often covered by different organizations:

- Project management, facilitation, and administration;
- Risk assessment and change management;
- Development and delivery of system/process training;
- Vendor and third-party management—especially if a consulting firm is involved; and
- Executive liaison for formally communicating project progress and business results on a regular basis.

The PMO also should communicate how the project is changing operational performance, ensuring that employees, customers, and suppliers associated with performance change have access to the measurements relevant to them.

3. ASSESS THE ORGANIZATION'S TECHNICAL MATURITY LEVEL BEFORE PROJECT LAUNCH

Companies design manufacturing and supply chain processes that optimize their own businesses. That's why no two enterprise software implementations are exactly alike. From an IT standpoint, companies begin implementations with different levels of skills and experience. This actually becomes one of the chief responsibilities of the project team: Design a meaningful plan that takes the organization's maturity and capabilities into account.

(continued)

Technology   *concluded*   5.1

When you consider the nature of application software—which ultimately embodies a company's business processes—implementation efforts must drive the cultural change required to fully tap the potential of the software's tools and processes. The magnitude of this change is characterized by the amount of process and technology change the new systems will require, and the degree of difficulty in getting users to modify behavior. Likewise, a savvy CEO is going to consider the incentive structures that exist, and whether they may actually inhibit the desire to alter the status quo.

4. APPOINT STRONG PROJECT MANAGERS

Projects as significant as an ERP system deployment need strong leaders, tough principles, and a fully involved staff that will ensure system benefits are delivered to predefined performance levels. These project managers need the skills to assess operational capability—especially process and data quality maturity. They must develop performance-management metrics and the environment that project teams will operate within as part of project delivery.

Some implementations may require a trained project professional—not just a key manager. Beyond thorough execution of project tasks, these professionals also must read and understand the changing environment—i.e., manage multiple constituencies across the project life cycle.

5. PAY CLOSE ATTENTION TO DATA QUALITY EARLY IN THE PROJECT

Missing or inaccurate data can be a true project killer. It's simple: Users will not trust a new system if they question the veracity of the information it generates. Unfortunately, the issue of data quality isn't a small one. Of companies responding to a recent PricewaterhouseCoopers survey, 75 percent reported significant problems as a result of defective data, and 33 percent had to delay or scrap new systems.

Other industry studies reveal that even smoothly run projects require teams that devote 20 percent to 30 percent of their time dealing with data consistency. Clean, reliable data is essential to the success of an enterprise software project, but it's a checklist item that often receives only cursory mention in project plans. Great project managers set data cleanup as a "must-do," early-stage activity.

These steps should be included in the work plan:

- An assessment of the company's data accuracy. Consider factors such as frequency of use, redundancy, and whether data is still at all relevant to the business processes.

- A remediation plan concerning scope and time. This could include generation of data, cleansing, consolidation, and transformation.

- Workflows and accountability for data-quality processes for ongoing accuracy.

- A validation process to ensure a clean start-up.

The data accuracy issue can become especially tricky when a project calls for a large amount of critical data to be moved from PC spreadsheets to a corporate database. A single user can be comfortable with the missing data or sloppy facts, but a corporation cannot.

6. USE VENDOR RESOURCES WISELY

Manufacturers embarking on enterprise system projects almost never have enough resources, so companies usually need to work with the software providers to get projects done. The challenge is: Just how much is right? The answer shows up in advantages in time, cost, and success of implementations.

Behind the question of how much of which resources—i.e., consulting, education, project management—a vendor can bring to a project, the real question is what in-house processes are in place to make the most of all the vendor can do. How will the manufacturer interact with the vendor to access capability, and what can be done to effectively leverage the services and tools that the vendor brings to the project?

On the other hand, relying too heavily on the vendor may result in projects that meet all of the implementation milestones, but don't do much to improve the way the manufacturer does business. Similarly, a company may not be privy to early warning signals that things need attention, or to key decisions that may have critical consequences for the business.

SUMMARY

While not perfect, conventional wisdom about enterprise software implementations is based on real experience. But it goes only so far. There's more to know and to do, and companies enjoying the rewards of success have pearls of wisdom to share. Neglecting such pragmatic insight can be risky to the health of your business.

Source: David Caruso, "Six Ways to Ensure an ERP Implementation Delivers Value," *Manufacturing Business Technology* (Volume 27; August 2007), p. 27.

more interested in territory and customer analyses and only secondarily interested in the territory sales broken out by product.

These sales breakdowns are not necessarily mutually exclusive in that the manager has to choose only one approach. Rather, sales analyses are most productive when they are done hierarchically, in the sense that one breakdown is carried out within another category. The categories are treated simultaneously instead of separately. For example, the analysis may end up showing that customer XYZ in the western region purchased so many units each of products A, B, C, and D. This illustrates a territory, customer, and product hierarchical breakdown.

The advantage of hierarchical breakdowns is illustrated later. For now, you should know that the typical sales analysis results not in a single report but in a family of reports, each reflecting a different level of aggregation, tailored to the person receiving it. Exhibit 5.16, for example, shows the types of sales reports used in a consumer food products company.

Illustration of a Hierarchical Sales Analysis

To illustrate some relevant comparisons and the process used in conducting a sales analysis, consider the example data in Exhibit 5.17 for the XYZ Company. Let's assume the XYZ

EXHIBIT 5.16
Sales reports in a consumer food products company

Report name	Purpose	Report access*
Region	To provide sales information in units and dollars for each sales office or center in the region as well as a regional total.	Appropriate regional manager
Sales office or center	To provide sales information in units and dollars for each district manager assigned to a sales office.	Appropriate sales office or center manager
District	To provide sales information in units and dollars for each account supervisor and retail salesperson reporting to the district manager.	Appropriate district manager
Salesperson summary	To provide sales information in units and dollars for each customer on whom the salesperson calls.	Appropriate salesperson
Salesperson customer/product	To provide sales information in units and dollars for each customer on whom the salesperson calls.	Appropriate salesperson
Salesperson/ product	To provide sales information in units and dollars for each product that the salesperson sells.	Appropriate salesperson
Region/product	To provide sales information in units and dollars for each product sold within the region. Similar reports would be available by sales office and by district.	Appropriate regional manager
Region/customer class	To provide sales information in units and dollars for each class of customer located in the region. Similar reports would be available by sales office and by district.	Appropriate regional manager

*To understand the rationale behind who was given access to each report, it is useful to know that salespeople were assigned accounts in sales districts. Salespeople were assigned one or, at most, a couple of large accounts and were responsible for all the grocery stores, regardless of geography, affiliated with these large accounts, or they were assigned a geographic territory and were responsible for all of the stores within that territory. All sales districts were assigned to sales offices or sales centers. The centers were, in turn, organized into regions.

EXHIBIT 5.17   Sales and sales quotas for XYZ company

Region	BPI (percentage of U.S.)	Sales quota ($ millions)	Sales ($ millions)	Difference ($ millions)	Performance index (PI= S/Q × 100)
New England	5.8193%	$ 24.44	$ 25.03	$ 0.59	102.4
Middle Atlantic	18.3856	77.22	78.19	0.97	101.3
East North-Central	20.1419	84.60	79.48	−5.12	94.0
West North-Central	7.3982	31.07	30.51	−0.56	98.2
South Atlantic	14.7525	61.96	64.07	2.11	103.4
East South-Central	5.2571	22.08	23.20	1.12	105.1
West South-Central	9.2022	38.65	38.42	−0.23	99.4
Mountain	4.2819	17.98	17.73	−0.25	98.6
Pacific	14.7613	62.00	64.60	2.60	104.2
Total United States	100.0000%	$420.00	$421.23	$ 1.23	100.3

Company previously determined its sales are highly correlated with population, income, and the general level of retail sales. As such, it has used the **Buying Power Index (BPI)** published by *Sales & Marketing Management* magazine to determine each region's market potential and has then multiplied these potentials by the company's expected market share to generate the regional quotas in Exhibit 5.17.

Note that although the annual quota was $420 million, total sales in all regions were $421.23 million. Not only has the total company met quota, but also so have most of the regions. The performance index, the ratio of sales to quota, is greater than 100 for five regions. Four regions fell short of their targets, but three of those came very close. Only the east north-central region fell short by any substantial amount (−5.12 percent), but it still had the highest absolute dollar value of sales of any of the major regions. Many sales managers might be tempted from this to assume all is well. At the most, they might send a letter to the manager of the east north-central region, urging him or her to push the salespeople in the region to do better. However, the best approach is to generate the sales breakdown for the east north-central region shown in Exhibit 5.18. The state quotas were determined by multiplying the BPI total U.S. percentages for each state by the $420 million total forecasted sales. In many cases, the firm might wish to convert each percentage to a percentage of the region rather than of the United States as a whole. Thus, the percentage for Illinois would be (6.0037 ÷ 20.1419) × 100 = 29.8. This percentage would then be applied to the $8.60 million quota for the region to get the quota for Illinois. Although the result is the same, this second alternative provides a clearer picture of the concentration of demand in

EXHIBIT 5.18   Sales breakdown for east north-central region of XYZ company

State	BPI (percentage of U.S.)	Sales quota ($ millions)	Sales ($ millions)	Difference ($ millions)	Performance index (PI= S/Q × 100)
Illinois	6.0037%	$25.22	$24.30	$−0.92	96.4
Indiana	2.4103	10.12	10.24	0.12	101.2
Michigan	4.6401	19.49	17.77	−1.72	91.2
Ohio	4.9764	20.90	20.43	−0.47	97.8
Wisconsin	2.1114	8.87	6.74	−2.13	76.0
Total region	20.1419%	$84.60	$79.48	$−5.12	94.0

the region. The benefit of this approach holds particularly when one works with smaller and smaller units of analysis.

Exhibit 5.18 shows a problem with sales throughout the region. Referring to the "Performance Index" columns, only the sales representatives in Indiana exceeded quota, and then only slightly. Note that the deviations about quota are larger than they were in Exhibit 5.17. This generally happens as one moves to smaller units of analysis. With larger aggregates—for example, regions versus states—the statistician's law of large numbers seems to apply in that the pluses and minuses about quota tend to balance each other. Thus, the performance indexes in the larger analysis tend to be closer to 100. A smaller deviation from quota should initiate further investigation when the analysis is based on large aggregates (regions) rather than on small ones (salespeople). Although some negative deviation in actual sales from standard is evident in Exhibit 5.18 among four of the five states, the deviation in Wisconsin is most pronounced. Only 76 percent of the quota was realized here.

Again, after examining this Wisconsin information, it would be very easy for a sales manager to take some immediate action. However, the savvy manager would recognize that more analysis is needed to uncover what is truly going on. The sales manager should review the tabulation of sales by sales representatives in the Wisconsin district. The eight areas into which the state is divided are shown in Exhibit 5.19, and the results of the tabulation of sales

EXHIBIT 5.19
XYZ company sales territories in Wisconsin

EXHIBIT 5.20 Sales by representative in the Wisconsin district of XYZ company

Area representative	BPI (percentage of U.S.)	Sales quota ($000)	Sales ($000)	Difference ($000)	Performance index ($PI = S/Q \times 100$)
1. T. Tate	0.0953%	$ 400.2	$ 392.6	$ −7.6	98.1
2. T. Bir	0.1332	559.4	501.0	−58.4	89.6
3. C. Holzem	0.1325	556.5	512.4	−44.1	92.1
4. A. Elliott	0.2021	848.8	768.7	−80.1	90.6
5. P. Martin	0.2596	1,090.3	969.3	−121.0	88.9
6. J. Campbell	0.3384	1,421.3	1,340.3	−81.0	94.3
7. L. Hutchins	0.6975	2,929.5	1,285.0	−1,644.5	43.9
8. B. Lessner	0.2528	1,061.8	970.5	−91.3	91.4
Total Wisconsin	2.1114%	$8,867.8	$6,739.8	$−2,128.0	76.0

by representative are shown in Exhibit 5.20. Sales are below quota in all sales areas in the state. This suggests that something may be fundamentally wrong. Perhaps economic conditions are poor and unemployment is high; perhaps competition is more intense than in other areas; or perhaps a problem exists with sales force morale and motivation. Although numerous plausible explanations exist for the sales manager to check, the core problem seems to be Hutchins. If he had done as well as the other sales reps in the state, sales for the district would have been much closer to target. The problem is particularly acute because Hutchins has the prime Milwaukee market for a sales territory. Before taking action about Hutchins, the sales manager should examine more specific information on his sales. Hutchins's sales by product are shown in Exhibit 5.21. Hutchins is below quota on the entire product line, but seems to be having the most problem with coffee makers and blenders/mixers/food processors.

So the fundamental question for the sales manager is the following: Is the problem Hutchins or these products? A further analysis of sales of these products by customer indicated the problem was concentrated among large department store buyers. Furthermore, the problem was not unique to Hutchins but was common to all reps in the east and west north-central regions. A major competitor had been attempting to improve its position in the north-central region through a combination of heavy advertising and purchase rebate offers on these products. This problem had been obscured in other sales territories because sales of other products had compensated for lost sales in coffee makers and blenders/mixers/food

EXHIBIT 5.21 Hutchins's sales by product

Product	Sales quota	Sales	Difference	Performance index ($PI = S/Q \times 100$)
Can openers/knife sharpeners	$ 212,000	$ 124,500	$ −87,500	58.7
Toasters	468,000	237,000	−231,000	50.6
Coffee makers	627,000	176,000	−451,000	28.1
Blenders/mixers/food processors	604,000	159,200	−444,800	26.4
Griddles/electric fry pans	573,000	340,000	−233,000	59.3
Other—electric carving knives/popcorn makers/hot trays, etc.	445,500	248,300	−197,200	55.7
Total	$2,929,500	$1,285,000	$−1,644,500	43.9

processors. Hutchins's sales of other products did not make up the deficit. The problem was compounded by an economic slowdown in the metal-working industry, a big employer in the Milwaukee area.

The Iceberg Principle

Our sales analysis indicates that the problem is not Hutchins; rather, it is the special competitive situation in the north-central region. This situation would not have come to light without this detailed sales analysis. One important principle illustrated by the preceding example is that aggregate figures can be deceiving. Another principle is that small, visible problems are often symptoms of large, unseen problems. The phenomenon has been linked to an iceberg—the **iceberg principle,** so named because only about 10 percent of an iceberg's mass is above the water level (analogous to the symptoms of a problem). The other 90 percent of the berg is below the surface (analogous to the real problem), and not always directly below the tip either. The submerged portion can be very dangerous to ships. So it is with much sales, marketing, and business data. Real problems are often obscured by visible symptoms.

The typical business engages in many varied activities and collects large volumes of data to support these activities. Thus, it is very common for difficulties or problems in one area to be submerged. The sales manager in our example would have succumbed to a misperception of the problem had the original aggregate sales analysis in Exhibit 5.17 been the stopping point. At that point, on the surface all appeared basically calm and peaceful, but more careful analysis revealed submerged problems with jagged edges that would continue to suboptimize business results if they are not attended to properly. Those analyzing the information that is collected need to be especially wary that the summaries they produce by aggregating and averaging data do not hide more than they reveal.

The iceberg principle is pervasive. The 80:20 rule or concentration ratio discussed earlier is one manifestation of it. Often, the concentration of sales within certain territories, products, or customers hides specific weaknesses. More than one company has shown satisfactory total sales, but when the total was subdivided by territories, customers, and products, serious weaknesses were uncovered.

The preceding sales analysis example also vividly illustrates the difference between a simple sales analysis and a comparative sales analysis, as well as the advantages of the latter. The simple raw sales analysis would have focused on the raw sales data in Exhibit 5.17—it would not have examined the differences from quota. In fact, simple sales analysis probably would not have generated any detailed investigation of the east north-central region because sales there were higher than in any other region. The comparison with quota, however, emphasized that the potential in this region was also greater than in any other and the firm was failing to get its share. The comparative analysis triggered the more intensive investigation and isolated the primary reason for the sales shortfall. The execution of the process depended on having sales quotas available on a very small basis. They had to be available by customer, by product, and by salesperson or the problem would never have come to light.

Quotas are sometimes difficult to generate on such a small basis. In our example, it was possible because detailed geographic statistics on the BPI were available. In situations where other data should be used, they need to be available by small geographic area. That is one reason the sales planning and sales evaluation questions are so intertwined. One must keep in mind the questions of evaluation and the comparisons needed when designing sales territories and sales quotas.

The Isolate-and-Explode Principle

Another concept the example illustrates is the principle of **isolate and explode,** in which the most significant discrepancies between actual and standard are identified, or isolated, and then examined in detail, or exploded. The detail this explosion reveals is then analyzed, the most significant discrepancies are again isolated, and these are exploded. The process continues until the "real" problems are isolated. Thus, in the example, the following were all isolated and exploded in turn: the east north-central region, the Wisconsin district, Hutchins's sales by product, and Hutchins's product sales by customer.

An alternative would have been to have masses of data available to the sales manager initially. For example, the information system could have supplied the sales manager with the detailed tabulations of sales by each salesperson of each product to each customer in the beginning. More than likely, such a tabulation would go unused because of its size and the time it would take to decipher its contents. The isolate-and-explode principle makes the task manageable. The sales manager can quickly localize trouble spots by focusing on the most substantial exceptions from standard and then hone in more efficiently on an effective cure.

The principle can also be used to isolate exceptional performances for the clues they might provide to what the firm is doing right. Investigating why the east south-central region was 5.1 percent over quota when the entire company was only 0.3 percent over quota might suggest effective competitive strategies and identify best practices that can be duplicated in other sales units.

The isolate-and-explode principle assumes the company's information system can provide sales data hierarchically. In the example, the sales manager could secure data broken out by customer, by product, by sales rep, by district, and by region. The breakdowns resemble a tree: Total U.S. sales are the trunk, regions are the main limbs, districts the next branches, and so on. Further, all combinations of these branches are possible. For example, it is possible to do a study by product and territory, or by customer and product. These alternative types of analysis can also be productive, as can simple one-way categorizing of sales data. The simple tabulation of sales by product, for example, is very useful in showing a firm's product line strengths. Similarly, the simple tabulation of sales by major classes of customers is often informative about the company's market strengths. Keep in mind that these sales analyses are diagnostics, not decision rules. They do not tell the manager what to do but only offer clues as to causes of problems. And sales analyses are only part of the story.

Summary

We have seen in the chapter that sales managers perform a vital role in the process of both using and generating information. The sales forecasts, quotas, territories, and sales analyses developed under the leadership of sales managers touch most every operational aspect of a firm. Aspects of organizational success at many levels are affected by the proficiency of sales managers in performing these information management roles. From the profitability brought by strategic marketing plans when a forecast proves accurate, to the satisfaction of a customer when a sales territory design allows for proper coverage, to the rewards afforded a salesperson for quota attainment—all these outcomes reflect on the sales manager's capability to effectively use information in the job.

Because of this impact, sales managers have a vested interest in becoming as proficient as possible in the information management aspect of their job as described in this chapter. The greater their mastery of these important facets of the position, the greater will be not only their own professional success but also the success of the firm and its salespeople.

Key Terms

market potential
sales potential
sales forecast
sales quotas
subjective forecasting
  methods
  user expectations
  sales force composite
  jury of executive opinion
  Delphi technique
objective forecasting
  methods
  market test

time-series analysis
moving average
exponential smoothing
decomposition
statistical demand analysis
scenario planning
North American Industry
  Classification System
  (NAICS)
sales volume quotas
activity quotas
financial quotas
sales force deployment

breakdown method
workload method
incremental method
account analysis
sales analysis
80:20 principle
enterprise resource
  planning (ERP)
Buying Power Index (BPI)
iceberg principle
isolate and explode

Breakout Questions

1. A common problem faced by those responsible for making sales forecasts is "selling" the predictions to others such as the vice presidents of marketing, production, and human resources, and to the CEO or the CFO. These parties hesitate to use forecasts that can have major implications, especially if they are wrong, on their functional area. What can those responsible for sales forecasting do to better sell their results to management? What forecasting guidelines should be followed to improve the predictions?

2. A survey of local business firms to determine how they forecast sales will produce a variety of answers. Some will claim they do not use any formal techniques to forecast sales. You know they must be using some approach, no matter how loosely defined. How do you know a business firm is making a sales forecast? What are the implications of not making a sales forecast?

3. For the following products, indicate what factor(s) you would use to estimate market potential:

    a. Yoplait yogurt
    b. Rolex watches
    c. Dell personal computers
    d. Toro power riding lawnmowers
    e. Ektelon racquetball racquets
    f. Nicole Miller designer ties
    g. SWATCH watches
    h. Tylenol
    i. Mary Kay cosmetics

4. To estimate market potential for the garden tractor division of the M–F Implement Co., Mark Haynes, the statistician, estimated the following relationship using multiple regression analyses:

$$Y = a + b_1 X_1 + b_2 X_2 + b_3 X_3 + b_4 X_4$$

    where

    Y = unit sales of U.S. garden tractors
    X_1 = number of single-family homes
    X_2 = disposable personal income
    X_3 = index of food prices
    X_4 = family size

Using data for 2002–2008, $R^2 = 65.0$ was obtained. Should this method be used to predict market potential?

5. A new cake mix is to be introduced by Miracle Foods. To develop territory potentials, a corollary index has been proposed. The index contains several factors, such as income, population, and retail food sales. Can you justify these factors? Does it make sense to use retail food sales, which means cake sales are a function of food sales?

6. Once a quarter, every six months, or annually, each salesperson should estimate the buying potential of each account for each major product or product line. Such a request usually causes the sales force to panic. What goals are likely to be achieved by having the sales force participate in sales forecasting? What are the potential pitfalls, if any? How could those pitfalls be overcome?

7. Most sales managers hesitate to modify sales territories unless supported by compelling reasons. Likewise, sales managers are reluctant to make major changes in the sales compensation package. On the other hand, reassigning salespeople from one territory to another is fairly common and often reflects a form of promotion. One expert contends that if a company's sales force knows the territory too well, then it's time to reassign territories. What are the pros and cons of this approach? What factors related to the salesperson, the company, and the external environment might drive a company to reassign a sales territory?

8. The chapter describes the process to follow to develop territories. After territories have been developed, changes may occur that indicate the territories need to be realigned. What changes can you identify that indicate the need for realignment? How would you go about the process of realigning territories? How would you implement the changes?

9. In the typical case, management by exception leads to a close examination of below-par situations. Only sales representatives who are not meeting objectives, products that are not selling according to expectations, and customers who are not buying products as predicted are carefully reviewed to determine corrective action. What arguments can be advanced for conducting a close examination of the opposite, above-par situations?

10. The use of scanner data collected at the time of checkout in supermarkets has increased dramatically in sales analysis. One company has recruited families nationwide to participate in a panel study. When a shopper enters the checkout lane, he or she gives the clerk a plastic card that is passed over the scanner. All items purchased that are scanned are recorded in the shopper's diary. Oscar Mayer, a Wisconsin-based producer of meat, turkey, and seafood, has used different advertising campaigns in several markets. Oscar Mayer analyzes scanner data to determine which ad campaign was most effective. How else could Oscar Mayer and other manufacturers use scanner data? Of what value would scanner data be to salespeople for a company such as Oscar Mayer? To food retailers? What are other industries that could benefit from the same type of data?

11. The Recall Computer Co. has six territories, each represented by one salesperson. After extensive planning, the company determines that each territory would be expected to achieve the following percentages of total company sales for 2008:

Territory 1	27%	Territory 4	12%
Territory 2	15%	Territory 5	20%
Territory 3	18%	Territory 6	8%

These figures are used as the standard for comparing each sales representative's actual 2008 sales. The company projected sales for 2008 of $18,500,000. Determine which sales representative's territory had the best performance, by using the performance index, if the actual sales for 2008 in each territory were $5,425,000, $3,205,000, $3,710,000, $2,400,000, $3,900,000, and $2,000,000, respectively, for territories 1–6.

12. In planning a sales analysis system, one must consider that information needs vary from district sales manager to regional sales manager to national sales manager. Give specific examples of how information needs vary among managers at these levels.

Leadership Challenge: A Quote by Any Other Name

Ralph Dickerson knew an adjustment was needed. In more than 20 years with Bright Right Plastics, he had been around for many changes, and as director of sales for the company, he had initiated a number on his own. Now Ralph knew that he had to re-evaluate the quota system that had been used at Bright Right for more than 15 years.

The system had been revised years ago to focus the sales force on financial goals, specifically sales volume. At the time, business was slow and senior management had wanted salespeople to drive sales for the company. It had worked as the company prospered and was now enjoying great success. Selling to large hardware stores, the company had built a reputation as a good supplier of quality plastic fittings and joints in the retail plumbing industry. At the same time, many aspects of the business environment had changed since the quota system was last revised. Most notably, foreign competitors had come in offering competitive prices and better service. Several of Bright Right's old competitors had been driven out of business, and Ralph knew that part of the problem was the quota system in place at the company.

Essentially, the system in place was based on sales volume. As it had evolved the system focused on unit sales. It involved a complex plan that allowed each salesperson to set unit sales goals for every product in the company's large inventory. Senior management considered quotas a critical element in their strategic planning. At the same time, they were used as motivational tools for the sales force. Each overall quota was set high, but within that the salesperson could develop individual product quotas based on his or her customer's needs.

The problem, as Ralph saw it, was that customers wanted greater coordination and support from their suppliers. Specifically, customers like Home Depot and Lowe's wanted salespeople to offer product demonstrations to their own sales force as well as help in arranging displays for the products. Ralph had heard complaints that Bright Right salespeople were less interested in doing these kinds of activities than salespeople from other companies. Unfortunately, he had heard these complaints for several years and was concerned they might be losing business, or soon would be.

He sat is his office pondering his next move. The CEO of the company had set up a meeting for tomorrow to discuss this issue and was looking to Ralph for answers.

Questions

1. What are the advantages and disadvantages of a sales volume–based quota system?

2. What are the advantages and disadvantages of an activity-based quota system?

3. What quota system would you recommend Ralph present to the CEO and why? What challenges would Ralph face in implementing your recommendation?

Role Play: Blue Tern Mills-B

Situation

This situation is a continuation of the situation presented in the Chapter 4 Role Play. Go back and read that Role Play and your notes from it to refamiliarize yourself with the scenario.

Agnes, Alan, and Penny have now had their meeting and have proposed a new sales force organization scheme for Blue Tern Mills postacquisition of the Hello line of healthy grain products. It is now time to begin the process of developing a sales forecast for the first year of operation of the combined companies. In order to begin this process. Agnes calls another meeting of the three for a few weeks later.

In advance of the meeting, she asks that each person come prepared with a set of notes listing their proposed combination of forecasting methods to employ along with their rationale for why each should be a part of the final approach to determining this first- year forecast. As you prepare these notes, keep in mind that especially this first year the forecast will be tricky because it will be difficult to determine in advance the full impact of the transition of the Hello line from the manufacturer's representatives to Blue Tern's own sales force, with the new organization scheme for it you developed earlier. Clearly, multiple methods of forecasting should be applied to reach a final forecasting decision and information will have to be effectively sourced and utilized from both firms.

The purpose of the meeting is to settle on methods to be employed in developing the first-year forecast, justify those methods, and list information needed and the sources of that information.

Characters in the Role Play

Agnes Klondyke, national sales manager for Blue Tern Mills

Alan Knorr, West Coast sales manager for Blue Tern Mills

Penny Pugsley, currently the director of sales for Hello Healthy Grain Foods and soon to be East Coast sales manager for Blue Tern Mills (note that Penny's job at Hello has been to supervise its network of manufacturer's representatives—Hello does not have its own sales force).

Assignment

Break into groups of three, with one student playing each character. It doesn't matter what the actual gender mix of your group is. Before you stage the meeting among Agnes, Alan, and Penny, work separately to come up with the information required: your ideas for methods to be employed in developing the first-year forecast, justification of why those methods, information that will be needed to drive your selected methods, and the sources of that information. Then get together and role-play the meeting. Share your ideas, especially discussing the pros and cons of different forecasting approaches proposed. After the discussion, come to agreement among yourselves on what will be the best mix of forecasting approaches, given the unique situation in the first year after the acquisition, and specify the needed information and sources. Note that you are not developing a forecast in the meeting—you are simply deciding on what approaches to be used, why, and what information is needed.

Minicase: Lasting Impressions

Lasting Impressions is a small Orlando, Florida, company that provides trade-show marketing solutions to customers of all sizes. The company offers to design a plan for trade-show exhibiting from start to finish, including developing a pre-and postevent marketing plan and branding strategy, creating the exhibit booth and corresponding collateral support materials, packaging and shipping all trade-show materials, and providing boothmanship training services.

Founded by CEO Rajiv Dembla in 1996, the company focuses its own sales efforts on customers within the state of Florida and has a team of four account executives—Mary Beth, Suzanne, Franco, and Syl—who act as the salespeople for the organization. Rajiv relies on the same territory design that he has for the past several years, in which he divides the state geographically into four equal-size regions, and the account executives are responsible for the cities within their respective region.

Rajiv is not an especially quantitative manager by nature, but he did acknowledge the need to do a sales forecast for the upcoming 2008–09 fiscal year. He used the sales force composite method by asking his account executives how much each expected to sell during the coming year and then totaling those estimates. This type of method has worked for the company in the past, but Rajiv is concerned that Syl acts in the spirit of the marketing adage "underpromise and overdeliver" by intentionally underestimating his sales expectations so that his quota will be lower. To be safe, Rajiv also determined the sales forecast by taking a moving average of the previous four years of sales (see Table FY 2008–09 Forecasted Sales and Quotas).

Based on an average of these two sales forecasts, Rajiv set out to develop the yearly sales quota for each of his account executives. As he usually did, he kept the quota as simple as possible by basing it on gross dollars brought into the firm from sales, and he made it equal for each account executive. To ensure that his sales team is aggressive, he set the quotas slightly higher than the forecasted sales. As further motivation, Rajiv put 25 percent of each account executive's compensation in the form of a bonus for meeting or beating sales volume quotas.

John Cook, Rajiv's executive assistant, is more sensitive to the needs of the staff than Rajiv and tends to be the one that people talk to freely. Mary Beth complains to him privately, "This quota system does not reward—and even punishes—me for doing what I do best, building relationships with customers through in-person consultations, field demonstrations, and attending trade-show events to ensure everything goes smoothly." She finds these activities invaluable for serving the customer and keeping her pipeline of business full in the long term, but they do not necessarily generate sales volume in the short term.

While Suzanne tells John, "I have no problem with the quota because my territory includes the home city of Orlando. I know all of the businesses there and have no problem generating sales," Franco comes to John upset. His region includes Tallahassee, Pensacola, and the rest of the Florida Panhandle, which is more rural, is farther away from home, and has fewer businesses. As a result, he says, "I am miserable! I can't meet these unfair quotas!"

Syl tells John, "I have the same problem generating sales at times in my north-central Florida territory because there are fewer large cities. "But," he whispers with a smile, "I don't worry about it. I recommend more expensive trade-show supplies and services to my customers at the end of the fiscal year to boost my short-term sales. And if I need more sales to meet my quota, I just do some creative accounting and record sales numbers for this year which should come due at the beginning of next year. It works every time."

John is in a quandary. He normally keeps the staff complaints confidential, but in this case he feels like he needs to tell Rajiv that all is not well at Lasting Impressions.

FY 2008–09 Forecasted Sales and Quotas		
Account executive	**Forecasted sales**	**Quota**
Mary Beth	$180,000	$200,000
Suzanne	180,000	200,000
Franco	180,000	200,000
Syl	180,000	200,000
Total	$720,000	$800,000

Questions

1. Based on the facts given, evaluate Rajiv's territory design. What other basic control unit might Rajiv have used besides cities? Why?

2. What other forecast method(s) should Rajiv have used besides the sales force composite moving average? Why?

3. What type of sales quota did Rajiv use? Did he set the appropriate quota level? Why or why not?

Suggested Readings

Darmon, Rene Y. "Selecting Appropriate Sales Quota Plan Structures and Quota-Setting Procedures." *Journal of Personal Selling & Sales Management* 17 (Winter 1997), pp. 1–16.

Georgoff, David M., and Robert Murdick. "Manager's Guide to Forecasting." *Harvard Business Review* 64 (January–February 1986), pp. 110–20.

Good, David J., and Robert W. Stone. "How Sales Quotas Are Developed." *Industrial Marketing Management* 20 (February 1991), pp. 51–55.

Grant, Ken, David W. Cravens, George S. Low, and William C. Moncrief. "The Role of Satisfaction with Territory Design on the Motivation, Attitudes, and Work Outcomes of Salespeople." *Journal of the Academy of Marketing Science* 29 (Spring 2001), pp. 165–78.

LaForge, Raymond W., and David W. Cravens. "Empirical and Judgment-Based Sales Force Decision Models: A Comparative Analysis." *Decision Sciences* 16 (Spring 1985), pp. 177–95.

LaForge, Raymond W., David W. Cravens, and Clifford E. Young. "Improving Sales-force Productivity." *Business Horizons* 28 (September–October 1985), pp. 50–59.

LaForge, Raymond W., David W. Cravens, and Clifford E. Young. "Using Contingency Analysis to Select Selling Effort Allocation Methods." *Journal of Personal Selling & Sales Management* 6 (August 1986), pp. 19–28.

Makridakis, Spyros. *Forecasting: Methods and Applications,* 3rd ed. New York: John Wiley & Sons, 1997.

Zoltners, Andris A., and Sally E. Lorimer. "Sales Territory Alignment: An Overlooked Productivity Tool." *Journal of Personal Selling & Sales Management* 20 (Summer 2000), pp. 139–50.

Comprehensive Cases for **Part One**

Case 1.1

The Valley Winery

Pat Waller, recently hired as sales manager of the San Francisco region's chain division, was lamenting the problems he inherited. Despite favorable sales results for the San Francisco region, turnover was so severe Waller could not understand how sales increased during the past several years. He was surprised to learn the average sales rep had been with the San Francisco division of Valley Winery for only seven months and sales force turnover neared 100 percent a year. In fact, only one sales rep had more than two years' experience. Waller had heard that high turnover was a problem nationwide but did not expect such high figures for San Francisco.

Waller supervises two area managers, who in turn direct nine district managers. District managers supervise five to six sales reps, of which there are 50 in the San Francisco division. Approximately 50 new sales reps are hired each year, but the sales force size remains relatively constant. Waller knew the increased competitiveness in the market would make it more difficult to continue to obtain future sales increases. The excessive turnover problem would command immediate attention.

THE COMPANY

The Valley Winery, founded in 1933 in Napa, California, is the largest domestic producer of wine in the United States. Started with only a $7,500 investment at the end of Prohibition, it has become the leading producer of low-priced, consistent-quality wines. Favorite brands include Santo Rey and Valley premium table wines, Astral sparkling wines, Valley brandy, and most recently the Cool Valley line of wine coolers. As is true with most other wineries, Valley produces a low-grade, fortified sherry known in the streets as "Sneaky Pete." This product appeals to a small market niche and receives virtually no marketing support. The Valley name does not even appear on the label, a practice followed by other wineries as well. Brand names for this low-end product include Snake-Eye, 20/20, and Acey-Deucy. Valley also bottles a line of pop wines, which have never achieved high

sales. Brands in the pop line are California Dream and Mile-High. The Valley Winery sells more than 40 percent of all wine produced in the United States each year.

The Valley Winery is also one of this nation's largest privately held companies. As such, it is not required to disclose any financial information. However, according to financial analysts who specialize in the wine and distilled spirits industry, 2007 sales were believed to have exceeded $1.5 billion. Of the various producers of wine and distilled spirits, the Valley Winery is believed to be the best managed and most innovative.

Valley's phenomenal growth and success can be traced to two broad factors. As already stated, it produces wines of consistently high quality at relatively low prices. Second, Valley's sales force, using a push strategy, is considered by many to be the most aggressive and innovative in the industry. As the manager of a San Francisco liquor store states, "Turn your back on a Valley sales rep, and your store becomes a Valley warehouse." Heading up the sales force is Carl Roman, whose passion for detail and success is well known.

Valley Winery distributes nationwide through liquor and beer distributors located in metropolitan areas. Valley owns roughly 50 percent of these distributors, mostly those that are larger and more profitable. Valley's field representatives call on noncompany liquor and beer wholesalers across the country. Valley uses a major account system with reps calling on the headquarters of large chain stores.

The organization of the San Francisco division is typical, especially in those market areas where Valley owns the distributor. There are three sales groups. The first group calls on liquor stores and bars. Career-type salespeople dominate this group and most are older. These sales reps are paid a straight commission of 6 percent on sales. Almost all, 95 percent, are male. The second group calls on restaurants, resorts, hotels, and motels. This predominantly female sales group is paid a straight salary ($39,532 to $46,233) plus a company car. The third group is the chain division. This group, 99 percent male, receives a straight salary plus car and a year-end bonus. Their salaries range from $45,563 to $52,263. The chain group is considered the major source of future sales managers.

Source: Neil M. Ford, 2007.

EXHIBIT 1   San Francisco division: chain store division organizational chart (December 2006)

EXHIBIT 2   San Francisco division: chain store division organizational chart (January 2007)

The San Francisco chain division sales organization has experienced numerous changes. Historically, the company had a wine division and a wine cooler division (Exhibit 1). Early in 2007, Carl Roman revamped the structure and created a product line division reflecting premium and vintage products. Within the premium division were the Valley wines, the aperitif wines, and the Astral sparkling wines. The vintage division carried the Estate wines, Santo Rey wines, the Cool Valley line of wine coolers, and the Valley brandy (Exhibit 2). Less

EXHIBIT 3   San Francisco division: chain store division organizational chart (June 2007)

than six months later, Roman introduced yet another modification reflecting the importance of key customers, which were classified as major accounts (Exhibit 3). Sales reps calling on major accounts represented the entire Valley line of wines and distilled spirits. The San Francisco division is responsible for sales to all of the major grocery headquarters, such as Safeway, Albertson's, and Cala Foods.

Forward integration decisions are a function of how well the independent distributor covers the market and the size of the market potential. Roman had been very concerned with the chain store sales performance in the San Francisco area for some time. The previous distributor assigned 15 sales reps to call on the chain outlets and had resisted Valley's pleas to increase the sales force to 30 to 35 reps. After Valley Winery bought out the San Francisco distributor, sales of Valley Wines increased dramatically, primarily due to the increased number of sales reps calling on chain stores—from 15 up to 50. None of the 15 reps who worked for the previous owner was retained after Valley purchased the distributorship.

The buying process for these major chain accounts is fairly standard. Each sales rep is personally responsible for a specific number of stores taken from all major grocery chains. Thus, a sales rep will call on Safeway, Albertson's, and Cala stores. The total number of outlets constitutes the sales rep's territory.

The sales rep is responsible for reaching monthly display quotas on each line of products. For instance, one month the representative is responsible for displaying 50 cases of Santo Rey wine in 1.5- and 4.0-liter sizes. The next month the rep may have a display quota of 50 cases of Santo Rey in 3.0-liter sizes. This pattern repeats itself throughout the year. Exhibit 4 illustrates monthly quota patterns for different display results by sales rep and the extent of the turnover problem.

Sales reps call on either the store manager or the wine clerk, using preprepared sales sheets. The store manager or wine clerk must then order the beverages from the chain's warehouse, where all wines and distilled spirits are stored. The sales rep is responsible for all merchandising, service, and anything else related to Valley Winery that is needed in the chain outlet.

Rumors are abundant about the aggressiveness displayed by sales reps in the wine and liquor industry, especially Valley sales reps, who have been accused of relocating competitive displays and products to obtain the best space for Valley wines. Sales reps from other

EXHIBIT 4   Cases on display: quota versus actual results by sales representative

Product: Cool Valley
Store: Safeway 711

Month	J	F	M	A	M	J	J	A	S	O	N	D	J	F	M	A	M	J	J	A	S
Quota	40	15	40	75	75	100	125	125	75	25	25	40	40	0	50	75	100	110	125	125	115
Mike Fisk	28	15	32	50	0	0	(terminated)														
Tom Rhea							22	45	39	25	30	27	0	45	62	94	94	96	100	120	70

Product: Santo Rey
Store: Albertson 42

Month	J	F	M	A	M	J	J	A	S	O	N	D	J	F	M	A	M	J	J	A	S
Quota	30	0	75	0	75	0	60	0	80	0	90	0	30	0	75	0	75	0	60	0	80
Stan Smith	0	0	12	0	50	0	60	(terminated)													
John Mahorn								0	21	0	28	(terminated)									
Steve Anderson												0	18	42	0	0	(terminated)				
Neil Johnson																	50	0	50	0	85

Product: Valley Wines
Store: Cala 572

Month	J	F	M	A	M	J	J	A	S	O	N	D	J	F	M	A	M	J	J	A	S
Quota	50	0	60	0	75	0	50	0	80	0	90	0	50	0	60	0	75	0	50	0	80
Paul Barling	30	0	27	0	60	0	45	0	45	0	50	0	(terminated)								
Mark Beringer													33	0	45	0	50	0	50	0	75

wineries dislike the "competitive spirit" shown by Valley reps, who have also been accused of such tactics as spraying hair spray on competitive displays and bottles so that they will gather dust and so discourage sales.

Waller's concern about the turnover problem led to a series of conclusions. First, recruiting and training costs approached $30,000 per year per representative. Waller knew that with less turnover, Valley Winery and the San Francisco division profitability would improve. Second, Waller believed sales would improve. The $30,000 figure does not include opportunity costs associated with lost sales resulting from not having accounts called on. And these costs do not include the time it would take for a new rep to adequately develop rapport with the accounts. Considering all these factors, Waller felt confident that decreasing turnover would improve sales and company profits. On the other hand, Waller knew Carl Roman was pleased with the division's improving performance.

Pat Waller decided at least to investigate the situation. As a start, he examined two possible sources to see if they were the crux of the problem. These included the recruiting and hiring process and the nature of the position. To research the recruiting and hiring process, Waller contacted the personnel office. To learn about the nature of the position, he traveled with a number of the sales reps.

Mike Wehner, personnel manager for the San Francisco division, was responsible for hiring all personnel for the division, including warehouse workers, truck drivers, office personnel, and the sales force. Wehner used a variety of methods to attract sales candidates. Recruiting college graduates from a number of area universities was common. This generally resulted in 10 to 15 new sales reps a year. Newspaper advertisements and posting job notices on selected job search Web sites usually produced 10 hires per year. The use of six local employment agencies, with fees of approximately $3,000 per hired individual, resulted in 15 to 20 new reps per year. Last, any employee recommending a friend or an acquaintance who was subsequently hired received a $300 finder's fee. This practice typically cost the company $3,000 per year. Wehner claims not to recruit personnel from competitors or customers. He thought those hired through employment agencies were the most successful, but he was not positive.

The hiring process generally followed a similar pattern. The selected applicant completes a simple application form and is then interviewed by Wehner or his assistant for approximately 30 minutes. During that time, if the candidate seems motivated and enthusiastic, and asks for the sales job, the applicant is asked back for additional interviews.

The candidate then interviews with the distributor-ship's top manager for no more than 10 minutes. The San Francisco distributor is owned by Valley, and the new sales rep works for the distributor. Valley can reassign the sales rep to wholly owned distributors. All sales reps interact with the area distributor and often participate in training programs with the other two sales groups. Waller learned the distributor's top manager regards youth and physical characteristics as the most important traits an applicant should have to pass this stage.

The next step involves an interview with Waller's predecessor, John Ruppert, who was promoted to a home office assignment as a major account manager. The recruit is then whisked off to spend a day in the field with an experienced salesperson. Waller questioned whether this day in the field, during which the recruit is "wined and dined," is an accurate representation of the job. If all of these hurdles are passed, the applicant is then offered the job.

Before being promoted to the sales manager position for the San Francisco division, Waller had moved through the ranks, starting as a sales rep in the Seattle division. As a sales rep, Waller served primarily in a missionary capacity, calling on liquor stores and taverns. He then advanced to district manager for the Seattle division. Next, Waller moved to the Phoenix division, where he served as area manager before accepting a home office assignment as a product manager assistant. This progression was typical for a person selected to move into sales management, except that most sales managers are promoted from the chain store sales force. Waller's new assignment represented his first exposure to major account management.

On September 8, 2007, Waller traveled with Marv Flanigan, a nine-month veteran. Although scheduled to meet at 7 A.M., Marv was late, stating his hour-long drive was delayed by a terrible accident. Flanigan said the latest territory change created a longer commute for him. Since he was late, they started to work immediately, forgoing the customary cup of coffee Waller intended to buy as a warm-up tactic to learn about Flanigan's plans for the day. Waller and Flanigan spent nearly the entire morning at an Albertson's store (#561) building a 50-case display for Valley wines, resetting the cold box, and servicing the shelves. After a 15-minute presentation to the wine clerk, Flanigan and Waller left for

the next call. When Waller congratulated Flanigan on the 50-case display, Flanigan quipped, "Thanks, but unfortunately it's not enough to make quota. Nobody, but nobody, ever makes quota. That's 25 cases short, and that store is one of my best accounts. And did you see my Santo Rey quota—90 cases—no way!"

During their afternoon together, Waller observed a very aggressive sales promotion that Flanigan presented to a wine clerk at a Safeway store (#724). Afterward, Waller questioned the tenuous sales figures Flanigan quoted to the wine buyer. He responded by claiming, "John [division's previous sales manager] and Rick [Marv's current area manager] told me to stretch the sales estimates." Continuing, he revealed, "They said it's the only way to make my numbers. Rick even told me to pump up the numbers on the recap I send to Napa."

Pumping up the numbers meant a salesperson would claim a 50-case display had been installed when the store manager or wine clerk would only order a 25- to 30-case display. The display would only look like a 50-case display; center boxes in the display would be empty.

On September 23, 2007, Waller worked with Bill Murphy. Murphy, a six-month veteran, arrived grumbling. He said his district manager called him at 10:30 the night before complaining about the condition of Safeway #507. After 30 minutes of specific instructions and other messages, Murphy had agreed to visit the store early that morning to correct the deficiencies. He mentioned that he received calls at night from his district manager about two to three times a week, often to check his progress on winery directives. These usually occurred, he claimed, during the hour or two he spent on preparation each night.

During lunch, Murphy discussed his desire to move into management. He said, "Although district managers are often considered to be no more than baby sitters for the new reps, I really think that I can do a great job. The pay doesn't even bother me. [District managers received $5,000 to $6,000 more.] I mean, with all the cases I've sold, if I were paid on commission, I'd already be rich. I think I can really train those new reps just as the manual says."

Pat Waller's work with the sales reps provided useful information. At this point, Waller thought he was starting to get a good sense of the situation. What do you think is happening at Valley Winery?

Case 1.2
Health Care Office Solutions, Inc.

Greg Braver, vice president of sales for Health Care Office Solutions (HCOS), has spent the last several weeks preparing for today. After receiving a call from John Marston, the founder and CEO of HCOS, two weeks ago he has been reviewing the company's overall marketing and, more specifically, sales strategy. Marston, Braver, and the entire senior management team at HCOS are meeting to chart the company's marketing strategy for the next several years. As vice president of sales, Braver is heading up the discussion and wants to be ready for any and all questions that might come up during the day. To help guide the company through this strategic analysis, HCOS has enlisted the services of Strategic Marketing Specialists (SMS), a consulting firm that worked with health care companies to develop effective strategic business plans. Grace Johnson, CEO of SMS and a well-respected consultant to the health care industry, is going to lead the discussion during the meetings.

Founded in Chicago by John Marston, HCOS began in 1980 as a printing company known as Printing Solutions, Incorporated, that worked with a wide variety of businesses in a number of industries. Despite being in a highly competitive industry, Printing Solutions developed a reputation for customer service and opened four other locations in the Chicago area over the next five years.

However, after only a couple of years the company realized that many of its best clients were doctors' offices. Small- to medium-sized doctors' offices (2–10 doctors) have very special printing needs due to the demands of internal record keeping for patients and insurance as well as government regulations. As a result, in 1985 the company made a strategic decision to focus exclusively on health care companies—specifically, doctors' offices and small clinics. The company had found a niche focusing on doctors' offices that did not have the expertise in-house to manage their printing needs. By providing excellent customer service and an understanding of the unique printing needs in health care, the company developed a local, regional, and finally a national reputation.

As part of the new strategic focus, the company changed its name to Health Care Office Solutions, Inc. The name change reflected, in part, a new reality for

Source: Mark W. Johnston, 2007.

EXHIBIT 1 Services offered by Health Care Office Solutions, Inc.

Printing
Statements
Super bills
Standard insurance forms
Design-it-forms
Checks
Stationery
Envelopes
Pegboard forms
Color-coded labels

Special Services
Marketing services and color printing
Mail and fulfillment services
Invoice and bill processing service

Miscellaneous Products and Services
File folders
Chart dividers
Folder design and assembly service
HIPAA forms, brochures, and cabinets

the company as it was now being approached to take on more office duties besides printing. For example, doctors' offices were interested in HCOS handling not only the printing but the stuffing, sorting, and fulfillment of their invoices, patient reminders, and other mailing tasks. HCOS started a new division to handle such responsibilities. Exhibit 1 delineates the business services currently offered by HCOS.

HCOS, as mentioned previously, has developed a national reputation working with small- to medium-sized doctors' offices (2–10 physicians and supporting staff that included office manager, nurses, nurse assistants, medical transcriptionist, insurance specialists, receptionists, and others). Doctors have come to realize that managing an office required a different set of skills and, more important, that managing an office took them away from their real mission: meeting and working with patients. A number of companies had been created to help support the operations of a physician's office. HCOS was one of those companies, and it has worked hard to understand the needs and demands of running a doctor's office.

In addition to printing, HCOS found a niche helping doctors manage two critical functions of their offices: (1) billing patients and insurance companies and (2) marketing. In the case of billing, the doctor's office transmits all patient data (procedure, insurance company, insurance coverage plan, and other relevant information) to HCOS, which then creates all the necessary forms, mails them, and even inventories the documents. The company charges a fee each month based on the number of transactions. In addition, HCOS prints the forms, providing a second significant revenue stream. Using this system, data can be put in once using an Excel-based program that inserts the data into the various forms easily. The information is then sent to HCOS, and the doctor's staff does not have to worry about the forms or mailing. This complete software and printing solution (known as the Total Solutions Package) has created even greater opportunities for the company.

Its marketing services operation is able to run an entire marketing campaign from creation through printing, mailing, and fulfillment, again using materials printed by HCOS. HCOS has several people trained in marketing communications to help develop the marketing collateral material. This value-added service has grown very quickly in recent years as doctors came to recognize how important it is to be connected to their existing patients while reaching out to new ones.

Greg Braver was hired in 1990 to build a national sales force. He had spent a career working for a number of companies in health care, and although his background in printing was limited, he knew the business process of doctors' offices, small clinics, and other health care providers. Starting as a pharmaceutical representative for Merck, Braver had fast-tracked to sales manager and district manager in just seven years. It was at this point he changed companies to become the regional sales manager at a hospital supply company. When he was approached about the vice president of sales position at HCOS, he immediately saw the potential for the company and the opportunity for him to build a national sales force.

The company developed a national sales force of 60 salespeople located in major cities around the United States. The company had two regions (East and West) that were headed up by Mike Towers (Eastern) and Jule Geiger (Western). Each region had four districts with approximately six to eight salespeople in each district. Exhibit 2 details the organizational structure of the sales force. Towers and Geiger had each been with the company more than seven years. Both had originally been hired as a salesperson and worked their way up to regional vice president.

EXHIBIT 2   Organizational structure of HCOS

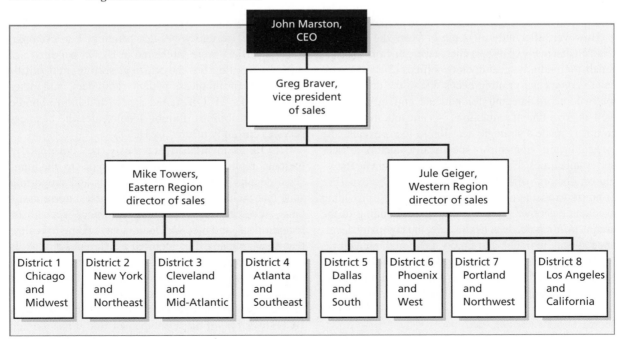

Early on, Braver focused on hiring salespeople with a background in health care. Marston and Braver felt it was more important for salespeople to understand the processes and procedures of doctors' offices than the printing business. Given his background, Braver was comfortable hiring pharmaceutical salespeople as well as salespeople from other health care suppliers such as Johnson & Johnson. These individuals knew the unique challenges doctors face running a complex office while maintaining a medical practice. As a result, their training time was shorter and focused more on the products and services offered by HCOS rather than a discussion of the customer. This meant they were productive sooner and training costs were lower.

On the down side, these individuals often came with established views of how to sell and the nature of the customer relationship. Braver found he had to retrain them on the importance of the customer relationship. HCOS built an excellent reputation on customer service, and its customer relationship was essential to the success of the company. In addition, hiring experienced salespeople was costly. Newly hired salespeople could expect to average $50,000 in salary and incentive compensation in their first year. Forty percent of the salespeople at HCOS had been with the company for at least 10 years and commanded salaries and incentive compensation of $80,000 on average. Incentive compensation usually took the form of bonuses based on hitting sales quotas for printing and the selling of the new, value added services offered by the company. Exhibit 3 details a typical compensation and benefits package for new and experienced (10 years or more) salespeople.

As the company's business consisted of small- and medium-sized physician offices, it had never created a national accounts sales team. Each salesperson has a protected territory and was responsible for the business in that area. The company did have different marketing programs for different types of medical practices (for example, pediatric versus orthopedic offices). In addition, the company's best accounts did receive additional attention from the salesperson in the territory. As physician offices grew larger, the demands on the salesperson became greater. In addition, as HCOS added more services like its Marketing Services Package, salespeople were spending more and more time with each client, particularly the larger ones.

As a result of an aggressive marketing campaign at physician conferences, advertising in medical journals, and, of course, a dedicated field sales force, the company had seen 26 years of growth. With salespeople in every major city, HCOS has a well-established network of offices to support its operations. As the company grew, senior managers had done their homework and identified new locations based on the amount of potential business as well as the ability to locate a printing facility at a reasonable cost. Marston believed and other senior managers agreed that it was critical for the company to maintain control over the customer's business from design to printing to order delivery. New services such as billing and mailing were subcontracted out to local companies in a given city, but HCOS works hard to identify quality vendors, and customers have not experienced any significant problems.

In the last year, however, Marston and Braver have begun to notice a change. While the company is still growing, the rate of growth has begun to slow down. Another trend also disturbed them: HCOS was losing new business at an increasing rate. With HCOS's focus on customer service and quality products/services, the company has always been able to do very well against the competition. Very few local or national printing companies can handle the unique challenges of working with doctors' offices. However, the company has noticed that companies like Administaff were winning contracts over HCOS. Finally, and this was the greatest concern for Marston and Braver, there seemed to be an increase in complaints from existing clients. While the company did not maintain a Customer Relationship Management (CRM) system, Braver was sure there were more complaints about late orders, poor quality, and lower customer service than in the past. Indeed, it was these issues that led to the series of meetings starting today.

Assess the current strategy of HCOS toward its most critical target market (mid-sized physician offices). Can you offer any suggestion on how HCOS can improve its relationships with existing customers and develop new business opportunities more effectively?

EXHIBIT 3   **Compensation/benefits package for new and experienced salespeople at HCOS**

	New	Experienced (10 years)
Salary	$40,000	$55,000
Incentive compensation (avg.)	10,000	25,000
Benefits	15,000	19,000
Health benefits	6,000	6,000
Retirement benefits	9,000	13,000
Total	$65,000	$99,000

Case 1.3

Microsoft Canada: Sales and Product Management Working Together

INTRODUCTION

Doug Taylor, national sales manager, Home & Entertainment Division (HED), for Microsoft Canada, was considering PC Marketing's move to launch a consumer education website. Barry Zeidenberg, group product manager for PC Marketing, believed that the Web site (his idea) was key to the long-term development of Microsoft's personal computer (PC) user base. The cost for the creation and maintenance of this site, "Microsoft Home Magazine," was estimated at $1 million per year, or 10 per cent of sales' and marketing's combined promotional budget. Taylor's initial reaction was that the money would be better spent in the sales channels, boosting overall sales.

MICROSOFT CANADA—HOME & ENTERTAINMENT DIVISION

The Home & Entertainment Division (HED) was the consumer side of Microsoft Canada's business (the other side, enterprise, dealt with the needs of corporations such as General Electric and Bell Canada). The HED division had two businesses: Xbox and PC. HED's PC business consisted of consumer software, commercial software and hardware. Consumer software consisted of brands such as Encarta, Money and Works. Commercial software included applications such as Windows, Office and Excel. Hardware included mice and keyboards. HED had performed extremely well, and Microsoft Canada depended on it for a significant portion of its revenue and profits from consumers.

Taylor and Zeidenberg had both worked in consumer packaged goods companies such as Coca-Cola and Unilever. Each had experience in both sales and marketing roles prior to their arrival at Microsoft. Although Taylor had been with Microsoft since 1998, Zeidenberg had more recently joined the company, in 2001. Both reported directly to Greg Barber, head of HED (see figure below).

Taylor, national sales manager, Home & Entertainment Division, managed national sales for both PC marketing and Xbox. His customers included mass merchandisers, such as Wal-Mart, Zellers and Toys "R" Us; electronics stores, such as Best Buy and Future Shop; and focused chains, such as EB Games. Taylor had annual base and stretch sales teams targets for both PC and Xbox sales. His annual compensation was a combination of base salary and incentives linked to volume and achievement of other objectives included in Microsoft's management by objectives (MBO) initiative. Although customers for both PC Marketing and Xbox were similar, there continued to be differences among customer priorities. One of Taylor's goals was to leverage PCs' advantage for Xbox sales and vice versa. For example, PC sales could have been higher at Wal-Mart if the retailer had been willing to focus its attention on serving the home-office space. Xbox's high-profile launch and channel support level allowed Taylor to improve his PC business at Wal-Mart. Taylor stated:

> I'm charged with getting the revenues for HED by selling product within the means I have, using channel budgets. To me, it does not matter whether I sell X number of Windows or Y number of optical mouse products. Topline revenue is my sole focus. Group Marketing Managers are charged with revenues on individual product lines.
>
> I'm a very data-focused person and enjoy mining databases for insights. I can see that the proposed Web site would help us build consumer interest in our PC products. I agree that cooperation with marketing requires an element of relationship management . . . but we also have to do what's best for the business.

Taylor, along with HED's two group product managers, shared a common promotional budget, deciding among themselves how best to allocate the dollars between channel spend (to support customers) and consumer spend (to educate the consumer and to drive demand). HED's annual promotional budget for the PC business was approximately $10 million.

Zeidenberg, the group product manager for PC marketing, coordinated the marketing activities for the PC business. His target market was Canadian consumers who used or were intending to use PCs. To reach this audience, Zeidenberg relied on a combination of advertising media, including print, television and online programs. Zeidenberg's goals included both annual product revenues and generating consumer interest in Microsoft's PC products, including Windows XP and Office. In addition to advertising to consumers, Zeidenberg explained,

> I am spending time with Taylor to educate our customer accounts on our marketing initiatives. And we're happy to see that our retail accounts are starting to recognize the value of our marketing initiatives and content. Two major electronics retailers have been saying to us that our marketing campaigns are great, and they want to work with us to leverage them in their own consumer communications strategy. While marketing is typically concerned with the a longer term view of the health of the business, we cannot ignore the shorter term impact of our marketing programs at the account level.

Zeidenberg's compensation was a combination of base salary and incentives. Relative to Taylor's compensation, Zeidenberg's performance incentives accounted for a smaller percentage of his overall compensation.

THE MICROSOFT HOME MAGAZINE WEB SITE

The objective of the proposed Web site, "Microsoft Home Magazine", was to "educate and excite" consumers in the "fight against PC apathy." "PC apathy" was defined by Microsoft as the tendency for consumers to use their PCs for only a limited number of activities, and thus put off upgrading their current computer system because they did not perceive the need for additional features.

On the Web site, consumers would be able to find articles on how to use their computer to organize their lives, tips on (legally) downloading and burning music to CDs, and advice columns on various computer-related topics. Third parties would be hired to write articles and manage website updates.

The site was expected to cost $1 million to develop and launch. The Web site's ongoing costs were also expected to be $1 million per year. For a screen shot of this proposed site, see Exhibit 1.

THE ISSUE

Taylor's main concern was that HED's PC business was expected to suffer double-digit percentage decreases in shipments from the previous year. He estimated that if he were to invest the same amount supporting his retail customers (in lieu of spending $1 million on a website), he could generate an additional $10 million in revenue next year. Taylor commented:

> On the positive side, incubating future customers is a good idea.

EXHIBIT 1   **The "Microsoft Home" Homepage**

Source: *www.microsoft.com/home*

On the negative side, this puts next year's sales goals at risk.

The Home & Entertainment Division held quarterly full-day meetings between sales and marketing in order to encourage collaboration and achieve alignment of individual product and total business objectives. Although Taylor and Zeidenberg had met several times on the "Microsoft Home Magazine" Web site initiative, both wondered if it would be valuable to solicit feedback from the other executives in HED on this proposed project.

On the positive side, Zeidenberg's Web site initiative would allow Microsoft to establish thought leadership for PC usage in Canadians' minds. It would highlight useful ways to integrate PC usage into everyday lives. On the other hand, competition at the retail level—which had always been aggressive—was not expected to abate. Site development and maintenance costs were a significant portion of HED's annual promotional budget. Could the division afford to invest in this initiative? Could it afford not to? The potential for conflict between sales and product management was clear.

Part **Two**

Implementation of the Sales Program

Sales Management Activities	Determinants of the Salesperson's Performance	Outcomes
	Salesperson's view of job requirements, role perceptions • Accuracy • Ambiguity • Conflict	
Supervision		
Selection of sales personnel	Aptitude	Performance Sales volume Percentage of quota Selling expenses Profitability Customer service Report
Sales training	Skill levels	
Motivating the sales force Compensation systems Incentive programs	Motivation level	

Chapter 1 suggested that sales management involves three interrelated processes: (1) formulation of a sales program, (2) implementation of the sales program, and (3) evaluation and control of the sales program. Part One of the book concentrated on the first of these processes. Part Two focuses on the second and explores the policies and procedures involved in implementing a firm's sales program. Chapter 6 provides a model that incorporates the main factors that affect a salesperson's performance and job behavior, including (1) environmental variables, (2) role perceptions, (3) aptitude, (4) skill levels, and (5) motivation. In addition, Chapter 6 discusses in greater detail an individual's role perceptions, a key element in the model. Role perceptions are the demands salespeople receive from their customers, managers, and families. Finally, the chapter discusses how supervisory policies can help salespeople deal with ambiguous and conflicting demands. Chapter 7 concentrates on another important factor in salesperson performance and behavior—motivation. Chapter 8 examines the personal characteristics related to sales aptitude and the ways in which recruiting and selection procedures can help build a sales force with the abilities needed to carry out essential selling tasks. The issues of sales force recruitment and selection are investigated in Chapter 9.

The sales manager must decide what aptitudes are required for the company's salespeople to sell the company's products and services. Selection criteria and recruiting techniques can then be developed to ensure that the company hires the right kind of people.

No matter how good a company is at selecting and recruiting salespeople, it still needs training programs to give new recruits and experienced veterans the necessary skills to remain successful in the rapidly changing sales environment. Sales training and a variety of training techniques are examined in Chapter 10.

Finally, a salesperson's motivation is largely a function of the amount and desirability of the rewards expected for a given job performance. The sales manager needs to identify what rewards are most attractive to the sales force and design compensation and incentive programs that will generate a high level of motivation. Chapter 11 concludes Part Two by examining how rewards can be incorporated into effective sales compensation and incentive programs.

The first three chapters focus on explaining the complex process of salesperson performance and behavior. The last three implement that understanding in sales management practice.

Chapter **Six**

Salesperson Performance: Behavior, Role Perceptions, and Satisfaction

The Changing Role of the Sellers

Sales effectiveness is often defined by sales revenue dollars. However, this data may oversimplify a complex situation. Many factors that drive sales are out of salespeople's control such as territory and regional differences, management policies, competitors, and the product itself. It takes a skilled salesperson to make a sales proposal that addresses a potential customer's needs. In fact, the salesperson's role has been changing from product developer to relationship manager and from "solution seller" to consultant. Increasingly, order taking, service, technical support, and product expertise are not even handled directly by the salesperson. As a result, the salesperson's status in the organization has changed. In 1992, all of the Chally's world-class sales forces represented their own products. In 2007 however, the top sales organizations are all specialized sales and service companies that do not manufacture any products themselves.

Clearly, there is a change to a more customer-driven marketplace that rewards companies with competitive advantages in product, technology, or research. Companies have therefore turned to "alternatives channels", be they efficient call centers, market segment distributors, or highly specialized "value added resellers" (VARS) that enable them to focus on core competencies more effectively. This leads to two important questions. How important are the sellers? Are they as important as the product?

Is the Product or the Seller the Key to Market Share?

The Chally World Class Sales Database (2007) sought to answer those questions. Analyzing data from over 17,000 customers in more than 15 different industries, Chally developed an overall rating of the vendor company, an overall rating of the sales representative, and the percent of total purchases from a particular supplier over a three-year period. We might call this third measure the "share of wallet". The goal of a company and salesperson is to be the only supplier to a customer, with 100 percent of the business.

The data was analyzed to determine what variables (which specific salesperson skills or vendor factors) account for the most "share of customer's wallet." The results found that the salesperson is more important than the product's price, quality or features and options. Interestingly, customers perceive an interaction between the effect of salesperson and their company that is not accounted for by the salesperson or company individually. This means that although a salesperson is slightly more important than company, when we consider company and salesperson together, the effect of the whole was greater than the sum of its parts. Put another way, the company and the salesperson were both important, but there was synergy if both were strong.

The role of salespeople in the sales function is more important than ever and represents a critical element in a company's overall marketing strategy. However, customer demand for better products, higher levels of customer support, and cutting-edge technology raises some interesting strategic questions for companies with a competitive advantage in product development or research. Do they invest in building a strong customer culture (focus on sales) or continue to invest heavily in product development and research. Given limited resources, most companies are likely to find it difficult to maintain a product focus while building a customer oriented culture with a strong sales function, which means the trend toward building strong customer relationships through alternative channels such as VARS distributors is likely to continue.

Source: HR Chally Group (2007).

LEARNING OBJECTIVES

How a salesperson performs is the result of a complex interaction of many factors. Many of those factors are the result of an individual's personal characteristics, motivation, and perceptions of the job. It is vital that sales managers have a clear understanding of salesperson performance so that they can maximize the performance potential of the salespeople in the organization. This chapter will present a model of salesperson performance and lay the groundwork for the information in Chapters 6 through 11. In addition, this chapter focuses on one of the key elements in the model: the salesperson's role perceptions.

After reading this chapter, you should be able to

- Understand the model of salesperson performance.

- Identify the various components that make up the model.

- Discuss the role perception process.

- Understand why the role of salesperson is susceptible to role issues.

- Discuss how role conflict, role ambiguity, and role accuracy influence a salesperson's role perceptions.

As the introductory scenario suggests, a number of factors can affect a salesperson's performance. When sales managers implement sales programs, they must motivate and direct the behavior of sales representatives toward the company's goals. Sales managers, therefore, must understand why people in the sales force behave the way they do. This chapter offers a model to understand sales force behavior. The model highlights the links between a salesperson's performance and the determinants of that performance. In addition, the chapter examines one of the key elements of the model, a salesperson's role perceptions. Put simply, salespeople operate in a unique environment where the nature of the roles is changing. The second part of the chapter will delineate how a salesperson's role perceptions affect his or her performance. Complete understanding of the model should develop as you study the remainder of this section, which discusses the basic components of the model in detail.

UNDERSTANDING SALESPERSON PERFORMANCE—WHY IS IT IMPORTANT FOR SALES MANAGEMENT?

Understanding the model of salesperson performance—as discussed over the next several chapters and presented in Exhibit 6.1—is extremely important to the sales manager because almost everything he or she does can influence it. For example,

- The way the sales manager organizes and deploys the sales force can affect salespeople's perceptions of the job.

- How the manager selects salespeople and the kind of training they receive can affect the aptitude and skill of sales personnel.

- The compensation program and the way it is administered can influence motivation levels and overall sales performance.

EXHIBIT 6.1   **Model of the determinants of a salesperson's performance**

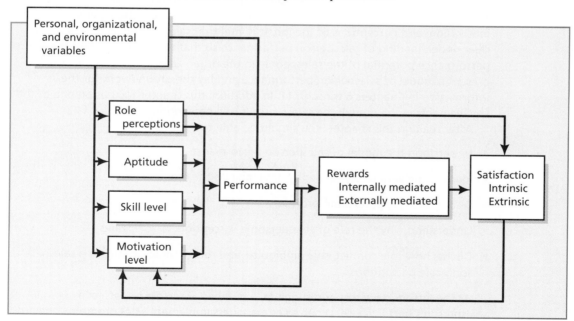

The model offers the sales manager a tool for visualizing the effects of his or her activities and for appreciating the interrelated roles of the options under his or her command. This chapter outlines the model and highlights the various components. In addition, it discusses a critical component of the model—role perceptions—and delineates the evidence supporting its effects and the influences on it.

THE MODEL

Research in industrial and organizational psychology suggests a worker's job performance is a function of five basic factors: (1) role perceptions, (2) aptitude, (3) skill level, (4) motivation, and (5) personal, organizational, and environmental variables.[1] Exhibit 6.1 presents an overall model of a salesperson's performance that includes these factors as primary determinants. The success of any salesperson is a complex combination of these forces, which can positively, or negatively, influence his or her performance.

Although not pictured in the model, substantial interaction occurs among the determinants. As a result, if a worker is deficient in any of these factors, he or she could be expected to perform poorly. If the salesperson has innate ability and the motivation to perform but lacks understanding of how the job should be done, for example, he or she could still perform below expectations. Similarly, if the salesperson has the ability and accurately perceives how the job should be performed but lacks motivation, he or she is likely to perform poorly.

One other note: The factors in the model are not independent of each other. It is not clear how the factors interact, and indeed, they almost certainly vary somewhat with each individual. However, it is fairly certain that the determinants are interrelated.

The Role Perceptions Component

The role attached to the position of salesperson represents the set of activities or behaviors to be performed by anyone occupying that position. While discussed in much greater detail later in the chapter, this role is defined largely through the expectations, demands, and pressures communicated to the salesperson by his or her role partners. These partners include people both outside and within the individual's firm who have a vested interest in how the salesperson performs the job—top management, the individual's supervisor, customers, and family members. The salesperson's perceptions of these expectations strongly influence the individual's definition of his or her role in the company and behavior on the job.

The role perceptions component of the model has three dimensions: role accuracy, perceived role conflict, and perceived role ambiguity. The term **role accuracy** refers to the degree to which the salesperson's perceptions of his or her role partners' demands—particularly those of company superiors—are accurate. **Perceived role conflict** arises when a salesperson believes the role demands of two or more of his or her role partners are incompatible. Thus, the individual cannot possibly satisfy them all at the same time. A salesperson suffers from role conflict, for example, when a customer demands a delivery schedule or credit terms the sales rep believes will be unacceptable to company superiors. **Perceived role ambiguity** occurs when salespeople believe they do not have the information necessary to perform the job adequately. The salespeople may be uncertain about what some role partners expect of them in certain situations, how they should satisfy those expectations, or how their performance will be evaluated and rewarded.

The model indicates the three role perception variables have psychological consequences for the individual salesperson. They can produce dissatisfaction with the job.

They can also affect the salesperson's motivation.[2] All these effects can increase turnover within the sales force and hurt performance. However, role stress (role conflict and role ambiguity) does not necessarily always imply a negative job outcome (e.g., increased turnover). Indeed, research suggests that a certain degree of role conflict and ambiguity enables salespeople to make creative decisions that can be beneficial to the customer and the organization. Business to business salespeople are particularly vulnerable to role inaccuracy, conflict, and ambiguity. Several personal and organizational variables can affect people's role perceptions. Fortunately, many of these variables can be controlled or influenced by sales management policies and methods, thus allowing the sales manager to influence the performance of individual salespeople.[3]

The Aptitude Component

The model of sales performance in Exhibit 6.1 treats an individuals sales aptitude largely as a constraint on the person's ability to perform the sales job. This assumes there is an adequate understanding of the role to be performed, motivation, and learned skills. In other words, two people with equal motivation, role perceptions, and skills might perform at very different levels because one has more aptitude or ability than the other.

There has been a lot of research on the effect of aptitude on sales performance. Sales aptitude includes a number of factors, such as verbal intelligence, mathematical ability, and sales expertise. In general, the results of the research have found there is a relationship between aptitude and performance. Unfortunately, broad measures of aptitude by themselves do not explain a very large proportion of the variation in sales performance.[4]

Broad measures of aptitude may not predict sales performance for several reasons. First motivation refers to the salesperson's desire to expend effort on very specific sales tasks such as calling on new accounts or preparing sales presentations, and it varies by sales position (experienced key account managers need to accomplish different tasks than new-account salespeople). As a result, the appropriate definition of aptitude, and the appropriate measures of the construct, may vary greatly from industry to industry, firm to firm, and product line to product line. For example, selling highly technical products requiring an engineering background (e.g., building construction) might demand math skills that an office supplies salesperson may not need to be successful.

Second, aptitude may affect performance in more ways than by simply moderating an individual's ability to do the job. It may also affect the salesperson's motivation to perform. For example, the salesperson's perceived ability to perform a task and his or her general self-confidence influence the individual's perceptions of whether increased effort will lead to improved performance. Furthermore, salespeople's intelligence and feelings as to whether they largely control their own destiny or whether this destiny is largely controlled by outside forces (internal versus external locus of control) affect whether they believe improved performance will lead to improvement in rewards they desire. All this suggests that objective measures of sales aptitude may be insufficient by themselves. The role of sales aptitude in salesperson performance as well as methods by which sales managers ascertain an individual's sales aptitude are discussed in Chapter 8.

The Skill-Level Component

Skill level refers to the individual's learned proficiency at performing the necessary tasks[5] and include such learned abilities as interpersonal skills, leadership, technical knowledge, and presentation skills. The relative importance of each of these skills, and the necessity of having other skills, depends on the selling situation. Different kinds of skills are needed for different types of selling tasks. Aptitude and skill levels are thus related constructs. Aptitude consists of relatively enduring personal abilities, whereas skills are proficiency levels that can change rapidly with learning and experience. The skill sets of a salesperson for i2 Technologies selling multimillion-dollar network systems are different from someone selling Lexus automobiles to consumers.

The salesperson's past selling experience and the extensiveness and content of the firm's sales training programs influence skill level. Although American companies spend large amounts of money on sales training, there is almost no research concerning the effects of these training programs on salespeople's skills, behavior, and performance. We will discuss training the sales force in much greater detail in Chapter 10.

The Motivation Component

Over the years, motivation has meant various, and often inconsistent, things in the literature, although some recent consensus seems to be emerging. For our purposes, **motivation** is viewed as the amount of effort the salesperson desires to expend on each activity or task associated with the job. These activities include calling on existing and potential new accounts, developing and delivering sales presentations, and filling out orders and reports.

The salesperson's motivation to expend effort on any task seems to be a function of the individual's (1) expectancies and (2) valences for performance. **Expectancies** are the salesperson's estimates of the probability that expending effort on a specific task will lead to improved performance on some specific dimension. For example, will increasing the number of calls made on potential new accounts lead to increased sales? **Valences for performance** are the salesperson's perceptions of the desirability of attaining improved performance on some dimension or dimensions. For example, does the salesperson find increased sales attractive?

A salesperson's valence for performance on a specific dimension, in turn, seems to be a function of his or her (1) instrumentalities and (2) valences for rewards. **Instrumentalities** are the salesperson's estimates of the probability that improved performance on that dimension will lead to increased attainment of particular rewards. For example, will increased sales lead to increased compensation? **Valences for rewards** are the salesperson's perceptions of the desirability of receiving increased rewards as a result of improved performance. Does the salesperson, say, find an increase in the compensation level attractive? A salesperson's expectancy, instrumentality, and valence perceptions can all affect the person's willingness to expend effort on a specific task or to engage in specific behaviors. Sales managers constantly try to find the right mix of motivation elements to direct salespeople in specific directions. The problem is particularly difficult because rewards that motivate one salesperson may not motivate another. There is the example of the manager at a leading consulting company in Chicago who gave his top performer a new mink coat. The only problem was that the individual did not wear fur. Rewarding the salesperson was a great idea, but the implementation of the reward led to problems for the sales manager. Moreover, what motivates a person at one stage in his or her career may not motivate the rep during some other period, as Leadership 6.1 indicates.

The salesperson's expectancy, instrumentality, and valence perceptions are not directly under the sales manager's control. But they can be influenced by things the sales manager does, such as how he or she supervises the salesperson or rewards the individual.[6] Since the salesperson's motivation strongly influences performance, the sales manager must be sensitive to the impact of various factors. These issues are explored more fully in the next chapter.

Leadership   Different Salespeople Require Different Drivers   6.1

Understanding salesperson performance is complicated. A number of factors can influence performance at any given moment. In addition, over time an individual's performance will fluctuate, meaning that attitudes, skills, and behaviors that lead to higher performance at one point will be different at another stage in the salesperson's career.

Managers must evaluate individual salespeople and identify drivers that motivate the person to do better at each stage in his or her career. As an example, when salespeople first start in their careers they are highly motivated, enthusiastic, and willing to "do whatever it takes." However, as they mature in their careers, the drivers that motivate them change—other things such as family become more important.

Successful sales managers are able to identify these drivers. One sales management expert identified six drivers that are often identified as keys to success in selling:

1. *Drive for a deeper meaning.* Really successful individuals always talk about a higher calling or meaning in their life that was important to their success. Put another way, focusing only on money and work will never sustain a person for his or her entire career. Indeed, research suggests that money becomes less and less of a motivating force as a person becomes more successful.

2. *Drive for joy.* There is a philosophy that speaks to "do what brings you joy." It's a simple but powerful idea. If you find fun in your work then work will be more fun. People can perceive when another person is friendly and happy. As a customer, if all things are equal, who would you rather buy from, a happy salesperson who enjoys what she does or a grumpy, sad individual who wishes he was doing something else?

3. *Drive for goals.* The new house, big vacation trip, or home entertainment system all represent specific goals that can be used as drivers, at least in the short run. Not all goals need to be related to personal objectives.

Salespeople can focus on professional goals such as being named "salesperson of the year." Goals are performance drivers because they allow salespeople to visualize what they are working hard to attain.

4. *Drive for team success.* Salespeople no longer operate "out in the cold." They are part of a team, and that team often has its own goals in addition to organizational goals. When salespeople learn that team goals are as important as individual goals, the result can be a performance driver. Salespeople learn that helping other people on the team (customer support, technical, logistics) ultimately benefits them because when the team succeeds the individual succeeds.

5. *Drive for leadership.* Salespeople can use leadership as an important performance driver. Successful salespeople invariably encourage managers to challenge their abilities and challenge them to be more productive. In some cases, it doesn't have to be a manager. Mentors can be performance drivers by teaching, coaching, encouraging, and even pushing the salesperson to do better.

6. *Drive for rewards.* Yes, it goes without saying that rewards are great performance drivers. The key is to never allow past rewards to substitute for future rewards. In other words, professional selling, more so than most professions, is about the future. The phrase "I used to be . . ." does not work as a driver of success in the future. It is important for the salesperson to enjoy success when it happens and use it as a springboard to future success.

Clearly, successful salespeople find the drivers that work for them. They are able to adopt new drivers as well as enhance and change old drivers. Sales managers must be aware of these drivers and identify which will work on each salesperson.

Source: Gschwandtner Gerhard, "Do You Have Enough Fuel to Win?" *SellingPower.com,* September, 2007.

The Personal, Organizational, and Environmental Variables Component

The sales performance model in Exhibit 6.1 suggests that personal, organizational, and environmental variables influence sales performance in two ways: (1) by directly facilitating or constraining performance and (2) by influencing and interacting with the other performance determinants, such as role perceptions and motivation.

Organizational Variables

Part One described how these variables can influence sales performance directly. The discussion of the organization of the sales force and the design of sales territories reviewed much of the evidence and logic supporting the relationship between performance and organizational factors. These factors include company advertising expenditures, the firm's current market share, and the degree of sales force supervision. There is a relationship between performance and environmental factors like territory potential, concentration of customers, the salesperson's workload, and the intensity of competition. The direct impact of the personal, organizational, and environmental variables on performance is thus rather clear.

Consider sales territory design, for example. Recent research suggests that as salespeople are more satisfied with their territory's design and structure, their performance increases. Including salespeople in the territory design process may seem intuitive, but managers sometimes find it difficult to balance the needs of the organization with the input of the salesperson. Sales managers have learned, however, that by including salespeople in the decision-making process on key issues such as territory design, the performance of the salesperson in that territory may increase over time.[7] The use of computer territory-mapping software has been helpful in enabling sales managers and salespeople to work together creating the most profitable and efficient territory configurations.[8] In the long term, this can lead to lower levels of role ambiguity and higher levels of job satisfaction as well as performance.

Personal Variables

A few studies have found significant relationships between personal and organizational variables—such as job experience, closeness of supervision, performance feedback, influence in determining standards, and span of control—and the amount of role conflict and ambiguity perceived by salespeople. Other studies related personal characteristics to variations in motivation by showing that salespeople's desires for different job-related rewards (e.g., pay, promotion) differ with such demographic characteristics as age, education, family size, career stage, or organizational climate.[9] Overall, though, many questions concerning the effects of personal, organizational, and environmental variables on the other determinants of sales performance remain unanswered. An important concern in recent years has been the effect of global sales responsibilities on individual salesperson performance. For example, are there unique issues faced by salespeople as they move into new international markets that affect their individual performance? Innovation 6.2 discusses this issue.

Personal Variables—Being a Good Corporate Citizen

As the role of salesperson changes from focusing on single transactions to building and maintaining a relationship with customers, salespeople have been asked to engage in a whole range of activities that can be described as **organizational citizenship behaviors (OCBs).** These focus on four basic types of behavior: (1) sportsmanship, (2) civic virtue, (3) conscientiousness, and (4) altruism. As Exhibit 6.2 demonstrates, these behaviors are directed at improving the overall effectiveness of the organization. Sportsmanship is an enthusiasm on the salesperson's part to endure suboptimal conditions without complaining to superiors or other salespeople (e.g., slow reimbursement of expenses or reduced administrative support). Civic virtue is a proactive behavior that includes making recommendations to management that will improve the overall performance of the organization (e.g., providing feedback from customers even though it may not be complimentary). Conscientiousness is the willingness to work beyond the "normal" expectations

Innovation Critical Global Sales Skills 6.2

Salespeople selling in a global environment need all the skills of a successful salesperson—and more. Increasingly, salespeople are being asked to build relationships with customers even as they move and expand around the world. At one time, servicing a global customer meant working primarily with the companies in the Fortune 1000. Today, however, small and medium companies are expanding into global markets, and salespeople must be able to work with those customers.

Several key skills are essential for salespeople to be successful selling in a global environment. They include

1. *Cultural sensitivity.* People are born and grow up in their own culture. It is natural for people to feel less comfortable in other cultures. However, successful selling in a global environment means having the ability to understand and adapt to different cultures. The ability to understand the selling process from the customer's perspective can help the salesperson adapt and adjust his or her presentation to the customer's unique cultural background.

2. *Flexibility.* Selling is about listening and responding to the customer's concerns, and this is magnified with global customers. Learning their business, responding to cultural differences, and making changes to a sales presentation based on the feedback from the customer

is essential to global sales success. Indeed, global salespeople know that being able to respond quickly to rapidly changing business and cultural conditions is often the difference between making and losing the sale.

3. *Patience.* In the United States, business relationships develop much more quickly than in the rest of the world. Salespeople are used to decisions based on the value proposition; however, in other cultures relationships develop more slowly and are based on a personal as well business connection.

4. *Technology friendly.* Sales in a global marketplace require the salesperson to be comfortable with technology. The cell phone, laptop, and wireless PDA are as important to the global salesperson today as the pen and paper of the twentieth century. Younger salespeople (Generation X and Y as well as younger baby boomers) are often the most comfortable using technology.

Although these are certainly not the only characteristics needed to be successful in a global environment, they are important for anyone considering a career in global sales.

Source: Frank Beeman, "Selling Around the World," *SellingPower.com,* October, 2007.

EXHIBIT 6.2

Components of organizational citizenship (sample items)

Source: This material drawn from Richard Netemeyer, James S. Boles, Daryl O. McKee, and Robert McMurrian, "An Investigation into the Antecedents of Organizational Citizenship Behaviors in Personal Selling Context," *Journal of Marketing,* July 1997, pp. 85–98; and Mel E. Schnake and Michael P. Dumler, "Levels of Measurement and Analysis Issues in Organizational Citizenship Behaviour Research," *Journal of Occupational and Organizational Psychology* 76, no. 3 (September 2003), pp. 283–301.

Sportsmanship

1. Consume a lot of time complaining about trivial problems (lack of sportsmanship).
2. Tend to make mountains out of molehills—make problems bigger than they are (lack of sportsmanship).
3. Always focus on what's wrong with my situation rather than the positive side of it (lack of sportsmanship).

Civic virtue

1. Keep up with developments in the company.
2. Attend functions that are not required but that help the company image.
3. Risk disapproval in order to express my beliefs about what is best for the company.

Conscientiousness

1. Conscientiously follow company regulations and procedures.
2. Turn in budgets, sales projections, expense reports, and so on earlier than required.
3. Return phone calls and respond to other messages and requests for information promptly.

Altruism

1. Help orient new agents even though it is not required.
2. Always ready to help or lend a helping hand to those around me.
3. Willingly give of my time to others.

of the job (e.g., working late or on weekends). Altruism refers to helping others in the organization (e.g., mentoring younger salespeople).

There is a growing understanding that salespeople who engage in these kinds of activities perform better on both outcome-based measures (sales volume) and behavior-based measures (customer satisfaction). Measuring salesperson performance will be discussed in Part Three. Engaging in activities that enhance the overall organization will most likely play an ever more important role in the salesperson's performance. As we have seen earlier in the text, the responsibilities of the salesperson are changing, and a greater focus on the organization and its relationship to customers is part of that process.

REWARDS

The performance model in Exhibit 6.1 indicates that the salesperson's job performance affects the rewards the representative receives. The relationship between performance and rewards is very complex, however. For one thing, firms often choose to evaluate and reward different dimensions of sales performance. Companies use a variety of performance based metrics to evaluate their salespeople including total sales volume, quota attainment, selling expenses, profitability of sales, new accounts generated, services provided to customers, performance of administrative duties, or some combination of these. Different firms are likely to use different dimensions. Even firms that use the same performance criteria are likely to have different relative emphases. A company can also bestow a variety of rewards for any given level of performance.

The model distinguishes between two broad types of rewards: extrinsic and intrinsic. **Extrinsic rewards** are those controlled and offered by people other than the salesperson, such as managers or customers. These include such things as pay, financial incentives, security, recognition, and promotion, rewards that are generally related to low-order human needs. **Intrinsic rewards** are those that salespeople primarily attain for themselves. They include such things as feelings of accomplishment, personal growth, and self-worth, all of which relate to high-order human needs.

As the model in Exhibit 6.1 suggests, salespeople's perceptions of rewards they will receive in return for various types of job performance, together with the value they place on those rewards, strongly influence their motivation to perform.

SATISFACTION

The **job satisfaction** of salespeople refers to all the characteristics of the job that representatives find rewarding, fulfilling, and satisfying, or frustrating and unsatisfying. As Exhibit 6.3 indicates, there are seven different dimensions to sales job satisfaction: (1) the job itself, (2) coworkers, (3) supervision, (4) company policies and support, (5) pay, (6) promotion and advancement opportunities, and (7) customers. Salespeople's total satisfaction with their jobs is a reflection of their satisfaction with each of these elements.[10]

How job satisfaction relates to motivation, performance, organizational citizenship behaviors, and turnover is a complicated issue. Chally interviewed individuals who left their organization and found they typically attribute their decision to leave to either supervision or career issues. People that find it difficult to get along with their managers often feel they can't take it any more and "get pushed" from their jobs. On the other hand, individuals dissatisfied because of career issues identify a combination of pay, promotion, and advancement opportunities within the company and "get pulled" to other employers. Thus, although job satisfaction is related to turnover, the relationship is complex and

EXHIBIT 6.3

Components of job satisfaction

Job Satisfaction Component	Sample Items
The job itself	My work is challenging. My work gives me a sense of accomplishment. My job is exciting.
Coworkers	My coworkers are selfish. My coworkers are intelligent. My coworkers are responsible.
Supervision	My sales manager is tactful. My sales manager really tries to get our ideas. My sales manager sees we have the things we need to do our job.
Company policies	Compared with other companies, company benefits are good. The company sales training is not carried out in a well-planned program. Management is progressive.
Pay	My income provides for luxuries. My compensation does not give me much incentive to increase my sales. My selling ability largely determines my earnings in this company.
Promotion	My opportunities for advancement are limited. Promotion in this company is based on ability. I have a good chance for a promotion.
Customers	My customers are fair. My customers blame me for problems over which I have no control. My customers respect my judgment.

involves variables within the company (supervision and advancement opportunities) as well as those external to the company (alternative jobs).

As Exhibit 6.1 suggests, the rewards received by a salesperson have a major impact on the individual's satisfaction with the job and the total work environment. The seven dimensions of satisfaction can be grouped, like rewards, into two major components: intrinsic and extrinsic. Extrinsic satisfaction is associated with the extrinsic rewards bestowed on the salesperson, such as satisfaction with pay, company policies and support, supervision, coworkers, chances for promotion, and customers. Intrinsic satisfaction is related to the intrinsic rewards the salesperson obtains from the job, such as satisfaction with the work itself and with the opportunities it provides for personal growth and accomplishment.

The amount of satisfaction salespeople obtain from their jobs is also influenced by their role perceptions.[11] Salespeople with high levels of conflict tend to be less satisfied than those who do not. So do those who experience great uncertainty in what is expected from them on the job.

Finally, a salesperson's job satisfaction is likely to affect the individual's motivation to perform, as suggested by the feedback loop in Exhibit 6.1. The relationship between satisfaction and motivation is, however, neither simple nor well understood. It is explored more fully in the next chapter.

As noted previously, the salesperson's role perceptions play a critical role in their overall performance. In the remainder of the chapter we will explore this variable in the model.

THE SALESPERSON'S ROLE PERCEPTIONS

The role component of the model has important implications for sales managers. Role perceptions affect salesperson performance in many ways. For example, feelings of ambiguity, conflict, and inaccurate role perceptions can cause psychological stress and job-related anxiety for salespeople. These, in turn, can lead to lowered performance. Fortunately, there are things the sales manager can do to minimize the negative consequences associated with role perceptions. The kind of salespeople that are hired, the way they are trained, the incentives used to motivate them, the criteria used to evaluate them, and the way they are supervised can all affect perceptions of role. These factors can also determine whether these perceptions are ambiguous, in conflict, or inaccurate. That is why the role components of the salesperson performance model are discussed in this chapter.

What makes understanding and managing role perceptions even more complicated is that not all the consequences of role ambiguity, role conflict, and role accuracy are negative. Eliminating ambiguity and conflict can reduce the challenge for a salesperson and actually limit long-term performance. The task for the sales manager is to create an environment that will stimulate and motivate the salesperson while reducing or at least minimizing the negative effects of role stress that are a natural part of selling.

STAGES IN DEVELOPING THE SALESPERSON'S ROLE

Every employee within the firm occupies a position to which a role is attached. This role represents the activities and behaviors that are to be performed by any person who occupies that position. The salesperson's role is defined through a three-step process.[12]

Stage 1: Role Partners Communicate Expectations

First, expectations and demands concerning how the salesperson should behave, together with pressures to conform, are communicated to the salesperson by members of that person's role set. The salesperson's role set consists of people with a vested interest in how the representative performs the job. These people include the individual's immediate superior, other executives in the firm, purchasing agents and other members of customers' organizations, and the salesperson's family. They all try to influence the person's behavior, either formally through organizational policies, operating procedures, and training programs, or informally through social pressures, rewards, and sanctions.

Stage 2: Salespeople Develop Perceptions

The second part of the role definition process involves the perceived role. This is salespeople's perceptions of the expectations and demands communicated by their role-set members. Salespeople perform according to what they think role-set members expect, even though their perceptions of those expectations may not be accurate. To really understand why salespeople perform the way they do, it is necessary to understand what salespeople think the members of the role set expect. At this stage of the role definition process, three factors can wreak havoc with a salesperson's job performance and mental well-being. As Exhibit 6.4 suggests, the salesperson may suffer from perceptions of role ambiguity, role conflict, or role inaccuracy.

EXHIBIT 6.4
Sales perceptions of the job

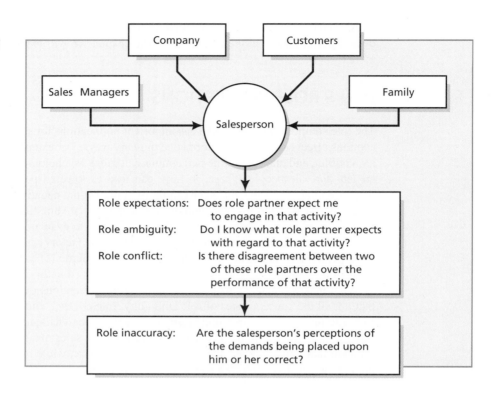

Perceived role ambiguity occurs when representatives do not think they have the necessary information to perform the job adequately. They feel uncertain about how to do a specific task, what the members of the role set expect in a particular situation, or how their performance is evaluated by members of the role set.

Perceived role conflict exists when a salesperson believes the role demands of two or more members of the role set are incompatible. A customer, for example, may demand unusually liberal credit terms or delivery schedules that are unacceptable to the salesperson's superiors. The representative's perception that it is not possible to simultaneously satisfy all members of the role set creates conflicting role forces and psychological conflict within the salesperson.

Perceived role inaccuracy arises when the salesperson's perceptions of the role partners' demands are inaccurate. Does the salesperson's idea about what the role partners desire correspond to their actual expectations? Role inaccuracy differs from role ambiguity in that, with role inaccuracy, the salesperson feels fairly certain about what should be done—except that the sales rep is wrong. It differs from role conflict in that the salesperson does not see any inconsistencies in that it is unrealized. The representative does not know that the perceptions held are inaccurate.

Stage 3: Salespeople Convert Perceptions into Behaviors

The final step in the role definition process involves the salesperson's conversion of these role perceptions into actual behavior. Both the salesperson's job behavior and psychological well-being can be affected if there are perceptions of role ambiguity or conflict or if these perceptions are inaccurate. There is a good deal of evidence, for example, that high levels of both perceived ambiguity and conflict are directly related to high mental anxiety and tension and low job satisfaction. Also, the salesperson's feelings of uncertainty and conflict and the actions taken to resolve them can have a strong impact on ultimate job performance.[13] At a minimum, the salesperson's performance is less likely to be consistent with management's expectations and desires when the representative is uncertain about what those expectations are, believes that the customers or family hold conflicting expectations, or has inaccurate perceptions of those expectations.

THE SALESPERSON'S ROLE IS VULNERABLE

Several characteristics of the salesperson's role make it particularly susceptible to role conflict, role ambiguity, and the development of inaccurate role perceptions:

1. Salespeople operate at the boundary of the firm.

2. A salesperson's performance affects the occupants of a large number of other positions.

3. The salesperson's role changes often, and the role itself is innovative.

Boundary Position

Salespeople are likely to experience more role conflict than other organization members because they occupy positions at the boundaries of their organization. Key members of each salesperson's role set—the customers—are in external organizations. As a result, the salesperson receives demands from organizations that have diverse goals, policies, and problems. Since each role partner (customers and the salesperson's own organization) wants the salesperson's behavior to be consistent with their own goals, the demands on the salesperson are diverse and often incompatible.

A customer, for example, may question the salesperson on the long-term commitment of the company to meet the needs of the customer. Recently, MCI representatives were questioned about the long-term viability of the company in light of accounting scandals and ethical lapses by top management. MCI representatives were told to be honest and explain to customers what the company was doing to earn back the customers' trust. The issue is to balance the amount of information given to the customer with the customer's legitimate concerns about the future ability of the company to meet existing product and customer service pledges.[14] The salesperson gets caught in the middle. To satisfy the demands of one role partner, the rep must deal with the concerns and demands of the other.

Another problem that arises from the salesperson's boundary position is that the role partners in one organization often don't appreciate the expectations and demands made by role partners in another. A customer, for example, may not know company policies or the constraints under which the salesperson must operate. Or the salesperson's superiors may formulate company policies without understanding the particular needs of some customers. Even a role partner who is aware of another's demands may not understand the reasoning behind them and consider them arbitrary or illegitimate.

A boundary position also increases the likelihood that the salesperson will experience role ambiguity or form inaccurate perceptions. Contact with many of the salesperson's role partners, (manager, other salespeoples) though regular, is probably infrequent and often brief. Under such conditions, it is easy for the salesperson to feel uncertain about what the company expects and how well he or she is performing.

The "Remote" Sales Force

Increasingly, salespeople operate from remote offices (often their home) and spend very little time in their company's offices. As they operate on the boundary of the organization role stress can occur leading to lower performance over time. While cost considerations are certainly a factor in the trend toward moving salespeople out of company offices, there are also potential benefits in improved customer relationship management as salespeople seek to get closer to the customer. Not surprisingly, however, being separated from the organization can lead to higher levels of alienation and isolation from the company. The end result of these negative attitudes can be lower levels of satisfaction and performance.

Recent research suggests that managers can play a significant role in mitigating the negative effect of a salesperson being located outside the company office. The key is for the manager to remain in contact with the salesperson, assuring them they are still a vital part of the organization. In addition, salespeople need to get feedback on their performance and how they can continue to improve their selling skills. Many companies, including Johnson & Johnson, Hewlett-Packard, and others, have salespeople who work remotely from their homes with great results, and there are valid reasons for companies to encourage salespeople to work away from the office.[15]

Large Role Set

The salespeople's role set includes many diverse individuals. The representative may sell to hundreds of customers, and each expects his or her own particular needs and requirements to be satisfied. In addition, people within the firm rely on the salesperson to execute company policies in dealings with customers and for the ultimate success of the firm's revenue-producing efforts. The specific design-performance criterion a product is supposed to satisfy, and the delivery and credit terms the salesperson quotes, can directly influence people in the engineering, production, and credit departments, for example. All these people may hold definite beliefs about how the salesperson should perform the job, and they will all pressure the individual to conform to their expectations.

The large number of people from diverse departments and organizations who depend on the salesperson increases the probability that at least some role demands will be incompatible. It also increases the probability that the salesperson's perceptions of some demands will be inaccurate and that the rep will be uncertain about others.

Selling in a Team

The complex nature of the relationship between company and customer has created a need for salespeople to work in teams that include specialists from many parts of the company (technical, manufacturing, logistics, and others). As a result, the role of salesperson has evolved in many cases from one of selling to the customer to one of managing the relationship between the company and the customer. Companies as diverse as Sun Microsystems, 3M, Siemens, and Sony have created sales teams managed by salespeople. In addition, in-house salespeople and customer service representatives create additional contact with the customer that often requires greater coordination with the salesperson. This can create role conflict for salespeople as they deal with the expectations and demands of many individuals within the sales team and the organization as a whole.

Innovative Role

The salesperson's role is frequently innovative because it is often necessary to produce new solutions to nonroutine problems. This is particularly true when the salesperson is selling highly technical products or engineered systems designed to the customer's specifications. The salesperson selling standardized products must also display creativity in matching the company's offerings to the customer's particular needs. With potential new accounts, this is an extremely difficult, but critical, task. Leadership 6.3 indicates another way in which

Leadership   Ethical Salespeople . . . Unethical Customers   6.3

Increasingly, salespeople are being put in difficult positions not by their own actions or those of management but rather by their customers. Corporate scandals such as those involving WorldCom, Enron, Global Crossing, and others have raised a number of concerns about the ethics of everyone in the organization.

Unfortunately, some customers continue to make unfair, unreasonable, and even illegal requests of salespeople. Many companies such as Dell, CNL Investments, and others have posted their ethics policies online and made them available to all their customers. They go on record as saying they (management, salespeople, everyone connected with the organization) will adhere to the highest ethical standards and will support ethical decisions by their salespeople.

Other companies have invested in ethical sales training to help educate their salespeople about the importance of ethics. IBM offers specific ethical training to their sales forces. This training is designed to provide salespeople with the tools and support to make better ethical decisions in the field.

It is critical for salespeople to know that as even though they operate on the boundary of the organization they are expected to adhere to the company's ethical standards. They also need to know they will be supported by management if they are asked to choose between an ethical decision and a customer's request. Finally, they need the tools to be able to make good ethical decisions. This begins with a clear understanding of the company's ethics policies and a process for handling ethical issues when they arise in the field.

salespeople can be caught in the middle between the demands of their customers and the expectations of their employers.

Occupants of innovative roles tend to experience more conflict than other organization members because they must have flexibility to perform their roles well. Such people must have the authority to develop and carry out innovative solutions. This need for flexibility often brings the salesperson into conflict with the company's standard operating procedures and the expectations of organization members who want to maintain the status quo. The production manager, for example, may frown on customized products because of increased production costs and negative effect on schedules, although marketing, and particularly the salespeople, might desire flexible production schedules that allow for greater customer input and more custom-designed products.

Occupants of innovative roles also tend to experience more role ambiguity and inaccurate role perceptions than occupants of noninnovative roles because they frequently face unusual situations where they have no standard procedures or past experience to guide them. Consequently, they are often uncertain about how their role partners expect them to proceed. The perceptions they do have are more likely to be inaccurate because of the nonroutine nature of the task. The flexibility that is needed to fulfill an innovative role can consequently have unforeseen, negative consequences.

Innovation in Communication Affects the Sales Role

The innovative nature of the sales role is changing very quickly. Salespeople interface with customers in a variety of new ways and customers connect with companies using the Internet and other electronic applications. As customers become "wired" to their suppliers, they expect even greater service, placing new demands on salespeople to know not only their own products but all the issues and concerns of their customers.

Cisco Systems, for example, created a B2B direct-order Web site for customers. Initially, salespeople expressed a great deal of concern about how such a site would affect their responsibilities. They experienced role conflict as their perception of the salesperson's job was changing based on the customer's ability to order directly from the Web site. However, once they understood the site actually represented an opportunity to engage in greater problem-solving and value-added activities, performance of the sales force went up dramatically.

ROLE CONFLICT AND AMBIGUITY

In discussing the causes and consequences of the various role perceptions, it is useful to separate the concepts of role conflict and role ambiguity, on the one hand, and inaccurate role perceptions, on the other.

Common Expectations and Key Areas of Conflict and Ambiguity

Different sales jobs require different tasks and place different demands on salespeople. The senior account executive for Liz Claiborne selling dresses to a head buyer at Macy's Department Stores will likely be most concerned with follow-up service to make sure the reorders for styles, colors, or sizes arrive in time for the current selling season. On the other hand, the salesperson for Baldor Electric Company Baldor selling oil pumps to a refinery is most concerned with making sure the equipment can handle the load, chemicals, and other harsh conditions to which it will be subjected. Thus, it is next to impossible to develop one set of expectations common to all sales jobs. Even firms within the same industry often place different demands on their salespeople. Nevertheless, the empirical evidence prompts several major conclusions:[16]

1. *Different role partners emphasize different types of expectations.* Salespeople see some role partners as being concerned with *what they do*—company superiors focus on the functional aspects of the job such as handling back charges and adjustments, expediting orders, and supervising installations. Others are more concerned with *how they do it*—family members are concerned about the salesperson's hours of work and customers are interested in the ability of the salesperson to get along with them.

2. *Perceived role expectations are consistent among salespeople.* Salespeople are consistent in their company's expectations as communicated by company superiors and sales managers. On the other hand, salespeople do not perceive similar role expectations regarding the demands of family members. These demands are much more likely to differ from salesperson to salesperson. This suggests that no matter what the company expects in hours of work, relations with customers, travel, and the like, a substantial number of its salespeople are likely to be in conflict with their family's expectations. That is becoming an increasingly serious problem for today's workers, as Leadership 6.4 indicates.

3. *Most business-to-business salespeople are plagued by ambiguity concerning some aspect of their job.* For example, salespeople indicate they are often uncertain about company policies, how company superiors are evaluating their performance, or what their sales managers expect. In comparison, very few are uncertain about the expectations or evaluations of customers or family members. This suggests customers and family members communicate their role expectations more effectively than company superiors do. Perhaps this is not surprising since a representative faces customers and family members almost daily, whereas company policies are communicated through infrequent sales meetings, e-mails, and other less effective means.

Leadership   Finding the Balance between Work and Family   6.4

As the demands of customers, management, and competitive selling environment continue to increase, finding the right balance between work and family becomes more difficult. Travel and entertaining are part of selling, and technology enables managers and customers to be in contact with salespeople all the time. It should not be surprising to learn that as the demands of the job increase, the conflict between work and family grows as well. In addition, recent research suggests that a trend toward working more hours continues, with men working almost 50 hours a week and women working nearly 44 hours.

Employers worry about productivity problems when work and family demands create conflict for an individual. A recent survey by the Families and Work Institute indicates that family bears a heavy burden. Two-thirds of the respondents indicated they didn't have enough time with their children, and almost that many (63 percent) felt that they were not able to spend enough time with their spouses. More than half the respondents felt they needed more time for themselves and were overworked in the last three months. In general, these same employees

- Experienced more conflict between the demands of home and work than in the past.

- Got less sleep.

- Experienced higher levels of stress.

The increased use of technology that enables employees, such as salespeople, to be in almost constant contact with the office and customers has also led to increases in work-related stress and conflict between job and home. Nearly 40 percent (38 percent) of the employees who indicated they are heavy users of technology reported being overworked. Indeed, there is growing feeling among employees that they are unnecessarily accessible. Among this group over half (51 percent) believe they are overworked and experience higher levels of job related stress.

All of this leads to some serious negative consequences for employers. More than 40 percent of employees who feel they are overworked also reported being angry with their employers often or very often. Nearly half (49 percent) indicated they were going to look for employment elsewhere in the next year. These two outcomes can have very negative consequences for sales organizations, as the salesperson represents the primary connection to the customer.

Though these are serious problems for employers, families are paying an even higher price. More than a quarter (26 percent) of the respondents indicated they are often or very often not in as good a mood as they would like when the get home at night. In addition, nearly one-third (28 percent) report they often or very often lack enough energy to do things with their families.

The findings, which echo those of similar studies by the institute, have major implications. One key finding is summarized as follows,

> Of particular concern are the negative spillover effects that demanding and hectic jobs can have on the quality of workers' personal lives and well being. This [negative job] spillover is reflected in high stress, poor coping, bad moods, and insufficient time and energy for people who are personally important, creating "problems" that, in turn, spill over into work and impair job performance. (p. 13, Executive Summary NSCW study)

Source: Ellen Galinsky, James T. Bond, Stacy S. Kim, Lois Backon, Erin Brownfield, and Kelly Sakai, "Overwork in America: When the Way We Work Becomes Too Much," Families and Work Institute, 2004. Ellen Galinsky, Stacy S. Kim, and James T. Bond, "Feeling Overworked: When Work Becomes Too Much," Families and Work Institute, 2001; "National Study of the Changing Workforce" (Executive Summary), Families and Work Institute, 1997.

4. *Most salespeople perceive conflicts between some company policies or expectations and their customers' demands.* Customers are usually seen as demanding more from their salesperson, more services, more honesty, more price concessions, and so forth. Sales managers and other company executives are seen as demanding that the salesperson hold down selling expenses and customer concessions. Most salespeople believe that their company superiors and customers expect them to travel, work flexible hours, and be available to customers in the evenings and on weekends. Unfortunately, they

also believe these expectations conflict with the desires of their families. Although job–family conflicts are not unique to salespeople, their pervasiveness in the sales force should be recognized as a major influence on job satisfaction and performance.

Consequences of Conflict and Ambiguity

Most people experience occasional role conflict and ambiguity. In small doses, role conflict and ambiguity may be good for the individual and the organization. When there are no disagreements and no uncertainty associated with a role, people can become so comfortable in the position that they constantly strive to preserve the status quo. Some role stress, therefore, can lead to useful adaptation and change. In sum, there is a level of hostility below which conflict and ambiguity may be benign but above which they will be negative. Excessive role stress can have dysfunctional consequences, both psychological and behavioral, for the individual and the organization, as Exhibit 6.5 indicates. Consider first the psychological consequences.

Psychological Consequences

When a salesperson perceives that role partners have conflicting expectations about how the job should be performed, the salesperson becomes the "person in the middle." How can they satisfy the demands of one role partner without incurring the wrath or disappointment of others? Take, for example, the customer-service representatives at Verizon Communications. A new performance evaluation program placed a great deal of emphasis on selling new products and services to customers who called in with questions (and often problems). Salespeople felt they had to put the sales function ahead of helping customers with problems and questions. Ultimately, they saw their role as problem solving and providing service to customers, while the company viewed them as salespeople. This situation can produce psychological conflict, which is uncomfortable for the individual. Job tensions

EXHIBIT 6.5   Causes and consequences of a salesperson's job perceptions

increase, and the salesperson tends to worry more about conditions and events at work than usual. The salesperson's overall feelings of anxiety increase, and the rep is likely to become less satisfied with role partners, the company, and the job.[17]

Perceived role ambiguity can have similar negative consequences. When salespeople feel they lack the information necessary to perform the job adequately, or they don't know what role partners expect of them, they lose confidence in their ability to perform the sales role successfully. Salespeople tend to worry a great deal about whether they are doing the right thing and about how role partners will react to their performance. They may also lose confidence in role partners and blame them for failing to communicate their expectations and evaluations adequately. Like conflict, then, perceived role ambiguity is likely to increase a salesperson's mental anxiety and decrease job satisfaction.[18]

Although both conflict and ambiguity affect job satisfaction negatively, they do so somewhat differently. Perceived role conflict primarily affects extrinsic job satisfaction but has little or no effect on the intrinsic satisfactions salespeople derive from the job. Salespeople's ability to obtain extrinsic rewards, such as more pay, a promotion, praise, and recognition, is influenced by role partners. Therefore, conflicts among the expectations and demands of those role partners not only make it more difficult for salespeople to satisfy their demands but also jeopardize the salesperson's ability to earn desired extrinsic rewards. On the other hand, such conflicts may not restrain their ability to obtain intrinsic satisfactions from the job. Even when two or more role partners cannot agree on how reps should perform, salespeople may still gain a sense of accomplishment from working or improving personal abilities.

Unlike perceived conflict, ambiguity has a negative impact on the intrinsic components of salespeople's job satisfaction as well as the extrinsic components.[19] When salespeople are uncertain about how they should be doing the job, whether they are doing it right, and how others are evaluating their performance, they are likely to lose self-confidence, and their self-esteem suffers. Ambiguity, therefore, reduces the ability to obtain intrinsic rewards and satisfactions from the job. Similarly, if salespeople are uncertain about how role partners are evaluating their performance, they become uncertain about their chances for promotion or pay increases. Finally, salespeople are likely to be dissatisfied with role partners who fail to make clear their expectations and evaluations, thus causing emotional discomfort in the sales force.

Behavioral Consequences

Perceived role conflict and ambiguity can produce dysfunctional behavior consequences among the sales force. It is naive to think that a happy worker is invariably a productive worker, but evidence collected from a variety of occupations suggests that a worker's satisfaction influences job behavior. For instance, a negative relationship consistently appears between job satisfaction and absenteeism and employee turnover. Low satisfaction is also related to turnover among salespeople, although the relationship is moderated by economic conditions and the availability of alternative jobs.[20]

Another relationship that appears in studies of other occupations is a positive correlation between satisfaction and performance, although there is controversy over the nature of the relationship. Some argue that high satisfaction leads to good performance; others argue that good performance makes workers more satisfied with their jobs. The available sales management literature seems to suggest a salesperson's job satisfaction is directly related to performance on the job and that conflict and ambiguity are negatively related to sales performance.[21] Role ambiguity and role conflict even affect whether sales managers and salespeople agree on how well the salesperson is doing the job.[22]

Managing Conflict and Ambiguity in a Salesperson

Given that conflict and ambiguity produce dysfunctional psychological and behavioral consequences for salespeople, the next question is: Can sales management do anything to hold conflicts and ambiguities at a reasonable level or help the salesperson deal with them when they occur? Evidence suggests that experienced salespeople perceive less conflict than less-experienced representatives.[23] Perhaps this is because salespeople who experience a great deal of conflict become dissatisfied and quit, whereas those who stay on the job do not perceive much conflict.

On the other hand, salespeople may learn with experience how to deal with conflict. They may learn demands that initially appear to be in conflict turn out to be compatible or they learn how to resolve conflicts so they are no longer stressful. Finally, salespeople may build up psychological defense mechanisms to screen out conflicts and ease the tension. If these hypotheses are correct, sales training programs can prepare new salespeople to deal with conflicts they will encounter on the job.

Perceived role conflict also seems to be affected by how closely salespeople are supervised. When sales managers structure and define their roles, salespeople seem to experience more conflict. Perhaps close supervision decreases flexibility in dealing with diverse role expectations. Another way to reduce role conflict, then, is to give salespeople a greater voice in what they do and how they do it.

There also seem to be things management can do to reduce role ambiguity. It also depends on experience, so sales training can help salespeople cope with it. Perhaps more importantly, it depends on the manager's supervisory style. Less ambiguity is experienced when salespeople are closely supervised and have some influence over the standards used to control and evaluate their performance.[24] Closely supervised salespeople are more aware of the expectations and demands of their supervisors, and inconsistent behaviors can be more quickly brought to their attention.

Similarly, salespeople who have input in determining the standards by which they are evaluated are more familiar with those standards, which tends to reduce role ambiguity. One direct way of affecting the closeness with which salespeople feel supervised is by altering the sales manager's span of control by changing the number of people reporting directly to the manager. An increase in the span of control tends to increase salespeople's perceived role ambiguity. Reducing it tends to allow closer supervision, which tends to make job-related issues clearer to salespeople.[25]

Close supervision can thus be a two-edged sword. While it can reduce ambiguity, supervision that is too close can increase a salesperson's role conflict and job dissatisfaction because the salesperson may no longer feel there is enough latitude to deal effectively with the customer or enough creativity to service the account. The problem is particularly acute when sales managers use coercion and threats to direct the salespeople under them.[26] Sales managers must walk a very fine line in how closely and by what means they supervise the people under them.

ROLE ACCURACY

The role component of the model contains three variables: role conflict, role ambiguity, and role accuracy. It is appropriate to highlight role accuracy separately for two reasons. First, role accuracy can be viewed both generally and from the standpoint of specific linkages. When it is viewed generally, its impact and antecedents are similar to those for role conflict and ambiguity. But additional insight is gained by looking at role accuracy with respect to specific linkages. Second, role accuracy specifically influences the motivation component of the model, and to understand role accuracy, it is necessary to assess its impact on the salesperson's motivation to perform.[27]

Nature of Role Accuracy

A salesperson has accurate role perceptions when he or she correctly understands what role partners expect when performing the job. Role accuracy involves such considerations as whether salespeople correctly think they can negotiate on price, promise shorter delivery times than normal, and handle back charges and adjustments for customers.

More specifically, role inaccuracy arises when the salesperson incorrectly perceives the relationships between activities and performance dimensions, or between performance dimensions and rewards. In terms of the model in Exhibit 6.1, this type of role inaccuracy relates to the motivation component and, more particularly, to the expectancy and instrumentality estimates. For example, a salesperson who does not accurately perceive how making more calls leads to more sales has linkage role inaccuracy with respect to this expectancy, or activity–performance, linkage. If the rep does not accurately perceive the relationship between more sales and a promotion, the person has linkage role inaccuracy with respect to this instrumentality, or performance–reward, linkage.

There is great potential for this type of specific linkage role inaccuracy among salespeople because all three components—activities, performance dimensions, and rewards— are multidimensional. There are consequently a great many linkages, which increases the chances a salesperson will have inaccurate perceptions about at least some of them. Some common activities in which salespeople are expected to engage, the criteria used to evaluate their performance, and the rewards typically used to motivate them are listed in Exhibit 6.6.[28] Not all salespeople in every firm are expected to engage in all these activities,

EXHIBIT 6.6   **Common activities, performance criteria, and rewards for industrial salespeople**

Activities*	
80s	**Now**
1. *Selling*	*Selling*
Plan selling activities	Plan selling activities
Qualify prospects	Qualify prospects
Present sales presentation	Present sales presentation
Handle objections	Handle objections
2. *Working with orders*	*Working with orders*
Correct, expedite orders	Correct, and expedite orders
3. *Servicing the product*	*Servicing the product*
Supervise installation	Supervise installation
Train customers	Train customers
4. *Information management*	*Information management*
Receive feedback from clients	Receive feedback from clients
Provide technical information to clients	Provide technical information to clients
Provide feedback to superiors	Provide feedback to superiors
5. *Servicing the account*	*Servicing the account*
Assist with inventory control	Assist with inventory control
Handle local advertising	Handle local advertising

(continued)

EXHIBIT 6.6 Common activities, performance criteria, and rewards for industrial salespeople *(concluded)*

Activities*

80s	Now
6. *Conference/meetings* Attend local/regional/national sales meetings	*Conference/meetings* Attend local/regional/national sales meetings
7. *Training/recruiting* Identify, recruit, and train new salespeople	*Training/recruiting* Identify, recruit, and train new salespeople
8. *Entertaining* Entertain clients consistent with company policies	*Entertaining* Entertain clients consistent with company policies
9. *Travel* Travel as required by customer demand	*Travel* Travel as required by customer demand
10. *Work with channel members* Maintain relationships with distributors NEW	*Work with channel members* Maintain relationships with distributors *Relationship management* Build relationships with customers Maintain relationship with current customers Networking inside customer operations
NEW	*Team management* Managing team interactions with customers Mentoring new salespeople inside sales team
NEW	*Technology management* Communication with customers using new technologies Incorporate new communication skills consistent with customer demands

Performance Criteria

Total sales volume and volume increase over last year
Degree of quota attainment
Selling expenses and their decrease versus last year
Profitability of sales and their increase over last year
New accounts generated
Improvement in service provided to customers
Customer satisfaction of sales relationship

Rewards

Pay
  Increased take-home pay
  Increased bonuses and other financial incentives
Promotion
  Higher level job
  Better territory
Nonfinancial incentives (contests, travel, etc.)
Special recognition (clubs, awards, etc.)
Job security
Feeling of self-fulfillment
Feeling of worthwhile accomplishment
Opportunity for personal growth and accomplishment
Opportunity for independent thought and action

*The list of activities in which salespeople commonly engage is developed from the articles by William C. Moncrief "Selling Activity and Sales Position Taxonomies for Industrial Salespeople," *Journal of Marketing Research* 23 (August 1986), pp. 261–70; William C. Moncrief, "Ten Key Activities and Industrial Salespeople," *Industrial Marketing Management* 15 (November 1986) pp. 309–17; and Greg W. Marshall, William C. Moncrief, and Felicia G. Lassk, "The Current State of Sales Force Activities," *Industrial Marketing Management* 28 (1999), pp. 87–98.

nor are they evaluated on each performance dimension. Neither do all firms provide the same rewards to the same degree. This makes it very difficult to discuss linkage inaccuracy in a way that is useful to sales managers in general. One has to get down to the level of the individual firm and the linkages operating there to discuss the concept.

In addition, the many roles of the salesperson change over time. As noted in Exhibit 6.6, salespeople are being asked to communicate with customers in new ways, employing new technologies. Equally important is the realization that in many cases the salesperson will no longer be the only person communicating with the customer. Indeed, the salesperson may only be one individual in a complex relationship that consists of technical specialists, customer service representatives, and others who interact with the customer on a regular basis. Salespeople become "relationship managers" in addition to holding the traditional roles associated with selling.

Summary

This chapter, the first on implementing the sales program, presented a model of salesperson performance. In addition, the chapter examined the critical component of the model, the salesperson's role perceptions.

The model suggests that a salesperson's performance is a function of five basic factors: (1) role perceptions, (2) aptitude, (3) skill level, (4) motivation, and (5) personal, organizational, and environmental variables. There is substantial interaction among the components. A salesperson who is deficient with respect to any one could be expected to perform poorly.

The role perceptions of the salesperson are defined largely through the expectations, demands, and pressures communicated by his or her role partners. Role partners are people both within and outside the company who are affected by the way the salesperson performs the job. Three major variables create an individual's role perceptions: role accuracy, perceived role ambiguity, and perceived role conflict. Role accuracy refers to the degree to which the salesperson's perceptions of his or her role partners' demands are accurate. Perceived role ambiguity occurs when the salesperson does not believe he or she has the information to perform the job adequately. Perceived role conflict arises when a salesperson believes that the demands of two or more of his or her role partners are incompatible.

The role of salesperson is particularly susceptible to feelings of ambiguity and conflict and to forming inaccurate perceptions. There are three reasons for this: (1) It is at the boundary of the firm, (2) the salesperson's relevant role set includes many other people both within and outside the firm, and (3) the position of sales rep often requires a good deal of innovativeness.

Aptitude refers to the salesperson's innate ability to do the job and includes such things as physical factors, mental abilities, and personality characteristics. Aptitude is a constraint on the person's ability to perform the sales job given an adequate understanding of the role to be performed, motivation, and learned skills and the absence of other constraints.

Skill level refers to the person's learned proficiency at performing the necessary tasks. It is different from aptitude. Whereas aptitude consists of relatively enduring personal abilities, skills are proficiency levels that can change rapidly with learning and experience.

Motivation refers to the effort the salesperson desires to expend on each activity or task associated with the job such as calling on potential new accounts or developing sales presentations. The motivation to expend effort on any particular task depends on (1) expectancy—the salesperson's estimate of the probability that expending effort on the task will lead to improved performance on some dimension—and (2) valence for performance—the salesperson's perception of the desirability of improving performance on that dimension. The valence for performance on any dimension is, in turn, a function of (1) instrumentality—the salesperson's estimate of the probability that improved performance on that dimension will lead to increased attainment of particular rewards—and (2) valence for rewards—the salesperson's perception of the desirability of receiving increased rewards as a result of improved performance.

The personal, organizational, and environmental variables influence sales performance in two ways: (1) by directly facilitating or constraining performance and (2) by influencing and interacting with other performance determinants, such as role perceptions and motivation.

The performance of the salesperson affects the rewards the individual receives. There are two basic types of rewards: extrinsic rewards, which are controlled and bestowed by people other than the salesperson, and intrinsic rewards, which are those that people primarily attain for themselves.

The rewards received by a salesperson have a major impact on the individual's satisfaction with the job and the total work environment. Satisfaction can also be of two types. Intrinsic satisfaction is related to the intrinsic rewards the salesperson obtains from the job, such as satisfaction with the work and the opportunities it provides for personal growth and sense of accomplishment. Extrinsic satisfaction is associated with the extrinsic rewards bestowed on the salesperson, such as pay, chances for promotion, and supervisory and company policies.

Key Terms

role accuracy
perceived role conflict
perceived role ambiguity
motivation
expectancies

valences for performance
instrumentalities
valences for rewards
organizational citizenship
  behavior (OCB)

extrinsic rewards
intrinsic rewards
job satisfaction

Breakout Questions

1. The president of Part-I-Tyme, manufacturer of salty snack foods, was dismayed over the dismal sales results reported for the first six months. A new product, a deluxe cookie, had been taste tested and consumers' responses were very positive. Part-I-Tyme's sales force consisted of 500 individuals in 25 sales districts around the country. They called on buyers for grocery chains and large restaurant chains. Over the years, the company had developed an excellent reputation with their customers. Part-I-Tyme's president was convinced the product would be well received by the company's customers and ultimately by consumers. However, it was obvious that something was wrong. The sales force had not really been enthusiastic about the product. How would you determine the nature of the problem? Can you use the model of salesperson performance in this situation?

2. Although many different kinds of tests exist, their ability to predict sales performance has been weak. How do you account for this?

3. A sales representative for the High Speed Technologies is faced with a demand from an important customer that is in direct conflict with company policies. The customer wants several product modifications with no change in price. What can the sales rep do to handle this conflict?

4. The sales force at Fire Protection Systems, a manufacturer of fire prevention systems for industrial applications, have been told they will now have to sell small fire extinguishers to the retail market. They have never sold in the retail market, and the company is going up against much larger competitors that have sold in that market for many years. What role problems are likely to occur?

5. Maria Gomez-Simpson, a customer service rep with GRA–JUS Associates, spends considerable time traveling to various customer offices. As a result, she often arrives home late. Maria asked her manager if she could rearrange her Thursday work schedule to allow her to attend an evening class at a local college. Which of the following statements best reflects how to manage the conflict created by Maria's request?

    a. "Since we're talking about only one night, go ahead, sign up for the course, and we'll work out the details."

    b. "We need to discuss this first to see if there is some way you can be back most of the Thursdays in time for your course and still get the job done as well."

    c. "We know that you get home late on certain days, but it is part of the job. Maybe you can take the course some other time."

Leadership Challenge: Tough Choices

Michael Yardley was worried as he hung up from a phone call with Megan Barnes, the most promising salesperson at Spring Board Technologies (SBT). Michael had hired Megan out of college only four years ago, and already Megan had distinguished herself as one of the best salespeople in the company. This was saying something as SBT had a worldwide sales force of more than 2,000 salespeople. Michael had already promoted Megan to senior sales account manager. In addition, Melissa Hendrix, executive vice president of sales for the company, had made it known to Michael and Megan that she was well aware of her performance and had targeted her for a fast track in the company.

Now Michael had just learned Megan was going to have her first baby, and he was having serious doubts about her future. Megan had married her college sweetheart soon after graduation. He was an engineer, and they had both come to enjoy the benefits of two incomes. Megan's sales success had surprised her. Her natural ability coupled with a focus on relationship selling had given her the opportunity to build significant partnerships with some of SBT's largest customers. At the same time, Megan had communicated to Michael that, at some point, she wanted to have a family. Megan was experiencing a great deal of role conflict. She wanted to take the time to start a family (she had thought she would take five years off while the baby was getting ready to start school) but also wanted to continue her career at SBT.

At the same time, Michael was concerned about losing his star salesperson, dealing with customer disappointment, and having to tell Melissa that a person she had felt was on the fast track at the company may be leaving to start a family. He knew there were no easy answers and was considering the options for Megan as well as SBT.

Questions

1. If you were Megan, what would you do and why? What factors should most influence her decision? Is this an either/or choice?

2. If you were Michael, how would you handle this situation? What advice would you offer to Megan?

3. If you were Melissa, would you get involved in Megan's decision? Why or why not?

Role Play: New England Green Sox

Situation

Jerry Momper loves sports. He just finished up a degree in sports marketing at Pinnacle University in the Northeast. And to his great pleasure, he is in his first month of his dream job: a salesperson (the title is account manager) for small and midsized accounts for the New England Green Sox. In general, he will be responsible for developing new customer relationships with firms in New England and the surrounding area, as well as working on enhancing relationships with firms that are already loyal customers of the Green Sox. His "product" is blocks of seats, special boxes, and special events at historic Fenway Park, as well as Green Sox promotions that can be held at various places of business as a marketing campaign for the customer's business.

The problem (actually it's more of an opportunity) is, this is a brand new position. Over the years, the team has had a major account position, similar to the one Jerry now has but more focused on big companies that might want to send a lot of people to games. The major account manager had also worked with smaller firms as needed, but Jerry's position allows the team to better tap into a lucrative market in the area. The person who continues to hold the major account manager position is Rex Wicke, a great guy about 40 years old who has been with the team in one administrative job or another for 19 years. Rex played ball in the minors for a short time and doesn't have any college experience. Rex is something of an icon in sports marketing in the New England area, and Jerry knows he can learn a lot from him.

Jerry has decided to set up a meeting to get a better feel for some important aspects of his new role at the Green Sox and more specifically some of the activities he may be asked to perform. Having had a sales management course at Pinnacle University, Jerry knows a lot about salesperson performance from the class but has never worked as a salesperson before.

Characters in the Role Play

Jerry Momper, small and medium account manager, New England Green Sox

Rex Wicke, major account manager, New England Green Sox

Assignment

Break into pairs, with one student playing each character. It doesn't matter what the actual gender mix of your pair is. Before you stage the meeting between Jerry and Rex, work separately to come up with a set of role issues you each believe will be important to discuss for Jerry's benefit in the new job. Also, jot down some of the more important sales activities you anticipate will be part of the new position. Then get together and role-play the meeting between Jerry and Rex. Share your ideas—especially pay attention to potential sources of role problems. To the extent possible, come to agreement between the two of you about some performance criteria and rewards that might be appropriate for this new position.

Minicase: Vaughn Manufacturing Company

Vaughn Manufacturing is a Detroit-based automobile parts manufacturer. Specifically, it manufactures crankshafts, a key component of the engine, and sells directly to automobile manufacturers (also known as original equipment manufacturers, or OEMs) like Ford or General Motors, as opposed to selling to engine manufacturers. While selling directly to OEMs grants Vaughn a higher "Tier 1" status in the automobile business and direct access to the biggest players, it also means Vaughn has very little leverage in negotiating with the much larger OEMs.

Detroit is by far the largest and most important sales territory for Vaughn, and its district sales manager is Keith Horton, a 26-year company veteran. Horton personally recruited several members of his team, who he calls "young guns," and takes great pride that the team's sales volume is consistently the highest in the company. Horton's managerial style can best be described as aggressive, and he often insults or pressures his salespeople in order to increase their performance. In his words, "auto-manufacturing is a cutthroat business, and I want my salespeople to be tough. I want to be the toughest thing that my salespeople ever face, so that customers will seem like pussycats by comparison." Although he closely watches the performance of the salespeople, the company provides little training or specific sales guidance. He feels that salespeople learn toughness by figuring things out for themselves.

The newest salesperson on the team is Raul Sajak, a 23-year-old recent college graduate. Raul is highly intelligent, graduating at the top of his class, sensitive, and extraordinarily good with relating to people. Although he could have worked in nearly any business, he wanted to join Vaughn, in part, because he was a successful retail automobile salesman throughout college and loved doing it. He is married and is preparing for the arrival of a new baby.

Although Raul started strong in his first year at Vaughn, he has struggled recently, being well below quota in nearly every sales category for the last quarter of the fiscal year. As the automobile market becomes more competitive, customers have been more difficult, making sales negotiations more complex, and creating further challenges for Raul. Vaughn's attorneys require that Raul and the other salespeople negotiate specific contract terms with respect to legal liability, but OEMs now require that suppliers sign their standard purchase agreement without negotiation if the supplier wants to sell at a given price. Furthermore, OEMs have very specific product specification requirements that Vaughn engineers tell Raul they will have trouble meeting. Raul often feels caught in the middle between the various interests inside the company. Compounding the problem is the feeling that he cannot go to Horton for guidance.

In addition, Raul is uncomfortable with the intimidation tactics of Horton and the OEMs. Horton has encouraged his sales team to bluff when asked about the wholesale cost of the crankshafts in order to make a sale and threaten to walk out of the sales negotiation with a "take it or leave it" approach. Raul is concerned that he cannot use the friendly, open, and intelligent sales approach to which he is accustomed.

Horton does not understand Raul's falling performance: "I don't get it. Raul is compensated on a 100 percent commission basis, so he has the incentive to sell more and make a great deal of money. I even offer free tickets to local professional sporting events like hockey, basketball, and baseball games when my salespeople meet or exceed sales goals. If he works as long as I have, he can be promoted to sales manager too."

Questions

1. Based on the model for salesperson performance, what are the possible causes for the diminished performance of Raul?
2. What can Horton do to improve the sales performance of Raul?

Suggested Readings

Bettencourt, Lance A., and Stephen W. Brown. "Role Stressors and Customer-Oriented Boundary Spanning Behaviors in Service Organizations." *Journal of the Academy of Marketing Science* 23, 4 (2003), pp. 394–408.

Boles, James S., John Andy Wood, and Julie Johnson. "Interrelationships of Role Conflict, Role Ambiguity, and Work Family Conflict with Different Facets of Job Satisfaction and the Moderating Effects of Gender." *Journal of Personal Selling & Sales Management* 23, 2 (2003), pp. 99–114.

Chonko, Lawrence B., Eli Jones, James A. Roberts, and Alan J. Dubinsky. "The Role of Environmental Turbulence, Readiness for Change, and Salesperson Learning in the

Success of Sales Force Change." *Journal of Personal Selling & Sales Management* 22, no. 4 (2002), pp. 227–46.

Chonko, Lawrence, and Eli Jones, "The Need for Speed: Agility Selling," *Journal of Personal Selling & Sales Management* 25 (Fall 2005), pp. 372–82.

Dixon, Andrea L., Rosann L. Spiro, and Lukas P. Forbes. "Attributions and Behavioral Intentions of Inexperienced Salespersons to Failure: An Empirical Investigation." *Journal of the Academy of Marketing Science* 31, (2003), pp. 459–67.

Donovan, D. Todd, Tom J. Brown, and John C. Mowen. "Internal Benefits of Service Worker Customer Orientation: Job Satisfaction, Commitment, and Organizational Citizenship Behaviors." *Journal of Marketing* 68, (2004), pp. 128–46.

Hartman, Katherine B., "Television and Movie Representations of Salespeople: Beyond Willy Loman," *Journal of Personal Selling & Sales Management* 26 (Summer 2006), pp. 283–92.

Homburg, Christian, and Ruth M. Stock. "The Link between Salespeople's Job Satisfaction and Customer Satisfaction in a Business-to-Business Context: A Dyadic Analysis." *Journal of the Academy of Marketing Science* 32, (2004), pp. 144–58.

Jaramillo, Fernando, Jay Prakesh Mulki, and Paul Solomon, "The Role of Ethical Climate on Salesperson's Role Stress, Job Attitudes, Turnover Intention, and Job Performance," *Journal of Personal Selling & Sales Management* 26 (Summer 2006), pp. 272–82.

Jong, Ad de, Ko de Ruyter, and Jos Lemmink. "Antecedents and Consequences of the Service Climate in Boundary-Spanning Self-Managing Service Teams." *Journal of Marketing* 68, (2004), pp. 18–35.

Krishnan, Balaji C., Richard Netemeyer, and James S. Boles. "Self-Efficacy, Competitiveness, and Effort as Antecedents of Salesperson Performance." *Journal of Personal Selling & Sales Management* 22, (2002), pp. 285–96.

Mantel, Susan Powell, "Choice or Perception: How Affect Influences Ethical Choices Among Salespeople," *Journal of Personal Selling & Sales Management* 25 (Winter 2005), pp. 43–55.

Mulki, Jay Prakesh, Fernando Jaramillo, and Greg W. Marshall, "Lone Wolf Tendencies and Salesperson Performance," *Journal of Personal Selling & Sales Management* 27 (Winter 2007), pp. 25–38.

Netemeyer, Richard G., Thomas Brashear-Alehandro, and James S. Boles. "A Cross-National Model of Job-Related Outcomes of Work Role and Family Role Variables: A Retail Sales Context." *Journal of the Academy of Marketing Science* 32, (2004), pp. 49–60.

Nonis, Sarath A., and Jeffrey K. Sager. "Coping Strategy Profiles Used by Salespeople: Their Relationships with Personal Characteristics and Work Outcomes." *Journal of Personal Selling & Sales Management* 23, (2003), pp. 139–50.

Pettijohn, Charles E., Linda S. Pettijohn, and A. J. Taylor. "Does Salesperson Perception of the Importance of Sales Skills Improve Sales Performance, Customer Orientation, Job Satisfaction, and Organizational Commitment, and Reduce Turnover?" *The Journal of Personal Selling & Sales Management* 27 (Winter 2007), pp. 75–88.

Ping, Robert, "Salesperson-Employer Relationships: Salesperson Responses to Relationship Problems and Their Antecedents," *Journal of Personal Selling & Sales Management* 27 (Winter 2007), pp. 39–57.

Workman, John P., Jr., Christian Homburg, and Ove Jensen. "Intraorganizational Determinants of Key Account Management Effectiveness." *Journal of the Academy of Marketing Science* 31, (2003), pp. 3–21.

Chapter **Seven**

Salesperson Performance: Motivating the Sales Force

Salesperson Motivators

Keeping each salesperson motivated is important in maintaining a high level of sales performance, so sales managers spend a great deal of time trying to recognize the psychological process of motivation. While there is no such job as "typical sales position," the Chally Assessment, based on the responses of more than 130,000 salespeople, does help sales managers discover salespeople's motivational profile and assists managers in working with salespeople. Here are six motivational characteristics of a salesperson as well as a Management Tip to help front line sales managers.

Salespeople

1. Prefer novel, nonroutine situations and

   - Like unique, and different situations and novel solutions, especially if seen as a breakthrough.

   - Tend to have a high tolerance for failure.

   - Welcome the challenge of trying or creating a new or different approach.

   - Enjoy field-testing a new solution or method by trial and error, make adjustments as necessary, and get momentum started while the idea or technology is still fresh and exciting.

   - See the opportunities to be gained rather than the potential for loss.

   - **Management Tip:** Encourage individuals to explore new challenges so that the salesperson does not feel like he or she is stuck in a rut or stuck in the same routine. Giving them freedom to try something different even though it may be risky or turn out to be a failure may keep them engaged.

2. See meeting people as opportunities and

- Prefer to ask questions of people who know rather than spend time reading a book. They like to surround themselves with people who they think are better at something than they are so they can ask questions of them.

- Like opportunities to learn from people who have different opinions or perspectives to share.

- Like opportunities to broaden their circle of acquaintances.

- Seek out people to have conversations with.

- **Management Tip:** Provide opportunities to meet and interact with new people that may not always blossom into a business relationship, but may have benefits in keeping a salesperson engaged.

3. Prefer a participative style and

- Look for solutions that work for everyone involved.

- Favor meetings where everyone can participate.

- **Management Tip:** Involve salespeople and give them a voice. Decisions handed down without input are not likely to be followed, and may lower morale.

4. Take pride in the depth of expertise acquired for their job.

- **Management Tip:** Give them an opportunity to develop their expertise. Coaching, training, and professional development opportunities are likely to be appreciated.

5. Prefer to avoid or minimize confrontation and

- Prefer to smooth over conflicts rather than choose a side.

- Would rather keep opinions to themselves rather than risk alienating power holders.

- **Management Tip:** Don't force salespeople to adopt one approach, rather, look for a "win-win" approach that leads to mutual satisfaction. You may get better compliance this way.

6. Enjoy sharing their expertise and

- Find gratification in the success of those who benefit from their assistance.

- Derive satisfaction from giving encouragement and support to others.

- Seek opportunities to volunteer information, knowledge, and expertise.

- Take pride in being a role model.

- Like serving as a mentor and personal coach to those needing individual guidance.

- **Management Tip:** Create opportunities for salespeople to experience how their expertise has benefited customers.

Source: HR Chally Group (2007).

LEARNING OBJECTIVES

Salespeople operate in a highly dynamic, stressful environment outside of the company. As we have already seen in Chapter 6, there are many factors that influence the salesperson's ability to perform. One of the most critical factors is motivation. It is very important that sales managers understand the process of motivation and be able to apply it to each individual in the sales force in such a manner as to maximize his or her performance potential.

After reading this chapter, you should be able to

- Understand the process of motivation.

- Discuss the effect of personal characteristics on salesperson motivation.

- Understand how an individual's career stage influences motivation.

- Discuss the effect of environmental factors on motivation.

- Discuss the effect of factors inside the company on motivation.

Unfortunately, many firms are not successful in developing systems or programs that are appropriate for the marketing challenges they face and the kinds of people they employ. Consequently, their salespeople are either undermotivated or stimulated to expend too much time and effort on the wrong tasks and activities. In either case, sales effectiveness and productivity suffer.

In view of the complicated nature of motivation and its critical role in sales management, the rest of this chapter as well as Chapter 11 (on compensation) are devoted to the subject. This chapter examines what is known about motivation as a psychological process and how a person's motivation to perform a given job is affected by environmental, organizational, and personal variables. Chapter 11 discusses compensation plans and incentive programs sales managers use to stimulate and direct salespeople's efforts.

THE PSYCHOLOGICAL PROCESS OF MOTIVATION

Most industrial and organizational psychologists view **motivation** as an individual's choice to (1) initiate action on a certain task, (2) expend a certain amount of effort on that task, and (3) persist in expending effort over a period of time.[1] For our purposes, motivation is viewed as the amount of effort the salesperson desires to expend on each activity or task associated with the job. This may include calling on potential new accounts, developing sales presentations, and managing technology. The psychological process involved in determining how much effort a salesperson will want to expend and some variables that influence the process are shown in Exhibit 7.1.

The conceptual framework outlined in Exhibit 7.1 is based on a view of motivation known as *expectancy theory*. A number of other theories of motivation exist,[2] and many of them are useful for explaining at least a part of the motivation process. However, expectancy theory incorporates and ties together, at least implicitly, important aspects of many of those theories, it has been the subject of much empirical research in sales management, and it also provides a useful framework for guiding the many decisions managers must make when designing effective motivational programs for a sales force. Consequently, the remainder of this discussion focuses primarily on expectancy theory, although several other theories are mentioned later when we examine how personal characteristics affect the motivation of different individuals.

EXHIBIT 7.1   The psychological determinants of motivation

Major Components of the Model

The model in Exhibit 7.1 suggests that the *level of effort expended* by a salesperson on each *job-related task* will lead to *some level of performance on some performance dimension.* These dimensions include, for example, total sales volume, profitability of sales, and new accounts generated. It is assumed the salesperson's performance on some of these dimensions will be evaluated by superiors and *compensated with one or more rewards.* These might be externally mediated rewards, like a promotion, or internally mediated rewards, such as feelings of accomplishment or personal growth.

A salesperson's *motivation* to expend effort on a given task is determined by three sets of perceptions: (1) *expectancies*—the perceived linkages between expending more effort on a particular task and achieving improved performance; (2) *instrumentalities*— the perceived relationship between improved performance and the attainment of increased rewards; and (3) *valence for rewards*—the perceived attractiveness of the various rewards the salesperson might receive.

Expectancies—Perceived Links between Effort and Performance

Expectancies are the salesperson's perceptions of the link between job effort and performance. Specifically, expectancy is the person's probability estimate that expending effort on some task will lead to improved performance on a dimension. Sales managers are concerned with two aspects of their subordinates' expectancy perceptions: magnitude and accuracy. The following statement illustrates an expectancy perception: "If I increase my calls on potential new accounts by 10 percent [effort], then there is a 50 percent chance [expectancy] that my volume of new account sales will increase by 10 percent during the next six months [performance level]." Key questions that arise from a salesperson's expectancies and their implications for sales managers are identified in Exhibit 7.2.

Accuracy of Expectancies

The **accuracy of expectancy estimates** refers to how clearly the salesperson understands the relationship between effort expended on a task and the resulting achievement on some performance dimension. When salespeople's expectancies are inaccurate, they are likely to misallocate job efforts. They spend too much time and energy on activities that have little impact on performance and not enough on activities with a greater impact. Consequently, some authorities refer to attempts to improve the accuracy of expectancy estimates as "trying to get salespeople to work smarter rather than harder."[3]

EXHIBIT 7.2
Important questions and management implications of salespeople's expectancy estimates

Question	Management Implications
Accuracy of Expectancy Estimates	
• Are salespeople's views of the linkage between activities and performance outcomes consistent with those of sales managers?	• If substantial variation exists, salespeople may devote too much effort to activities considered unimportant by management, and vice versa. This might indicate a need for the following: —More extensive/explicit sales training. —Closer supervision. —Evaluation of salesperson's effort and time allocation as well as performance.
• Are there large variations in expectancy perceptions between high performers and low performers in the sales force?	• If high-performing salespeople hold reasonably consistent views concerning which activities are most important in producing good performance, those views might be used as a model for sales training/professional development programs.
Magnitude of Expectancy Estimates	
• All other things equal, the higher the salesperson's expectancy estimates, the greater the individual's motivation to expend effort. —Do personal characteristics of salespeople influence the size of their expectancies? Overall self-esteem? Perceived competence? Mental ability? (Intelligence?) Previous sales experience?	• If such relationships are found, they may suggest additional criteria for recruitment/selection.
—Do perceptions of uncertainty or constraints in the environment (e.g., materials shortages, recession, etc.) reduce salespeople's expectancy estimates?	• During periods of economic uncertainty, management may have to change performance criteria, evaluation methods, or compensation systems to maintain desired levels of effort from the sales force (e.g., lower quotas, reward servicing rather than selling activities).

Working smarter requires that the salesperson have an accurate understanding of what activities are most critical—and therefore should receive the greatest effort—for concluding a sale. Of course, a single activity might be carried out in a number of ways. For instance, a salesperson might employ any of several different sales techniques or strategies when making a sales presentation. Therefore, working smarter also requires an ability to adapt the techniques used to the needs and preferences of a given buyer.

As a result of the war on terrorism and events in the Middle East, salespeople have learned to adapt to a new selling environment. For example, due to security concerns as well as higher travel costs customers and salespeople are considering other ways of communicating with one another. As a result, presentation skills are more important than ever as Web-conferencing and teleconferencing are replacing the one-on-one presentation. As one management consultant put it, "If I do a teleconference, I'll have to prepare much more of a presentation." These kinds of changes have led to new skills and the reinforcement of existing ones. It is important that management motivate salespeople to expend effort on appropriate activities or approaches that can increase performance and lead to greater satisfaction within the sales force.

Unfortunately, it is possible for a salesperson to misjudge the true relationship between the effort expended on a particular task and resulting performance. When this happens, the salesperson misallocates efforts. The rep spends too much time and energy on activities that have relatively little impact on performance and not enough on activities with greater impact.

Research suggests that a salesperson's immediate superior, with presumably greater knowledge and experience, will more accurately perceive the linkages between effort and performance. If this is true, then inaccurate expectancy perceptions can be improved through closer contact between salespeople and their supervisors. Expanded sales training programs, closer day-to-day supervision of the sales force, and periodic review of each salesperson's time and effort by the supervisor should improve the accuracy of expectancy estimates.

Salespeople often complain that supervisors have an unrealistic view of conditions in the field. In addition, they do not realize what it takes to make a sale.[4] If these complaints are valid, managers' perceptions of the linkages between effort and performance may not be appropriate criteria for judging the accuracy of salespeople's expectancies. It may be better to use the expectancy estimates of the highest performing salesperson in the company as a model for sales training and supervision.

Magnitude of Expectancies

The **magnitude of expectancy estimates** reflects the salesperson's perceptions of his or her ability to control or influence his or her own job performance.

Several individual characteristics are likely to affect these expectancies. Some psychologists suggest that a salesperson's overall level of self-esteem and perceived ability to perform necessary tasks are positively related to the magnitude of the person's expectancy estimates.[5] Similarly, the salesperson's general intelligence and previous sales experience may influence the individual's perceived ability to improve performance through personal efforts. If these relationships are true, they may be useful supplementary criteria for the recruitment and selection of salespeople.

Environmental characteristics also influence a salesperson's perceptions of the linkages between effort and performance. How the salesperson perceives general economic conditions, territory potential, the strength of competition, restrictions on product availability, and so forth are all likely to affect his or her thoughts on how much sales performance can be improved by simply increasing efforts. The greater the environmental constraints a salesperson sees as restricting performance, the lower the rep's expectancy estimates will be. Turbulence in financial markets, and fluctuations in leading global economies have created a great deal of economic uncertainty in many global markets. This has led companies to reevaluate their purchases, and consequently, salespeople are faced with a much more complex and difficult selling environment. Therefore, managers may find it desirable to change performance criteria or evaluation methods during periods of economic uncertainty to maintain desired levels of effort from the sales force.

As Exhibit 7.3 indicates, personal and organizational characteristics affect the magnitude and accuracy of salespeople's expectancy perceptions. Managers must consider these factors when deciding on supervisory policies, compensation, and incentive plans so their subordinates' expectancies will be as accurate as possible. The factors that affect salespeople's expectancy estimates, along with their managerial implications, are discussed later in this chapter.

Instrumentalities—Perceived Links between Performance and Rewards

Like expectancies, **instrumentalities** are probability estimates made by the salesperson. They are the individual's perceptions of the link between job performance and various rewards. Specifically, an instrumentality is a salesperson's estimate of the probability that an improvement in performance on some dimension will lead to a specific increase in a

EXHIBIT 7.3   **Factors influencing the motivation process**

particular reward. The reward may be more pay, winning a sales contest, or promotion. As with expectancies, sales managers should be concerned with both the magnitude and the accuracy of their subordinates' instrumentalities.

Accuracy of Instrumentalities

The **accuracy of instrumentality estimates** refers to the true linkages between performance on various dimensions and the attainment of rewards as determined by management practices and policies on sales performance evaluation and rewards for levels of performance.[6] Exhibit 7.4 identifies some important questions for sales management regarding a salesperson's instrumentality estimates and their implications. These policies and practices may be misperceived by the salesperson leading the individual to concentrate on improving performance in areas that are less important to management and ultimately become disillusioned with his or her ability to attain rewards.

Thus, it is important to compare salespeople's instrumentality perceptions with stated company policies and management perceptions of the true or desired linkages between

EXHIBIT 7.4

Important questions and management implications of salespeople's instrumentality estimates

Question	Management Implications
Accuracy of Instrumentality Estimates	
• Are salespeople's views of the linkage between performance on various dimensions and the rewards they will receive consistent with those of sales managers?	• If substantial variation exists, salespeople may concentrate on aspects of performance considered relatively unimportant by management, and vice versa. This might indicate the need for the following: —More extensive/explicit sales training. —Closer supervision. —More direct feedback to salespeople concerning how performance is evaluated and how rewards are determined.
Magnitude of Instrumentality Estimates	
• How are salespeople's instrumentality estimates influenced by their compensation system (salary versus commission)? —Do salespeople on commission have higher instrumentality estimates for performance dimensions related to short-term sales volume? —Do salaried salespeople have higher instrumentalities for performance dimensions not directly related to short-term sales volume?	• If such relationships are found, managers should select the type of compensation plan that maximizes instrumentality estimates for those performance dimensions considered most crucial.
• Do personal characteristics of salespeople influence the size of their instrumentality estimates? —Feelings of internal control? —Mental ability? —Sales experience?	• If such relationships are found, they may suggest additional criteria for recruitment/selection.

performance and rewards. If salespeople do not accurately perceive how performance is rewarded in the firm, management must improve the accuracy of those perceptions. This is done through closer supervision and more direct feedback about evaluation and the determination of rewards.

Magnitude of Instrumentalities

One variable that has a notable impact on the **magnitude of instrumentality estimates** is the firm's compensation plan. For example, a salesperson compensated largely or entirely by commission is likely to perceive a greater probability of attaining more pay by improving performance on the dimensions directly related to total sales volume (increase in total sales dollars or percentage of quota). On the other hand, the salaried salesperson is more likely to perceive a greater probability of receiving increased pay for improving performance on dimensions not directly related to short-term sales volume (new-account generation, reduction of selling expenses, or higher customer satisfaction).

The salesperson may also be rewarded with promotion, recognition, and feelings of accomplishment and value these other rewards more highly than an increase in pay. In any case, the company's compensation plan is unlikely to affect the salesperson's perceptions of the linkages between performance and these nonfinancial rewards. Therefore, a compensation plan by itself is inadequate for explaining differences in motivation among salespeople.

The salesperson's personal characteristics also influence the magnitude of instrumentality estimates. For example the individual's perception of whether he or she controls life's events or whether these events are determined by external forces beyond the individual's control. Specifically, the more salespeople believe they have internal control over their lives, the more likely they are to believe improved performance will result in the attainment of rewards.

Besides the firm's compensation policies, other organizational factors and the personal characteristics of the salespeople can influence both the magnitude and the accuracy of their instrumentality estimates and are explored in a later section of this chapter and in Chapter 11.

Valences for Rewards

Valences for rewards are salespeople's perceptions of the desirability of receiving increased rewards from improved performance. One question about valences that has always interested sales managers is whether there are consistent preferences among salespeople for specific kinds of rewards. Are some rewards consistently valued more highly than others?

Historically, many sales managers assume monetary rewards are the most highly valued and motivating rewards. They believe recognition and other psychological rewards are less valued and spur additional sales effort only under certain circumstances. Very little research has tested whether salespeople typically desire more pay than other rewards. Thus, the assumption is based largely on the perceptions of sales managers rather than on any evidence obtained from salespeople themselves.

There is evidence to suggest that other rewards are at least as important as financial compensation. A vice president at Bebco Industries, a hazardous waste equipment company based in Texas, puts it this way, "You can throw money at people—bonuses, incentives, rewards, additional skills training—and they're all important parts of what the manager offers. But praise is number one. It goes a long way when you give them that pat on the back." Recent research suggests that more and more companies consider other factors as or even more important than compensation. According to one sales executive,

"Good management equals better performance and better motivation." The use of cash as an incentive has actually been declining. Companies are incorporating other forms of incentives such as debit/gift cards and leisure trips.[7]

An even more extreme view of financial rewards argues that linking pay to performance can have a negative effect on employees' motivation over time.[8] In this view, when pay is tied to performance, employees become less interested in what they are doing and more interested in simply capturing the reward. Intrinsic motivation is eaten away by extrinsic motivators like commissions and incentive contests, and employee creativity and quality of work may suffer as a result.

In light of these contradictory arguments and research results, is the conventional wisdom that salespeople desire money more than other rewards wrong? Or do salespeople simply desire a greater variety of rewards and work-related options than individuals in other kinds of jobs? Several studies focused on business-to-business salespeople generally support the conventional view. Their findings suggest that, on average, salespeople place a higher value on receiving more pay than any other reward, including intrinsic rewards like feelings of accomplishment or opportunities for personal growth. More recently, research in a nonsales setting confirms the importance of financial incentives as the primary reward, although recognition among peers was also found to be a significant motivator.[9] Informal surveys affirm that, while there are many different ways to motivate salespeople, compensation is still dominant. Overall, sales executives favor money, but offering other incentives makes sense in some cases. The national retail sales manager for Vita Health Products summarized the view of many executives, "I'll go with cash [as the best incentive]. People can't always get away for trips. Besides, cash gives them a choice."[10]

No universal statements can be made about what kinds of rewards are most desired by salespeople and most effective for motivating them. Salespeople's valences for rewards are likely to be influenced by their satisfaction with the rewards they are currently receiving. Their satisfaction with current rewards, in turn, is influenced by their personal characteristics and by the compensation policies and management practices of their firm.

CAN THE MOTIVATION MODEL PREDICT SALESPERSON EFFORT AND PERFORMANCE?

Several studies have tested the ability of motivation models such as the ones outlined in Exhibits 7.1 and 7.3 to predict the amount of effort workers will expend on various job activities. The findings support the validity of such expectancy models of motivation.[11]

The salesperson model of performance suggests motivation is only one determinant of job performance. Thus, it seems inappropriate to use only motivation to predict differences in job performance. However, several studies have attempted to do just that, with surprising success reporting that an individual's motivation to expend effort can explain up to 40 percent of the variation in the overall job performance.[12]

It is nice to know that models like Exhibit 7.1 are valid descriptions of the psychological processes that determine a salesperson's motivation. However, there is a question of even greater relevance to sales managers as they struggle to design effective compensation and incentive programs: How are the three determinants of motivation—expectancy perceptions, instrumentality perceptions, and valences for rewards—affected by (1) differences in the personal characteristics of individuals, (2) environmental conditions, and (3) the organization's policies and procedures? The impact of each of these variables on the determinants of motivation is now examined in greater detail.

THE IMPACT OF A SALESPERSON'S PERSONAL CHARACTERISTICS ON MOTIVATION

When placed in the same job with the same compensation and incentive programs, different salespeople are likely to be motivated to expend widely differing amounts of effort. People with different personal characteristics have divergent perceptions of the links between effort and performance (expectancies) and between performance and rewards (instrumentalities). They are also likely to have different valences for the rewards they might obtain through improved job performance. The personal characteristics that affect motivation include (1) the individual's satisfaction with current rewards, (2) demographic variables, (3) job experience, and (4) psychological variables, particularly the salesperson's personality traits and attributions about why performance has been good or bad. Let's examine the impact of each of these sets of variables on salespeople's expectancies, instrumentalities, and valences.

It should also be noted that many of these personal characteristics change and interact with one another as a salesperson moves through various career stages. For instance, when people begin their first sales job, they are likely to be relatively young and have few family responsibilities, little job experience, and low task-specific self-esteem. Later in their careers, those salespeople will be older and have more family obligations, more experience, and more self-esteem. As a result, their valences for various rewards and their expectancy and instrumentality estimates are all likely to change as their careers progress. Consequently, a later section of this chapter examines how salespeople's motivation is likely to change during their careers and addresses some managerial implications of such changes.

Satisfaction

Is it possible to pay a salesperson too much? After a salesperson reaches a certain satisfactory level of compensation, does he or she lose interest in working to obtain still more money? Does the attainment of nonfinancial rewards similarly affect the salesperson's desire to earn more of those rewards? The basic issues underlying these questions are whether a salesperson's satisfaction with current rewards has any impact on the desire for more of those rewards or on different kinds of rewards. The relationship between satisfaction and the valence for rewards is different for rewards that satisfy lower-order needs (e.g., pay and job security) than for those that satisfy higher-order needs (e.g., promotions, recognition, opportunities for personal growth, self-fulfillment). Maslow's theory of a need hierarchy,[13] Herzberg's theory of motivation,[14] and Alderfer's existence, relatedness, and growth theory[15] all suggest that lower-order rewards are valued most highly by workers currently dissatisfied with their attainment of those rewards. In other words, the more dissatisfied a salesperson is with current pay, job security, and other rewards related to lower-order needs, the higher the desire to increase those rewards. In contrast, as salespeople become more satisfied with their attainment of lower-order rewards, the value of further increases in those rewards declines.

The theories of Maslow, Herzberg, and Alderfer further suggest that high-order rewards are not valued highly by salespeople until they are relatively satisfied with their low-order rewards. The greater the salesperson's satisfaction with low-order rewards, the higher the desire for high-order rewards.

Perhaps the most controversial aspect of Maslow's and Alderfer's theories is the proposition that high-order rewards have increasing marginal utility. The more satisfied a salesperson is with the high-order rewards received from the job, the higher the value he or she places on further increases in those rewards.

Research in industrial psychology provides at least partial support for these suggested relationships between satisfaction and the valence of low-order and high-order rewards. Some of the evidence is equivocal, though, and some propositions—particularly the idea that high-order rewards have increasing marginal utility—have not been tested adequately.

In general, research suggests that salespeople who are relatively satisfied with their current income (a lower-order reward) have lower valences for more pay than those who are less satisfied. Most of these studies also report salespeople who are relatively satisfied with their current attainment of higher-order rewards, such as recognition and personal growth, tend to have higher valences for more of those rewards than those who are less satisfied. However, the evidence is mixed concerning whether salespeople who are relatively satisfied with their lower-order rewards have significantly higher valences for higher-order rewards than those who are less satisfied, as the theories would predict.[16]

Demographic Characteristics

Demographic characteristics, such as age, family size, and education, also affect a salesperson's valence for rewards. At least part of the reason for this is that people with different characteristics tend to attain different levels of rewards and are therefore likely to have different levels of satisfaction with their current rewards. Although there is only limited empirical evidence regarding salespeople, some conclusions can be drawn from studies in other occupations.[17] These conclusions are summarized in Exhibit 7.5.

Generally, older, more experienced salespeople obtain higher levels of low-order rewards (e.g., higher pay, a better territory) than newer members of the sales force. Thus, it could be expected that more experienced salespeople are more satisfied with their lower-order rewards. Consequently, they should have lower valences for lower-order rewards and higher valences for higher-order rewards than younger and less experienced salespeople.

A salesperson's satisfaction with their current level of lower-order rewards may also be influenced by the demands and responsibilities he or she must satisfy with those rewards. A salesperson with a large family to support, for instance, is less likely to be satisfied with a given level of financial compensation than a single salesperson. Consequently, the more family members a salesperson must support, the higher the valence for more lower-order rewards.

Finally, individuals with more formal education are more likely to desire opportunities for personal growth, career advancement, and self-fulfillment than those with less education. Consequently, highly educated salespeople are likely to have higher valences for higher-order rewards.

Job Experience

As people gain experience on a job, they are likely to gain a clearer idea of how expending effort on particular tasks affects performance. Experienced salespeople are also more likely to understand how their superiors evaluate performance and how particular types of

EXHIBIT 7.5
The influence of demographic characteristics on valence for rewards

Demographic Variable	Valence for Higher-Order Rewards	Valence for Lower-Order Rewards
Age	+	−
Family size		+
Education	+	

performance are rewarded in the company than their inexperienced counterparts. Consequently, a positive relationship is likely between the years a salesperson has spent on the job and the accuracy of his or her expectancy and instrumentality perceptions.

In addition, the magnitude of a salesperson's expectancy perceptions may be affected by experience. As they gain experience, salespeople have opportunities to sharpen their selling skills; and they gain confidence in their ability to perform successfully. As a result, experienced salespeople are likely to have larger expectancy estimates than inexperienced ones.[18]

Psychological Traits

An individual's motivation also seems to be affected by psychological traits. Various traits can influence the magnitude and accuracy of a person's expectancy and instrumentality estimates, as well as valences for various rewards, as summarized in Exhibit 7.6. People with strong achievement needs are likely to have higher valences for such higher-order rewards as recognition, personal growth, and feeling of accomplishment. This is particularly true when they see their jobs as being relatively difficult to perform successfully.[19]

The degree to which individuals believe they have internal control over the events in their lives or whether those events are determined by external forces beyond their control also affects their motivation. Specifically, the more salespeople believe they have internal control over events, the more likely they are to think they can improve their performance by expending more effort. They also believe improved performance will be appropriately rewarded. Therefore, salespeople with high *internal locus of control* are likely to have relatively high expectancy and instrumentality estimates.[20]

There is evidence that intelligence is positively related to feelings of internal control.[21] Those with higher levels of intelligence—particularly, verbal intelligence—are more likely to understand their jobs and their companies' reward policies quickly and accurately. Thus, their instrumentality and expectancy estimates are likely to be more accurate.

Finally, a worker's general feeling of self-esteem and perceived competence and ability to perform job activities (task-specific self-esteem) are both positively related to the magnitude of expectancy estimates.[22] Since such people believe they have the talents and abilities to be successful, they are likely to see a strong relationship between effort expended and good performance. Also, people with high levels of self-esteem are especially likely to attach importance to, and receive satisfaction from, good performance. Consequently, such people probably have higher valences for the higher-order, intrinsic rewards attained from successful job performance, although the lone study to examine the impact of self-esteem on salespeople's reward valences failed to support this proposition.[23]

EXHIBIT 7.6   **The influence of psychological traits on the determinants of motivation**

	Motivational Variables					
	Expectancies		Instrumentalities		Valences	
Personality Trait	**Magnitude**	**Accuracy**	**Magnitude**	**Accuracy**	**Higher Order**	**Lower Order**
High need achievement					+	
Internal locus of control	+		+			
Verbal intelligence	+	+	+	+		
General self-esteem	+				+	
Task-specific self-esteem	+				+	

Performance Attributions

People try to identify and understand the causes of major events and outcomes in their lives. These are called **performance attributions.** A given individual might attribute the cause of a particular event—such as good sales performance last quarter—to the following:

1. **Stable internal factors** that are unlikely to change much in the near future, such as personal skills and abilities.

2. **Unstable internal factors** that may vary from time to time, such as the amount of effort expended or mood at the time.

3. **Stable external factors,** such as the nature of the task or the competitive situation in a particular territory.

4. **Unstable external factors** that might change next time, such as assistance from an unusually aggressive advertising campaign or good luck.

The nature of a salesperson's recent job performance, together with the kind of causes to which the rep attributes that performance, can affect the individual's expectancy estimates concerning the likelihood that increased effort will lead to improved performance in the future.[24] Various attributions' likely effects on the magnitude of a salesperson's expectancy estimates are summarized in Exhibit 7.7.

As Exhibit 7.7 indicates, expectancy estimates are likely to increase if recent successful sales performance is attributed to either stable or unstable internal causes or to stable external causes. For instance, salespeople are likely to attach even higher expectancies to future performance where they take credit for past success, as the result of either superior skill (stable internal cause) or personal effort (unstable internal cause). Salespeople's expectancies are also likely to increase where past success is attributed to a perception that the task is relatively easy (stable external cause). However, if past successful performance is attributed to an unstable external cause that could change in the next performance period—such as good luck—there is no basis for salespeople to revise their expectancy estimates in any systematic way.

Suppose a salesperson performed poorly last quarter. Exhibit 7.7 indicates the impact of that poor performance on the individual's expectancy estimates is influenced by the causal attributions of the person. If the salesperson attributes poor past performance to stable causes that cannot be changed in the foreseeable future, such as low ability (stable internal cause) or a difficult competitive environment (stable external cause), his or her expectancy

EXHIBIT 7.7

The influence of performance attributions on the magnitude of a salesperson's expectancy estimates

Performance Attribution	Impact on Magnitude of Salesperson's Expectancy Estimates
Good Performance Attributed to:	
Stable internal cause	+
Unstable internal cause	+
Stable external cause	+
Unstable external cause	0
Poor Performance Attributed to:	
Stable internal cause	−
Unstable internal cause	+
Stable external cause	−
Unstable external cause	0

estimates are likely to be lower. Interestingly, research suggests that when salespeople attribute poor performance to stable internal causes (such as low ability), they blame themselves for the failure and may seek help from others in order to improve their performance next time. However, if the poor performance is attributed to an unstable internal cause—such as not expending sufficient effort to be successful—the person's expectancies may actually increase. The person may believe performance can be improved simply by changing the internal factor that caused the problem last time—by expending more effort.

A key to the application of attributions to performance is the accurate analysis of the salesperson's behavior and attitudes. If, for example, the salesperson consistently blames the customer, the competition, or the economic situation for poor performance when, in fact, the poor performance is due to internal factors (lack of effort or ability), then it is unlikely the problem can be easily corrected. Fortunately, research suggests that in most cases salespeople are realistic of their assessment of the attributing success or failure to specific external and internal factors.

Management Implications

The relationships between salespeople's personal characteristics and motivation has two broad implications for sales managers. First, people with certain characteristics are likely to understand their jobs and their companies' policies especially well. They also perceive higher expectancy and instrumentality links. Such people should be easier to train and motivated to expend greater effort and achieve better performance. Therefore, as researchers and managers gain a better understanding of these relationships, it may be possible to develop improved selection criteria for hiring salespeople who are easy to train and motivate.

Second, and more important, some personal characteristics are related to the kinds of rewards salespeople value. This suggests sales managers should examine the characteristics of their salespeople and attempt to determine their relative valences for various rewards when designing compensation and incentive programs. Also, as the demographic characteristics of the sales force change, a manager should be aware that salespeople's satisfaction with rewards and their valences for future rewards might also change. There is little doubt that understanding the nature of the relationship between the salesperson's personal characteristics and motivation is difficult and requires a unique understanding of each individual. Leadership 7.1 highlights how important it is to understand each individual in order to maximize their motivation.

CAREER STAGES AND SALESPERSON MOTIVATION

The previous discussion of the personal factors affecting motivation also suggests that salespeople's expectancy estimates and reward valences are likely to change as they move through different stages in their careers. As a person grows older and gains experience, demographic characteristics and financial obligations change, skills and confidence tend to improve, and the rewards he or she receives—as well as satisfaction with those rewards—are likely to change. We have seen that all of these factors can affect an individual's expectancies and reward valences.

Career Stages

Research has identified four **career stages** through which salespeople go: **exploration, establishment, maintenance,** and **disengagement.**[25] Typical paths of progression through these four career stages are diagrammed in Exhibit 7.8.

Leadership   Understanding the Role of Your Sales Force   7.1

One size does not fit all when it comes to motivating a sales force. Every individual is unique and requires a different motivational program to maximize performance. Using a personality tool called the Enneagram and applying modern management techniques to this ancient Greek personality assessment can help sales managers develop motivational programs for specific salespeople.

Type 1   Perfectionist

Traits
Driven to do the right thing, very critical of themselves and others, have a strong sense of responsibility, and have a strong potential to express anger.

How to motivate
Recognize them when they do things in accordance with the rules; it is important when using incentive plans to be consistent and to clearly explain the criteria for success.

Type 2   Helper

Traits
Will seek to take care of others at their own expense, very concerned with relationships; they seek personal relationships with their managers.

How to motivate
Respond well to plaques, awards, and the more "pat on the back" kind of recognition; however, they appreciate this one-on-one rather than in the group.

Type 3   Achiever

Traits
Focus on efficiency, goal driven, and identify with being a winner; they have a strong need for success and for being recognized as being successful.

How to motivate
Look for public recognition (recognizing them in the company newsletter as salesperson of the month); also respond well to gifts and other types of recognition that enable them to display their success.

Type 4   Individualist

Traits
Sensitive to beauty and seek to find the meaning in things; they are complex people who can be prone to mood swings, feelings of inadequacy, and envy.

How to motivate
Recognize their unique contribution to the company and make them aware of their importance in the organization; they often find themselves frustrated by the "process" of selling, so help them make the process easier.

Type 5   Observer

Traits
Think outside the box, able to look at things in new ways, and are often more comfortable working with ideas rather that making an emotional contact with people.

How to motivate
Need time and space to work alone; difficult for them to be motivated by performance goals; and it is essential to give them sufficient time to get the job done; they do not respond well to emotional connection and prefer a more detached relationship.

Type 6   Team Player

Traits
Loyal and engaging with customers and other employees; however, they are also worriers and full of their own doubts about their ability.

How to motivate
Not surprisingly, it is critical for them to feel a part of the team either working directly within a team or at least be a part of the larger work team; have a need for validation and belonging to the company.

Type 7   Enthusiast

Traits
Always focused on the positive; have a high energy level and as such have a high need for action; they can also lose sight of the key goals.

How to motivate
Team them with someone who is more focused on accomplishing stated goals; they appreciate awards that are fun and activity based such as sporting events or parties.

(continued)

Leadership   *concluded*   7.1

Type 8   Leader

Traits   Tendency to be dominating and protective of other employees; while tough on the outside, these individuals often have a very tender heart on the inside.

How to motivate   Allow them to be in charge but don't necessarily feel the need to publicly reward them; create a project or account that will enable them to control and lead.

Type 9   Peacemaker

Traits   Can see all points of view and consequently seek to make peace with everyone in the organization; want to be a part of the group and shy away from confrontation.

How to motivate   Do not seek out personal recognition but rather want the entire organization to be successful; would rather see recognition spread throughout the company than directed at them.

Source: Based on information from The Enneagram Institute, visit *www.enneagraminstitute.com,* September 2007.

Exploration Stage

People in the earliest stage of their careers (typically individuals in their 20s) are often unsure about whether selling is the most appropriate occupation for them and whether they can be successful salespeople. To make matters worse, underdeveloped skills and a lack of knowledge tends to make people at this early stage among the poorest performers in the sales force. Consequently, people in the exploration stage tend to have low psychological involvement with their job and low job satisfaction. As Exhibit 7.8 indicates, this can cause some people to become discouraged and quit and others to be terminated if their performance does not improve.

Because salespeople in the exploration career stage are uncertain about their own skills and the requirements of their new jobs, they tend to have the lowest expectancy and instrumentality perceptions in a firm's sales force. They have little confidence that expending more effort will lead to better performance or that improved performance will produce increased rewards. But they do have relatively high valences for high-order

EXHIBIT 7.8
Sales career path

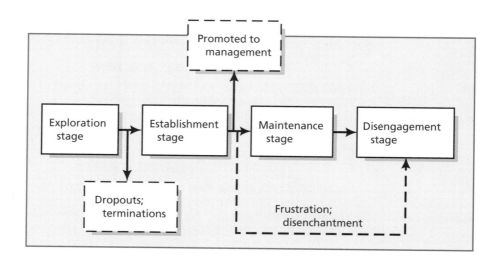

rewards, particularly for personal growth and recognition. They seek reassurance that they are making progress and will eventually be successful in their new career. Consequently, good training programs, supportive supervision, and a great deal of recognition and encouragement are useful for motivating and improving the performance of salespeople at this formative stage of their careers.

Establishment Stage

Those in the establishment stage—usually in their late 20s or early 30s—have settled on an occupation and desire to build it into a successful career. Thus, the major concerns of salespeople at this stage involve improving their skills and their sales performance. As they gain confidence, these people's expectancy and instrumentality perceptions reach their highest level. People at this stage believe they will be successful if they devote sufficient effort to the job and their success will be rewarded.

Because people at this career stage are often making other important commitments in their lives—such as buying homes, marrying, and having children—their valences for increased financial rewards tend to be relatively high. However, their strong desire to be successful—and in many cases the desire to move into management—makes their valences for promotion higher at this stage than at any other. They also have very high valences for recognition and other indications that management approves of their performance and considers them worthy of promotion.

However, the strong desire for promotion at this stage can have negative consequences. As shown in Exhibit 7.8, some successful people may win promotions into sales or marketing management, but many others will not, at least not as soon as they hoped. Some of these individuals become frustrated by what they consider to be slow progress and quit for jobs in other companies that promise faster advancement or they move prematurely into a disengagement stage. To help prevent this, managers should guard against building unrealistic expectations concerning the likelihood and speed of future promotions among their establishment-stage salespeople. Research interviewing people who have left a company finds one of the most common reasons cited is dissatisfaction with career opportunities such as pay, promotion, and advancement opportunities.

Maintenance Stage

This stage normally begins in a salesperson's late 30s or early 40s. The individual's primary concern at the maintenance stage is with retaining the present position, status, and performance level within the sales force, all of which are likely to be quite high. For this reason, people in the maintenance stage continue to have high valences for rewards that reflect high status and good performance, such as formal recognition and the respect of their peers and superiors.

By this stage, though, both the opportunity and desire for promotion diminish. Consequently, instrumentality estimates and valences concerning promotion fall to lower levels. But salespeople at this stage often have the highest valences for increased pay and financial incentives of anyone in the sales force. Even though such people are among the highest-paid salespeople, they tend to want more money due to both increased financial obligations (e.g., children getting ready for college, large mortgages) and a desire for a symbol of success in lieu of promotion.

Disengagement Stage

At some point, everyone must begin to prepare for retirement and the possible loss of self-identity that can accompany separation from one's job. This usually begins to happen when people reach their late 50s or early 60s. During this disengagement stage, people psychologically withdraw from their job, often seeking to maintain just an "acceptable" level of performance with a minimum amount of effort in order to spend more time developing interests outside of work. As a result, such people have little interest in attaining more high-order rewards—such as recognition, personal development, or a promotion—from their jobs. Because they tend to have fewer financial obligations at this stage, they are also relatively satisfied with their low-order rewards and have low valences for attaining more pay or other financial incentives. Not surprisingly, then, salespeople at this career stage have average performance levels lower than any others except new recruits in the exploratory stage. And their low valences for either high- or low-order rewards make it difficult to motivate them.

What is most disconcerting about disengagement, however, is that it does not occur only among salespeople at the end of their careers. As mentioned earlier, long before they approach retirement age, people may become bored with their jobs and frustrated by a failure to win promotion. Such people may psychologically withdraw from their jobs rather than search for a new position or occupation. They are commonly referred to as *plateaued salespeople*—people who have stopped developing, stopped improving, and often stopped showing an interest. In summary, the individual concerns, challenges, and needs associated with each career stage—together with the implications for motivating a salesperson at that stage—are presented in Exhibit 7.9.

The Problem of the Plateaued Salesperson

Plateauing, or early disengagement, is not an isolated phenomenon among salespeople. Indeed, it has been suggested that 96 percent of all companies have a problem with plateaued salespeople.[26] Moreover, as many as 25 percent of all salespeople operate in a comfort zone that reduces or eliminates the motivation to be a high performer.

Causes of Plateauing

The primary causes of early disengagement are the boredom and frustration that arise when a relatively young person is kept in the same job too long and sees little likelihood of a promotion or other expansion in job responsibilities in the near future. Among the reasons frequently cited for plateauing are (1) lack of a clear career path, (2) boredom, and (3) failure to manage the person effectively. It appears that the same factors hold for both men and women.

One factor, however, may be a more important cause of plateauing among saleswomen than salesmen, burnout. Although the reasons are not fully understood, it could be due to the demands of their multiple roles (mother, wife) in addition to those of their jobs. It has also been suggested the opportunity to earn high levels of pay provided by commission-based compensation systems can increase the rate of plateauing in a sales force. Managers indicate salespeople compensated by commission may more easily earn sufficient pay to meet their economic needs and thereby become less motivated by the chance to earn still higher financial compensation. We explore this issue in more detail in Chapter 11.

Possible Solutions

All of this suggests that one way of reducing the plateauing problem in a sales force—and of remotivating salespeople who have reached a plateau—is to develop clearly defined career paths for salespeople who are good performers but are not promoted into management early in their careers. Such alternative career paths typically involve promotions to positions within the sales force that involve additional responsibility and more demanding challenges.

EXHIBIT 7.9   **Characteristics of different stages in a salesperson's career**

Sources: Adapted from William L. Cron, "Industrial Salesperson Development: A Career Stages Perspective," *Journal of Marketing* Fall 1984, p. 40; and William L. Cron, Alan J. Dubinsky, and Ronald E. Michaels, "The Influence of Career Stages on Components of Salesperson Motivation," *Journal of Marketing*, January 1988, pp. 78–92.

	Exploration	**Establishment**	**Maintenance**	**Disengagement**
Career concerns	Finding an appropriate occupational field	Successfully establishing a career in a certain occupation	Holding on to what has been achieved Reassessing career, with possible redirection	Completing one's career
Developmental tasks	Learning the skills required to do the job well Becoming a contributing member of an organization	Using skills to produce results Adjusting to working with greater autonomy Developing creativity and innovativeness	Developing broader view of work and organization	Establishing a stronger self-identity outside of work Maintaining a high performance level
Personal challenges	Must establish a good initial professional self-concept	Producing superior results on the job in order to be promoted Balancing the conflicting demands of career and family	Maintaining a high performance level Maintaining motivation though possible rewards have changed Facing concerns about aging and disappointment over what one has accomplished Maintaining motivation and productivity	Acceptance of career accomplishments Adjusting self-image
Psychosocial needs	Support Peer acceptance Challenging position	Achievement Esteem Autonomy Competition	Reduced competitiveness Security Helping younger colleagues	Detachment from organization and organizational life
Impact on motivation	Low expectancy and instrumentality perceptions High valences for higher-order rewards, such as personal growth and recognition Supportive supervision is critical	Highest expectancy and instrumentality perceptions High valences for pay, but highest valences for promotion and recognition Must avoid generating unrealistic expectations	Instrumentality and valence for promotion fall Valences for recognition and respect remain high Highest valences for increased pay	Lowest instrumentality perceptions and valences for both higher-order and lower-order rewards Still desires respect, but that is unlikely to motivate additional effort

Leadership   Dealing with the Plateaued Salesperson   7.2

Plateauing or early disengagement is a serious problem, and sales managers consider a wide range of tools to help keep salespeople motivated. Recently, a sales expert offered the following ideas on motivating the sales force:

1. *Accountability.* Require salespeople to account for the time and activities. This applies not only to salespeople but to management as well.

2. *Compensation.* Salespeople need to be rewarded on the basis of their performance; if they perform well, they should receive higher rewards. This is not to say that commission-based programs are the best way to reward salespeople all the time (as you will see in Chapter 11).

3. *In the field.* Salespeople who get complacent often spend more time in the office than in the field.

4. *Positive attitude.* It is human nature for a salesperson to want to be in a positive environment. If management is constantly negative, this will have a negative effect on the salesperson.

5. *Information.* While unnecessary reports are a burden for salespeople, it is critical to keep accurate records of customer contacts and the relationship (order status, problems) between the customer and company.

6. *Selection.* Hire individuals who want to sell and work hard. It is important to take the time to hire the right candidates. One old adage states it this way, "Hire slowly, fire quickly."

7. *Training.* Spend the time to develop good, effective training, and use sufficient resources to accomplish the training objectives.

Source: Alan Test, "Motivating Your Salesperson," *American Salesman,* 49, no. 5 (2004), pp. 3– 8.

For instance, a firm might develop a career path involving frequent promotions to increasingly lucrative and challenging territories or assignments to larger and more high profile accounts or promote high-performing salespeople into national account management positions. The idea is to provide opportunities for frequent changes in job duties and responsibilities to increase job variety. Simultaneously, job changes can be used as rewards for good performance to motivate salespeople and show they are valued employees even though they do not move into management.

To be effective, however, promotions along the sales career path must be real and not simply changes in title. They must involve actual changes in duties and responsibilities, and offered on the basis of good past performance.

Another closely related approach to revitalizing plateaued salespeople is to enrich their current jobs by finding ways to add variety and responsibility without developing a complicated system of hierarchical positions and promotion criteria. This is a more viable approach in smaller firms, and will probably become more popular as firms reduce the number of sales managers and adopt flatter sales force structures. For example, plateaued salespeople might be asked to devote time to training and mentoring new recruits, gathering competitive intelligence, or becoming members of cross-functional account management or product development teams. A number of other suggestions for dealing with disengaged salespeople offered by sales managers are discussed in Leadership 7.2.

THE IMPACT OF ENVIRONMENTAL CONDITIONS ON MOTIVATION

Environmental factors such as variations in territory potential and strength of competition can constrain a salesperson's ability to achieve high levels of performance. Such environmental constraints can cause substantial variations in performance across salespeople. In addition to placing actual constraints on performance, however, environmental conditions can affect salespeople's perceptions of their likelihood of succeeding and thus their willingness to expend effort.

Although management can do little to change the environment faced by its salespeople (with the possible exception of rearranging sales territories), an understanding of how and why salespeople perform differently under varying environmental circumstances is useful to sales managers. Such an understanding provides clues about the compensation methods and management policies that will have the greatest impact on sales performance under specific environmental conditions.

In some industries, the pace of technological change is very rapid, and salespeople must deal with a constant flow of product innovations, modifications, and applications. Salespeople often appreciate a constantly changing product line because it adds variety to their jobs, and markets never have a chance to become saturated and stagnant. For example, it is common in the laptop computer industry to speak of product life cycles in months not years. One leading manufacturer replaces its entire line of laptop computers every nine months. However, a rapidly changing product line can also cause problems for the salesperson. New products and services can require new selling methods and result in new expectations and demands from role partners. Consequently, an unstable product line may lead to less accurate expectancy estimates among the sales force.

In some firms, salespeople must perform in the face of output constraints, which can result from short supplies of production factors, including shortages of raw materials, plant capacity, or labor. Such constraints can cause severe problems for the salesperson. In one paper-products firm a few years ago, salespeople were penalized for exceeding quotas. In general, salespeople operating in the face of uncertain or limited product supplies are likely to feel relatively powerless to improve their performance or rewards through their own efforts. After all, their ultimate effectiveness is constrained by factors beyond their control. Therefore, their expectancy and instrumentality estimates are likely to be low.

There are many ways of assessing the strength of a firm's competitive position in the marketplace. One might look at its market share, the quality of its products and services as perceived by customers, or its prices. Regardless of how competitive superiority is defined, though, when salespeople believe they work for a strongly competitive firm, they are more likely to think selling effort will result in successful performance. In other words, the stronger a firm's competitive position, the higher its salespeople's expectancy estimates are likely to be.

Sales territories often have very different potentials for future sales. These potentials are affected by many environmental factors, including economic conditions, competitors' activities, and customer concentrations. Again, though, the salesperson's perception of the unrealized potential of the territory can influence his or her motivation to expend selling effort. Specifically, the greater the perceived potential of a territory, the higher the salesperson's expectancy estimates are likely to be.

THE IMPACT OF ORGANIZATIONAL VARIABLES ON MOTIVATION

Company policies and characteristics can directly facilitate or hinder a salesperson's effectiveness. Such organizational variables may also influence salespeople's performance indirectly, however, by affecting their valences for company rewards and the size and accuracy of their expectancy and instrumentality estimates. These relationships between organizational variables and the determinants of motivation are summarized in Exhibit 7.10.

EXHIBIT 7.10   Influence of organizational variables on the determinants of motivation

Organizational Variables	Motivational Variables					
	Expectancies		Instrumentalities		Valences	
	Magnitude	Accuracy	Magnitude	Accuracy	Higher Order	Lower Order
Closeness of supervision		+		+		
Span of control		−		−		
Influence over standards				+		
Frequency of communication		+		+		
Opportunity rate					Curvilinear	
Recognition rate					Curvilinear	
Compensation rate						−
Earnings opportunity ratio						+

Supervisory Variables and Leadership

According to one highly regarded theory of leadership, a leader attains good performance by increasing subordinates' personal rewards from goal attainment and by making the path to those rewards easier to follow—through instructions and training, by reducing road-blocks and pitfalls, and by increasing the opportunities for personal satisfaction.[27]

This theory suggests that effective leaders tailor their style and approach to the needs of their subordinates and the kinds of tasks they must perform. When the subordinates' task is well defined, routine, and repetitive, the leader should seek ways to increase the intrinsic rewards of the task. This might be accomplished by assigning subordinates a broader range of activities or by giving them more flexibility to perform tasks. When the subordinate's job is complex and ambiguous, that person is likely to be happier and more productive when the leader provides relatively high levels of guidance and structure. Alan Mulally, CEO of Ford, regarded as one of the best managers in corporate America takes a very simple approach. He does not focus on mistakes but, rather, seeks to build confidence and trust which provides a great example for everyone at Ford.[28]

In most occupations, workers perform relatively well defined and routine jobs, and they prefer to be relatively free from supervision. They do not like to feel their superiors "breathing down their necks." Business to Business salespeople, however, are different. They occupy a position at the boundary of their companies, dealing with customers and other nonorganization people who may make conflicting demands. Salespeople frequently face new, nonroutine problems. Consequently, evidence shows B-2-B salespeople are happier when they feel relatively closely supervised, and supportive supervision can increase their expectancy and instrumentality estimates for attaining extrinsic rewards.[29] Closely super-vised salespeople can learn more quickly what is expected of them and how they should perform their job. Consequently, such individuals should have more accurate expectancies and instrumentalities than less closely supervised salespeople. But, as we discussed, close supervision can increase role conflict since it can reduce flexibility in accommodating and adapting to customers' demands.

Another organization variable related to the closeness of supervision is the firm's first-level sales managers' span of control. The more salespeople each manager must supervise (the larger the span of control), the less closely the manager can supervise each person. Therefore, the impact of span of control on role perceptions and motivation variables should be the opposite of the expected impact of close supervision, although this is chang-ing as the result of technology.

Another related supervisory variable is the frequency with which salespeople communicate with their superiors. The greater the frequency of communication, the less role ambiguity salespeople are likely to experience and the more accurate their expectancy and instrumentality estimates should be. Again, however, frequent contact with superiors may increase the individual's feelings of role conflict.

Incentive and Compensation Policies

Management policies and programs concerning higher-order rewards, such as recognition and promotion, can influence the desirability of such rewards in the salesperson's mind. For these rewards, there is likely to be a curvilinear relationship between the perceived likelihood of receiving them and the salesperson's valence for them. For example, if a large proportion of the sales force receives some formal recognition each year, salespeople may think such recognition is too common, too easy to obtain, and not worth much. If very few members receive formal recognition, however, salespeople may believe it is not a very attractive or motivating reward simply because the odds of attaining it are so low. The same curvilinear relationship is likely to exist between the proportion of salespeople promoted into management each year (the opportunity rate) and salespeople's desire for promotion.[30]

Another issue is preferential treatment for "stars." The goal of recognition and other forms of incentives is to motivate people to do better, but what happens when one star demands and receives much more than the average or even much more than the company's other top performers, when Alex Rodriquez was on the market one of the teams recruiting Rodriquez (A-Rod) was the New York Mets. However, the Mets withdrew from consideration when they realized that while they could afford A-Rod, the end result on team morale would be negative. Steve Phillips, the general manager of the Mets at the time, put it this way, "It's not about an individual. It's about 25 players that join together as a team, which is something that when compromised becomes difficult to win." The same is true in the sales force.

A company's policies on the kinds and amounts of financial compensation paid to its salespeople are also likely to affect their motivation. As seen, when a person's lower-order needs are satisfied, they become less important and the individual's valence for rewards that satisfy such needs, such as pay and job security, is reduced. This suggests that in firms where the current financial compensation is relatively high, salespeople will be satisfied with their attainment of lower-order rewards. They will have lower valences for more of these rewards than people in firms where compensation is lower.

The range of financial rewards currently received by members of a sales force also might affect their valences for more financial rewards. If some salespeople receive much more money than the average, many others may feel underpaid and have high valences for more money. The ratio of the total financial compensation of the highest-paid salesperson to that of the average in a sales force is the **earnings opportunity ratio.** The higher this ratio is within a company, the higher the average salesperson's valence for pay is likely to be.

Finally, the kind of reward mix offered by the firm is a factor. Reward mix is the relative emphasis placed on salary versus commissions or other incentive pay and nonfinancial rewards. It is likely to influence the salesperson's instrumentality estimates and help determine which job activities and types of performance will receive the greatest effort from that salesperson. The question from a manager's viewpoint is how to design an effective reward mix for directing the sales force's efforts toward the activities believed to be most important to the overall success of the firm's sales program. This leads to a discussion of the relative advantages and weaknesses of alternative compensation and incentive programs, the topic of Chapter 11.

Summary

The amount of effort the salesperson desires to expend on each activity or task associated with the job—the individual's motivation—can strongly influence job performance. This chapter reviewed the factors that affect an individual's motivation level. The chapter suggested an individual's motivation to expend effort on any particular task is a function of that person's (1) expectancy, (2) instrumentality, and (3) valence perceptions.

Expectancy refers to the salesperson's estimate of the probability that expending a given amount of effort on some task will lead to improved performance on some dimension. Expectancies have two dimensions that are important to sales managers—magnitude and accuracy. The magnitude of a salesperson's expectancy perceptions indicates the degree to which the individual believes that expending effort on job activities will directly influence job performance. The accuracy of expectancy perceptions refers to how clearly the individual understands the relationship between the effort expended on a task and the performance on some specific dimension that is likely to result.

Instrumentalities are the person's perceptions of links between job performance and various rewards. Specifically, an instrumentality is a salesperson's estimate of the probability that a given improvement in performance on some dimension will lead to a specific increase in the amount of a particular reward. A reward can be more pay, winning a sales contest, or promotion to a better territory. As with expectancies, sales managers need to be concerned with both the magnitude and accuracy of their subordinates' instrumentalities.

The salesperson's valence for a specific reward is the individual's perception of the desirability of receiving increased amounts of that reward. This valence, along with the individual's valence for all other attractive rewards and the person's instrumentality perceptions, determines how attractive it is to perform well on some specific dimension.

Several factors influence salespeople's expectancy, instrumentality, and valence perceptions. Three major forces are (1) the personal characteristics of the individuals in the sales force, (2) the environmental conditions they face, and (3) the company's own policies and procedures. The chapter reviewed some major influences and their likely impacts on each of the three categories.

Key Terms

motivation
expectancies
  *accuracy of expectancy
  estimates*
  *magnitude of expectancy
  estimates*
instrumentalities
  *accuracy of instrumentality
  estimates*

*magnitude of instrumentality
  estimates*
valences for rewards
performance attributions
  (stable, unstable, internal,
  external)
career stages (exploration,
  establishment,

maintenance,
  disengagement)
plateauing
earnings opportunity ratio

Breakout Questions

1. Sales support personnel include customer service reps, account coordinators, sales assistants, and others whose efforts have a critical impact on a sales force's success. The chapter discusses motivation from the perspective of the sales force. How would you apply the concepts discussed in the chapter to sales support personnel? What can a company do to motivate sales support personnel?

2. "What's all this stuff about different pay packages and different incentive plans based on how long a sales rep has been with the company?" demanded the irate sales manager. "Around here, everybody gets the same treatment. We're not offering customized compensation packages." What are the problems associated with motivating sales reps on the basis of their stage in the career cycle?

3. How do you motivate sales representatives when money is not effective? What can a sales manager do to motivate the successful salesperson?

4. Most sales reps dislike inputting data into the company's CRM system. They think their time could be spent more profitably, such as calling on accounts. Using Exhibit 7.3, trace the thought process sales reps go through as they consider applying more effort to putting customer data into the computer. Do the same for applying more effort to calling on accounts.

5. How would you respond to a salesperson who says the following? "You are asking me to spend more time calling on new accounts, but I do not see the point in doing so; most of my business comes from my existing accounts."

Leadership Challenge: What Have You Done for Me Lately?

Terri Ann Masters, sales manager for Rudolph Manufacturing, was wrestling with a critical issue related to one of her longtime and, until recently, most talented salespeople, Jason Benjamin. With the company for nearly 15 years, Jason had been one of its top salespeople for 11 of those years. At first, Terri Ann thought it was just "bad luck" and Jason would be able to turn it around. Now, however, after four years of seeing Jason miss sales targets and hearing increasing complaints from customers, Terri Ann knew something was wrong.

This was especially critical for Rudolph because Jason called on some of the company's biggest clients. Jason had worked his way up in the company and been given these accounts seven years ago. During his first three years with the accounts, Jason generated substantial new business from his clients. Management at the customers had actually gone to the trouble of calling Terri Ann and complimenting Rudolph on the relationship Jason had established. The end result was that Jason frequently exceeded his sales quotas and received healthy bonuses.

In the last few years, however, there was very little new business coming from Jason's accounts. At the same time, Terri Ann knew these companies were growing and were taking business to other competitors. It was not that Jason had lost the accounts; they were still doing a reasonable business with Rudolph. Rather, Terri Ann recognized there was additional business the company was not getting for some reason.

Of even greater concern was the number of complaints about Jason that had been coming in to Terri Ann. Jason certainly did not have the greatest number of complaints, but given his history, they were high. In addition, Jason seemed to be less motivated. When Terri Ann would call his office on Friday afternoons, she would find that he had already left for the weekend. The "old" Jason was one of the hardest-working salespeople in the company.

The problem was coming to a head. Management had a big push on inside the company to increase productivity. Terri Ann also had several younger salespeople who were eager to move into larger, more demanding and higher potential accounts.

Questions

1. You are Terri Ann Masters. What would you do about Jason Benjamin?

2. What would you do with these younger salespeople who are looking for new opportunities inside the company?

3. Offer ideas on why Jason's performance might have slipped after all these years with the company?

Role Play: Maven Software

Situation

Maven Software provides unique solutions for dental offices that want to fully integrate their patient records, billing, insurance filing, and outbound patient correspondence. Maven started out in 1974 in St. Louis as a local provider of forms utilized by doctors and dentists for record-keeping. Bob Perkins (Bob Sr.) started the firm, and when he retired in 2002 Bobby (Bob Jr.) took over as CEO. In an amazing evolution, the company has become a leading provider in the United States of integrated software solutions for dentists (they made the decision in 1996 to fully devote their efforts to that one market).

Arthur Grabber is one of the three original employees hired by Bob Sr. Arthur was the original salesperson for Maven and for years devoted his time and energy to "beating the bushes" for business—originally largely by phone and, where possible, by face-to-face sales calls. The transition to a technology product focus was a little rough for Arthur, but his relationships with key clients he developed and nurtured over many years helped him overcome the product transition. Arthur is 55 and plans to retire at age 60. Instead of being "the" salesperson for Maven, he is now one of 23 client executives who live in geographically dispersed locations throughout the United States. The sales director is a very competent woman named Leona Jones, who came to Maven in 2006 after a 10-year career in sales management with Merck.

Lately, Leona has been thinking a lot about Arthur, his history with the company, and his enormous contributions to its success over 30+ years. In a way, she is in awe of his accomplishments. On the other hand, he has been rather slow to adopt technological aids to the sales process (he still is reluctant to choose e-mail as a source of client communication, for example). And she is cognizant of the fact that at this stage in Arthur's career, piling more salary and incentive pay onto him is very unlikely to motivate him to change his basic sales approach. Don't misunderstand—it's not that Arthur is a "problem" salesperson; he brings in slightly better sales results annually than the average. But she would like to find a way to address his impending move from the maintenance stage to the disengagement stage of the career cycle.

She picks up the phone and calls Arthur, who is working in his in-home office in a suburb of St. Louis. She asks him to schedule a meeting to catch up on a few things related to planning business for the remainder of the year. During that meeting, she also plans to open up a nonthreatening, friendly dialogue about how Arthur would like to see his last five years with Maven unfold.

Characters in the Role Play

Arthur Grabber, client executive for Maven Software, based in St. Louis

Leona Jones, sales director for Maven Software, based in St. Louis

Assignment

Break into pairs, with one student playing each character. The student playing Arthur simply needs to get into the character of a salesperson at his stage of the career cycle. The student playing Leona needs to develop a set of issues to bring up with Arthur about important aspects of how to enhance his productivity and satisfaction as he moves into the last few years of employment with the company. The dialogue should be positive, with the goal to come out of the meeting with some specific items for follow-up and implementation.

Minicase: Land Escape Vacation Club	Land Escape Vacation Club sells fractional interests in time-share vacation properties at various beach locations. For example, an owner will purchase an interest of four weeks a year at a Land Escape property in a place like Hilton Head, South Carolina. Prospective buyers are offered a free weekend stay at a Land Escape resort if they listen to a sales presentation while they are there.

Sales at the La Jolla, California, location have been inconsistent over the past two years, and the sales manager, Denise London, has been asked by Land Escape's vice president of sales to review the profiles of her three salespeople in order to come up with a plan to improve sales.

Catalina Curtis

Catalina is a woman in her 30s with a husband and two small children at home. She was once a television weather forecaster (she would say "meteorologist") but got fired and was forced to do something else. She thought that working in sales would be for the short term until another television opportunity came about, but she has now been in Land Escape sales for about three years. Trying to make the best of a bad situation, she was very enthusiastic when she first began selling, but her enthusiasm and energy level have been waning as she has realized that she will probably continue doing sales for the long term. She and her husband feel some financial pressure because of their decision to put their children in private school, which is very costly. The economy has been difficult, and Catalina is beginning to believe she cannot succeed no matter what she does.

She is somewhat insecure and sensitive but conscientious and a team player. She likes people and seeks personal relationships with customers and takes a long-term approach. Her philosophy is "if potential customers don't want to buy right away, I don't pressure them. I will keep in contact with them and eventually they will come back and buy." Denise does not care for Catalina's style and tends to let her operate without supervision, because, frankly, she doesn't know what to tell her to do better.

Zach Jones

Zach is 25 years old, just two years out of college. He has been with Land Escape for approximately eight months now. He is a perfectionist and highly competitive. Before he came to Land Escape, he had no previous sales experience, but he does have a natural selling skill. He is a little bit of a loose cannon and is not afraid to bend or even break the rules. Needless to say, he is not the least bit self-conscious. Some find him friendly and like his engaging style; however, some are turned off by it and see him as a stereotypical "slick" salesperson.

His goal is to make as much money as possible in a short amount of time. He will decide later whether he wants to stay in sales for the long term; right now he just wants to be young and have fun. He is favored by the sales manager, Denise, who sees him as a potential star because of his early success. As a result, she gives him closer supervision and guidance.

John Sargent

John is the dean of the group at age 53. He has been in Land Escape sales since its inception 12 years ago and was in sales for 10 years before that time. He is good at what he does. He says, "I've pretty much mastered the art of time-share selling, and I'm cruising along. I know exactly how much effort to make to get the sale, so why should I do any more than that?"

His art-collecting hobby now interests him more than selling, and he has no desire to be promoted to sales manager or move to a different location. John is somewhat resentful that he has a female manager who has less experience than he does and has made it known that he needs no supervision from her. He does well enough that Denise complies and just lets him sell without a close watch.

Denise knows she needs to make some changes, but is not sure what to do. She feels the current compensation plan of 70 percent commission and 30 percent salary is fairly generous, and she even runs the occasional sales contest to boost numbers during the slower months. She had better think of something quickly before the VP gives her a "permanent vacation."

Questions

1. In what career stage would you place each of the three salespeople?
2. If you were the sales manager, how would you motivate each salesperson? Explain your recommendations.
3. What measures might you use to motivate them as a group?

Suggested Readings

Motivation

Brown, Steven P., Kenneth R. Evans, Murali K. Mantrala, and Goutam Challagalla. "Adapting Motivation, Control, and Compensation Research to a New Environment." *Journal of Personal Selling & Sales Management* 25 (Spring 2005) pp. 155–67.

Dixon, Andrea L., Rosann Spiro, and Lukas P. Forbes. "Attributions and Behavioral Intentions of Inexperienced Salespersons to Failure: An Empirical Investigation." *Journal of the Academy of Marketing Science* 31, no. 4 (2003), pp. 459–67.

Jaramillo, Fernando, William B. Locander, Paul E. Spector, and Eric G. Harris. "Getting the Job Done: The Moderating Role of Initiative on the Relationship Between intrinsic Motivation and Adaptive Selling." *Journal of Personal Selling & Sales Management* 27 (Winter 2007) pp. 59–74.

Johnson, Mark S. "A Bibliometric Review of the Contribution of Attribution Theory to Sales Management." *Journal of Personal Selling & Sales Management* 26 (Spring 2006), pp. 181–95.

Krishnan, Balaji, Richard Netemeyer, and James S. Boles. "Self-Efficacy, Comptitiveness, and Effort as Antecedents of Salesperson Performance." *Journal of Personal Selling & Sales Management* 22, no. 4 (2002), pp. 285–95.

Leach, Mark, P., Annie H. Lui, and Wesley J. Johnston. "The Role of Self-Regulation Training in Developing the Motivation Management Capabilities of Salespeople." *Journal of Personal Selling & Sales Management* 25 (Summer 2005) p. 269–81.

Nonis, Sarath A., and Jeffrey K. Sager. "Coping Strategy Profiles Used by Salespeople: Their Relationships with Personal Characteristics and Work Outcomes." *Journal of Personal Selling & Sales Management* 23, no. 2 (2003), pp. 139–50.

Silver, Lawrence S., Sean Dwyer, and Bruce Alford. "Learning and Performance Goal Orientation of Salespeople Revisited: The Role of Performance-Approach and Performance-Avoidance Orientations." *Journal of Personal Selling & Sales Management* 26 (Winter 2006) pp. 27–38.

Leadership and Motivation

Brashear, Thomas G., James S. Boles, Danny N. Bellenger, and Charles M. Books. "An Empirical Test of Trust-Building Processes and Outcomes in Sales Manager–Salesperson Relationships." *Journal of the Academy of Marketing Science* 31, no. 2 (2003), pp. 189–200.

Brashear, Thomas G., Danny N. Bellenger, James S. Boles, and Hiram C. Barksdale. "An Exploratory Study of the Relative Effectiveness of Different Types of Sales Force Mentors." *Journal of Personal Selling & Sales Management* 26 (Winter 2006) pp. 7–18.

Ingram, Thomas N., Raymond W. LaForge, William B. Locander, Scott B. MacKenzie, and Phillip M. Podsakoff. "New Directions in Sales Leadership Research." *Journal of Personal Selling & Sales Management* 25 (Spring 2005) pp. 137–54.

Ramaswami, Sridhar. "Influence of Control Systems on Opportunistic Behaviors of Salespeople, a Test of Gender Difference." *Journal of Personal Selling & Sales Management* 22, no. 3 (2002), pp. 173–88.

Rouzies, Dominique, and Anne Macquin. "An Exploratory Investigation of the Impact of Culture on Sales Force Management Control Systems in Europe." *Journal of Personal Selling & Sales Management* 22, no. 1 (2002), pp. 61–72.

Career Stages and the Problem of Plateaued Salespeople

Dixon, Andrea L., Lukas P. Forbes, and Susan M. B. Schertzer. "Early Success: How Attributions for Sales Success Shape Inexperienced Salesperson's Behavioral Intentions." *Journal of Personal Selling & Sales Management* 25 (Winter 2005) pp. 67–77.

Flaherty, Karen E., and James M. Pappas. "The Influence of Career Stage on Job Attitudes toward a Contingency Perspective." *Journal of Personal Selling & Sales Management* 22, no. 3 (2002), pp. 135–43.

Lopez, Tara, and Amy McMillan-Capehart. "How Outgroup Salespeople Fit in or Fail to Fit in: A Proposed Acculturation Effects Framework." *Journal of Personal Selling & Sales Management* 22, no. 4 (2002), pp. 297–309.

Pullins, Ellen Bolman, and Leslie M. Fine. "How the Performance of Mentoring Activities Affects the Mentor's Job Outcomes." *Journal of Personal Selling & Sales Management* 22, no. 4 (2002), pp. 259–71.

Chapter Eight

Personal Characteristics and Sales Aptitude: Criteria for Selecting Salespeople

The War for Talent

A company's employees are its single greatest asset—and investment. Currently, there is a war for talent as organizations compete vigorously to attract and retain high performance individuals. One consequence of this war is that companies are substantially increasing their resources in both time and money to train, develop, and compensate their best employees. Like any investment, however, there is a risk and, unfortunately, some individuals turn out to be a poor match for the position. When employees leave an organization (whether voluntarily or involuntarily), a significant portion of the company's investment in those individuals is lost. Chally provides an online tool to identify the costs of losing valuable employees—The Employee Turnover Cost Calculator.

Using the Employee Turnover Cost Calculator, it is possible to determine, position by position, the cost of turnover in an organization. To calculate the cost of turnover, the follow information is needed:

- Number of employees who hold the position.

- Annual percentage of turnover within the position.

- Annual compensation within the position.

- Average tax and benefit cost (as a percentage of salary).

- Average number of candidates interviewed per opening.

- Average number of candidates assessed per opening.

Based upon this information, three categories of costs are combined to estimate a total cost of turnover.

- Separation costs, such as those associated with exit interviews, separation pay, increases in unemployment taxes, and administrative expenses.

- Replacement costs—consists of the funds a company commits for attracting new applicants to fill the vacancies, then interviewing, assessing, and checking backgrounds of the candidates. While the costs associated with these two categories can be significant, even combined they are usually far less than those associated with the final category.

- Training costs. Typically, while new employees are being trained, they are not making a direct contribution to the company's business. However, during this time the companies pay the trainee's full salaries and benefits, as well as those for any trainers who might be employed. After training is complete, a probationary period usually follows wherein the new hire's productivity can expected to be around 50 percent of an established employee's level (that is to say those individuals who left the company).

Winning the War

To minimize high turnover costs, the first step is to evaluate hiring procedures. Many companies continue to use traditional interviewing in the sales force selection process, inviting candidates to meet with a sales manager as well as other members of the sales team. Unfortunately, individuals responsible for hiring often get little or no training, causing them to rely on standard inquiries instead of guided, behavioral-based interview questions. Chally's data indicates the probability of hiring the right candidate increase only 1 percent using such interviewing practices, which is essentially no better than flipping a coin. Including background and reference checks improves accuracy by 3 percent, while interviewing a candidate with guided, behavioral-based questions adds about 7–8 percent better precision to the hiring decision.

Managers who make the right hiring decision less than 60 percent of the time have little chance of minimizing turnover costs. However, they can dramatically increase their hiring success rate (up to 35 percent better) by identifying critical success skills associated with a particular sales role and employing a predictive tool to help select appropriate candidates. Chally has identified 14 distinct sales roles, ranging from new business development (Hunter) to account management (Farmer) based on research that discovered the characteristics present in top performers that were lacking in the bottom performers with the same job requirements. From there a predictive tool was developed that identifies a candidate's natural capacity for these differentiating skills, giving hiring decision makers insight during the interview process. Selecting candidates with a natural capacity for key job requirements yields faster ramp-up time and reduces turnover.

Source: HR Chally Group (2007).

LEARNING OBJECTIVES

What makes a good salesperson? This question is the focus of Chapter 8. Perhaps no other question faced by sales managers is more important because it has such a profound effect on every aspect of a manager's job. From recruiting and selecting to motivating and evaluating a sales force, one of the important questions—if not the most important—is, What makes that person successful (or not successful)? Sales managers are constantly looking for those characteristics that consistently define success or failure.

At the end of this chapter, you should be able to

- Understand the answer to the question, Are good salespeople born or made?

- Define the characteristics of successful salespeople.

- Explain the role of sales aptitude in sales performance.

- Understand the different success characteristics for different sales positions.

ARE GOOD SALESPEOPLE BORN OR MADE? THE DETERMINANTS OF SUCCESSFUL SALES PERFORMANCE

Stable, self-sufficient, self-confident, goal-directed, decisive, intellectually curious, accurate—these are personal traits one major personnel testing company says an individual should have to be a successful salesperson. A crucial question, though, is whether the presence or absence of such traits is determined by a person's genetic makeup and early life experiences, or whether they can be developed through training, supervision, and experience after the person is hired for a sales position. In other words, are good salespeople born or made?

Many companies in the pharmaceutical industry believe that successful salespeople are both born and made. They spend a great deal of time and energy identifying characteristics and **selection criteria** for success in a sales position at the company. Firms gather information about potential new hires through interviews, references, and tests to determine which candidates have the traits and characteristics they believe are important determinants of future sales success. But these same companies also devote substantial resources to training and supervisory programs aimed at further developing each new salesperson's skills, knowledge, and motivation.

Many sales executives have somewhat mixed feelings concerning what it takes to become a successful salesperson. In a study several years ago, a majority of managers indicated they believe good salespeople are made rather than born. Sales and marketing executives said training and supervision are more critical determinants of selling success than the inherent personal characteristics of the individual.[1] However, these same executives also described men and women they knew as being "a born salesperson." And a minority argued that personal traits were critical determinants of good sales performance. For example, one executive asked, "Can they teach ego, train it into an individual? Can they teach personal drive or persistence that gets the sale?"[2]

Thus, while most managers believe that the things a firm does to train and develop its salespeople are the most critical determinants of their future success, many also believe that a firm cannot put in the salesperson all the elements of success and that certain basic personal traits—such as a strong ego, self-confidence, decisiveness, and a need for achievement—are necessary requirements. Is it possible that both sets of factors play crucial roles in shaping a salesperson's performance? A review of past empirical research on this issue can help provide a more definitive answer.

A Review of Past Research

A research technique known as meta-analysis has been used to integrate and evaluate the findings of a large number of past research studies examining relationships between the performance of individual salespeople and a variety of personal and organizational factors that might influence that performance.[3] Based on summary of the analysis, variables were grouped into the six categories shown in Exhibit 8.1. The exhibit also shows the actions a sales manager or top executive might take to influence or control each

EXHIBIT 8.1   Variables that cause differences in performance across individual salespeople and the actions management can take to influence them

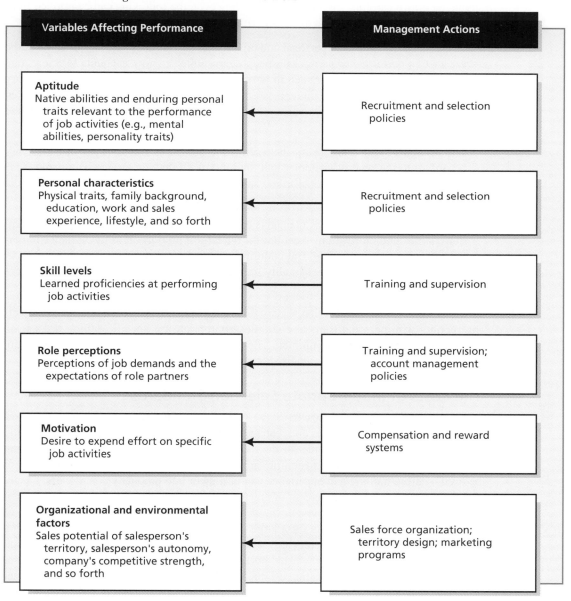

group of determinant variables. Note that two of the categories—aptitude and personal characteristics—contain enduring personal traits and past experiences of the salesperson. These variables are impossible for the manager to influence or change, except by choosing salespeople with desirable traits. A third category—skill levels—includes personal abilities that can change and improve as the salesperson gains knowledge and experience. Thus, skill variables can be influenced by management through effective training programs and supervision. The remaining three categories of determinant variables—role perceptions, motivation, and organizational characteristics—are also directly influenced by management through such means as supervision, compensation and reward systems, and other company policies and programs.

Due to the nature of the analysis, it is important to remember that specific conclusions should be drawn carefully. With this in mind, however, the following can be implied from the analysis of the determinants of sales performance:

- While all six categories of personal and organizational variables account for some of the variance in performance across salespeople, no single category accounts for more than about 8.5 percent of the variance in performance. This means that no single category does a very good job of explaining performance and suggests the performance of a given salesperson is a function of a variety of influences, including both personal traits and organizational factors.

- The strengths of the relationships between some categories and sales performance vary according to the type of customer and the kind of product or service being sold. This suggests that different personal traits, aptitudes, and skills are required for success in different kinds of sales jobs.

- On average, factors that sales managers can control or influence—such as role perceptions, skills, and motivation—account for the largest proportion of the variance in performance across salespeople. But enduring personal characteristics—such as aptitude, personal background, and personality traits—are also related to individual differences in performance.

These conclusions suggest that successful salespeople are both born and made. Selecting recruits with personal traits and abilities appropriate for specific selling tasks is an important determinant of their ultimate sales performance but, how those salespeople are managed is even more crucial to their success.

The Costs of Inappropriate Selection Standards

Although personal characteristics may have less influence on a salesperson's long-term performance than company policies and management actions, firms should pay close attention to hiring the right kinds of people for their sales forces for another reason. People lacking the appropriate personal traits and abilities are more likely to become frustrated and quit—or be fired—before training and experience can turn them into productive employees. Chally estimates that as much as 65 percent of unwanted turnover is a result of job dissatisfaction stemming from frustrated employees hired into poorly fitting jobs. Reducing the cost of turnover can have huge benefits for a large company. Global Imaging Systems (GIS) is a provider of copiers, video conferencing, network integration and other imaging solutions to middle market companies. It was listed by Forbes as one of the 400 Best Big Companies in America in 2007. Global Imaging estimated that turnover costs them $11.25 million per year. By changing their selection process, GIS experienced a 25 percent reduction in turnover which translated into savings of $2.8 million. Reducing turnover also benefits small companies. Connecticut Business Systems, a subsidiary of GIS, lowered their turnover from 89 percent a year to 13 percent, which translates into substantial savings in a company of only 200 employees.

Research suggests that on average, about 15 percent of a firm's sales force will quit or be terminated in a given year[4] and the odds that a given salesperson will either quit or be fired during his or her first five years of employment approach 50–50. From this one may conclude that companies are not always successful in identifying and hiring people with the necessary personal characteristics and abilities for success.[5]

Because firms spend a great deal of money and time training new salespeople, mistakes in recruitment and selection that lead to high early turnover rates can be very costly. Firms with high-tech products or broad and complex product lines can spend more than $100,000 a year training a salesperson. Across a broader range of consumer and industrial goods and service industries, firms spend an average of four months and more than $7,000 training each new sales rep.[6] In addition, it takes from three months to a year before new sales reps generate enough sales to cover their compensation and expenses.[7] Thus, when a frustrated salesperson quits in the first year or two of employment, the firm never recoups the cost of recruiting and training that individual.

Because mistakes in recruitment and selection can be costly in the short term and lead to lower productivity in the long term, many sales managers consider the evaluation and selection of new recruits to be among the most important aspects of their jobs. As a result, the remainder of this chapter examines some of the personal and psychological characteristics related to a person's ability to carry out different types of sales jobs.

CHARACTERISTICS OF SUCCESSFUL SALESPEOPLE

Aptitude and personal characteristics are typically thought to place an upper limit on an individual's ability to perform a given sales job. Two people with equal motivation, role perceptions, and training might perform at different levels because one does not have the personal traits or abilities necessary to do the job as well as the other. The questions to consider are these: What specific personal traits and abilities enable a person to achieve good sales performance? What are the determinants of sales aptitude?

Characteristics Sales Managers Look For

One way to answer these questions is to identify the personal characteristics that sales managers look for when selecting new salespeople. Research indicates that enthusiasm consistently ranks among the personal attributes sales manager consider most important in recruiting. Other characteristics considered relatively important are good organizational abilities, ambition, and the two related attributes of persuasiveness and communication skill. Although many executives consider previous sales experience to be important in indicating the sales aptitude of new employees, general experience in selling is typically viewed as more relevant than specific product or industry experience.[8]

Surveys asking executives what they look for when hiring new salespeople are instructive, but they do not provide a definitive answer to the question of what personal characteristics make some individuals better salespeople than others. For one thing, the studies cited above reflect only the opinions of American managers concerning what characteristics are related to selling success in the U.S. market. As firms become strong global competitors, managers wrestle with the question of whether different characteristics are related to successful sales performance in different countries. The question of cross-cultural characteristics is examined in Leadership 8.1.

Leadership   German–American Cross-Cultural Business Differences   8.1

As we will see in the next chapter, many companies have identified specific criteria for evaluating and hiring potential new salespeople. In some cases, those criteria have been validated by comparing the characteristics of high performing salespeople with low performers who have quit or been dismissed.

When those same companies expand operations into other countries, however, it is often more difficult to find sales recruits who fit the established criteria. In addition, those criteria can change as companies move into new areas of the world. Cultural differences cause some personal traits and characteristics to be more critical for success in certain countries than others. Consequently, many global companies have had to adapt their salesperson selection criteria to the cultural and social conditions that exist in different countries.

Consider the cross-cultural business differences between Germany and the United States. Germans have a strong deference for leaders and people in authority. As a result, the casual leadership style of many American managers would be more uncomfortable for German salespeople. At the same time Germans are much more respectful of titles and, in general, would take a more formal approach in their relationships with management and customers. For example, it is much more customary in Germany for salespeople to address customers with formal, "Herr" (Mister), "Frau" (Madame), or "Fraulein" (Miss).

Americans are also more likely to mix work and play. It is much more common for an American salesperson to meet a customer for dinner and a social event than their German counterpart. Similarly, German salespeople tend to be more formal in their dress and mannerisms (no shirt sleeve shirts). Finally, Germans frequently learn English as their second language and are very comfortable doing business globally. Even small firms look for international business opportunities.

These and other cultural differences encourage companies to adapt their selection criteria to meet the needs of local customers as they move into new markets around the world. They also make changes in their training to support the skill sets required in individual countries. While identifying individuals with appropriate cultural sensitivities is difficult, companies understand the importance of finding salespeople with the ability to adapt their personal style to fit unique selling situations in front of any customer, whether that customer is in the United States, Germany, or anywhere else.

Source: "Seven German–American Cross Cultural Business Differences," *SellingPower.com,* October 2007.

Also, manager surveys merely reflect the opinions and perceptions of those sales executives who responded. Although those perceptions may be based on years of practical experience, they can still be inaccurate, biased, or based on knowledge of only a limited range of industries or types of selling jobs. A more objective way to determine what specific personal characteristics are most strongly related to selling success is to study a large cross section of salespeople. To this end, it would be very useful to examine in more detail the specific variables included in the aptitude, skill levels, and personal characteristics categories of the meta-analysis of past research that we discussed earlier. Fortunately, there is research that has done exactly that.[9]

Research Concerning the Personal Characteristics of Successful Salespeople

One limitation of the meta-analysis of factors related to differences in sales performance discussed earlier was that the six categories of variables were very broadly defined. Each category contained a large number of more specific items, some of which may be much more strongly related to differences in sales performance than the average for the whole category. Consequently, a second analysis was done after breaking up the broad aptitude, skill levels, and personal characteristics categories into more narrowly defined subcategories of closely related variables.

It is important to note, though, that some of the variables reported in Exhibit 8.2 can no longer be legally collected for use in the selection process. For example, potentially discriminatory information about such **physical characteristics** as age, sex, and race cannot be included on applications. These and other legal and social concerns related to cultural diversity in the workforce are discussed later in this chapter and in Chapter 9.

A number of variables are related to salespeople's **psychological traits** and abilities. The exhibit defines seven subcategories of personality traits, five groups of other enduring aptitude factors or mental abilities, and five groups of skills. Note that the aptitude, personality, and **skills variables** must be measured explicitly during the selection process through the use of formal, scored tests or assessment techniques.[10]

Overview of Findings

As expected, this detailed analysis uncovered specific personal characteristics and traits that can better distinguish between high- and low-performing salespeople—and some that are even worse predictors of performance—than the broad categories of variables examined earlier. Although no single trait could account for a majority of the variance in performance across salespeople, Exhibit 8.2 shows that some personal variables (such as an individual's personal history and family background, current marital and family status, and vocational skills) can account for as much as 20 percent of the variance in selling success. Some traits on which sales managers commonly rely to evaluate new recruits (such as educational attainment, intelligence test scores, or sociability) have not proven effective in accounting for difference in sales performance. Thus, the following sections discuss these widely varying relationships between personal variables and sales performance in depth.

One finding was consistent, however, across all the research. Different types of selling situations appear to require salespeople with different personal traits and abilities. Consequently, the last section of this chapter examines the evidence concerning what personal traits and abilities are best suited to different types of sales jobs.

Demographic and Physical Variables

The meta-analysis results in Exhibit 8.2 indicate those demographic factors, such as sex and age, and physical characteristics, such as height and appearance, account for much less than 5 percent of the difference in performance across salespeople. The lack of any strong relationships between these variables and sales performance is a very important finding. It has implications for public policy regarding equal employment opportunities for women and minorities, and it refutes the conventional wisdom espoused by some sales managers in the past.

Gender and Race   Like many other job categories, business-to-business selling was predominantly a white male occupation for many decades and employment opportunities for women and racial minorities were severely limited. The most recent U.S. Census data indicate that while blacks accounted for about 12 percent of the population, less than 9 percent of all sales jobs were held by black workers. Similarly, women accounted for less than 25 percent of people selling manufactured goods.

One major reason for this unequal employment was the widely held misperception that some customers would be reluctant to deal with or buy from minority salespeople. Similarly, many sales managers thought women were too emotional and lacking in aggressiveness and self-confidence to be effective salespeople. Some managers thought turnover rates would be higher for women due to marriage and childbirth. The view of many older

EXHIBIT 8.2
Summary of the effect of variables on salesperson performance

Variable	Percentage of Variance in Performance Explained
Demographic and physical characteristics—physical traits	
Age*	Less than 5%
Gender*	Less than 5%
Physical appearance	Less than 5%
Height, weight, neatness, and general appearance	
Background and experience—developmental education and work experience	
Personal history and family background*	Almost 21%
Father/mother occupation, number of siblings, family responsibilities	
Level of educational attainment	Less than 5%
Years of school, degrees earned, grade average	
Educational content	Less than 5%
College major, number of business courses	
Sales experience	Less than 5%
Years of sales experience, number and types of sales jobs, promotions	
Nonsales work experience	Less than 5%
Work history, including military service, length of time in past jobs	
Current status and lifestyle—present marital, family, and financial status	
Marital/family status*	Almost 12%
Current marital status, number and ages of dependents	
Financial status	Approximately 6%
Past and current income levels, family income, home ownership	
Activities/lifestyle*	Less than 5%
Church attendance, club memberships, hobbies, interests	
Aptitude—enduring personal characteristics that determine an individual's overall ability to perform a sales job	
Intelligence	Less than 5%
Measure of mental abilities, score on intelligence tests	
Cognitive ability	Almost 7%
Mental flexibility, ideational fluency, spatial visualization, inductive and logical reasoning, associative and visual memory	
Verbal intelligence	Less than 5%
Comprehension and manipulation of words, verbal skills	
Math ability	Less than 5%
Comprehension of quantitative relationships	
Sales aptitude	Less than 5%
Enduring personal characteristics and abilities thought to be related to the performance of specific sales tasks	
Personality—enduring personal traits that reflect an individual's consistent reactions to situations encountered in the environment	
Responsibility	Less than 5%
Dependability, emotionally stable, punctual, adjusts well to frustration, keeps promises, and follows plans	
Dominance	
Takes command, exerts leadership, pushes own ideas, wants power versus being submissive	

(continued)

EXHIBIT 8.2
Summary of the
effect of variables
on salesperson
performance
(*concluded*)

Variable	Percentage of Variance in Performance Explained
Sociability	Less than 5%
Enjoys social activities and interaction, likes to be around other people, and is talkative and gregarious	
Self-esteem	Less than 5%
Physically, personally confident and can stand criticism, believes others have a positive attitude toward him or her	
Creativity/flexibility	Less than 5%
Innovative, flexible, ready to entertain new ideas and ways of doing things, individualistic	
Needs for achievement/intrinsic reward	Less than 5%
Wants to do his or her best, seeks success in competition, gains satisfaction from accomplishment and personal development	
Need for power/extrinsic reward	Less than 5%
Motivated primarily by desires for money or advancement, has strong need for security, desires increased power and authority	

Skills—learned proficiencies and attitudes necessary for effective performance of specific job tasks (these can change with training and experience)

Vocational skills	Almost 9.5%
Job and company specific skills, technical knowledge, knowledge of the company and its policies	
Sales presentation	Almost 5%
Skills related to identifying and evaluating customer needs, presentation style, ability to handle objections, close the sale	
Interpersonal	Less than 5%
Skills related to understanding, persuading, and getting along with other people	
General management	A little over 9%
Skills related to organizing, directing, and leading other people	
Vocational esteem	Less than 5%
Degree of preference for the tasks and activities associated with the sales job	

*These areas are considered inappropriate or illegal in selecting a job candidate.

sales managers could be summarized by the following quote, "I'm not sure exactly how I'd manage a woman if I did hire one."[11] Fortunately, these managers have, for most part, retired or been replaced over the last several years.

Social Changes Have Improved Employment Opportunities   Women and minorities are moving into senior positions and are demonstrating tremendous skill and ability in business-to-business selling, but there is still work to be done. Based on the most recent data shown in Exhibit 8.3 women account for less than 25 percent of sales reps and hold about 14 percent of the sales management positions. It is important to note, however, that women have achieved greater acceptance in some industries, such as communications, publishing, insurance, and business services, than in more traditionally male-dominated industries such as construction, machinery, and primary metals.

Another issue women face in many professions, including sales, is compensation relative to their male counterparts. Again, while progress has been made, there is still a gap between compensation levels for men and women in the same positions. As Exhibit 8.4 indicates, at the vice president of sales level the gap between men and women, on average, is a little more than $34,000 ($170,619 for men versus $136,250 for women). While the

EXHIBIT 8.3
**Women in sales and
sales management
positions:
percentages by
industry**

Source: Christen P. Heide,
*Dartnell's 30th Sales Force
Compensation Survey*
(Chicago: Dartnell Corporation,
1999), p. 171.

Industry Group	Percentage of Women Sales Reps	Percentage of Women Sales Managers
Agriculture	4.7%	0.0%
Banks	24.7	23.3
Business services	30.3	21.5
Chemicals	9.1	5.7
Communications	34.7	15.3
Construction	20.0	20.0
Electronic components	10.8	14.2
Electronics	19.6	5.4
Fabricated metals	5.9	10.3
Food products	28.5	43.8
Instruments	10.7	8.2
Insurance	27.4	14.0
Machinery	8.2	3.8
Manufacturing	17.6	6.8
Office equipment	24.1	7.4
Paper/allied products	1.8	12.5
Printing/publishing	38.9	23.2
Rubber/plastics	17.7	20.8
Wholesale (consumer)	19.5	4.8
Average	24.3%	14.3%

EXHIBIT 8.4
**Compensation levels
of men and women in
sales and marketing
careers**

Source: Erin Strout, "Tough
Sell," *Sales & Marketing Man-
agement,* July 2001, p. 52 and
Laine Chroust Ehmann "Great
Opportunities: How the Future
Looks for Women in Sales and
Management," *SellingPower
.com,* October 2007.

Average total compensation of respondent by title	Men	Women
Vice president sales and marketing	$138,525	$122,689
Director or manager sales and marketing	109,315	70,670
Vice president sales only	170,619	136,250
Director or manager sales only	116,500	108,599
Overall, women in managerial and professional positions earn 70% of their male counter parts.		

Average total compensation of respondent against the number of years in sales and marketing		
Under two years	$ 67,914	$ 57,275
3–5 years	83,114	65,869
6–10 years	105,181	79,050
11–25 years	132,303	102,228
Over 25 years	134,137	103,886

discrepancies in income vary throughout an individual's career, there is a consistent gap between the income levels of men and women in sales. Historical trends suggest the gap is closing, but clearly it is still present in sales.

Until recently, there has been a perception that older salespeople lack the energy and are too inflexible to be successful in the highly competitive world of sales. Researchers suggest that this may not be true and that older salespeople work at least as hard and are just as committed to their jobs as younger salespeople. Exhibit 8.5 details the results

EXHIBIT 8.5
The aging sales force

Source: Katherine Kaplan, "Better with Age," *Sales & Marketing Management,* July 2001, pp. 58–62.

On a scale of 1 to 5, salespeople were evaluated by 300 sales and marketing executives. Results suggest that older salespeople score as well as younger salespeople on some dimensions and higher in several areas such as commitment and emotional stability. Younger salespeople on the other hand score higher in areas such as the ability to understand technology and adaptiveness to travel demands.

Characteristic	Ages 25–39	Ages 40–54	Ages 55–65+
Energy level	4.15	3.49	2.90
Knowledge of products/services	3.07	4.35	4.29
Enthusiasm for the job	3.83	3.56	3.46
Commitment to serving clients	3.21	4.23	4.19
Creativity in problem solving	3.08	4.03	3.69
Aggressiveness in getting the sale	3.75	3.78	3.37
Adaptiveness in travel demands	3.83	3.32	2.82
Ability to meet sales goals	3.33	4.10	3.76
Use and understanding of technology	4.16	3.20	2.69
Emotional stability	2.85	4.21	4.15
Commitment, dedication to the company	2.58	4.10	4.15
Honesty and commitment to clients	3.08	4.19	4.33
Ability to develop trust among clients	3.03	4.37	4.42

of a survey that indicate that older salespeople were more committed to serving clients and their company than their younger counterparts. As one sales consultant put it, "Stereotypes of older salespeople have definitely lost their thunder." The issue of age will become even more critical as baby boomers (born between 1946 and 1963) begin to retire in great numbers.

The positive trends in the employment of women and minorities in recent years have resulted from a variety of social changes, including pressures exerted by the civil rights movement, changing attitudes concerning women's roles, increasing career orientation among women, and legal requirements. The rights of women and minorities to equal employment opportunities in selling, as well as in other occupations, are protected by federal laws. Title VII of the Civil Rights Act prohibits discrimination in hiring, promotions, and compensation. It covers all private employers of 15 or more persons. The Equal Employment Opportunity Commission administers Title VII. Since 1972, it has had broad enforcement powers. While enforcement policies have fluctuated with political changes in the executive branch of the federal government over the years, the commission's guidelines prohibit withholding jobs or promotions because of either customer preferences for salespeople of a particular race or sex or presumed differences in turnover rates. They also prohibit separate promotional paths or seniority lists. Additional legislation has outlawed discrimination on the basis of age and physical disabilities. These important pieces of employment legislation and their implications for sales force recruitment and hiring decisions are examined in more detail in Chapter 11.[12]

Cultural Diversity and Changing Attitudes Have sales managers' attitudes changed as more women and minorities have been added to their sales forces? Unfortunately, there has been little relevant empirical research comparing the job performance of minority salespeople with that of other ethnic groups; however, the growing number of successful minority salespeople and sales managers provides strong anecdotal evidence of their performance capabilities. In addition, many leading firms such as IBM and Procter & Gamble are extremely active in recruiting minorities for their sales forces.

The experiences of these companies suggest that, given adequate training and solid company support, minority salespeople have no major difficulties gaining access to customers. Also, their job performance is not systematically different from that of the rest of the sales force. Furthermore, increasingly minority salespeople are the sales leaders.

As for saleswomen, there is no evidence of consistent differences in the productivity of men and women in business-to-business sales. While men and women are seen as sharing the potential for sales success, both groups are still often perceived to have unique job requirements and concerns and special strengths that enable them to perform better on different aspects of the sales job. For instance, the etiquette involved in traveling with male colleagues or entertaining male clients can still pose uncertainties for some saleswomen. Recent comments from a sales manager exemplify the problem, "Sales involves a lot of travel—I'd feel uncomfortable subjecting a woman to that. What if something happened—would the company be liable?"[13] Similarly, surveys suggest some sales managers and purchasing agents judge salesmen as being better than saleswomen on some dimensions of job performance, such as technical assistance, but perceive saleswomen to be superior on other attributes, including preparation for sales presentations and follow-through.[14]

One must question such generalizations concerning the comparative strengths and weaknesses of salesmen and saleswomen, however. Research suggests variations in sales performance are probably much greater within each group than between them.[15] Thus, there is little that is inherently and unalterably either "male" or "female" about any aspect of good sales performance.

Physical Characteristics and Customer Similarity   While demographic and physical attributes are not strongly related to sales performance in general, particular characteristics may enable a salesperson to deal more effectively with some types of customers than with others. Consequently, some research studies have taken a *dyadic* approach to try to explain variations in performance among salespeople.

Most of the studies test a very simple hypothesis: Salespeople are more likely to be successful when they are dealing with prospects similar to themselves in demographic characteristics, personality traits, and attitudes than when their prospects have characteristics different from their own. It is a natural tendency to understand, have empathy for, and be attracted to other people more like us. Therefore, a salesperson may be better able to understand a customer's problems and needs, communicate a sales message, and persuade the prospect to make a purchase when the rep has physical characteristics, personality traits, and attitudes similar to those of the prospect.[16]

The implications of this hypothesis seem simple and straightforward: Managers should hire salespeople with demographic and personality characteristics as similar as possible to those of the prospects upon whom they will be calling. However, there are two fundamental problems with this prescription. For one thing, it is often impossible to implement. Because buyers and purchasing agents come in all shapes and sizes and vary widely in characteristics, it can be difficult to match a salesperson's attributes with those of all or even most potential customers. A second much more fundamental problem is that research does not support the validity of the similarity hypothesis. For example, one study found that a very small percentage of the differences (less than 2 percent of the variance) in the amount purchased by different customers could be explained by salesperson–customer similarity.[17]

While it may be difficult, at best, to find salespeople with demographic and personality characteristics similar to their customers, this does not mean that physical appearance and image are not important. As detailed in Leadership 8.2, image is important in maintaining

Leadership The Importance of Image 8.2

Lawrence Mandel, sales executive with a financial services company in the Pacific Northwest, strode into the prospective customer's office full of confidence but was greeted with, "Just get back from the links?" At that point Mr. Mandel knew he was in trouble. He was wearing a golf shirt and khaki pants. Trying to recover from the awkward moment he responded, "Uh—We're business causal in our office." While he spent the next 30 minutes going over his presentation it was clear from the prospect's continuous glancing at his watch that he was not going to get the sale. As Mandel explains, "I lost all credibility by not coming in there in a suit. This guy wasn't looking to buy something from some chump in a short sleeved shirt. I totally projected the wrong image."

While it may seem superficial, it is a fact of human nature that what people look like and how they present themselves does matter. Dawn Waldrop, a consultant who teaches executives how to dress, puts it this way, "Lets face it: Humans are very visual beings. If you walk in the door and don't look your best your client may not get past that, no matter how great your presentation is." The problem is many sales managers don't feel comfortable giving sales people feedback about personal issues such as dress. While not all consultants agree on the most appropriate dress, the consensus is it is better to be slightly overdressed relative to the customer than underdressed. Sam Parker, a sales consultant in Virginia, illustrates, "If he [client] is wearing a sport coat, you put on a suit. Nobody is going to look at you poorly because you are slightly overdressed."

Image is important both in relationships with the customer and in the hiring process. Consider the following:

What type of sales representative has a tougher time making sales? (percent of respondents indicating it was an issue)

A sloppily dressed sales rep	94%
An unstylish sales rep (haircut, out of style outfit)	75
A physically unattractive sales rep	59
An overweight sales rep	54
A sales rep with a heavy accent	54
A very young looking sales rep	32
An older looking sales rep	8

What type of sales representative would you avoid hiring? (percent of respondents indicating it was an issue)

Any sales rep who was a sloppy dresser	80%
Any sales rep who used salty language	78
Any sales rep who had visible body piercing or tattoos	77
Any sales rep who looked unstylish	51
Male sales rep who was overweight	37
Female sales rep who was overweight	23
Any sales rep with a heavy regional or foreign accent	20
Female sales rep who was very unattractive	20
Male sales rep who was very unattractive	13
Any sales rep who had a very youthful appearance	12
Any sales rep who appeared to look older	2

One result of the focus on image is improved self-confidence. Research suggests that when people dress more professionally they feel better about themselves. Burt Smith, vice president of marketing for MediaBin, a high-tech firm in Atlanta, states, "I'm more comfortable standing in front of a client when I'm dressed up and well groomed." The old adage "when you look good, you feel good" may in fact be true.

Source: Melinda Ligos, "Does Image Matter?" *Sales & Marketing Management,* March 2001, pp. 52–56.

a successful relationship with customers. It also plays a critical role in the hiring process, as managers are not as likely to hire someone who is sloppily dressed or presents a less than professional image.

Background and Experience

One of the surprises in the findings presented in Exhibit 8.2 is that personal history and family background variables are among the best predictors of sales success, accounting for an average of about 20 percent of the variance in performance across salespeople.

This suggests that information about such things as whether a person held part-time jobs or had substantial family responsibilities as a youngster provides a good indication of likely emotional maturity and motivation. These traits, in turn, are important determinants of sales performance, particularly for young recruits. Increasingly, it is also beneficial, if not essential, for salespeople to be multilingual, especially in some professions and in certain geographic areas. For example, Spanish is spoken widely in parts of Texas, California, Florida, and many urban areas in the Northeast and Midwest. Salespeople who have mastered Spanish can find greater opportunities in many sales careers such as real estate.

More surprising, perhaps, is that some of the background factors on which sales managers most commonly rely when evaluating potential recruits—such as the person's educational attainment, course of study, and general work experience—do not show much relationship with sales performance. Companies still seek individuals with a college education. Innovation 8.3 speaks to the issue of education and its importance in sales success.

Even a person's past sales experience—a factor that receives primary emphasis in some firms' recruitment and selection—does not do a good job of explaining differences in performance across salespeople. Surprisingly, companies continue to focus on hiring sales representatives with prior experience. One study reported that nearly half of the companies preferred hiring individuals with one to three years experience, and 40 percent wanted even more experience (more than three years). Only 10 percent indicated they hire new salespeople with less than one year of experience. More recently, high-tech companies have looked to recruit sales professionals with proven track records that can make a difference immediately. In light of the rapidly changing technology landscape many companies feel they do not have the time to train a salesperson to be successful.[18]

Current Status and Lifestyle Variables

As was the case with personal history and family background, a person's current marital and family status, income level, and financial obligations (e.g., a large mortgage) are relatively good predictors of sales performance. Variables related to marital and family status account for about 12 percent of the variance in performance across salespeople (Exhibit 8.2). However, be aware that it is not appropriate for interviewers to ask about marital status or specific issues related to family status (number of kids). As we see later, though, these relationships are much stronger for some kinds of sales jobs than for others. At the same time, a person's lifestyle does not appear to be closely related to sales performance, accounting for less than 5 percent of individual differences in sales performance.

Aptitude Variables

Despite the variety of tests of sales aptitude developed specifically for selecting salespeople, such measures explain less than 5 percent of differences in sales performance. Once again, however, the ability of sales aptitude to predict performance varies greatly across different types of sales jobs. We explore this in more detail in the next section of this chapter.

Most tests of general mental aptitude or abilities—such as general intelligence tests, measures of verbal ability and fluency, and tests of math ability—are all relatively uncorrelated with sales performance. But a person's ability to think logically and display flexibility in solving problems—an ability measured by tests of cognitive ability—is a relatively good indicator of likely success in selling. Cognitive ability measures explain nearly 7 percent of the variance in performance across salespeople.

Innovation The Educated Sales Force 8.3

The level of education in the sales force of the twenty-first century has never been higher. Almost two-thirds of all salespeople have a college degree and more than 6 percent have a postgraduate degree. As noted below, there is a great deal of variance in the percentages by industry. However, overall the percentages speak to a profession where education is important even though it has not been shown to be a significant predictor of performance.

Industry	College Degree (%)	Post-graduate Degree (%)
Health services	100%	
Pharmaceuticals	100	
Air transportation	100	
Printing/publishing	84	5.3%
Rubber/plastics	83	
Manufacturing	78	6
Electronics	77	22
Chemicals	73	18
Business services	72	8
Electronic components	67	8
Communications	56	6
Banking	46	10
Construction	40	
Trucking/warehousing	33	
Real estate	33	
Retail	29	
Transportation equipment	28	

The percentage number does not equal 100 percent, as only two categories were included in the table.

Source: Christen P. Heide, *Dartnell's 30th Sales Force Compensation Survey* (Chicago: The Dartnell Corporation, 1999), p. 173.

As the table suggests some industries (e.g., pharmaceuticals) recruit college educated salespeople exclusively while others (e.g., retail and transportation equipment) have less than one third of the sales force with a college degree. Not surprising, sales managers have a variety of opinions on the issue. Consider how three executives responded to the question.

Would you hire a salesperson who doesn't have a college degree?

No. The risk in hiring the candidate without the degree is that by not having the experience in the industry or the savvy that comes from a business degree, he might get himself in way over his head and blow the reputation of the company. A college degree means focus, discipline, and sweat equity. I do have someone on my team without a college degree, but she has 25 years experience.

Mary Platt, regional sales manager,
Wells Fargo, Los Angeles, California

The lack of a college degree would not automatically preclude an applicant's otherwise strong resume. But I would scrutinize the person's resume much more carefully.

Jeffrey Slack, national account manager,
Computer Associates, Tampa, Florida

I would. There are many people out there who haven't had the opportunity for a higher education, but do have experience from working internships.

Juan Rivera, director of guest relations,
Hotel Del Monico, New York, New York.

Source: *Sales & Marketing Management,* May 2001, p. 14.

Personality Variables

More studies have attempted to explain individual variations in sales performance by examining personality trait differences than any other personal characteristic. Also, much of the conventional wisdom to which sales managers and consultants have adhered over the years has stressed the importance of such personality traits as self-esteem, extraversion, sociability, dominance, and a strong need for achievement as determinants of sales success. It is rather disappointing, then, to discover that individual personality traits explain a very small percentage of the differences in salespeople's performance (less than 5 percent of the variance).

Recent research has found the type of sales job must be considered. For example, extraversion is measured using items like, "I am the life of the party." For years conventional wisdom believed that an extravert would perform well in all sales roles. However, recent research suggests extraversion is positively related to sales roles such as retail and call centers (inside sales), but negatively related to performance in business-to-business sales roles. Potential B2B customers felt that extraverts did a poor job of relating a product to their business needs. As good B2B salespeople say, "It isn't about talking, it's about listening." The research concluded that using a personality test to predict sales success is best achieved when the test is designed for a specific sales role.

More recent research suggests that cooperative behavior is a key characteristic for success. At this point, the best predictors of a person's willingness to be cooperative are past tendencies of cooperativeness or specific personality tests that focus on measuring cooperative attitudes and behavior. However, some personality tests that focus on only a few broad, stable traits—such as extroversion, openness to experience, and conscientiousness—may be more strongly related to sales success.[19]

Skill Variables

Vocational skills encompass a salesperson's acquired knowledge and abilities directly related to the company, its products, and customers. Not surprising, the more skill a salesperson has, the better the performance is likely to be. Vocational skills account on average for more than 9 percent of the variance in sales performance. It is also no surprise that differences in salespeople's skill at preparing and delivering good sales presentations can explain as much as 5 percent of the differences in their performance. Sales managers also evaluate how well individuals use technology in their presentations. As the technology and customers become more sophisticated, the quality of the presentation must get better. Consequently, the ability to deliver quality presentation becomes more important.

General management skills, such as organizational and leadership abilities, account for approximately 9 percent of the variance in performance across salespeople. This is to be expected since most salespeople have the freedom to manage their own time and to organize their efforts within their territories. Also, some salespeople must work closely and coordinate their efforts with a customer's personnel to carry out such tasks as sales engineering, installation of equipment, and training of the customer's employees. Interestingly, interpersonal skills related to understanding and getting along with people are not strongly related to ultimate sales performance. This runs counter to the conventional wisdom offered by many authorities.

Finally, the lack of significant sales performance predictors is not surprising. Customers and salespeople cannot even agree on which skills are critical for sales success. Exhibit 8.6 highlights the problems in identifying characteristics that build trust between customer and salespeople. While salespeople indicate listening skills are most critical in building trust with the customer, customers themselves rank product knowledge number one.

JOB-SPECIFIC DETERMINANTS OF GOOD SALES PERFORMANCE

It is clear that different types of sales jobs require salespeople to perform different tasks and activities under different circumstances. It would seem to make sense, then, to develop task-specific definitions of sales aptitude and ability, since the traits and skills needed to be successful in one type of sales job may be irrelevant to another. As discussed in Chapter 9, this kind of task-specific, or *contingency,* approach is the one sales managers should use when determining what traits and abilities to look for in new sales recruits. Unfortunately,

EXHIBIT 8.6
The characteristics of salespeople who win customer trust

Source: *Sales & Marketing Management,* February 2001, p. 90.

Customers and salespeople were asked, What kind of rep is most trustworthy? Salespeople indicated listening skills were most important in building trust with the customer while customers believe product knowledge was the key in winning trust.

Characteristic	Percent of Customers Responding	Percent of Salespeople Responding
Product knowledge	79.5%	79.6%
Understands business	63.9	73.1
Reliable	63.1	75.9
Understands needs of customer	63.1	85.3
Confidence in product	54.1	63.8
Likable	53.3	55.6
Positive attitude	50.8	71.2
Good listening skills	44.3	87.2
Intelligent	41.8	40.3
Asks good questions	39.3	65.9
Self-confident	22.1	45.6
Well-dressed	14.8	29.1

little published research is available to guide sales managers in deciding what personal characteristics are most important in enabling salespeople to perform well in specific types of sales jobs.[20] The findings of research to date are examined below.

Selling Different Types of Products and Services

The previous research discussed earlier found that the strength of the relationships between some personal characteristics and sales performance varied widely across studies. Some of the variation was because different studies examined samples of salespeople engaged in selling different types of products. Thus, a given trait might bear a strong relationship with performance in studies where the respondents were selling business-to-business goods to organizational customers, but the same trait might have only a weak relationship to performance in studies focused on people selling consumer goods or services.

Overall, the following variables have been shown to be different across different kinds of selling environment:

- Personal history and family background

- Marital and family status

- Sales aptitude

- Dominance

- Self-esteem

- Sales presentation skills

- Interpersonal skills

The findings suggest that for people selling business-to-business products to institutional customers, "professional" skills and traits—such as sales aptitude, sales presentation skills, interpersonal skills, and self-esteem—are relatively good predictors of successful performance.

However, for jobs involving the sale of services, such job-related skills appear to be relatively less important. Traits related to aggressiveness and motivation, such as a dominant personality and family obligations, are better indicators of success in selling services than they are for jobs involving either consumer or business-to-business goods.

Different Types of Sales Jobs

One study directly compared the characteristics of successful and unsuccessful salespeople in specific sales jobs across a large number of organizations. These firms were classified according to the type of selling in which their salespeople were primarily engaged.

The four categories of Business to Business sales jobs were used: (1) trade selling, (2) missionary selling, (3) technical selling, and (4) new-business selling. The study then compared personal characteristics of successful and unsuccessful salespeople in each of the four kinds of sales jobs. The results of this survey are summarized in Exhibit 8.7.[21] While it is not appropriate to draw specific conclusions about each type of sales job, it is clear that different types of sales positions require different kinds of sales skills and abilities.

IMPLICATIONS FOR SALES MANAGEMENT

What has this review of the knowledge accumulated through experience and published research taught us about the personal characteristics that are related to sales aptitude and the potential for selling success? For one thing, no general physical characteristics, mental abilities, or personality traits appear to be consistently related to sales aptitude and performance in all companies and selling situations. Also, the evidence suggests it is probably neither wise nor practical for a sales manager to try to select salespeople with characteristics that match those of their potential customers. The possible exception is in selling to consumers. Instead, the most potentially useful approach to defining sales aptitude and evaluating a person's potential is first to determine the kinds of tasks involved in a specific sales job. Then, one can evaluate the relevance of particular characteristics and abilities for enabling a person to carry out those tasks successfully.

Unfortunately, very little research has either analyzed the tasks and activities unique to particular types of selling or identified the personal traits and abilities important for success in different sales jobs. For the time being, then, sales executives must develop their

EXHIBIT 8.7
Characteristics related to sales performance in different types of sales jobs

Type of Sales Job	Relatively Important Characteristics	Relatively Less Important Characteristics
Trade selling	Age, maturity, empathy, knowledge of customer and business methods	Aggressiveness, technical ability, product knowledge, persuasiveness
Missionary selling	Youth, high energy and stamina, verbal skill, persuasiveness	Empathy, knowledge of customers, maturity, previous sales experience
Technical selling	Education, product and customer knowledge—usually gained through training, intelligence	Empathy, persuasiveness, aggressiveness, age
New-business selling	Experience, age and maturity, aggressiveness, persuasiveness, persistence	Customer knowledge, product knowledge, education, empathy

own specifications concerning what to look for in new sales recruits. Those specifications should be developed after a careful analysis and description of the tasks and activities involved in selling the firm's products to its target market. There should also be an evaluation of the characteristics and qualifications that new salespeople must have to perform those tasks and activities. Therefore, Chapter 9 examines the methods and procedures involved in sales force recruitment and selection. It begins with a discussion of how to carry out a job analysis and develop a list of qualifications to use in evaluating recruits.

Summary

This chapter, the first of two dealing with salesperson selection, sought to review the evidence regarding what personal and psychological characteristics are related to an individual's likely performance as a salesperson. Personal traits and aptitude are typically thought to place an upper limit on an individual's ability to perform a given sales job.

Several sets of personal factors are thought to affect a salesperson's ability to perform, including the following:

1. Demographic and physical characteristics—such as age, sex, and physical appearance.

2. Background and experience factors—such as a person's personal history and family background, educational attainment, and sales experience.

3. Current status and lifestyle variables—including a person's marital and financial status and activities outside of the job.

4. Aptitude variables—enduring mental characteristics such as intelligence, cognitive abilities, and sales aptitude.

5. Personality traits—including such characteristics as sociability, dominance, and self-esteem.

6. Skill levels—learned proficiencies, such as vocational skills (e.g., product knowledge), interpersonal skills, sales presentation skills, and general management skills.

Although a number of reasons can be advanced as to why these factors might be related to sales performance, the available evidence suggests that none is consistently related to performance when examined across industries and job settings.

One of the more persuasive reasons for these inconsistent relationships is that particular characteristics of salespeople enable them to deal more effectively with some kinds of customers than with others. Consequently, some studies have used a dyadic approach to explain variations in performance among salespeople. The basic hypothesis is that salespeople are more likely to be successful when they deal with prospects who are similar to themselves in terms of demographic characteristics, personality traits, and attitudes. The implication of the dyadic perspective for sales managers is that they should hire salespeople with characteristics similar to the customers on whom they will call. But such a strategy can be hard to implement in business to business selling, and it is likely to become even more difficult as both sales recruits and customer organizations become more culturally diverse. Also, the existing research evidence does not consistently support the proposition.

The most important conclusion regarding salespeople selection is that there are many different types of selling jobs. Each type requires the salesperson to perform a variety of different tasks and activities under different circumstances. Consequently, the most useful approach to defining sales aptitude and evaluating a person's potential for future success is, first, to determine the kinds of tasks involved in a specific sales job. Then one can evaluate the relevance of particular characteristics and abilities for enabling a person to carry out those tasks successfully.

Key Terms

selection criteria   psychological traits
physical characteristics   skill variables

Breakout Questions

1. Mark and Cynthia had just finished a long session that produced a heated discussion concerning hiring people who are overweight. Mark stressed that overweight people are considered lazy, sloppy, and lacking in self-esteem. He insisted that no sales manager would overlook these features and hire such a person. "What a waste of money, since customers don't want to do business with a tubbo," argued Mark. Cynthia countered with equal conviction, accusing Mark of stereotyping all people who are overweight. She asked Mark if he knew that for some people the problem was genetic and not over-indulgence. "Besides," she stressed, "not hiring someone because of their weight just happens to be illegal." Is it legal not to hire a person because of his or her weight?

2. As we saw in the chapter, women are playing an increasingly important role in selling both as salespeople and as sales managers. What are the challenges facing women and other minorities as they become involved in a sales career?

3. Enthusiasm is one of the more important attributes sales executives look for in new salespeople. How would you measure or determine whether an applicant possessed enthusiasm? If an applicant lacks enthusiasm but shows a positive interest in sales, would it be possible to teach enthusiasm?

4. The sales manager of a company manufacturing orthopedic medical equipment attempts to hire salespeople based on the personalities of the customers. The sales manager uses the same process when assigning salespeople to customers. In other words, the similarity hypothesis discussed earlier is being applied. Does this process make sense? As a sales manager, would you use the similarity theory in hiring salespeople or assigning salespeople to customers? Why or why not?

Leadership Challenge: Characteristics of the Great Salesperson

Thad Williams had the kind of problem many sales managers wish they could experience more often. He just came out of a strategic planning meeting with senior management at his company, Logistics Logic (a leading supplier of logistics solutions for manufacturing companies). The emphasis in many organizations on supply chain management had created huge demand for the products and services offered by Logistics Logic. Started by Eric and Jody Lemaster in 1981, the company had developed an excellent reputation by helping companies become more efficient and effective in managing the flow of goods in and out of the organizations. Logistics Logic worked with key players in the supply chain management industry (FedEx, UPS, DHL, and others) to develop custom-designed hardware and software for unique logistics solutions. The company had found a great niche for its products by focusing on medium-sized companies around the world.

Thad had been with the company for 10 years and worked his way up to vice president of sales. Revenue exceeded $200 million last year, and the company had a worldwide sales force of 130. At this meeting, Thad had been given the go-ahead to hire 30 new salespeople, all of them in the United States. This would represent the largest increase of salespeople in the company's history and was based on the goal of taking the company to $260 million in the next two years.

The typical salesperson was a male in his early forties with a technical background in logistics. Interestingly, however, Thad had noticed that most of the new salespeople (those hired in the last three years) were women (8 out 10). Salespeople needed a very good knowledge of logistics and the fundamentals of relationship selling. The compensation system allowed salespeople to earn a good living, with many earning in excess of $100,000 per year.

Thad had also noticed the typical customer had changed in recent years. When he started, customers were often men in their fifties who had little formal education in logistics. Now customers were most often experienced men and women with formal training in supply chain management.

Logistics Logic, and more specifically Thad Williams, knew the company's new salespeople were critical to the organization's continued success; the question was, What would make a successful Logistics Logic salesperson in the twenty-first century?

Questions

1. What qualities and characteristics do you think are important for a new salesperson at Logistics Logic? Why?
2. What kind of person would you recruit (experienced versus less experienced, age, education, background, etc.)?

Role Play: Bass Brokers, Inc.—A

Situation

National sales manager Roscoe Lee slammed his fist down on the desk in his office, startling human resources manager Pat Tollford. "Sales District 5 has got to get control of their turnover," Roscoe exclaimed. "Why is the turnover rate among salespeople in that district running 20 percent annually when the company average is less than 3 percent per year?"

Roscoe and Pat work at the home office of Bass Brokers, Inc., a sales brokerage firm that represents lines of fishing equipment sold in a variety of retail outlets across the United States and Canada. Bass Brokers was started in 1977 by avid fisherman Pug Pike, who literally sold fishing lures out of the trunk of his car to mom-and-pop tackle shops in Louisiana and Mississippi. Bass Brokers now represents some of the top lines of lures and other fishing equipment supplies and has grown to a sales force of 60 spread across six sales districts in the United States and Canada. Each district is led by a district sales manager who reports directly to Roscoe.

The fact that one of Bass Brokers' sales districts is experiencing high turnover is quite troubling, as the firm prides itself on really understanding the selection criteria necessary to ensure that the salespeople it hires will have a high likelihood of success with the company. Among the core values of Bass Brokers are building customer relationships, fair and civil treatment of all employees, and involvement of all employees in the process of company planning and decision making. Bass Brokers salespeople are compensated by a combination of base salary and commission on products sold. Because the firm has such a positive culture and tries hard to use selection criteria that are a good match to the firm, turnover has never been a problem—in fact, historically nearly all of the company's new salespeople have been hired to fill opening's created in three ways: retirements, promotions, or salespeople leaving Bass Brokers on good terms to take a more lucrative sales position elsewhere. Over the past two years, District 5 has lost four salespeople, each of whom had left the company within a short time of being hired, and each of whom seemed to never really fit in well with the needs of Bass Brokers.

This history has led Roscoe and Pat to conclude that a problem exists with the selection criteria used in District 5. The district manager there, Jason Queen, is the newest district manager at Bass Brokers, having been promoted from a sales job in another district of the firm three years ago. The district has 10 sales positions reporting to Jason. Six of these are long-term Bass Brokers salespeople who continue to do well and enjoy working for Jason. The other four were new people who have turned over during the past 24 months. In Jason's estimation, and Roscoe and Pat concur, these four individuals never really caught on to the Bass Brokers way of doing business.

Despite its success in the sales area, Bass Brokers has never formalized selection criteria for its salespeople. Nowhere in either the HR department or the sales department does any documentation of the specific personal characteristics and sales aptitude criteria for selecting salespeople exist. Because of the turnover problem in District 5, before anymore new salespeople are hired Roscoe and Pat must brainstorm and develop a list of these criteria.

Characters in the Role Play

Roscoe Lee, national sales manager for Bass Brokers, Inc.

Pat Tollford, human resource manager for Bass Brokers, Inc.

Assignment

Break into pairs, with one student playing each character. It doesn't matter what the actual gender mix of your pair is. Before you stage the continuation of the above-mentioned meeting between Roscoe and Pat, work separately using the material in your chapter to come up with a logical set of selection criteria you each believe will be important to discuss in the meeting. Then get together and role-play the meeting between Roscoe and Pat. Think about the various types of clients Bass Brokers is likely to sell fishing products to—essentially, any type of retail outlet that carries such products. Also consider what you learned above about the culture and values of the company. Roscoe and Pat's goal is to compare their ideas and come up with a list of selection criteria that are most important to apply in hiring Bass Brokers salespeople. For the criteria that make your final list, be sure to note why you two agree each is important.

Minicase: J.P. Reynolds Investments

Raymond Baker is J.P. Reynolds Investments' district sales manager for the Southeastern Region (covering Florida, Georgia, South Carolina, Tennessee, and Alabama). J.P. Reynolds sells a variety of mutual funds and other investment products to financial services companies that are retailer sellers of such products. It generally offers its investment products to small- and medium-sized customers, such as regional banks, as opposed to large financial services companies.

Raymond recently lost his best salesperson and must replace him immediately. This morning he interviewed two job candidates, Dag Wicklo and Katharine Bryant, for the position of sales representative, level II (three to six years of experience), for about 45 minutes each. Dag is 26, tall, athletic, enjoys outdoor activities, is not married, has no children, and is clearly from the South. He came to the interview with very short-cropped hair and a slightly wrinkled suit. He scored slightly below average on the test of general mental aptitude administered by the HR department. Katharine is 36, shorter than average, not athletic, is married to a wealthy financier, has two children, and is originally from New York. She is wearing a very formal black suit and expensive-looking shoes. She scored well on the test of general mental aptitude.

Here are a few excerpts from the respective interviews:

RB: How would you describe your selling style?

DW: Ray, I'm a go-getter. I'm young, enthusiastic, and I love selling. I also love money, so I love working with investment products and love the commission-based nature of the business. Most of all I love people, and they respond well to me. By the end of a meeting, I feel like I'm with a friend, and the sale happens so naturally, it doesn't even feel like selling.

KB: Mr. Baker, I try to know my product inside and out and present a clear, logical case as to why my customer should purchase it. However, I don't get down and beg for the sale. If the customer does not want to buy, I simply go to the next prospect. Also, I try to stay as professional as possible and not get too close to the customers.

RB: What strengths and weaknesses would you bring to this position?

DW: My number-one strength is that I'm very likable. I speak Spanish, Portuguese, and English, so I can talk to almost anyone. Also, despite my young age, I have five years of sales experience in the investment field and have received high performance evaluations. I'm confident, resilient, and creative. I find a way to solve a problem. Finally, I'm a good presenter and like to speak without any prepared speech or remarks.

My biggest weakness is that I can be less than organized. I sometimes let my creative energy get the better of me, and I'm not always the most professional or polished guy. I get the job done in my own way, I guess. Also, I don't have much formal college education and don't understand the technology as well as I would like. I'm sure I can learn it, though.

KB: I take command of a room or a situation well and don't let anyone intimidate me. I have a master's degree in art history and have the intelligence to handle myself well and understand the products. Also, I am extremely organized. If you asked them, my children can verify what a tight ship I run at home. Although I do not have sales experience in selling investment products, my husband is an investment banker, as was my father, so I can speak the language.

My main weakness is that I have only two years of sales experience, but I have owned and managed my own business before. Also, I don't need the money, so I'm not as aggressive as some of these young bucks in terms of sales volume. However, I feel that I can relate well to the customer and will understand them better because of my other business experience.

Joanna Baer, the vice president of sales and Raymond's immediate boss, just interviewed each applicant this afternoon and has called Raymond into her office to discuss the situation. Because of the pressing need, the company needs to make an offer to one of the two candidates. Raymond knows he must evaluate the applicants quickly and make a recommendation to Joanna.

Questions

1. What categories of variables affecting performance can you identify?
2. Within each category, which variables do you think are relevant to a salesperson's performance at J.P. Reynolds? Why?
3. If you were Raymond, which applicant would you recommend to Joanna to hire? Why?

Suggested Readings

Determinants of Sales Performance

Cron, William L., Greg W. Marshall, Jagdip Singh, Rosann L. Spiro, and Harish Sujan. "Salesperson Selection, Training, and Development: Trends, Implications, and Research Opportunities." *Journal of Personal Selling & Sales Management* 25 (Spring 2005) pp. 123–36.

DeCarlo, Thomas E., Sanjeev Agarwal, and Shyman B. Vyas. "Performance Expectations of Salespeople: The Role of Past Performance and Casual Attributions in Independent and Interdependent Cultures." *Journal of Personal Selling & Sales Management* 27 (Spring 2007) pp. 133–47.

Dixon, Andrea L., Rosann L. Spiro, and Lukas P. Forbes. "Attributions and Behavioral Intentions of Inexperienced Salespersons to Failure: An Empirical Investigation." *Journal of the Academy of Marketing Science* 31, no. 4 (2003), pp. 459–67.

Jelinek, Ronald, and Michael Ahearne. "The Enemy Within: Examining Salesperson Deviance and its Determinants." *Journal of Personal Selling & Sales Management* 26 (Fall 2006) pp. 327–44.

Kidwell, Blair, Richard G. McFarland, and Ramon A. Avila. "Perceiving Emotion in the Buyer-Seller Interchange: The Moderated Impact on Performance." *Journal of Personal Selling & Sales Management* 27 (Spring 2007) pp. 119–32.

Krishnan, Balaji C., Richard G. Netemeyer, and James S. Boles. "Self-Efficacy, Competitiveness, and Effort as Antecedents of Salesperson Performance." *Journal of Personal Selling & Sales Management* 22, no. 4 (2002), pp. 285–95.

Nonis, Sarath A., and Jeffrey K. Sager. "Coping Strategy Profiles Used by Salespeople: Their Relationships with Personal Characteristics and Work Outcomes." *Journal of Personal Selling & Sales Management* 23, no. 2 (2003), pp. 139–50.

Pelham, Alfred. "An Exploratory Model and Initial Test of the Influence of Firm-Level Consulting-Oriented Sales Force Programs on Sales Force Performance." *Journal of Personal Selling & Sales Management* 22, no. 2 (2002), pp. 97–110.

Schwepker, Charles H., Jr. "Customer-Oriented Selling: A Review, Extension, and Directions for Future Research." *Journal of Personal Selling & Sales Management* 23, no. 2 (2003), pp. 151–71.

Sivadas, Eugene, Susan Bardi Kleiser, James Kellaris, and Robert Dahlstrom. "Moral Philosophy, Ethical Evaluations, and Sales Manager Hiring Intentions." *Journal of Personal Selling & Sales Management* 23, no. 1 (2002–3), pp. 7–21.

Women and Cultural Diversity

Boles, James S., John Andy Wood, and Julie Johnson. "Interrelationships of Role Conflict, Role Ambiguity, and Work-Family Conflict with Different Facets of Job Satisfaction and the Moderating Effects of Gender." *Journal of Personal Selling & Sales Management* 23, no. 2 (2003), pp. 99–113.

Piercy, Nigel F., David W. Cravens, and Nikala Lane. "Sales Manager Behavior Control Strategy and Its Consequences: The Impact of Manager Gender Differences." *Journal of Personal Selling & Sales Management* 23, no. 3 (2003), pp. 221–37.

Ramaswami, Sridhar. "Influence of Control Systems on Opportunistic Behaviors of Salespeople: A Test of Gender Differences." *Journal of Personal Selling & Sales Management* 22, no. 3 (2002), pp. 173–88.

Stevens, Charles D., and Gerrard Macintosh. "Personality and Attractiveness of Activities within Sales Jobs." *Journal of Personal Selling & Sales Management* 23, no. 1 (2003), pp. 23–37.

Chapter Nine

Sales Force Recruitment and Selection

The Real Value of Hiring Good Employees

As we discussed in Chapter 8, organizations often claim employees are their most valuable resource, but just how valuable are they? More often than not, the value added by employees is difficult to assess; however, sales positions are unique because their value can be determined by actual sales in dollars or product units. Once individual employee value is determined, other important questions arise: what is the difference to the bottom line of selecting a good hire versus a poor hire? How does a company hire the right person? Can a selection assessment increase the probability of choosing a good hire?

In an effort to address these questions, Chally studied salesperson performance data over four years from a leading financial services provider. The average annual sales per sales representative was nearly $1.1 million. However, performance across the sales force was highly variable, with poor hires averaging about $300,000 in annual sales. Thus, if the company had hired an "average" salesperson instead of a poor performer, it would have generated almost $800,000 in additional sales. Multiply this figure by the number of below average performers and the number of years a salesperson is expected to stay with the company, and it becomes apparent that avoiding hiring mistakes can dramatically increase profitability. Each time a territory is filled with a poor performer, the company loses a great deal of potential revenue.

Next, Chally investigated whether selection tests can significantly help a company identify the right people. Chally's research found a company using a standardized test that wasn't even a strong predictor of success (for example, a typical "personality" or "style" test such as Edwards Personal Preference Survey or Myers-Briggs) could increase average annual sales to $1.2 million, a gain of $100,000 over the average. However, if they incorporated a highly predictive, empirically validated test, average annual sales jump to $1.4 million or *nearly $300,000 more* than the average sales. In sum, increasing the output per employee and the average number of years an employee stays on the job results in large financial gains for a company.

Hiring better performers means hiring people that fit the job better and are likely to stay longer. Employing a validated selection assessment has significantly lowered turnover and increased revenue for a number of companies including:

• CopyMax and Media 24 each experienced a 32 percent reduction in turnover.

• Association of Financial Planners experienced a 27 percent increase in revenue one year and a 33 percent increase in year two after changing their hiring tools.

It is not uncommon for employers to reduce turnover by 30 percent while simultaneously increasing productivity by 30 percent by changing their personnel selection tools. These reductions in turnover and increases in productivity have an enormous impact on a company's bottom line. As Bill Gibson, director of GM fleet and commercial sales, reports, GM was able to increase sales by 50–60 thousand units while simultaneously improving customer retention, which translated into a $1 billion revenue increase. Clearly, employees are an organization's most valuable resource.

Source: HR Chally Group (2007).

LEARNING OBJECTIVES

Perhaps more than any other function of the sales manager, successfully recruiting new salespeople into the company is critical to the long-term success of the organization. As markets expand both domestically and internationally, companies continue to seek qualified new candidates to fill sales positions. At the same time, it is likely that talented people in the organization are being recruited, often by competitors, and leaving for other opportunities. Finally, competition for talented candidates is fierce and the cost of poor recruiting is high, in both direct and indirect costs. For all these reasons, recruiting and selecting salespeople has become a very important part of the sales manager's job. This chapter will outline the process of recruiting new salespeople into the organizations.

At the end of this chapter, you should be able to

• Understand the key issues that drive the recruitment and selection of salespeople.

• Identify who is responsible for the recruitment and selection process.

• Understand a job analysis and how selection criteria are determined.

• Define the sources for new sales recruits.

• Explain the selection procedures.

• Understand the equal opportunity requirements for selecting salespeople.

RECRUITMENT AND SELECTION ISSUES

The Real Value of Hiring Good Employees opener illustrates the variety of important issues that must be resolved when recruiting and selecting new salespeople. These issues are diagrammed in Exhibit 9.1.

The first decision to be made concerns who in the company will have the responsibility for hiring new salespeople. While it is common to assign this responsibility to field sales

EXHIBIT 9.1

The decision process for recruiting and selecting salespeople

Establish policy concerning responsibility
 for recruitment and selection.

• Who will participate in the process?
• Who has authority to make hiring decisions?

Analyze the job and determine
 selection criteria.

• Conduct a job analysis.
• Write a job description.
• Develop a statement of job qualifications.

Find and attract a pool of applicants.

• Internal sources.
• External sources.

Develop and apply selection procedures
 to evaluate applicants.

• Application blanks.
• Interviews.
• Reference checks.
• Formal tests.

managers, top sales executives or personnel departments play a more active role and bear more of the burden for this important function in some firms.

Regardless of who has the responsibility for recruiting new sales reps, certain procedures should be followed to ensure that new recruits have the aptitude for the job and the potential to be successful. As discussed in Chapter 8, there do not seem to be any general characteristics that make some people better performers across all types of sales jobs. Therefore, a thoughtful recruitment process includes a thorough analysis of the job and a description of the qualifications that a new hire should have. The company then seeks to find and attract a pool of job applicants with the proper qualifications. The objective, in other words, is not to maximize the number of job applicants but to attract a few good applicants. This is because of the high costs involved in attracting and evaluating candidates. For instance, a large industrial services firm estimates that it spent more than $750,000 for want ads, employment agency fees, psychological tests, and sales manager's time interviewing and evaluating candidates in order to hire 50 new salespeople. And it cost another $1 million to train those new recruits. The final stage in the hiring process is to evaluate each applicant using personal history information, interviews, reference checks, and formal tests. The purpose is to determine which applicants have the characteristics and abilities for success. During this stage of the evaluation and selection process, managers must be especially careful not to violate equal employment opportunity laws and regulations.

The remaining sections of this chapter discuss the specific methods and procedures managers might use at each stage of the recruitment and selection process. The recruiting process is complex, and the selection of the right candidate is a function of many different criteria. As demonstrated in Innovation 9.1, companies use a variety of tools to help

Innovation The Hiring Quiz   9.1

Managers are always searching for tools that will enable them to make better hiring decisions. Here is a quiz for managers to help in defining the right candidate.

The right candidate is a function of the score to the quiz.

1. Are you in an industry with
   a. Relatively few well-known competitors and few changes in relation to new products and service? (1 point)
   b. New competition entering the market and rapid changes to products and services introduced? (2 points)

2. What category fits your product?
   a. Capital equipment (1 point)
   b. Consumer (2 points)
   c. Service (3 points)

3. If your product is technical in nature, what is your level of technical sales support?
   a. Strong (1 point)
   b. Average (2 points)
   c. Weak (3 points)

4. How do you market your product?
   a. Heavily (1 point)
   b. Very little (2 points)
   c. Rely on sales staff to do it (3 points)

5. Are you interested in
   a. The development of additional business within existing accounts? (1 point)
   b. The management of an existing line of business within mature accounts? (2 points)
   c. The promotion of a new product to prospective customers? (3 points)

6. How much time can you afford to hire and train new sales staff before receiving a return on your investment?
   a. 30–90 days (1 point)
   b. 91–180 days (2 points)
   c. 181 days or more (3 points)

7. Will your sales staff work in an office where
   a. Direct supervisor is present? (1 point)
   b. No direct supervisor is present? (3 points)

8. Will your sales staff
   a. Rely on other sales personnel to prospect and qualify potential customers? (2 points)
   b. Qualify prospects themselves? (0 points)

9. How much time will you spend training your new hire?
   a. 81 hours or more (1 point)
   b. 41–80 hours (2 points)
   c. 0–40 hours (3 points)

10. How much time will you spend coaching and counseling your new sales staff?
    a. 21 hours or more per week (1 point)
    b. 11–20 hours per week (2 points)
    c. 0–10 hours per week (3 points)

Add your total points and then refer to the description below to determine the best type of individual for your sales efforts.

HOW TO SCORE

1. Add your total points from questions 1–10.

2. Match your point total to the corresponding point totals below.

3. Your ideal candidate will possess the characteristics indicated for the point total.

PRIMARY CHARACTERISTIC OF SALESPERSON

13 points or less	Tenacity, rapport building, work standards, oral communication, ability to learn
14–18 points	Leadership, planning and organization, job motivation, presence
19–28 points	Persuasiveness, negotiation, analysis, initiative, written communication

(continued)

Innovation   *concluded*   9.1.

SECONDARY CHARACTERISTIC OF SALESPERSON		SOURCE OF SALES RECRUITS	
13 points or less	Planning and organization, listening, job motivation, initiative, written communication	13 points or less	New college graduate or hire from within
14–18 points	Analysis, tenacity, oral communication, written communication, rapport building	14–18 points	Hire from within or competitive hire
19–28 points	Independence, listening, oral communication, presence, planning	19–28 points	Competitive hire

Source: Walt Shedd, "Ten Steps to Top Sales Professionals," *www.sellingpower.com*, October 2007.

them identify the right candidates. Although the primary focus is on "how to do it" from a manager's point of view, some material in this chapter should be useful for learning what is expected if you ever apply for a sales job.

WHO IS RESPONSIBLE FOR RECRUITING AND SELECTING SALESPEOPLE?

Several years ago, an MBA student at the authors' school was recruited for a sales job with a major manufacturer of outdoor and garden equipment. She was interviewed extensively and wined and dined, not only by the sales manager, who was her prospective supervisor, but also by higher-level executives in the firm, including the vice president of marketing. All this attention from top-level managers surprised the candidate. "After all," she said, "it's only a sales job. Is it common for so many executives to be involved in recruiting new salespeople?"

The student's question raises the issue of who should have the primary responsibility for recruiting and selecting new salespeople. The way in which a company answers this question typically depends on the size of the sales force and the kind of selling involved. In firms with small sales forces, the top-level sales manager commonly views the recruitment and selection of new people as a primary responsibility. In larger, multilevel sales forces, however, the job of attracting and choosing new recruits is usually too extensive and time-consuming for a single executive. In such firms, authority for recruitment and selection is commonly delegated to lower-level sales managers or staff specialists.

In companies where the sales job is not very difficult or complex, new recruits do not need any special qualifications, and turnover rates in the sales force are high—as in firms that sell retail consumer goods—first-level sales managers often have sole responsibility for hiring. When a firm must be more selective in choosing new recruits with certain qualifications and abilities, however, a recruiting specialist may assist first-level managers in evaluating candidates and making hiring decisions. These staff positions are usually filled by sales managers who are being groomed for higher-level executive positions.

In some firms, members of the personnel department—or outside personnel specialists—assist and advise sales managers in hiring new salespeople instead of assigning such duties to a member of the sales management staff. Companies like Ritz-Carlton use outside consultants to help them screen and isolate certain individuals with the specific skill sets needed for success. This approach helps reduce duplication of effort and avoids friction between the sales and personnel departments. One disadvantage is that personnel specialists may not be as knowledgeable about the job to be filled and the qualifications necessary as a member of the sales management staff. When the personnel department or outside specialist is involved in sales recruiting and hiring, they usually help attract applicants and aid in evaluating them. The sales manager, however, typically has the final responsibility for deciding whom to hire.

Finally, when the firm considers the sales force a training ground for sales and marketing managers, human resource executives or other top-level managers may participate in recruiting to ensure new salespeople have management potential. This was the situation in the firm that interviewed our MBA student. Although it wanted to hire her for "just a sales job," company executives saw that job as a stepping-stone to management responsibilities.

JOB ANALYSIS AND DETERMINATION OF SELECTION CRITERIA

Research relating salespeople's personal characteristics to sales aptitude and job performance suggests there is no single set of traits and abilities sales managers can use as criteria in deciding what kind of recruits to hire. Different sales jobs require different skill sets, and this suggests people with different personality traits and abilities should be hired to fill them. The first activities in the recruitment and selection process thus should be the following:

1. Conduct a job analysis to determine what activities, tasks, responsibilities, and environmental influences are involved in the job to be filled.

2. Write a job description that details the findings of the job analysis.

3. Develop a statement of job qualifications that determine and describe the personal traits and abilities a person should have to perform the tasks and responsibilities involved in the job.

Most companies, particularly larger ones, have written job descriptions for sales force positions. Unfortunately, those job descriptions are often out of date and do not accurately reflect the current scope and content of the positions. The responsibilities of a given sales job change as the customers, the firm's account management policies, the competition, and other environmental factors change. Unfortunately firms often do not conduct new analyses and prepare updated descriptions to reflect those changes. Also, firms create new sales positions, and the tasks to be accomplished by people in these jobs may not be spelled out.

Consequently, a critical first step in the hiring process is for management to make sure the job to be filled has been analyzed recently and the findings have been written out in great detail. Without such a detailed and up-to-date description, the sales manager will have more difficulty deciding what kind of person is needed. In addition, prospective recruits will not really know for what position they are applying.

Who Conducts the Analysis and Prepares the Description?

In some firms, analyzing and describing sales jobs are assigned to someone in sales management. In other firms, the task is assigned to a job analysis specialist, who is either someone from the company's personnel department or an outside consultant. Regardless of who is responsible for analyzing and describing the various selling positions within a company, however, it is important that the person collect information about the job's content from two sources: (1) the current occupants of the job and (2) the sales managers who supervise the people in the job.

Current job occupants should be observed or interviewed, or both, to determine what they actually do. Sales managers at various levels should be asked what they think the job occupant should be doing in view of the firm's strategic sales program and account management policies. It is not uncommon for the results of the job analysis to discover salespeople doing things management does not know and not performing activities management believes are important. Such misunderstandings and inaccurate role perceptions illustrate the need for accurate and detailed job descriptions.[1]

Job descriptions written to reflect a consensus between salespeople and their managers can serve several useful functions in addition to guiding the firm's recruiting efforts. They can guide the design of a sales training program to provide new salespeople with the skills to do their job more effectively. Similarly, detailed job descriptions can serve as standards for evaluating each salesperson's job performance, as discussed in Chapter 13.

In many companies, there are a variety of sales positions. In some cases, the job title may not even include the word *sales,* even though the responsibilities are primarily those of a sales representative. Exhibit 9.2 presents the job descriptions for several different types of sales positions at Dell Corporation. Note that in each description, the company seeks to delineate many of the items covered in the next section. It is also important to be aware that, while both positions are sales related, they require different skills and experience levels. While not all companies provide this kind of detailed job description, it is extremely beneficial to the probability of long-term success for the candidate if both the company and potential salesperson know exactly what the expectations are before employment.

Content of the Job Description

Good job descriptions of sales jobs typically cover the following dimensions and requirements:

1. The nature of product(s) or service(s) to be sold.

2. The types of customers to be called on, including the policies concerning the frequency with which calls are to be made and the types of personnel within customer organizations who should be contacted (e.g., buyers, purchasing agents, plant supervisors).

3. The specific tasks and responsibilities to be carried out, including planning tasks, research and information collection activities, specific selling tasks, other promotional duties, customer servicing activities, and clerical and reporting duties.

4. The relationships between the job occupant and other positions within the organization. To whom does the job occupant report? What are the salesperson's responsibilities to the immediate superior? How and under what circumstances does the salesperson interact with members of other departments, such as production or engineering?

5. The mental and physical demands of the job, including the amount of technical knowledge the salesperson should have concerning the company's products, other necessary skills, and the amount of travel involved.

6. The environmental pressures and constraints that might influence performance of the job, such as market trends, the strengths and weaknesses of the competition, the company's reputation among customers, and resource and supply problems.

EXHIBIT 9.2 **Job description—Dell Corporation**

Account Executive IV Global Alliances

Description

Identifies and pursues strategic business opportunities through partnerships and/or strategic alliances.
- Responsible for selling Dell's products and services through large application and outsourcing vendors.
- May be responsible for special programs and/or solutions.
- Sells Dell Managed Service (DMS) and Dell Professional Service (DPS) lines.
- Teams with internal Dell resources and leads the cross-functional team in making the best business decisions.
- Focuses on delivering a positive customer experience according to Dell standards.

Responsible for building strong, complex alliances with global System Integrators (SI).
  - SIs who take advantage of the Dell direct model and help create new innovative approaches to the outsourcing market place.
- Responsible for global, strategic, coordination of "go-to-market" strategies that help drive exponential sales growth into the outsourcing market place.

Qualifications

Sales thought leader, influencing how segment functions/engages client set.
  - Leveraged to serve as coach/mentor.
- Creates superior relationships with senior level executives and influential stakeholders to sustain a long-term relationship.
- Has boardroom/executive presence.
- Significant complexity through both SI relationships and Enterprise product/service solutions.

Strong history of complex relationship building.
- Sales history showing ability to sell solutions in complex environments.
- Strong understanding of operational issues and solutions.
- Proven strength in outsourcing and complex service environments.
- Ability to build solid virtual teams.
- Very strong negotiation skills and financial strength.
- Establishes organizational initiatives that enable greater focus on customers.
- Organizes Dell-wide teams in response to SI/customer needs/ opportunities 15+ years of sales experience or related, industry or segment experience.
  - Five years or more specialty sales (System Integrator, Alliance Experience).

ESL (Education, State, and Local Government) Large Business—Account Executive

Description

Principal Duties and Responsibilities :
Responsible for Education, State and Local Government Middle Market account penetration, customer satisfaction and sales growth for long-term results.
1. Ability to act as a Territory Manager by organizing and leveraging all Dell resources to meet territory needs.
2. Develops and plans territory strategies and activities for education accounts such as, selecting accounts, selecting products for calls, identifying buyer influences, overcoming objections, introducing new products, selling all lines of business, making sales presentations and negotiating.
3. Provide customer and competitor feedback to management.
4. Attend and participate in industry sales conferences and trade shows.
5. Requires complex selling skills and responsibility.

(continued)

EXHIBIT 9.2 **Job description—Dell Corporation** *(concluded)*

Qualifications

Knowledge, Skills, Education and Abilities:
Strong knowledge of industry, service and enterprise products, and proactive selling skills.
Experience dealing with objections.
Strong organizational and planning skills.
Strong verbal and written communication skills.
Ability to operate remotely and travel.
Bachelor's degree desired, with a minimum of seven years of related experience.
Requires proven selling ability in previous positions.
8–10 years of sales experience.
5–7 years of related, industry or segment experience.

Determining Job Qualifications and Selection Criteria

Determining the qualifications a prospective employee should have to perform a given sales job is the most difficult part of the recruitment and selection process. The sales manager—perhaps with assistance from a workforce planning specialist or a vocational psychologist—should consider the relative importance of all the personal traits and characteristics discussed previously. These include physical attributes, mental abilities and experience, and personality traits.

The problem is that nearly all these characteristics are at least somewhat important in choosing new salespeople. No firm, for instance, would actively seek sales recruits who are unintelligent or lacking in self-confidence. At the same time, it is unlikely that many job candidates possess high levels of all the desirable characteristics. The task, then, is to decide which traits and abilities are most important in qualifying an individual for a particular job and which are less critical. Also, consideration should be given to trade-offs among the qualification criteria. Will a person with a deficiency in one important attribute still be considered acceptable if he or she has outstanding qualities in other areas? For example, will the firm be willing to hire someone with only average verbal ability and persuasiveness if that person has an extremely high degree of ambition and persistence?

Methods for Deciding on Selection Criteria

Simply examining the job description can assist decision makers making choices about the key qualifications in new salespeople. If the job requires extensive travel, for instance, management might look for applicants who are younger, have few family responsibilities, and want to travel. Similarly, statements in the job description concerning technical knowledge and skill can help management determine the educational background and previous job experience to look for when selecting from a pool of candidates. For example, in the Dell Corporation job descriptions in Exhibit 9.2, one of the positions (ESL Large Business Account Executive) required extensive travel and work experience. Criteria like these will often serve to limit the number of candidates.

Larger firms go one step further and evaluate the personal histories of their existing salespeople to determine what characteristics differentiate between good and poor performers. As seen in Chapter 8, this analysis seldom produces consistent results across different jobs and different companies. It can produce useful insight, however, when applied to a single type of sales job within a single firm.

Current sales people might be divided into two groups according to their level of performance on the job: one group of high performers and one of low performers. The characteristics of the two groups are then compared on the basis of information from job application forms, records of personal interviews, and intelligence, aptitude, and personality test scores. Alternatively, statistical techniques might be used to look for significant correlations between variations in the personal characteristics of current salespeople and variations in their job performance. In either case, management attempts to identify personal attributes that differ significantly between high-performing and low-performing salespeople. The assumption is that there may be a cause-and-effect relationship between such attributes and job performance. If new employees are selected who have attributes similar to those of people who are currently performing the job successfully, they also may be successful.[2]

In addition to improving management's ability to specify relevant selection criteria for new salespeople, a firm should conduct a personnel history analysis for another compelling reason. Such analyses are necessary to validate the selection criteria the firm is using, as required by government regulations on equal employment opportunity in hiring. This issue is discussed later in this chapter. Besides comparing the characteristics of good and poor performers in a particular job, management might also try to analyze the unique characteristics of employees who have failed—people who either quit or were fired. One consulting firm, the Klein Institute for Aptitude Testing, suggests that the following characteristics are frequently found among salespeople who fail:

1. Instability of residence.

2. Failure in business within the past two years.

3. Unexplained gaps in the person's employment record.

4. Recent divorce or marital problems.

5. Excessive personal indebtedness; for example, bills could not be paid within two years from earnings on the new job.

The firm might attempt to identify such characteristics by conducting exit interviews with all salespeople who quit or are fired. However although this sounds like a good idea, it seldom works well in practice. Salespeople who quit are often reluctant to discuss the real reasons for leaving a job, and people who are fired are not likely to cooperate in any research that will be of value to their former employer. However, some useful information about ex-salespeople can often be obtained from the application forms and test scores recorded when they were hired. They may also have spoken with the managers who were their supervisors at the time they left the company.

On the basis of these kinds of information, a written statement of job qualifications should be prepared that is specific enough to guide the selection of new salespeople. These qualifications can then be reflected in the forms and tests used in the selection process, such as the interview form in Exhibit 9.3.[3]

RECRUITING APPLICANTS

Some firms do not actively recruit salespeople. They simply choose new employees from applicants who come to them and ask for work. Although this may be a satisfactory policy for a few well-known firms with good products, strong positions in the market, and attractive compensation policies, today's labor market makes such an approach unworkable for most companies.

EXHIBIT 9.3 Applicant interview form

Business Division
Applicant Interview Form

Applicant name: _____ Date:_____

Interview with: Time:

1. _____ _____

2. _____ _____

3. _____ _____

4. _____ _____

Rating:
5—Excellent
4—Above average
3—Average
2—Fair
1—Poor

Directions: Check square that most correctly reflects characteristics applicable to candidate. An outstanding candidate would score 95 to 100.

General appearance   1   2   3   4   5
  1. Neatness, dress
  2. Business image

Impressions
  3. Positive mannerisms
  4. Speech, expressions
  5. Outgoing personality
  6. Positive attitude

Potential sales ability
  7. Persuasive communication
  8. Aggressiveness
  9. Sell and manage large accounts
  10. Make executive calls
  11. Organize and manage a territory
  12. Work with others
  13. Successful prior experience
  14. Potential for career growth

Maturity
  15. General intelligence, common sense
  16. Self-confidence
  17. Self-motivation, ambition
  18. Composure, stability
  19. Adaptability
  20. Sense of ethics

General comments:_____

_____

Overall rating (total score):_____

Would you recommend this candidate for the position?_____

Why or why not?_____

As was the case throughout the 90s and into the first decade of the twenty-first century, firms that seek well-educated people for sales jobs must compete with many other occupations in attracting such individuals. To make matters worse, people with no selling experience frequently tend to have negative attitudes toward sales jobs. Also, the kinds of people who do seek employment in sales often do not have the qualifications a firm is looking for, particularly when the job involves relatively sophisticated selling, such as technical or new-business sales. Consequently, the company may have to evaluate many applicants to find one qualified person.

This is one area in which some firms try to be efficient but end up being inefficient and often ineffective. They attempt to hold down recruiting costs on the assumption that a good training program can convert marginal recruits into solid sales performers. As we saw in the last chapter, however, some of the determinants of sales success, such as aptitude and personal characteristics, are difficult or impossible to change through training or experience. Therefore, spending the money and effort to find well-qualified candidates is a profitable investment. In certain industries, and when environmental conditions make the job market tight for recruiting companies, even finding sufficient numbers of qualified individuals can be a challenge. For example, the life insurance industry reports that it must interview between 60 and 120 people to find one hire.[4]

In view of the difficulties in attracting qualified people to fill sales positions, a well-planned and effectively implemented recruiting effort is usually a crucial part of the firm's hiring program. The primary objective of the recruiting process should not be to maximize the total number of job applicants. Too many recruits can overload the selection process, forcing the manager to use less thorough screening and evaluation procedures. Intel, for example, receives thousands of applications every day. Besides, numbers do not ensure quality. The focus should not be on how many recruits can be found but on finding a few good ones.

Therefore, the recruiting process should be designed to be the first step in the selection process. Self-selection by the prospective employees is the most efficient means of selection. The recruiting effort should be implemented in a way that discourages unqualified people from applying. For example, many companies have adopted the Internet as a recruiting source for potential candidates. Often companies like Cisco Systems and IBM have a screening procedure by which candidates can provide certain key pieces of data about themselves, and the company will search its job openings to look for a match. It is important that recruiting communications point out both the attractive and unattractive aspects of the job to be filled, specify the job qualifications, and state the likely compensation. This will help ensure that only qualified and interested people apply for the job. Also, recruiting efforts should be focused only on sources of potential applicants where fully qualified people are most likely to be found.

Sales managers can go to a number of places to find recruits or leads concerning potential recruits. **Internal sources** consist of other people already employed in other departments within the firm, whereas **external sources** include people in other firms (who are often identified and referred by current members of the sales force), educational institutions, advertisements, and employment agencies.

Each source is likely to produce candidates with somewhat different backgrounds and characteristics. Therefore, while most firms seek recruits from more than one source, a company's recruiting efforts should be concentrated on sources that are most likely to produce the kinds of people needed. Research suggests that firms use many different sources for finding recruits, depending on the type of sales job they are trying to fill. When the job involves missionary or trade selling, firms rely most heavily on a variety of external sources, such as advertisements, employment agencies, and educational institutions. When the job involves technical selling requiring substantial product knowledge and industry

Leadership The Challenge of Recruiting a Global Sales Force 9.2

What makes one salesperson successful and another a failure? This is a question sales professionals have been trying to answer for years. Indeed, as we have been discussing in earlier chapters, the characteristics of sales success are difficult, if not impossible, to identify. Consider then the challenge of a company recruiting a global sales force. Not only is it faced with the significant challenge of trying to determine the qualities to look for in a salesperson, but it must also deal with social and cultural differences.

Sales experts suggest that rather than focus on differences, firms should focus on the similarities. This is not too say that all salespeople should be the same, but rather, the focus should be on the sales tasks. Specifically, as companies seek to build long-term customer relationships, the basic qualities needed by the salesperson are the same whether they are selling in Orlando or Osaka, New York or New Delhi.

Empathy, communication, and the ability to be self-motivating are characteristics that salespeople need in today's selling environment, no matter where they work. In addition, the ability to understand, work with, and feel comfortable using technology is becoming a critical success factor in selling. Since salespeople are equipped with cell phones, and laptops, they need to be able to use the technology to maximize the customer relationship.

Focusing on the fundamental qualities needed to build a successful customer relationship rather than social and cultural differences enables companies to develop a more consistent pool of potential salespeople around the world. Coupled with effective ways of measuring the individual's abilities, this approach can give global sales managers a useful strategy in sales force recruitment.

experience, firms focus more heavily on employees in other departments within the company and on personal referrals of people working for other firms in the industry.[5] The relative advantages and limitations of each of these sources of new recruits are discussed in more depth in the following sections.

All of the recruiting issues faced by sales managers are magnified as companies expand globally and seek to hire salespeople in new international markets. Cultural differences, language barriers, and legal restrictions create additional concerns about hiring the right people for the sales position. The key is for a company to have done its homework and research each new market before making the decision to enter it. For example, in many European countries it is much more difficult to terminate an employee than in the United States. This makes the hiring decision much more difficult. It is important for a company to understand the legal requirements of hiring new salespeople before hiring them. Leadership 9.2 discusses the challenges of recruiting a global sales force.

People in nonsales departments within the firm, such as manufacturing, maintenance, engineering, or the office staff, sometimes have latent sales talent and are a common source of sales recruits. Past surveys suggest that more than half of U.S. industrial goods producers hire at least some of their salespeople from other internal departments.

Recruiting current company employees for the sales force has distinct advantages:

1. Company employees have established performance records, and they are more of a known quantity than outsiders.

2. Recruits from inside the firm should require less orientation and training because they are already familiar with the company's products, policies, and operations.

3. Recruiting from within can bolster company morale, as employees become aware that opportunities for advancement are available outside of their own departments or divisions.

To facilitate successful internal recruiting, the company's personnel department should always be kept abreast of sales staff needs. Because the personnel staff is familiar with the qualifications of all employees and continuously evaluates their performance, they are in the best position to identify people with the attributes necessary to fill available sales jobs.

Internal recruiting has some limitations. People in nonsales departments seldom have much previous selling experience. Also, internal recruiting can cause some animosity within the firm if supervisors of other departments think their best employees are being pirated by the sales force.

External Sources

Although it is often a good idea to start with internal sources when recruiting new salespeople, most of the time there will not be enough qualified internal candidates to meet the human resource needs of a firm's sales force. As a result, the vast majority of companies must expand the search to cover external sources.

Referral of People from Other Firms

In addition to being potential sales employees themselves, company personnel can provide management with leads to potential recruits from outside the firm. Current salespeople are in a good position to provide their superiors with leads to new recruits. They know the requirements of the job, they often have contacts with other salespeople who may be willing to change jobs, and they can do much to help "sell" an available job to potential recruits. Consequently, many sales managers make sure their salespeople are aware of the company's recruiting needs. Some companies offer bonuses as incentives for their salespeople to recruit new prospects. Such referrals from current employees must be handled tactfully so as not to cause hard feelings if the applicant is rejected later.

Customers can also be a source of sales recruits. Sometimes a customer's employees have the kinds of knowledge that make them attractive as prospective salespeople. For instance, department store employees can make good salespeople for the wholesalers or manufacturers that supply the store because they are familiar with the product and the procedures of store buyers. Cosmetics companies such as Estée Lauder and L'Oréal recruit from the ranks of department store personnel.

Customers with whom a firm has good relations may also provide leads concerning potential recruits who are working for other firms, particularly competitors. Purchasing agents know what impresses them in a salesperson, they are familiar with the abilities of the sales reps who call on them, and they are sometimes aware when a sales rep is interested in changing jobs.

The question of whether a firm should recruit salespeople from its competitors, however, is controversial. Such people are knowledgeable about the industry from their experience. They also might be expected to "bring along" some of their current customers when they switch companies. This does not happen frequently, however, since customers are usually more loyal to a supplier than to the individual who represents that supplier.

On the other side of the argument, it is sometimes difficult to get salespeople who have worked for a competing firm to unlearn old practices and to conform to their new employer's account management policies. Also, some managers think recruiting a competitor's personnel is unethical. They believe it is unfair for firm B to recruit actively someone from firm A after A has spent the money to hire and train that person. Such people may be in a position to divulge A's company secrets to B. Consequently, some firms refuse to recruit their competitor's salespeople, although whether such policies are due to high ethical standards, the expense of retraining, or fear of possible retaliation is open to question.

Advertisements

A less selective means of attracting job applicants is to advertise the available position. When a technically qualified or experienced person is needed, an ad might be placed in an industry trade or technical journal. More common, advertisements are placed in the personnel or marketplace sections of local newspapers to attract applicants for relatively less demanding sales jobs that don't require special qualifications. A well-written ad can be very effective for attracting applicants. As suggested, however, this is not necessarily a good thing. When a firm's advertisements attract large numbers of applicants who are unqualified or only marginally interested, the firm must engage in costly screening to identify legitimate candidates.[6] If a firm does use newspaper ads in recruiting, it must decide how much information about the job it should include in the ads. Many sales managers argue that *open ads,* which disclose the firm's name, product to be sold, compensation, and specific job duties, generate a more select pool of high-quality applicants, lower selection costs, and decreased turnover rates than ads without such information. Open ads also avoid any ethical questions concerning possible deception.

However, for less attractive, high-turnover sales jobs—such as telemarketing selling—some sales managers prefer *blind ads,* which carry only minimal information, sometimes only a phone number. These maximize the number of applicants and give the manager an opportunity to explain the attractive features of the job in a personal meeting with the applicant.[7]

Employment Agencies

Employment agencies are sometimes used to find recruits, usually for more routine sales jobs such as retail sales. However, executive search firms such as Heidrick and Struggles specialize in finding applicants for more demanding sales jobs. Some sales managers have had unsatisfactory experiences with employment agencies. They charge that agencies are sometimes overzealous in attempting to earn their fees, and send applicants that do not meet the job qualifications. Others argue, however, that when a firm has problems with an employment agency, it is often the fault of the company for not understanding the agency's role and not providing sufficient information about the kinds of recruits it is seeking. When a firm carefully selects an agency with a good reputation, establishes a long-term relationship, and provides detailed descriptions of job qualifications, the agency can perform a valuable service. It locates and screens job applicants and reduces the amount of time and effort the company's sales managers must devote to recruiting.

In recent years, new online companies such as monster.com have taken the concept of employment agency in a new direction. Increasingly, employment Web sites provide a valuable service, enabling employers to learn about potential candidates over the Internet. At the same time, individuals can learn about thousands of positions efficiently and effectively online.

Educational Institutions

College and university placement offices are a common source of recruits for firms that require salespeople with proven intellectual ability or technical backgrounds. Most educational institutions in fact allocate resources to "career management" departments that enhance the development of careers for their graduates. Educational institutions are a particularly effective source when the sales job is viewed as a first step toward a career in management. College graduates are often more socially poised than people of the same age without college training, and good grades provide evidence the person can think logically, budget time efficiently, and communicate reasonably well.

But younger college graduates seldom have much selling experience, and are likely to require more extensive orientation and training in selling fundamentals. Also, college-educated sales recruits have a reputation for "job hopping," unless the jobs are challenging and promotions are rapid. One insurance company, for instance, stopped recruiting college graduates when it found that such recruits did not stay with their jobs very long. Such early turnover is sometimes more the fault of the company than of the recruits. When recruiters paint an unrealistic picture of the job demands and rewards of the position to be filled, or when they recruit people who are overqualified for the job, high turnover is often the result.[8]

There is, however, a growing movement to professionalize the sales career, with a number of colleges and universities creating comprehensive sales programs, led by a group of schools in the University Sales Center Alliance. Currently there are more than a dozen schools offering a four-year degree in sales and many more that give students the opportunity to earn a certificate or minor in sales. These programs often require an internship to acquire real-world sales experience and provide valuable insight into various sales career options. Graduates of these programs are highly sought after by companies, as the time it takes for a graduate to become productive is reduced by 50 percent over other graduates. Moreover, they are 35 percent less likely to leave their employer. Although professional sales programs are valued by employers, universities are just now embracing them, primarily due to the outdated and incorrect belief that personal selling is not a true academic discipline.

Junior colleges and vocational schools are another source of sales recruits that has expanded rapidly in recent years. Many such schools have programs explicitly designed to prepare people for selling careers. Thus, companies do not have to contend with the negative attitudes toward selling they sometimes encounter in four-year college graduates. Junior colleges and vocational schools are particularly good sources of recruits for sales jobs that require reasonably well-developed mental and communications abilities, but where advanced technical knowledge or a four-year degree is not essential.

Internet

Increasingly, companies are seeking applications over the Internet. Indeed, as seen in Exhibit 9.2, companies such as Dell Corporation are posting jobs and requesting that candidates submit their applications over the Internet and appropriate action is taken. In many cases, younger candidates are as comfortable submitting Internet applications as they are filling them out on paper. In addition, by targeting the Internet application to specific job postings, the company can direct the information to the right people very efficiently. For example, Internet applications to Dell include a unique job reference so that the information can be sent to the right people at a specific geographic location.

While the use of the Internet to recruit salespeople is clearly increasing, the unique aspects of the sales position coupled with the need to meet and interview individuals in person make it a difficult tool for recruiting purposes. However, as a screening device it is effective since a large number of applications can be processed easily. Some companies, such as IBM, receive thousands of applications per day for positions throughout the company. By using the Internet, they can process these applications to the right people efficiently and effectively.

SELECTION PROCEDURES

After the qualifications necessary to fill a job have been determined and some applicants have been recruited, the final task is to determine which applicants best meet the qualifications and have the greatest aptitude for the job. To gain the information needed to evaluate each prospective employee, firms typically use some combination of the following **selection tools and procedures:**[9]

1. Application blanks

2. Personal interviews

3. Reference checks

4. Physical examinations

5. Psychological tests

   a. Intelligence

   b. Personality

   c. Aptitude/skills

Past research studies suggest that, on average across all occupations, composites of psychological test scores have the greatest predictive validity for evaluating a potential employee's future job performance, whereas evaluations based on personal interviews have the lowest. In other words, test scores have the highest correlations with candidates' subsequent performance on the job and account for about 28 percent of the variance in subsequent performance across new hires. Ratings based on personal interviews, on the other hand, account for only about 2 percent of variance in subsequent performance.[10] Given the ability of psychological tests to do a better job of predicting sales performance, it is surprising that firms actually use personal interviews much more frequently. A survey of selection procedures followed by 121 industrial firms suggests personal interviews are almost universally employed, while psychological tests are the least-used selection tool, although their use is increasing again. However, large firms are somewhat more thorough in their use of psychological tests—and the development of detailed job descriptions—than smaller firms.

Application Blanks

Although professional salespeople often have résumés to submit to prospective employers, many personnel experts believe a standard company application form makes it easier to assess applicants. A well-designed application blank helps ensure that the same information is obtained in the same form from all candidates.

The primary purpose of the application form is to collect basic information about the recruit's personal history. Forms typically ask for facts about the candidate's physical condition, education, business experience, military service, and outside interests/activities and can be used to screen for basic qualifications such as educational experience.

A second function of the application form is to help managers prepare for personal interviews with job candidates. Often a recruit's responses to items on the application raise questions that should be explored during an interview. If the application shows that a person has held several jobs within the past few years, for example, the interviewer should attempt to find out the reasons for these changes. Perhaps the interviewer can determine whether the applicant is a "job hopper" who is unlikely to stay with the company very long. Indeed, a study conducted at one pharmaceutical firm found that common application information—such as candidates' tenure in their previous jobs and their amount of sales experience—was able to distinguish salespeople more likely to stay with the hiring company over time from those who were more likely to quit.[11]

Personal Interviews

In addition to probing into the applicant's history, personal interviews enable managers to gain insight into the applicant's mental abilities and personality. An interview provides a manager with the opportunity to assess a candidate's communication skills, intelligence, sociability, aggressiveness, empathy, ambition, and other traits related to the qualifications necessary for the job. Different managers use many different interviewing approaches to accomplish these objectives. These methods of conducting personal interviews, however, can all be classified as either structured or unstructured.

In **structured interviews,** each applicant is asked the same predetermined questions. This approach is particularly good when the interviewer is inexperienced at evaluating candidates. The standard questions help guide the interview and ensure that all factors relevant to the candidate's qualifications are covered. Also, asking the same questions of all candidates makes it easier to compare their strengths and weaknesses. To facilitate such comparisons, many firms use a standard interview evaluation form on which interviewers rate each applicant's response to each question together with their overall impressions of the candidate.

One potential weakness of structured interviews is that the interviewer may rigidly stick to the prepared questions and fail to identify or probe the unique qualities of each candidate. In practice, though, structured interviews are often not as inflexible as the criticism implies. As a manager gains interviewing experience, he or she often learns to ask additional questions when an applicant's response is inadequate without disturbing the flow of the interview.[12]

At the other end of interviewing techniques is the **unstructured interview.** Such interviews seek to get the applicant talking freely on a variety of subjects. The interviewer asks only a few questions to direct the conversation to topics of interest, such as the applicant's work experiences, career objectives, and outside activities. The rationale for this approach is that significant insight into the applicant's character and motivations can be gained by allowing the applicant to talk freely with a minimum of direction. Also, the interviewer is free to spend more time on topics where the applicant's responses are interesting or unusual.

Successful, unstructured interviewing requires interviewers with experience and interpretive skills. Because there is no predetermined set of questions, there is always a danger that the interviewer will neglect some relevant topics. It is also more difficult to compare the responses of two or more applicants. Consequently, since most firms' sales managers have relatively little experience as interviewers, structured interviews are much more common in selecting new salespeople than unstructured approaches.

Within the interview itself, particularly those that are relatively unstructured, some sales managers use additional techniques to learn as much as possible about the applicant's character and aptitude. One such technique is the stress interview. The interviewer puts the applicant under stress in one of many ways, ranging from silence to constant, aggressive probing and questioning. The rationale for this technique is that the interviewer may learn how the applicant will respond to the stress encountered in selling situations.

Another approach is for the interviewer to ask the applicant to sell something. "Hand the prospect a stapler, a laptop computer, or any other object that's handy and ask him to 'sell' it. . . . A pro should be able to sell anything," says one sales manager. "The one thing he's got to do is to ask for the order. Seven of ten fail to do so."[13]

Techniques like these can be useful to assess a candidate's character and selling skills, but they should be used as only one part of the interview. Sometimes sales managers become so obsessed with finding the "one best way" to assess candidates that they allow

Leadership   Selecting Salespeople Face to Face: The Role of Personal Interviews   9.3

Personal interviews are the most commonly used method of selecting salespeople. Despite research to the contrary and perhaps, in part, because it is intuitively obvious, sales managers believe that meeting a candidate face to face is essential in assessing that individual's personal selling skills.

Sales managers often take a more pragmatic view. Cynthia Braun, northeast regional sales manager for Lepel Corporation, focuses on the candidate's presentation skills. She suggests, "See how prepared they are. Do they bring visual aids or give interesting anecdotes to set themselves apart?" Personality is another characteristic that can be assessed in a personal interview. Dave Hinkes, Xerox sales executive in Florida, puts it this way, "I look for creativity." He also looks for candidates willing to take risks. As an example, Hinkes tells of an applicant who had been doing well until the critical Q&A time. The applicant then took the opportunity to focus entirely on benefits and "safety nets." Hinkes notes, "A salesperson should not be security conscious. A preoccupation with security is a red flag that they're not going to be out there putting it all on the line."

Unfortunately, while we have seen how important it is to recruit the right kind of person, sales managers have received very little training in recruitment policies and techniques. They are briefed on legal aspects of what they can and cannot say or do but never given much in the way of training to help them identify the best people for a new sales position. Learning how to conduct a good job interview is a learned behavior. For example, in order to make good recruiting decisions managers need to know how and when to use structured versus unstructured questions and how to identify key characteristics in an individual.

Front line sales managers are critical in the recruiting process and should play an active role rather than relying on employment agencies, human resource personnel, or the Internet. The interviewer should seek to draw out basic information about the candidate, such as communication skills, key personality traits, and interest in the job. If a candidate passes initial screening and moves to a second interview, the managers should "drill down" with the candidate to assess and, hopefully, validate that individual's potential. While personal interviews should not be the only tool used in assessing a candidate, they are still the most effective tool for managers in making the critical sales-person hiring decision.

Sources: Bob Ayrer, "Hiring Salespeople—Getting behind the Mask," *American Salesperson* 49, no. 2 (2004), p. 20; and Audrey Bottjen, Interview with a Salesperson," *Sales & Marketing Management,* April 2001, p. 70.

interviewing gimmicks to get in the way of real communication. After all, another purpose of job interviews is to provide candidates with information about the job and company so they will be interested in taking the job. One real danger with gimmicky interviewing techniques is that the applicant will be turned off and lose interest in working for the firm. Regardless of the interviewing technique more managers rely on interviews to evaluate sales candidates than any other selection tool. Yet as we saw earlier, there is some evidence that evaluations based on personal interviews are among the least-valid predictors of job performance. Does this mean many firms are doing a less than optimal job of evaluating and selecting new salespeople? Are there ways to improve the accuracy of impressions gained from interviews? These questions are explored in Leadership 9.3.

If an applicant makes it past the face-to-face interviews, a reference check is often the next step. Some sales managers question the value of references because "they always say nice things." However, with a little resourcefulness, reference checks can be a valuable selection tool.

Checking references can ensure the accuracy of factual data about the applicant. It is naive to assume that everything a candidate has written on a résumé or application form is true. Facts about previous job experiences and college degrees should be checked. As we have seen, individuals do not always tell the truth on their résumés (George O'Leary and his application for the head football coaching position at the University of Notre Dame).

The discovery of false data on a candidate's application raises a question about basic honesty as well as about what the candidate is trying to hide. References can supply additional information and opinions about a prospect's aptitude and past job performance. Calling a number of references and probing them in depth can be time-consuming and costly, but it can also produce worthwhile information and protect against making expensive hiring mistakes.[14]

Physical Examinations

One typically does not think of selling as physically demanding, yet sales jobs often require a great deal of stamina and the physical ability to withstand lots of stress. Consequently, even though physical examinations are relatively expensive compared with other selection tools, many sales managers see them as valuable aids for evaluating candidates.

However, managers should be very cautious in requiring medical examinations, including specific tests for such things as drug use or the HIV virus, for prospective employees. Under the Americans with Disabilities Act (discussed in more detail later in this chapter), it is no longer advisable to use a standard physical examination for all positions. If used, the physical exam should focus only on attributes directly related to the requirements of the job to be filled. For example, in many sales positions, conditions such as diabetes or epilepsy would have little or no impact on the candidate's ability to perform. Therefore, questions concerning such conditions should be avoided, and any information collected for emergency situations should be kept confidential. Under the law's guidelines, a physical examination should be performed only after a job offer has been extended. And the job offer cannot be made conditional on the results of the physical exam unless all new hires for a position are subjected to the same physical exam and the results of those exams are treated as confidential medical records.[15]

Tests

A final set of selection tools used by many firms consists of tests aimed at measuring an applicant's mental abilities and personality traits. The most commonly used tests can be grouped into three types: (1) intelligence, (2) aptitude, and (3) personality tests. Within each category, there are a variety of different tests used by different companies.

Intelligence Tests

Intelligence tests are useful for determining whether an applicant has sufficient mental ability to perform a job successfully. Sales managers tend to believe these are the most useful of all the tests commonly used in selecting salespeople. General intelligence tests are designed to measure an applicant's overall mental abilities by examining how well the applicant comprehends, reasons, and learns. The Wonderlic Personnel Test is one common general intelligence test. It is popular because it is short; it consists of 50 items and requires only about 12 minutes to complete. The WPT can be administered using paper, PC, or over the Internet. Finally, it is available in more than 15 languages, including Chinese and Russian.

When the job to be filled requires special competence in one or a few areas of mental ability, a specialized intelligence test might be used to evaluate candidates. Tests are available for measuring such things as speed of learning, number facility, memory, logical reasoning, and verbal ability.

Aptitude Tests

Aptitude tests are designed to determine whether an applicant has an interest in, or the ability to perform, certain tasks and activities. For example, the Strong Interest Inventory asks respondents to indicate whether they like or dislike a variety of situations and activities.

This can determine whether applicants' interests are similar to those of people who are successful in a variety of different occupations, including selling. Other tests measure skills or abilities, such as mechanical or mathematical aptitude, that might be related to success in particular selling jobs.

One problem with at least some aptitude tests is that instead of measuring a person's innate abilities, they measure current level of skill at certain tasks. At least some skills necessary for successful selling can be taught, or improved, through a well-designed training program. Therefore, rejecting applicants because they currently do not have the necessary skills can mean losing people who could be trained to be successful salespeople.

Personality Tests

Many general personality tests evaluate an individual on numerous traits. For example, the Edwards Personal Preference Schedule—offered by many testing organizations,—measures 24 traits such as sociability, aggressiveness, and independence. Such tests, however, contain many questions, require substantial time to complete, and gather information about some traits that may be irrelevant for evaluating future salespeople. Consequently, more limited personality tests have been developed in recent years that concentrate on only a few traits thought to be directly relevant to a person's future success in sales.[16] These are often designed and administered by individual testing services. For example, Walden Testing has a specific test to assess an individual's selling skills.

Concerns about the Use of Tests

During the 1950s and early 1960s, tests—particularly general intelligence and sales aptitude tests—were widely used as selection tools for evaluating potential salespeople. However, due to a number of legal concerns and restrictions posed by civil rights legislation and equal opportunity hiring practices, companies had cut back the use of these tests until recently. Now, current evidence suggests that properly designed and administered tests are valid selection tools, which has spurred an increase in their popularity, although they are somewhat more widely used in large firms than in smaller ones.[17]

Despite the empirical evidence, however, managers continue to be leery of tests, and many firms do not use them as part of their evaluation of sales recruits. There are a number of reasons for these negative attitudes.

For one thing, despite the evidence that tests have relatively high predictive validity on average, some managers continue to doubt that tests are valid for predicting the future success of salespeople in their specific firm. As discussed in Chapter 8, no personality traits have been found to positively affect performance across a variety of selling jobs in different firms. Thus, specific tests that measure such abilities and traits may be valid for selecting salespeople for some jobs but invalid for others. Also, tests for measuring specific abilities and characteristics of applicants do not always produce consistent scores. Some commercially available tests have not been developed using established scientific measurement procedures; as a result, their reliability and validity are questionable. Even when a firm believes a particular trait, such as empathy or sociability, is related to job performance, there is still a question about which test should be used to measure that trait.

A related concern, particularly in the case of personality tests, is that some creative and talented people may be rejected simply because their personalities do not conform to test norms. Many sales jobs require creative people, particularly when those people are being groomed for future management responsibilities. Yet these people seldom fit an average personality profile because the "average" person is not particularly creative.

Another concern about testing involves the possible reactions of the people who are tested. A reasonably intelligent, "test-wise" person can "fudge" the results of many tests by selecting answers he or she thinks management will want. These answers may not accurately reflect that person's feelings or behavior. Also, many prospective employees view extensive testing as a burden and perhaps an invasion of privacy. Therefore, some managers fear that requiring a large battery of tests may turn off a candidate and reduce the likelihood of accepting a job with the firm.

Finally, a given test may discriminate between people of different races or sexes, and the use of such tests is illegal. Consequently, some firms have abandoned the use of tests rather than risk a legal challenge.

Guidelines for the Appropriate Use of Tests

To avoid, or at least minimize, the preceding testing problems, managers should keep the following guidelines in mind:

1. Test scores should be considered as a single input in the selection decision. Managers should not rely on them to do the work of other parts of the selection process, such as interviewing and checking references. Candidates should not be eliminated solely on the basis of test scores. The best approach is to incorporate information from multiple sources (such as a test, interview, and selection process). The different types of data increase confidence by using multiple sources to corroborate the decision. Chally's "How to Select a Sales Force that Sells" (2005) provides a lot of guidance on how information from a written test, interview, and reference check can be integrated to select a salesperson.

2. Applicants should be tested on only those abilities and traits that management, on the basis of a thorough job analysis, has determined to be relevant for the specific job. Broad tests that evaluate a large number of traits not relevant to a specific job are probably inappropriate.

3. When possible, tests with built-in internal consistency checks should be used. Then the person who analyzes the test results can determine whether the applicant responded honestly or was faking some answers. Many recently designed tests ask similar questions with slightly different wording several times throughout the test. If respondents are answering honestly, they should always give the same response to similar questions.

4. A firm should conduct empirical studies to ensure the tests are valid for predicting an applicant's future performance in the job. This kind of hard evidence of test validity is particularly important in view of the government's equal employment opportunity requirements. Often this requires hiring an expert consultant in employment testing such as an industrial-organizational psychologist or using a testing firm that has such expertise on staff.

5. It is important to include both high and low performers in a validation study. Simply benchmarking and identifying top employees will not identify the traits and skills that differentiate good from poor performers.

EQUAL EMPLOYMENT OPPORTUNITY REQUIREMENTS IN SELECTING SALESPEOPLE

The number of federal lawsuits alleging workplace discrimination is large and growing.[18] The primary basis for these suits is Title VII of the 1964 Civil Rights Act, which forbids discrimination in employment on the basis of race, sex, religion, color, or national origin. A number of federal laws have extended this protection against job discrimination to include such factors as age and physical and mental disabilities, as summarized in Exhibit 9.4. Consequently, extreme care should be taken to ensure the selection tools a firm uses in hiring salespeople—especially its interviewing and testing procedures—are not biased against any subgroup of the labor force. Exhibit 9.5 offers guidelines concerning the kinds of illegal or sensitive questions managers should avoid when conducting employment interviews or designing application forms.

Requirements for Tests

Section 703(h) of the 1964 Civil Rights Act approves the use of "professionally developed ability tests," provided such tests are not "designed, intended, or used to discriminate because of race, color, religion, sex, or national origin." Suppose, however, an employer innocently uses a test that does discriminate by having a larger proportion of men than women, or a larger percentage of whites than blacks, receive passing scores. Has the employer violated the law? Not necessarily.

In such cases, the employer must prove the test scores are valid predictors of successful performance on the job in question. In other words, it is legal for a firm to hire more men than women for a job if it can be proven that men possess more of some trait or ability that will enable them to do the job better. This requires that the employer have empirical evidence showing a significant relationship between scores on the test and actual job performance. The procedures a firm might use to produce this kind of evidence were described earlier in this chapter when discussing how to determine whether particular job qualifications are valid.[19]

Requirements for Interviews and Application Blanks

Because it is illegal to discriminate in hiring on the basis of race, sex, religion, age, and national origin, there is no reason for a firm to ask for such information on its job application forms or during personal interviews. It is wise to avoid all questions in any way

EXHIBIT 9.4
Legislation affecting recruitment and selection

Legislative Act	Purpose
Civil Rights Act of 1866	Gives blacks the same rights as whites and has since been extended by the courts to include all ethnic groups.
Civil Rights Act of 1964 (Title VII)	Prohibits discrimination in employment based on race, color, religion, national origin, or sex.
Age Discrimination in Employment Act (1967)	Prohibits discrimination against people ages 40 to 70.
Fair Employment Opportunity Act (1972)	Founded the Equal Employment Opportunity Commission to ensure compliance with the Civil Rights Act.
Rehabilitation Act of 1973	Requires affirmative action to hire and promote handicapped persons if the firm employs 50 or more workers and is seeking a federal contract in excess of $50,000.
Vietnam Era Veterans Readjustment Act (1974)	Requires affirmative action to hire Vietnam veterans and disabled veterans of any war by firms holding federal contracts in excess of $10,000.
Americans with Disabilities Act (1990)	Prohibits discrimination based on handicaps or disabilities—either physical or mental. Applied to all employers with 25 or more employees beginning July 26, 1992, and extended to employers with 15 or more workers on July 26, 1994.

EXHIBIT 9.5 **Illegal or sensitive questions that should be eliminated from employment applications and interviews**

Category	Illegal or Sensitive Topics
Nationality or race	It is not permissible to make comments or ask questions related to the race, color, national origin, or descent of an applicant (or even his or her spouse). An applicant should not be asked to provide a photograph. An applicant can be asked to demonstrate proficiency in another language if that is a requirement of the job, but he or she cannot be asked if that is his or her native language. An applicant may be asked if he or she is a U.S. citizen but not whether he or she is a native or naturalized citizen. It is permissible ask if the individual has the legal right to remain and work in the United States.
Religion	It is not permissible to ask about an individual's religious beliefs. In addition, do not ask whether the company's schedule would interfere with the individual's religion.
Sex and marital status	An applicant's gender should not be a part of the hiring discussion, unless it is directly related to the job itself. In addition, questions about the spouse (for example, spouse's employment status) are not permitted. Finally, no questions regarding family size (currently or planned in the future) are permitted.
Age	It is permitted to ask if the individual is a minor or over the age of 70; however, the applicant should not be asked specific questions about his or her age or date of birth.
Physical characteristics, disabilities, health problems, disabilities	Avoid all questions related to an individual's personal health situation. However, once a description of the job has been provided, the applicant may be asked whether or not he or she has any physical or mental condition that would limit his or her ability to perform the job.
Height and weight	It is important to be sensitive to questions about height and weight because, while they are not illegal, they could provide the basis for discrimination on certain demographic and or ethnic groups (women, Asians, and others).
Financial situation (bankruptcy)	Questions about an individual's financial situation should be avoided as it is illegal to deny employment to someone solely on the basis of whether or not he or she has filed for bankruptcy.
Arrests and convictions	It is illegal to ask about prior arrests; however, it is permissible to ask about convictions provided the employer provides a statement about how the information will be used in the selection process.

related to such factors. Then there will be no question in the applicant's mind about whether the hiring decision was biased or unfair. This is easier said than done, however, because some seemingly innocent questions can be viewed as attempts to gain information that might be used to discriminate against a candidate.

Summary

This chapter reviewed the issues that surround the recruitment and selection of new salespeople. The issues discussed ranged from who is responsible for these tasks to the impact of federal legislation barring job discrimination on selection procedures.

Two factors are primary in determining who has the responsibility for recruiting and selecting salespeople: (1) the size of the sales force and (2) the kind of selling involved. In general, the smaller the sales force, the more sophisticated the selling task; and the more the sales force is used as a training ground for marketing and sales managers, the more likely it is that higher-level people, including the sales manager, will be directly involved in the recruitment and selection effort. To ensure that recruits have the aptitude for the job, it is useful to look at the recruitment and selection procedures as a three-step process. The steps are (1) a job analysis and description, (2) the recruitment of a pool of applicants, and (3) the selection of the best applicants from the available pool.

The job analysis and description phase includes a detailed examination of the job to determine what activities, tasks, responsibilities, and environmental influences are involved. This analysis may be conducted by someone in the sales management ranks or by a job analysis specialist. Regardless of who does it, it is important for that person to prepare a job description that details the findings of the job analysis. Finally, the job description is used to develop a statement of job qualifications, which lists and describes the personal traits and abilities a person should have to perform the tasks and responsibilities involved.

The pool of recruits from which the firm finally selects can be generated from a number of sources, including (1) people within the company, (2) people in other firms, (3) educational institutions, (4) advertisements, and (5) employment agencies. Each source has its own advantages and disadvantages. Some, such as advertisements, typically produce a large pool. The key question the sales manager needs to address is which source or combination of sources is likely to produce the largest pool of good, qualified recruits.

Once the qualifications necessary to fill a job have been determined and applicants have been recruited, the final task is to determine which applicant best meets the qualifications and has the greatest aptitude for the job. To make this determination, firms often use most, and in some cases all, of the following tools and procedures: (1) application blanks, (2) face-to-face interviews, (3) reference checks, (4) physical examinations, and (5) intelligence, aptitude, and personality tests. Although most employers find the interview and then the application blank most helpful, each device seems to perform some functions better than the other alternatives. This may explain why most firms use a combination of selection tools.

Title VII of the 1964 Civil Rights Act forbids discrimination in employment on the basis of race, sex, color, religion, or national origin. A firm must be careful, therefore, about how it uses tests, how it structures its application form, and the questions it asks during personal interviews so as not to be charged with noncompliance with the act. A firm that uses tests, for example, must be able to demonstrate empirically that the attributes measured are related to the salesperson's performance on the job.

Key Terms

job description
internal sources
external sources
selection tools and
  procedures
structured interview
unstructured interview

Breakout Questions

1. The sales manager for one of the nation's largest producers of consumer goods has identified eight factors that appear to be positively related to effective performance. The manager of human resources, who is concerned about high turnover rates among the sales force, would like to use this information to improve the company's recruiting and hiring process. The key factors are

(*a*) priority setting, (*b*) initiative and follow-through, (*c*) working effectively with others, (*d*) creativity and innovation, (*e*) thinking and problem solving, (*f*) leadership, (*g*) communication, and (*h*) technical mastery.

How could these factors become part of the company's recruiting and hiring process? How would you define these factors and determine if applicants for sales positions possess these factors?

2. In a recent discussion on the use of the Internet to generate applications, the following quote was made and illustrates the application of the Internet to the recruiting and selection process:

It doesn't care whom you know, what kind of suit you're wearing, or whether you have a firm handshake. Salespeople looking for a job may soon have to face their toughest interview yet—with a computer.

What are the advantages of using the Internet to conduct preliminary job interviews? What problems is a company that uses computer-aided interviewing likely to encounter?

3. College recruiters were discussing some of the students they had interviewed that day. One interviewer described a female applicant with excellent credentials as follows: "She looked too feminine, like she would need someone to take care of her, and she was not all that serious about a sales job with us." When asked to explain her comments, the interviewer said, "Under her jacket she wore a flowery blouse with little flowing sleeves and a lace collar." The other recruiter countered and asked, "What do a flowery blouse, flowing sleeves, and a lace collar have to do with performance?" Comment.

4. One potential source of applicants for sales positions are sales representatives who work for competitors. One sales manager indicated, "Pirating sales representatives from other companies makes sense. Let them do the training, then we'll hire them." Is this ethical? Is this legal? Does this practice make good business sense?

Leadership Challenge: Internet or Interview

Ron Deaple considered all his options. As key account sales manager for Cutting Edge Technology, he was responsible for sales and support of the company's most important customers. The company's most significant business was to manufacturers such as Dell and HP as well as other product companies (PalmOne, Blackberry). Ron's position made him ultimately responsible for the relationship with these customers.

Key account managers at Cutting Edge were often younger, highly motivated individuals. While a technology background was helpful, Ron found it was even more important for these individuals to have an understanding of relationship selling. He believed if an individual knew about relationship building he could train them on the technical aspects of the job. Ron had personally recruited nearly all of the 50 key account managers. Up to now, Ron had recruited from other companies, hiring individuals with at least five years experience. In addition, Ron believed that it was critical for applicants to go through at least three interviews including with himself, the executive vice president of marketing, and at least one other key account manager.

It had become clear to Ron and others at Cutting Edge, however, that the old methods of relying on word of mouth and industry contacts were not going to be sufficient sources of new applicants in the future. Ron knew a logical source of new applicants would be the Internet. They were a technology company, and looking for potential new sales people on the Internet would expand the list of possible candidates. His concern was the lack of direct contact with the person applying for the position. Sure he could generate a lot of applicants, but how would he be sure to get the *right* applicants. In addition, he believed the interview process was essential to identifying good candidates and that was not possible over Internet.

Questions

1. What are the strengths and weaknesses of recruiting on the Internet? What are the strengths and weaknesses of face-to-face interviews in the recruiting process?
2. How would you address Ron Deaple's concerns of using the Internet in his recruiting process?
3. Design a program that would enable you to incorporate both the Internet and personal interviews in the recruiting process.

Role Play: Bass Brokers, Inc.—B

Situation

This situation is a continuation of the situation presented in the Chapter 8 role play. Go back and read that role play and your notes from it to refamiliarize yourself with the scenario.

Now that Roscoe Lee and Pat Tollford have agreed on the key selection criteria Bass Brokers, Inc., should use when selecting new salespeople, they have decided that they can further help the district sales managers, and especially District 5 sales manager Jason Queen, by developing some guidelines for recruiting sales position applicants and by developing a more formalized selection procedure for salespeople. As Bass Brokers' newest district manager, Jason is delighted that he will benefit from these new guidelines and procedures as he works to hire replacement salespeople and reduce his district's turnover. Roscoe and Pat have invited Jason into the home office to secure his input on these issues.

Characters in the Role Play

Roscoe Lee, national sales manager for Bass Brokers, Inc.

Pat Tollford, human resource manager for Bass Brokers, Inc.

Jason Queen, District 5 sales manager for Bass Brokers, Inc.

Assignment

Break into groups of three, with one student playing each character. It doesn't matter what the actual gender mix of your pair is. Before you stage the meeting, work separately using the material in your chapter to come up with your recommendations for (1) a logical plan for recruiting Bass Brokers salespeople, especially focused on the right *sources* of recruits, and (2) a selection process, especially focused on the right *selection tools and procedures.* You will need to be prepared to justify your recommendations in the meeting. Then, get together and role-play the meeting with Roscoe, Pat, and Jason. The group should first discuss approaches to recruiting and come to a consensus. Then the group should discuss selection tools and procedures and come to a consensus. Be sure everyone shares their own recommendations and justifies them. In the end, you want to come out of the meeting with a unified plan so that Jason and the other district sales managers at Bass Brokers can implement the ideas with their next hiring process.

Minicase: Digital Age Games

Digital Age Games is a video game publisher that took gaming to a new level in the early 1990s with its well-known "Sack Attack—Extreme Football" game. Unfortunately, it has not had a popular game title since that time and is attempting to make a comeback with its new game "Drop-Kick—Extreme Wrestling." However, Digital Age has found that there is "extreme" competition for space on retailer shelves, as the top three game publishers (Digital Age is not one of them) have a 90 percent share of the market and a corresponding share of shelf space. Therefore, Digital Age's sales group is an area of key concern.

To address this concern, Digital Age's management has hired Shirley Hill, job analysis consultant, to conduct a job analysis of the company's sales positions and give overall advice on how to improve the recruitment process for those positions.

Shirley began her analysis by doing research on the gaming industry as a whole, reviewing the sales structure and job descriptions of Digital Age's major competitors and determining goals and objectives of Digital Age's management. Management told her that it wants to focus on customer prospecting and product demonstration by increasing in-person salesperson attention (and therefore, salesperson travel). It also wants employees with gaming knowledge who will better understand product detail and be able to communicate it to customers.

She spoke at length with the sales managers to determine what the salespeople actually *do,* as well as which are high performers and which are low performers. On her office visits with management, she perceived the tension her presence brought to the sales representatives, who were concerned that their jobs may be at stake, so she spared them and herself by not talking with them directly.

Because the job descriptions had not been updated since 1997, her next order of business was to create a new description for the sales representative position. Her draft job description is as follows:

Sales Representative

The *Digital Age Games* North American sales organization drives the placement, retail marketing, and retail advertising support for consumer goods in its established retail and distribution channels.

The sales representative must:

- Manage U.S. video game distributors and other regional accounts for both video game and PC game products.
- Achieve quarterly sell-in objectives and revenue targets.
- Maintain established accounts through regular customer contact in pursuit of follow-on sales.
- Provide crisp and consistent feedback/communication to manager and others as required.

Selection criteria:

- 2–3 years of experience in sales of entertainment products.
- Bachelor's degree.
- Team player who can deal with ambiguity.
- Customer-service-oriented.
- Strong presentation and communication skills.
- Excellent organizational skills and attention to detail.

Finally, Shirley made recommendations as to sources for new sales recruits. Because knowledge of gaming and the product is central to the position, she recommended that the company primarily look to applicants who are existing employees in the company. Similarly, Shirley reasoned, by advertising positions on the Internet, both on Digital Age's Web site and other third-party job sites, Digital Age would attract tech-savvy applicants. Shirley insisted that these two sources would provide more than enough quality applicants.

Shirley was quite satisfied with her analysis and recommendations, but management has some concerns and has scheduled a feedback meeting with her.

Questions

1. From the facts given, did Shirley do a proper job analysis? What else could she have done to evaluate the current positions? Explain.

2. Evaluate the job description. Is there anything you would have added, deleted, or changed?

3. Besides those recommended by Shirley, what other source(s) of applicants might Digital Age use for recruiting new salespeople? Why?

Suggested Readings

Cron, William L., Greg W. Marshall, Jagdip Singh, Rosann L. Spiro, and Harish Sujan. "Salesperson Selection, Training, and Development: Trends, Implications, and Research Opportunities." *Journal of Personal Selling & Sales Management* 25 (Spring 2005) pp. 123–36

DelVecchio, Susan, and Earl D. Honeycutt, Jr. "An Investigation of African-American Perceptions of Sales Careers." *Journal of Personal Selling & Sales Management* 20, no. 1 (2000), pp. 43–52.

Lopez, Tara, and Amy McMillan-Capehart. "How Outgroup Salespeople Fit in or Fail to Fit in; A Proposed Acculturation Effects Framework." *Journal of Personal Selling & Sales Management* 22, no. 4 (2002), pp. 297–309.

Marshall, Greg W., Thomas H. Stone, and I.M. Jawahar. "Selection Decision Making by Sales Managers and Human Resource Managers: Decision Impact, Decision Frame, and Time of Valuation." *Journal of Personal Selling & Sales Management* 21, no. 1 (2001), pp. 19–28.

Sivadas, Eugene, Susan Bardi Kleiser, James Kellaris, and Robert Dahlstrom. "Moral Philosophy, Ethical Evaluations, and Sales Manager Hiring Intentions." *Journal of Personal Selling & Sales Management* 23, no. 1 (2002–03), pp. 7–21.

Testing and Assessment: An Employer's Guide to Good Practices, Dept. of Labor, 2000.

Wiles, Michael A., and Rosann L. Spiro. "Attracting Graduates to Sales Positions and the Role of Recruiter Knowledge: A Reexamination." *Journal of Personal Selling & Sales Management* 24, no. 1 (2004), pp. 39–48.

Chapter Ten

Sales Training: Objectives, Techniques, and Evaluation

Military Training and Sales Success

Assembling the right skills in a sales force can involve a number of decisions. For example, should salespeople be recruited who already possess the desired skills, or should the focus be on training the existing sales force? Managers have to decide what skills

- *can* be trained

- *must* be trained

- are a requirement for the sales candidate prehire

In some situations, previous training may be very beneficial. However, many companies, managers, and leaders might not see or understand the transferability of unique training backgrounds to their specific sales environments.

To help sales leaders better understand the effect of unique training backgrounds on sales success, Chally investigated the degree to which military training develops critical sales skills. A second question was also studied: if military training does enhance sales skills, would skills differ on the basis of military rank and service length? Chally compared archival data from 80,849 salespeople scored on 156 competencies measured by the Chally Assessment to a sample of 250 recent veterans from RecruitMilitary, a Cincinnati, Ohio, based full-service military-to-civilian recruiting firm. Results were compared for (1) veterans and civilian salespeople, (2) veteran officers and veteran noncommissioned officers, and (3) short-tenured veterans and long-tenured veterans.

Chally found that military training does enhance important sales skills and gives veterans several advantages over the general salesperson. As a result, companies should consider veterans for jobs that require the following sales skills:

- Cordial style of communication (willingness to listen and respond is a friendly manner).

- Focus on resolving customer problems (relationship building).

- Competitive approach (motivation to win).

- Accountability for core business results (directed behavior that leads to defined goals).

- Focus on near-term results through incremental gains (do the little things that lead to sales success).

The research found differences between commissioned and non-commissioned officers and suggests that commissioned officers are likely be more comfortable in sales roles where (1) quick decisions are part of the sales process, (2) innovation is valued, (3) the selling process involves a team approach, and (4) the organization's goals match individual personal success objectives. By contrast, non-commissioned officers are a better fit in sales positions where (1) decision-making is slower, (2) salespeople have the ability to work alone, (3) individuals have the opportunity to emerge as a leader, and (4) success is defined by individual goals.

Key differences were also identified when length of service was considered (long-term veterans were defined by 20 years or more of service while short-term veterans had 5 years or less). The results imply long-term veterans are more likely to use early attempts at closing, while short-term veterans are likely to wait longer before asking for customer commitment. Long-term veteran/salespeople also prefer (1) taking sufficient time to prepare sales presentations, (2) cutting through administrative red tape to find a solution, (3) sharing their expertise with those who seek advanced learning (coaching), and (4) evaluating success by the *quality* of results. By contrast, short-term veteran/salespeople prefer (1) off-the-cuff presentations, (2) working within the company's current systems and procedures, (3) teaching new, inexperienced salespeople, and (4) evaluating success by the *quantity* of results.

In conclusion, Chally's research demonstrates the value of military training in providing veterans with many sales skills that will benefit any organization. For a company faced with the challenge of recruiting for candidates' skills and/or training the skills in current salespeople, the key is to begin by focusing on which sales competencies are critical for success in the role.

Source: HR Chally Group (2007).

LEARNING OBJECTIVES

Salespeople operate in a highly competitive and dynamic environment. In addition, new salespeople must assimilate a great deal of information about the company, products, and customers. A key element in enhancing the success of current salespeople and preparing new salespeople is training. Companies in the twenty-first century realize that good training is an essential component of success for the sales force. This chapter will examine the objectives, techniques, and methods of evaluating training in the sales force.

After reading this chapter, you should be able to

- Identify the key issues in sales training.

- Understand the objectives of sales training.

- Discuss the development of sales training programs.

- Understand the training of new sales recruits and experienced salespeople.

- Define the topics covered in a sales training program.
- Understand the various methods for conducting sales training.
- Discuss how to measure the costs and benefits of sales training.

ISSUES IN SALES TRAINING

Training salespeople is a huge industry. In 2006, the most recent year for which data are available, American companies spent more than 50 billion on training. Exhibit 10.1 lists the top 10 training organizations in 2006 as determined by Training Magazine. It is not surprising then the subject of sales training usually produces considerable interest among managers at all levels of the company. Sales managers—national, regional, and district—have a variety of objectives for training. National account managers want the sales training to provide specific details about certain industries and teach the sales reps to develop close relationships with customers—a critical issue, especially with large national accounts. Market managers are interested in how much training sales representatives receive in dealing with the complex customer problems. Product managers, of course, hope the salespeople have been well schooled in product knowledge, specifications, and applications. Even managers external to the marketing function, such as human resource managers, have a stake in the sales training process. Recruiters know that highly regarded sales training programs enhance the firm's ability to recruit and retain salespeople. A few firms have developed such strong sales training programs that participants who complete the program liken the process to having earned a second degree or an MBA.

When determining sales training needs, three issues must be considered:[1]

- *Who should be trained?* In most organizations new sales recruits receive a combination of training and orientation to company policies and procedures. But this raises the issues of training for different types of salespeople and, depending upon how market or competitive changes may have altered the nature of sales tasks, training for different stages of the same salesperson's career.

- *What should be the primary emphasis in the training program?* Sales training can encompass the following: product knowledge, company knowledge, customer knowledge, or selling skills (e.g., time management or presentation skills). All of these may be important, but the relative importance of each type of training differs depending upon the selling situation, the feasible scope and costs of sales training, and the nature of the company's marketing strategy.

EXHIBIT 10.1
Training Magazine's Top Training Companies

Source: *Manage smarter.com* October, 2007.

Organization
Booz-Allen Hamilton
IBM
Ernst & Young
Ritz Cartton Hotel Co.
Lockheed Martin
Verizon Wireless
Wyeth Pharmaceuticals
Pfizer
KLA-Tencor
General Mills

- *How should the training process be structured?* The following methods are options: On-the-job training and experience versus a formal and more consistent centralized program; Web-based or instructor-based, and in-house training versus outside expertise.

The points raised above clearly indicate that sales training is ongoing and not likely completed in a onetime event. Ideally, sales training for new recruits will instill, in a relatively short period of time, a vast amount of knowledge that has taken skilled sales representatives years to acquire. Sales training for experienced salespeople, on the other hand, may be the result of new product offerings, changes in market structure, new technologies, competitive activities, and so on, plus a desire to reinforce and upgrade critical selling skills. Although some sales managers have a narrow view about the objectives of sales training—for example, to increase motivation—others identify a variety of objectives.

OBJECTIVES OF SALES TRAINING

Although the specific objectives of sales training may vary from firm to firm, there is some agreement on the broad objectives. Sales training is undertaken to increase productivity, improve morale, lower turnover, improve customer relations, and produce better management of time and territory.

Increase Productivity

One objective of sales training is to provide valuable skills that will have a positive effect on selling performance. In a relatively short time, sales training attempts to teach and enhance critical selling skills. The time it takes for a new member of the sales force to achieve satisfactory levels of productivity is thus shortened considerably. Lucent Technologies, for example, credits much of its success in the industry to having a well-trained sales force. Over the last several years, the telecommunications industry has experienced significant decline globally; however, Lucent has done better than the industry average due in part to its additional sales force training. Indeed, the company is projecting good growth, with revenue in excess of $8 billion and a return to profitability after several years of losses.[2]

Improve Morale

How does sales training lead to better morale? One of its objectives is to prepare trainees to improve their productivity as quickly as possible. If sales trainees know what is expected of them, they will be less likely to experience the frustration that arises from trying to carry out a job without adequate preparation. Without sales training, sales representatives may not be able to answer questions that customers have, increasing the salesperson's aggravation and lowering morale. Evidence indicates salespeople who are uncertain about their job requirements tend to be less satisfied with their jobs. Conversely, this same evidence shows salespeople who are well aware of the job requirements are also more satisfied with their company's sales training activities.

Creating the right format for sales training is a challenging task. Refer to Leadership 10.1 for a discussion on creating the most effective training experience. Competent sales training is not a function of motivational hype but rather delivering specific skills and techniques designed to enhance the salesperson's ability to be successful in the field.[3]

Lower Turnover

If sales training can lead to improved morale and greater job satisfaction, then the result should be lower turnover in the sales force. Young, inexperienced salespeople are more

Leadership The Challenge of an Effective Training Experience: Follow-up 10.1

Many training professionals will tell you the toughest audience is salespeople. Motivational pep talks and PowerPoint presentations that do not provide real tools now will anger salespeople and waste money for the company. Salespeople tend to be more independent and more critical of the information they receive in training. Consequently, salespeople demand training that is geared toward them and their unique needs. However, delivering an effective training experience is only half the problem.

Research suggests that salespeople retain only—or put another way, they forget—half of what they have been taught in training within five weeks. This suggests it is important not only to create positive and valuable training but to reinforce the training with follow-up after the experience.

Management has identified post-training follow-up as a major issue. Of the top five issues reported by sales training managers in a recent study, three were related to post-training:

- *Issue 1. Poor implementation of training program.* Not implementing the sales training after the program had been given was the number-one reason, with more than half the managers identifying this issue as significant.

- *Issue 2. Lack of measurable results.* It is not possible to know how well the training has worked without clearly defined metrics for success.

- *Issue 4. Lack of refresher courses or materials.* Following up with additional materials is essential for the original training program to really be effective.

Interestingly, the third-ranked issue, *lack of management support,* has been a problem in sales training for many years. Recently, however, as we saw in the Lucent example, senior managers are realizing how important a well-trained sales force is to achieving overall company goals and objectives.

So the question remains, How can a company best provide the follow-up after the training experience? The following were identified as the most effective tools for bolstering sales training:

1. Sharing sales experiences and practices among the sales team (59%).

2. Coaching by the sales manager (46%).

3. Follow-up training classes (43%).

4. A concise statement by management detailing expectations of the training (39%).

5. Incentive compensation for new sales behaviors (36%).

Clearly, for training to be effective, management must commit to follow-up and use tools that will reinforce the training for salespeople.

Source: "Half Life of Sales Training," *American Salesman* 49, no. 1 (2004), p. 23.

likely to get discouraged and quit as a result of not being prepared for the job. Turnover can also lead to customer problems, since many customers prefer continuity with their sales representative. A customer called on by a salesperson who suddenly quits may transfer business to other suppliers rather than wait for a new representative. Sales training, by leading to lower turnover, alleviates such problems. The pharmaceutical industry has focused a great deal of effort on improving its sales training programs. The industry estimates that turnover can cost as much as 200 percent of a salesperson's total compensation package and cites training as the most significant factor in improving the retention rate of high-performing salespeople. Given that U.S. pharmaceutical companies have almost doubled their sales forces over the last 10 years, it is not surprising they now focus on sales training programs designed to improve retention and performance.[4]

Improve Customer Relations

One benefit of sales training that accompanies lower turnover is continuity in customer relationships. Having the same sales representative call on customers on a regular basis promotes customer loyalty, especially when the salesperson can handle customer questions, objections, and complaints. Customers place orders for their own benefits. Inadequately trained salespeople are usually not able to provide these benefits, and customer relations suffer.

Improve Selling Skills

Many companies believe that improving basic selling skills can lead to improved performance in the field. For example, time and territory management is a subject in many sales training programs. How much time should be devoted to existing accounts versus how much to call on potential new accounts? How often should each class of account be called on? What is the most effective way of covering the territory with respect to miles driven and time spent? Many sales training programs provide salespeople with answers to these questions.

In addition, over time research on the relationship between salesperson and customer can lead to new approaches in sales training. For example, recent research suggests that it can be beneficial for salespeople to provide more structure to the sales presentation in dealing with inexperienced customers. A focused selling strategy designed to create an "agenda" for the customer as they move through the decision-making process can be helpful for new customers who are unaware of the product/services performance characteristics or benefits. This kind of information can be conveyed to salespeople very effectively in a sales training program.[5]

THE DEVELOPMENT OF SALES TRAINING PROGRAMS

There is no question that sales training is an important function. However, there are numerous problems when trying to implement sales training programs. Recently, senior training managers from more than 30,000 organizations were asked to identify their most important training issues and priorities. They identified linking training programs with business strategy as the top priority over the next several years. This means training salespeople to be customer-focused and providing them with tools necessary to build strong customer relationships by adding value to the customer's business. These senior managers, however, cited some very significant obstacles in achieving their training goals. These obstacles included,

- Top management not dedicated to sales training.

- Lack of buy-in from frontline sales managers and salespeople.

- Salespeople's lack of understanding of what the training is supposed to accomplish (objectives).

- Salespeople's lack of understanding regarding the application of the training to their everyday tasks (lack of connection between training and specific sales tasks).[6]

These issues raise an important question. What is management doing that allows some of these problems to occur? Two problems exist. First, management too often expects sales training to solve all the company's sales problems when, in fact, the problem with sales might not even be connected with the sales force (for example, poor product quality or an inefficient supply chain that is unable to deliver products on time). Providing more training to the sales force will not help the company's sales if the product or service does not add value for the customer. If the sales problems are not resolved, budget-cutting activities often start with the sales training program. In addition, too often management fails to understand sales training. Sales training is viewed as a cost of doing business rather than as an investment that pays future dividends. Why are only costs evaluated and not the other

Innovation Sales Training Failure: Causes and Cures 10.2

Why do so many sales training programs fail? Sales professionals have been trying to answer that question for years. Recently, a study suggested four reasons for the failure of sales training programs:

- Too much emphasis on providing the current fad in training without considering the real training needs of the sales force.

- Too many programs are delivered "off the shelf." The program is given without tailoring the training to the specific needs of the salespeople or the company.

- Time demands limit the salesperson's ability to practice the skills learned in the training.

- As noted in Leadership 10.1, very little time is spent reinforcing the sales training.

While these reasons certainly provide insight on the problems of sales training, it is even more important to provide some ideas on how to improve sales training programs. A focused approach that emphasizes specific training tools and measured results includes the following steps.

1. Gain commitment by involving leaders in designing the rollout process.

2. Focus training on the top needs areas.

3. Make training relevant to different groups by customizing the content and presentation.

4. Quantify the pain of not changing.

5. Incorporate new behaviors into everyday tools and processes.

6. Use managers and those who catch on quickly to coach other team members.

7. View training as change management; create an environment that encourages and rewards change behaviors.

8. Encourage implementation of new skills immediately.

9. Ask salespeople to report successes to managers at the end of the quarter. Publicize and celebrate these results.

10. Measure results.

Source: Heather Baldwin, "Rethinking Sales Training," *SellingPower.com,* August 2006 online issue.

half of the operating statement? (Additional revenue generated from effective training)[7] The second problem rests within the sales training function: namely, the evaluation of sales training programs. Historically, too many sales training programs have been conducted without measuring the benefits. Although companies are spending more time and effort on measuring the results of training, the problem of measurement persists. Evaluation is difficult, but considering the millions of dollars devoted to sales training, it is not unreasonable to expect some attempt to measure the benefits.

We will discuss in greater detail how to evaluate sales training programs later in the chapter. Innovation 10.2 discusses the failure of sales training programs and a phased approach to enhancing their success.

Creating Credibility in Sales Training

Many sales trainers believe their programs lack credibility. Budget-cutting efforts are too often directed at existing sales training programs.[8] This may reflect management's feelings that these programs are accomplishing little and are expendable. Sales training programs have to fit the long-term goals and objectives of the organization, and just like the company's own products and services, they must deliver value to the organization.

Analyze Needs

The starting point in creating credibility is to conduct a **sales training analysis** that analyzes the training needs of the sales force (see Exhibit 10.2). One way to do this is

EXHIBIT 10.2
**Analyzing the
training needs
of the sales force**

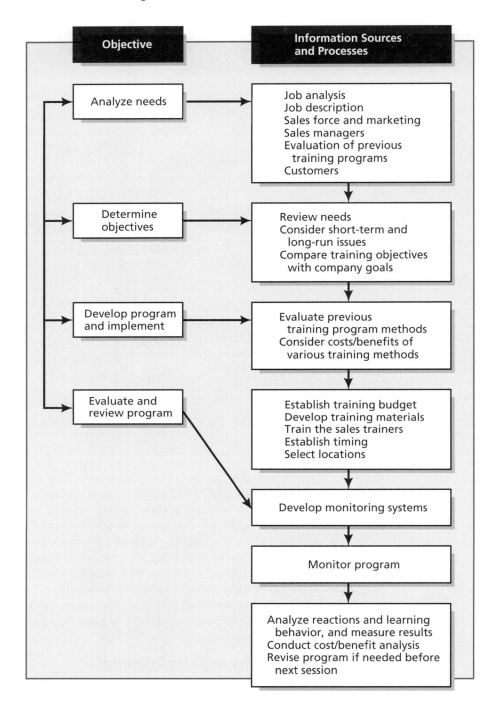

to travel with sales reps, observe and ask them what they need to know to perform their
jobs more effectively. Field sales managers are an excellent source of information because
they are closest to sales people. Interviews with key members of management can also
identify training needs. One expert advocates sending anonymous questionnaires to customers asking, What do you expect of a salesperson in the industry? How do salespeople
disappoint you? Which company in the industry does the best selling job? In what ways

are its salespeople better? Other sources include company records showing turnover data, performance evaluations, and sales and cost analyses. Attitudinal studies conducted with the sales force provide additional insights. This analysis of needs answers three basic questions: Where in the organization is training needed? What should be the content of the training program? Who needs the training? Chally recommends that to get the most out of their training dollar managers should (1) train the right personnel for the right jobs, (2) focus on the highest potential personnel, (3) identify those that can benefit most from training, and (4) realize skills training that maximizes strengths can be more effective than training aimed at overcoming weaknesses.

Determine Objectives

It is important to set realistic objectives. Chally estimates that even effective training cannot improve a person's skills by more than 20 percent. Thus, people in the wrong positions cannot be trained to become top performers, only their "bad" skills can be improved to "not quite as bad." As a result setting specific, realistic, and measurable objectives for the sales training program is critical. The objectives may include learning about new products, sales techniques, or company procedures. Keep the objectives simple, for example, management may want a 10 percent sales increase, which then becomes the broad objective of the training program. The specific objective might be to teach sales reps how to call on new accounts, which will help lead to the broad objective. Measurability is critical in sales training. More will be said about this later.

Develop and Implement Program

At this point, a decision has to be made concerning developing the training program or hiring an outside organization to conduct it. Many companies, both large and small, outsource at least a part of their sales training. Small companies often outsource most of their training. Large companies usually develop most of their own programs and use outside agencies to handle specific or special training needs. When considering an outside training supplier it is critical to conduct a careful investigation. One sales manager mentioned how embarrassed he was by retaining a company that put on an "entertaining song-and-dance routine" that cost $65,000 but failed to have any lasting effect. Use of outside sources is encouraged only if they meet the objectives of the company.

Evaluate and Review Program

Designing a measurement system is the next step. Here are some questions that need to be asked:

- What do we want to measure?

- When do we want to measure?

- How do we do it? What measuring tools are available?

Using tests to measure learning is not difficult; however, measuring the application of training in the field is very difficult. Whether a salesperson can demonstrate a product can be evaluated during a training session. But whether that same individual demonstrates the product effectively in front of a customer is harder to assess. This is why field sales managers are an important link: They can provide follow-up and feedback information on the salesperson's ability to retain and use sales training takeaways in the field. The field sales managers can also coach the salesperson if there is a need for follow up.

Finally, evaluations of sales performance provide additional evidence on the value of training, although such information must be used carefully. Changes in performance, like sales increases, may be due to factors not related to sales training; and when training managers claim they are, it casts doubts on the sales training efforts.

Larger companies must decide which group to train. Most of the time some groups are targeted for training before others. It is also important to remember that not everyone in the sales force needs training. Certainly, newly hired recruits need training, whether it's on the job at first, more centralized, or some other arrangement. When procedures or products change, everyone needs training. If certain salespeople are having specific problems related to performance or attitude, the training needs to be directed at them individually. To include the entire force wastes resources and creates problems, especially among those not experiencing the same issues. When a new training method is being tested, it is wise to use a group that will be receptive. This increases credibility, creating a favorable climate for continuation.

Since measurement is crucial, the sales trainer needs to collect data before training starts. The needs analysis discussed earlier provides relevant information pertaining to program content. For example, if management knew some salespeople had difficulty managing their sales calls, observation by the trainer or the field sales manager after the program should provide data indicating the value of the training. Call reports would be another source of information. Follow-up must continue beyond the initial check because the use of new skills may drop off as noted in Leadership 10.1. If this happens, reinforcement is necessary.

The data collection process should provide sales trainers with information that will justify the program. Top management wants to know if the benefits exceed or equal the costs. Keeping top management informed about the success of training programs contributes to the overall credibility.

Sales training programs, whether being sold to the sales manager or top management, must be credible. Management can always find other alternatives for spending resources.

TRAINING NEW SALES RECRUITS

Larger companies have specific programs for training new sales recruits. These programs differ considerably in length and content, however. The differences often reflect variations in company policies, the nature of the selling job, and types of products and services. Even within the same industry, sales training programs vary in length, content, and technique.

Although a few companies have no set time for training sales recruits, most firms have embraced the notion of a fixed period for formal training. The time varies from just a couple of days in the office, followed by actual selling combined with on-the-job coaching, to as long as two or three years of intensive training in a number of fields and skills.

What accounts for this variation? First, training needs vary from firm to firm and even within a firm. For example, one manufacturer of drugs has a seven-week program for new recruits who will sell conventional consumer products. For those recruits destined to sell more technical products, the training lasts two years.

Second, training needs vary because of differences in the needs and aptitudes of the recruits. Experienced recruits have less need for training than inexperienced recruits, although most large firms require everyone to go through some formal training. One B2B firm requires a one-week program for experienced recruits, but inexperienced recruits may require a two-to three-year program.

A final reason for variation in the length of training programs is company philosophy. Some sales managers believe training for new recruits should be concentrated at the beginning of a sales career, but others think it should be spread over a longer time, including

EXHIBIT 10.3
Length and cost of sales training for new hires

Source: Christen P. Heide, *Dartnell's 30th Sales Force Compensation Survey:* (Chicago: Dartnell Corp., 1999), p. 143.

	Training Period for New Hires (months)	Cost
Company Size		
Under $5 million	4.4	$5,500.0
$5–24.9 million	4.2	8,141.1
$25–99.9 million	3.7	8,090.9
$100–250 million	1.7	7,400.0
Over $250 million	3.6	7,000.0
Product or Service		
Consumer products	3.4	5,354.2
Consumer services	3.3	4,537.3
Industrial products	4.8	9,893.5
Industrial services	4.8	9,060.5
Office products	3.8	6,269.4
Office services	3.2	6,200.0
Type of Buyer		
Consumers	3.3	4,220.6
Distributors	3.9	7,256.5
Industry	4.3	8,234.2
Retailers	3.2	6,711.0
Overall	**3.9**	**$7,079.8**

a large dose of learning by doing. Exhibit 10.3 illustrates the differences in the length of sales training programs for new hires. While a few years old the Dartnell study represents one of the most recent, comprehensive study on sales training. The study suggests the following shifts have taken place (Keep in mind that these costs have undoubtedly gone up in recent years):

- Smaller companies, those with less than $5 million in annual sales, are spending more on sales training per new hire than indicated by earlier data. This translates to $5,500 worth of training per salesperson.

- The length of training in smaller companies has increased from 3.3 months to 4.4 months.

- The data suggest that smaller companies are placing a great deal more emphasis on training than they were several years ago.

- Companies say they are spending time and money on training experienced salespeople, indicating a strong commitment to a well-trained sales force.

- Large companies, those with more than $5 million in annual sales, reported spending less money on training than in the last survey period.[9]

TRAINING EXPERIENCED SALES PERSONNEL

After new salespeople are assigned to a field position, they quickly become involved in customer relationships, competitive developments, and other related matters. Over time, their knowledge of competitors and market conditions becomes dated. Even their personal

EXHIBIT 10.4   Length, type, and cost of sales training for experienced reps

Source: Christen P. Heide, *Dartnell's 30th Sales Force Compensation Survey:* (Chicago: Dartnell Corp., 1999), p. 145.

	Hours per Year of Ongoing Training	Type of Training		Cost
		Selling Skills (%)	Product (%)	
Company Size				
Under $5 million	30.1	40.7%	60.0%	$3,752
$5–24.9 million	36.1	44.6	53.3	3,947
$25–99.9 million	31.0	45.4	47.6	3,902
$100–250 million	25.2	43.4	56.9	5,365
Over $250 million	38.0	44.2	51.3	4,824
Product or Service				
Consumer products	35.8	44.1	50.1	4,039
Consumer services	33.9	49.3	47.5	3,623
Industrial products	31.6	37.1	58.9	5,149
Industrial services	30.8	41.8	53.9	4,867
Office products	41.8	38.0	59.0	4,261
Office services	33.3	45.2	56.0	3,470
Type of Buyer				
Consumers	36.2	45.3	53.4	3,142
Distributors	35.7	40.2	55.1	4,168
Industry	31.5	43.2	55.2	4,605
Retailers	32.9	43.7	51.9	4,181
Overall	**32.5**	**43.6%**	**54.0%**	**$4,032**

selling styles may become stereotyped and less effective. Also, because of changes in company policies and product line, salespeople require refresher or advanced training programs. Almost without exception managers believe the need to learn is a never-ending process and even the most successful salespeople can benefit from additional training. Exhibit 10.4 shows the length, type, and cost of sales training for experienced sales reps. Dartnell's research suggests the following observations:

- Experienced sales reps are given, on average, 32.5 hours of ongoing training per year at a cost of $4,032 per rep.

- The fact that experienced reps continue to receive increasing amounts of training reflects a continuing commitment on the part of management to provide ongoing learning opportunities for their senior salespeople.

- Companies are spending an increasing amount of time on product training and less on training in selling skills.[10]

Additional training often occurs when a sales representative is being considered for promotion. In many companies, a promotion is more than moving from sales to district sales manager. A promotion can include being assigned better customers, transferring to a better territory, moving to a staff position, or being promoted to sales management. Whenever salespeople are assigned better customers or better territories, additional sales training acquaints them with their increased responsibilities.

Many companies decentralize the training for experienced salespeople. Lucent, IBM, and Cisco Systems are among those that get training into the field using Internet based programs.

Training experienced salespeople is viewed as providing insurance for a company's major asset. Debbie Brady, director of learning and organizational effectiveness at Edward Jones, financial services company, notes that the company's focus on training allows it to "thrive in the chaos." She states, "By cultivating our next generation of leaders and preserving the company culture, we are allowing our employees to truly learn and grow."[11]

SALES TRAINING TOPICS

For new salespeople, the content of sales training tends to remain relatively constant over time. Product or service knowledge appears in the majority of programs as well as an orientation on the market/industry, company, and basic selling skills. Beyond these standard topics, there exists a vast array of different subjects that range from the logical, such as training sales reps in how to build successful customer relationships, and team selling, to some questionable topics, such as training the sales force to modify their sales presentation based on whether the customer is "left-brained" or "right-brained."

Product Knowledge

Although product knowledge is one of the most important topics, knowing when and how to discuss the subject in a sales call is probably even more important. More time is typically spent on product knowledge than any other subject, although the time spent varies with the product sold.

Companies that produce technical products, such as technology companies, spend more time on this subject than manufacturers of nontechnical products. Hewlett-Packard, Microsoft, and others allocate a great deal of time educating salespeople on their products and services to better service customers. It is critical that the right product or service be applied to each customer's unique application.

Product knowledge involves knowing not only product specifications but also how the product is used and, in some cases, how it should not be used. One producer of network computer servers gives newly hired sales engineers extensive in-plant exposure to technical and engineering matters. Before field assignment, they spend time in a customer's operations, where they learn about the customer's business processes and operations under realistic conditions.

Product knowledge is not limited to the company's products. Customers often want to know how competitive products compare on price, construction, performance, and compatibility with each other. Customers expect reps to show them how the seller's products can be coordinated with competitive products, such as in a computer installation that involves a number of products by different manufacturers. One manufacturer of power tools that supplies tools to the construction industry exposes sales trainees to competitors' tools so they will know which best handles the customer's demands.

A major objective in product knowledge training is to enable a salesperson to provide potential customers with the information needed for rational decision making. Some benefits that accrue to salespeople as they acquire product knowledge include,

1. Pride and confidence in product quality.

2. Self-assurance emanating from technical knowledge of product makeup.

3. Communication with customers through the use of the operational vocabulary peculiar to the industry.

4. Understanding of product functioning that allows effective diagnosis of customer problems.[12]

All these benefits contribute to improved salesperson–customer interaction.

Market/Industry Orientation

Sales training in the market/industry orientation covers both broad and specific factors. From a broad viewpoint, salespeople need to know how their particular industry fits into the overall economy. Economic fluctuations affect buying behavior, which affects selling techniques. Information about inflationary pressure, for example, may be used to persuade prospective buyers to move their decision dates ahead. If the sales force is involved in forecasting sales and setting quotas, knowledge of the industry and the economy is essential.

From a narrower viewpoint, salespeople must have detailed knowledge about present customers. They need to know their customers' buying policies, patterns, and preferences and the products or services these companies produce. In some cases, sales reps need to be knowledgeable about their customers' customers. This is especially true when sales representatives sell through wholesalers or distributors that often want salespeople to assist them with their customers' problems. These salespeople are expected to know the needs of both wholesalers and retailers, even though the retailers buy from the wholesalers.

Company Orientation

New salespeople need to learn company policies that affect their selling activities. Like all new employees, they are made aware of personnel policies on a variety of items such as salary structure and company benefits.

Salespeople expect customers to request price adjustments, product modifications, faster delivery, and different credit terms. Most companies have policies on such matters arising from legal requirements or industry practices. Too often, however, avoidable delays and lost sales result when salespeople are not made aware of important company policies.

Two different learning environments provide salespeople with knowledge of company policies. The first places sales trainees inside the home office working in various departments, such as credit, order processing, advertising, sales promotion, or shipping. The second method has the new salesperson working as an inside sales coordinator or customer service representative processing customer orders, maintaining e-mail and telephone contact with customers, and sometimes serving as the company contact for a group of customers.

Major corporations provide the sales force with on-line manuals or CDs that cover product line information and company policies. A well-prepared sales manual can give a sales representative a quick answer to a customer's question.

Time and Territory Management

New salespeople frequently need assistance in managing their time and territories. A survey by Learning International suggests that salespeople perceive this as an important problem. Management also considers time management a critical issue. Blue Cross and Blue Shield instituted Internet-based learning for the salespeople to provide more time for them to spend with their customers. Dan Goettsch, sales training manager, states, "One of the big issues here is the notion that selling time is a very precious commodity. Any time [out of the field] is costly for sales folks."[13]

The familiar 80–20 ratio, where 20 percent of a company's customers account for 80 percent of the business, applies to time and territory management in the reverse direction. It is not unusual to find sales representatives who are skilled in all areas except

Leadership   Ethics Training Becomes Part of Sales Training   10.3

The insurance industry has been plagued by deceptive sales practices for years. Indeed, the industry as a whole has suffered from a bad reputation as a small percentage of salespeople follow unethical, even illegal, sales techniques. A number of leading insurance companies recognized this issue and created the Insurance Marketplace Standards Association (IMSA) to help establish, enforce, and promote ethical standards in the insurance industry.

For a company to be certified by the IMSA, it must follow established policies and practices to ensure its salespeople pursue ethical sales practices. Training on ethical practices is a critical element in the certification process. All sales agents and support staff are required to take an ethics course that is taught by agency managers. The sales professionals are given study materials on ethics and take an exam.

The organization and its members subscribe to a tough set of ethical standards that can be summarized as the IMSA's Principles of Ethical Market Conduct:

1. Conduct business according to high standards of honesty and fairness and render that service to its customers which, in the same circumstances, it would apply to or demand for itself.

2. Provide competent and customer-focused sales and service.

3. Engage in active and fair competition.

4. Provide advertising and sales materials that are clear as to purpose and honest and fair as to content.

5. Provide for fair and expeditious handling of customer complaints and disputes.

6. Maintain a system of supervision and review that is reasonably designed to achieve compliance with these Principles of Ethical Market Conduct.

As of 2007, less than 20% of 1,000 companies selling life insurance in the United States have been awarded membership in the IMSA. This is not surprising given the rigorous assessment and certification process. However, those companies that do gain membership possess a competitive advantage.

Source: IMSA, *www.imsaethics.org,* Fall 2007.

efficient time management spending 80 percent of their time with customers who account for only 20 percent of sales. In addition, assigning a salesperson too many accounts or a territory that is too large leads to time and territory management problems.

A manufacturer of micrographic equipment trains salespeople to "plan your work—work your plan." Although some instruction in time management is provided by this company during classroom training, the major responsibility rests with the district sales managers. Sales representatives turn in their projected activities every two weeks and review their district sales manager's past plans and performance. The district sales manager helps them modify the projected plans for greater efficiency. The desire for more effective time and territory management has led to greater telephone and e-mail usage.

Legal/Ethical Issues

Statements—or, rather, misstatements—made by salespeople have legal and ethical implications. Leadership 10.3 describes a company's response to ethical problems.

Lapses in ethical conduct have been known to lead to legal problems. The example in the Leadership box stems from problems confronted by major insurance companies that allowed sales representatives to engage in unethical practices, such as selling whole life insurance policies as annuities. In one case, the legal settlement ran into millions of dollars. An article in *BusinessWeek* makes the following point:

> After years of scandals involving some of the biggest names in life insurance, consumers are finally waking up to churning. This abusive sales practice occurs when agents dupe customers into replacing perfectly good cash-value policies.[14]

Technology   Internet Training Comes of Age   10.4

Companies and salespeople are under increasing pressure to deliver added value to customers faster and better. This has led many companies to explore and implement Web-based training. Not surprising, it has taken several years for companies to first understand how and what to deliver over the Internet. For example, Perfect Commerce, a leading provider of business-to-business e-commerce solutions, studied Web-based training for several years before deciding on a format and structure of its training program.

Entire industries are also looking to the Internet to deliver critical training. The Credit Union National Association (CUNA; 30) provides extensive training to its members using CPDonline, a training program that emulates the classroom learning environment. The Association encourages its members to provide more online training and provides tools to help them implement such training programs.

Retailers have also found the Internet to be an excellent tool for delivering training. Companies like Home Depot are using the Internet to deliver product information to their sales associates. PetsMart incorporates a wide range of topics in its online training programs, including ideas on how to meet and greet customers.

Using Web-based training allows companies to maintain more control over the content and spend less money on training. In addition, by controlling the content, they need to hire fewer outside training consultants. Some estimates put the amount of training done online at about 15–20 percent of all training. However, that figure is expected to grow to nearly 50 percent of all training over the next five years.

Technology

Most companies issue salespeople laptop computers. In addition, many companies, such as IBM, also create "home offices" for their sales force that eliminate the need to go into an office at all. With a high-speed network connection, laptop or desktop computer, printer, and cell phone, a salesperson is almost totally self-sufficient. Salespeople use PCs to plan their call activities, submit orders, send reports, check on inventory and price levels, receive messages, and present product and service demonstrations. In some cases, the sales rep can access the company's decision support system (DSS) to learn what products have been selling in an area or for a specific customer.

Companies have found that proper use of technology allows their salespeople more face-to-face customer contact time. It also enables salespeople to respond much faster to the customer. The cell phone puts the customer in contact with the salesperson almost all the time. Coupled with direct network connections that companies such as General Motors and Ford have with their suppliers, it is no wonder that many customers report much better communication between themselves and the salespeople who call on them. Technology 10.4 talks about the use of Internet technology in training.

Specialized Training Topics

Companies are frequently coming to the conclusion that training is most effective when it is specialized and tailored to individual job functions. For example, price objections are common in sales transactions, and sales managers are not pleased if they feel that sales reps offer discounts too quickly. Recently, Johnson Controls Inc., a manufacturer of automated control systems based in Atlanta, instituted a six-month training program to address the issue of price negotiations. Linda DeMars, regional sales manager for Johnson Controls, reports, "What we notice is that our salespeople find it more comfortable, or it looks like the only option, to erode market pricing as opposed to 'bundling' or building value." One solution adopted by Johnson Controls was to provide salespeople with detailed financial information to help them make more profitable decisions.[15]

Many companies, like Caterpillar Inc., spend substantial sums of money each year on trade shows. Increasing cost pressures have forced management to be more concerned about the return from trade shows and other similar expenditures. As a result, Caterpillar personnel selected to staff trade show exhibits undergo a training program to increase their effectiveness in the unique trade show enviornment. Most salespeople selected have the training and experience to make in-depth presentations in their specialties. But even though they're very good, they are not necessarily skilled at working a trade show. They don't always know how to engage and qualify new prospects, handle big crowds, or weed out the buyers from the "tire kickers."[16]

Other subjects addressed in training programs include body language, eye movement, and even attempts to determine if the prospect is right-brained or left-brained. Indicators of left- or right-brained people might be whether or not a customer wears a watch or carries a calculator.[17] It should be noted, however, that there is no evidence to support this concept in a sales context.

Sales training is also effective in helping salespeople work through problems or issues that may limit their performance. Recently, researchers have reported that sales call anxiety (SCA) can lead to real problems in both a salesperson's effectiveness and efficiency. One of the results of the research is a focus on better training methods to reduce SCA before it becomes a problem for salespeople.[18]

SALES TRAINING METHODS

The most commonly used methods of sales training are on-the-job training, individual instruction, in-house classes, and external seminars. Companies use a variety of techniques, recognizing that different subjects require different methods (Exhibit 10.5). Overlap exists within a given method. On-the-job training includes individual instruction (coaching) and in-house classes held at district sales offices. In addition, companies currently seem more willing than in the past to seek outside help when it comes to solving their training/motivation problems.[19] Finally, companies are realizing that sales training does not need to be boring. Innovation 10.5 illustrates how companies use creative ideas to help train their salespeople.

EXHIBIT 10.5
Common instruction methods

Common Instructional Methods

Classroom with instructor
Workbooks/manuals
Public seminars
Videotapes
CD-ROM
Self-assessment
Role-play
Noncomputer, self-study
Case studies
Internet
Intranet
Non-computer-based games
Computer-based games
Audiocassettes
Teleconferencing
Videoconferencing: groups

Innovation   Creative Sales Training 101   10.5

Who says sales training has to be boring? Many companies are taking a new approach to sales training. While the focus is still on providing the knowledge and selling skills necessary to be successful, companies are also finding that it is possible to deliver the training in a unique and memorable experience.

Whirlpool for example sends its salespeople to a home filled with Whirlpool appliances. They spend several months learning about the products and how to use them in a real-world setting. When consumers complain about soiled clothes or dirty dishes, salespeople have a new and better appreciation of their problems. Black and Decker also believes in putting its salespeople in real settings and created a facility that lets them get "hands on" with the tools. They use the tools to build and work on projects that will help them learn how their customers interact with the products.

Other companies hire outside training specialists to deliver a unique training experience. One distinctive training experience puts groups of salespeople in the kitchen to learn team-building skills by working together as a group to plan, cook, and serve a meal to senior managers. Other training experiences range from boot camps in the mountains to safaris in Africa. Many are designed to build teamwork and take salespeople out of their normal work environment.

The bottom line is that sales training can be more than classrooms, computers, and product information. It is critical however, that management has a clear understanding of the objectives and goals of this kind of training. Simply sending salespeople off for a week of boot camp in the Rockies without a clear understanding of deliverables is expensive and will not lead to greater performance or more satisfied salespeople.

As has been noted, companies continue to use external sources for a lot of their sales training needs (Exhibit 10.6). However, the use of outside sources is not without some controversy. Jack Falvey, sales consultant, indicates, "The design, development, and sale of training materials is a big business these days." Companies question if they should spend money on outside sales training sources. Falvey's response is, "Only if you have lots of discretionary money to spend and don't know what to do with it."[20]

"Selling," according to Falvey, "is an interactive skill that must be acquired in combination with the knowledge of how both you and your customers do business. It can't be separated out into a generic system that can later be recombined in some way with your business."[21]

Dr Pepper/Seven Up, like many other companies, has established outsourcing partnerships that provide training programs for all types and levels of employees. The company hired an outside training company, Acclivus, to help improve the customer problem-solving skills of its sales and customer service staff. However, the outsourcing partnership did not eliminate the training function at Dr Pepper/Seven Up. The net effect was to enhance the training capabilities of the company.[22]

On-the-Job Training

The mere mention of **on-the-job training (OJT)** sometimes scares new sales recruits. The thought of "learning by doing" is psychologically discomforting to many. Often, this is due to their incorrect perceptions of what is involved in OJT. On-the-job training is not a sink-or-swim approach in which the new salesperson is handed a sales manual and told to "go out and sell." OJT should be a carefully planned process in which the new recruit learns by doing and, at the same time, is productively employed. Furthermore, a good OJT program contains established procedures for evaluating and reviewing a salesperson's progress. Critiques should be held after each sales call and summarized daily. The critiques cover effectiveness, selling skills, communication of information in a persuasive manner, and other criteria.

EXHIBIT 10.6 **Sales training methods**

Source: Christen P. Heide, *Dartnell's 30th Sales Force Compensation Survey:* (Chicago: Dartnell Corp., 1999), p. 141.

	Percentage of Companies Using					
	Individual Instruction	Home Assignments	In-House Class	On the Job	External Seminars	Other
Company Size						
Under $5 million	72.3%	13.1%	43.1%	78.5%	59.2%	6.2%
$5–24.9 million	71.2	16.9	64.4	85.0	72.5	8.8
$25–99.9 million	65.1	17.4	69.8	87.2	80.2	7.0
$100–250 million	54.2	20.8	75.0	91.7	79.2	4.2
Over $250 million	76.5	38.2	79.4	91.2	79.4	0.0
Product or Service						
Consumer products	75.7	21.3	61.8	89.7	72.1	6.6
Consumer services	74.3	16.9	62.5	85.3	69.1	7.4
Industrial products	66.0	20.0	62.5	83.0	71.5	6.5
Industrial services	66.9	18.2	60.4	79.2	76.0	7.8
Office products	70.9	25.6	65.1	93.0	74.4	4.7
Office services	69.0	19.5	62.8	88.5	71.7	7.1
Type of Buyer						
Consumers	73.6	18.2	56.6	87.4	69.8	6.3
Distributors	69.6	18.7	62.6	85.4	74.9	5.8
Industry	69.7	18.1	62.3	83.2	72.6	7.1
Retailers	72.4	20.0	60.0	91.0	71.7	7.6
Overall	**69.8%**	**17.7%**	**60.8%**	**84.3%**	**71.0%**	**6.7%**

Research over the last few years suggests that informal on-the-job training is an effective way of learning for salespeople. Indeed, it is suggested that the majority of all learning at work takes place informally. The Education Development Center identified five keys for effective on-the-job informal training:

1. *Teaming.* Bringing together people with different skills to address issues.

2. *Meetings.* Setting aside times when employees at different levels and positions can get together and share thoughts on various topics.

3. *Customer interaction.* Including customer feedback as part of the learning process.

4. *Mentoring.* Providing an informal mechanism for new salespeople to interact and learn from more experienced ones.

5. *Peer-to-peer communication.* Creating opportunities for salespeople to interact together for mutual learning.[23]

A key aspect of on-the-job training is the coaching salespeople receive from trainers, who may be experienced sales personnel, sales managers, or personnel specifically assigned to do sales training. On-the-job training and coaching often occur together; this is referred to as *one-on-one training.* Observation is an integral part of the process. Managers are aware that helping a salesperson reach his or her full potential means spending time with the person one on one. One consultant specializing in sales performance states, "Managers play an essential role in cultivating talent. They need to take on a coaching role." In addition, providing individual feedback can lead to greater salesperson satisfaction. One salesperson sums up the benefits of one-on-one feedback this way, "For my entire sales career, my manager went on calls with me at least two days every month. The [sales] classes never would have had an impact without coaching."[24] OJT often involves job rotation— assigning trainees to different departments where they learn about such things as manufacturing, marketing, shipping, credits and collections, and servicing procedures. After on-the-job training, many sales trainees proceed to formal classroom training.

Classroom Training

For most companies, formal classroom training is an indispensable part of sales training, although very few of them rely solely on it. Classroom training has several advantages. First, each salesperson receives standard briefings on such subjects as product knowledge, company policies, customer and market characteristics, and selling skills. Second, formal training sessions often save substantial amounts of executive time because executives can meet an entire group of salespeople at once. Third, lectures, presentations, and case discussions can be programmed into a classroom setting. The opportunity for interaction between salespeople is a fourth advantage.

Such interaction is beneficial, since reinforcement and ideas for improvement can come from other salespeople. Interaction is so important that many companies divide salespeople into teams for case presentations, which results in interaction and forces salespeople to become actively involved.

Classroom training also has its disadvantages. It is expensive and time-consuming. It requires recruits to be brought together and facilities, meals, transportation, recreation, and lodging to be provided for them. Sales managers, who are cognizant of these costs and time demands, sometimes attempt to cover too much material in too short a time. This results in less retention of information. Many sessions become mere cram sessions. Sales managers must avoid the natural tendency to add more and more material, because the additional exposure is often gained at the expense of retention and opportunity for interaction.[25]

Role-Playing

A popular technique used in many companies has the salesperson act out the part of a sales rep in a simulated buying session. The buyer may be either a sales instructor or another trainee. **Role-playing** is widely used to develop selling skills, but it can also be used to determine whether the trainee can apply knowledge taught via other methods of instruction. The salesperson, trainer, and other salespeople critique the trainee's performance immediately following the role-playing session.

Role-playing where a sales trainee performs in front of others and where that performance is subsequently critiqued can be harsh. Some of these problems disappear if the critique is conducted only in the presence of the sales trainee and then only by the sales instructor. When role-playing is handled well, most trainees can still identify their own strengths and weaknesses.

Electronic Training Methods

Electronic training methods, and more specifically the Internet, have revolutionized the delivery of training, not just in sales but across the entire organization. Companies even deliver quality learning experiences to their customers over the Internet. Companies find the Internet to be not only effective in delivering just-in-time information but also very efficient. Online training is growing at a rapid rate. International Data Corporation reports that online training was a $18 billion industry in 2006.[26]

Perhaps not surprising, IBM is investing a great deal of time and resources into the delivery of online training to its sales force of more than 300,000 worldwide. Its Internet-based training strategy involves delivering small incremental packets of information on products and customers just in time to complete specific projects currently on the salesperson's activity list. In addition, online chat groups enable the salesperson to gather even more information or provide feedback on current activities.

IBM believes this has led to greater effectiveness in the sales efforts and seeks to make online training a vital part of its overall sales training program. Plans call for 35 percent of IBM sales training to be done over the Internet. The key is to deliver the information when and where the salesperson can use it most. Nancy Dixon, consultant in corporate learning, believes this trend will continue: "People are learning all the time. It's up to the company to make sure they have the tools they need in order to focus that learning on their jobs." One other significant benefit of the program is the cost saving. IBM estimates it will save $200 million in reduced travel and hotel costs alone.[27]

In addition to online training, companies are delivering a great deal of training using CD-ROM and disk programs. Indeed, the number-one delivery mechanism for computer-based training is CD-ROM.[28] In addition, while many companies are using open delivery systems directly over the Internet, the most dominant form of online training is the internal company network, with 30 percent of training coming through internal networks.[29]

Do these programs work? Can they train salespeople to effectively interact with customers? Answers to these questions have not been well documented. As with all methods, be it understanding body language or eye movements, there is a great deal of information salespeople need in order to be effective. Online training can be very effective in delivering certain kinds of information but will not likely eliminate the need for one-on-one training for salespeople.[30]

MEASURING THE COSTS AND BENEFITS OF SALES TRAINING

Sales training is a time-consuming and very costly activity. Is all this effort worth the cost? Are **sales training costs** justified by the benefits produced? If done properly, sales training can be one of the most helpful tools used to increase the satisfaction and performance of salespeople. However, as discussed in Leadership 10.6, there are many obstacles in the way of a successful training strategy.

Sales training and increased profits have an obscure relationship at best. In the beginning of this chapter, we identified some broad objectives of sales training: improved selling skills, increased productivity, improved morale, lower sales force turnover, better customer relations, and better time and territory management. Unfortunately, pinning down the relationship between sales training and these broad objectives is not easy. Very little research has been done to determine what effect, if any, sales training has on the sales force. Most sales organizations simply assume on blind faith that their sales training programs are successful. After all, if a company has high sales and high profits, why should a sales manager assume sales training is anything but effective?

Sales Training Costs

Business firms spend millions of dollars each year on sales training in hopes of improving overall productivity. A look back at Exhibit 10.3 suggests that only the largest companies can afford to support a full-scale training program, yet all firms need sales training, regardless of size. The statistics suggest that business has a relatively generous attitude toward

Leadership   Successful Sales Training Road Blocks   10.6

It's 8:30 and 30 minutes into an all-day seminar costing $1,000 per person. The salesperson already knows that she has heard it all before, which means another day of training with little or nothing to show for it. Companies spend billions on training and find it difficult, at best, to determine the real value of it.

Unfortunately, there are many problems associated with the development of effective training programs. Below is a list of nine common problems that inhibit qualified training success in many sales organizations.

1. *Training can't solve the problem.* The real cause of many problems inside the sales force is often something that will not be solved by more training.

2. *Busy, jaded salespeople are not open to learning new skills.* Salespeople are faced with a fundamental problem, not enough time. When they are away from their customers, sales performance takes the hit. Consequently, they want to see results immediately.

3. *Managers don't support the training program.* Not surprising, salespeople are reluctant to actively participate in training if management does not support it.

4. *Conflicting methods and philosophies are taught at each session.* When salespeople are subjected to training, it is critical that everyone be familiar with what has gone on before so that conflicting information is not presented to the sales force.

5. *The training isn't relevant to the company's pressing needs.* It is crucial to have frontline managers provide at least some input into the content of training programs.

6. *The training format doesn't fit the need.* Many companies fail to match the need with the format. For example, using a half-day seminar to change salesperson attitudes might work, but to provide detailed information about a new product will almost never be successful. A common problem is a failure to build in practice time by which salespeople can try out what they have learned in the training. If you give them a half-day seminar on new selling skills and then let them go, the likelihood those skills will work is very low.

7. *E-learning is overused, or used in wrong situations.* While e-learning can be successful, many companies use it without considering if it is the right methodology to deliver the training.

8. *There's no follow-up after training.* Companies spend millions on training and never follow up. The result is that salespeople don't feel compelled to use it.

9. *The trainer can't relate to the sales team.* It is a fact of human nature, if a person is not interesting, people lose interest. A trainer must be able to connect with his or her audience.

sales training. It allocates funds for training with minimal regard for the results. Clearly, measuring the benefits of sales training needs some attention.

Is the measurement process that difficult? After all, if sales training is supposed to lead to better productivity, improved morale, and lower turnover, then why not measure changes in these variables after training has occurred? Some sales managers have done just that. They have assumed: We instituted sales training and shortly afterward sales increased. Therefore, sales training was the reason. Right? Wrong! Unless appropriate procedures are used to design the research by which the benefits are assessed, it is hard to say what caused the sales increase. Sales may have increased as a result of improved economic conditions, competitive activity, environmental changes, seasonal trends, or other reasons. Consequently, research must be carefully designed to isolate these contaminating effects to identify the benefits directly attributable to training.

Measurement Criteria

Even though intervening variables such as changes in competitive activities make evaluation of sales training programs difficult, it is still important to measure training effectiveness. This

EXHIBIT 10.7 **Evaluation options matrix**

Source: Thomas Atkinson and Theodore L. Higgins, "Evaluation Obstacles and Opportunities," *Forum Issues,* February 1988, p. 22.

Evaluation Level: What Is the Question?	Information Required: What Information to Collect?	Method: How to Collect?
Reaction		

Did participants respond favorably to the program?	Attitudinal	Evaluation
		    Questionnaires
		    Comments
		    Anecdotes
		    Interviews with participants

Learning		
Did participants learn concepts or skills?	Understanding of concepts, ability to use skills	Before-and-after test
Behavior		
Did participants change their on-the-job behavior?	On-the-job behavior	Behavior ratings, before and after Critical incident technique Time-series analysis
Results		
What personal or organizational results occurred?	Changes in sales, productivity, or other performance	Cost–benefit methods

raises the question, What characteristics of sales training should be assessed? Exhibit 10.7 to illustrates an evaluation options matrix. Often companies choose one of the criteria shown in Exhibit 10.7 to measure effectiveness, however a strong argument can be made that several criteria should be used in assessing the results of any sales training program. Measuring what was learned, for example, does not mean much if the company does not also measure changes in behavior. However, it is important to assess sales training programs, because the program should deliver value to the salesperson and organization. The solution rests in properly specifying the objectives and content of the sales training program, the criteria used to evaluate the program, and the proper design of the research so benefits can be unambiguously determined.

Measuring Broad Benefits

Broad benefits of sales training include improved morale and lower turnover. Morale can be partially measured by studies of job satisfaction. Suppose, for instance, a company measured job satisfaction as part of a needs analysis and found evidence of problems. A follow-up job satisfaction study after the corrective sales training program would determine if morale changed noticeably.

Measuring reactions and learning is important in sales training for both new and experienced personnel. Most companies measure reactions by asking those attending the training to complete an evaluation form either immediately after the session or several weeks later. Emotions and enthusiasm may be high right after a session, but sales training effectiveness is much more than a "warm feeling." Measuring what was learned requires tests. To what extent did salespeople learn the facts, concepts, and techniques included in the training session? Objective examinations are appropriate.

Measuring Specific Benefits

Liking the program and learning something are not enough. Specific measures to examine behavior changes and results are needed to assess effectiveness. The effectiveness of a sales training program aimed at securing more new customers, for example, is assessed, in part by examining call reports to see whether there are more new customers. Results are measured by tracking new-account sales to see whether they have increased. If the specific objective of sales training is to increase the sales of more profitable items, evidence that this has been accomplished provides a partial measure of training effectiveness. Finally, if reducing customer complaints was the objective, then the appropriate specific measure is whether customer complaints decreased.

The measurement of specific and broad benefits is predicated on the assumption the sales training program is designed to achieve certain goals. The goals should be established before sales training begins. When specific objectives have been determined, the best training program is developed to achieve these objectives. Most training programs have several objectives. Multiple measurements of the effectiveness of the training program are then a necessary part of evaluating the benefits.

Recent studies reveal that most sales training evaluation measures are simple, consisting primarily of reactions to the program. Meaningful evaluation measures, such as learning, behavior, and results, are used much less frequently. Often, the easiest-to-collect measures—staff comments and feedback from supervisors and trainees—are used the most. Bottom-line evaluation (e.g., changes in sales volume) is used less frequently or not at all.

Exhibit 10.8 shows how sales managers rank the various measures by both importance and frequency of use.[31] Interestingly, the most frequently used measure is course evaluation, but it is only ranked ninth on importance. Course evaluation is a reaction measure that fails to reveal learning, behavioral, and results changes associated with the sales training.

Evaluating the benefits of sales training is difficult. One study asked sales managers to identify the most important restrictions against sales training evaluation. The most common restrictions were time and money and difficulty in gathering the data or gaining access to data.[32]

Recent Trends in Sales Training Evaluation

In recent years there has been a surge of interest in sales training evaluation. Managers are no longer willing to rest on the assumption that sales training must be effective since sales

EXHIBIT 10.8
Overall ranking of evaluation measures

Approach	Type	Importance	Frequency
Trainee feedback	Reaction	1	2
Supervisory appraisal	Behavior	2	6
Self-appraisal	Behavior	3	7
Bottom-line measurement	Results	4	9
Customer appraisal	Behavior	5	10
Supervisory feedback	Reaction	6	4
Performance tests	Learning	7	5
Training staff comments	Reaction	8	3
Course evaluations	Reaction	9	1
Subordinate appraisal	Behavior	10	12
Pre- vs. post-training measurements	Learning	11	11
Coworkers appraisal	Behavior	12	13
Knowledge tests	Learning	13	8
Control group	Learning	14	14

are rising. Managers are now being asked to provide concrete evidence that sales training makes a difference. Evidence based on salesperson reactions or testing what was learned is useful but no longer sufficient proof. If sales training is to be viewed as an investment rather than a cost, then managers must be able to document the benefits in order to calculate a return on investment.

What's behind this movement toward more accountability? According to Beverly Geber, former special projects editor of *Training* magazine, "Blame TQM or downsizing or impatient managers. Fact is, trainers are being pressured to evaluate training courses at much deeper levels."[33] A dilemma facing many sales training managers is that while management wants evidence that supports the value of training, funds needed for evaluation, especially measuring actual changes in sales levels, have not been budgeted. This kind of measurement usually requires using a control group, a rare activity in most companies. "In the businesses I've been in, nobody, especially in sales, wants to volunteer to be in the control group," says Mark Faber, research and measurement manager of sales planning for Microsoft Corporation. "The military has no trouble getting control groups: 'You guys go out with guns and you other guys go out without them.' Nobody in sales wants to go out without guns."[34]

Faber and others have been able to achieve the ends of a control method without actually using control groups. "You can implement training in one site and see a change," suggests Dan Baitch, research project manager for Learning International in Stamford, Connecticut "Then you implement it in another site and see another change. Meanwhile, nothing is changing in the other sites, so each acts as a control group for the one before it."[35]

There are problems, of course, in equating sales increases with sales training. There are too many variables that could have had a positive effect on sales: introduction of a new product, failure of a competitor, increase in advertising, or improvement in price competitiveness. Regardless of the evaluation method employed, sales training managers face increasing demands as to the value of their programs.

Summary

Sales training is a varied and ongoing activity that is time-consuming and expensive. Most companies engage in some type of sales training. In fact, most sales managers feel that sales training is such an important activity that they require it for everybody, regardless of their experience. Some common objectives of sales training are to teach selling skills, increase productivity, improve morale, lower turnover, improve customer relations, and improve time and territory management.

Considerable variability exists in the length of sales training programs. Industry differences account not only for variations in length but also for variations in program content. Company policies, the nature of the selling job, and the types of products and services offered also contribute to differences in time spent and on topics covered.

Product knowledge receives the most attention, followed by selling techniques, market/industry orientation, and company orientation. This allocation is the subject of considerable criticism.

As a result of various environmental changes, the content and method of sales training has changed. Standard issue for salespeople today is a cell phone and laptop computer. In addition, they are as likely to receive training via the Internet and CD-ROM as they are by another person.

Sales training is very expensive and generally considered beneficial. Accurate measurement of the benefits is difficult. It is hard to isolate the effects produced solely by sales training from those that might have been produced by other factors, such as changes in the economy or the nature of competition. Sales training provides managers with the opportunity to convey their expectations to the sales force. A well-designed training program shows the sales force how to sell. Sales managers can communicate high performance expectations through training and equip the force with the skills needed to reach high performance levels.

Key Terms

sales training analysis
on-the-job training (OJT)

role-playing
electronic training methods

sales training costs

Breakout Questions

1. The response from a few of the sales reps from Marlow Technologies toward the new sales training topic was not encouraging. Geoff Marlow, national sales manager, was dismayed at what he perceived to be a total lack of social graces on the part of the 15-person sales force. To rectify this situation, he retained a consulting firm that specializes in etiquette training to provide a day-long session on the subject. Frank Casey, one of Marlow's sales trainees, was not pleased and said, "What's this? Now we have to go to charm school too! Next thing you know, they'll want to teach us how to dress." Are such topics as etiquette and dress appropriate for sales training? How would you evaluate the effectiveness of this kind of training?

2. The newly assigned sales representative was perplexed about her inability to learn about consumers' needs. She contends her customers are not willing to tell her what problems they are experiencing. After making several joint calls with her, the district sales manager agreed she was not receiving informative responses to her questions. What are the characteristics of good questions? How can sales reps be trained to ask better questions?

3. One expert contends that sales training is not at all complicated as some would claim. He predicts that regardless of the advances in communication, resources, technology, and training tools, the basic selling skills that trainers teach salespeople will change very little from those that have been successful during the past 50 years. What will change, according to the expert, is how salespeople are trained to use these skills effectively. Do you agree with this prediction?

Leadership Challenge: Train What?

As Susan Jamison, director of sales training at O&F Products (a leader in consumer packaged products), leaned back in her chair, she was thinking about the upcoming semiannual sales training sessions for the sales force at O&F. These sessions took place over three days, and while regional directors could alter some of the content to fit local needs, Susan was responsible for putting together the overall outline and content of the training. O&F placed a lot of emphasis on training, and these training sessions were a major element in the company's ongoing commitment to having the best sales force in the industry.

After a series of meetings with senior sales managers as well as input from other top management in the company, she was unclear regarding the content of the training this year. Senior sales managers were calling for a focus on new-product information. The company had introduced a number of new products in the last several years, and sales for some of them had not met the company's projections. Senior sales personnel felt it was due, in large part, to a lack of training. In addition, these same individuals felt salespeople would benefit from additional training on some of the existing products, particularly those in which O&F did not enjoy a market leadership position. At the same time, senior management, particularly the General Counsel for the company, wanted the focus to be on sales ethics. Recently, the industry had been under attack for unfair and perhaps illegal sales practices to retailers. Senior management wanted the three-day training session to provide salespeople with a better understanding of ethical decision making at the company.

Susan was in a tough position. She felt both groups had legitimate information to be presented during the training seminar. Unfortunately, there was only sufficient time to focus on one of the areas: ethics or product knowledge.

Questions

1. What are the benefits and limitations of focusing on only product knowledge in training?
2. Do you think you can really train sales ethics?
3. You are Susan Jamison. What would you choose to do in this situation and why?

Role Play: Bass Brokers, Inc.—C

Situation

This situation is a continuation of that presented in the Chapters 8 and 9 role plays. Go back and read those and your notes from them to refamiliarize yourself with the scenario.

It is now six months later, and Jason Queen has made two outstanding hires of new salespeople in District 5. The emphasis on proper selection criteria, recruiting sources, and selection tools and procedures seems to have paid off. Bass Brokers' national sales training manager, Gloria Long, has just returned from a full week working with Jason and several of his salespeople, including the two new hires. She has scheduled an appointment with Roscoe Lee, her boss and national sales manager, to debrief her "work-with" in District 5.

"I'm pleased with the new hires out in District 5," she tells Roscoe as she sits down across the desk from him. "We've made great progress on institutionalizing our recruiting and selection. Now, what about taking a closer look at our training?" Gloria goes on to explain that, while the typical on-the-job training new Bass Brokers salespeople receive obviously serves its purpose, perhaps it is time to provide some additional companywide training opportunities beyond just the hands-on approach used by the district managers. Roscoe is well aware that Bass Brokers has always relied on district managers to do most of the training and that it usually takes the form of periodically riding with salespeople on client calls and providing constructive feedback for improvement. This approach has been augmented by visits from Gloria, who focuses on riding with each salesperson at least once a year and visiting each district manager quarterly.

"I've thought about this too," Roscoe says. "I agree with you that we should step back and evaluate whether we could do a better job of training our salespeople by using more varied approaches. Especially, I would like us to focus on preparing new salespeople and on providing career enhancing professional development opportunities for all our salespeople. Let's you and I talk now about what the options might be, then we will throw some suggestions out to the district managers for their input."

Characters in the Role Play

Roscoe Lee, national sales manager for Bass Brokers, Inc.

Gloria Long, national sales training manager for Bass Brokers, Inc.

Assignment

Break into pairs, with one student playing each character. It doesn't matter what the actual gender mix of your pair is. Before you stage the continuation of the meeting, work separately using the material in your chapter to come up with your recommendations for a mix of sales training methods that you believe would be best for Bass Brokers. You will need to be prepared to justify your recommendations in the meeting. Then get together and role-play the continuation of the meeting between Roscoe and Gloria. Be sure each of you share your ideas and justify them. In the end, you want to come out of the meeting with a unified proposal for sales training at Bass Brokers that could be forwarded to the district managers for their input.

Minicase: Fletcher Ball Bearings

Fletcher Ball Bearings, based in Lewiston, Maine, is one of the world's leading manufacturers of precision bearings and bearing products. Fletcher sells its products to many industries, including aerospace, communications, health care, and defense. Ball bearings have many uses within these industries, such as gas turbine engines, fuel pumps, aircraft instruments, gyros, dental and surgical hand pieces, and electric motors. As one might expect, these are very complicated products and require a technical knowledge not only of the bearings themselves but also of the products of which they are an integral part.

The company is divided into several divisions, each with its own specialized sales force. The Aero division manufactures and sells bearings for use in end products such as rotary-wing aircraft (helicopters), fixed-wing aircraft, jet engines, missiles, actuators, landing gear, starters, and satellites. The Aero division attempts to hire salespeople with an aerospace or engineering education and relevant work experience. However, the level of expertise varies drastically among its 150 salespeople, and even those with the highest expertise do not know everything because the technology changes so quickly.

A new director of sales, Gordon Chase, joined the company a year ago, and immediately began preaching the need for training in order for salespeople to stay up to date with product knowledge. However, the senior board of the company voted down his one-year training budget request of $8,000 per salesperson and instead reduced it to $2,000 per salesperson. The board's complaint was that the company had spent a great deal of money on training in the past but could not identify any tangible benefits.

So Chase proceeded as best he could under the approved budget and set up a training program that provided five hours of classroom training per month for each salesperson. This included company orientation information, information on specifications of the ball bearings sold by the Aero division, and some information about the prime industry players and their products. The training was administered by internal company managers who were very knowledgeable as to the bearing products and specifications. They also were members of industry associations and had a good working knowledge of aerospace manufacturing operations at key account customers like Lockheed Martin, Boeing, and NASA. The classes were designed to have "something for everyone," so each contained both basic and advanced information.

Chase was pleased that he was able to squeeze so many hours of training from his limited budget. However, not everyone shared his positive assessment. Joe Rodgers, one of the more senior salespeople, commented, "This one-size-fits-all approach of the training frustrates me to no end because in order to get a few nuggets of new, worthwhile information I have to sit through two hours of things I already know!" He and others began to rebel and stopped going to training altogether. Conversely, the new salespeople felt like they were not getting enough introductory training and could not understand some of the more advanced technology updates because they were still trying to master the basics of being a salesperson. Also, the information on the customers and the end products was helpful but not nearly as detailed as the salespeople would have liked it to be.

Chase started a feedback program of collecting anonymous written evaluations after each classroom training session and began to see a trend of negative feelings from the employees. He was concerned that these negative assessments would be the death knell for his fledgling training program and knew he had to make some improvements before the next budget year.

Questions

1. What should Chase have said to the senior board to have received a higher training budget? How can Fletcher measure the benefits of a training program to justify its costs?
2. What additional topics should the training cover?
3. What training methods or trainers other than classroom instruction by internal trainers might Chase consider using to improve the training? Why?
4. What changes would you recommend to help Aero division better satisfy the needs of new personnel versus experienced ones? Why?

Suggested Readings

Anderson, Rolph, Rajiv Mehta, and James Strong. "An Empirical Investigation of Sales Management Training Programs for Sales Managers." *Journal of Personal Selling & Sales Management,* Summer 1997, 17 no. 3, pp. 53– 66.

Artis, Andrew B. and Eric G. Harris. "Self-Directed Learning and Sales Force Performance: An Integrated Framework." *Journal of Personal Selling & Sales Management* 27 (Winter 2007) pp. 9–24.

Attia, Ashraf M. Earl D. Honeycutt Jr., and Mark P. Leach "A Three-Stage Model for Assessing and Improving Sales Force Training and Development" *Journal of Personal Selling & Sales Management* 25 (Summer 2005) pp. 253–68.

Barksdale, Hiram C., Jr., Danny N. Bellenger, James S. Boles, and Thomas G. Brashear. "The Impact of Realistic Job Previews and Perceptions of Training on Sales Force Performance and Continuance Commitment: A Longitudinal Test." *Journal of Personal Selling & Sales Management* 23, no. 2 (2003), pp. 125–38.

Darmon, Rene. "Controlling Sales Force Costs through Optimal Recruiting and Training Policies." *European Journal of Operational Research* 154, no. 1 (2004), p. 291.

Honeycutt, Earl D., Jr, Kiran Karande, Ashraf Attia, and Steven D. Maurer. "An Utility Based Framework for Evaluating the Financial Impact of Sales Force Training Programs." *Journal of Personal Selling & Sales Management* 21, no. 3 (2001), pp. 229–38.

Leach, Mark P., and Annie H. Liu. "Investigating Interrelationships among Sales Training Evaluation Methods." *Journal of Personal Selling & Sales Management* 23, no. 4 (2003), pp. 327–39.

Leach, Mark P. Annie H. Liu, and Wesley J. Johnston, "The Role of Self-Regulation Training in Developing the Motivation Management Capabilities of Salespeople," *Journal of Personal Selling & Sales Management,* 25 (Winter 2005), pp. 269–81.

Lopez, Tara, and Amy McMillan-Capehart. "How Outgroup Salespeople Fit In or Fail to Fit In: A Proposed Acculturation Effects Framework." *Journal of Personal Selling & Sales Management* 22, no. 4 (2002), pp. 297–309.

Rich, Gregory. "Selling and Sales Management in Action: The Constructs of Sales Coaching and Supervisory Feedback, Role Modeling and Trust." *Journal of Personal Selling & Sales Management,* Spring 1998, 18 no. 2, pp. 53–64.

Wilson, Philip H., David Strutton, and M. Theodore Farris II. "Investigating the Perceptual Aspect of Sales Training." *Journal of Personal Selling & Sales Management* 22, no. 2 (2002), pp. 77–86.

Chapter Eleven

Salesperson Compensation and Incentives

Characteristics of Great Sales Compensation Plans

You will learn in this chapter that compensating salespeople is more complex than many other professions. Several important components of salesperson compensation exist that often include combinations of salary, commission, bonus, sales contests, nonfinancial rewards such as recognition programs, and expense accounts, among others. Based on research by H.R. Chally, there are 16 characteristics of compensation plans that, if present, increase the chances that a plan will prove successful in contributing to high salesperson performance.

- Characteristic #1: *Calibrate the plan with the firm's overall profit objectives.* In Chapter 3 you learned about the importance of effectively integrating sales with other functional areas in a firm. For planning purposes, the sales forecast and associated compensation plan and budget must be developed in conjunction with the overall organizational planning process. Successful sales managers don't do compensation planning in a vacuum.

- Characteristic #2: *Make sure the compensation plan focuses on motivating salespeople to meet not just tactical sales objectives but also to contribute toward strategic company objectives.* Too many salespeople are compensated devoid of any connection to unit or organizational profit, growth, market share, new product revenue, and other strategic organizational issues. Worse, some compensation plans actually direct salesperson behavior *away* from organizational objectives!

- Characteristic #3: *Ensure the plan is directly tied to* measurable criteria *that represent the important tactical and strategic objectives as mentioned above.* Gross sales volume as a measure of salesperson performance misses many nuances of issues like customer satisfaction, customer retention, new customer development, competitive advantage, and profitability.

- Characteristic #4: *It is usually best to include both fixed and variable elements within the compensation plan.* Designing a combination of these elements is a central topic in this chapter.

- Characteristic #5: *Keep the plan simple yet thorough.* Ensure that it strikes a proper balance between being sophisticated enough to capture all the elements of performance that need to be compensated but not so overly complicated that the salesperson cannot determine for what he or she is (or isn't) being rewarded.

- Characteristic #6: *Reward securing, building, and maintaining long-term relationships with profitable customers.* Relationship—or consultative—selling takes a long time and generally necessitates a heavy fixed salary component to a compensation plan.

- Characteristic #7: *Consider salespeople a mission-critical asset.* Salesperson turnover costs too often are neglected in budgeting. Replacement costs include recruitment, selection, training, and opportunity costs of vacant territories often approach $40,000–$60,000. The compensation plan should be a factor that discourages turnover among the salespeople you want to keep—such a compensation plan is likely cheaper than the turnover costs from a poor plan.

- Characteristic #8: *Ensure you are rewarding salesperson efforts according to their worth (contribution), not just the level of activity.* The best salespeople tend to work smarter, not necessarily harder.

- Characteristic #9: *Ensure payouts are clearly differentiated for top, average, and inadequate performers.* Effective plans motivate all salespeople—stars to continue, average producers to improve, and poor performers to leave. Undifferentiated plans end up retaining poor performers and also causing top performers to leave for greener pastures elsewhere.

- Characteristic #10: *Distinguish between performing tasks and achieving results.* Then, the balance of fixed versus variable compensation types in the plan must be crafted depending on the balance in focus between rewarding tasks and results.

- Characteristic #11: *Avoid direct competition between salespeople.* Excellent plans do not pit one salesperson in your company directly against another for a limited pot of compensation. Rather, they focus only on rewarding salespeople for concentrating on customers or, at the very least, outselling competitors. Sales contests are notorious for violating this characteristic of great compensation plans.

- Characteristic #12: *Reduce role conflict, ambiguity, and stress.* You've seen that these potential elements of the sales role can be quite deleterious to salesperson performance. Make the compensation plan transparent and use it to enhance salesperson control over their jobs.

- Characteristic #13: *If you want to change the plan, generally don't change too quickly.* Top sales organizations don't pull the rug out from under their salespeople with what may appear to be arbitrary, capricious, and frequent changes to the compensation plan. If the plan must be changed, involve salespeople in the process and generally take it slow. An exception to this advice is provided next.

- Characteristic #14: *When the time is right to change the plan quickly, do so.* Exciting new products, company acquisitions, new markets, and other conditions can warrant quick changes in a compensation plan so that salespeople can properly participate in the bonanza.

- Characteristic #15: *Permit every salesperson with above-adequate performance to seek his or her desired compensation potential without penalty.* Great sales compensation plans ensure each successful salesperson can find a comfortable level of income, and this may vary widely by type of sales job and by individual.

- Characteristic #16: *The acid test is how the plan impacts the customer marketplace.* Customers get strong signals when a vendor firm is having compensation difficulties. Disparaging comments from salespeople, turnover, and reductions in service quality can all damage the customer relationship. Great compensation plans negate such problems.

Source: HR Chally Group (2005), *Principles of Sales Compensation.* Dayton, OH: HR Chally Group.

LEARNING OBJECTIVES

This chapter provides an overview of key issues related to compensating salespeople. The key issues to understand involve the types of compensation, and especially incentive forms of compensation, available and when each might be most effectively offered.

After reading this chapter, you should be able to

- Discuss the advantages and limitations of straight salary, straight commission, and combination plans.

- Explain how and why a bonus component to compensation might be used as an incentive.

- Understand the effective use of sales contests, as well as the potential pitfalls of their use.

- Identify key nonfinancial rewards, and how and why they might be important.

- Recognize key issues surrounding expense accounts in relationship selling.

- Discuss making decisions on the mix and level of compensation.

OVERVIEW OF COMPENSATION AND INCENTIVES

Chapter 6 introduces the concept of rewards. The way the reward structure is implemented in a sales organization is through the **compensation plan** afforded to salespeople. Three basic questions drive successful compensation programs:

1. Which compensation method is most appropriate for motivating specific kinds of selling activities in specific selling situations?

2. How much of a salesperson's total compensation should be earned through incentive programs?

3. What is the appropriate mix of financial and nonfinancial compensation and incentives for motivating the sales force?

The opening vignette of the chapter provides a wide array of testimonials from salespeople about what types of rewards motivate them to higher levels of performance. Perusal of their comments reveals that everything from salary to commission potential to various nonfinancial factors motivate those salespeople. Their examples provide a microcosm of what it is like to try to develop compensation and incentive plans for salespeople today—sales managers find many different preferences among their salespeople and have to find a way to balance those preferences with the needs of the firm.

In most firms, the total financial compensation paid to salespeople comprises several components, each of which may be designed to achieve different objectives. The core of sales compensation plans consists of a salary and incentive payments. A **salary** is a fixed sum of money paid at regular intervals. The amount of salary paid to a given salesperson is usually a function of that person's experience, competence, and time on the job, as well as the sales manager's judgments about the quality of the individual's performance. Salary adjustments are useful for rewarding salespeople for performing customer relationship building activities that may not directly result in sales in the short term, such as prospecting for new customers or providing postsale service. They can also help adjust for differences in sales potential across territories.

Many firms that pay their salespeople a salary also offer additional **incentive payments** to encourage good performance. Those incentives may take the form of commissions tied to sales volume or profitability, or bonuses for meeting or exceeding specific performance targets (e.g., meeting quotas for particular products within the company's line or for particular types of customers). Such incentives are useful for directing salespeople's efforts toward specific strategic objectives during the year, as well as providing additional rewards for the top performers within the sales force. A **commission** is a payment based on short-term results, usually a salesperson's dollar or unit sales volume. Since a direct link exists between sales volume and the amount of commission received, commission payments are particularly useful for motivating a high level of selling effort.

A **bonus** is a payment made at the discretion of management for achieving or surpassing some set level of performance. Whereas commissions are typically paid for each sale that is made, a bonus is typically not paid until the salesperson surpasses some level of total sales or other aspect of performance. When the salesperson reaches the minimum level of performance required to earn a bonus, however, the size of the bonus might be determined by the degree to which the salesperson exceeds that minimum. Thus, bonuses are usually *additional incentives* to motivate salespeople to reach high levels of performance rather than part of the basic compensation plan. Bonuses are almost never used alone as a form of compensation; rather, they are combined with one or more other compensation elements. Attaining **quota** is often the minimum requirement for a salesperson to earn a bonus. Quotas can be based on goals for sales volume, profitability of sales, or various account-servicing activities. To be effective, quotas (like goals) should be specific, measurable, and realistically attainable. Therefore, bonuses can be offered as a reward for attaining or surpassing a predetermined level of performance on any dimensions for which quotas are set.

In addition to the above incentives, many firms conduct **sales contests** to encourage extra effort aimed at specific short-term objectives. For example, a contest might offer additional rewards for salespeople who obtain a specified volume of orders from new customers or who exceed their quotas for a new product during a three-month period. Contest winners might be given additional cash, merchandise, or travel awards.

Finally, a foundation of most compensation plans is a package of **benefits.** These are designed to satisfy the salesperson's basic needs for security. They typically include such things as medical and disability insurance, life insurance, and a retirement plan. The types and amount of benefits included in a compensation plan are usually a matter of company policy and apply to all employees. However, the benefit package a firm offers its salespeople should be reasonably comparable to those offered by competitors to avoid being at a disadvantage when recruiting new sales talent.

The key forms of financial compensation of salespeople are summarized in Exhibit 11.1. It is important to know that beyond financial compensation, a variety of forms of **nonfinancial incentives** exist. These might take the form of opportunities for promotion or various types of recognition for performance such as special awards and publications in company newsletters. Nonfinancial incentives will be discussed in more detail later in the chapter.

EXHIBIT 11.1
Components and objectives of financial compensation plans

Components	Objectives
Salary	• Motivate effort on nonselling activities • Adjust for differences in territory potential • Reward experience and competence
Commissions	• Motivate a high level of selling effort • Encourage sales success
Bonuses	• Direct effort toward strategic objectives • Provide additional rewards for top performers • Encourage sales success
Sales contests	• Stimulate additional effort targeted at specific short-term objectives
Benefits	• Satisfy salespeople's security needs • Match competitive offers

STRAIGHT SALARY, STRAIGHT COMMISSION, AND COMBINATION PLANS

The three primary methods of compensating salespeople are (1) straight salary, (2) straight commission, and (3) a combination of base salary plus incentive pay in the form of commissions, bonuses, or both. In recent years, a steady trend has developed away from both straight salary and straight commission plans toward combination plans. Today, combination plans are by far the most common form of compensation.

In essence, managers seek to create a "pay for performance" plan that rewards people using both salary and incentive programs to maximize the salesperson's performance. Unfortunately, creating such programs is very complex, and companies often choose a program based on convenience or cost effectiveness rather than actual benefits to the company.[1] And, as highlighted by the testimonials of salespeople in the opening vignette to this chapter, much variety exists of preferences of rewards among salespeople.

The following sections highlight the three principal compensation approaches. Exhibit 11.2 summarizes this discussion.

Straight Salary

Two sets of conditions favor the use of a straight salary compensation plan: (1) when management wishes to motivate salespeople to achieve objectives other than short-run sales volume and (2) when the individual salesperson's impact on sales volume is difficult

EXHIBIT 11.2   **Characteristics of compensation methods for salespeople**

Compensation method (Frequency of use)	Especially useful	Advantages	Disadvantages
Straight salary	When compensating new sales reps; when firm moves into new sales territories that require developmental work; when sale reps must perform many nonselling activities	Provides sales rep with maximum security; gives sales manager more control over sales reps; is easy to administer; yields more predictable selling expenses	Provides no incentive; necessitates closer supervision of sale reps' activities; during sales declines, selling expenses remain at same level
Straight commission	When highly aggressive selling is required; when nonselling tasks are minimized; when company cannot closely control sales force activities	Provides maximum incentive; by increasing commission rate, sales managers can encourage reps to sell certain items; selling expenses relate directly to selling resources	Sales reps have little financial security; sales manager has minimum control over sales force; may cause reps to provide inadequate service to smaller accounts; selling costs are less predictable
Combination	When sales territories have relatively similar sales potential; when firm wishes to provide incentive but still control sales force activities	Provides certain level of financial security; provides some incentive; selling expenses fluctuate with sales revenue; sales manager has some control over reps' nonselling activities	Selling expenses are less predictable; may be difficult to administer

to measure in a reasonable time. Because relationship selling may involve both of these conditions, it is not uncommon for sales jobs with heavy customer care to be compensated by straight salary.

Advantages

The primary advantage of a straight salary is that management can require salespeople to spend their time on activities that may not result in immediate sales. Therefore, a salary plan or a plan offering a large proportion of fixed salary is appropriate when the salesperson is expected to perform many customer service or other nonselling activities. These may include market research, customer problem analysis, product stocking, customer education, or sales promotion. Straight salary plans are also common in industries where many engineering and design services are required as part of the selling function, such as in high technology industries.

Straight salary compensation plans are also desirable when it is difficult for management to measure the individual salesperson's actual impact on sales volume or other aspects of performance. Thus, firms tend to pay salaries to their sales force when (1) their salespeople are engaged in missionary selling, as in the pharmaceutical industry; (2) other parts of the marketing program, such as advertising or dealer promotions, are the primary determinants of sales success, as in some consumer packaged goods businesses; or (3) the selling process is complex and involves a team or multilevel selling effort, as in the case of computers. Career counselors often advise college students interested in taking a first job in relationship selling to try to make that first experience heavier in salary component versus incentive pay. This gives the new salesperson some time to learn the ropes and hone his or her skills while earning a steady income. Because straight salary plans provide salespeople with a steady, guaranteed income, they are often used when the salesperson's ability to generate immediate sales is uncertain, as in the case of new recruits in a field-training program or when a firm is introducing a new product line or opening new territories.

Finally, salary plans are easy for management to compute and administer. They also give management more flexibility. It is easy to reassign salespeople to new territories or product lines because they do not have to worry about how such changes will affect their sales volumes. Also, since salaries are fixed costs, the compensation cost per unit sold is lower at relatively high levels of sales volume.

Limitations

The major limitation of straight salary compensation is that financial rewards are not tied directly to any specific aspect of job performance. Management should attempt to give bigger salary increases each year to the good performers than those given to the poor ones. However, the amount of those increases and the way performance is evaluated are subject to the whims of the manager who makes the decision. Also, salaries do not provide any direct financial incentive for improving sales-related aspects of performance. Consequently, over the long run salary plans appeal more to security-oriented rather than achievement-oriented salespeople.

Straight Commission

A commission is payment for achieving a given level of performance. Salespeople are paid for results. Usually, commission payments are based on the salesperson's dollar or unit sales volume. However, it is becoming more popular for firms to base commissions on the *profitability* of sales to motivate the sales force to expend effort on the most profitable products or customers. The most common way is to offer salespeople variable commissions, where relatively high commissions are paid for sales of the most profitable products or sales to the most profitable accounts. Such a **variable commission rate** can also be used to direct the sales force's efforts toward other straight sales objectives, such as paying a higher commission on a new product line being introduced.

Advantages

Direct motivation is the key advantage of a commission compensation plan, as a clear and direct link exists between sales performance and the financial compensation the salesperson earns. Consequently, salespeople are strongly motivated to improve their sales productivity to increase their compensation, at least until they reach such high pay that further incremental increases become less attractive. Commission plans also have a built-in element of fairness (assuming that sales territories are properly defined, with about equal potential), because good performers are automatically rewarded, whereas poor performers are discouraged from continuing their low productivity.

Commission plans have some advantages from a sales management viewpoint. Commissions are usually easy to compute and administer. Also, compensation costs vary directly with sales volume. This is an advantage for firms that are short of working capital because they do not need to worry about paying high wages to the sales force unless it generates high sales revenues.

Limitations

Straight commission compensation plans have some important limitations that have caused many firms, especially those engaged in relationship selling, to abandon them. Perhaps the most critical weakness is that management has little control over the sales force. When all their financial rewards are tied directly to sales volume, it often can be difficult to motivate salespeople to engage in relationship building activities that do not lead directly to short-term sales. Consequently, salespeople on commission are likely to "milk" existing customers rather than work to develop new accounts and sustain long-term relationships. For example, they may overstock their customers and neglect service after the sale. Finally, they have little motivation to engage in market analysis and other similar functions that take time away from actual selling activities.

Straight commission plans also have a disadvantage for many salespeople. Such plans make a salesperson's earnings unstable and hard to predict. When business conditions are poor, turnover rates in the sales force are likely to be high because salespeople find it hard to live on the low earnings produced by poor sales. To combat the inherent instability of commission plans, some firms provide their salespeople with a **draw,** or drawing account. In a draw, money is advanced to a salesperson in months when commissions are low to ensure he or she will always take home a specified minimum amount of pay. The amount of the salesperson's draw in poor months is deducted from earned commissions when sales improve. This gives salespeople some secure salary, and it allows management more control over their activities. A problem arises, however, when a salesperson fails to earn enough commissions to repay the draw. Then the person may quit or be fired, and the company must absorb the loss.[2]

Combination Plans

Compensation plans that offer a base salary plus some proportion of incentive pay are the most popular because they have many of the advantages but avoid most of the limitations of both straight salary and straight commission plans. The base salary provides the salesperson with a stable income and gives management some capability to reward salespeople for performing customer service and administrative tasks that are not directly related to short-term sales. At the same time, the incentive portion of such compensation plans provides direct rewards to motivate the salesperson to expend effort to improve sales volume and profitability.

Combination plans bring together a base salary with commissions, bonuses, or both. When salary plus commission is used, the commissions are tied to sales volume or profitability, or both, just as with a straight commission plan. The only difference is that the commissions are smaller in a combination plan than when the salesperson is compensated solely by commission. As described earlier, adding a bonus component typically recognizes the achievement of some specific performance goal.

Whether base salary is combined with commission payments or bonuses, managers must answer several other questions when designing effective combination compensation plans. These include, (1) What is the appropriate size of the incentive relative to the base salary? (2) Should a ceiling be imposed on incentive earnings? (3) When should the salesperson be credited with a sale? (4) Should team incentives be used, and if so, how should they be allocated across members of a sales team? and (5) How often should the salesperson receive incentive payments?

Proportion of Incentive Pay to Total Compensation

What proportion of total compensation should be incentive pay? A sales manager's decision concerning what proportion of the overall compensation package is represented by incentive pay should be based on the degree of relationship selling involved in the job. When the firm's primary selling approaches are directly related to short-term sales (such as increasing sales volume, profitability, or new customers), a large incentive component should be offered. When customer service and other nonsales objectives are deemed more important, the major emphasis should be on the base salary component of the plan. This gives management more control over rewarding the sales force's relationship selling activities.

When the salesperson's selling skill is the key to sales success, the incentive portion of compensation generally should be relatively large. However, when the product has been presold through advertising and the salesperson is largely an order taker, or when the salesperson's job involves a large proportion of missionary or customer service work, the incentive component should be relatively small.

If a particular combination plan is not very effective at motivating salespeople, one of the most common reasons is that the incentive portion is too small to generate much interest. Companies are always challenged to hire and retain the best salespeople. One approach is to open up the incentive component to negotiation on a salesperson-to-salesperson basis, thus creating a very individualized combination plan. In this way, salespeople who seek greater compensation security can focus on more fixed compensation (salary), while others can opt for the potential to earn even higher total compensation by taking greater risks through placing more of their compensation on incentive-based rewards.[3] Such individualized approaches must allow a salesperson to change his or her compensation allocation periodically, perhaps annually.

Incentive Ceilings

Should there be a ceiling or cap on incentive earnings to ensure top salespeople do not earn substantially more money than other employees? This is an issue that is dealt with in very different ways across companies and industries, and for which strong arguments can be made on both sides. Part of the differences in how different firms handle this issue seems to reflect variation in average compensation levels, with firms in relatively low paying industries being more likely to impose caps than those in higher-paying lines of trade.

Arguments in favor of using ceilings include that they ensure top salespeople will not make such high earnings that other employees in the firm, sometimes even managers, suffer resentment and low morale. Ceilings also protect against windfalls, such as increased sales due to the introduction of successful new products, where a salesperson's earnings might become very large without corresponding effort. Finally, ceilings make a firm's maximum potential sales compensation expense more predictable and controllable.

A strong counterargument can be made, however, that such ceilings ultimately have a bad effect on motivation and dampen the sales force's enthusiasm. Also, when ceilings are in place, some salespeople may reach the earnings maximum early in the year and be inclined to take it easy for the rest of the year.

The issue of incentive ceilings has become a growing problem in relationship selling, and in particular when compensating a salesperson in a team-selling environment. As team selling brings individuals from around the company to help with a customer, the question becomes how much the sales representative should make in a sale that is the result of the efforts of many individuals inside his or her firm. This problem is made worse as the size of each sale grows larger and larger and is especially relevant when dealing with key accounts. Another problem with incentive ceilings occurs as customers move around the world. How much should the sales representative be compensated for a sale in another part of the world even though that person is servicing the customer's headquarters in his or her territory? The solution to these problems that many companies have chosen is limiting or capping a salesperson's incentive compensation.[4]

Some desired effects of ceilings can be accomplished without arbitrarily limiting the motivation of the sales force by having management pretest any new or revised compensation plan before it is implemented. Sales managers can do this by analyzing the historical records of sales performance by selected salespeople to see how they would have come out under the proposed compensation system. In this test, particular attention should be given to the amount of compensation that would have been earned by the best and poorest performers to ensure that the compensation provided by the plan is both fair and reasonable.

When Is a Sale a Sale?

When incentives are based on sales volume or other sales-related aspects of performance, the precise meaning of a sale should be defined to avoid confusion and irritation. Most incentive plans credit a salesperson with a sale when the order is accepted by the company, less any returns and allowances. Occasionally, though, it makes good sense to credit the salesperson with a sale only after the goods have been shipped or payment has been received from the customer. This is particularly true when the time between receipt of an order and shipment of the goods is long and the company wants its salespeople to maintain close contact with the customer to prevent cancellations and other problems. As a compromise, some plans credit salespeople with half a sale when the order is received and the other half when payment is made.

Team versus Individual Incentives

The increasing use of sales or cross-functional teams to win new customers and service major accounts raises some important questions about the kinds of incentives to include in a combination compensation plan. Should incentives be tied to the overall performance of the entire team, should separate incentives be keyed to the individual performance of each team member, or both? If both group and individual incentives are used, which should be given the greatest weight? These questions have to be addressed successfully by sales managers when designing team-based incentives.

Leadership   Maritz Plans Ahead: New Recognition Tool   11.1
Suite Puts Focus on Manager Training

In a classic incentive program, a company dangles a big reward, like a trip or a television, as inducement to drive up sales figures. The objective is clear, the reward is universal, the results are easily measured. The problem is that fewer programs today fit that classic model. Instead, more companies want to drive murky concepts, like brand awareness or better health, and employees want award options that aren't listed in a catalogue. "Our studies had shown that only one in ten people in America are recognized in ways that are meaningful to them," says Melissa Van Dyke, employee engagement consultant for Fenton, Mo.–based rewards company Maritz. "We started thinking that there was a side of the story that was missing."

To fill this perceived gap, Maritz has partnered with recognition guru Bob Nelson, author of *1001 Ways to Reward Employees,* to develop its new Recognition Studio, a set of tools that helps companies centralize their incentive objectives and functions, integrating formal and informal rewards as well as communications, marketing, measurement, and tracking into one reward solution.

The process begins with robust assessments that poll both employees (about their reward preferences) and managers (about their views on recognition). The second step involves training managers to use recognition to meet strategic goals. The client can choose to have Maritz consultants either train individual managers or their own trainers in a two-day session that teaches the philosophy behind using rewards, incorporating market data and research, and hands-on tactics.

Maritz also has changed its approach toward award categories. Rather than the usual dichotomy between travel and merchandise options, clients of the Recognition Studio can incorporate nontraditional rewards—like extra time off, cultural events, educational opportunities or even a better parking space—into typical points programs. Maritz uses the results of the assessments to determine which awards will be most effective for the type of initiative planned. "Motivation is more than merchandise or travel," says Van Dyke. "That's been the old debate, but the workforce has moved right past that. The trend is moving more to individual preferences."

Maritz also wanted to respond to clients who needed a program that could better integrate all their reward programs with marketing and human resource objectives. The challenge was to find a way to formally organize awards without losing the spontaneity and personal touch of the most effective reward systems. By incorporating managerial training, the program ensures managers are both empowered to implement programs and knowledgeable about getting the results the company needs. "We talk about centralizing the effort, but decentralizing the ownership," says Van Dyke. "You don't want to diminish the creativity of the program."

This arrangement is the first phase in what Maritz sees as a transformation of corporate approach to rewards, and Van Dyke expects the program will keep evolving. "There is an inherent change in how businesses are going to engage their employees," she says. "The incentive industry is going to be called upon to provide solutions, and be more of a consultative partner to HR."

Source: A.E. Smith, "Maritz Plans Ahead," *Incentive* (June, 2007), p. 7.

When Should the Salesperson Receive Incentive Payments?

A survey of more than 500 compensation plans found that 21 percent paid salespeople incentive earnings on an annual basis, 3 percent paid semiannually, 24 percent paid quarterly, and 52 percent made monthly payments. In general, plans offering salary plus commission are more likely to involve monthly incentive payments, whereas salary plus bonus plans more often make incentive payments on a quarterly or annual schedule.

Shorter intervals between performance and the receipt of rewards increase the motivating power of the plan. However, short intervals add to the computation required, increase administrative expenses, and may make the absolute amount of money received by salespeople appear so small they may not be very impressed with their rewards. Consequently, quarterly incentive payments are an effective compromise.

Leadership 11.1 shows how rewards consultancy Maritz is helping firms better align and manage their incentive programs.

SALES CONTESTS

Sales contests are short-term incentive programs designed to motivate sales personnel to accomplish specific sales objectives. Although contests should not be considered part of a firm's ongoing compensation plan, they offer salespeople the opportunity to gain financial, as well as nonfinancial, rewards. Contest winners often receive prizes in cash, merchandise, or travel. Winners also receive nonfinancial rewards in the form of recognition and a sense of accomplishment.

Successful contests require the following:

- Clearly defined, specific objectives.

- An exciting theme.

- Reasonable probability of rewards for all salespeople.

- Attractive rewards.

- Promotion and follow-through.[5]

Contest Objectives

Because contests *supplement* the firm's compensation program and are designed to motivate extra effort toward some short-term goal, their objectives should be very specific and clearly defined. Equally important, incentive compensation needs to be consistent with stated corporate objectives. Unfortunately, although companies may believe an objective is important, they do not always create incentives for salespeople that reflect those objectives.

The time frame within which the contest's objectives are to be achieved should be relatively short. This ensures that salespeople will maintain their enthusiasm and effort throughout the contest. But the contest should be long enough to allow all members of the sales force to cover their territories at least once and to have a reasonable chance of generating the performance necessary to win. Therefore, the average duration of sales contests is about three months.

Contest Themes

A sales contest should have an exciting theme to help build enthusiasm among the participants and promote the event. The theme should also be designed to stress the contest's objectives and appeal to all participants. Companies are getting more and more creative in creating themes for contests.

Probability of Winning

Three popular contest formats are available. In the first, salespeople compete with themselves by trying to attain individual quotas. Everyone who reaches or exceeds quota during the contest period wins. A second form requires that all members of the sales force compete with each other. The people who achieve the highest overall performance on some dimension are the winners, and everyone else loses. A third format organizes the sales force into teams, which compete for group and individual prizes.

Historically, individual sales quotas have been the most popular of the three formats. This reliance on individual quotas allows firms to design contests that focus salespeople's effort on specific objectives, do not put representatives in low-potential territories at a disadvantage, and do not undermine cooperation in the sales force by forcing salespeople to compete against each other.

Whichever format is used, it is essential that every member of the sales force have a reasonable chance of winning an award. If there are to be only one or a few winners, many salespeople may think their chances of coming out on top are remote and thus completely give up on the contest. In addition, average or below-average performers may automatically assume the top performers will win the award and not try as hard to hit sales goals. In this respect, contests that provide rewards to everyone who meets quotas during the contest period are desirable. Increasingly, companies are focusing on incentive programs, including contests, that seek to reward more rather than fewer salespeople.

Types of Contest Rewards

Contest rewards can take the form of cash, merchandise, or travel. All three types of rewards are commonly used, and a company may vary the kinds of rewards offered from contest to contest. Companies are also realizing that one size does not fit all. More and more rewards are being tailored to individual salesperson "hot buttons." Once the dollar value of the reward is established, the winner may choose from several rewards. Or the manager may simply ask what kind of reward the salesperson wants to receive from the company. The idea is to find rewards that motivate each salesperson within the constraints of the budget. As one consultant states, "Tom, your top salesperson, learns that the reward for achieving success in the new sales contest is a set of MacGregor golf clubs. However, Tom's wife just bought him a new set of Callaways complete with the new Big Bertha driver. Chances are that Tom will not be motivated to win another set of clubs."[6]

An Incentive Federation survey found that on average 79 percent of respondents found noncash reward programs to be extremely effective in motivating participants to achieve sales goals.[7] "Cash is great," says a sales and marketing manager for a major insurance company. "But we like to give merchandise so the winner has some boasting rights when they win. And, if we award money, the rep generally won't spend the money on something for themselves—even if it's something they really want." One of the company's salespeople was awarded a suede jacket for a contest he won. "I wear it all the time, and every time I get a compliment, I tell them I won it," he says.

Merchandise also gives management an opportunity to make the reward presentation as part of a ceremony celebrating success. "When you present someone with a watch with all their colleagues around, they can congratulate the winner and, at the same time, see what they can win if they hit their next target," the manager says. And the salesperson agrees: "Merchandise gets me going. A check isn't as tangible as merchandise. You can't really show someone a check—it's not interesting. When you get money, you just mentally lump it in with your paycheck."[8]

Lexington, Kentucky–based printer manufacturer Lexmark International, adjusted its incentive program to allow for changing preferences among salespeople. Rather than offering a one-size-fits-all reward, Lexmark adopted a points-based program in which salespeople can select gifts from a catalog. So far, the most popular items have been useful products for the home.[9]

Whatever form of reward is used, the monetary value must be large enough to be attractive to the participants, given their level of compensation. A portable DVD player, for example, may be more attractive when the average salesperson makes $40,000 per year than when the average compensation is $100,000.

Today, some companies are turning to online approaches to aid sales managers in administering contest and other incentives for their salespeople. Innovation 11.2 provides an example of how this works.

Innovation   Online Incentive Programs   11.2

Sales organizations are increasingly trying new tools to administer incentives to the sales force, and some have turned to online incentive providers to help out.

Rob Sowers, regional manager at Netopia, a manufacturer of broadband equipment, software, and services in San Francisco, turned to innergE, an online incentive program developed by Hinda Incentives, a Chicago-based performance improvement company. "We wanted to motivate our resellers to push Netopia's products to their customers over those of our competitors," Sowers says. "But we didn't want to spend valuable time, resources, and manpower to do it." With the innergE platform, the company didn't have to.

Hinda set up a customized Web site for Netopia—complete with a catalog of more than 2,000 rewards, ranging from DVD players and digital cameras to travel certificates—that could be accessed by more than 200 participants in the program. The points reps earned for moving Netopia merchandise were logged on the site, as were those they redeemed for rewards. "Normally, I'd have to keep track of this myself," Sowers says. "It's like the computer ran the entire thing, soup to nuts." In the end, Netopia saw sales jump 15 percent for the first quarter that the program was underway.

On average, clients pay an annual fee of $5,000 for Hinda to set up and administer innergE. In comparison, companies that use traditional offline incentive programs tend to spend considerably more, often just on flashy and lengthy product brochures alone. "There's really no downside to online motivational programs," says Mark Bondy, president of Viktor Incentives & Meetings, an incentive firm headquartered in Traverse City, Michigan. "They're being used more and more, and will become the norm within a year or so."

Sarah Camp, who has often relied on incentive programs to motivate sales reps in the past, is getting her feet wet with eChoice Points, an online points-based program developed by All Star Incentive Marketing in Sturbridge, Massachusetts. Camp, a marketing projects coordinator with Bendix Brakes in Troy, Michigan, is hoping the program will encourage brake pad installers to think of Bendix first.

Clients such as Camp pay approximately $7,500 for eChoice Points, which is a good deal for her, mostly because the new program is bringing in results. "The goal of going online was to reach more of our resellers around the country." With upward of a thousand program participants—significantly more than in years past—Camp says, "So far, so good."

Source: Michelle Gillan, "E-Motivation," *Sales & Marketing Management,* April 2003, p. 50.

Contest Promotion and Follow-through

To generate interest and enthusiasm, contests should be launched with fanfare. Where possible, firms should announce contests at national or regional sales meetings. Follow-up promotion is also necessary to maintain interest throughout the contest period. Special Web sites where salespeople can enter password-protected personal pages facilitate this. As the contest proceeds, salespeople should be given frequent feedback concerning their progress so they know how much more they must do to win an award. Finally, winners should be recognized within the company, and prizes should be awarded promptly.

Criticism of Sales Contests

Although many sales managers believe contests are effective for motivating special efforts from salespeople, contests can potentially cause a few problems, particularly if they are poorly designed or implemented.

Some critics argue that contests designed to stimulate sales volume may produce results that are largely fleeting, with no lasting improvement in market share. Salespeople may "borrow" sales from before or after the contest to increase their volume during the contest. They may hold back orders before the start of the contest and rush orders that would normally not be placed until after the contest. As a result, customers may be overstocked, causing sales volume to fall off for some time after the contest is over.

Contests may also hurt the cohesiveness and morale of the company's salespeople. This is particularly true when contests force individual salespeople to compete with one another for rewards and when the number of rewards is limited.

Finally, some firms tend to use sales contests to cover up faulty compensation plans. That is, salespeople should not have to be compensated a second time for what they are already being paid to do. Thus, contests should be used only on a short-term basis to motivate special efforts beyond the normal performance expected of the sales force. If a firm finds itself conducting frequent contests to maintain an acceptable level of sales performance, it should reexamine its entire compensation and incentive program.

NONFINANCIAL REWARDS

Most sales managers consider opportunities for promotion and advancement second only to financial incentives as an effective sales force motivator. This is particularly true for young, well-educated salespeople who tend to view their jobs as stepping-stones to top management. One common career path is from salesperson to district sales manager to top sales management. Thus, if a person has been with a firm for several years without making it into sales management, the individual may start to believe such a promotion will never happen. Consequently, veteran salespeople may begin to concentrate solely on financial rewards, or they may lose motivation and not work as hard at their jobs.

To overcome this problem, some firms have instituted two different career paths for salespeople. One leads to management positions, while the other leads to more advanced positions within the sales force. The latter usually involves responsibility for dealing with key accounts or leading sales teams. In this system, even though a salesperson may not make it into management, he or she can still work toward a more prestigious and lucrative position within the sales force. To make advanced sales positions more attractive as promotions, many firms provide people in those positions with additional **perquisites,** or **perks,** including higher compensation, a better automobile, and better office facilities.

Recognition Programs

Contest awards and promotions to positions with more responsibility provide recognition for good performance, but many firms also have separate recognition programs to provide nonmonetary rewards. As with contests, effective recognition programs should offer a reasonable chance of winning for everyone in the sales force. But if a very large proportion of the sales force achieves recognition, the program is likely to lose some of its appeal because the winners feel no special sense of accomplishment.

Consequently, effective recognition programs often recognize the best performers across several different performance dimensions. For example, winners might include persons with the highest sales volume for the year, the biggest percentage increase in sales, the biggest dollar increase, the highest number of new customers, the largest sales per account, and the best customer retention record. Recognition is an attractive reward because it makes a salesperson's peers and superiors aware of the outstanding performance. Communicating the winner's achievements, through recognition at a sales meeting, publicity in the local press, announcements in the company's internal newsletter, or other ways, is an essential part of a good recognition program. Also, firms typically give special awards as part of their recognition program, and these are often awards with low monetary but high symbolic value, such as trophies, plaques, or rings. Finally, as Exhibit 11.3 points out, objectivity and good taste are also important ingredients of effective recognition programs, as they are for contests and other incentives.

EXHIBIT 11.3
Guidelines for effective formal recognition programs

Regardless of its size or cost, any recognition program should incorporate the following features:

- *The program must be strictly performance-based,* with no room for subjective judgments. If people suspect that it is in any way a personality contest, the program will not work. The winners should be clear to anyone looking at the data.

- *It should be balanced.* The program should not be so difficult that only a few can hope to win or so easy that just about everyone does. In the first case, people will not try; in the second, the program will be meaningless.

- *A ceremony should be involved.* If rings are casually passed out or plaques sent through the mail, a lot of the glamour of the program will be lost.

- *The program must be in good taste.* If not, it will be subject to ridicule and, rather than motivate people, it will leave them uninspired. No one wants to be part of a recognition program that is condescending or tacky. The program should make people feel good about being part of the company.

- *There must be adequate publicity.* In some cases, sales managers do such a poor job of explaining a program or promoting it to their own salespeople that no one seems to understand or care about it. Prominent mention of the program in company publications is the first step to overcoming this handicap.

EXPENSE ACCOUNTS

Expense items incurred by sales reps in the field—travel, lodging, meals, and entertaining customers—can be substantial. Depending on the industry and type of sales job, it is not unusual for field selling expenses to approach $25,000 or more per salesperson, and in some cases they are much higher. The growing trend of creating home offices for salespeople has increased expenses related to technology (e.g., laptops, cell phones, PDAs, fax machines, teleconferencing) but reduced some travel expenses such as company-leased automobiles. Many firms have experimented with a variety of expense reimbursement plans. Such plans range from unlimited reimbursement for all "reasonable and allowable" expenses to plans where salespeople must pay all expenses out of their total compensation. Obviously, access to an **expense account** represents an enhancement to a salesperson's compensation.

When deciding which form of expense reimbursement to use, sales managers must make trade-offs between tight control aimed at holding down total expenses and the financial well-being—and the subsequent motivation level—of salespeople. Some expense items—such as entertainment expenses, club dues, and the costs of personal services while the salesperson is away from home—can be considered either legitimate business expenses that should be reimbursed by the company or personal expenses that the salesperson should pay. Obviously, company policies and reimbursement plans that treat such costs as business expenses increase the salesperson's total financial compensation but also increase the firm's total selling costs. Different reimbursement plans have an impact on the effective financial compensation received by, and the motivation level of, a firm's salespeople. Three key types of plans are direct reimbursement, limited reimbursement, and no reimbursement.

Direct Reimbursement Plans

One popular type of expense reimbursement plan involves direct and unlimited reimbursement of all "allowable and reasonable" expenses. The primary advantage is that direct reimbursement plans give the sales manager some control over both the total magnitude of sales expenses and the kinds of activities in which salespeople will be motivated to engage. If a particular activity, such as entertaining potential new accounts, is thought to be an important ingredient of the firm's account management policies, salespeople can be encouraged to engage in that activity by being informed that all related expenses will be reimbursed. On the other hand, managers can discourage their subordinates from spending time on unimportant tasks by refusing to reimburse expenditures for such activities.

Thus, company policies concerning reimbursable expenses can be a useful tool for motivating and directing sales effort. Some firms report they adjusted their expense reimbursement policies according to the differences in the territories covered or the job activities required of different members of their sales forces. For example, some firms reimburse a broader range and higher levels of expenses for their national account managers than for members of their regular field sales force.

Reimbursement under such plans is contingent on the salesperson submitting receipts or detailed records justifying expense claims, so the processing and evaluation of expense claims add to the firm's sales administration costs.

Limited Reimbursement Plans

Some firms limit the total amount of expense reimbursement, either by setting maximum limits for each expense item (such as a policy that limits reimbursement for restaurant meals to $40 per person) or by providing each salesperson with a predetermined lump-sum payment to cover total expenses. This approach keeps total selling expenses within planned limits—limits that are often determined by the sales expense budget set at the beginning of the year. In some cases, budgeted expense amounts may vary across members of the sales force, depending on the past or forecasted sales volume or the requirements of the territories.

Unless the budgeted limits are based on an accurate understanding of the costs associated with successful sales performance in each territory, however, limited reimbursement plans can hurt motivation and sales performance. Individual salespeople may believe their ability to do a good job is constrained by tightfisted company expense reimbursement policies. Rather than pay for necessary activities out of their own pockets, salespeople are likely to avoid or cut back on certain expense activities to keep their costs within their budgets.

No Reimbursement Plans

Some firms require salespeople to cover all of their own expenses. Such plans usually involve paying the salesperson a relatively higher total financial compensation to help cover necessary expenses and thus represent a variation of the predetermined lump-sum approach. Such plans are most commonly associated with straight commission compensation plans involving high-percentage commissions. The rationale is that salespeople will be motivated to spend both the effort and money necessary to increase sales volume so long as the resulting financial rewards are big enough to be worthwhile.

As with limited reimbursement plans, such approaches help the firm limit sales expenses or, in the case of commission plans, make them a totally variable cost that moves up and down with changes in sales volume. However, they also sacrifice management control over the motivation and types of activities engaged in by members of the sales force.

MAKING COMPENSATION AND INCENTIVE PROGRAMS WORK

The many complex issues involved make designing and implementing an effective compensation and incentive program difficult. Many managers wonder whether their company's program is as effective as possible in motivating the kinds and amounts of effort they

Leadership   Dumb Down Your Pay Programs   11.3

An exasperated sales rep recently handed me a 20-page document and said, "Just look at this compensation plan. I can't make any sense out of this." His confusion was warranted. There was way too much complexity to grasp within the encyclopedia-sized compensation plan. Unfortunately, this is often the norm. So how can sales departments keep their compensation plans from becoming so convoluted?

To be successful, any compensation plan must have a clear link between sales performance and sales rewards. The number-one complaint from the field is that this link is either too hard to understand or missing altogether. The more complex the plan, the less likely salespeople are to recognize the link. Here are five ways to fix a compensation plan and ensure that salespeople are actually motivated by it.

1. *Clean up the jobs.* Decontaminate the sales jobs by measuring time and eliminating nonselling and non-productive activities. Executives at one major telecommunications company were shocked to learn that the largest use of their sales reps' time was internal meetings. With more focused sales jobs, management can substantially reduce the need for complex sales compensation plans.

2. *Three is the magic number.* Give yourself a goal: no more than three performance measures in your sales compensation plan. Too many measures dilute the impact of the incentive dollars. When asked to describe how the sales compensation plan worked at a major transportation company using six measures, a leading salesperson dismissed the plan by saying, "Frankly, I don't understand how it works. I sell what I can, and they send me a check."

3. *Exclude inappropriate measures.* A vice president of sales for a major computer company recently lamented

how departments such as marketing wanted to add "pet" measures to the sales compensation plan. Also, the CEO wanted to add a measure related to customer service. The sales compensation plan can't be a parking place for every company measure. Only use measures the salesperson can affect, because it's not right to hold salespeople's pay hostage to corporate performance numbers.

4. *Hold supervisors accountable.* Don't try to use the sales compensation plan to "supervise" the sales force, and don't expect it to terminate poor performers or to teach good selling habits. You are reaching a crisis stage when field managers reject a sales initiative because it isn't rewarded in the sales compensation plan.

5. *Tighten sales credit rules.* Which salesperson gets credit for which sales is always a critical issue in compensation plans. Limit credit splits, duplicate crediting, and credit following. Eliminating these wherever possible makes crediting easier for your salespeople to understand. Avoid the common crediting errors such as "landlording," where sales reps get credit for all sales in their territories regardless of who sold the customer. And never double credit simply for appeasement purposes.

Increased complexity in sales compensation plans most often occurs because of the good intentions of management. But with each effort to serve various objectives, the pay plan becomes more complex. Simplifying sales compensation plans is sure to yield higher motivation and better sales results.

Source: David Cichelli, "Dumb Down Your Pay Programs," *Sales & Marketing Management,* September 2003, p. 88.

desire from salespeople. And sometimes, as reflected in Leadership 11.3 compensation plans just get so complicated that they have to be retooled to make them understandable to the sales force.

To make matters worse, even well-designed motivational programs can lose their effectiveness over time. As we discussed earlier in the book, the characteristics of relationship selling are different from other approaches to selling, and this fact along with the changing nature of the market environment can cause motivation programs to lose their effectiveness. As salespeople become satisfied with the rewards offered by a particular incentive plan, for instance, the requirements of the job or the customer may change. Leadership 11.4 describes a possible result when reward systems do not match current job needs.

Leadership The Perils of Rewarding A while Hoping for B 11.4

Steven Kerr coined the phrase "Rewarding A while Hoping for B" way back in 1975 in an article in the *Academy of Management Review*. His premise was this: Very frequently, organizations establish reward systems that pay off one behavior even though the rewarder hopes dearly for some other behavior." This concept has strong application in sales force compensation plans, especially in today's complex environment of relationship selling.

Sales managers who wonder why their salespeople's behaviors do not seem to match their organization's goals might do well to consider that their reward systems pay off salespeople for behaviors other than those sought by the firm. In the past, rewarding salespeople was easier. Then, the focus was on individual salespeople approaching customers on a transaction-to-transaction basis. The focus today is on not just the salesperson but the whole organization working together toward developing long-term customer relationships. Do straight commission plans make sense in this environment? Not likely, as such approaches are the epitome of motivating individual sales efforts and not teamwork.

As an example, take hypothetical salesperson Chris. To achieve goals that yield desired results, Chris often has to rely in part on the performance of teammates who represent other functional areas of the firm. Unlike many salespeople of the past, Chris cannot individually and directly control much of the relationship selling process. Chris can serve as to marshal internal resources and apply them to the relationship-building process and can certainly serve as a point person for managing the relationship, but he *cannot* directly control the actions of the whole team. Clearly, in such a situation standard compensation and incentive systems are inadequate.

Firms cannot expect salespeople to focus on operating effectively within a team or on securing, building, and maintaining long-term relationships with profitable customers if the reward system doesn't recognize and compensate them for these behaviors. That is, the "Hoping for B" should be matched by "Rewarding B." In the relationship selling environment, incentives must be rethought and performance appraisal instruments must be refashioned to reflect the goals and behavior required for success today.

Steven Kerr had it right in 1975: "For an organization to act upon its members, the formal reward system should positively reinforce desired behaviors, not constitute an obstacle to be overcome."

Kerr's original article was updated and republished as follows: Steven Kerr, "On the Folly of Rewarding A, while Hoping for B," *Academy of Management Executive,* 9:1 (1995), pp. 7–14.

Recognizing such problems, an increasing number of firms frequently review their compensation and incentive policies. Many firms adjust their total compensation levels at least annually, and they are increasingly willing to make more substantial adjustments in their programs when circumstances demand. Some firms have established compensation and incentive committees to regularly monitor sales motivation programs for fairness and effectiveness. Two major issues involve (1) assessing the firm's relationship selling objectives and (2) determining which aspects of job performance to reward.

Assessing the Relationship Selling Objectives

A major purpose of any sales compensation program is to stimulate and influence the sales force to work toward accomplishing the objectives of securing, building, and maintaining long-term relationships with profitable customers. As a first step in deciding what job activities and performance dimensions a new or improved motivation program should stimulate, a manager should evaluate how salespeople are allocating their time. On what job activities do they focus, and how much time do they devote to each? How good are their current outcomes on various dimensions of performance, such as total sales volume, sales to new customers, or retention of existing customers? Much of this information can

Leadership   How to Tell if Your Quota System Isn't Working   11.5

Your sales force's performance isn't up to snuff. Before you pour more resources into additional training, sales contests, or cash prizes, try looking at your quota system. Many of the most common quota measures—such as evenly dividing the sales department's total goal by its number of salespeople, or increasing quota by the same percentage as a projected industry growth rate—are often ineffective or inaccurate, says Paul DiModica, CEO of Atlanta-based sales training firm DigitalHatch Inc. This can result in a vicious cycle of wrong forecasts, unreasonable quotas, and frustrated salespeople. Act fast if you spy these clues that your quota system isn't working:

1. NOBODY MAKES GOAL

Perhaps the most obvious sign that your quota system isn't working is if no one can meet it. When that happens, it's likely that the numbers are based on what executive management is striving for, rather than on real-world calculations. DiModica's firm worked with one $40 million software company with a 30-person sales force that missed its quota two years in a row, resulting in layoffs. "Management thought they needed to implement more sales training, but that was not the biggest issue. Their sales quota was based on a guesstimate, not factual information," DiModica says. The managers of the company set goals based on what investors wanted them to do, on the previous year's numbers, and on how they thought their competitors were doing. DiModica helped the firm recalculate its quotas based on such concrete numbers as existing market demand, regional demand, sales closing ratios, and the number of proposals needed to get in front of the customer. As a result, the sales force met its quota exactly, even though it had lost some of its salespeople. "Most quotas are done in a back room," DiModica says. "It's a management number based on what management thinks it needs to keep the company growing."

2. THERE ARE NO OVERACHIEVERS

"When you notice your top reps are hitting quota early and not overachieving, that's one sign your quota system is sorely lacking," says Eric Meerschaert, managing director for the Denver office of business consulting firm Charter Consulting. A good quota system should always have salespeople striving for more, he says. One of Charter's clients, a large industrial firm, was finding that its most competitive performers were reaching quota midyear and then basically quitting after they met their set goal. Whatever additional deals they closed went toward meeting next year's quota. Meerschaert's team helped the company institute a compensation system that was based more on a salesperson's year-to-year improvement and reaching an upside goal rather than giving them an absolute number that capped performance. As a result, sales increased by 15 percent during a year when the sales force had been cut by 10 percent.

3. ONLY SUPERSTARS MAKE GOAL

Sales managers who make the mistake of setting quotas based on their top sellers' performance run the risk of demotivating the rest of their salespeople. Setting a goal with no account of such variables as region or experience—and without letting your salespeople know how it's calculated—may make your reps question the quota's fairness. "You shouldn't have a high number of high performers and low performers. About 50 percent should be in the fat part of the bell curve," says John Buie, executive vice president of sales for Synygy, a suburban Philadelphia sales consultancy and provider of quota-calculation software.

Meerschaert says if 10 percent of your sales force constantly makes 90 percent of sales, then managers won't see the overall performance of their sales force increase over time. "The team is not just the top 20 sales reps," he says. "Let's say the top rep closes 10 million dollars on the average. You want more people to get to that, rather than have the one person get to 25 million," he says. If most team members don't make goal, managers risk seeing discouraged salespeople leave when they actually have the potential to perform very well.

Source: Julia Chang, "Numbers Crunching," *Sales & Marketing Management*, February 2003, p. 49.

be obtained from job analyses the firm conducts as part of its recruitment and selection procedures, as well as from performance evaluations and company records.

This assessment of the sales force's current allocation of effort and levels of performance can then be compared to the firm's specific objectives for relationship selling. Such comparisons often reveal that some selling activities and dimensions of performance are receiving too much emphasis from the sales force, while others are not receiving enough. This situation necessitates an adjustment in the incentive plan; in particular, it requires an immediate look at the quotas salespeople are working against. An important sales management function is monitoring whether the compensation and incentive plan, as well as associated quotas, continue to be effective over time in motivating the sales force. Remember, to be effective, quotas (which are goals for attaining some aspect of the sales job) must be specific, measurable, and realistically attainable. Leadership 11.5 provides three clues to watch for that might indicate a quota system isn't working.

Determining Which Aspects of Job Performance to Reward

When the firm's relationship selling objectives are misaligned with its sales force's allocation of time, the compensation and incentive program can be redesigned to more strongly reward desired activities or performance outcomes, thus motivating the sales reps to redirect their efforts.

Exhibit 11.4 lists specific activities and performance dimensions that can be stimulated by a properly designed compensation and incentive program. Of course, managers would like their salespeople to perform well on all of these dimensions, and as we saw earlier in the chapter, different components of a compensation program can be designed to reward different activities and achieve multiple objectives.

It is a mistake to try to motivate salespeople to do too many things at once. When rewards are tied to numerous different aspects of performance, (1) it becomes difficult for a salesperson to focus on improving performance dramatically in any one area, and (2) the salesperson is more likely to be uncertain about how total performance will be evaluated and about what rewards can be obtained as a result of that performance. In short, complex compensation and incentive programs may lead to great confusion by salespeople. Thus, it is better for compensation and incentive plans to link rewards to only the key aspects of job performance. They should be linked to those aspects consistent with the firm's highest-priority relationship selling objectives.

The complex relationship between today's customers and their suppliers has created the need for salespeople to cooperate and work with many individuals within their own firm as well as within the customer's business. Many of the performance outcomes identified in Exhibit 11.4 will not be achieved unless salespeople cooperate with others. Linking financial compensation programs with the need for salesperson cooperation is critical in building long-term relationships with customers.[10] Oracle's Siebel CRM applications, for example, and others link sales force compensation with customer-oriented metrics such as customer satisfaction. One reason for the reluctance of many firms to base rewards on customer satisfaction is the difficulty of measuring changes in satisfaction over time. Also, while there is some evidence that strong satisfaction-based incentives improve customer

EXHIBIT 11.4
Sales activities and performance outcomes that might be encouraged by compensation and incentive programs

- Sell a greater overall dollar volume.
- Increase sales of more profitable products.
- Push new products.
- Push selected items at designated seasons.
- Achieve a higher degree of market penetration by products, kinds of customers, or territories.
- Secure large average orders.

- Secure new customers.
- Service and maintain existing business.
- Reduce turnover of customers.
- Encourage cooperation among members of sales or account management teams.
- Achieve full-line (balanced) selling.
- Reduce direct selling costs.
- Increase the number of calls made.
- Submit reports and other data promptly.

Innovation   Linking CRM and the Sales Force Compensation Plan   11.6

In the back of a London cab, a European sales manager once regaled me with anecdotes about how salespeople really use their companies' customer relationship management software (CRM)—the salespeople who were subjects of the anecdotes alternately gamed and ignored what the software asked them to do.

He was so unimpressed with CRM that the first thing he did after joining a huge British company was kill off a planned enterprise CRM implementation. "I earned my pay for that alone," he laughed.

But as we arrived at our meeting, he said something that made me rethink my assumptions about sales force automation software: The most successful implementation he had seen was built around the online sales force compensation and performance evaluation system.

In other words, CRM and sales force compensation and incentives were integrated and linked. Salespeople couldn't access their expense reimbursements, compensation status, and outstanding incentives unless they filled out their online field reports. By aligning the system with what salespeople were most interested in, the quantity and quality of response rates dramatically improved.

To make CRM functionality more valuable, I've heard that a few technology and capital goods companies have programmed the system so that prospects get a copy of the rep's field report. In effect, the potential client gets to see what the sales team thought of the meeting, along with promised next steps, questions, concerns, and perceived resistance. The kicker to this is that the copy sent to prospects contains an e-mail address for private comments sent only to the home office. What an intriguing "market mechanism" to encourage disclosure, transparency, and feedback.

Of course, most off-the-shelf sales force automation (SFA) software doesn't have this kind of functionality, or it's baked in a form that's awkward or inaccessible to many salespeople. Consequently, there have been numerous bootleg efforts to use e-mail and customized Web pages to complement, or substitute for, enterprise CRM. You can see with the rise of salesforce.com that the burgeoning ability of the Web to be a low-cost, easy-to-modify sales services platform is growing over time. And efforts to get salespeople and Web masters together to create highly focused, easy-to-use Web sites to support sales in the field are getting better. They seem to argue against off-the-shelf systems and toward semicustom, Net-centric Web sites.

The ability of a savvy firm to recognize those aspects of its sales culture it wishes to reinforce, and repress, can be readily played out on Web-based SFA systems. One company spent millions on an off-the-shelf SFA package and replaced it less than eight months later with a Web-based knockoff that delivered 80 percent of the functionality at 20 percent of the price.

The core issue here, though, isn't the cost. It's the problem identified by the European sales manager: CRM that tries to dictate how salespeople behave always fails. CRM that respects how salespeople really behave has a decent shot at success. That reality requires a willingness to creatively customize and not cheaply standardize.

Source: Michael Schrage, "Software That's Actually Useful," *Sales & Marketing Management,* August 2003, p. 25.

service by salespeople, some managers worry that such incentives may distract sales reps from the tasks necessary to capture additional sales volume in the short term. To offset this problem, some firms combine customer-satisfaction–based incentives with bonus or commission payments tied to sales quotas or revenue. Unfortunately, such mixed-incentive plans can sometimes add additional confusion in the sales force and even lead to *reductions* in customer service levels.[11] The bottom line, then, is that although rewarding customer service is an attractive goal, it can present some thorny measurement and design issues for the sales manager that will have to be worked out.

Adding rewards for good customer service, although an important step, means that compensation of consultative selling approaches will likely be even more challenging. Sixty-five percent of sales managers believe that building consulting competencies in their sales force is a key to driving their company's growth. As such, managers cannot reward their sales force merely for what products they want pushed, but rather for how well they build a profitable relationship for both parties. According to Craig Wilson, Director of Corporate Marketing at International Paper, "There is a difference between selling and value managing. Selling is about what you want the customer to hear about your product and your features. Value managing is about understanding what the customer needs, providing the benefits the customer is looking for, and having that customer understand how those benefits translate into a better top-line or a better bottom-line. It's no longer about what we want to push, it's got to be about what fulfills the customer need and what will do that profitably for both parties." It may not yet be clear how to best compensate salespeople for consulting skills, but without doubt the issue is a top priority for sales organizations today.[12]

As we learned in Chapter 3, many firms have turned to CRM systems to help manage their overall customer relationship activities. A critical issue arises as to how the CRM system, which as we know is an important tool for the sales force, fits in with the firm's compensation plan. Innovation 11.6 and Technology 11.7 provide vivid examples of how CRM and sales force compensation and incentives can be integrated and linked.

DECIDING ON THE MOST APPROPRIATE MIX AND LEVEL OF COMPENSATION

All salespeople do not find the same kinds of rewards equally attractive. Needs and preferences for a particular reward vary, depending on personalities, demographic characteristics, and lifestyles of different salespeople. Consequently, no single reward—including money—is likely to be effective for motivating all of a firm's salespeople. Similarly, a mix of rewards that is effective for motivating a sales force at one time may lose its appeal as the members' personal circumstances and needs change and as new salespeople are hired. In view of this, a wise preliminary step in designing a sales compensation and incentive package is for a firm to determine its salespeople's current preferences for various rewards.[13]

The decision about how much total compensation (base pay plus any commissions or bonuses) a salesperson may earn is crucial in designing an effective motivation program. The starting point for making this decision is to determine the gross amount of compensation necessary to attract, retain, and motivate salespeople who can manage the firm's customer relationships. This also depends on the specific type of sales job in question, the size of the firm and the sales force, and the resources available to the firm.

In Chapter 2 we introduced several different types of sales jobs, and it is important to note that average compensation varies substantially across these. In general, more complex and demanding sales jobs, which require salespeople with special qualifications, offer higher pay than more routine sales jobs. To compete for the best talent, a firm should determine how much total compensation other firms in its industry or related ones pay people in similar jobs. Then the firm can decide whether to pay its salespeople an amount that is average in relation to what others are paying or above average. Few companies consciously pay below average (although some do so without realizing it) because below-average compensation generally cannot attract the right level of selling talent.

The decision about whether to offer total compensation at an average or premium level depends in part on the size of the firm and its sales force. Large firms with good reputations in their industries and large sales forces generally offer only average compensation. Such firms, such as Intel or Cisco, can attract sales talent because of their reputation in the marketplace and because they are big enough to offer advancement into management.

Technology   Is Your Compensation Plan Undermining Your CRM Initiative?   11.7

Incentive compensation plans are designed to motivate sales and service professionals to achieve goals and strive for excellence. But the disturbing truth is that these same compensation plans are often in opposition to the corporate strategy and CRM initiative. The effect is that employees will lose sight of what's important: their customers. "Compensation is the first litmus test for a company's seriousness about the customer," says Lior Arussy, president of call center consultancy Strativity Group.

It may seem impossible to design compensation plans that keep sales and service reps motivated and focused on the customer while supporting corporate goals. But companies like DirecTV and Hologic have succeeded in doing so. Here are four strategies that will help your comp plan succeed, too.

PAY FOR THE RESULTS YOU WANT

In sales, as in life, you get what you pay for. If, for example, your organization needs to increase sales of a new product line, but reps receive incentives that favor existing product lines, the reps won't bother to pursue sales for the new product line.

According to Brad Brown, principal at sales compensation consultancy Reward Strategies, companies must make sure they're paying for the most important activities, and that those activities are connected to their business strategy and flow to the bottom line. Compensation should pay sales and service reps to achieve those specific results.

Rewarding reps for the wrong results can prove especially deleterious to customer service efforts. A common call center mistake, Arussy warns, is to reward agents based on performance during peak hours. For example, a company may pay bonuses to agents who answer more calls during a peak time. However, this can lead to unscrupulous, yet commonly used, techniques that frustrate customers. In an effort to reach their call volume goals, agents may place customers back in the call queue, pass the caller to another agent, or simply hang up—all in an effort to quickly get to the next caller. This behavior can severely decrease customer satisfaction levels and lead to an increase in customer attrition.

A better strategy is to reward agents not simply for volume, but also for meeting customer-focused goals. Arussy suggests that call center managers set up bonus structures based, for example, on the creation and accumulation of new ideas from customers. So instead of having an electronic board on the wall that shows the number of calls waiting, the board can show scores for the number of ideas generated or implemented, or savings and revenue numbers based on ideas generated for the company.

SHARE OWNERSHIP

In complex sales environments one customer may require several salespeople at different stages in the customer's life cycle. But each salesperson must have his own reward structure. "The compensation system must be well aligned with the job," says David Cichelli, author of *Compensating the Sales Force: A Practical Guide to Designing Winning Sales Compensation Plans.*

Hologic, a provider of medical imaging products, found that rewarding salespeople and field engineers for their specific role in the sales cycle not only improved performance, but also boosted incremental sales. Hologic's imaging systems include both hardware and software components that can be quite costly, running in excess of $500,000. The company has a growing service business that represents roughly 25 percent of the company's overall revenue of $204 million. An important component of Hologic's service business is extended product warranties.

Hologic sales professionals are compensated for selling the imaging systems themselves. But the company's 120 field engineers, deployed throughout the United States, are in the best position to sell extended contracts as customers approach the end of their original one-year warranty. The field engineers are rewarded separately for customer retention efforts when they sell extended contracts or cross-sell or upsell other products.

To support the field engineers, Hologic is using Oracle's Contract Renewal application, part of Oracle's E-Business Suite. The application notifies field engineers approximately two months prior to a local client's warranty expiration date, giving clients fair warning to avoid any lapse in coverage. Previously, warranty renewals often slipped through the cracks, says David Rudzinsky, chief information officer at Hologic.

As a result of the compensation strategy and the software to support it, "we have noticed an uptick in contract

(continued)

Technology   *concluded*   11.7

renewals and we can renew contracts faster, eliminating any lapse in coverage," Rudzinsky says.

AUTOMATION: LET REPS TRACK THEIR PAY

Many organizations still use basic, homegrown systems like spreadsheets to track compensation. But these systems provide little to no visibility for sales and service professionals to determine what is owed to them and when. So they try to figure it out on their own, which causes two major problems: overpayment and frustration.

"The system is a black box: There's no information being provided to them, and you have a complete environment of shadow accounting, where sales reps track their own efforts to determine compensation," says Greg Wynne, director of product marketing at Callidus Software, a developer of enterprise incentive-management software. "It's a huge drag on productivity, which takes time away from being in the field and trying to generate business."

So inefficient are these manual systems that it may take three or more months after the target date to reward sales and service professionals, which can lead to the costly problem of overpayment. DirecTV, for example, was taking too long to pay its distributors the sales compensation owed to them. As a result, the satellite communications company received many double submissions for compensation credit. "DirecTV wasn't turning around compensations quickly enough," Wynne says. "What's most important to any company is that they don't lose the relationship with that [sales] channel. So they'll err on the side of overpaying [rather] than underpaying."

To correct the problem DirecTV implemented the Callidus TrueComp incentive compensation management (ICM) system. DirecTV is now able to provide its payees with up-to-date, Web-based reports of both daily and pay-period results. This has significantly reduced its administrative time lag and provided visibility into its compensation program, which has helped the company reduce compensation overpayment.

Unnecessary overpayment on sales compensation plans can be costly. Research firms like Gartner and Forrester Research estimate that, on average, organizations overcompensate their sales professionals between 3 and 10 percent annually.

Just as problematic is underpayment. If sales and service professionals don't clearly understand their rewards structure and, as a result, incorrectly calculate their rewards, they will be unpleasantly surprised when they receive less than they had anticipated. This creates frustration and dissatisfaction. One solution is to use an ICM application, which can minimize these problems by providing up-to-date visibility into the rewards accumulated and the status of payments.

KEEP IT SIMPLE AND UP-TO-DATE

Business strategies change and compensation plans must change with them. Outdated comp plans become difficult to track, and "suddenly you find yourself micromanaging the sales compensation program," Cichelli says. To help minimize compensation overhauls, he says, managers should keep performance measures down to three metrics or less, and they should be easy for employees to understand.

To establish the most appropriate metrics, Cichelli suggests interviewing senior management to determine future sales objectives, headquarters staff to learn what is currently working and what areas need improvement, and field sales management and sales personnel for their understanding of the existing program and suggestions for improvement.

After gaining input from the appropriate employees, create new sales metrics that are in line with both corporate goals and sales professionals' desires. The sales metrics should be challenging, achievable goals that at least 50 percent of the sales force should achieve, and an additional 15 percent should surpass, according to Reward Strategies' Brown.

Brown also suggests simplifying payment methods. Bonus plans are preferable to commissions, because they're easier to administer and keep cost-of-sales and cost-of-labor in check, he says.

Finally, be patient. Cichelli says that it can take large organizations four to five months to fully implement a compensation plan. Organizations with 10 to 50 sales reps should start their redesign efforts at least two months in advance of the implementation date. Sales organizations with fewer than 10 salespeople should allow at least one month for the redesign efforts.

And when you think you're done with your compensation plan, think again. Zig Ziglar, author and motivational speaker, says, "People say that motivation doesn't last. Well, neither does bathing. That's why you need to do it every day."

Source: David Myron, "Is Your Compensation Plan Undermining Your CRM Initiative?" *CRM Magazine* (Volume 8, May 2004), pp. 40–43.

Also, such firms can hire younger people, often just out of school, as sales trainees and put them through an extensive training program. This allows them to pay relatively low gross compensation because they do not have to pay a market premium to attract older, more experienced salespeople. In contrast, smaller firms often cannot afford extensive training programs. Consequently, they must often offer above-average compensation to attract experienced sales reps from other firms.

Dangers of Paying Salespeople Too Much

Some firms, regardless of their size or position in their industries, offer their salespeople opportunities to make very large amounts of financial compensation. The rationale for such high incomes is that opportunities for high pay will attract the best talent and motivate members of the sales force to continue working for higher and higher sales volumes. This leads some sales managers to be ambivalent about the potential for paying their salespeople too much, since in their view salesperson compensation relates directly to their volume of sales.

Unfortunately, overpaying salespeople relative to what other firms pay for similar jobs and relative to what other employees in the same firm are paid for nonsales jobs can cause major problems. For one thing, compensation is usually the largest element of a firm's selling costs. Therefore, overpaying salespeople unnecessarily increases selling costs and reduces profits. Also, it can cause resentment and low morale among the firm's other employees and executives when salespeople earn more money than even top management. It then becomes virtually impossible to promote good salespeople into managerial positions because of the financial sacrifice they would have to make. Finally, it is not clear that offering unlimited opportunities to earn higher pay is always an effective way to motivate salespeople to continually increase the selling effort—that is, at some compensation level, the next dollar earned would almost have to begin to show diminishing returns in terms of salesperson motivation.

Dangers of Paying Salespeople Too Little

Overpaying salespeople can cause problems, but it is critically important not to underpay them. Holding down sales compensation may appear to be a convenient way to hold down selling costs and enhance profits, but this is usually not true in the long run. When buying talent in the labor market, a company tends to get what it pays for. If poor salespeople are hired at low pay, poor performance will almost surely result. If good salespeople are hired at low pay, the firm is likely to have high turnover, with higher costs for recruiting and training replacements and lost sales.

In the high flying days of the e-commerce boom of the late 1990s, many technology companies offered low salaries but stock options that offered salespeople (and everyone else in the firm) the promise of great wealth when the options were cashed in later. However, as the technology sector fell on more difficult economic times, the ability of these companies to reward salespeople with stock options diminished to the point where many technology companies have gone back to financial compensation as the primary motivator.[14] This raises a question of cause and effect. Do firms perform well because they create the opportunity for the big payday, which does not always happen, or are they more successful if they pay people what they are worth plus an incentive for outstanding performance? In either case, paying what it takes to attract and keep a competent sales force seems a more likely path to high performance in relationship selling than being overly creative with the latest financial gimmicks designed to recruit but not necessarily retain the best people. Leadership 11.8 provides insights on why sales force incentive plans must also contribute to the success of the overall firm.

Leadership   Maximize Incentive ROI: Tips to Keep Your Reward and Recognition Programs in the Black   11.8

It's the start of a new year, which means sales managers are reviewing last year's incentive programs to determine whether they're worth repeating. And in a climate where businesses are looking for places to trim the fat, managers are likely being asked to justify the expense of even long-standing incentive programs.

"If you haven't been asked to justify your program, consider yourself lucky," says Michelle Smith, vice president of business development for O.C. Tanner, a provider of employee recognition and incentive solutions based in Salt Lake City. Demonstrating return-on-investment (ROI) isn't easy, as increased revenue does not necessarily yield greater ROI. But here are a few fundamental steps to ensure you get your money's worth from your 2006 programs:

CLEARLY DEFINE ALL PROGRAM GOALS

Evaluating an incentive program aimed at increasing sales can prove difficult, because a simple percentage increase is not a good-enough measure; you must know what sales are now, and what is expected. Do you want a 10 percent increase in revenue or in products sold? "Quantify your goal as much as possible," Smith says. An incentive program to boost productivity must also be defined. For instance, in a call center, determine whether your goal is to have customer service reps answer more calls per hour or reduce the time spent on each call.

INVOLVE ALL STAKEHOLDERS

A sales incentive program encompasses more than just the sales force. In determining who the stakeholders are, ask, "Who can help us achieve our goal and who can hurt us?"

Smith says. Should sales support and customer service be involved? How about the sales distribution channel? Can inventory support our goal, or does manufacturing need to be beefed up? How about shipping? Can our suppliers keep up with our growing demand? Without buy-in from all stakeholders, the salespeople may not get the support of the departments that they need, Smith says. Constant communication will also help keep all the stakeholders engaged; having everyone track the progress can keep the stakeholders motivated and involved in the program.

IDENTIFY POTENTIAL PITFALLS

Anticipating problems can make the difference between a successful program and one that was merely well-intentioned. With a sales incentive, numbers can be skewed by several factors. For example, a sale could have been recorded and entered into the ROI calculation, but then the product may have been returned, or heavy discounts can be eroding your profit margin. Set specific and consistent parameters regarding when a sale is recorded, and institute limits on discounts. Also, take note of the market: If it is unusually strong, set your goal higher; if the trend is downward, make your expectations more realistic.

In addition, make sure that whatever incentives you use—even nonsales incentives, such as productivity incentives—aren't accidentally alienating customers. A decline in product or service quality due to new practices could drive customers to competitors.

Source: Mary Litsikas, "Maximize Incentive ROI: Tips to Keep Your Reward and Recognition Programs in the Black." *Sales & Marketing Management* (Volume 158, January/February 2006), p. 16.

Summary

To effectively manage the relationship selling function, sales managers must be concerned with the firm's compensation system. Which rewards do salespeople value? How much of each is optimum? How should the rewards be integrated in a total compensation system? This chapter provides insights to these issues.

In determining the most effective form of financial compensation, the firm must decide whether it should use (1) straight salary, (2) straight commission, or (3) a combination of base salary and incentive pay such as commissions, bonuses, or both. Most companies today use a combination approach. The base salary provides the salesperson with a stable income while allowing the company to reward its salespeople for performing tasks not directly related to short-term sales. The incentive portion of combination plans provides direct rewards to motivate salespeople to expend effort to improve their sales volume or profitability. To be effective, the incentive pay portion of the combination plan has to be large enough to generate the necessary interest among salespeople. Sales contests are often part of the incentive portion of compensation systems. To be successful, a sales contest needs to have (1) clearly defined, specific objectives, (2) an exciting theme, (3) a reasonable probability of rewards for all salespeople, (4) attractive rewards, and (5) effective promotion and follow-through.

Nonfinancial incentives can play an important role in a firm's compensation system. Opportunities for salesperson promotion and advancement, recognition programs and other forms of nonfinancial incentives can be effective sales motivators. For recognition programs to be effective, the salesperson's peers and superiors must be made aware of his or her outstanding performance. This can be done through recognition at a sales meeting, publicity in the local press, announcements in the company's internal newsletter, or other ways. Because all salespeople cannot possibly move into sales management positions, some companies have dual career paths to maintain the motivating potential of promotion and advancement. One path leads to positions in the sales management hierarchy; the other leads to greater responsibilities in sales positions such as a larger territory or key account position.

Expense accounts can enhance a salesperson's overall compensation. Three common means of handling salesperson expenses are direct reimbursement, limited reimbursement, and no reimbursement. When everything else is said and done, the sales manager must determine an appropriate mix and level of compensation for salespeople that maximizes the compensation plan's motivational value, is fair, and also is consistent with the firm's resource capabilities.

Key Terms			
	compensation plan	quota	draw
	salary	sales contests	perquisites (perks)
	incentive payment	benefits	expense account
	commission	nonfinancial incentives	
	bonus	variable commission rate	

Breakout Questions

1. We know that the use of selling teams, sometimes including both salespeople and others from the firm, to accomplish relationship selling is common practice today. As with individual salespeople, the success of these teams depends, in part, on the reward systems used to motivate and recognize performance. How would you develop a compensation plan that motivates members of a selling team? How can you ensure the plan is fair for everybody involved?

2. The Ruppert Company needed to build market share quickly. To motivate sales growth, Ruppert installed a straight commission compensation plan: The more the sales reps sold, the more they made. This strategy seemed to work—sales volume climbed and the Ruppert Company captured more market share. After two years on this program, sales growth flattened out and Ruppert began to lose market share. Sales

reps continued to earn $85,000 to $90,000 on average in commissions through developing and penetrating current key accounts in their territories. Studies showed the sales force was not overworked and further territory penetration was clearly possible. What do you think was happening?

3. When OfficeSolutions, a software producer, went into business, it needed to establish market share quickly. To accomplish this, it decided to pay the sales force on a commission basis. After two years, however, the company had a large base business and customers began to complain that salespeople were not spending enough time with them on postsale service and problem solving, important relationship selling activities. The salespeople said they did not make any money on problem solving and they would rather spend their time finding new customers. What's more, salespeople spent little or no time selling the new products on which OfficeSolutions was staking its future. The salespeople said they could sell the old products more easily and earn more money for both themselves and the company. How might the company rework its compensation plan to begin to resolve this issue?

4. When designing sales compensation plans, it is important to meet the relationship selling objectives and at the same time appropriately reward the person who has to meet those objectives. How would you design sales compensation plans to match the following different company objectives and sales environmental situations?

   a. Company has a high revenue growth objective in a sales environment characterized by frequent product introductions, boom markets, and a loose competitive structure.
   b. Company has a protect-and-grow revenue objective in a sales environment characterized by slow growth, many competitors, and few product introductions. The firm's primary source of differentiation is it's excellent sales force.
   c. Company's objectives are to have an overall revenue growth and balanced product mix sales. The sales environment has multiple customer markets, many product groups, high-growth and low-growth products, and high and low sales intensity.
   d. Company's objective is to maintain revenue and have new account sales growth (that is, conversion selling by taking customers from the competition). The sales environment is a moderate-to-slow–growth marketplace.

5. Sales contests, although very popular, raise questions concerning their value. Questions asked include, Don't they simply shift into the contest period sales volume that would have occurred anyway? How can everyone be equally motivated when certain territories have a built-in edge because of customer and market characteristics? Won't the contest backfire if people feel they haven't had a fair chance to win? Will all sales reps participate with equal enthusiasm when there can be only a few winners? Respond to each of these objections.

6. A sales manager says, "You can never hold enough sales contests for your salespeople. The more the merrier . . . they are guaranteed to increase your business." Evaluate this statement.

7. Things are tough at Morgan, Inc. For the last several months, sales reps, who are paid on a commission basis, have barely covered their monthly personal expenses. To help the sales force through these tough times, Morgan executives decided to introduce monthly draws. Sales reps whose commission earnings fall below a specified monthly amount receive a special loan, or draw, against commissions. When sales and commissions improve, the sales reps will repay the cash advance from future earnings. Under what conditions will this plan help Morgan achieve its sales strategy? Under

what conditions is it likely to fail? (Hint: Think about what might happen in the future in terms of sales volume.)

8. Assume you are taking a job in relationship selling right out of college. What would be your own ideal compensation mix? Why do you prefer the one you propose?

9. What are the pros and cons of placing ceilings on salesperson incentives? If you were a sales manager, would there ever be a situation where you would advocate the use of incentive ceilings? If so, in what situation and why?

10. Veteran salespeople can pose unique challenges in terms of compensation. Why? What would you suggest in terms of designing a compensation plan that would motivate a veteran sales rep?

Leadership Challenge: One for All, All for One

Danielle Drexel was getting ready to make some important decisions for her company, Dynamic Printing. She had started the company in Chicago and in a little more than 12 years it had become one of the area's largest printers. With more than 50 salespeople in the Chicago area, the company had built a reputation for quality printing, great service, and fair prices.

Over the years the printing business had changed. When Danielle started the company, salespeople called on customers. Once a relationship had been established, customers would send the work to the shop. Often the salespeople would handle the pick up and delivery or the customers would have a courier do the job. Salespeople oversaw the job and the customer had little contact with anyone other than the salesperson.

As customers demanded more and better service, Dynamic Printing had created customer service representatives (CSRs) who handled problems and inquiries over the phone. These CSRs were responsible for a group of customers and worked closely with salespeople to enhance the customer's relationship with the company. In the last few years, Dynamic had seen the need for a third group, Inside Support Personnel (ISP), to help with the flow of orders and other issues that came up inside the company. ISPs worked for the CSRs and helped support the overall customer service experience.

As a result of these changes, each customer (particularly those who were regular customers of Dynamic Printing) had a sales team. Unfortunately, the compensation system at Dynamic Printing had not changed in 10 years. Specifically, salespeople received a 10 percent commission on gross sales for each of their customers. It made no difference how the sales were generated (by the salesperson or by calling into the store and talking with a CSR). CSRs and ISPs were paid a straight salary (with the CSRs making about 30 percent more, on average, than the ISP employees).

As Danielle sat in her office, she came to realize that this system was no longer valid. Over the last five years the sales mix had changed and sales generated in house now accounted for 50 percent of all sales for many customers. The CSRs and ISPs had expressed frustration that they were responsible for a lot of business and they received no credit. Indeed, they argued, the salespeople were receiving money for work they did with the customer. Danielle knew something had to change, but what?

Questions

1. As a CSR, what do you think is a fair solution to the compensation problem?

2. As a salesperson, what do you think is a fair solution to the compensation problem?

3. You are Danielle. What would you do about the compensation system at Dynamic Printing and why?

Role Play: Cannonball Express

Situation

"Lordy, lordy, Big Jim's forty" the e-mail birthday card screamed out from the monitor on the computer stand in his office in the Buckhead district of Atlanta. Well, Cannonball Express VP of sales (and birthday boy) Jimmy "Big Jim" Cooley didn't need to be reminded. In fact, he has been thinking a lot lately not so much about his own trek into middle age, but more about the fact that most of his sales force are, to put it delicately, no longer spring chickens. In fact, at 40 Big Jim is seven years younger than the average age of his sales force!

Cannonball Express, based in Atlanta, operates an intracity fast delivery small package and parcel service network throughout the southern United States. In Big Jim's business, "intracity" means that he doesn't try to compete directly with UPS, FedEx, DHL, or Express Mail who focus on intercity (between-city) delivery. To the contrary, Cannonball Express's business is totally focused on getting packages from point A to point B *within a metropolitan area,* so that the item is received the same day it is shipped. Attorneys, physicians, bankers, real estate professionals, and insurance agents are typical users. However, any person or business can call Cannonball Express's toll-free number for a pickup guaranteed to be within two hours of the phone call. The firm operates in 14 separate metropolitan areas and has been in business since 1990. Big Jim started as a delivery driver in Charlotte and worked his way up the company ladder to regional sales manager and then VP of sales in 2000, a position in which he has had a phenomenally successful run. Under his leadership, sales have grown an average of 9 percent per year, although lately the growth has been more in the 3–4 percent range.

Across the company, Cannonball Express has 34 salespeople and three sales managers. The sales force focuses exclusively on the B2B market, both in securing new customers and in nurturing existing customers. An astounding 87 percent of this team has been with the company 10+ years, and the average age of the group is 47. Big Jim has always been a believer in providing a strong mix of compensation and incentives, including a salary component, commission, and financial bonuses for achieving specific goals, which might vary over time depending on business trends. Given the very low turnover, it is not surprising that the salespeople are generally quite satisfied with all aspects of their job and very dedicated to the firm and its success. However, this past year Big Jim has for the first time begun to hear some grumbling in the ranks about the compensation plan. Between this and the declining sales increases, Big Jim has decided it is time to act.

Two weeks ago, Big Jim pulled in the three regional sales managers for a meeting about this topic in Atlanta. Carlos Rivera came up from Florida, Judy Bentley flew down from Arlington, Virginia, and Max Moncrief hopped on the MARTA train for the short ride over to Buckhead from the other side of Atlanta. From this day-long meeting, it was decided that a new compensation plan needs to be developed that takes into account (*a*) the changing preferences for incentives of an older sales force and (*b*) the need for rejuvenating the annual growth rate percentage. Big Jim has charged each of the three regional managers to come up with their own ideas with justifications. He has scheduled another meeting at headquarters in two weeks to go over the options and make a decision.

Characters in the Role Play

Jimmy "Big Jim" Cooley, VP of sales

Carlos Rivera, regional sales manager for Florida, Alabama, Mississippi, and Louisiana

Judy Bentley, regional sales manager for Virginia, the District of Columbia, Kentucky, and Tennessee

Max Moncrief, regional sales manager for Georgia and the Carolinas

Assignment

Break into groups of four, with one student playing each character. It doesn't matter what the actual gender mix of your group is. Before you stage the meeting, work separately using the material in your chapter to come up with your own recommendation for a new compensation and incentive plan for Cannonball Express that you believe will best address the issues identified above. Be prepared to justify why you believe each element in your plan is appropriate. Then get together and role-play the meeting among Big Jim, Carlos, Judy, and Max. In the end, you want to come out of the meeting with agreement on a new incentive and compensation plan.

Minicase: Forrest's Bike World

Forrest Powell established Forrest's Bike World, a retailer of bicycles and related parts and gear, in 2000 in Portland, Oregon. The company saw steady growth in its first few years and had opened eight stores throughout Portland by the year 2005. Forrest is the owner and acts as the general manager for all stores. Each store has one manager and four to six salespeople, with two to three working on the sales floor at any given time. Forrest himself is a bike enthusiast and rides more than 100 miles per week. He encourages his sales staff to do the same and looks for fellow bike enthusiasts when hiring. As a result, the sales staff generally loves to buy equipment from the store, especially since Forrest gives an employee discount of 10 percent.

Forrest's sales revenues increased by almost 15 percent each year for the first five years of the company's existence. But since that time, sales revenues and profits have declined at approximately the same rate. According to Forrest's analysis, the decline did not seem to have a single cause: a down economy, opening too many stores too quickly, rise of price from suppliers. He has tried to reduce costs to maintain consistent profits but has cut them to the point where the only remaining reductions would be to begin closing stores, which he does not want to do.

Forrest has always prided himself on having a top-notch sales staff. Although the staff shares a common bond of love for cycling, they are a heterogeneous group in other ways. About one-half are in their 20s, one-quarter in their 30s and one-quarter in their 40s. Some have families, some do not. Some are married, some are single. Some rely solely on the job income to live, some do not. For the first six years, Forrest paid his staff a straight salary in the range of $22,000 to $34,000, depending on sales experience, with an annual bonus of $500 if the salesperson met the standard sales quota for the year. Forrest liked the stability the salary provided his staff, especially those with families. However, after the sales began to drop in 2005. Forrest decided that the staff would sell more if they were better motivated. So he instituted a new compensation plan that paid the sales staff on 100 percent commission. To allow for some stability, there was a system of a "draw" where employees could borrow against future commissions. This plan has now been in place for almost four years, but sales are still declining. Forrest recently sat down with his best store manager, Adam Gifford, to assess the commission-based compensation plan.

They started with Forrest's business goals in order of importance: (1) Increase sales revenues relative to quota, (2) increase customer satisfaction and customer loyalty, (3) increase sales for certain product lines, (4) take advantage of bike knowledge of the sales staff, and (5) encourage bicycle riding in local events.

Then they examined the staff. Adam's first observation was that the sales skills of his staff vary greatly. For example, top performer Kim Hillbauer has no trouble meeting her monthly quota; she even makes it so early in the month that she can relax for the remaining time. However, other salespeople like Michael Carmichael do not sell as easily and feel pressure because they support big families. Moreover, Michael and others have taken money from the draw but then felt even more pressure for being far behind. Several have even quit to eliminate their debt, leaving Forrest with a loss and having to incur the added expense of training new hires. In addition, the sales approach has evolved into one of pressuring the customer to buy rather than building a relationship and taking the true needs of the customer into account. Also, there has been little effort to follow up with customers after a sale, assist with bike maintenance, or even clean up the store. As a result, customer loyalty and retention have been down. Furthermore, the old team environment, where a salesperson with a customer would call over a more knowledgeable salesperson to answer a customer question, has been replaced with an "every person for her- or himself" mentality.

Forrest and Adam decided that things must change, and the compensation plan was the place to start.

Questions

1. Did Forrest and Adam do a good job of assessing the situation with respect to the compensation plan? What other information would you like to have that is not given?

2. What were the advantages and disadvantages of Forrest's straight salary compensation plan? What were the advantages and disadvantages of his straight commission plan?

3. Given the facts above, recommend to Forrest a combination compensation plan that would best suit his situation. What other compensation devices might you use in addition to bonus, salary, and commission? Explain your recommendation.

Suggested Readings

Brown, Steven P., Kenneth R. Evans, Murali K. Mantrala, and Goutam Challagalla. "Adapting Motivation, Control, and Compensation Research to a New Environment." *Journal of Personal Selling & Sales Management* 25 (Spring 2005) pp. 155–67.

Chang, Julia. "Trophy Value." *Sales & Marketing Management,* October 2004, pp. 24–29.

Colletti, Jermoe A., Mary S. Fiss, Ted Briggs, and S. Scott Sands. *Sales Compensation Essentials: A Field Guide for the HR Professional.* Scottsdale, AZ: World at Work Press, 2006.

Kornik, Joseph. "What's it All Worth? - Annual Compensation Survey." *Sales & Marketing Management* (May 2007) pp. 27–39.

Lopez, Tará Burnthorne, Christopher D. Hopkins, and Mary Anne Raymond. "Reward Preferences of Salespeople: How Do Commissions Rate?" *Journal of Personal Selling & Sales Management* 26 (Fall 2006) pp. 381–90.

Menguc, Bulent, and A. Tansu Barker. "The Performance Effects of Outcome-Based Incentive Pay Plans on Sales Organizations: A Contextual Analysis." *Journal of Personal Selling & Sales Management* 23 (Fall 2003), pp. 341–58.

Pullins, Ellen Bolman. "An Exploratory Investigation of the Relationship of Sales Force Compensation and Intrinsic Motivation." *Industrial Marketing Management* 30 (July 2001), pp. 403–13.

Sarin, Shikhar, and Vijay Mahajan. "The Effect of Reward Structures on the Performance of Cross-Functional Product Development Teams." *Journal of Marketing* 65 (April 2001), pp. 34–53.

Widmier, Scott. "The Effects of Incentives and Personality on Salesperson's Customer Orientation." *Industrial Marketing Management* 31 (October 2002), pp. 609–15.

Yilmaz, Cengiz, and Shelby D. Hunt. "Salesperson Cooperation: The Influence of Relational, Task, Organizational and Personal Factors." *Journal of the Academy of Marketing Science* 29 (Fall 2001), pp. 335–57.

Zoltners, Andris A., Prabhakant Sinha, and Sally E. Lorimer. *The Complete Guide to Sales Force Incentive Compensation: How to Design and Implement Plans that Work.* New York: AMACOM, 2006.

Comprehensive Cases for **Part Two**

Case 2.1

California Credit Life Insurance Group

Diane Flanagan, vice president of human resources at California Credit Life Insurance Group (CCLI), had just returned to her office after a lengthy conversation with Kevin Stark, vice president of sales. Flanagan and Stark had spent many hours reviewing the results of several reports that described the problems and opportunities experienced by women in sales.

The reports came from a variety of sources and were based on one-on-one discussions between women and men in sales and another person such as a reporter or a human resource manager. In some cases, the information resulted from focus group interviews. Flanagan and Stark hoped to gain a comprehensive understanding of the environment faced by women in sales.

Toward the end of their meeting, Flanagan received a rather urgent telephone call from Shelley Ryan, a lawyer from CCLI's legal staff. Ryan was calling to inform Flanagan that Suzette Renoldi, a sales rep in the southeastern region, had just filed a sexual discrimination suit against James Bradford, CCLI area sales manager from the southeastern region. Ryan called to Flanagan's attention that this was not the first complaint of sexual discrimination involving Bradford. Flanagan was aware of this and, in addition, knew of another situation that could have led to sexual harassment charges being brought against Bradford. The person involved, Ilse Riebolt, declined to pursue the matter for a variety of reasons. Diane Flanagan had been unable to assure Ilse Riebolt that bringing charges would be very reasonable, based on the description of the events. After an excellent start with CCLI, Riebolt quit in 1997 and took a position with a competitor.

California Credit Life prided itself on being an equal opportunity employer and wanted to avoid any adverse publicity. Flanagan was very concerned about the veracity and implications of the suit. On the other hand, she was not interested in any attempts to cover up the situation if the charges were true.

According to company policy and advice provided by Shelley Ryan, the first action to be taken should be a thorough investigation of the charges and of all available

Source: Neil M. Ford, 2007.

data. Ryan urged Flanagan to gather the necessary information as quickly and as quietly as possible.

Initially, Flanagan determined she would need a vast amount of information. CCLI's computerized customer relationship management system (CRM) would be a source of much of the needed data. The CRM system contained such files as sales performance, quotas, expenses, salaries, and commissions for all of CCLI's sales reps across the country. A separate data management system in the human resources department contained the data from studies conducted on such subjects as job satisfaction, role conflict, role ambiguity, and other subjects.

THE COMPANY

California Credit Life Insurance Group was incorporated in Los Angeles in 1961. CCLI's initial product line included all types of life insurance. Since its inception, CCLI has expanded its product line to include all types of insurance such as health, automobile, professional liability, pension and retirement programs, commercial packages, and related financial services.

In 1997, CCLI decided to open an office in the southeastern area of the United States as soon as all staffing and physical details could be resolved. The southeastern region became a reality in 2001, with James Bradford selected to be area sales manager. Bradford had been a sales rep in the Dallas region and had been selected for the new position based on his excellent sales performance and his strong interpersonal skills. Shortly after Bradford accepted the position, it became apparent to Diane Flanagan that he did not wholeheartedly support CCLI's position concerning equal opportunity. In fact, it became necessary to instruct Bradford that one-third of his sales force would be female, a figure in line with CCLI's experience in its other regional offices.

California Credit Life Insurance has 15 regional offices and 230 sales representatives. Area sales managers typically supervise 15 people, a large number but manageable given the nature of the selling job. The sales reps work independently and do not need day-to-day supervision or contact with their area sales manager.

CCLI requires two performance evaluations each year. Area sales managers have hiring authority and can set base salaries with approval from CCLI. Promotional opportunities are limited, and turnover among the area sales managers has been very low.

Area sales managers can recognize excellent performance by increasing the base salary and modifying a sales rep's territory to cover better accounts. Sales reps receive a 3 percent commission on sales in addition to their base salaries. Yearly bonuses are distributed by the area sales manager based on a sales rep's performance. Records indicated Bradford's bonus allocation did not reflect sales volume and seemed to be determined by taking the total bonus award and dividing it by 15. This process added an average of $1,750 to each sales rep's income.

THE SUZETTE RENOLDI MATTER

Renoldi joined CCLI in 2001 after graduating with a business degree from the University of South Carolina. Her initial performance was strong, and she made quota each year except for the last two years. Quotas are set by the area sales manager based on guidelines handed down from Kevin Stark, vice president of sales, and negotiations between the area sales manager and each sales representative.

Diane Flanagan contacted Shelley Ryan to determine what was behind Renoldi's legal action against CCLI and Bradford. Ryan informed her that she had not seen the actual complaint but knew that Renoldi had asked for territory changes so that her sales opportunities would be greater, a request that Bradford denied. Bradford allegedly told Renoldi that her unwillingness to entertain clients, especially males, was the reason her sales had fallen off and not because of a lack of sales potential. Renoldi refuted this accusation and claimed Bradford's territory assignment was discriminatory from the start. Flanagan knew she would need to see the complete complaint and personally discuss the situation with both Renoldi and Bradford. Meanwhile, Flanagan started compiling as much information as possible from company sources.

The first documents received by Flanagan revealed sales volumes for each sales representative (Exhibit 1), expense account data (Exhibit 2), number of performance evaluations (Exhibit 3), and base salaries (Exhibit 4). Her office conducts various personnel studies, and she had available the summary results of a recent job satisfaction survey for the entire company. She requested a breakout based on region and sex, knowing that the small number of women in the southeastern region posed a statistical problem. Exhibit 5 presents job satisfaction scores for the sales representatives by sex for the southeastern region and the entire company. Flanagan was somewhat pleased with the results for the entire company but disappointed with the southeastern region's showing. At this juncture, Flanagan decided to summarize some of the studies she and Stark had been reviewing.

The first study, conducted by HBRS (a research company), was based on a series of focus group interviews with women sales reps from a variety of selling positions. HBRS also conducted focus group sessions with men. No attempt was made to conduct sessions with both men and women because it was believed this would limit discussion. Flanagan read the following verbatim comments:

Karen R. (computer sales): *I really enjoy the challenge of selling high-priced, high-tech computers. It feels great to help somebody solve a problem. But I still get questions from my friends when I tell them about my travel demands.*

Margaret M. (medical equipment sales): *I don't mind the travel, but at times it is all lumped together. Making child care arrangements can be a hassle.*

Sherry W. (office equipment sales): *This travel thing is bad news at my house. My husband becomes aloof the minute I mention that I have to be gone overnight. He's still aloof after I return. I know he wants me to quit and get a job with no travel.*

Martha W. (cosmetics sales): *I don't have a husband to contend with, but with my travel schedule I don't have much of a social life either. My biggest problem was deciding what to pack and lost luggage. I'm supposed to carry a sample case that weighs 35 pounds plus a garment bag and my briefcase.*

Deirdre B. (insurance sales): *I rarely travel outside of the city. My major headache is the guy who thinks that I should be home sewing and cooking or, if I have to work, in the typing pool.*

Karen R. (computer sales): *I've made quota every year for the last five years only to confront men who say I'm lucky. One guy told me that I*

EXHIBIT 1 Total sales and sales to quota, 2001–2007*

	2001 Total Sales	Percent to Quota	2002 Total Sales	Percent to Quota	2003 Total Sales	Percent to Quota	2004 Total Sales	Percent to Quota	2005 Total Sales	Percent to Quota	2006 Total Sales	Percent to Quota	2007 Total Sales	Percent to Quota
Suzette Renoldi	$228,800	101.4	$247,104	102.1	$261,930	101.4	$267,169	102.3	$264,340	101.1	$282,844	99.6	$288,500	98.5
Stuart Pletz	215,600	97.3	219,912	99.4	230,908	99.9	242,453	101.1	245,442	101.6	262,623	98.4	288,885	100.2
Alvin Polard	100,000	96.7	101,000	97.2	103,020	100.0	106,111	100.3	107,500	100.6	115,025	100.3	124,227	100.6
Ted Hervington	350,000	100.3	346,500	95.4	343,035	99.6	T							
Tim Hart	264,900	99.8	270,198	100.4	275,602	100.9	281,114	100.8	282,445	101.2	302,216	102.0	326,395	102.7
Brett Moore	234,000	98.9	231,660	96.7	231,660	99.0	232,818	98.1	T					
Shari Swaggert	375,000	105.3	397,500	103.5	413,400	102.6	417,534	102.1	410,890	99.8	T			
Mark Hoffton	189,000	101.2	192,780	100.6	198,563	101.1	204,520	100.8	204,800	100.7	219,136	100.1	230,093	100.4
Bob Pizzano	250,100	100.1	257,603	101.0	265,331	101.8	273,291	101.2	275,364	101.6	294,639	102.1	318,210	102.0
Felicia Abler	289,650	100.8	309,926	104.5	325,422	103.2	326,724	103.4	322,745	101.9	345,337	102.9	348,790	98.7
Kathy Levenhagen	190,000	103.8	209,000	106.2	223,630	103.5	230,339	103.9	225,990	102.1	241,809	100.1	265,990	99.0
Jeff Birdest	195,640	95.4	205,422	100.4	211,585	102.9	217,932	101.6	218,500	101.7	233,795	101.4	252,110	101.7
Larry Green	320,000	99.6	326,400	99.7	336,192	102.4	347,959	102.3	348,660	102.0	373,066	103.1	414,103	102.5
Chris Brackett	296,430	101.3	311,252	102.4	326,815	103.6	339,887	103.0	342,110	103.4	366,057	104.1	406,323	103.8
Ilse Rieboldt	287,500	102.4	296,125	105.3	T									
Mike Peck					100,412	102.3	253,117	101.6	241,553	99.1	281,313	101.8	305,014	102.4
Jeff Martin							213,419	99.1	235,017	100.2	279,106	101.2	312,844	102.8
Cliff Arlen									185,442	97.1	214,877	99.3	264,651	98.1
Kim Babler											204,913	98.4	278,228	100.2

*Terminations are noted by T.

EXHIBIT 2 Expense account data, 2001–2007*

	2001	2002	2003	2004	2005	2006	2007
Suzette Renoldi	$1,800	$1,875	$1,820	$1,830	$1,790	$1,933	$1,905
Stuart Pletz	1,100	1,367	1,450	1,690	1,855	2,078	2,210
Alvin Polard	1,250	1,462	1,667	1,723	1,775	1,988	1,995
Ted Hervington	1,790	1,890	1,993	T			
Tim Hart	2,000	2,134	2,177	2,189	2,950	3,304	3,380
Brett Moore	2,500	2,578	2,673	2,774	T		
Shari Swaggert	1,540	1,603	1,615	1,672	1,715	T	
Mark Hoffton	1,778	1,800	1,829	1,950	2,059	2,306	2,384
Bob Pizzano	1,892	1,966	1,998	2,150	2,331	2,611	2,673
Felicia Abler	1,224	1,250	1,282	1,354	1,332	1,439	1,461
Kathy Levenhagen	1,452	1,466	1,562	1,432	1,455	1,571	1,543
Jeff Birdest	1,970	1,980	2,155	2,245	2,778	3,111	3,260
Larry Green	2,145	2,256	2,347	2,355	2,679	3,000	3,114
Chris Brackett	2,234	2,457	2,679	2,789	2,887	3,233	3,211
Ilse Rieboldt	1,234	1,423	T				
Mike Peck			1,131	2,046	2,811	2,270	2,413
Jeff Martin				1,548	2,060	2,316	2,385
Cliff Arlen					1,440	2,119	2,376
Kim Babler						1,804	2,223

*Terminations are noted by T.

EXHIBIT 3 Performance evaluations, 2001–2007*

	2001		2002		2003		2004		2005		2006		2007	
	1st	2nd	1st	2nd	1st	2nd	1st	2nd	1st	2nd	1st	2nd	1st	2nd
Suzette Renoldi	Y	N	Y	Y	Y	Y	Y	Y	N	Y	Y	N	Y	Y
Stuart Pletz	Y	Y	Y	Y	Y	Y	Y	Y	Y	Y	Y	Y	Y	Y
Alvin Polard	Y	Y	Y	Y	Y	N	Y	Y	Y	Y	Y	Y	Y	Y
Ted Hervington	Y	Y	Y	Y	Y	Y	T							
Ted Hart	Y	Y	N	Y	Y	Y	Y	Y	Y	Y	Y	Y	Y	Y
Brett Moore	Y	Y	Y	Y	Y	Y	Y	Y	T					
Shari Swaggert	Y	Y	Y	Y	Y	Y	Y	Y	N	Y	T			
Mark Hoffton	Y	Y	Y	Y	Y	Y	Y	Y	Y	Y	Y	N	Y	Y
Bob Pizzano	Y	Y	Y	Y	Y	Y	Y	Y	Y	Y	Y	Y	Y	Y
Felicia Abler	Y	Y	N	Y	Y	Y	Y	Y	Y	Y	N	Y	N	Y
Kathy Levenhagen	Y	N	Y	Y	N	Y	Y	Y	N	Y	Y	Y	N	Y
Jeff Birdest	Y	N	Y	Y	Y	Y	Y	Y	Y	Y	Y	Y	Y	Y
Larry Green	Y	Y	Y	Y	Y	Y	Y	Y	Y	Y	Y	Y	Y	Y
Chris Brackett	Y	Y	Y	N	Y	Y	Y	Y	Y	N	Y	Y	N	Y
Ilse Rieboldt	Y	Y	N	Y	T									
Mike Peck						Y	Y	Y	Y	Y	Y	T	Y	Y
Jeff Martin							Y	Y	Y	Y	Y	Y	Y	Y
Cliff Arlen									Y	Y	Y	Y	Y	Y
Kim Babler											Y	Y	N	Y

*Terminations are noted by T.

EXHIBIT 4   Base salaries for all sales reps in the SE region, 2001–2007*

	2001	2002	2003	2004	2005	2006	2007
Suzette Renoldi	$25,000	$27,600	$29,200	$29,200	$29,250	$29,300	$30,750
Stuart Pletz	25,000	27,300	28,900	29,150	29,860	30,580	32,750
Alvin Polard	25,000	28,930	29,600	29,990	30,650	31,320	33,850
Ted Hervington	25,000	26,000	26,700	T			
Tim Hart	25,000	25,780	26,750	26,890	26,900	27,000	29,700
Brett Moore	25,000	25,900	26,200	26,750	T		
Shari Swaggert	25,000	29,000	29,500	29,750	29,800	T	
Mark Hoffton	25,000	26,200	27,150	27,450	27,900	28,500	30,500
Bob Pizzano	25,000	27,100	28,450	28,600	28,770	28,900	31,300
Felicia Abler	25,000	28,750	29,200	29,450	29,500	29,750	31,500
Kathy Levenhagen	25,000	28,450	28,750	28,950	29,340	29,750	31,500
Jeff Birdest	25,000	25,700	26,500	27,800	29,100	31,000	33,750
Larry Green	25,000	25,900	28,000	28,750	30,100	31,500	34,000
Chris Brackett	25,000	27,000	27,800	28,900	29,900	31,000	33,750
Ilse Rieboldt	25,000	26,200	T				
Mike Peck			26,000	27,500	28,300	28,750	30,000
Jeff Martin				26,500	27,500	28,250	29,500
Cliff Arlen					27,000	27,500	28,250
Kim Babler						27,250	28,000

*Terminations are noted by T.

EXHIBIT 5   Job satisfaction summary, 2007*

	Southeastern Region			Total Company		
	Male	Female	Total	Male	Female	Total
1. Job	54.06	45.13	52.16	53.84	50.19	53.61
2. Fellow workers	58.35	49.63	55.82	57.98	51.11	57.39
3. Supervisor	59.91	41.24	57.33	54.13	48.54	51.43
4. Company policy and management support	61.58	52.28	60.17	58.91	53.28	56.46
5. Pay	49.31	52.39	50.07	49.88	51.65	49.92
6. Promotion and advancement	59.41	48.37	57.30	58.28	49.87	57.06
7. Customer	53.70	48.44	51.19	54.07	48.56	52.09
Total	59.47	48.14	59.12	58.19	50.23	57.48

*All scores are standardized at a mean of 50. The higher the score, the more sales representatives are satisfied.

make more sales because customers want to see what a female sales rep looks like; then when I'm making my presentation, I rely on my feminine wiles to make the sale.

Cherie I. (aluminum sales):   *I've had the credibility problem too. One purchasing agent informed me that my predecessor stood 6 feet, 2 inches, weighed 195 pounds, and had a beard. I was really flustered with that comment and*

even more so when he asked me if I was busy in the evening. No doubt he wanted to explain the intricacies of aluminum to me.

Laura W. (advertising sales):   *Being hassled comes with the territory. And I don't have to leave the office either. But I've adapted. I either play naive or ignore the comments. I told one fellow laughingly that he could do better than me. But I do get tired of the hassle.*

Candace S. (commercial lending):   *The surprises never end. My first attempt at customer entertaining was a shocker. The customer said he would join me for dinner if he could bring his wife along. I was dumbfounded. Do I take both and report the expenses? I did, but business talk was very limited. I got the account, but it was weird.*

Laura W. (advertising sales):   *Entertaining has been a problem with me too, especially when it comes to paying the check. Some men must feel threatened by this.*

Brenda S. (building supply sales):   *Remember when we were girls? The boys wouldn't let us join their stupid clubs. Not much has changed, has it? Now it's the country club where decisions are made. And, damn it, don't tell me that I have to take up golf. I may get good and win. I remember my boss's reaction when I clobbered him in tennis.*

Roseann S. (textbook sales):   *Speaking of bosses, my manager's evaluation of my performance is an embarrassment. He is absolutely unable to criticize my performance. Most reviews have been late too.*

Karla H. (software programs):   *This is my second sales job. My first put me into a "pioneer" situation, industrial equipment. To succeed with that company you had to be a "superwoman" and become "one of the guys." I was told that I could not succeed without experience. What a catch-22! I can't get experience without succeeding.*

Peggy T. (chemical sales):   *You know, I've experienced a lot. This is my tenth year with _____. And I've been hassled, rejected, had to cancel a sales call due to a sick child, but I wouldn't trade it for anything. Your sales manager is really key. Mine treats me the same as he treats everybody else, but he does recognize that there are gender differences.*

The male commentators had this to say:

Bill M. (computer sales):   *Well, I can tell you this much. When the first women showed up, I was really surprised. Not that women cannot sell computers, after all many of my customers are women and most of them are really sharp, but we weren't informed that a woman had been hired.*

Joe M. (machine tool sales):   *Yeah, I was surprised too. But this "little thing" wanted to set*

the pace. You know, be the first woman ever to sell heavy-duty machinery costing $250,000 and up. She just didn't look the part, flowery dresses, heels, perfume. One of her customers called my boss and asked him to send a man the next time.

Frank C. (office furniture sales):   *We have several women in my district. Like everybody else, some are super, some are average. I think that it has been a good move. We are now selling accounts that we were unable to sell before. And our national sales manager had us attend several company training sessions on how to integrate women into the sales force.*

John R. (tractor sales):   *I know this is going to sound strange, but I don't like it. A woman's place is in the home, not out selling and taking up space that some man could occupy. They have no business selling tractors!*

Mike R. (pharmaceutical sales):   *Talk about problems. We now have several women in our sales force. You should have seen the other reps when the first one was introduced at a sales meeting. You would have thought that she was the first gal these guys had ever seen. But I just about lost it when she comes up to me one day and asks if I would help her carry some boxes to her car. "Carry them yourself" is what I should have said.*

Paul T. (building materials sales):   *The thing that bugs me is the equal rights stuff, or should I say unequal rights. I'd like to see what happens if I call the boss or a customer and tell them I can't keep an appointment because my babysitter is sick. Not only that, Susan just got back from maternity leave—something I'll never get—and I had to cover her accounts while she was gone.*

Mack H. (stockbroker):   *I don't want to play "Can You Top This," but we have a similar situation. Karen comes back off of maternity leave (this was her second child) and then decides that full-time is too much for her. She asks (and gets it too) to work only from Tuesday to Thursday. And she still gets full benefits but at a reduced salary.*

Calvin H. (chemical sales):   *We have a few women in the sales force, and the problems have been minimal. Management handled it well. They even had discussions with the sales force about how to call on customers who are women.*

Our purchasing agents, production engineers—they're all men—have had sessions on how to deal with women sales reps.

Brad M. (food product sales):   *Well, with women in my group we've had the usual mess. Office romance, you know. He was married—was, that is—and now he's divorced, and she is working for another company. I think she was fired, but nobody will admit it.*

Bob R. (aluminum sales):   *Yeah, I can identify with that. It almost caused a divorce in my house. I was expected to travel with Beth and show her the ropes. Well, my wife wanted to know what "ropes" I was going to show her. All I had to do was mention that I was going to travel with Beth, and things went to hell. It's OK now, but it was shaky for a while.*

Todd B. (commercial lending sales):   *I've made joint calls with Katherine, and I've learned a lot. I thought I knew all the answers, but watching Kate interact with customers has been a real treat. She's good and really has a knack for finding out customer needs. My own sales have increased as a result, I'm sure.*

Flanagan finished her review of the HBRS report and thought that most of the comments reinforced what she suspected were the major problems confronting women in sales. Other reports she reviewed supported the findings of the HBRS report. She wondered if she could get the remaining women in the southeastern region to discuss their feelings, attitudes, and problems with her or with a neutral third party. She knew the legal proceedings might prevent her from contacting the women. Shelley Ryan and CCLI's legal staff suggested she could bring in several women from different regions for a focus group or one-on-one sessions. Ryan told her to bring in some men too since their perceptions will be valuable. Flanagan decided to adopt this strategy. After all, regardless of the outcome of the Renoldi case, CCLI should learn as much as possible about the subject to avoid future incidents.

Flanagan decided to retain a research firm to conduct the focus group interviews with samples of women and men sales reps. Six groups of 10 sales reps each participated in the project. The sessions lasted approximately two hours. Dana Moore and Bill Carson moderated the focus groups and reported to Flanagan that they felt very positive about the process and the results. The report was

accompanied with videotapes so Flanagan could see and hear the proceedings. To remain objective, Flanagan did not review the tapes and asked Moore and Carson to prepare their verbatim comments without identifying the respondent.

Flanagan reviewed the report, hoping to find some insight as to how CCLI might avoid future problems such as the one existing in the southeastern region. Many of the comments coincided with those from the HBRS report, although a few provided additional insight concerning the problem in the southeastern region. Flanagan read with great interest the following verbatim comments from the women:

Sales rep #1:   *Basically, I like my job a lot. But it has taken me much time to get to that point. And it's been my doing, all the way, especially with the limited support that I get from my manager.*

Sales rep #2:   *Speaking of support, some of the guys I work with view me as a threat to their precious power structure. One guy told me that I should be home making soup and not taking up space that a man could fill.*

Sales rep #3:   *I can relate to that. My manager at my last sales job was the only woman district sales manager in the company. She was told that she should not take credit for work done by the men who worked for her.*

Sales rep #4:   *It's not just how I relate to my manager but the whole support issue. I don't feel like I'm part of the company. Why just the other day, a customer asked about a new policy that he knew about but nobody told me about. I asked one of the men in our office, and he knew.*

Sales rep #5:   *I had a similar situation just the other day, and I don't like having to say, "I don't know the answer, but I'll find out for you." But I knew that the customer expected an answer then, not later.*

Sales rep #6:   *I'd like to think that if I needed an answer my manager would be the logical source. But in my office I ask one of the other women.*

Sales rep #7:   *I really question the ability of the higher-ups to tell me what's going on. It would be great to have a mentor or someone that I could rely on for the straight scoop.*

Sales rep #8:   *Hey, I don't want to seem odd, but my manager is really supportive. I told him about my problem taking a customer to dinner and getting into the hassle about who pays the bill. The customer just would not let a woman buy him dinner. My manager said I should join the Capital Club and take customers there where the bill doesn't come to the table. It works like a charm.*

Sales rep #9:   *I've had a similar experience. A customer, a good one, sent me a bottle of Passion perfume and a cashmere sweater. I was dumbfounded and asked my manager what to do, since I didn't recall hearing anything about receiving gifts during our training program. He gave me several suggestions, and I decided which one to try. It worked, and I still have the account.*

Sales rep #10:   *My manager is pretty supportive. But he can't eliminate the hassling that goes on with some customers. Do the purchasing agents and others with CCLI treat women sales reps the same?*

Sales rep #11:   *I'd really like a chance to move into sales management. That's why I got into sales to begin with. Now, all I have to do is figure out what it takes to get promoted. It's a big mystery at CCLI. And if something doesn't happen soon, I'll go elsewhere.*

Sales rep #12:   *This whole performance evaluation process is a joke. My manager is usually late, and on top of it the review is so general and vague that I have no idea what I'm supposed to do to better myself. And our annual bonuses show no relation to contribution. We all get the same bonus.*

The comments from the men did not add anything to her understanding of CCLI's problems. They were very similar to those provided by HBRS, plus they duplicated many of the comments made by the women concerning performance evaluations and promotion policies.

The report suggested to Diane Flanagan that CCLI has much work ahead if it is going to avoid problems similar to those in the southeastern region. Although names were not given in the report, Flanagan thought she could associate many of the comments with James Bradford, CCLI's problem sales manager. She did not learn anything from the focus groups that would help with the legal proceedings in the Suzette Renoldi matter. But, for certain, she wanted to change things to avoid future problems.

Case 2.2

On-Time Package Delivery

Sitting in his office Wayne Jacobson, Senior Vice President of Sales, was getting ready for his meeting tomorrow with Justin Spencer, President and Chief Operating Officer at On-Time Package Delivery (OTPD). Jacobson had spent the last several weeks talking with district managers, salespeople, and customers gathering information. He knew there were several issues facing the OTPD sales force, and his job was to identify them and develop solutions to solve the problems.

ON-TIME PACKAGE DELIVERY, INCORPORATED

On-Time Package Delivery is a regional package delivery service based in New York. With sales of just more than $50 million, the company is overshadowed by the big names in package delivery: UPS, FedEx, and the U.S. Postal Service. However, OTPD has carved out a niche by focusing on express intracity package delivery. In large cities like New York, Boston, and Philadelphia there are many documents and small packages that need to get across town in a hurry. OTPD was projected to hit its overall sales goals for the year. However, Jacobson also knew that OTPD was targeting only 4 percent sales growth, which was significantly below industry average growth of 8 percent.

In 1980, Ron Young founded OTPD as the solution to a problem he had been encountering as an attorney— getting important legal documents to clients quickly, reliably, and cost effectively. Young and a group of investors developed a business model that included highly trained "delivery specialists" (package pickup and delivery people). Another key to success was that OTPD was among the first intracity package delivery services to maximize technology in the package delivery business. A high level of customer service coupled with excellent technology helped establish a loyal client following among professional business services (law firms, consulting services).

Very early, OTPD realized the need for a sales force to build and maintain client relationships. Over the years, senior management believed the sales force represented a real competitive advantage for the company. The

Source: Mark W. Johnston, 2007.

company currently had four sales districts, all in major eastern U.S. cities (Exhibit 1 details the structure of the OTPD sales force).

THE OTPD SALES FORCE

The OTPD sales force consisted of two categories of salespeople. With approximately 45 salespeople in the company, nearly 75 percent were classified as sales representatives. These individuals had two primary job responsibilities: (1) generate new business and (2) maintain a good customer relationship with smaller established accounts. The second of the two categories, key account managers, were senior salespeople responsible for the largest accounts. For this group, success was measured by the increase in sales for each account as well as customer satisfaction scores collected twice a year. Each district had two to three key account managers.

The sales force consisted of men (60 percent of the sales force) and women (40 percent) in their 30s and 40s. Sales representatives tended to be younger (30s), while key account managers were older (40s). When a key account manager position became open, the policy of the company was to promote a sales representative.

The compensation and benefits package was above average for the industry. Experienced sales representatives could earn $81,000–92,000 a year in salary and bonuses, key account manager compensation was $92,000–95,000, and district managers averaged $145,000. In addition, each member of the sales force was given a laptop and cell phone with unlimited usage. In reality, many salespeople used the cell phone as the primary phone for work and personal activities. Each salesperson was also given a car and enrolled in a retirement plan with the company.

A CONVERSATION WITH DAN GUNTHER, DISTRICT MANAGER IN BOSTON

One of the first people Jacobson contacted was Dan Gunther, district manager in Boston. Dan, a 15-year veteran with OTPD, had started out as a sales

EXHIBIT 1   **Organizational chart for on- time package delivery, December 2007**

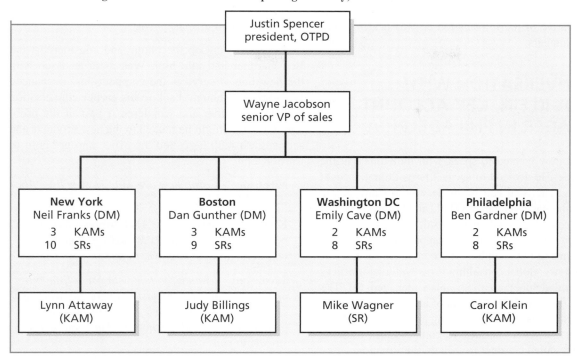

KAM = key account manager
SR = sales representative
DM = district manager

representative after graduation. He had been promoted to key account manager and finally been given the Boston district almost three years ago. Boston was the second-largest market for OTPD, after New York, and Gunther had done a good job with the district. When he took over, the Boston district was stagnant, with little or no growth, and through his leadership sales had risen 25 percent in two of the three years he had been manager. Indeed, Boston had been the number-one district at OTPD for two of the three previous years. After the usual small talk Jacobson got down to business:

Jacobson: *I noticed sales are flat for the last six months in Boston, what do you think is the problem?*

Gunther: *Don't worry; it is a short-term issue. Everything is fine. My salespeople are working hard. We have just had a run of bad luck. You know sometimes things don't go your way for a while but we will turn it around.*

Jacobson: *Dan I think it may be more than that. There has been an increase in client complaints. For example, I got a call from Craig McMillan,*

managing partner at Clark, Burton, and Bowers, about the lack of service. As you know, Clark, Burton, and Bowers have been with us for many years and are one of our largest customers with offices in New York, Boston, and Washington D.C. While you are not responsible for New York or D.C., McMillan indicated that Judy Billings, our key account manager in Boston, has been slow in responding to questions and not as responsive as she used to be.

Gunther: *Look Wayne, we are working hard here in Boston. Judy is one of my best salespeople and consistently hits her sales goals. It's not her fault if the folks at Clark, Burton, and Bowers make unreasonable demands.*

Dan did have a point. Judy was a solid performer and, as a result, she had been promoted to key account manager two years ago. One of her largest accounts was Clark, Burton, and Bowers. With more than 100 attorneys in Boston, they generated a lot of business for OTPD. Clark, Burton, and Bowers had been a customer for a long time and Jacobson did not believe them to be overly demanding. He spoke with several other district managers, but his conversation with Dan Gunther was representative of the information he was hearing from all the managers.

A CONVERSATION WITH CAROL KLEIN, KEY ACCOUNT MANAGER IN PHILADELPHIA

Jacobson now wanted to speak with individuals in the sales force. He decided to speak first with key account managers. The final call he made was to Carol Klein. She is a nine-year veteran of OTPD and followed the traditional path of promotion from sales representative to key account manager. Carol is responsible for the largest accounts in Philadelphia. These included several law firms and two global consulting firms with major offices in the Philadelphia area. She also managed OTPD's business for two of the three major hospitals in the area.

Jacobson was sensitive to going around the local district manager, Ben Gardner, to contact Carol directly, so he first called Gardner to explain the situation.

Jacobson: *Hi Ben, I wanted to give you a heads up on something.*

Gardner: *Sure Wayne, what's up?*

Jacobson: *I am going to give Carol Klein a call about why her sales numbers have been flat over the last year.*

Gardner: *Wayne, you know Carol had a hard time introducing our new line of value added services to her clients. Indeed, many of our salespeople found their clients resistant to our new products and services. After the initial training on the new services our salespeople have not had any follow up.*

Jacobson: *I understand Ben and I want to make it clear that I am not singling Carol out so don't be concerned. The reason I want to give Carol a call is that I respect her opinion and want to ask her what she thinks is going on with the sales force in general. I am calling you because I wanted you to know about the call from me first. In addition, I wanted you to know that this is not directed at you or the Philadelphia district in particular. Rather, it is information for me to consider for the entire company.*

Gardner: *Great, well thanks for the call. I believe Carol will be in the office after 4:00 this afternoon if you want to give her a call.*

Jacobson hung up the phone and considered what Ben Gardner had told him. Was there an issue with the new line of services the company had introduced last year? He thought back to his earlier conversation with Dan Gunther and wondered if part of the problem in Boston might be related to the new products and services. At 4:30 he called the office and got hold of Carol Klein:

Jacobson: *Carol, how are you? How is little Alice doing these days?*

Klein: *Things are busy. Alice is great and almost two years old now, thanks for asking. Ben told me you were going to call, what's up?*

Jacobson: *I wanted to talk with you a little bit about your sales for the last year. You are usually among our top salespeople. Ben tells me you are a great colleague and has nothing but good things to say about you.*

Klein: *I appreciate that and want to say that I very much enjoy working for Ben; he is a terrific manager.*

Jacobson: *So, why are your sales numbers flat or even a little down?*

Klein: *To be honest Wayne, the job is getting difficult. When I started with OTPD, Jeff (Carol's husband) and I were both really involved with our careers and I was able to dedicate a lot of time and effort to my work. When Alice arrived I made the decision to keep working. OTPD has been great and I have enjoyed my success here as a key account manager. However, I find myself being torn between doing an outstanding job at OTPD and being a mom to Alice. I know that this has affected my effort and commitment to clients over the last six to eight months.*

Jacobson (surprised by Klein's comments):
Well Carol, I know I speak for Ben and the entire company in saying we only want what is best for you and your family. Perhaps you need to consider your options and talk to Ben about this in more detail. We can certainly talk about this again soon. Well, I need to get going but please feel free to contact me if and when you want to talk about this further.

Klein's comments had taken Jacobson by surprise. It had not occurred to him that Carol would be talking about family issues; however, as he began to consider the issues facing the company he realized that family and personal issues could be a factor for the sales force.

A CONVERSATION WITH MIKE WAGNER, SALES REPRESENTATIVE IN THE WASHINGTON D.C. DISTRICT

Jacobson next wanted to talk with several sales representatives. He followed the same procedure as before, contacting Emily Cave, district manager for the Washington D.C. area, and explaining the reason for his call to Wagner. In the brief conversation, Cave mentioned that Wagner remained one of the district's better salespeople. He consistently met sales goals and customers were generally satisfied with his service. Mike Wagner is single, in his late 30s and a six-year veteran of OTPD. He is currently in line for promotion to key account manager. Jacobson caught up with Wagner in the office late in the day:

Jacobson: *Hi Mike, how are you?*

Wagner: *I am well Wayne, thanks. How are things with you?*

Jacobson: *Good; things are very busy as usual. Mike, I wanted to give you a call and chat a little about your sales figures for the last six months. First, I want you to know that I am not here to be negative about your performance. Emily tells me you are a good performer. My call is to get a better understanding of the issues and problems facing the sales force today.*

Wagner: *Fire away. As you know Wayne, I will tell you what I think.*

Jacobson: *I know you will and that is what I am looking for. So, why do you think your sales growth is down from recent years?*

Wagner: *I can only speak for me; however, in talking with other salespeople I think we are all facing the same issues. Primarily, the competition is really pushing hard these days. I recently visited First Call Medical Centers and they told me that Gold Package Delivery Services was offering a similar package of services to ours at a lower cost. To be honest, I didn't have a good answer for them, and unfortunately, that has been happening a lot lately.*

Jacobson: *Do you feel you needed more information on the competition in order to respond the questions from First Call Medical?*

Wagner: *Yes, I did not have a good understanding of how our products and services compared with Gold Package Delivery.*

Jacobson: *Thanks, Mike. I appreciate your feedback. Good luck and please feel free to contact me anytime.*

Jacobson considered the phone call and began to formulate some ideas on improving the performance of the sales force. However, there was still an important group he needed to hear from—customers.

A CONVERSATION WITH CARMELLA STRINGER, DIRECTOR OF ADMINISTRATIVE SERVICES FOR THE LAW FIRM OF STRAWN, NIGHT, AND SQUIRES

Jacobson wanted to complete his research by hearing from a few customers. After speaking with three clients, several issues began to emerge. He thought he would call one more customer, Carmella Stringer at Strawn, Night, and Squires (SNS), before his meeting with Justin Spencer. Strawn, Night, and Squires is the largest law firm in the Northeast and OTPD's biggest client. Indeed, Ron Young was an attorney with the firm when he started OTPD, and the law firm was among the company's first clients. SNS is a New York account and Lynn Attaway is the key account manager. However, Jacobson had been responsible for SNS when he was a key account manager and had always maintained an interest in the account. Indeed, he often made sales calls with Lynn, and while the relationship was unusual, Jacobson maintained it because (1) SNS was the company's largest and most important account and (2) he wanted to stay close to the customer and be involved in selling.

Carmella had been the director of administrative services for 10 years, and Jacobson had a very good working relationship with her. She had never been afraid to offer suggestions or criticisms in the past, and he felt she would give him straight answers. He picked up the phone and called her:

Jacobson: *Hi Carmella, how are things at Strawn, Night, and Squires?*

Stringer: *Good thanks; it seems like everyone needs an attorney!*

Jacobson: *I wanted to check in and see how OTPD was treating you. Have we been doing a good job for you?*

Stringer: *Wayne, I am glad you called because, to be honest, we had a serious problem the other day. As you know Lynn has been working hard to introduce your new services into our firm. She was very persuasive and we have been using some of those services such as express delivery. Well, two days ago SNS had a client across town wait more than five hours for a package that was promised in two hours. As you know, I am charged extra for express service and OTPD did not deliver.*

Jacobson (in shock):   *Carmella, first let me apologize for the missed delivery time. Let me assure you that we will deal with this issue internally and that this will not happen again. I will follow up on this and get back with you by the end of the day.*

Stringer: *Thanks Wayne, I would appreciate that very much.*

Jacobson was not happy. This kind of service was unacceptable with any customer, let alone OTPD's biggest. He decided to first call Neil Franks, district manager in New York, to get his take on the situation. Neil indicated that he was aware of the incident and suggested he call Lynn Attaway to find out the specifics of what happened.

Jacobson: *Hi Lynn, I just got off the phone with Carmella Stringer from Strawn, Night, and Squire.*

She is not happy about something that happened a few days ago.

Attaway: *Wayne, I know and I am glad you called. I had been meaning to call you because I know you are very interested in what happens at SNS. Essentially, there was a mistake in how the package was entered into the system. Carmella notified the package delivery specialist about the express delivery request but did not mark it on the newly revised "package expedite form" (PEF). The package delivery specialist never noted it, and the package went through the normal same-day delivery sorting procedure. In all honesty Wayne, I am at fault here as I was not aware of the changes to the PEF and did not notify Carmella that she needed to note "express delivery" on the form.*

Jacobson: *I am glad to hear we have found out what happened. You need to follow up with Carmella. In addition, do whatever is necessary to keep her and SNS happy. I heard you mention that you were not aware of the changes to the PEF. Did you not see the e-mail I sent last month regarding the new forms?*

Attaway: *Wayne, I get dozens of e-mails every day and that one must have slipped by me. There have been so many changes to our services, forms, pricing, and overall business model that it is difficult to keep up with them. It won't happen again.*

Attaway was a good key account manager, and if she was missing important information then others were probably doing the same thing. He got back with Carmella Stringer and assured her this would not happen again and Lynn would be in touch with her to make sure everything is taken care of with SNS.

All the data he collected certainly gave Jacobson a lot to think about. He began to prepare his presentation for Justin Spencer tomorrow. Given everything that has happened what do you think that report should say?

Case 2.3

Spectrum Brands, Inc.— The Sales Force Dilemma

IVEY

Richard Ivey School of Business
The University of Western Ontario

> We are in the business of building our strengths by
> managing brands . . . as retailers get bigger . . . we get
> bigger to fight fire with fire. I'm now in the business
> of managing BRANDS, not simply PRODUCTS!

It was November 2005, and Bob Falconi, vice-president of sales and marketing for the Canadian division of Spectrum Brands Inc., was sitting in his new Brantford, Ontario office, pondering his next steps regarding his sales force. During the course of the last year, the company had gone through a number of changes at the global level. Spectrum Brands (Spectrum), a global consumer products company formerly known as Rayovac Corporation, had made a number of acquisitions to diversify and expand its product and brand portfolio. With these changes, Spectrum had become a leading supplier of consumer batteries, lawn and garden care products, specialty pet supplies, and shaving and grooming products.

Falconi, charged with the task of creating a national sales force from the teams of the newly merged companies, sat in his office trying to make sense of the new business. He knew that creating an effective sales team—one which would capitalize on the synergies across the various businesses—would be very difficult, since these companies each operated differently with regards to the role of their sales forces, customers targeted and products sold. Knowing the importance of the sales function to each of these companies, Falconi wanted to ensure, despite the differences amongst the diverse groups, that he still maintained a team that would effectively and

Source: Joe Falconi wrote this case under the supervision of Professor Don Barclay solely to provide material for class discussion. The authors do not intend to illustrate either effective or ineffective handling of a managerial situation. The authors may have disguised certain names and other identifying information to protect confidentiality.

efficiently continue to increase the sales of each business unit.

The task ahead of him was big, but Falconi knew that a plan needed to be implemented immediately to avoid disrupting the growth momentum of the company's individual brands, to maintain customer relationships, and to preclude competition from taking advantage of any perceived disruptions during this time of change.

THE CONTEXT

The consumer brands industry had become highly competitive on a global basis. Numerous acquisitions and mergers had taken place over the past decade, resulting in a select group of large companies with extensive brand portfolios. These companies had developed numerous product lines that allowed them to compete in a variety of markets and product categories, and also strengthened their relationships with retailers.

With the growth of large retail chains across North America through retail consolidation, the balance of power had shifted away from manufacturers. Small players could no longer compete effectively, as strong relationships with retailers had become essential in order to compete for limited and valuable shelf space within stores. Manufacturers built alliances with other consumer brand companies in order to gain strength and power in the retail market. As a result, companies such as Procter & Gamble (P&G), Unilever, S.C. Johnson, and others with large portfolios of popular consumer brands, dominated the shelves in traditional retail channels including Grocery (e.g. Loblaw, Dominion), Drug stores (e.g. Shoppers Drug Mart, Katz Group), Hardware retailers (e.g. Home Hardware), Home and Garden retailers (e.g. RONA, The Home Depot) and Mass Merchandisers (e.g. Wal-Mart). Internet and direct-to-consumer sales had not proven to be valuable alternate channels for these companies, as retailers would retaliate by de-listing products of those manufacturers who tried to go in this direction.

Companies competing against the brands under the umbrellas of these large companies continued to struggle for position and, ultimately, for market share, mainly because of the established relationships that these large firms had with the retailers. The trend was towards companies such as Spectrum Brands who had a presence in batteries, shaving and grooming products, lawn and garden products, and specialty pet supplies.

CONSUMER BRANDS MARKETS

BATTERY MARKET

North American consumers of household batteries (AAA, AA, C, D and 9-volt standard batteries) sought convenience and quality when purchasing batteries and tended to gravitate towards the brand names they knew and trusted. Duracell and Energizer continued to dominate the market due to their brand recognition, their relationships with distributors and retailers, and their established presence in the large one-time-use alkaline battery category. These two firms were leaders in this market for decades because of their ability to adapt to consumer needs and to merge with other consumer goods companies to create brand portfolios, thus gaining valuable negotiating power with retailers. For example, the Duracell battery brand was owned by the largest and most recognized consumer products company in the world—Procter & Gamble (P&G)—while the Energizer battery brand was owned by Energizer Holdings Inc., which also owned the Shick Razors brand. Each company held a 40 percent market share within the battery industry.

Household batteries were sold through wholesalers, distributors, professionals and OEMs, but the large majority were sold through traditional retail channels. Of these retailers, mass merchandisers, home and garden centers and niche electronic stores accounted for more than 60 percent of sales.

As of 2005, the alkaline battery was the predominant type of household battery in North America, and was offered by all major competitors in all sizes. The growth within this segment had become relatively flat, at only one to two percent annually, yet, due to its size, it was expected to dominate the market for the next five to 10 years. In 2005, the overall battery market in Canada was estimated to be $300[1] million, with the alkaline category representing 70 percent, the rechargeable category making up 10 percent, and other battery chemistries, including zinc, representing 20 percent.

The market for household batteries was highly seasonal. The large majority of sales occurred during the months leading up to and following Christmas sales of electronics and other battery-operated devices. Close to 70 percent of battery sales occurred during this period.

SHAVING AND GROOMING PRODUCTS MARKET

The shaving and grooming products industry was dominated by a select group of companies selling electric shavers and accessories, electric grooming products and hair care appliances. Electric shavers included both rotary and foil designs for men and women, and accessories included replacement parts, pre-shave products and cleaning agents for shavers. Electric grooming products included beard/moustache trimmers, nose and ear trimmers, haircut kits and related accessories. Hair care appliances included hair dryers, setters, curling irons, crimpers, straighteners and hot air brushes.

The shaving and grooming products market was growing at a rate of three to four percent annually, and this trend was likely to continue. The market for electronic shaving and grooming products was highly seasonal with peaks during the months leading up to and following the Christmas holiday season and around Father's Day and Mother's Day weekends. The majority of these products were purchased as gifts, and thus the sales cycle followed these gift-giving seasons.

The primary competitors in the shaving market included: Norelco, Braun and Remington. Norelco was a division of Koninklijke Philips Electronics (Philips), which was one of the world's biggest electronics companies and the largest one in Europe. Braun was a member of the Gillette family of products which was now part of P&G, while Remington was part of Spectrum. Norelco only sold rotary shavers, Braun only offered foil shavers, while Remington was the only company competing in both segments. Quality, price and brand awareness were the main factors influencing sales in this segment.

The major competitors in the hair care market were Remington, Norelco, Conair Corporation and Helen of Troy Limited. Each company offered a complete line of hair care products and accessories and competed on quality and price within this category.

Competitors within both of these segments sold their products largely through traditional retail channels with a heavy emphasis on mass merchandisers and specialty retailers such as salons and hair and body care shops. Like all consumer product companies, those firms able to maintain or increase the amount of retail shelf space

---

[1] All funds are in Canadian dollars unless otherwise indicated.

allocated to their respective products could gain share of mind and, potentially, a share of the market.

LAWN AND GARDEN MARKET

The lawn and garden market was a US$4 billion industry in North America, with an additional US$1 billion in sales of household insect control products. Companies manufactured and marketed fertilizers, herbicides, outdoor insect control products, rodenticides, plant foods, potting soil, grass seeds and other growing media. The lawn and garden industry had been driven largely by affluent baby boomers who enjoyed gardening and also by increasing home ownership levels. Growth in this market had been between 4 and 5 percent annually and was expected to continue at this pace. In North America, more than 80 percent of households were participating in at least one lawn and garden activity in 2004.

The main competitors within the lawn and garden segment included: United Industries (United)/Nu-Gro, Scotts Miracle-Gro Company (Scotts) and Central Garden &Pet Company (CGPC). Scotts marketed products under the Scotts and Miracle-Gro brand names. They led this market with a 30 percent market share. CGPC sat behind United with a 17 percent market share. They sold garden products under the Amdro, Image and Pennington Seed brand names.

Growth in the insect control market had been generated by population growth in the insect-prone Sunbelt region and the heightened awareness of insect-borne diseases such as West Nile virus. Growth in this market had been slightly higher than historical levels since 2002 with a 7 to 8 percent annual growth rate.

In the insect control market, the major competitors included United, Scotts and S.C. Johnson & Son, Inc. Scotts, once again the market leader, sold products under the Ortho and Roundup brand names, while S.C. Johnson marketed their insecticide and repellent products under the Raid and OFF! brands.

Competitors within both of these markets sold mainly through mass merchandisers, home centers, independent nurseries and hardware stores. Home centers and mass merchandisers typically carried one or two premium brands and one value brand on their shelves. Obtaining and maintaining share of shelf within these retailers was critical as 50 to 60 percent of sales passed through these two channels.

The lawn and garden market was also highly seasonal. Products were shipped to distributors and retailers beginning as early as March in preparation for the spring season. Demand for products typically peaked during the first six months of the calendar year. This seasonality created a major risk within this industry, as there was a heavy dependence on weather to drive sales. A poor season greatly hindered the bottom line.

SPECIALTY PET SUPPLY MARKET

The specialty pet supply industry had historically been one of the fastest growing consumer product categories with annual growth between six and eight percent. This category consisted of aquatic equipment (i.e. aquariums, filters, pumps), aquatic consumables (i.e. fish food, water treatments, conditioners) and specialty pet products for dogs, cats, birds and other small domestic animals. In North America, this was an US$8 billion market in 2004, and was expected to grow to over US$11 billion by 2007.

Much of this growth could be attributed to the increasing levels of pet ownership. On average, households with children under the age of 18, and adults over 55 (who were typically "empty nesters"), tended to keep pets as companions and had more disposable income and leisure time to spend with them. In North America, both of these categories have expanded rapidly with the aging of the baby boomer population. As of 2004, 62 percent of households in the United States owned a pet, and 46 percent owned two or more pets. In addition to these trends, the growing movement towards pet humanization— the tendency of pet owners to treat pets like cherished members of the family—had also factored greatly into this market expansion.

The specialty pet supply industry was highly fragmented. There were over 500 manufacturers in North America, consisting of both small companies with limited product lines and larger firms. No company held a market share of greater than 10 percent. The largest competitors included: CGPC, United Pet Group/Tetra and the Hartz Mountain Corporation. CGPC led the market with a nine percent market share.

Products within this segment were sold through specialty pet stores, independent pet retailers, mass merchants, grocery stores and through various professional outlets. Mass merchandisers, supermarkets and discounters increasingly supplied pet products, but they focused mainly on a limited selection of items such as pet food. The majority of sales were made through pet supply stores, of which there were over 15,000 in the United States and more than 5,000 in Canada. There were only two national retailers in this industry: PetsMart and PetCo. PetsMart accounted for 10 percent of North American pet product net sales in fiscal 2004. PetCo reflected similar statistics, but no other retailer accounted for more than eight percent of industry retail sales.

Sales in this segment remained fairly stable throughout the year since pets needed to be maintained continuously.

COMPETITIVE CONTEXT

In all of these industries, some competitors had gained significant market share and had explicitly committed significant resources to protecting share and/or stealing share from others. In some product lines, competitors had lower production costs and higher profit margins, enabling them to compete more aggressively through advertising and by offering retail discounts and other promotional incentives to retailers, distributors and

wholesalers. This aggressive strategy obviously provided additional strength in attracting retailers and consumers. The ability to retain or increase the amount of retail shelf space allocated to their respective products provided competitive advantages in each of these market spaces.

SPECTRUM BRANDS, INC.

Spectrum brands products were available through the world's top 25 retailers, in over one million stores throughout North America, Europe, Asia Pacific, the Middle East, Africa, Latin America and Brazil. Overall, the company was generating US$2.8 billion in annualized revenues from its brand portfolio (see Exhibits 1 and 2 for Spectrum pre-merger and consolidated financial information).

EXHIBIT 1   (**Numbers based on fiscal year ending September**)

Rayovac Corporation Net Sales Breakdown

Consolidated Net Sales by Product line (US$ millions)	2005	2004*
Batteries	$ 968	$ 939
Lights	94	90
Shaving & Grooming	271	272
Personal Care	143	116
Lawn and Garden	447	N/A
Household Insect Control	150	N/A
Pet Products	286	N/A
Totals	**$2,359**	**$1,417**

*United/Nu-Gro was acquired by Rayovac mid 2005.

Rayovac & Remington

(US$ millions)	Rayovac 2004	Rayovac 2003	Remington 2004	Remington 2003*
Net Sales	$1,029	$922	$388	N/A
Gross Profit	42.8%	38.1%	47.0%	N/A
Operating Income	109	$ 60	47	N/A
Net Income	$ 39	$ 15	$ 17	N/A

*Remington was acquired by Rayovac mid 2003.

United Industries and Tetra

North America (US$ millions)	United 2005	Tetra 2005
Net Sales from External customers	$787	$96
Segment Profit	$ 79	$10
SP as % of Net Sales	10.0%	10.4%

Similar to its competitors, Rayovac had acquired other consumer brand companies to enhance its ability to gain retail presence. Beginning in 2003, Rayovac acquired Remington Products Inc., a company specializing in consumer shaving and grooming products. In February 2005, Spectrum Brands was created when the Rayovac Corporation acquired United Industries Corporation (a leading U.S. manufacturer of consumer lawn and garden care, and insect control products), Nu-Gro Corporation (the Canadian subsidiary of United, specializing in lawn and garden care products) and Tetra Holdings Inc. (a leading supplier of fish and aquatics supplies). Continued growth and strategic acquisitions allowed the company to leverage global distribution channels, purchasing power and operational processes. These mergers provided the company with an extended brand portfolio. This allowed all of the brands to access a number of new retailers where they had not previously been able to gain shelf space. In turn, this increased the ability for each brand to compete within its given markets. Spectrum became the global leader in aquatic supplies; the number two player in the lawn and garden industry, the household insect control market, and the shaving and grooming supplies industry; and the third largest global company in the battery industry (see Exhibit 3 for a list of brand names under the Spectrum label).

RAYOVAC

Rayovac was the third largest global consumer battery manufacturer in the world—third largest in North America and second largest in Europe. The company sold batteries and flashlights for various household and industrial uses and was the largest worldwide seller of hearing aid batteries. Their battery product line included one-time-use alkaline and Nickel Metal Hydride (NiMH) rechargeable batteries available in all standard sizes (AAA, AA, C, D, 9-Volt) to compete in the highly saturated but lucrative household market. Globally, Rayovac held a 14 percent market share, with a 20 percent share of the Canadian market. The division generated US$1.5 billion in annual global revenues in 2004.

The company began operations in 1906, but did not introduce the Rayovac name until the 1930s. Their

EXHIBIT 2

SPECTRUM BRANDS, INC. AND SUBSIDIARIES CONSOLIDATED STATEMENTS OF OPERATIONS (years ended Septemeber 30, 2005, 2004) (US$ 000s)		
	2005	**2004**
Net Sales	$2,359,447	$1,417,186
Cost of goods sold	1,465,096	811,894
Restructuring and related charges	10,496	(781)
Gross Profit	883,855	606,073
Operating Expenses:		
Selling	473,834	293,118
General and Administration	160,382	121,319
Research and Development	29,339	23,192
Restructuring and related charges	15,820	12,224
	679,375	449,853
Operating Income	204,480	156,220
Interest expense	134,053	65,702
Other income, net	(856)	(14)
Income from continuing operations before taxes	71,283	90,532
Income tax expense	24,451	34,372
Income from continuing operations	46,832	56,160
Loss from discontinued operations, net of tax benefits	-	380
Net Income	$ 46,832	$ 55,780

(continued)

EXHIBIT 2   *(concluded)*

SPECTRUM BRANDS, INC. AND SUBSIDIARIES CONSOLIDATED BALANCE SHEETS
(years ended Septement 30, 2005, 2004)
(US$ 000s)

	2005	2004
Assets		
Current Assets:		
Cash and cash equivalents	$ 29,852	$ 13,971
Receivables:		
Trade A/R, net of allowances	$ 362,399	$ 269,977
Other	$ 10,996	$ 19,655
Inventories	$ 451,553	$ 264,726
Deferred income taxes	$ 39,231	$ 19,233
Assets held for sale	$ 108,174	$ 9,870
Prepaid expenses and other	$ 45,762	$ 51,262
Total Current Assets	$1,047,967	$ 648,694
Property, plant and equipment, net	$ 304,323	$ 182,396
Deferred charges and other	$ 47,375	$ 35,079
Goodwill	$1,429,017	$ 320,577
Intangible assets, net	$1,154,397	$ 422,106
Debt issuance costs	$ 39,012	$ 25,299
Total Assets	$4,022,091	$1,634,151
Liabilities and Shareholder's Equity		
Current Liabilities:		
Current maturities of LT debt	$ 39,308	$ 23,895
Accounts payable	$ 281,954	$ 226,234
Accrued liabilities:		
Wages and benefits	$ 47,910	$ 40,138
Income taxes payable	$ 40,468	$ 21,672
Restructuring and related charges	$ 16,978	$ 8,505
Accrued interest	$ 31,529	$ 16,302
Liabilities held for sale	$ 22,294	$ —
Other	$ 76,935	$ 60,094
Total Current Liabilities	$ 557,376	$ 396,840
Long-term debt, net of current maturities	$2,268,025	$ 806,002
Employee benefit obligations, net of current portion	$ 78,510	$ 69,246
Deferred income taxes	$ 208,251	$ 7,272
Other	$ 67,199	$ 37,368
Total Liabilities	$3,179,361	$1,316,728
Minority interest in equity of consolidated subsidiary	$ —	$ 1,379
Shareholders' equity:		
Common Stock	$ 666	$ 642
Additional paid-in capital	$ 671,378	$ 224,962
Retained earnings	$ 267,315	$ 220,483
Accumulated other comprehensive income (loss)	$ 10,260	$ 10,621
Notes receivable from officers/shareholders	$ —	$ (3,605)
	$ 949,619	$ 453,103
Less treasury stock, at cost	$ (70,820)	$ (130,070)
Less unearned restricted stock compensation	$ (36,069)	$ (6,989)
Total Shareholders' equity	$ 842,730	$ 316,044
Total Liabilities and Shareholders' equity	$4,022,091	$1,634,151

Source: 2005 Spectrum Brands Inc. Annual Report.

EXHIBIT 3

BATTERY & LIGHTING PRODUCTS

SHAVING, GROOMING & HAIR CARE PRODUCTS

LAWN & GARDEN CARE

INSECT CONTROLPRODUCTS

AQUARIUM PRODUCTS & SUPPLIES

PET PRODUCTS & SUPPLIES

initial focus was on manufacturing specialty batteries for use in such devices as their patented vacuum tube hearing aids. The company expanded and grew through their continued development of state-of-the-art flashlights and non-traditional batteries, including their successful hearing aid battery line. They eventually entered the competitive household battery market through key acquisitions and by capitalizing on existing distributor and retailer relationships. This was long after the market leaders, Duracell and Energizer, had become well-established within this market. Rayovac made great strides over its last few years in an attempt to gain ground. Acquisitions had been made to gain access to international markets including Europe (Varta Battery Corporation acquired in 2002), China (Ningbo Baowang acquired in 2004) and Brazil (Microlite acquired in 2004).

The leaders in this industry had leading brands and thus greater control over distribution channels, retailers and prices. Rayovac had only been able to secure shelf space in a small number of retailers, including Wal-Mart (making up 40 percent of sales), Canadian Tire (15 percent of sales), Home Hardware (10 percent of sales), and other chains and smaller niche retailers such as Toys R' Us, Radio Shack and others (35 percent of sales).

REMINGTON PRODUCTS COMPANY

Remington was a leading designer and distributor of consumer shaving and personal care products in North America and the United Kingdom. They marketed a broad line of electric shaving and grooming products for both men and women, as well as hair care products and other personal care items.

Beginning operations in 1936 as a division of Remington Rand, Remington captured a strong position as a global player in the market by developing new innovative shaving products. Before being bought by Rayovac Corporation in 2003, the Remington Electric Shaver Division had been involved in various mergers: merging with the Sperry Corporation in 1955; being bought by entrepreneur Victor Kiam in 1979; and then acquiring Clairol Inc.'s worldwide personal care appliance business in 1993. Through all of these moves, Remington was able to command a 30 percent market share in North America and a 21 percent share in the United Kingdom, with the number one position in men's foil shavers, women's foil shavers, and men's grooming products, and the number two position in men's rotary

shavers globally. Remington had become an established name in the industry, achieving global revenues of US$350 million in 2003.

Remington, like Rayovac, sold its products largely through traditional retail channels. The breakdown of retailers was similar to that of Rayovac, with the niche retailers being salons and specialty hair and body care shops.

UNITED INDUSTRIES CORPORATION

United Industries Corporation was a leading manufacturer and marketer of professional and consumer lawn and garden care and insect control products. It produced a wide variety of products, including brand name items and private label products for individual retail chains. United also produced and distributed controlled release nitrogen and other fertilizer technologies to the consumer, professional and golf industries worldwide under various brand names.

United competed in the United States under the United name. In Canada, the company operated under the Nu-Gro Corporation (Nu-Gro) name. United, which began operations in the early 1950s, acquired Nu-Gro in April 2004 to serve as the Canadian arm of the company. Nu-Gro was established in 1988 as an exclusively Canadian lawn and garden company. Both were leaders within their marketplaces, maintaining a number of top-selling brands including Vigoro, Shultz and CIL.

Within the lawn and garden industry in North America, United/Nu-Gro was the number two company, holding a 23 percent market share. The company targeted consumers who wanted products comparable to and at lower prices than premium-priced brands, and thus positioned their brands as the value alternatives. In 2004, United/Nu-Gro together generated sales of US$550 million in this market.

In the household insect control industry, United/Nu-Gro generated US$150 million in sales in 2004. With their insect control brands, it was again the number two company, with 24 percent market share in North America.

The consumer division for both of these categories sold its products through various retail outlets, including home and garden centers, large home supply retailers, and general mass merchandisers. The sales breakdown was as follows: Canadian Tire (13 percent), Home Depot (9 percent), Rona (seven percent), Lowe's (6 percent), Home Hardware (five percent), Wal-Mart (3 percent), independent garden retailers (5 percent), other small retailers and garden stores (12 percent) and their professional division made up 40 percent.

The United/Nu-Gro professional division served two major markets: Professional Turf Care Products for golf courses and lawn care companies, and Professional Pest Control Products and Animal Health Products for pest control operators and farms (making up 25 and 15 percent respectively of the company's overall sales). This division had its own dedicated sales force and marketing team to manage the diverse needs of the professional customers.

United was also a leading supplier of quality products to the pet supply industry in the United States, under the United Pet Group (UPG) name. UPG operated in the fragmented U.S. pet supply market, manufacturing and marketing premium-branded pet supplies for dogs, cats, fish, birds and other small animals. Products included: aquarium kits, stand-alone tanks, filters and related items, and other aquarium supplies and accessories, as well as pet treats and supplies. This division was number two in North America, with an 8 percent market share and annual revenues in 2004 totalling US$250 million (figure includes Tetra sales). This division sold its products through large mass merchandisers, while also targeting the larger pet supply chains of PetsMart and PetCo, and the considerable number of independent pet supplies stores.

TETRA HOLDINGS

Tetra Holdings was a global supplier of fish and aquatic supplies, operating in over 90 countries worldwide and holding leading market positions in Germany, Japan, the United States and the United Kingdom. They manufactured, distributed and marketed a comprehensive premier line of foods, equipment and care products for fish and reptiles, along with accessories for home aquariums and ponds.

Tetra was founded in Germany in the early 1950s, pioneering the development of flake fish foods. The company grew into one of the most recognized global brand names in the pet supplies industry. In addition to the products they offered, they also published hundreds of books on aquarium fish keeping, reptile and amphibian keeping, and water gardening.

Tetra was acquired by United Industries in early 2004, joining the UPG division. Despite the merger, United maintained separate operations for each brand with the exception of combining administrative functions. UPG only operated in the United States, while Tetra operated globally. These groups together held the number two position in the North American pet supply market, with 8 percent market share. Like UPG, Tetra sold its products through large mass merchandisers, while also targeting the larger pet supply chains (PetsMart and PetCo) and smaller pet supplies stores in the countries in which it operated.

BOB FALCONI

Bob Falconi completed his Executive MBA program at the Richard Ivey School of Business in 1990. He had been involved in the battery business for 27 years, working his first 16 with Duracell, where he became vice-president of sales. He left Duracell in 1995 for a new start-up battery company, Pure Energy Battery Corporation, which introduced a revolutionary new rechargeable alkaline battery system. He left Pure Energy in 1999 to serve as country manager for Rayovac Canada, and had then taken on the role of vice-president of sales and marketing for Spectrum. Throughout his career, he had developed a keen understanding of brand management, and had been given the responsibility within Spectrum to leverage his experiences.

REASONS FOR THE ACQUISITIONS

Through the evolution into Spectrum Brands, Rayovac had become a channel marketer, and purveyor of specialty brands. The Rayovac Corporation had been painted into a corner in the competitive battery market due to its lack of retail strength. In order to compete on a larger scale, greater power within retail channels was required. The company had continually looked for potenztial acquisitions where it felt that it could add value to the company's operations while at the same time creating a larger and more powerful combined company. Rayovac's goal was to grow through acquisitions that diversified and increased its revenue base while leveraging its strengths and capabilities in global merchandising and distribution.

With the Remington merger, there were many similarities between the two companies in terms of marketing and channel strategies. However, the systems Remington had in place to manage logistic processes were outdated and inefficient. Rayovac saw this as an opportunity to add value to this company through the sharing of best practices. Rayovac acquired Remington and was able to update the company's logistic processes and systems and improve the overall operations of the firm. Through this merger, Rayovac was able to drive US$35 million in annual costs out of the combined enterprise while adding the Remington revenues to Rayovac's top line.

With the recent United/Nu-Gro/Tetra acquisitions, Rayovac was looking to continue its growth and expand into new product categories. New products would provide increased negotiating strength with the larger retailers while diversifying the company's revenue base. For example, with this merger, worldwide battery sales represented approximately 40 percent of revenue as compared to the 2004 level of 67 percent. More importantly, the merger served to balance out the sales cycle for the firm given the different seasonalities of the various categories—this meant no down time for the sales force. Finally, Spectrum Brands had at least one brand in all of the major retailers in the world, a situation they hoped to leverage into having other brands in many retailers (see Exhibit 4 for annualized revenues by product category).

THE ISSUE

As Falconi looked through his notes on his individual Canadian business units and their competitive markets, he questioned how best to organize the new sales force in order to capitalize on the strengths of each brand, given the similarities and differences between them. He knew that with the recent acquisitions, the company was looking to leverage any synergies created and reduce costs where possible. However, as overarching objectives, he wanted to make sure that customers would be serviced in the same fashion, if not better, and that sales would not be affected. Falconi decided to take a look at how each business unit currently operated, and how some of their major competitors were organized (see Exhibit 5 for a post-merger organizational chart).

EXHIBIT 4

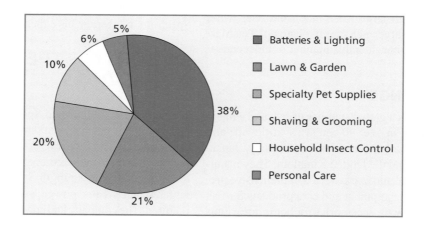

- Batteries & Lighting
- Lawn & Garden
- Specialty Pet Supplies
- Shaving & Grooming
- Household Insect Control
- Personal Care

EXHIBIT 5

THE CURRENT SALES FORCES

RAYOVAC AND REMINGTON

In Canada, the Rayovac/Remington sales force was currently organized by distribution channel. The eight sales representatives serving this division were responsible for selling all products under both the Rayovac and Remington brand names to their assigned retailers. This was a small sales team, but it had tremendous support from the U.S. office for large accounts, as well as for marketing and trade promotion campaign design. Sales targeted towards hearing aid professionals and industrial and OEM distributors were handled from the U.S. office.

These sales representatives were organized geographically as well. The allocation was as follows: six in Toronto, and one in each of Vancouver and Montreal. Each representative was responsible for the retailers in their regions. Toronto had a greater number of corporate head offices, thus requiring more representatives to service these accounts.

The average base salary for these sales reps was approximately $70,000, with an overall employee expenditure budget of around $900,000 annually, including bonuses. With these representatives, this division was able to generate a 2004 sales volume of over $50 million in Canada.

Overall, this sales force had worked well for the company. The division had been able to minimize the size of the sales force while still achieving their sales goals in an effective and efficient manner.

NU-GRO

In a similar fashion, Nu-Gro operated customer-focused teams made up of 30 consumer sales reps. Logistics were a very important element within the lawn and garden industry, as shipping costs for these products were significant. For example, a trailer shipment of fertilizer could have a maximum of 1,500 bags valued at $3 a bag, while the same trailer could ship $1 million worth of batteries. As a result, sales reps for Nu-Gro needed to plan carefully with customers in order to minimize costs by ensuring full truck shipments.

As with Rayovac/Remington, sales representative were distributed geographically to service key Canadian locations: 17 in Ontario, six in Vancouver, three in Montreal, and two in each of Calgary and Winnipeg.

The average base salary for these sales reps was slightly lower than for Rayovac/Remington representatives at $60,000, with an overall employee expenditure budget of approximately $2 million annually, including bonuses. With these sales reps, this division was able to generate a 2004 sales volume of more than $105 million in Canada.

Nu-Gro, however, had been struggling as the company's operations and product offerings were extremely unfocused. Over the past five years, the company had acquired a large number of their smaller competitors and had accumulated their associated brands under the Nu-Gro umbrella. As a result, Nu-Gro experienced a proliferation of products and brands (see Exhibit 6). There were strong arguments to stay in under-performing categories, including contribution toward fixed manufacturing costs, improved transportation economics and account control. On the other hand, the significant working capital required to support these under-performing products could not justify keeping them. Brand and SKU rationalization was needed, and a target of up to a 50 percent reduction over a one year period was being considered. Ultimately, a more focused product portfolio would facilitate the efforts of the sales force.

In addition to the large SKU offerings, the sales team was forced to target a wide variety and large number of customers with these brands, including both the

EXHIBIT 6

Major	#SKU's	Revenue By Type/Category		Contribution Margin %	
		$M	% Total	$M	% Sales
Fertilizers	752	29.8	36.40%	3.9	13.20%
Pesticides	234	21.9	26.80%	5.5	25.20%
Soils	176	12.3	15.00%	0.2	1.30%
Seed	143	9	11.00%	0.2	1.80%
Other	92	8.8	10.80%	0.3	10.40%
Grand Total	**1,397**	**$ 82**	**100.00%**	**$10**	**12.30%**

large mass retailers and the small "mom and pop" garden stores. These efforts were very time-consuming and uneconomical for the sales team, as the majority of stores were of the smaller garden shop variety that ordered limited quantities.

The professional division that served the two major lawn and garden markets had been fairly successful in the past through its strong established relationships. The sales force for this division had and would continue to remain independent from Spectrum's consumer (retail) sales division. Nu-Gro maintained a separate sales force beyond the 30 consumer representatives exclusive to this division.

Overall, Nu-Gro's consumer sales operations needed adjustment. A strategy that refocused the sales team's efforts on their large and more important areas, while still finding a way to reach their current customer base, was required to turn this division around.

TETRA/UNITED PET GROUP

The sales force for this division in the United States was regionally based so that each sales rep could ensure an ample supply of product for their distributors and dealers. These sales representatives were responsible for the large accounts such as PetsMart and PetCo, mass merchandisers such as Wal-Mart, and the large number of smaller specialty retailers.

However, in Canada, sales for this division were handled by distributors. These distributors were responsible for the sales to the highly fragmented Canadian specialty pet retailer market. They offered the same services that an internal sales force could provide, including organizing special promotions and setting up in-store displays. Ultimately, they were able to generate sales from a large number of smaller players more economically than a small internal sales team could. The sales managers for Rayovac/Remington and Nu-Gro were responsible for managing these distributors. The larger retail accounts were managed by the U.S. sales team but serviced by these distributors.

SALES MANAGEMENT

Of the 38 sales reps between the Rayovac/Remington and Nu-Gro divisions, four of them filled the roles of sales manager, two managers for each division. Each rep/manager was responsible for the various representatives in their specific geographic regions. They spent 65 percent of their time selling to their own individual accounts. The remaining 35 percent was spent managing

reps, managing distributors, forecasting, strategic planning and analysing their market. For each division, one rep/manager was responsible for the sales reps in the large Ontario market, while the other managed the sales reps in the rest of the country. Regardless of structure of the sales operation going forward, Falconi would likely organize around three regions: the West, Ontario and the East, with one manager responsible for the sales reps within each region. This, of course, raised the issue of the surplus manager and would provide an opportunity to reconsider the incumbents.

COMPETITOR ORGANIZATIONS

Falconi wanted to look at how some of Spectrum's competitors organized their sales forces within Canada. He decided to select a few of the major players from each industry as comparison points. Koninklijke Philips Electronics and P&G operated their sales divisions by product category. Each category had its own dedicated sales force further divided by specific retail channels and/or customer, depending on the size of the retailer. For example, Norelco's sales force was responsible exclusively for shaving and grooming products and did not cross-sell other Philips brands such as televisions. Similarly, Braun sales reps would sell both the Braun and Gillette shaving brands, Duracell would have its own sales team, but neither group would cross-sell other P&G brands. In certain circumstances, one purchasing manager for a retailer such as Wal-Mart might deal with a sales rep from each product category but these sales reps would deal exclusively with Wal-Mart as a customer. In other circumstances, the sales reps would interface with different purchasing managers in those retailers where the purchasing function was organized by category.

Both Scotts and CGPC operated their sales divisions in a different manner. Their sales forces were organized by product category, but covered all retail channels. Thus, they had specific sales reps for categories such as fertilizers, soils and seeds, insect control products, and pet supplies (CGPC only), but each sales rep would service clients across multiple channels. Like Philips and P&G, these companies had developed a sales force with product category expertise, yet they did not concentrate an individual sales rep on a specific retailer.

Due to the size and strength of each of these companies, they had been successful at developing a "pull" strategy with the consumers. Retailers were almost mandated to support and sell these companies' products because of the consumer demand created. In addition, the sales forces had developed strong relationships with retailers, the "push" component.

SALES FORCE OPTIONS

Looking forward, Falconi wanted to evaluate his options regarding how to organize his sales force to see what alternatives or combinations made sense to Spectrum's operations and the market characteristics.

SEPARATE SALES FORCES

Maintaining a separate sales force for each brand line would offer Spectrum the greatest degree of expertise on each brand. These sales reps were already familiar with, and had extensive knowledge about, their brands and would require little, if any, additional training. Sales reps could continue to operate as they already did, and maintain the momentum they had already generated for their product lines. Ultimately, such an organization would allow for a more focused sales force in that representatives would be in a better position to answer product-related questions and offer product educational services.

On the other hand, maintaining separate sales forces would not take advantage of the synergies that the recent merger had created for the company. There would be little to no expense reduction, as the existing sales rep levels would likely be maintained. In addition, this organization would not offer any efficiency improvements in the use of sales reps during slower seasonal periods. Finally, there would be a significant duplication of efforts as Spectrum would have multiple sales reps calling on the same retailer at any given time.

MERGED SALES FORCE

With a merged sales force, Spectrum would essentially move to a "one bag" sales rep approach, in that each representative would be responsible for becoming an expert on all product lines and selling every brand to their specified customers. With this option, Falconi would have to define each sales rep's responsibilities relating to whether or not the representative would cover all customers in a geographic area, or be responsible for a specific retail group or nationwide chain.

As with the separate sales force option, the "one bag" sales rep would offer Spectrum numerous benefits. First,

Spectrum would be able to capitalize on the potential synergies of the merger as Rayovac did with the Remington acquisition and integration. With each representative selling the entire Spectrum product line, there would be the opportunity to cross-promote brands, leveraging the strong relationships that certain brands have with particular retailers to sell and promote the other lines. This is especially important as Spectrum tries to gain presence for all their lines within each major retailer across the country.

Additionally, Falconi would be able to consolidate the existing teams into a smaller unit. Responsibilities for individual retailers could be handled by one or two sales reps selling the entire portfolio of brands, rather than one representative for each individual brand. For example, there are certain customers to whom each business unit has been selling products, including Wal-Mart, The Home Depot, RONA, Canadian Tire, as well as many others across the country. Overall, by merging the sales force, it is estimated that Spectrum would be able to reduce the salaries and bonus expense to approximately $2 million for the entire Canadian sales division.

Finally, a merged sales force would create a more efficient team to cope with the seasonality issues inherent in the industries in which Spectrum operates. Sales reps would always have something going on with one of the portfolio brands, allowing them to be in constant contact with retail purchasers.

While there are many benefits to this approach for a diversified company like Spectrum, there could be great difficulty in creating an effective and efficient merged team. First, with the addition of numerous new brands to the company's portfolio, sales reps would need to develop an expertise for a large number of brands and products. In addition, the new products they would be selling are completely different from the current brand category they have experience with (i.e. a battery sales rep selling fertilizer). Additional training would be required for all sales reps to educate them on the unfamiliar brands. This training could ultimately be costly and take a substantial amount of time.

Given the variety of products and brands under the Spectrum name, a merged sales force may prove to be highly unfocused. A representative may be incapable of attaining a sufficient knowledge base about every product line, or have too much going on to give each brand the necessary focus needed to sustain its current sales levels. This could hinder sales and effectively kill the existing momentum of the brands.

DISTRIBUTORS

Distributors provide sales and logistic services to firms in exchange for commission fees. Such firms are typically hired by smaller companies with limited sales reach, or by companies who are entering new geographic markets but do not yet have a sales team in place. They usually have an advantage over these types of companies as they are well-established, they have existing relationships with retailers, and they operate large sales groups that can service a large number of customers. They typically serve a variety of manufacturers, and thus are able to operate such a sales process in an efficient manner. As a result, distributors are typically given the task of reaching the large number of smaller retailers that prove to be too costly for a small sales force to target, while the manufacturer's internal sales team targets the smaller number of large customers that contribute greater individual sales.

Though there are many benefits to using professional distributors as the company's sales force, there are drawbacks as well. The costs associated with these services can be substantial relative to an internal sales force. The cost of sales through a distributor is approximately 15 percent against revenues, while it is two to 3 percent with an internal sales person. As a result, successful firms that are able to establish large sales teams can ultimately generate sales at a lower cost.

OTHER ALTERNATIVES AND CONSIDERATIONS

While each of these alternatives would provide Spectrum with benefits in particular areas, Falconi knew that creating a sales force based on a combination of one or more of these elements might generate greater returns for the company. For example, one option would be to use a combination of a merged sales force and distributors in order to reach both large and small retailers more effectively. Another option could be to create "platform teams," where one business manager would be responsible for maintaining the relationships with the retailers, while a group of product experts support the manager during sales pitches. Falconi wanted to further explore these opportunities, and others, to see what benefits might be derived.

Falconi knew that before any changes could be made to the sales strategy, selecting his sales managers would be the first essential step. He would need to ensure that he had the right people in this role, whether they were the current managers or new ones. These individuals would serve as the leaders for the overall sales force, ensuring continued momentum and performance of the representatives. They would also be the "change agents" responsible for implementing the plans developed by Falconi for any reorganization. If there was a new strategy implemented, Falconi would have to decide how to judge these managers and how best to use them given the chosen system.

Falconi realized he would have to consider the impact that this major change would have on the current employees. The employees recognized that, with such a merger, the company would look for potential synergies to reduce overall company expenses. Other companies in similar situations have typically looked to consolidate employee positions as one option to reduce costs. If there was to be a merger of the sales teams, Falconi would be responsible for selecting the best candidates for the new organization, meaning that nobody's job was safe. As a result, employees from both the Rayovac/Remington and Nu-Gro divisions would be feeling very apprehensive at this point. People are often averse to change and the sales reps would be concerned about their future employment status and the implications of any forthcoming changes to the company.

Falconi knew that dealing with the sensitivities of his employees would be crucial to achieving a successful implementation of a new sales strategy, if, indeed, the company chose to proceed with that option. Changes would need to be made while the company was still in operation; thus, care needed to be given to these issues in order to avoid potential disturbances and to preserve the current momentum of the business. Falconi realized that change management skills would definitely be required to implement a new structure, or to alleviate concerns if no changes were planned, but he wondered how best to deal with these issues moving forward.

Finally, Falconi needed to decide how many sales reps should be kept if a new strategy was to be implemented and by what criteria he should be judging his representatives. He knew that the sufficient number of sales reps would depend on the chosen direction of the sales force strategy, but he wondered what his team would look like once the dust had settled.

DECISION

Given the nature of the new company, and the industries each business unit competed in, Falconi was unsure what sales force structure would offer the company the greatest benefits, at the same time allowing it to grow its sales and gain a greater retail presence for the entire Spectrum brand portfolio. How should the new company be structured in terms of reporting, responsibilities and the size of the sales force? Should Spectrum try to structure itself similarly to its competitors, or did their operation require a different approach?

Additionally, depending on which sales force structure was selected, Falconi would have to consider how to organize the teams relative to Spectrum's retail customers. He could organize them by geography, by retail channel, by individual retailers, by some combination of these or by another method altogether. Falconi would have to explore the benefits of the options and determine what made the most sense.

The board of directors was meeting next week and Falconi wanted to present them with a full report outlining his proposed strategy regarding the sales force, and why the other alternatives were dismissed. Overall, Falconi knew that a decision would need to be made quickly in hopes that the new sales force strategy could be implemented prior to the peak period for the lawn and garden industry. Falconi knew that sufficient time would be needed to implement changes and initiate any training that might be required for the sales team.

Part **Three**

Evaluation and Control of the Sales Program

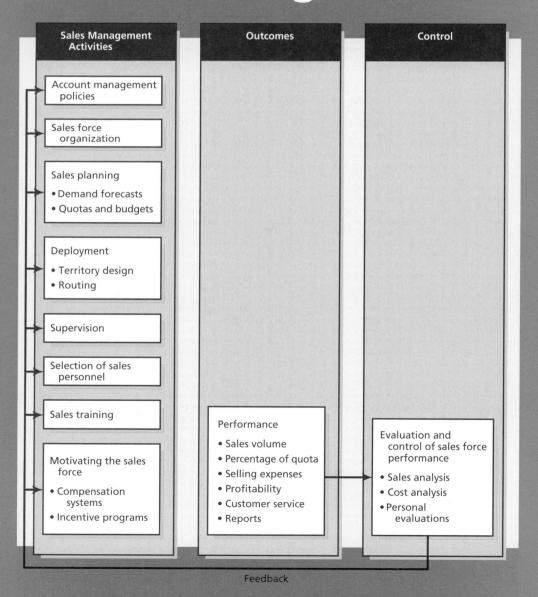

Sales Management Activities	Outcomes	Control
Account management policies		
Sales force organization		
Sales planning • Demand forecasts • Quotas and budgets		
Deployment • Territory design • Routing		
Supervision		
Selection of sales personnel		
Sales training		
Motivating the sales force • Compensation systems • Incentive programs	Performance • Sales volume • Percentage of quota • Selling expenses • Profitability • Customer service • Reports	Evaluation and control of sales force performance • Sales analysis • Cost analysis • Personal evaluations

Feedback

Chapter 1 suggested that sales management involves three interrelated processes: (1) formulation of a sales program, (2) implementation of the sales program, and (3) evaluation and control of sales force performance. Part One of the book concentrated on the first of these processes. Part Two focused on the second and explored the policies and procedures involved in implementing a firm's sales program. Finally, in Part Three, we give attention to evaluation and control of sales force performance.

Chapter 12 discusses cost analysis and demonstrates how sales managers employ cost data in the evaluation and control process. The costs of various selling functions can be monitored across individual salespeople, districts, products, and even customers. When combined with sales analysis data, it is possible to judge the profitability of various products and customer types. However, cost analysis presents some difficult technical questions concerning how certain costs—such as administrative salaries and overhead—should be allocated (for example, between salespeople and products).

Chapter 13 focuses on behavioral and other analyses that are critical components for assessing performance in the twenty-first century. A salesperson's ability to achieve a certain sales volume is sometimes constrained by factors beyond the rep's control, such as competition or economic conditions. Therefore, some managers believe it is necessary to evaluate the actual behavior of salespeople as well as their ultimate performance (sales data). A number of techniques attempt to measure and evaluate various aspects of a salesperson's job behavior, including self-rating scales, supervisor ratings, field observations, and surveys of customer satisfaction.

Chapter Twelve

Cost Analysis

Real Cost Analysis Leads to Real Benefits

In order to address today's business challenges and remain competitive in an ever-changing marketplace, operational excellence, cost control, and a customer focus are essential. Sales managers are addressing these challenges by adopting more complex accounting and cost projection methods. Activity-based costing, as discussed in the chapter, enables managers to determine the profitability of individual customers and products, different distribution channels, or geographic areas.

Chally research suggests the top three capabilities sales executives most need to develop are:

- Operational excellence that brings together an attention to quality, and cost control (see Chapter 12).

- Talent acquisition and retention (see Chapter 9).

- Employee and customer focus (see Chapter 2).

The intersection of these can be summed up by Gary Tubridy, senior vice president of the Alexander Group,

> The challenge will be to grow revenues in a profitable and productive way. Revenues are going to have to grow at a faster rate than expenses. Sales executives are going to need to improve the productivity of their organizations. They're going to have to get smarter with how they use both human resources and alternative sales channel resources, because they're going to have to introduce alternative channels to develop leads, to improve service, and to improve coverage on small business and middle market that they're not covering well today, and lead all of this additional channel resource into existing sales organizations to improve productivity. And when it's done right, then an organization is going to have a finely working machine that will separate itself from its rivals. That's what I think the best sales executives are going to be up to in the next few years.

A Chally case study demonstrates how thinking carefully about a company's resources and how to employ them most effectively can improve the bottom line. An established product/service company wanted to improve the customer service of their sales team. The company employed field sales personnel as well as sales service support staff available to customers through a 1–800 number. In an effort to improve customer service, the company decided to dedicate some of the sales service support staff to particular field sales personnel and individual customers.

Chally's research found those customers with a "dedicated" sales service support representative had higher satisfaction with the company and were better customers.

In comparison with customers with "nondedicated" support, "dedicated" support customers had

- 18 percent higher customer service ratings (higher company satisfaction).

- 15 percent higher probability of being a repeat customer.

- 23 percent higher sales volume (they bought more products and services).

- 30 percent higher purchases on lower dollar cost/high volume "standard" consumable products (lower sales costs on higher margin products).

As a result, assigning the sales service support staff to particular customers rather than a 1–800 number pool enabled the sales support staff to build better customer relationships. This restructuring led to better customer service and increased sales.

Source: HR Chally Group (2007).

LEARNING OBJECTIVES

Many students of sales and marketing like to focus on the revenue side. They migrate to sales positions because making things happen is an essential function of creating business. But costs are important, too, and managing costs carefully is often the difference between a thriving business and one that struggles to exist.

After completing this chapter, you should be able to

- Select the appropriate cost allocation method for various sales management situations.

- Describe how such methods would be implemented.

- Discuss the importance of return on assets managed (ROAM) and be able to calculate ROAM.

- Apply financial cost analysis to sales management situations in order to make decisions.

Not too long ago, a company (which asked to remain nameless) set a sales goal for a particular product of 100,000 new units. It dropped two products that were similar and increased sales for the preferred product from 70,000 units to three times the goal, or 300,000 units. The sales force had their best year ever, making more money per salesperson than ever before. Yet, every unit they sold cost an average $2.00 in losses. How could this happen?

Over a half-million dollars were lost because information concerning performance wasn't gathered and shared on a timely basis. Increasing competition in a global marketplace makes avoiding such mistakes all the more imperative. More than half of top Sales Executives see operational excellence, quality, and cost control as the most valuable strength a company will need to have in order to compete in the new Millennium.[1] Costs were higher than expected, prices were lower than expected as more buyers took advantage of quantity discounts, and, worse, the information didn't reach decision makers in time.

Cost analysis is complementary to sales analysis in sales force management. While sales analysis focuses on the results achieved, cost analysis looks at the costs incurred in producing those results and whether the returns justify the expenditures. Companies

Innovation   Learning about the Lifetime Value of the Customer   12.1

Putting together and maintaining a sales force is expensive. Successful companies know they need to assess how best to use such a valuable resource. One tool being used by more and more companies is a measure of the Lifetime Value of the Customer. This is a measure of each customer's long-term value, or profitability. Companies have come to realize that not all customers are created equal. Some customers thought to be very profitable turn out to be a lot less profitable than first imagined. Interestingly, sometimes the largest customers in terms of sales generated are among the least profitable in terms of gross margin. Why? Because big customers demand more and better service and often drive harder deals on price, which leads to lower profit margins.

As you can see, critical to an assessment of a customer's lifetime value is an analysis of the costs associated with doing business with that customer. The first step is to have up-to-date information on the real costs of doing business with that customer. Often this means assigning a number of costs that might normally be left as overhead to specific customers. In addition, and this is key to sales cost analysis, it is essential to determine the real cost of maintaining the customer relationship. Of course, this includes not only the salesperson's time but the amount of customer service contact, sales terms, and payment schedules.

The final assessment of a customer's value is based on short- and long-term company objectives. While some companies are not generating highly profitable sales now, it may be possible to increase profitability by applying more and better resources to the customer. Companies almost always want to have potential new big customers in development to ensure company growth and protect against the loss of current big customers.

Banks such as Bank of America have been aggressive in assessing lifetime customer value. As a result, they evaluate each customer in terms of the business they currently have with the bank, the costs of providing those services, and the potential for new business. In some cases, the results have been surprising. For example, Bank of America found that nearly half its retail customers were unprofitable based on the services provided, funds deposited, and current fees being charged to customers. At the other end, banks are also targeting their best customers by offering more and better services such as platinum credit cards and low-interest home equity lines.

sometimes implement systems and procedures that are intended to increase sales but do not always produce profit increases. To determine whether the returns justify the expenditures, it is necessary to gather, classify, compare, and study marketing cost data, which is the essence of marketing cost analysis. (See how companies need cost data to assist them in calculating important customer analysis in Innovation 12.1)

Marketing cost analysis can help identify opportunities for increasing the effectiveness of marketing expenditures. Sales are achieved at some cost, and marketing productivity focuses on the sales or profit output per unit of marketing effort input. Unfortunately, it is often difficult for a firm to know what the output/input relationships are without detailed analyses.

Most firms today produce many products, which they sell in multiple markets. For each product and market, the mix of marketing elements differs. Only by analyzing specific relationships among these products and markets can the firm hope to identify situations where marketing input should be increased or altered, where it should remain at historic levels, and where it should be decreased. These insights are simply not produced by the information that flows from normal accounting operations. Similarly, to deploy the firm's salespeople most effectively, the sales manager needs to appreciate the output/input relationships by product, territory, customer, channel of distribution, and so on. Marketing cost analysis estimates these relationships.

COST ANALYSIS DEVELOPMENT

Sales management has been somewhat slower to adopt cost analysis (or as it is sometimes called, profitability analysis) than sales analysis for managing the sales function. The empirical evidence indicates that if they do it at all, firms are more likely to conduct product profitability analyses and less likely to do it for customers. Only about half of all companies do it at all, and less than a third analyze costs by products, territories, salespeople, and customers. Interestingly, companies do focus on a salesperson's pricing authority which is a key factor in determining the overall profitability of each customer.[2]

Historically, one reason for this was that most accounting systems were not designed to meet the needs of marketing management but, rather, to report the aggregate effects of a firm's operations to creditors and stockholders. They were subsequently modified to provide a better handle on the production operations of the firm. Even today many accounting systems are still oriented toward external reporting and production cost analysis.

However the integration of company information systems over the last 10 years enable accounting systems to identify and include the types of cost and profitability data needed by sales executives. For a sales manager, the key is to understand how costs are allocated so that the true profitability of any particular customer, geographic area, product, or market can be determined. Any accounting system can take the direct cost of supplies and components and add those together to come up with the cost of a product. The challenge is adding management costs, office supplies, warehousing, IT and so forth. There are three approaches to cost allocation: full costing, contribution analysis, and activity-based costing (ABC). The choice of which costing approach to use is very important to sales managers. For example, territories have been mistakenly cut because the accounting information used by managers didn't allocate costs appropriately.

Full Cost versus Contribution Margin

The more popular and traditional accounting methods are the **full-cost** (or as it is sometimes called, net profit) approach and the **contribution margin** approach. The argument over which should be used has generated controversy through the years.[3] To appreciate the controversy fully, it is helpful to understand the differences between direct and indirect costs as well as specific and general expenses.

A direct cost can be specifically identified with a product or a function.[4] The cost is incurred because the product or function exists or is contemplated. If the product or function were eliminated, the cost would also disappear. An example is inventory carrying costs for a product.

An indirect cost is a shared cost because it is tied to several functions or products. Even if one of the products or functions were eliminated, the cost would not be. Rather, the share of the cost previously borne by the product or function that was eliminated would shift to the remaining products or functions. An example of an indirect cost is the travel expenses of a salesperson selling a multiple product line. Even if one product the rep sells is eliminated, the travel cost would not be.

The *profit/loss or net income statement* typically distinguishes between costs and expenses. The term *cost* is often restricted to the materials, labor, power, rent, and other miscellaneous items used in making the product. The cost of goods sold on the following conceptual net income statement reflects these costs.

	Sales
	Sales
Less:	Cost of goods sold
Equal:	Gross margin
Less:	General administrative and selling expenses
Equal:	Profit or net income before taxes

The expenses reflect the other costs incurred in operating the business, such as the cost of advertising and of maintaining branches. Expenses cannot be tied nearly as well as costs to specific products, since they are general expenses associated with doing business. In marketing cost analysis, the distinction between costs and expenses is not nearly so clear, and the terms are often used interchangeably.

Just like costs, expenses can be classified into two broad categories: specific and general expenses. A specific expense is just like a direct cost—it can be identified with a specific product or function. The expense would be eliminated if the product or function were eliminated. If the product were eliminated, for example, the specific expense of the product manager's salary need not be incurred.

A general expense is like an indirect cost—it cannot be identified directly with a specific object of profit measurement such as a territory, salesperson, or product. Thus, the expense would not be eliminated if the specific object were eliminated. An example is the sales manager's salary when the object of measurement is a product in a multiple-product company. The elimination of the product would not eliminate this salary.

A particular cost or expense may be direct for some measurement purposes and indirect for others. The object of the measurement determines how the cost should be treated.

If it is a product line, costs directly associated with the manufacture and sales of the product line are direct. All other costs in the business are indirect. If the object of measurement shifts to a sales territory, some of the costs of product-line measurement, which were direct, will remain direct costs now associated with the territory; some will become indirect; and others that were indirect will become direct. For example,[5]

	Object of Measurement	
Cost	**Product**	**Territory**
Sales promotion display	Direct	Direct
Sales rep compensation	Indirect	Direct
Product-line manager's salary	Direct	Indirect
Corporate president's salary	Indirect	Indirect

As mentioned, there is controversy about whether one should use a full-cost or contribution margin approach in marketing cost analysis. Proponents of the full-cost or net profit approach argue that all costs should be assigned and somehow accounted for in determining the profitability of any segment (e.g., territory, product, and salesperson) of the business.

Under this approach, each unit bears not only its own direct costs but a share of the company's cost of doing business, referred to as indirect costs. Full-costing advocates argue that many of the indirect costs can be assigned to the unit being assessed on the basis of a demonstrable cost relationship. If a strong relationship does not exist, the cost must be prorated on a reasonable basis. Under the full-costing approach, a net income for each marketing segment can be determined by matching the segment's revenue with its direct and indirect costs.[6]

Contribution margin advocates argue, on the other hand, that it is misleading to allocate costs arbitrarily. They suggest that only those costs that can be specifically identified with the segment of the business should be deducted from the revenue produced by the segment to determine how well the segment is doing. Any excess of revenues over these costs contributes to the common costs of the business and thereby to profits. The contribution margin approach does not distinguish where the costs are incurred but rather simply whether they are variable or fixed. Thus, the difference between sales and all variable costs, whether they originate in manufacturing, selling, or some administrative function, are subtracted from revenues or sales to produce the contribution margin of the segment.

The net profit approach does attempt to determine where the costs were incurred. The difference in perspectives is highlighted in Exhibit 12.1. Not only is segment net income derived differently in the two approaches, but also advocates of the contribution margin approach do not even focus on net income when evaluating the profitability of a segment of the business. Rather, they focus on the contribution produced by the segment after subtracting the costs directly traceable to it from its sales.

The contribution margin advocates are winning the controversy. Although the early emphasis in accounting for distribution costs was on full-cost allocation, the recent emphasis is on the contribution margin approach.[7] The contribution margin approach has unmistakable logic. If the costs associated with the segment are not removed with the elimination of the segment, why should they be arbitrarily allocated? That just confuses things and provides a blurred, distorted picture for management decision making. The costs still have to be borne after the segment is eliminated, but they must be borne by other segments of the business. Such allocation can simply tax the ability of these other segments to remain profitable. Exhibits 12.2 and 12.3 illustrate this phenomenon.

The example involves a department store with three main departments. The administrative expenses in Exhibit 12.2 are all fixed costs; they were allocated to departments on the basis of the total percentage of sales accounted for by each department. This is a common allocation basis about which more will be said later. Those who embrace the full-cost approach would argue that Department 1 should be eliminated because of the net loss of $12,500.

Note what would happen if this were pursued. First, the sales of the department would be lost, but $12,500 of selling expenses would also be eliminated. However, the $25,000 of fixed costs must now be borne by the other departments. Allocating these costs on the

EXHIBIT 12.1   **Differences in perspective between full-cost and contribution margin approaches to marketing cost analysis**

Full-Cost Approach		Contribution Margin Approach	
	Sales		Sales
Less:	Cost of goods sold	Less:	Variable manufacturing costs
Equal:	Gross margin	Less:	Other variable costs directly traceable to the segment
		Equal:	Contribution margin
Less:	Operating expenses (including the segment's allocated share of company administration and general expenses)	Less:	Fixed costs directly traceable to products Fixed costs directly traceable to the market segment
Equal:	Segment net income	Equal:	Segment net income

EXHIBIT 12.2

Profit and loss statement by department using a full-cost approach

	Totals	Department 1	Department 2	Department 3
Sales	$500,000	$250,000	$150,000	$100,000
Cost of goods sold	400,000	225,000	125,000	50,000
Gross margin	100,000	25,000	25,000	50,000
Other expenses				
Selling expenses	25,000	12,500	7,500	5,000
Administrative expenses	50,000	25,000	15,000	10,000
Total other expenses	75,000	37,500	22,500	15,000
Net profit (loss)	25,000	(12,500)	2,500	35,000

EXHIBIT 12.3

Profit and loss statement if department 1 were eliminated

	Total	Department 2	Department 3
Sales	$250,000	$150,000	$100,000
Cost of goods sold	175,000	125,000	50,000
Gross margin	75,000	25,000	50,000
Other expenses			
Selling expenses	12,500	7,500	5,000
Administrative expenses	50,000	30,000	20,000
Total other expenses	62,500	37,500	25,000
Net profit (loss)	12,500	(12,500)	25,000

basis of percentage of sales suggests that Department 2 is unprofitable (see Exhibit 12.3). If one used the same argument as before, it too should be considered for elimination. Then the $50,000 of administrative expenses would be borne entirely by Department 3, making Department 3 (the entire store) unprofitable. That would suggest the store be closed, meaning management would close a profitable store simply because one department displayed a small dollar loss—a loss that could be attributed to an arbitrary allocation of fixed costs. Department 1, in fact, makes a positive contribution to profits, as the contribution margin statement in Exhibit 12.4 shows.

A contribution margin versus a full-cost profitability analysis is also supported by the recognition that most marketing phenomena are highly interrelated. For example, the demand for one product in a multiproduct company is often influenced by the availability of others, while the absence of a product may cause the sale of another product to decline.

EXHIBIT 12.4

Contribution margin by departments

	Totals	Department 1	Department 2	Department 3
Sales	$500,000	$250,000	$150,000	$100,000
Variable costs				
Cost of goods sold	400,000	225,000	125,000	50,000
Selling expenses	25,000	12,500	7,500	5,000
Total variable costs	425,000	237,500	132,500	55,000
Contribution margin	75,000	12,500	17,500	45,000
Fixed costs				
Administrative expenses	50,000			
Net profit	25,000			

The entire product line may be greater than the sum of its parts in terms of sales and profits. The same argument applies to other elements of the marketing mix. They have interdependent effects. The contribution margin approach implicitly recognizes this synergy through its emphasis on the contribution of each segment or part.

In sum, allocations of indirect costs for segment performance evaluation are generally inappropriate. That is, any measure of segment performance that includes allocated shares of indirect costs includes factors that do not really reflect performance in the segment as a separate entity. Hence, indirect cost allocations should not be made if the purpose is to measure true performance.

ABC Accounting

Over the last decade there has been a significant shift in the way accountants and managers view costs. Rather than focus on the reason for the cost (labor hours to produce a product), this new approach identifies and delineates the cause-and-effect relationship between costs and desired organizational outcomes. As a result, marketing decision makers can get answers to questions such as, How profitable is it to do business with this customer? or What level of customer service will make this customer unprofitable?

Activity-based costing (ABC) is based on the simple premise that almost all company activities are in support of manufacturing (or producing), marketing, and delivering goods and services to the customer. As presented in Exhibit 12.5, an ABC system consists of three basic informational components related to the company: resources, activities, and

EXHIBIT 12.5 **A diagram of activity-based costing**

Source: Adapted from James M. Reeve, "Activity-Based Cost Systems for Functional Integration and Customer Value," in *Competing Globally through Customer Value: The Management of Strategic Suprasystems,* eds. Michael J. Stahl and Gregory M. Bounds (New York: Quorum Books, 1991), p. 501.

EXHIBIT 12.6
Comparison of contribution and ABC methods

Source: Robert A. Dwyer and John F. Tanner, Jr., *Business Marketing: Connecting Strategy Relationships and Learning* (New York: McGraw-Hill, 1999).

	Digital Wamometer			Tricometer
Sales	$545			$545
Less variable costs*	320			335
Contribution margin	$225			$210
		Contribution Method		
Less fixed mfg. costs†	85	50	50	15
Less fixed selling costs‡	30	25	25	20
Income using ABC	$110			$185
Income using contribution		$150	$135	

*Includes commission paid to salespeople as well as direct manufacturing and shipping costs.
†Total fixed manufacturing costs = $100, but allocated based on complexity of setup and other activities in manufacturing process in ABC.
‡Total fixed selling costs (administrative overhead and sales office expenses) = $50, but allocated on the basis of digital wamometer requiring six calls to every four for the tricometer using ABC.

cost objects. Cost objects are associated with products, channels, and customers, all of which are particularly relevant to marketers. Critical to the analysis is an understanding that company resources (people, money, and organizational assets) are used to drive the activities that are needed to develop, produce, market, and service products for the customer. As an example, to make a sales call on a customer several resources are needed, such as salesperson's time (a human resource) and organizational assets (car, computer, cell phone, and other supplies). After resources have been identified they are assigned to activities. For example, consider the number of service calls a company makes on a customer. Intuitively, it makes sense that customers requiring frequent service calls cost the company more than the customer who rarely requests service. Unfortunately, it was not possible for traditional cost accounting systems to capture those differences.[8]

Let's consider an example: Suppose a sales office is responsible for selling two products and has only one team of salespeople selling both products. Each product represents 50 percent of the office's sales. The important activity in this situation would be the number of sales calls per product. If digital wamometers (DW) take three sales calls to close and tricometers take two sales calls to close, then the total calls to close two sales (one of each product) is five. Using activity-based costing, the DW is allocated 60 percent of the office's costs because it is more difficult to sell, and the tricometer gets 40 percent. Contribution or full-cost approaches would allocate 50 percent of fixed costs to each product on the basis of sales volume. Note the difference in income in Exhibit 12.6; would management decisions be the same using ABC versus the contribution approach?

PROCEDURE

The general procedure followed in conducting a cost or profitability analysis first involves specifying the purpose for which the cost study is being done. Knowing the purpose helps to determine the functional cost centers. The next step is to spread the natural account costs to these functional cost centers. Then the functional costs are allocated to appropriate segments using some reasonable basis. Finally, the allocated costs are summed, and the contribution of the segment is determined. Incidentally, the term *segment* is used here to mean a portion of the business, not in the normal sense of market segment.

The process is shown in Exhibit 12.7. Although the diagram is simple, its execution is difficult. Hard decisions about what **sales costs** or expenses are to be treated as fixed, semifixed, or variable and how various costs should be allocated to segments must be made.

EXHIBIT 12.7

Steps in conducting a marketing profitability analysis

Step 1 — Specify purpose and determine functional cost centers

↓

Step 2 — Spread natural account costs to functional cost centers

↓

Step 3 — Allocate functional costs to appropriate segments using some reasonable basis

↓

Step 4 — Sum allocated costs to determine contribution of the segment

As mentioned, the first step in a marketing profitability analysis is to determine the purpose for which it is being done. Is it designed to investigate the profitability of the various products in the line? Or is it designed to determine the profitability of sales branches, customers, or individual salespersons? The decision is essential because the treatment of the various costs and expenses depends on the purpose.

Ideally, the firm would want to break all its costs or revenues into small building blocks or modules. These elements would be as small as possible and yet still be meaningful.[9] Such a breakdown allows the firm to aggregate these building blocks as needed to produce profitability analyses for various segments of the business. An example of a basic building block or module of cost is a regional sales manager's salary, which is a general expense when the profitability of various product lines is at issue. But that same sales manager's salary is a specific expense and needs to be considered when determining the contribution to profit of the region.

Thus, good profitability analyses require that the various costs be partitioned into direct and indirect expenses so the proper aggregations can be made. What is properly treated as direct and what should be treated as indirect or general depend on the study's purpose. Sales managers typically are most concerned with the profitability of various regions, branches, salespeople, and customers; they are only remotely concerned with the profitability of various products. Thus, a salesperson's salary is more likely to be treated more of a direct than an indirect expense, whereas a product manager's salary is likely indirect, when the profitability of regions, branches, salespeople, and customers is at issue. Investigation of the profitability of the product line requires just the opposite treatment, which again illustrates the importance of specifying the purpose of the study.

In the second step of a profitability analysis, natural account costs need to be spread to the functional cost centers. Natural accounts are the categories of cost used in the normal accounting cycle. These costs include such things as salaries, wages, rent, heat, light, taxes, auto expenses, raw materials, and office equipment/supplies. They are called *natural accounts* because they bear the name of their expense categories.

Natural accounts are not the only way of classifying costs. In manufacturing cost accounting, for example, costs are often reclassified according to the purpose for which they were incurred. Thus, production wages might be broken into the cost categories of forging, turning, grinding, milling, polishing, and assembling. These categories are functional account categories because they recognize the function performed, which is the purpose for incurring the cost.

Marketing cost analysis has a similar orientation. It recognizes that marketing costs are incurred for some purpose, and it recognizes general selling and administrative expenses according to their purposes or functions. As Edmund D. McCarry stated so elegantly years ago, "The term *function* should be defined so as to meet the purpose for which it is used. The function of the heart is not simply to beat, which is its activity, but rather to supply the body with a continuous flow of blood."[10]

The salaries paid in a branch office, for example, could go to perform such functions as direct selling, advertising, order processing, and customer service. A functional cost analysis would involve spreading the total salaries paid in the office to these various functions. Exhibit 12.8 lists the major functional accounts that are useful in marketing cost analyses.

As Exhibit 12.7 indicates, the third step in conducting a cost or profitability analysis is to allocate the functional costs to the various segments of the business. One needs to recognize immediately that the bases for allocation are not fixed. Rather, they depend on the discretion of the decision maker and what he or she feels are "reasonable" bases.

One basis often used is to divide the expenses according to volume attained, which is in line with traditional cost accounting. Thus, if a regional sales manager was responsible for six branch offices, and one office produced 25 percent of the sales in the region, it would be charged with one-fourth of the sales manager's salary and expenses. This method is often used because of its simplicity.[11]

Allocating costs by sales volume is an erroneous method, however, in that it fails to recognize the purpose for which the regional sales manager's costs were incurred, which is the reason for a functional cost analysis. Maybe the branch was troublesome to manage and consumed 50 percent of the manager's time. In this case, it should bear half his salary. Alternatively, it may have run smoothly. The manager rarely had to get involved with the branch activities, so it consumed only 10 percent of his time and effort. In this case, only one-tenth of the regional sales manager's salary should be charged against the branch in determining its profit contribution. As Horngren, the eminent cost accountant, stated years ago, "The costs of efforts are independent of the results actually obtained, in the sense that the costs are programmed by management, not determined by sales. Moreover, the allocation of costs on the basis of dollar sales entails circular reasoning."[12] Thus, the trend is toward activity-based cost allocations.

The causal relationships used can, and most likely will, be different for different questions. Exhibit 12.9 shows some common bases for allocating functional costs to product

EXHIBIT 12.8
Major functional accounts that are useful in marketing cost analysis

- Direct selling
- Advertising and sales promotion
- Product and package design
- Technical product services
- Sales discounts and allowances
- Credit extension
- Warranty costs
- Marketing research
- Warehousing and handling
- Inventory
- Packaging, shipping, and delivery
- Order processing/information technology
- Customer service
- Billing and recording of accounts receivable
- Returned merchandise

EXHIBIT 12.9   Functional cost groups and bases of allocation

| Functional Cost Group | Basis of Allocation | | |
	To Product Groups	To Account Size Classes	To Sales Territories
1. Selling—Direct Costs Personal calls by salespeople and supervisors on accounts and prospects; sales salaries, incentive compensation, travel, and other expenses	Selling time devoted to each product, as shown by special sales call reports or other special studies	Number of sales calls times average time per call, as shown by special sales call reports or other special studies	Direct
2. Selling—Indirect Costs Field supervision, field sales office expense, sales administration expenses, sales personnel training, sales management; market research, new-product development, sales statistics, determining services, sales accounting	In proportion to direct selling time, or time records by project	In proportion to direct selling time, or time records by project	Equal charge for each sales rep
3. Advertising Media costs such as TV, radio, billboards, internet, newspaper, magazine; advertising production costs; advertising department salaries	Direct, or analysis of space and time by media, other costs in proportion to media costs	Equal charge to each account, or number of ultimate consumers and prospects in each account's trading area	Direct, or analysis of media circulation records
4. Sales Promotion Consumer promotions such as coupons, patches, premiums; trade promotions such as price allowances, point-of-purchase displays, cooperative advertising	Direct, or analysis of source records	Direct, or analysis of source records	Direct, or analysis of source records
5. Transportation Railroad, truck, barge, etc., payments to carriers for delivery of finished goods from plants to warehouses and from warehouses to customers; traffic department costs	Applicable rates times tonnages	Analysis of sampling of bills of lading	Applicable rates times tonnages
6. Storage and Shipping Storage of finished goods inventories in warehouses; rent (or equivalent costs), public warehouse charges, fire insurance and taxes on finished goods	Warehouse space occupied by average inventory; number of shipping units	Number of shipping units	Number of shipping units

(continued)

EXHIBIT 12.9   Functional cost groups and bases of allocation *(concluded)*

| Functional Cost Group | Basis of Allocation | | |
	To Product Groups	To Account Size Classes	To Sales Territories
inventories, etc; physical handling, assembling, and loading out of rail cars, trucks, barges for shipping finished products from warehouses and mills to customers; labor, equipment, space, and material costs.			
7. **Order Processing** Checking and processing of orders from customers, shipping dates, coordination with production planning, transmittal to production, pricing customer invoices; freight accounting; credit and collection; handling cash receipts; provision for bad debts; salary, supplies, space, and equipment costs (computers, printers, etc.)	Number of order lines	Number of order lines	Number of order lines

groups, account size classes, and sales territories. Leadership 12.2 shows how important appropriate breakdowns can be in managing salespeople's activities.

The fourth step in the process is to sum the costs allocated to the segment. Costs for which there is no direct causal relationship remain unallocated in determining the contribution of the segment. A comparison of the contributions of like segments then indicates the remedial action that might be taken, if any.

THE PROCESS ILLUSTRATED

To illustrate the process of conducting a cost or profitability analysis, consider the situation encountered by the Hurricane Performance Bicycle Company, in Exhibit 12.10, which was faced with a loss in its Orlando branch of more than $160,000.[13] Suppose the sales manager is interested in further analyzing the branch to see whether the loss can be traced to particular sales reps or customers.

The sales manager has completed the first step in a cost analysis—the manager has decided the purpose of the analysis is to isolate the profit contributions of the various sales representatives in the branch. The next thing the manager must do is spread the general selling and administrative expenses incurred by the branch in the profit and loss statement to the various functional accounts. To keep the example simple, the costs incurred in manufacturing will not be separated, although a more sophisticated contribution margin analysis would reflect such differences. Rather, the cost of goods sold is assumed to be a fixed charge to the Orlando branch, meaning the manager needs to concentrate on spreading only the selling and administrative expenses of functional cost groups.

Leadership   Ripping Off the Company Using the T&E Expense Account

12.2

Susan Yeaple never meant to eavesdrop on her employees, but as she casually sat at her desk on that Friday afternoon she could not help but overhear a conversation that gave her great concern. To her surprise, she learned it was common practice for salespeople to apply the "10 percent rule" in completing their expense reports for the company. Put simply, the rule meant that all expenses (meals, mileage, etc.) were increased by 10 percent. She pondered her options and chose to remain quiet; however, she went to payroll and asked that 10 percent be withheld from each salesperson's paycheck to send the message that this practice would not be tolerated in the future.

Ms. Yeaple's experience is much more common than many people think, as almost every sales manager has at least one story about salespeople cheating on their expense reports. Indeed, fraud related to travel and entertainment (T&E) expenses has grown more than 200 percent since 1996 and exceeds the growth of all other types of corporate fraud. More specific, nearly 60 percent of sales managers report catching a salesperson cheating on an expense report. Interestingly, nearly one-quarter (22 percent) report that they have had a salesperson list a "strip bar" as a restaurant.

Not surprising, managers believe it is critical to review expense reports. Fifty-eight percent review expense reports every month for their entire sales force, while another third do it occasionally. Only 5 percent indicated they never evaluate the expense reports of their salespeople.

There are two common frauds associated with T&E accounts. The first is *mischaracterized expenses.* This occurs when salespeople have a personal dinner or buy a personal item and charge it as a business expense. Companies have instituted detailed analyses of call reports and work schedules against T&E expenses. Increasingly, managers are also requiring a comprehensive explanation of expenses that includes what, when, and where the item was purchased. If the expense is a dinner or some other entertainment, the customer's name should be identified in the report. The second T&E fraud is *overstated expenses.* As the name implies, it means making a $50 dinner a $100 expense on the T&E report. Of course, requiring a receipt goes a long way to minimizing this kind of problem.

Source: Jay Boehmer, "Expense Fraud Explodes," *Business Traveler News,* August 11, 2003, pp. 1, 68–69.

EXHIBIT 12.10
Example profit and loss statement

Profit and Loss Statement for HURRICANE PERFORMANCE BICYCLE COMPANY Orlando Office		
Sales		$4,963,500
Cost of goods sold		4,061,000
Gross margin		902,500
Selling and administrative expenses		
Salaries	$309,000	
Commissions	49,635	
Advertising	254,000	
Postage and office supplies	980	
Packaging materials	60,840	
Transportation charges	182,520	
Travel expenses	76,000	
Rent	130,000	
Total selling and administrative expenses		1,062,975
Net profit (loss)		$ (160,475)

EXHIBIT 12.11   **Allocation of natural accounts to functional accounts**

Natural Accounts		Direct Selling	Advertising	Warehousing and Shipping	Order Processing and Billing	Transportation
				Functional Accounts		
Salaries	$ 309,000	$257,000		$ 24,000	$28,000	
Commissions	49,635	49,635				
Advertising	254,000		$254,000			
Postage and supplies	980				980	
Packaging materials	60,840			60,840		
Transportation charges	182,520					$182,520
Travel expenses	76,000	76,000				
Rent	130,000	28,000		95,000	7,000	
	$1,062,975	$410,635	$254,000	$179,840	$35,980	$182,520

Exhibit 12.11 lists the functional cost categories across the top and the natural account categories along the side. The individual entries indicate how a total natural cost is apportioned according to purpose. Note that the sum of all the functional costs in a row equals the natural cost for that row; that is, all natural costs are accounted for in the spread.

The details in the division of costs depend on the operation of the branch. In this case, the branch in the previous year paid $309,000 in salaries. They were distributed in the following way: branch manager—$78,000; four salespeople—$179,000; warehouse clerk—$24,000; and a clerical person handling order processing and billing—$28,000. The salaries of the branch manager and salespeople are charged against direct selling expenses because that is the purpose for which they were incurred.

Similarly, the office and warehouse clerk salaries are charged against their main functions. The functional account direct selling is also charged with the commissions earned by the four representatives; in addition to their base salaries, all salespeople were paid a commission equal to 1 percent of sales. Advertising charges reflect both a natural account cost and a functional account cost. Advertising charges are typically maintained in a separate category in the normal accounting cycle, and their name speaks to their purpose. The same is true of transportation charges.

The postage and supplies the office consumed were used to support the order processing and billing functions, and thus they are assigned to this category. Similarly, packaging material costs are assigned to warehousing and shipping because that is the function for which they are used. Travel expenses reflect the food, lodging, and other expenses incurred by the sales representatives in carrying out their main function of selling; thus, these costs are so assigned.

Perhaps the one natural account cost that requires the most explanation is rent. The company was paying $70 per square foot for office space and $20 per square foot for warehouse space. These costs are spread to the functional accounts in proportion to the space used by each activity. More particularly, the order processing and selling functions used 100 of the 500 square feet of office space the company rented; the salespeople and sales manager used the remainder. The $95,000 assignment of rent to warehousing and shipping costs reflects the 4,750 square feet of warehouse space the company rented at $20 per square foot.

To assess the profit contribution of each salesperson, it is necessary to allocate all relevant functional costs to salespeople. Costs that bear some causal relationship to the level

EXHIBIT 12.12 **Basic data used for allocations**

A. Information by Product

Products	Selling Price per Unit	Cost per Unit	Gross Margin per Unit	Number Sold in Period	Sales in Period	Advertising Expenditures
A	$230	$180	$50	6,450	$1,483,500	$120,000
B	180	150	30	10,060	1,810,800	80,000
C	120	100	20	13,910	1,669,200	54,000
				30,420	$4,963,500	$254,000

B. Information by Salesperson

Salesperson	Number of Sales Calls	Number of Orders	Number of Units Sold			
			A	B	C	Total
Nicholls	75	50	1,400	2,210	3,410	7,020
Pogue	125	65	1,725	2,725	3,515	7,965
Vilwock	100	50	1,711	2,609	3,506	7,826
Tucker	100	80	1,614	2,516	3,479	7,609
	400	245	6,450	10,060	13,910	30,420

of activity should be allocated; these include salaries, commissions, and travel expenses. Conversely, costs that are not affected by the level of activity are not allocated. Office rent is an example. Even if one salesperson were fired, this cost would not change; thus, it should not be allocated.

Exhibit 12.12 provides much of the data on which the allocations to generate the profitability analysis by salesperson in Exhibit 12.13 are based. Exhibit 12.13 lists the gross margin by salesperson. From this, all direct expenses are subtracted to derive the contribution to profit by salesperson. Let us consider each expense category.

Direct Selling

For **direct selling,** the salary and commission items need little explanation; they reflect what each representative is paid and the 1 percent commission each earned on what was sold. Travel expenses per sales rep were determined by dividing total travel expenses by the number of calls to generate the cost per call, or $190. Branch accounting records allowed the identification of travel expenses by sales representative. Contact management software, such as GoldMine enables sales managers and salespeople to track their sales calls by type (such as new account calls, cold calls, customer calls), so sales managers can use the software to track the time they spend with field salespeople. This cost is not allocated in the example because this information was not available, and in its absence, there is not reasonable cause-and-effect basis for making the allocation.

Advertising

Panel A of Exhibit 12.12 lists the amount spent on advertising for each product. When these amounts are divided by the number of units sold, the following advertising charges per unit are generated:

A. $120,000 ÷ 6,450 units = $18.60/unit

B. $ 80,000 ÷ 10,060 units = $ 7.95/unit

C. $ 54,000 ÷ 13,910 units = $ 3.88/unit

EXHIBIT 12.13   **Profitability analysis by salesperson**

	Total	Nicholls	Pogue	Vilwock	Tucker
Sales					
Product A	$1,483,500	$ 322,000	$ 396,750	$ 393,530	$ 371,220
Product B	1,810,800	397,800	490,500	469,620	452,880
Product C	1,669,200	409,200	421,800	420,720	417,480
Total Sales	4,963,500	1,129,000	1,309,050	1,283,870	1,241,580
Cost of Goods Sold					
Product A	1,161,000	252,000	310,500	307,980	290,520
Product B	1,509,000	331,500	408,750	391,350	377,400
Product C	1,391,000	341,000	351,500	350,600	347,900
Total COGS	4,061,000	924,500	1,070,750	1,049,930	1,015,820
Gross Margin	902,500	204,500	238,300	233,940	225,760
Expenses					
Direct selling					
Salary	179,000	40,000	45,000	46,000	48,000
Commissions	49,635	11,290	13,091	12,839	12,416
Travel	76,000	14,250	23,750	19,000	19,000
Advertising					
Product A	120,000	26,047	32,093	31,833	30,028
Product B	80,000	17,575	21,670	20,748	20,008
Product C	54,000	13,238	13,646	13,611	13,506
Warehousing and shipping	60,840	14,040	15,930	15,652	15,218
Order processing	980	200	260	200	320
Transportation	182,520	42,120	47,790	46,956	45,654
Total Expenses	802,975	178,759	213,229	206,837	204,149
Contribution to Profit (Loss)	$ 99,525	$ 25,741	$ 25,071	$ 27,103	$ 21,611

The advertising expenses borne by each salesperson are determined by multiplying these per-unit advertising charges by the number of bicycles of each model that each rep sold.

The number of units of the product sold is a very common basis for allocating advertising expenses. Two other common bases are the number of prospects secured and the number of sales transactions. The decision to allocate advertising expenses on the basis of the number of units sold is controversial. While the per-unit-of-product-sold approach is popular, it is not hard to develop an argument against it. One could argue, for example, that advertising expenses are fixed for a period, and since they are fixed costs, productive salespeople should not have to assume a larger advertising burden than unproductive salespeople. One could also argue that the per-unit approach treats advertising as a consequence of sales, rather than as a cause, and therefore the scheme violates the control principle alluded to earlier that one should search for factors that control the functional cost.

While both of these arguments have merit, we will use the per-unit-of-product basis for allocating advertising expenses below for three reasons: (1) the per-unit approach is one of the most popular; (2) there is no clearly preferred alternative in the literature; (3) the example is designed to illustrate the cost analysis process, not to provide the last word on all possible nuances. Yet you should be aware that the decision as to how to allocate advertising expenses or any of the expense categories can change the fundamental conclusions one draws about the profitability of a particular segment.

Warehousing and Shipping

In regard to **warehousing and shipping** costs, the profitability analysis by sales representatives does not include an allocation for the warehouseperson's salary because that salary would continue regardless of what the sales rep sold. Rather, all that is allocated to the salespeople are the packaging costs per unit, which amounted to $2 per bicycle.

Order Processing

The office clerk's salary is not allocated to salespeople because there is no causal link between an individual representative's sales and that salary. The office rent charged to this activity is similarly not allocated. The **order processing** costs that are allocated are the direct expenses for postage and supplies. Order processing costs are most directly linked to the number of orders, which produces an allocation of $4 per order.

Transportation

Transportation charges amounted to $6 per bike. These are charged against the individual sales representatives according to the number of bicycles each sold. When all these expenses are aggregated and subtracted from gross margin, it is found that each representative is contributing to profits. Such a result poses a dilemma for the company sales manager. The branch is not profitable, but each salesperson in the branch is contributing to profits. Admittedly, the sales reps may not be making a large enough contribution. If there were a profit standard for each salesperson, performance could be compared to the standard. This example demonstrates the difference between a performance analysis in which a standard of comparison is established beforehand and a straight cost and profitability analysis.

   The company sales manager could compare the contributions to profit of the representatives in the Orlando branch with those of other sales representatives by doing a similar analysis for other branches. If the Orlando salespeople were found to be low, it might indicate the payroll in the Orlando branch was too high for the number of bicycles sold. The sales manager might then consider removing one or more reps from the territory. Alternatively, the manager might consider increasing the number of calls or changing the salary/commission mixture in the salespeople's compensation package. Still other strategies would be to close the warehouse associated with the branch or to close the branch. The profit implications of each strategy would be different. They could be calculated, however, if the company maintains sales and cost records by small units. Conversely, when basic records are aggregated into larger totals and are stored that way in the company's accounting system, such isolate-and-explode analyses are precluded.

   Suppose the sales manager felt that for strategic reasons, she did not wish to close the branch or the warehouse. Rather, she wished to consider reassigning one representative in the branch to another office and territory. Since there are typically significant company costs and personal disruptions to the rep in such a switch, the sales manager did not take these reassignments lightly. Suppose, therefore, she wanted to ascertain the profitability of each account to the salesperson and the company.

   Exhibit 12.14 and Exhibit 12.15 contain, respectively, the activity levels of Tucker, the worst-performing representative in terms of the analysis contained in Exhibit 12.12,

EXHIBIT 12.14
Activities of Tucker
broken down by
account

Customers of Tucker	Number of Sales Calls	Number of Orders	Number of Units Purchased			
			A	B	C	Total
Allen	50	35	807	1,258	1,567	3,632
Brown	25	20	645	880	1,043	2,568
Cooper	25	25	162	378	869	1,409
Total	100	80	1,614	2,516	3,479	7,609

EXHIBIT 12.15
Profitability analysis
for Tucker broken
down by customer

	Total	Allen	Brown	Cooper
Sales				
Product A	$ 371,220	$185,610	$148,350	$ 37,260
Product B	452,880	226,440	158,400	68,040
Product C	417,480	188,040	125,160	104,280
Total Sales	1,214,580	600,090	431,910	209,580
Cost of Goods Sold				
Product A	290,520	145,260	116,100	29,160
Product B	377,400	188,700	132,000	56,700
Product C	347,900	156,700	104,300	86,900
Total COGS	1,015,820	490,660	352,400	172,760
Gross Margin	225,760	109,430	79,510	36,820
Expenses				
Direct selling				
Salary	48,000	24,000	12,000	12,000
Commissions	12,416	6,001	4,319	2,096
Travel	19,000	9,500	4,750	4,750
Advertising				
Product A	30,028	15,014	12,000	3,014
Product B	20,008	10,004	6,998	3,006
Product C	13,506	6,083	4,049	3,374
Warehousing and shipping	15,218	7,264	5,136	2,818
Order processing	320	140	80	100
Transportation	45,654	21,792	15,408	8,454
Total Expenses	204,149	99,798	64,740	39,611
Contribution to Profit (Loss)	$ 21,611	$ 9,632	$ 14,770	$ (2,791)

broken down by account and the resulting profit contribution of each account based on the same allocation criteria used previously. The analysis illustrates the operation of the iceberg principle.

Although Tucker overall contributes to profit, one account is generating a loss. The loss can be traced to the number of bicycles ordered by Cooper. Cooper orders every time Tucker calls, but the average order size is very low. Less frequent calls might be the answer; fewer calls might produce the same net sales but reduce Tucker's travel expenses charged to Cooper. The analysis also reveals that although Allen purchased the most bikes,

Brown was the most profitable account Tucker had. Again, these insights would be impossible to generate if Hurricane Performance Bicycle Company did not use modularized marketing cost analyses.

The profitability analyses by marketing segment do not tell the sales manager of Hurricane Performance Bicycle Company or any other manager what to do. They do, however, provide managers with some basic information for making intelligent choices.

Promise and Problems

The preceding example, while basic, reveals both the promise and some of the problems associated with marketing cost analysis. The real benefit is the opportunity it provides managers to isolate segments of the business that are most profitable as well as those that generate losses. This information allows those involved to improve their planning and control of the firm's activities. When combined with proper sales analysis techniques discussed in Chapter 13, it provides sales managers with a formidable analytical weapon for managing the personal selling function.

The example also illustrates the problems associated with the technique. Sales analysis requires that data be available in the proper detail. Some data can be costly to generate and expensive to maintain, but sophisticated information systems like enterprise software and contact management software can lower the cost. The system must be able to select and aggregate only those inputs appropriate to the segment of the business being analyzed. As the example indicates, there is often a question as to which costs should be allocated and what bases should be used to allocate these costs. The most appropriate allocation bases can generate spirited discussion among those involved. Allocations cannot be taken lightly because they ultimately affect the profitability of a segment; at the same time, however, there are usually no perfect answers as to how costs should be allocated. Thus, setting up a good marketing cost system can take a good deal of expensive executive time.

The benefits outweigh the higher costs. A growing number of companies are profiting from implementing market cost analysis.[14]

Return of Assets Managed

Sales and cost analyses provide the sales manager with two important financial techniques for controlling the personal selling function. The first measures the results achieved and the second the cost of producing those results. The important financial ingredient left out of those analyses is the assets needed to produce those results. At a minimum, the company will be committing working capital in the form of accounts receivable and inventories to support the sales function.[15] The return produced on the assets used in each segment of the business provides sales managers with a useful variation of more traditional cost analysis procedures for evaluating and controlling various elements of the personal selling function.

The formula for **return on assets managed (ROAM)** reflects both the contribution margin associated with a given level of sales and asset turnover.[16] It is as follows:

$$\text{ROAM} = \text{Contribution as a percentage of sales} \times \text{Asset turnover rate}$$

The formula indicates that the return to a segment of the business can be improved either by increasing the profit margin on sales or by maintaining the same profit margin and increasing the asset turnover rate. The formula can then be used to evaluate segments or to select the best alternative from strategies being considered.

Think of, for example, the use of ROAM to evaluate the performance of two sales branches. Exhibit 12.16 contains the basic financial data. Note that Branch A sold more

EXHIBIT 12.16

Analysis of return on assets managed

	Branch A	Branch B
Sales	$2,500,000	$1,500,000
Cost of Goods Sold	2,000,000	1,275,000
Gross Margin	500,000 (20%)	225,000 (15%)
Less variable branch expenses		
Salaries	155,000	80,000
Commissions	25,000	10,000
Office expenses	30,000	20,000
Travel and entertainment	40,000	20,000
	250,000	130,000
Branch contribution to profit	250,000	95,000
Branch investments		
Accounts receivable	500,000	150,000
Inventories	750,000	225,000
	1,250,000	375,000
Earnings as a percentage of sales	10.0%	6.3%
Turnover	2.0	4.0
Branch percent return on assets managed	20.0%	25.2%

than Branch B and the gross margin on these sales was higher, both in total and as a percentage of sales, because of the mix of products. Furthermore, the contribution to total company profits was higher for Branch A than for Branch B, and earnings as a percentage of sales were 10.0 percent in Branch A and only 6.3 percent in Branch B. By all these standards, Branch A performed better.

These criteria, however, ignore the assets needed to produce these results. Consider that when the investment in assets, which in the example consists of accounts receivable and inventories for each branch, is factored into the analysis, the picture changes. Branch B required a smaller commitment of the firm's capital. Consequently, Branch B was able to affect an asset turnover twice as large as Branch A, so the return on investment was higher in Branch B than in Branch A.

While the basic ROAM formula can be used to provide useful management information, the managerial insights it affords can be magnified by breaking the basic formula down by its components. The first component—contribution as a percentage of sales—equals the ratio of net contribution divided by sales. The second component—the asset turnover rate—equals sales divided by the assets needed to produce those sales. Each of these second-level components could be expanded. One could, for example, break down the sales component by product or salesperson and could similarly break down the assets to assess the impact of each product or salesperson on profitability. Alternatively, one might choose to explode into its detailed elements only one of the second-level components of net contributions, sales, and assets. Exploding one or more of the components of the equation allows management to trace the impact of a number of "what if" scenarios.

Exhibit 12.17, for example, diagrams the return on assets model, with the asset component exploded. Each of the boxes applies to the segment of the business being analyzed. Previously, we saw, for example, that Branch B produced a higher ROAM than Branch A. With the exploded model, management can quickly explore what might be done to

EXHIBIT 12.17   **Expanded return on assets managed (ROAM) model**

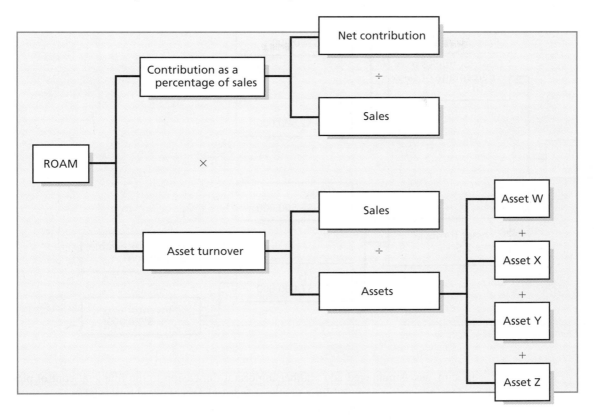

bring the returns into line. Exhibit 12.16 indicates, for example, that the amount invested in receivables and inventories as a percentage of sales varies across the two branches and that, in particular,

	Branch A		Branch B	
Receivables as a percentage of sales	$\dfrac{500,000}{2,500,000}$	$= 20\%$	$\dfrac{150,000}{1,500,000}$	$= 10\%$
Inventories as a percentage of sales	$\dfrac{750,000}{2,500,000}$	$= 30\%$	$\dfrac{225,000}{1,500,000}$	$= 15\%$

   Management might logically ask what would happen to ROAM in Branch A if receivables or inventories as a percentage of sales or both were reduced to the levels existing in Branch B. Exhibit 12.18 traces the implication of what a reduction in accounts receivables to 10 percent of sales (to $250,000) in Branch A through better billing and follow-up procedures might do for its profitability. The example, which assumes no lost sales because of these billing efforts, demonstrates the returns could be brought directly in line with this one change. Management could just as easily assess the profit implications of, say, 5, 10, and 15 percent declines in sales to determine how sensitive the branch returns might be to a change in the billing procedures.

EXHIBIT 12.18   **Impact of a reduction in accounts receivable to $250,000 in branch A**

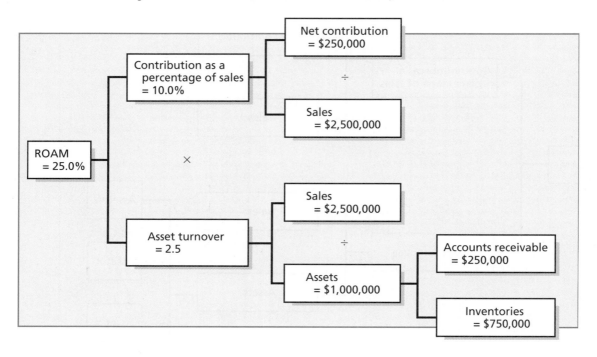

In sum, assets managed add another important dimension to the financial control picture. The investment required for a venture needs to be recognized because long-run profits can be maximized only if the optimal level of investment in each asset is achieved. Unfortunately, the point was made earlier that marketers have been slower to embrace cost analysis than sales analysis. Clearly, despite their compelling intuitive appeal, cost or profitability analysis and asset return analysis have a way to go before they match the popularity of sales analysis in managing the personal selling function.

Summary

Marketing cost analysis attempts to isolate the costs incurred in producing various levels of sales to determine the profitability of sales by segment of the business. Marketing cost analysis can be used to advantage by sales managers to investigate the profitability of regions, branches, territories, customers, or various channels of distribution.

Most firms have been slower to embrace cost analysis than sales analysis for studying their marketing activities. Part of this lag can be explained by the fact that many costs associated with doing business are not entered in the firm's accounting system in their most useful form for decision making. Thus, it is necessary to rework these costs so they are more useful. The adoption of activity-based cost (ABC) accounting systems is helping to increase the use of cost analysis.

A marketing cost analysis can be conducted using either a full-cost, a contribution margin, or an activity-based cost approach. The full-cost approach allocates all the costs of doing business, even fixed costs, to one of the operating segments. The contribution margin approach holds that only those costs that can be specifically identified with the segment of the business should be deducted from the revenue produced by the segment. The contribution margin approach is more logically defensible from a decision-making perspective. An activity-based cost approach is similar to contribution, but the cost of each activity is defined and allocated.

There are four steps in conducting a marketing cost analysis. First, the purpose of the study must be specified. Second, the natural account costs must be spread to functional cost centers. Next, the functional costs must be allocated to appropriate operating segments using some reasonable bases. Here one looks for those factors that bear a cause-and-effect relationship with the cost. Finally, the allocated costs are summed so the contribution of the segment can be determined.

Return on assets managed provides the sales manager with still another financial tool for controlling the personal selling function. Return on assets managed is the product of contribution to profit as a percentage of sales multiplied by asset turnover. Asset turnover is found by dividing sales by the assets needed to produce those sales. The formula recognizes that the sales manager has only limited assets with which to work. He or she can maximize the profits produced by the personal selling function only if each asset is put to its highest and best use. Return on assets managed is currently less popular than either sales or cost analysis in managing the personal selling function.

Key Terms

full-cost accounting
contribution margin
  accounting
activity-based costing
  (ABC)

sales costs
  direct selling
  advertising
  warehousing and shipping

order processing
transportation
return on assets managed
  (ROAM)

Breakout Questions

1. "Our costs are out of control," claimed Rosemary Harper, chief financial officer of Broadway United. "In particular, I am really concerned about the level of marketing costs, especially for the sales force." With a 235-person sales force, Broadway sells computer hardware and software packages to financial institutions. Harper supports the recommendations of a sales consulting firm to reduce the sales force by 50 percent and to hire a new "sales force" consisting of manufacturer's agents who would be paid on a straight commission basis. The reduction in the sales force would mean that 10 district sales managers would lose their jobs. The sales training manager position would be eliminated as well since manufacturer's agents do not need training according to the sales consultant. Harper intended to keep only the best sales reps and eliminate the others in the 50 percent reduction process. "Those experienced sales reps that remain with Broadway will not need enough training to justify keeping Broadway's training department," noted Harper. What are the advantages and disadvantages of the sales consultant's proposal? Is it possible for a company to cut costs too far?

2. Advertising has a synergistic effect. For example, in the Hurricane Performance Bicycle Company case, the $254,000 advertising expenditure for product A had a positive impact on products B and C and on the company as well. Besides, dollars spent in one period have a carryover effect to future periods. What recommendations would you make to handle these situations?

3. The Rite-Way Corporation, a manufacturer of a line of writing instruments, has completed a ROAM analysis for all products. The deluxe model in its line of fountain pens sells for 5.50 but produces a ROAM of 8.3 percent, well below the 23.5 percent average for the other products. Management believes rising raw material costs, such

as gold and silver prices, are beyond Rite-Way's control. Should Rite-Way drop its deluxe product? Should Rite-Way eliminate commissions paid to sales representatives for deluxe sales?

4. The sales manager of Branch A (Exhibit 12.16) was dismayed with the results. The 20 percent ROAM for the branch was below expectations. The sales manager's response was "OK, they want better results, then we'll increase sales by at least 10 percent. But we'll have to cut prices by 5 percent to do this." Will this benefit Branch A?

5. Accounts receivable are too high for Branch A in Exhibit 12.16. One sales analyst recommends giving credit and collection responsibilities to the sales force. Sales reps would be provided with delinquency objectives aimed at reducing accounts receivables by 20 percent. Those meeting their objectives would earn an additional 1 percent of sales for commission. Will this work? Another analyst contends that since the sales force has no training in credits and collections, accounts receivable should be excluded from ROAM calculations. Do you agree? What would happen to Branch A's ROAM if accounts receivable were excluded?

6. Given the following profit and loss statement for the XYZ Company, allocate the natural accounts to the functional accounts:

XYZ Company
Profit and Loss Statement
2007

Sales		$1,676,000
Cost of goods sold		1,003,000
Gross margin		$ 673,000
Selling and administrative expenses		
Salaries		
Salespeople	120,000	
Sales manager	30,000	
Office personnel	38,000	
Warehouse personnel	30,000	
Commissions	16,760	
Advertising	93,800	
Postage	450	
Supplies		
Office	200	
Warehouse	500	
Packaging	30,000	
Transportation	80,290	
Travel expenses	40,000	
Rent		
Sales	15,000	
Warehouse	35,000	
Order processing	10,000	
Heat and electricity		
Sales	7,000	
Warehouse	18,000	
Order processing	5,000	
Total selling and administrative expenses:		$ 570,000
Net profit (loss)		$ 103,000

7. Nancy Troyer, the sales manager for InterCraft, a manufacturer and distributor of picture frames and supplies, was in the midst of a heavy discussion with representatives from the company's accounting department. The discussion revolved around the new cost system the accounting department was developing so the sales function could be managed more effectively. The topic at the moment was how each salesperson's automobile expenses should be allocated, given that salespeople were handling eight product lines and selling to three different types of outlets—office supply stores, book stores, and arts and crafts specialty supply outlets. The situation was complicated further because sales reps were also expected to prospect for new accounts and attend trade shows in their own and contiguous territories. How would you recommend the costs be allocated if Troyer wanted to determine the profitability of each salesperson? Each product line? Each customer?

8. You are given the following information on two salespeople: Salesperson A earns a $22,000 salary; salesperson B earns $23,000. Both earn 1 percent commission. Advertising costs $3 per unit. Shipping expenses are $2 per unit. Order processing costs total $1 per order. Travel expenses amount to $0.50 per call. Your task is to calculate the contribution to profit (loss) made by each salesperson.

Sales-person	Number of Calls	Number of Orders	Units Sold	Total Sales	Cost of Goods Sold
A	200	250	15,000	$750,000	$600,000
B	295	230	18,000	900,000	720,000

9. As the sales manager of the M.N.O. Company, you are trying to evaluate the performance of two districts. You have decided to look at how each district has managed its assets employed in the selling function. Your task is to determine each district's ROAM.

		District 1		District 2
Sales		$800,000		$500,000
Cost of goods sold		624,000		390,000
Gross margin		176,000		110,000
Variable district expenses:				
Salaries	$49,600		$31,000	
Commissions	8,000		5,000	
Office expenses	9,600		6,000	
Travel	12,800		8,000	
Total expenses		80,000		50,000
Net profit (loss)		96,000		60,000
District investment in assets:				
Accounts receivable		120,000		45,000
Inventories		200,000		80,000
Earnings as a percent of sales		0.12		0.12
Turnover		2.5		4.0

10. Sylvie Faivre, sales analyst for the Bouvre Cheese Company had completed her analysis of one of the southern districts. The district was a candidate for consolidation because management believed sales were not as expected. Sylvie suggested she

should first determine the district's return on assets managed before any decisions were made concerning territory modification. The following provides the data needed to calculate ROAM for the district:

Sales		$4,500,000
Cost of goods sold		4,000,000
Gross margin		500,000
Less variable branch expenses		
Salaries		$ 175,000
Commissions		30,000
Office expenses		35,000
Travel and entertainment		55,000
		295,000
District contribution to profit	$ 205,000	
District investments		
Accounts receivable	750,000	
Inventories	900,000	
	$1,650,000	

Determine the ROAM for the district. What would happen if inventories were reduced by 20 percent? How much would sales have to increase to obtain the company average ROAM of 25 percent? Bouvre's management believes salaries are too high and is considering a 15 percent reduction. Assuming no impact on sales, how would this affect district ROAM?

Leadership Challenge: That Sale Was Expensive, I Think

Barry Jefferson could not understand why he was having a problem getting the information. As the western regional vice president of sales for Digital Dimension Manufacturing he wanted to know how much it was costing the company for a salesperson to make a customer call. Certainly the company would know how much it costs to make a sales call. Unfortunately, the more he investigated the problem, the more he realized Digital Dimension did not have a good handle on its sales costs.

Digital Dimension was an established manufacturer of high-technology components. Its products were used in a variety of products from computers to high-technology appliances (refrigerators, dishwashers, etc.). Practically any product that required a computer chip could use the products offered by the company. As such, the company dealt with a wide range of customers, from the very large to medium-sized companies. At this point, Digital Dimension did practically all of its business in the United States, even though some of its customers were among the largest global companies.

Barry had 150 salespeople in 10 districts west of the Mississippi. He knew the cost of making a sale varied a great deal across the sales force. Nearly half of the sales force was assigned to single customers; indeed, some even had offices inside their customer's business. For the very largest customers, Digital Dimension had as many as four salespeople dedicated to a single account. Others, mostly new salespeople, were responsible for calling on smaller, less-established customers as well as generating new business from potential clients.

He had spoken with his counterpart, Kim Reese, eastern region VP of sales, and she had confirmed her frustration with the current lack of information as well. She indicated support for a meeting with Grace Hart, executive vice president of sales, to discuss how

Digital Dimension could get a better handle on the cost of doing business. As Barry sat in his office he considered how the meeting would go.

Questions

1. You are Barry Jefferson. What do you think would be important to discuss in a meeting with Grace Hart about the sales costs at Digital Dimension?

2. What information would you need to know in order to estimate the cost of making a sales call at the company?

3. If you were Grace Hart, what questions would you ask Barry Jefferson about implementing a cost analysis plan?

Role Play: CanDo Coffee Service

Situation

Levita Wampley assumed the position of vice president of sales for the CanDo Coffee Service seven months ago. Before joining CanDo, Levita served for 12 years in various selling and sales management positions for a major restaurant food service provider. CanDo serves principally medium to large offices and factories, providing coffee pots, coffee, filters, and cups to various break rooms at their clients' places of business. The geographic area served is the state of Florida, with concentrations in the major metropolitan areas. In total, CanDo has about 2,100 established clients and a sales force of 25, plus two sales managers. Salespeople typically call on each client once every two weeks to ensure everything is going well with the service, to clean the equipment as needed, and to replenish supplies. Salespeople drive a CanDo van, which they must keep stocked appropriately from their local CanDo warehouse. CanDo operates with a very healthy margin of profit, as it is essentially providing a turnkey service to its clients—who are quite willing to pay well for avoiding the bother of performing this task.

Levita has become convinced that she must address the following problem. It seems that because of differing travel requirements for salespersons' routes, varying distances from salespersons' homes to the local CanDo warehouse, differences in the nature of the facilities of clients (size, layout, ease of access, etc.), and variation in the number of break rooms in each facility that must be serviced, a growing feeling of inequity is being experienced by the CanDo sales force. The salespeople are paid on a combination of salary and commission, and the commission is based on the profitability of each sales territory. Fixed and variable costs associated with the territory are allocated to arrive at the profit component. And to complicate things more, there is also a potential for a bonus component based on signing up new customers. This compensation mix is not the problem: the problem is effectively arriving at the territory profit figure monthly so that commission payments are fair and equitable across the different client situations and travel requirements.

In the past, the bottom-line profit has been calculated using a contribution margin approach with indirect costs allocated on the basis of overall sales volume of the territory as a percentage of total sales. Levita certainly realizes this is potentially problematic and has recently been reading up on activity-based costing as one way of dealing with issues such as this. She calls a meeting with the two sales managers, Ryan Roan and Fernando Perez, to discuss how they might restructure the calculations of the profit component of the salesperson incentive plan.

Characters in the Role Play

Levita Wampley, VP of sales for CanDo Coffee Service

Ryan Roan, sales manager for northern Florida (roughly from I-4 northward)

Fernando Perez, sales manager for southern Florida (roughly everything south of I-4)

Assignment

Break into groups of three, with one student playing each character. It doesn't matter what the actual gender mix of your group is. Before you stage the meeting, work separately using the material in your chapter to come up with your own recommendation for a new approach to calculating the territory profit figures monthly. You can make some assumptions about the potential bases for allocation, and you can be creative in your solutions, so long as they are realistic. You will need to be prepared to justify your recommendations in the meeting. Then get together and role-play the meeting among Levita, Ryan, and Fernando. In the end, you want to come out of the meeting with a unified plan for changing this important input to their incentive program. Above all else, be sure your new system for calculating the territory profit component is fair and equitable to the CanDo salespeople. Note: Do not recommend changing their compensation/incentive plan. Assume that you are to simply fix the profit calculation.

Minicase: Takamatsu Sports

Takamatsu Sports is a Japanese sporting goods company based in Osaka, Japan, that manufactures and sells tennis equipment. It sells three different tennis racquets: the Nomo, the Ichiro, the Matsui. The company experienced a loss last year for the first time, and founder and CEO Hiroshi Takamatsu is interested in analyzing the company's financial data to determine a cause for the loss. Takamatsu's profit and loss statement for last year is as follows:

Profit and Loss Statement for Takamatsu Sports (in USD)

Sales		$2,253,370
Cost of goods sold		1,754,630
Gross margin		$ 498,770
Selling and administrative expenses		
Salaries	$156,000	
Commissions	22,534	
Advertising	176,890	
Postage and office supplies	342	
Packaging materials	20,527	
Transportation charges	51,318	
Travel expenses	42,000	
Rent	120,000	
Total selling and administrative expenses		589,611
Net profit (loss)		($90,871)

Takamatsu Sports has three sales representatives: Daisuke Chimura, Akihide Fujita, and Yoko Ota. Mr. Chimura and Mr. Fujita, both men, had been with the company for years and had successful sales records. However, the newest sales representative, Ms. Ota, is female and yet unproven, and the decision to hire her was a big change from traditional Japanese culture, because in the past it was rare for women to hold such positions. Mr. Takamatsu felt when hiring her that she was highly qualified, but he was concerned that she would have a challenge in communicating to customers because the customers may be uncomfortable working with a woman. In fact, early indications are that Ms. Ota is not making as many sales calls as the other two representatives. This troubles Mr. Takamatsu because at

Takamatsu Sports, and in Japan in general, selling is based on a relationship-selling model, where relationships between seller and customer are paramount and may be built for months before an overture of buying products even is made.

Mr. Takamatsu decided to do a cost analysis with the purpose of determining the profitability of the three sales representatives. He then allocated natural accounts to functional accounts as follows:

Natural Accounts		Functional Accounts				
		Direct Selling	Advertising	Warehousing	Orders/ Billing	Transportation
Salaries	$156,000	$120,000		$ 19,000	$17,000	
Commissions	22,534	22,534				
Advertising	176,890		$176,890			
Postage and supplies	342				342	
Packaging materials	20,527			20,527		
Transportation charges	51,318					$51,318
Travel expenses	42,000	42,000				
Rent	120,000	32,800		82,000	5,200	
Totals	$589,611	$217,334	$176,890	$121,527	$22,542	$51,318

He then gathered the following sales data to use in the profitability analysis:

A. Information by Product

Products	Selling Price per Unit	Cost per Unit	Gross Margin per Unit	Number Sold in Period	Sales in Period	Advertising Expenditures	Advertising Expenditures Per Unit
Nomo	$ 45	$ 35	$ 10	16,742	$ 753,390	$ 29,500	$ 1.76
Ichiro	70	55	15	10,543	738,010	60,210	5.71
Matsui	110	85	25	6,927	761,970	87,180	12.59
				34,212	$2,253,370	$176,890	

B. Information by Salesperson

Salesperson	Number of Sales Calls	Number of Orders	Number of Units Sold			
			Nomo	Ichiro	Matsui	Total
Chimura	45	30	5,902	3,409	2,410	11,721
Fujita	40	20	5,100	3,510	1,890	10,500
Ota	35	30	5,740	3,624	2,627	11,991
	120	80	16,742	10,543	6,927	34,212

Mr. Takamatsu also determined the following data for making the cost allocations:

- Each salesperson was paid $40,000 salary with a 1 percent commission on what was sold.
- Each salesperson was allotted an annual travel expense budget of $14,000, which was fully used by each salesperson.
- Advertising cost was allotted by the number of units sold by each salesperson.

- Packaging and shipping for the warehousing cost is $0.60 per unit sold.
- Order processing cost is $.01 per unit sold.
- Transportation cost is $1.50 per unit sold.

Mr. Takamatsu has now come to you, his trusted managerial accountant, with the above data and has asked you to perform the profitability analysis for the three sales representatives.

Questions

1. Develop a profitability analysis by salesperson based on the model of Exhibit 12.12 in the textbook.
2. Who is the most profitable sales representative? The least? Are Mr. Takamatsu's concerns about Ms. Ota's performance valid?
3. Based on your analysis, what recommendation(s) can you give to Mr. Takamatsu to return his company to profitability?

Suggested Readings

Challagalla, Goutam N., and Tasadduq A. Shervani. "Dimensions and Types of Supervisory Control: Effects on Salesperson Performance and Satisfaction." *Journal of Marketing* 60 (January 1996), pp. 89–105.

Goebel, Daniel, J., Greg W. Marshall, and William B. Locander. "Activity Based Costing." *Industrial Marketing Management* 27 (1998), pp. 497–510.

Hunter, Gary K., and William D. Perreault Jr. "Sales Technology Orientation, Information Effectiveness, and Sales Performance" *Journal of Personal Selling & Sales Management* 26 (Spring 2006) pp. 95–113.

Kissan, Joseph. "On the Optimality of Delegating Pricing Authority to the Sales Force." *Journal of Marketing,* 65 (January 2001), pp. 62–70.

Ness, Joseph A., Michael J. Schroeck, Rick A. Letendre, and Willmar J. Douglas. "The Role of ABM in Measuring Customer Value." *Strategic Finance* 82 (April 2001), pp. 44–49.

Chapter **Thirteen**

Evaluating Salesperson Performance

The Case for a Focus on Sales Force Performance Management Systems

An effective salesperson performance management system (1) informs your sales force of the way you want them to sell; (2) provides sales management with a framework from which to manage; and (3) enables measurement and continuous improvement of the sales force's performance.

Performance management has come into sharp focus as a key issue for world-class sales organizations. Over time, sales organizations have tended to remain a bit of a holdout in implementing various new-age approaches to evaluation and control. Somehow, the entire business process reengineering (BPR) and total quality management (TQM) movements of the last 25 years largely passed right through the world without leaving much of a mark on the sales force. Perhaps credit for the current interest goes to the widespread adoption of customer relationship management (CRM) and sales force automation (SFA). That is, after years of expensive, chaotic software implementations, sales executives are finally clueing in to the fact that without fundamental business processes underpinning their information systems, they have invested enormously in what are essentially large databases with input screens and output reports. By adding comprehensive performance management systems with proper milestones, workflow, business logic, and controls to the systems, sales managers can actually bring order to the chaos and begin to proactively manage their productivity as manufacturing and other areas of the firm have for decades.

Numerous executives interviewed for the 2007 HR Chally report highlighted major milestones in integrating performance management systems, defined their key performance metrics, and discussed how the processes influence everything from selling, to coaching, to managing, to measuring and rewarding. World-class sales forces have come to acknowledge two key truths that now usher in a new era in sales force management. First, sales is no longer the domain of individualist mavericks who succeed through inherent personal ability and brute force of will. Professional selling is a highly complex affair that involves the participation of many team contributors.

Long, extended sales cycles now commonly involve roles such as inside salespeople, major account managers, technical specialists, business partners, customer service, and other internal resources. Explicitly defining the responsibilities of each and coordinating customer touchpoints is impossible to accomplish without a structured process to assign ownership, timing, and performance accountability to the people and associated tasks.

A second truth is that senior executives are now demanding accountability from *all of the functional areas* inside their companies—and sales is certainly not excluded. Sales can no longer remain the black box that it has been to many CEOs, most of whom have no front-line sales experience. Research by State Farm in 2006 identified only 15 of the Fortune 500 CEOs as having had front-line sales experience. Consequently, the pressure for sales forces to perform is increasing, and average tenure of Chief Sales Officers (CSOs) is falling. According to Jim Dickie of CSO Insights, in 2004 the average tenure of a CSO had fallen to just over 23 months. Given these conditions, sales executives are no longer satisfied to wait and see how their sales force is performing—they must aggressively engage in performance management. This desire to manage, coupled with enhanced information technology capability to collect and report data in an accurate and timely manner, has driven sales management to take control of their sales forces. But you can't manage what you can't measure, and you can't measure without formal performance management processes.

The bottom line is that world-class sales forces are focusing on comprehensive performance management systems and processes for the first time in earnest. They have the motive, they have the capability, and they are making it happen. Looking forward, you can bet that such processes will continue to rise in stature as the performance gap widens between firms who have them and firms who don't.

Source: HR Chally Group (2007), *The Chally World Class Excellence Research Report: The Route to the Summit.* Dayton, OH: HR Chally Group.

LEARNING OBJECTIVES

Performance evaluations should be a process that provides a forum for dialogue between a salesperson and the sales manager, focused on gaining the impetus for future professional development and performance success. In order to successfully execute a performance review, sales managers must have a strong working knowledge of different measures of performance that are appropriate to a particular selling situation. Then they must conduct the appraisal in a manner that allows the salesperson to build on current strengths and proficiencies and make performance improvements where warranted.

After reading this chapter, you should be able to

- Explain the difference between performance and effectiveness.

- Identify objective measures of salesperson performance, both output and input.

- Utilize ratio analysis as an objective approach to salesperson performance measurement.

- Discuss key issues related to subjective measurement of salesperson performance and the forms that might be used to administer such an evaluation.

- Understand how a sales manager can make the performance review process more productive and valuable for the salesperson.

PERFORMANCE VERSUS EFFECTIVENESS

A key issue in evaluating the performance of salespeople is the distinction among the concepts of behavior, performance, and effectiveness.[1] Although role perceptions, aptitude, skill level, and motivation level were discussed in Chapter 6 as being directly linked to performance, it is also important to understand that they are directly linked to behavior as well.

Behavior refers to what salespeople do—that is, the tasks on which they expend effort while working. These tasks might include calling on customers, writing orders, preparing sales presentations, sending follow-up communication, and the like. These are the sales activities discussed in Chapter 2.

Think of **performance** as behavior evaluated in terms of its contribution to the goals of the organization. In other words, performance has a normative element reflecting whether a salesperson's behavior is good or bad, appropriate or inappropriate, in light of the organization's goals and objectives. Note that behavior and performance are both influenced by relevant sales activities. Of course, these activities in turn depend on the types of sales jobs in question.

Before we discuss salesperson evaluation further, let's also distinguish between performance and effectiveness. By definition, **effectiveness** refers to some summary index of organizational outcomes for which an individual is at least partly responsible. Examples include sales volume, market share, profitability of sales, and customer retention rate. The crucial distinction between performance and effectiveness is that the latter does not refer to behavior directly; rather, it is a function of additional factors not under the individual salesperson's control. These include such things as top management policies, sales potential or difficulty of a territory, and actions of competitors.

It is generally agreed that salespeople should be evaluated solely on those phases of sales performance over which they exercise control and should not be held responsible for factors beyond their control. If a company's method of measuring salesperson performance is to result in valid comparisons, serious consideration must be given to distinguishing between factors within a salesperson's control versus those outside his or her control in developing yardsticks for objective or subjective evaluation. Leadership 13.1 presents a classic theory of motivation, **attribution theory,** that is quite relevant to this managerial dilemma.

One could argue that a sales manager's careful specification of performance standards by territory should eliminate inequities across territories. For example, percentage of quota attained should be an acceptable measure of performance because quotas supposedly consider variations in environmental factors across territories. Admittedly, a comparison of salespeople with respect to percentage of quota attained is a better measure of their performance than is a comparison that simply looks at each representative's level of absolute sales or market share, assuming the quotas were done well. However, assuming that quotas are done well is a big "if"—sometimes quotas are not so well developed. In some instances, they are arbitrary and are not necessarily based on an objective assessment of all the factors that facilitate or constrain a salesperson's ability to make a sale. This is especially true if quota development relies too heavily on historical trends and not enough on emerging trends in a given sales territory.

Even when quotas are done well, the measure "percentage of quota attained" still omits much with respect to a salesperson's performance. For one thing, it ignores the profitability of sales. Sales reps can be compared with respect to profitability, or the return they produce on the assets under their control. Establishing quotas that accurately consider the many factors affecting the level of sales a representative should be able to produce in a

Leadership Attributions and Salesperson Performance Evaluation 13.1

Evaluating the performance of a salesperson is all about the sales manager attributing causes of that performance. That is, managers seek out *why* a salesperson's effectiveness is diminished or enhanced so that appropriate reinforcing or remedial actions may be taken. This process of attributing causes of outcomes has been studied extensively under the rubric of *attribution theory,* an approach quite relevant to sales management practice.

Psychologist Fritz Heider developed the cornerstone concept that evaluators tend to operate as "naïve psychologists" when they observe and analyze the behavior of others. He classified variables used by evaluators to interpret the actions of others into three categories: (1) a performance variable (i.e., task success, or effectiveness); (2) environmental variables (task difficulty and luck); and (3) person, or dispositional, variables (ability and effort). Heider proposed that evaluators assess performance based on the following relationships among these factors:

1. Ability = Task difficulty/Effort

2. Performance = (Ability × Effort) ± Task difficulty

According to equation 1, if two salespeople put forth the same amount of effort, the one who performs the more difficult task is expected to have the greater ability. Also, if two salespeople accomplish the same task with equal levels of performance, the one who expends the least effort is expected by the rater to have the higher ability. According to equation 2, a sales manager's perception of a salesperson's performance is a function of ability times effort, plus or minus the effects of differing task difficulty.

In the context of salesperson evaluation, Heider's concept of task difficulty may be easily translated to territory difficulty. Territory difficulty is important because rarely, if ever, in professional selling does one find any two territories that are equal in all respects. Therefore, sales managers must adjust performance ratings by taking into account the differences in territory difficulty among the salespeople they supervise. Unfortunately, this if often

neglected when sales managers complete performance evaluations. A phenomenon known as the *fundamental attribution error* predicts that contextual or background information (such as differences in territories among salespeople in a sales manager's unit) will be systematically ignored by evaluators, and instead their ratings will be based on "person" factors such as perceived ability and effort. Heider proposed that background situational (contextual) information is less salient to evaluators than is person (appraisee) information, which is analogous to the Gestalt concept of figure against ground. In the context of salesperson evaluations, such thinking suggests that an evaluation bias may arise in which sales managers focus on dispositional factors, such as the salesperson's ability and effort (the "figure") and ignore contextual factors (the "ground"), such as territory difficulty and luck.

Sales organizations must work hard to guard against this form of evaluation bias. Assuming equal performance, over time a salesperson who is evaluated equally or lower than a peer whose territory is less difficult may become dissatisfied and feel unfairly treated, resulting in a very effective salesperson leaving the company. Firms must train their sales managers to fully consider all contextual and person factors when making their evaluations. By doing so, sales managers can avoid succumbing to the fundamental attribution error.

Sources: Thomas E. DeCarlo, Sanjeev Agarwal, and Shyman B. Vyas. "Performance Expectations of Salespeople: The Role of Past Performance and Casual Attributions in Independent and Interdependent Cultures." *Journal of Personal Selling & Sales Management* 27 (Spring 2007), pp. 133–47l; Andrea L. Dixon, Lukas P. Forbes, and Susan M. B. Schertzer. "Early Success: How Attributions for Sales Success Shape Inexperienced Salesperson's Behavioral Intentions." *Journal of Personal Selling & Sales Management* 25 (Winter 2005), pp. 67–77; Andrea L. Dixon, and Susan M. B. Schertzer. "Bouncing Back: How Salesperson Optimism and Self-Efficacy Influence Attributions and Behaviors Following Failure." *Journal of Personal Selling & Sales Management* 25 (Fall 2005), pp. 361–69.

territory is difficult, but determining the appropriate standards of profitability for each territory is even more difficult.

Even if good sales and profit standards could be developed, the problem of evaluating salespeople would not be solved because neither measure incorporates activities that may have no short-term payout but still have substantial consequences to the firm in the long run. These include the time devoted to laying the groundwork for a long-term client relationship, particularly when developing a potentially large account. Other activities that often go unmeasured are building long-term goodwill for the company and developing a detailed understanding of the capabilities of the products being sold. Thus, other measures beyond sales and profits are needed to more directly reflect salesperson performance.

The other measures firms use to evaluate salespeople fall into two broad categories: (1) objective measures and (2) subjective measures.[2] *Objective measures* reflect statistics the sales manager can gather from the firm's internal data. These measures are best used when they reflect elements of the sales process. *Subjective measures* typically rely on personal evaluations by someone inside the organization, usually the salesperson's immediate supervisor, of how individual salespeople are doing. Subjective measures are generally gathered via direct observation of the salesperson by the manager but may involve input from customers or other sources.

OBJECTIVE MEASURES

Objective measures fall into three major categories: (1) output measures, (2) input measures, and (3) ratios of output or input measures. Exhibit 13.1 lists some of the more common output and input measures, and Exhibit 13.2 (later in the chapter) provides some of the more commonly used ratios.

The use of outputs, inputs, and ratios to measure salesperson performance is a recognition of the nature of the relationship selling process. As we have learned, some sales

EXHIBIT 13.1
Common output and input measures used to evaluate salespeople

Output measures	Input measures
Orders	Calls
Number of orders	Total number of calls
Average size of orders	Number of planned calls
Number of canceled orders	Number of unplanned calls
Accounts	Time and time utilization
Number of active accounts	Days worked
Number of new accounts	Calls per day (call rate)
Number of lost accounts	Selling time versus nonselling time
Number of overdue accounts	Expenses
Number of prospective accounts	Total
	By type
	As a percentage of sales
	As a percentage of quota
	Nonselling activities
	E-mails to prospects
	Phone calls to prospects
	Number of formal proposals developed
	Advertising displays set up
	Number of meetings held with distributors/dealers
	Number of training sessions held with distributor/dealer personnel
	Number of calls on distributor/dealer customers
	Number of service calls made
	Number of overdue accounts collected

processes, especially those experienced by salespeople seeking to secure, build, and maintain long-term relationships with profitable customers, can take months or years. Within the relationship selling process, salespeople engage in activities with (or in pursuit of) the prospect or buyer. The manager can measure those activities and compare the activities with results for each stage. By examining this performance evidence, managers can pinpoint potential areas for improvement by each salesperson, or identify changes that should be made in the sales strategy so that it is aligned with how buyers want to buy.

Output Measures

Output measures represent the results of the efforts expended by the salesperson.

Orders

The number of orders each salesperson secures is often used to assess the rep's ability to ultimately close sales. Although the number of orders a salesperson secures is important, the average size of those orders is equally so. Having many orders may mean the orders are small and may indicate the person is spending too much time calling on small, low-potential customers and not enough time calling on large, high-potential customers.

Still another related measure is the number of canceled orders. A salesperson who loses a large proportion of total orders to subsequent cancellation may be using high-pressure tactics in sales presentations rather than engaging in relationship selling.

Accounts

The various account measures provide a perspective on the equity of territory assignments and also on how the salesperson is handling the territory. Attention to these measures can help the sales manager overcome the tendency to discount territory difficulty information as discussed in Leadership 13.1. One popular measure focuses on the number of active accounts in the salesperson's customer portfolio. Various definitions of an active account are used. For example, it may be any customer that has placed an order in the past six months or in the past year. A salesperson's performance in one year may be compared with performance in past years by contrasting the number of active accounts. Closely related to this yardstick is a measure that tracks the number of new accounts a salesperson develops in a given time. Some companies even establish new-prospect quotas for salespeople that allow a ready comparison of performance to standard in this area of evaluation.

As with the number of new accounts, the number of lost accounts can be a revealing statistic, since it indicates how successfully the salesperson is satisfying the ongoing needs of the established accounts in the territory. Still other account measures by which salespeople can be compared are the number of overdue accounts, which might indicate the level to which the salesperson is following company procedures in screening accounts for their creditworthiness, and the number of prospective accounts, which assesses the salesperson's ability to identify potential target customers.

Input Measures

Many objective measures of performance evaluation focus on the efforts sales representatives expend rather than the results of those efforts. These efforts are **input measures** of performance. Input measures are important for two key reasons. First, efforts or desirable behaviors are much more directly controllable than results in the short term. If a rep's sales fall short of quota, the problem may lie with the person, the quota, or a change in the environment. On the other hand, if the number of calls a salesperson makes falls short of the target, it is much clearer that the problem lies more directly with the individual.[3] Second, in relationship selling a time lag frequently exists between inputs and outputs. A particularly large sale may be the result of several years of effort. Thus, a focus on the efforts (behaviors) themselves affords the sales manager the opportunity to evaluate and coach the salesperson during the relationship selling process into making changes that can positively affect the output (results).

Calls

The number of current customer or prospect calls is often used to decide whether a salesperson is covering the territory properly. The number of calls on each account is an important factor in the design of territories and also should be used to evaluate the salesperson assigned to the territory. After all, sales calls are a resource with finite supply—they represent a resource that is time-sensitive in that the time available to make them evaporates if it is not used.

CRM software systems integrate customer contacts by salespeople into their information collection, analysis, and reporting capabilities. Also, contact and customer management software, such as GoldMine and Act! by Sage, automates the call report process. In a record established for each account, the salesperson can input information about each call. This information can be summarized by the software for a report made available to the sales manager either by e-mail or Web access. Of course, if the CRM software resides on a shared network, the sales manager can access the information directly. Such technological advances minimize the time spent preparing paperwork and help salespeople maximize their time in front of buyers; they also serve as a great aid to sales managers in performance evaluation.

Time and Time Utilization

The number of days worked and the calls per day (or call rate) are routinely used by many companies to assess salespeople's efforts since the product of the two quantities provides a direct measure of the extent of customer contact. If the amount of customer contact by a salesperson is low, one can look separately at the components to see where the problem lies. Perhaps the salesperson has not been working enough because of extenuating circumstances, a situation that would show up in the number of days worked. Alternatively, perhaps the salesperson's total time input was satisfactory, but the salesperson was not using that time wisely and, consequently, had a low call rate.

Comparing salespeople's division of time between sales calls, traveling, office work, and other job aspects offers a useful perspective. For the most part, the firm would want salespeople to maximize the time in face-to-face customer contact at the expense of the other two factors. Sales organizations want salespeople to minimize unproductive time. Of course, *telecommuting,* or working from a home office, is not new in the field of professional selling. Through necessity (e.g., no company facility from which to work in the salesperson's headquarter's city) or convenience, many salespeople maintain their primary office space in their home.

Analysis of time utilization requires detailed input on how each salesperson is spending time, and collecting and analyzing this data can be expensive and can itself be time-consuming. Some companies, however, routinely conduct such analysis because the benefits are deemed to outweigh the costs.

Expenses

The objective inputs discussed so far for evaluating salespeople (calls; time and time utilization) focus mainly on the extent of a salesperson's efforts. Another key emphasis when evaluating salespeople is the cost of those efforts. Many firms keep records detailing the total expenses incurred by each salesperson. Some break these expenses down by type, such as automobile expenses, lodging expenses, entertainment expenses, and so forth. Sales managers might look at these expenses in total or as a percentage of sales or quota by salesperson and then use these expense ratios as part of the salesperson's performance evaluation.

Nonselling Activities

In addition to assessing the direct contact of salespeople with customers, some firms monitor indirect contact. They use indexes such as the number of letters written, number of telephone calls made, and number of formal proposals developed.

As we have learned, in relationship selling a salesperson's activities go beyond what might be considered a pure selling emphasis. For example, companies that sell to retailers may ask salespeople to help monitor and stock shelves, create displays, help retailers advertise, and engage in a number of other nonselling activities as part of an ongoing client relationship . In such instances, firms often try to monitor the extent of these duties, using such indexes as the number of promotional or advertising displays set up, the number of dealer meetings, the number of training sessions for distributor personnel held, the number of calls the salesperson made on dealer customers, the number of service calls made, the number of customer complaints received, and the number of overdue accounts collected. Some of this information can be gathered from the salesperson's reporting system, but it is becoming increasingly commonplace to gain feedback on elements of salesperson performance directly from customers. This trend is discussed in a later section of this chapter on 360-degree performance feedback.

Ratio Measures

As we have learned, a focus on outputs other than straight sales volume and profit can provide useful information on how salespeople are performing. So can analysis of input factors. Additional insights may also be gathered by combining the various outputs or inputs in selected ways, typically in the form of various **ratio measures.** As mentioned earlier, Exhibit 13.2 lists some of the ratios commonly used to evaluate salespeople. These are grouped by expense ratios, account development and servicing ratios, and call activity or productivity ratios.

Expense Ratios

The sales expense ratio combines both salespeople's inputs and the results produced by those inputs in a single number. Salespeople can affect this ratio either by making sales or by controlling expenses. The ratio can also be used to analyze salesperson expenses by type. Thus, a sales/transportation expense ratio that is much higher for one salesperson than others might indicate the salesperson is covering his or her territory inefficiently. However, it is important that the sales manager recognize territory difficulty differences when comparing these ratios, as the salesperson who has an out-of-line ratio may simply have a larger, more geographically dispersed sales territory to cover.

The cost per call ratio expresses the costs of supporting each salesperson in the field as a function of the number of calls the salesperson makes. The ratio can be evaluated using total costs, or the costs can be broken down by elements so that ratios such as expenses per call and travel costs per call can be computed. Not only are these ratios useful for comparing salespeople from the same firm, but they can also be compared with those of other companies in the same industry to assess the efficiency of the firm's selling effort. Such comparative data may be available from trade or professional associations.

EXHIBIT 13.2

Common ratios used to evaluate salespeople

Expense ratios

- Sales expense ratio $= \dfrac{\text{Expenses}}{\text{Sales}}$

- Cost per call ratio $= \dfrac{\text{Total costs}}{\text{Number of calls}}$

Account development and servicing ratios

- Account penetration ratio $= \dfrac{\text{Accounts sold}}{\text{Total accounts available}}$

- New-account conversion ratio $= \dfrac{\text{Number of new accounts}}{\text{Total number of accounts}}$

- Lost account ratio $= \dfrac{\text{Prior accounts not sold}}{\text{Total number of accounts}}$

- Sales per account ratio $= \dfrac{\text{Sales dollar volume}}{\text{Total number of accounts}}$

- Average order size ratio $= \dfrac{\text{Sales dollar volume}}{\text{Total number of orders}}$

- Order cancellation ratio $= \dfrac{\text{Number of canceled orders}}{\text{Total number of orders}}$

- Account share $= \dfrac{\text{Salesperson's business from account}}{\text{Account's total business}}$

Call activity or productivity

- Calls per day ratio $= \dfrac{\text{Number of calls}}{\text{Number of days worked}}$

- Calls per account ratio $= \dfrac{\text{Number of calls}}{\text{Number of accounts}}$

- Planned call ratio $= \dfrac{\text{Number of planned calls}}{\text{Total number of calls}}$

- Orders per call (hit) ratio $= \dfrac{\text{Number of orders}}{\text{Total number of calls}}$

Account Development and Servicing Ratios

A number of ratios concern accounts and orders that reflect on how well salespeople are capturing the potential business that exists in their territories. The account penetration ratio, for example, measures the percentage of accounts in the territory from which the salesperson secures orders. It provides a direct measure of whether the salesperson is simply skimming the cream of the business or is working the territory systematically and hard. It can also aid management in identifying both underperforming accounts and accounts that have low lifetime value to the sales organization.

The new-account conversion ratio similarly measures the salesperson's ability to convert prospects to customers. The lost account ratio measures how well the salesperson maintains active customers, reflecting how well the rep is serving the established accounts in the territory.

The sales per account ratio indicates the salesperson's success per account on average. A low ratio could indicate the salesperson is spending too much time calling on small, less profitable accounts and not enough time calling on larger ones. One could also look at the sales per account ratios by class of account, which can reveal the strengths and weaknesses of each salesperson. For example, a salesperson who has a low sales per account ratio for large, high-potential accounts might need help in learning how to sell to a buying center.

The average order size ratio can also reveal the salesperson's patterns of calling on customers. A very low average order size might suggest that calls are too frequent and the salesperson's productivity could be improved by spacing them more. The order cancellation ratio reflects on the salesperson's method of selling. A very high ratio could mean the salesperson is using high-pressure tactics to secure orders rather than pursuing relationship selling approaches and handling customers in a consultative manner.

A key measurement in some types of businesses, particularly those that provide supplies and raw materials, is account share. Account share is the percentage of the account's business that the salesperson gets. Many buyers will split their business among a number of vendors, believing (often erroneously) that they get better service and lower prices when sellers have to compete for the business. In industries where such buying practices are prevalent, the number of accounts is less important to salespeople than the share of each account. As account share increases, economies of scale increase, which raises the profit of the account. Similarly, the measure is an indication of the strength of the relationship with the account.

Call Activity or Productivity Ratios

Call activity ratios measure the effort and planning salespeople put into their customer call activities and the successes they derive from it. The measures might be used to compare salesperson activities in total—such as when using calls per day or when using calls per total number of accounts, or by type of account. The planned call ratio could be used to assess if the salesperson is systematically planning territory coverage or whether the representative is working the territory without an overall game plan. The orders per call ratio bears directly on the question of whether the salesperson's calls on average are productive. This ratio is sometimes called the hit ratio or batting average, since it captures the number of successes (hits or orders) in relation to the number of at-bats (calls).

Summary of Objective Measures

As Exhibits 13.1, 13.2, and the above discussion indicate, many objective output measures, input measures, and ratio measures are available by which salespeople may be evaluated and compared. As you probably sense, many of the measures are somewhat redundant in that they provide overlapping information on salesperson effectiveness. A number of other ratios could be developed by combining the various outputs, inputs, or ratios in different ways. For example, one combination that is often used to evaluate salespeople is the following equation:

$$\text{Sales} = \text{Days worked} \times \frac{\text{Calls}}{\text{Days worked}} \times \frac{\text{Orders}}{\text{Calls}} \times \frac{\text{Sales}}{\text{Orders}}$$

or

$$\text{Sales} = \frac{\text{Days}}{\text{worked}} \times \frac{\text{Call}}{\text{rate}} \times \frac{\text{Batting}}{\text{average}} \times \frac{\text{Average}}{\text{order size}}$$

The equation highlights nicely what a salesperson can do to increase sales. The representative can increase the (1) number of days worked, (2) calls made per day, (3) level of success in securing an order on a given call, and (4) size of those orders. Thus, the equation can be used to isolate how an individual salesperson's performance could be improved. Such an equation, though, focuses on the results of the salesperson's efforts and ignores the cost of those efforts. Similarly, many of the other measures that have been reviewed could be combined via similar equations, but these too would probably ignore one or more elements of salesperson success. Bottom line: No single measure exists that can fully capture the scope of salesperson effectiveness.

In concluding this discussion of objective measures of salesperson performance, two essential points deserve mention. First, just as measuring straight sales volume and profit have advantages and disadvantages for use in evaluating salespeople, so do all of these other objective measures of performance. Rather than relying on only one or two of the measures to assess performance, the methods are more productively used in combination. Second, and also very important, all of the indexes are an aid to judgment, not a substitute for it. For example, the United States Army Recruiting Command (the part of the Army that sells young people on joining) once overrelied on conversion ratios (the percentage of prospects who actually ended up joining the army) to evaluate recruiters' performance. Orders were issued that calls of certain types had to be increased by a high percentage. The problem was that while the calls could be increased, quality could not be maintained. Recruiting effectiveness not only did not increase but actually went down as recruiter morale declined. The comparisons allowed by the various indexes should be the beginning, not the conclusion, of any analysis aimed at assessing how well individual salespeople or the entire sales force are doing.

SUBJECTIVE MEASURES

A useful conceptual distinction exists between the quantitative nature of objective measures of performance discussed in the preceding section and the qualitative nature of the **subjective measures** discussed here. Quantitative measures of performance focus on the outputs and inputs of what salespeople do, whereas qualitative measures reflect behavioral or process aspects of what they do and how well they do it. This difference in what is being measured creates some marked differences in the way objective and subjective measurements are taken and how they are used.

In many ways, it is more difficult to assess the quality rather than the quantity of a salesperson's performance. Quantity measures can require a detailed analysis of a salesperson's call report, an extensive time utilization analysis, or an analysis of the type and number of nonselling activities employed. However, once the measurement procedure is set up, it typically can be conducted with less bias and inconsistency than can quality measurement. On the other hand, when assessing qualitative performance factors, even a well-designed measurement process that is firmly in place leaves much more room for bias in the evaluation. **Bias** refers to performance evaluations that differ from objective reality, usually based on errors by the evaluator. Even well-designed systems must invariably rely on the personal judgment of the individual or individuals charged with evaluation, in our case, the sales manager. Typically, these judgments are secured by having the manager rate the salesperson on a performance appraisal form on each of a number of attributes using some type of rating scale. The attributes most commonly evaluated using performance evaluation forms include,

1. *Sales results.* Volume performance, sales to new accounts, and selling the full product line.

2. *Job knowledge.* Knowledge of company policies, prices, and products.

3. *Management of territory.* Planning of activities and calls, controlling expenses, and handling reports and records.

4. *Customer and company relations.* The salesperson's standing with customers, associates, and company.

5. *Personal characteristics.* Initiative, personal appearance, personality, resourcefulness, etc.

Note that these include a mix of objective and subjective performance measures. In fact, it is true that most formal performance evaluations of salespeople involve a combination of these two types of evaluative criteria.

Forms Used for Subjective Measurement

Exhibit 13.3 shows a typical salesperson evaluation form for various subjective performance criteria. The specific evaluative criteria should match those identified as key success factors for the position (see Chapter 2 for a discussion of the identification of key success factors for sales positions). Such evaluations may be completed annually, semiannually, or quarterly, depending on the firm's human resource management policies. These evaluations supplement the objective performance data generated for the same time frame to provide an overall evaluation of salesperson performance. The form in Exhibit 13.3 is better than many of those in use because it contains anchors or verbal descriptors for the various points on the scale. Another favorable feature of this example form is the space provided for comments, which can enhance understanding of the ratings supplied. The form contains a section where needed improvements and corrective actions may be detailed. All in all, the form should facilitate a constructive dialogue between the salesperson and sales manager and help the salesperson understand his or her strengths and weaknesses and develop approaches to improve performance.

The worst type of rating forms simply list the attributes of interest along one side of the form and the evaluation adjectives along the other. Little description is provided, thus the potential for much ambiguity exists in the evaluation. Exhibit 13.4 illustrates such a poor form. Of course, this type of form can be completed very easily since the evaluator simply checks the box for the adjective that most clearly describes his or her perceptions of the salesperson's performance on each attribute. Unfortunately, such forms are quite common in sales organizations, and they work very poorly in practice and do little to stimulate a constructive dialogue between the salesperson and sales manager. Salespeople typically receive little useful information on improving performance when forms such as Exhibit 13.4 are used.

Problems with Subjective Performance Measurement

Some common problems with performance appraisal systems that rely on subjective rating forms, particularly those using the simple checklist type, include the following:[4]

1. *Lack of an outcome focus.* The most useful type of performance appraisal highlights areas of improvement and the actions that must be taken to implement such improvements. For this to occur, the key behaviors in accomplishing the tasks assigned must be identified. Unfortunately, many companies have not taken this step. Rather, they have simply identified attributes thought to be related to performance, but they have not attempted to systematically assess whether the attributes are key. One type of performance appraisal called BARS (behavioral anchored rating scale) helps overcome this weakness. A BARS system attempts to identify behaviors that are more or less effective with respect to the goals established for the person. BARS will be discussed in more detail shortly.

EXHIBIT 13.3   **Sample subjective performance evaluation form**

SALES PERSONNEL
INVENTORY

Employee's Name _____   Territory _____

Position Title _____   Date _____

INSTRUCTIONS (Read Carefully)
1. Base your judgment on the previous six-month period and not on isolated incidents alone.
2. Place a check in the block that most nearly expresses your judgment on each factor.
3. For those employees who are rated at either extreme of the scale on any factor—for example, outstanding, deficient, limited—please enter a brief explanation for the rating in the appropriate space below the factor.
4. Make your rating an accurate description of the person rated.

FACTORS TO BE CONSIDERED AND RATED:

1. Knowledge of work
(includes knowledge of product, knowledge of customers' business)

☐ Does not have sufficient knowledge of products and application to represent the company effectively.

☐ Has mastered minimum knowledge. Needs further training.

☐ Has average amount of knowledge needed to handle job satisfactorily.

☐ Is above average in knowledge needed to handle job satisfactorily.

☐ Is thoroughly acquainted with our products and technical problems involved in this application.

Comments _____

2. Degree of acceptance by customers

☐ Not acceptable to most customers. Cannot gain entry to their offices.

☐ Manages to see customers but not generally liked.

☐ Has satisfactory relationship with most customers.

☐ Is on very good terms and is accepted by virtually all customers.

☐ Enjoys excellent personal relationship with virtually all customers.

Comments _____

3. Amount of effort devoted to acquiring business

☐ Exceptional in the amount of time and effort put forth in selling.

☐ Devotes constant effort in developing business.

☐ Devotes intermittent effort in acquiring moderate amount of business.

☐ Exerts only minimum amount of time and effort.

☐ Unsatisfactory. Does not put forth sufficient effort to produce business.

Comments _____

(continued)

EXHIBIT 13.3   Sample subjective performance evaluation form *(continued)*

4. Ability to acquire business	☐ Is able to acquire business under the most difficult situations.	☐ Does a good job acquiring business under most circumstances.	☐ Manages to acquire good percentage of customer's business if initial resistance is not too strong.	☐ Able to acquire enough business to maintain only a minimum sales average.	☐ Rarely able to acquire business except in a seller's market.

Comments _____
_____

5. Amount of service given to customers	☐ Rarely services accounts once a sale is made.	☐ Gives only minimum service at all times.	☐ Services accounts with regularity but does not do any more than called on to do.	☐ Gives very good service to all customers.	☐ Goes out of the way to give outstanding service within scope of company policy.

Comments _____
_____

6. Dependability— amount of supervision needed	☐ Always thoroughly abreast of problems in the territory, even under most difficult conditions. Rises to emergencies and assumes leadership without being requested to do so.	☐ Consistently reliable under normal conditions. Does special as well as regular assignments promptly. Little or no supervision required.	☐ Performs with reasonable promptness under normal supervision.	☐ Effort occasionally lags. Requires more than normal supervision.	☐ Requires close supervision in all phases of job.

Comments _____
_____

7. Attitude toward company— support given to company policy	☐ Does not support company policy—blames the company for factors that	☐ Gives only passive support to company policy—does not act as member of a team.	☐ Goes along with company policy on most occasions.	☐ Adopts and supports company policy in all transactions.	☐ Gives unwavering support to the company and company policy to

(continued)

EXHIBIT 13.3 Sample subjective performance evaluation form *(continued)*

affect customers unfavorably.

customers even though he/she personally may not agree with the policy.

Comments _____

_____

8. Judgment

☐ Analyses and conclusions subject to frequent error and are often based on bias. Decisions require careful review by supervisor.

☐ Judgments usually sound on routine, simple matters but cannot be relied on when any degree of complexity is involved.

☐ Capable of careful analyzing of day-to-day problems involving some complexity and rendering sound decisions. Decision rarely influenced by prejudice or personal bias.

☐ Decisions can be accepted without question except when problems or extreme complexity are involved. Little or no personal bias enters into judgment.

☐ Possesses unusual comprehension and analytical ability. Complete reliance may be placed on all judgments irrespective of degree of complexity. Decisions and judgments are completely free of personal bias or prejudice.

Comment _____

_____

9. Resourcefulness

☐ Work is consistently characterized by marked originality, alertness, initiative, and imagination. Can be relied on to develop new ideas and techniques in solving the most difficult problems.

☐ Frequently develops new ideas of merit. Handling of emergencies is generally characterized by sound decisive action.

☐ Meets new situations in satisfactory manner. Occasionally develops original ideas, methods, and techniques.

☐ Follows closely previously learned methods and procedures. Slow to adapt to changes. Tends to become confused in new situations.

☐ Requires frequent reinstruction. Has failed to demonstrate initiative or imagination in solving problems.

Comments _____

_____

(continued)

EXHIBIT 13.3 **Sample subjective performance evaluation form** *(concluded)*

1. Be given additional instruction on _____
_____

2. Be given additional experience such as _____
_____

3. Study such subjects as _____
_____

4. Change attitude as follows _____
_____

5. There is nothing more that I can do for this employee because _____
_____

6. Remarks _____
_____
_____

EXHIBIT 13.4
Sample of a poorly constructed subjective performance evaluation form

	Poor	Fair	Satisfactory	Good	Outstanding
Knowledge of work	☐	☐	☐	☐	☐
Degree of acceptance by customers	☐	☐	☐	☐	☐
Amount of effort devoted to acquiring business	☐	☐	☐	☐	☐
Ability to acquire business	☐	☐	☐	☐	☐
Amount of service given to customers	☐	☐	☐	☐	☐
Dependability, amount of supervision needed	☐	☐	☐	☐	☐
Attitude toward company, support for company policies	☐	☐	☐	☐	☐
Judgment	☐	☐	☐	☐	☐
Resourcefulness	☐	☐	☐	☐	☐

2. *Ill-defined personality traits.* Many performance evaluation forms contain personality factors as attributes. In the case of salespeople, these attributes might include such things as initiative and resourcefulness. Although these attributes are intuitively appealing, their actual relationship to performance is open to question.[5]

3. *Halo effect.* A halo effect is a common phenomenon in the use of any performance evaluation form. It refers to the fact that the rating assigned to one characteristic may significantly influence the ratings assigned to all other characteristics, as well as the overall rating. The halo effect holds that a sales manager's overall evaluations can be predicted quite well from their rating of the salesperson on the single performance dimension they believe is the most important. Different branch or regional managers might have different beliefs about what is most important, compounding the problem.

4. *Leniency or harshness.* Some sales managers rate at the extremes. Some are very lenient and rate every salesperson as good or outstanding on every attribute, whereas others do just the opposite. This behavior is often a function of their own personalities and their perceptions of what comprises outstanding performance, and no fundamental differences may exist in the way the salespeople under each of the managers are actually performing. The use of different definitions of performance depending on the manager can seriously undermine the whole performance appraisal system.

5. *Central tendency.* Some managers err in the opposite direction in that they never, or very rarely, rate people at the ends of the scale. Rather, they use middle-of-the-road or play-it-safe ratings. One learns very little from such ratings about true differences in performance, and such ratings can be particularly troublesome when a company attempts to use a history of poor performance as the basis of a termination decision.

6. *Interpersonal bias.* Interpersonal bias refers to the fact that our perceptions of others and the social acceptability of their behaviors are influenced by how much we like or dislike them personally. Many sales managers' evaluations of sales reps are similarly affected. Furthermore, research suggests a salesperson can use personal influence or impression management strategies on the manager to bias evaluations upward.

7. *Organizational uses influence.* Performance ratings are often affected by the use to which they will be put within the organization. If promotions and monetary payments hinge on the ratings, a tendency may exist toward leniency on the part of the manager who values the friendship and support of subordinates who press for higher ratings. It is not difficult to imagine the dilemma of a district sales manager if other district sales teams received consistently higher compensation increments and more promotions than his or her sales group. On the other hand, when appraisals are used primarily for the development of subordinates, managers tend to more freely pinpoint weaknesses and focus on what is wrong and how it can be improved.[6]

By now, it should be clear that performance evaluation may be fraught with opportunities for biases and inaccuracies to creep into the process. Leadership 13.2 describes one form of potential evaluator bias in more detail, the **outcome bias.** An outcome bias occurs when a sales manager allows the outcome of a decision or a series of decisions made by a salesperson to overly influence the performance ratings made by the manager.

Avoiding Errors in Performance Evaluation

To guard against the distortions introduced in the performance appraisal system by problems such as those listed above, many firms provide extensive training and guidelines to sales managers on completing the forms and conducting the appraisal process. Some common instructions issued with such forms include,

1. Read the definitions of each trait thoroughly and carefully before rating.

2. Guard against the common tendency to overrate.

3. Do not let personal likes or dislikes influence your ratings. Be as objective as possible.

4. Do not permit your evaluation of one factor to influence your evaluation of another.

5. Base your rating on the observed performance of the salesperson, not on potential abilities.

Leadership Outcome Bias in Salesperson Performance Evaluations 13.2

By nature, professional selling is focused on bottom-line results. Persons who are successful in sales tend to like meeting tough goals and thrive on the immediacy, regularity, and visibility of feedback on their results. Thus, it is common for results (or *outcomes*) in sales to be viewed by management as a surrogate for the behavioral side of salesperson performance. In short: Make your quota, you must be doing things right; but miss your quota and, boy, are you ever doing the wrong things.

These "things" we are talking about are all the process steps that go into the job of selling. On a very basic level, they are all the decisions made by the salesperson over the course of a day, week, month, quarter, and year that add up to that person's performance (remember, earlier in this chapter we defined performance in terms of behavior evaluated in the context of its contributions to the goals of the organization).

Sometimes the outcomes and the process leading to those outcomes match: for example, a salesperson has a great sales quarter and also was great at doing all the things that are part of the sales job (presentations, customer care, administration, etc.). Clearly, the sales manager should recognize and reward this achievement. And in the opposite case, where a salesperson has a lousy sales quarter and also is struggling with the process elements of the job, clearly the sales manager needs to document the poor performance and a developmental plan needs to be put in place.

But what about the mixed cases? Consider the salesperson who has a great sales quarter but is not cutting the mustard in the day-to-day elements of the job. Maybe the favorable outcome was due to an unexpected windfall from a client, an easy territory, or some other event not directly attributable to much of anything the salesperson actually did to earn the business. Evaluating this salesperson favorably overall, based strictly on his or her performance outcome, can open a huge can of worms in a sales unit, as peer salespeople will see this person as a slacker who got lucky. And finally, perhaps the worst case of all, consider the salesperson who has a lousy sales quarter but who absolutely has done everything right. If this salesperson is evaluated as a poor performer, based strictly on the outcome, chances are the organization will lose him or her.

The *outcome bias* is that evaluators tend to overlook process and rate performers based on outcomes. As illustrated in the mixed-case examples above, this tendency of outcome to overwhelm process can lead poor morale, ill will, and turnover within the sales force.

It should be mentioned, however, that one school of thought in sales is that a bias toward outcomes isn't really a bias at all. That is, salespeople know when they get into the profession that bottom-line sales volume is the key to success. This perspective may be somewhat valid in straight commission selling situations. But in most of today's relationship-driven professional sales jobs, it is folly to utilize performance evaluation systems that ignore good, or bad, behavioral aspects of performance in favor of just the short-run bottom line. As we have learned, much of what constitutes success in relationship-driven sales organizations involves a complex set of actions inside and outside the selling firm, and the true outcome of these activities may not be realized for a long time. Fortunately, most modern sales organizations understand the threat of the outcome bias and work to integrate multiple aspects of performance into the evaluation process. One approach that addresses this is the BARS system, which is discussed in this chapter.

For recent treatments on the outcome bias see: Nidhi Agrawal and Durairaj Maheswaran, "Motivated Reasoning in Outcome Bias Effects," *Journal of Consumer Research* 3 (March 2005), pp. 798–805; Philip J. Mazzocco, Mark D. Alicke, and Teresa L. Davis, "On the Robustness of Outcome Bias: No Constraint by Prior Culpability," *Basic and Applied Social Psychology* 26 (2/3 2004), p. 131.

6. Never rate an employee on several instances of good or poor work, but rather on general success or failure over the whole period.

7. Have sound reasons for your ratings.[7]

These admonitions can help, particularly when the evaluator must supply the reasons for ratings. However, they do not resolve problems related to the selection of attributes for evaluation and how the resulting items are presented on the form. A trend in performance appraisal directed at resolving this issue is the **BARS (behaviorally anchored rating scale).**

Using a BARS System

A BARS system attempts to concentrate on the behaviors and other performance criteria that can be controlled by the individual. The system focuses on the fact that a number of factors affect any employee's performance. However, some of these factors are more critical to job success than are others, and the key to evaluating people is to focus on these *critical success factors* (CSFs).[8] Implementing a BARS system for evaluating salespeople requires identifying the behaviors that are key to their performance. Also, the subsequent evaluation of a salesperson's performance must be conducted by rating these key behaviors using the appropriate descriptions.[9]

The process of developing a BARS system goes as follows. First, the key behaviors with respect to performance are identified using critical incidents. *Critical incidents* are occurrences that are vital (critical) to performance. To use the critical incident technique, those involved could be asked to identify some particularly outstanding examples of good or bad performance and to detail the reasons why.[10] The performances identified are then reduced to a smaller number of performance dimensions.

Next, the group of critical incidents is presented to a group of sales personnel who are asked to assign each critical incident to an appropriate performance dimension. An incident is typically kept in if 60 percent or more of the group assigns it to the same dimension as did the instrument development group. The sales personnel group is also asked to rate the behavior described in the critical incident on a 7- or 10-point scale with respect to how effectively or ineffectively it represents performance on the dimension. Incidents that generate good agreement in ratings, typically indicated by a low standard deviation, are considered for the final scale. The particular incidents chosen are determined by their location along the scale, as measured by the mean scores. Typically, the final scale has six to eight anchors. An example of a BARS scale that resulted from such a process for the attribute "promptness in meeting deadlines" is shown in Exhibit 13.5.

EXHIBIT 13.5
A BARS scale with behavioral anchors for the attribute "promptness in meeting deadlines"

Very high This indicates the more-often-than-not practice of submitting accurate and needed sales reports.	10.0 — 9.0 —	Could be expected to promptly submit all necessary field reports even in the most difficult of situations.
	8.0 — 7.0 —	Could be expected to promptly meet deadlines comfortably in most report completion situations.
	6.0 —	Is usually on time and can be expected to submit most routine field sales reports in proper format.
Moderate This indicates regularity in promptly submitting accurate and needed field sales reports.	5.0 — 4.0 —	Could be expected to regularly be tardy in submitting required field sales reports.
	3.0 — 2.0 —	Could be expected to be tardy and submit inaccurate field sales reports.
Very low This indicates irregular and unacceptable promptness and accuracy of field sales reports.	1.0 —	Could be expected to completely disregard due dates for filling almost all reports.
	0.0 —	Could be expected to never file field sales reports on time and resist any managerial guidance to improve this tendency.

A key advantage of a BARS system is that it requires sales managers to consider in detail a wide range of components of a salesperson's job performance. It must also include clearly defined anchors for those performance criteria in specific behavioral terms, leading to thoughtful consideration by managers of just what comprises performance. Of course, by nature a BARS emphasizes behavior and performance rather than effectiveness. When used in tandem with appropriate objective measures (sales and profit analyses and output, input, and ratio measures), a BARS approach provides an attractive means of handling subjective evaluation criteria and thus providing as complete a picture as possible of a salesperson's overall performance and effectiveness.

BARS systems are not without their limitations, though. For one thing, the job-specific nature of the scales they utilize suggests they are most effective in evaluating salespeople performing very similar functions. They might be effective in comparing one national account rep to another national account rep or two territory representatives against each other, but they could suffer major shortcomings if used to compare a national account rep against a territory salesperson because of differences in responsibilities in these positions. BARS systems also can be relatively costly to develop since they require a good deal of up-front time from multiple people.[11]

360-DEGREE FEEDBACK IN PERFORMANCE EVALUATION

As we learned in Chapter 3, one important attraction of CRM systems to firms is the inherent capability of such systems to provide feedback from a wide range of constituents and stakeholders. Although the usage focus of much of this information is on product development and formulation of the overall marketing message, CRM systems typically also facilitate the gathering, analysis, and dissemination of a great deal of information directly relevant to the performance of the sales force.

In order for a sales organization to take full advantage of the available information generated by enterprise software such as CRM, the firm as a whole must embrace the philosophy that the customer is a customer of the *company,* not just of the individual salesperson. We have seen that the complex and often lengthy process of developing and managing customer relationships almost always involves more than just a salesperson and purchasing agent. An effective CRM system should be gathering data at all the important touchpoints where members of a selling organization interact with members of a buying organization, or members of a selling organization interact internally in order to forward a business relationship with a customer.

Such a comprehensive information management process allows for a rethinking of the nature of input data for use in salesperson performance evaluation. Rather than relying on purely objective measures or on subjective measures generated by one person (the sales manager), information for performance evaluation may come from multiple sources simultaneously. This concept of **360-degree performance feedback** opens the door to a new era in using the performance appraisal process as an effective tool for salesperson development and improvement. Among the sources of feedback that would be useful to salespeople are external customers, internal organization members who serve as resources in serving external customers (this group is often referred to as **internal customers**), other members of the salesperson's selling team, any direct reports the sales manager may have (such as sales assistants), and of course the sales manager.[12] Integrating feedback from these and other relevant sources of performance information into the formal evaluation process (and thus onto the evaluation form) can provide the impetus for a more productive dialogue between the sales manager and salesperson when performance review time comes around.

One other issue deserves mention related to 360-degree feedback—**self-evaluation.** Sales organizations should encourage salespeople to prepare an honest assessment of their own performance against the established objective and subjective performance criteria, and this should be prepared *prior* to the formal performance review session with the sales manager.[13] The best sales organizations use this process to begin the dialogue of sales unit goal-setting for the next period, and especially to establish a professional development program to help move the salesperson toward the fulfillment of his or her personal goals on the job. We learned in Chapter 11 that intrinsic rewards are among the most powerful motivators—things such as feelings of accomplishment, personal growth, and self-worth. Allowing the salesperson to have direct input in establishing personal growth goals on the job, and then institutionalizing the achievement of those goals via the formal performance evaluation process, goes a long way toward providing a workplace atmosphere in which intrinsic rewards may be realized by salespeople.

It is particularly important to involve salespeople directly in all phases of the performance appraisal process. When appraisals provide clear criteria, the criteria meet with the salesperson's approval, and the appraisals are perceived as fair and used in determining rewards, salesperson job satisfaction increases. Thus, the critical determinants of appraisal effectiveness are not purely criteria-driven but rather are largely determined by appraisal process factors that managers can influence, such as buy-in by those being appraised and fairness with which the appraisal process is administered.[14]

An old adage in human resource management holds that if an employee is surprised by anything he or she is told during a formal performance review, the manager providing the evaluation is not doing a very good job. Performance evaluation should not be simply one cathartic event that happens periodically. Such a view can cause great trepidation on the part of both employees and managers, and it often results in managers procrastinating in conducting the review and minimizing the time spent with the employee during the review. In contrast, great sales organizations use the performance evaluation process to facilitate *ongoing* dialogue between salespeople and their managers. The key goal of the process should be facilitating professional and personal development—providing the salesperson the feedback and tools necessary to achieve his or her goals in the job. To make this happen, sales managers must be prepared to carry on the dialogue beyond just the periodic formal appraisal event and into day-to-day communication with the salesperson. Importantly, this developmental perspective on performance evaluation requires that sales managers not just *give* feedback but also listen and respond to feedback and questions from the salesperson. Innovation 13.3 provides insight on how sales managers can utilize the performance evaluation meeting to the salesperson's benefit.

Ultimately, sales organizations need to work toward developing a **performance management system** along the lines of the discussion in the chapter opener. To do so requires a commitment to integrating all the elements of feedback on the process of serving customers so that performance information is timely, accurate, and relevant to the customer management aspects of the firm.[15] The pieces of the performance puzzle are integrated in such a way that the salesperson does not have to wait on the manager for a formal validation of performance. Instead, under a performance management approach, salespeople take the lead in goal setting, performance measurement, and adjustment of their own performance.[16] The concept of performance management is analogous to TQM approaches that advocate the empowerment of employees to take ownership of their own jobs and conduct their own analyses of performance against goals, creating a culture of self-management. To successfully implement a performance management system, sales managers must shift their leadership style to that of a partner in a mutually shared process.

Innovation   Appraising Your Appraisals   13.3

Regardless of evaluation frequency, if your appraisals don't include the correct components, you are wasting everyone's time. To make salesperson performance evaluations as effective as possible, follow these tips (stated from the sales manager's perspective):

- *Analyze the data beforehand.* Make sure to review hard sales numbers closely before the meeting. Encourage the salesperson to do likewise. If you and the salesperson know the statistics going in, you can spend the time together focusing on the reasons behind the figures and how you can help him or her improve.

- *Let the salesperson talk first.* "Typically people will be more critical of themselves than you will be of them," says Rollie Waters, president of the Waters Consulting Group Inc., a Dallas-based management and compensation consulting firm. By allowing your salespeople to have the first word, you can learn what they're thinking and tailor your comments accordingly.

- *Provide constructive criticism.* Waters suggests planning ahead by creating a list of three areas in which the salesperson could improve. "Don't overwhelm them with a long list," Waters says. When you sit down with your salespeople, discuss goals they should try to achieve to become better salespeople. Also, set clear follow-up dates to check on their progress.

- *Accentuate their successes.* "Characteristically, sales reps thrive on affirmation," says Reg Ellis, president of Toronto-based Ellis Associates Inc. "They need to hear that the organization knows they are doing things well." And don't just praise your best reps—learn from their techniques so you can pass them on to those who need some performance improvement. Not only will their advice help others, but they will feel more valued and appreciated.

- *Focus on specifics.* Telling a salesperson that he or she "doesn't have enough fire in the belly" won't help spur on greatness. Rather, draw attention to specific examples of what the salesperson does well and what needs to be worked on. "If you initially define the job in behavioral terms, then you can give meaningful feedback on how to do it better, such as making more calls," Ellis says.

- *Ask what you can do better.* Salesperson performance evaluations are a two-way street. Although a key purpose is to help the salesperson improve, you can benefit from them as well. Ask your salespeople, "What can we do to make your job better?" Their answers can help increase communication, improve the total sales effort, and even make you aware of your own shortcomings.

Source: Jordana Mishory, "Appraising Your Appraisals," *Sales & Marketing Management* 156 (July 2004), p. 38.

Summary

Performance and effectiveness are different concepts. Performance may be thought of as a salesperson's behavior evaluated in terms of its contribution to the goals of the organization. On the other hand, effectiveness is an organizational outcome for which a salesperson is at least partly responsible, usually examined across a variety of indices.

Salespeople may be evaluated on the basis of objective and subjective criteria. Objective measures reflect statistics a sales manager can gather from a firm's internal data and other means and may be categorized as output measures (the results of the efforts expended by the salesperson) and input measures (the efforts they expend in achieving the results). Objective measures also may take the form of ratios that combine various outputs or inputs. On the other hand, subjective measures typically rely on personal evaluations of how the salesperson is doing, usually as viewed by the sales manager. In most cases, sales managers should pay attention to both objective and subjective measures in evaluating salespeople.

A variety of potential pitfalls exist in performance measurement, particularly utilizing subjective measures. These problems frequently take the form of various errors or biases in the evaluation, which result in an inaccurate performance appraisal that is perceived (rightly so) as unfair by the salesperson. Sales organizations and their managers must take great care to ensure that the performance evaluation process is conducted in as fair and accurate a manner as possible. Utilizing 360-degree feedback in the performance review, including a strong component of self-evaluation by the salesperson, can be very helpful in improving the usefulness of the performance evaluation process.

Key Terms	behavior	subjective measures	self-evaluation
	performance	bias	performance management
	effectiveness	outcome bias	system
	attribution theory	BARS (behaviorally	
	objective measures	anchored rating scale)	
	output measures	360-degree performance	
	input measures	feedback	
	ratio measures	internal customers	

Breakout Questions

1. Kevin Harrison, sales rep for Allied Steel Distributors, had an appointment with his sales manager to discuss his first-year sales performance. Kevin knew that the meeting would not go well. One of Allied's major accounts had changed suppliers due to problems with Kevin. The purchasing agent claimed that "personality differences" were so serious that future business with Allied was not possible. Kevin knew that these so-called personality differences involved his unwillingness to entertain in the same style as the previous sales rep. The previous sales rep frequently took the purchasing agent and others to a local topless bar for lunch. The rep told Kevin that this was expected and that if he wanted to keep the business, it was necessary. Besides, tickets to the professional basketball games didn't count anymore. What are the short- and long-range implications of this type of customer entertaining? What would you do in a similar situation? How should Kevin's sales manager react?

2. A large corporation notices an irregular decrease in the sales of a particular representative. The sales rep, normally in very high standing among other salespeople and quotas, has of late failed to achieve her own quota. What can be done by the sales manager to determine whether the slump in the sales curve is the responsibility of the representative or due to things beyond her control?

3. Given the following information from evaluations of the performance of different sales representatives, what possible conclusions can be made about why the sales reps are not achieving quota (assume each is not making quota)?

   a. *Representative 1:* Achieved goals for sales calls, telephone calls, and new accounts; customer relations good; no noticeable deficiencies in any areas.

   b. *Representative 2:* Completed substantially fewer sales calls than goal. Telephone calls high in number, but primarily with one firm. Time management analysis shows the sales rep to be spending a disproportionately large amount of time with one firm. New accounts are low; all other areas good to outstanding.

   c. *Representative 3:* Number of sales calls low, below goal. Telephone calls, letters, proposals all very low and below goal. Evaluation shows poor time utilization. Very high amount of service-related activities in sales representative's log; customer relations extremely positive; recently has received a great deal of feedback from customers on product function.

4. Is sales "just a numbers game," as one sales manager states? She believes that all you have to do is make the right number of calls of the right type, and the odds will work in your favor. Make 10 calls, get one sale. So to get two sales, make 20 calls. Is this the right approach? Why or why not?

5. Jackie Hitchcock, recently promoted to district sales manager, faced a new problem she wasn't sure how to resolve. The district's top sales rep is also the district's number-one problem. Brad Coombs traditionally leads the company in sales but also leads the company in problems. He has broken every rule, bent every policy, deviated from guidelines, and been less than truthful. Jackie knew Brad had never done anything illegal, but she was worried that something serious could happen. Other problems with Brad include not preparing call reports on time, failing to show up at trade shows, and not attending sales training programs. How should Jackie handle this problem? How does a sales manager manage a maverick sales rep? Specifically, how can the performance evaluation process help Jackie deal with Brad?

Leadership Challenge: Understanding Salesperson Performance

Mike Hunt had been in sales for 20 years, and, as sales manager for Market First Distributors, he was confident of his ability to evaluate salespeople. Market First was a regional distributor of food products to restaurants. It competed with large distributors such as Sysco and had developed a very good reputation for great service and reasonable prices.

The company had a sales force of 70 in six districts across five midwestern states. A formal evaluation process had been implemented nine years ago. The process focused on salespeople meeting specific targets on account development (sales per account and average order size) and call activity (calls per account). However, while the process had been successful in the past and everyone understood the expectations under the current system, Mike felt that something was missing.

Market First had begun to notice an increase in complaints with customers across all the sales districts. While the specific nature of the complaints varied, some themes showed up consistently. Customers were complaining that salespeople did not spend as much with them as they used to and were not as interested in the relationship.

Mike as well as senior management believed that it was time to broaden the performance evaluation process. They felt that by setting standards for territory management and customer satisfaction, the company could assess how well the sales force was doing in these critical areas. At this point, however, he was unsure how to set up such a system. As he sat in his office considering the options, he wondered if this would do more harm than good in the long run.

Questions

1. You are Mike Hunt. How would you measure a salesperson's territory management skills and his or her relationship with the customer?

2. Mike has asked you to come in and explain the strengths and weaknesses of objective versus subjective measures for territory management and relationship with customers. What would you say?

Role Play: Harvey Insurance Agency

Situation

Harvey Insurance Agency sells an extensive line of policies, representing several major insurance companies. Principal agent Bill Harvey started the business in 1993 with one office assistant, and since then the company has grown to become one of the largest independent insurance agencies in the Los Angeles area. Besides the original office, Bill now has two satellite offices around the metro area, each with a managing agent. Across the three locations he also employs 14 other agents and 27 staff people who primarily assist with clerical duties and follow-up.

Bill has always treated his people well, and as the agency has grown he has continued to pride himself on the family feeling of the business. Yet recently he has begun to question whether his performance evaluation system is appropriate. Yes, sales have continuously grown and he has had very little turnover, but success in the industry (which has always been oriented toward relationship selling) is becoming more and more about securing, building, and maintaining long-term relationships with profitable customers. Relationship selling necessitates many activities on the part of the agents to support sales.

Until now, Bill's annual performance review of his agents has focused almost exclusively on a few objectives: principally, sales volume, number of new customers, number of calls per week, and number of policies sold by line versus goals. The agents make commission and bonuses, plus a base salary. Bill likes this compensation plan because it allows him to financially reward agents for volume and for selling specific items, and it still affords him the opportunity, through the salary component, to have influence on their nonselling activities.

Bill sees his present challenge as follows: The focus on relationship selling necessitates maintaining the current compensation plan with the salary component. But his performance evaluation system doesn't match up well with the realities of his business, because it focuses only on a few objective performance measures. He sees the opportunity to incorporate some appropriate subjective measures of performance into the evaluation process and perhaps even add or change some of the objective measures. Bill calls a meeting with Chip Landers and Connie Perez, the managing agents of his satellite offices, to brainstorm ideas for changing the performance evaluation system for the agents.

Characters in the Role Play

Bill Harvey, principal agent for Harvey Insurance Agency

Chip Landers, managing agent for the San Fernando Valley office

Connie Perez, managing agent for the Orange County office

Assignment

Break into groups of three, with one student playing each character. It doesn't matter what the actual gender mix of your group is. Before you stage the meeting, work separately using the material in your chapter to come up with your own recommendation for a new set of objective and subjective measures of agent performance. You will need to be prepared to justify your recommendations in the meeting. Then get together and role-play the meeting among Bill, Chip, and Connie. In the end, you want to come out of the meeting with a unified plan for changing the performance evaluation system for agents at Harvey Insurance Agency.

Minicase: Massachusetts Restaurant Appliances

Massachusetts Restaurant Appliances (MRA), headquartered in Somerville, Massachusetts (in the Boston area), sells large, industrial appliances such as refrigerators, freezers, and dishwashers to restaurants all over the United States. For several years, the company has been second in market share to industry leader New York's Ruth Restaurant Services, but it has been gaining share in recent years.

MRA is especially optimistic about catching Ruth this year because of the rise of its star sales manager, David Epstein, an energetic 31-year-old, who has been with the company since he was 22. Epstein is popular with the sales staff, but he also is aggressive and demands high performance. One of his initiatives is to make all salespeople accountable by strictly evaluating performance using ratios as well as purely objective measures. In particular, he has collected performance data for each of his seven sales representatives as follows:

Sales rep	Previous sales	Current sales	Current quota	Number of accounts	Number of orders	Expenses	Number of calls	Number of days worked
Derek Francona	$480,000	$481,000	$575,000	1,100	780	$ 9,300	1,300	235
Johnny Schilling	750,000	883,000	835,000	1,600	1,970	12,300	1,800	223
Daphne Gellar	576,000	613,000	657,000	1,150	1,020	7,500	1,650	228
Robert Smythe	745,000	852,000	850,000	1,350	1,650	11,000	1,700	230
Jennifer McCarver	765,000	860,000	850,000	1,300	1,730	11,300	1,750	232
Manuel Lopez	735,000	835,000	825,000	1,400	1,790	11,500	1,750	220
Samantha Kerrey	665,000	670,000	720,000	1,600	960	10,800	1,550	200
Erin McCloud	775,000	925,000	875,000	1,700	1,910	12,800	1,850	225

Epstein would like to see an analysis of salesperson performance using the following ratios: sales growth, sales to quota, sales per account, average order, sales expense, calls per day, orders per call.

Most of the salespeople are happy to be evaluated, but a few are dubious and fearful of the consequences. Robert Smythe, for one, feels that his territory, which includes the Western mountain states as well as Alaska, is more difficult to sell in because there are fewer restaurants and he has only been a salesperson for about a year. In addition, one of Derek Francona's largest customers recently went out of business, and he feels that his numbers slipped as a result. Both are close to quitting because they feel they are being evaluated unfairly.

Epstein wants to beat Ruth very badly this year and feels that improving salesperson performance is the key. Therefore, his performance evaluation system is of the utmost importance.

Questions

1. Using the data given, calculate the performance ratios requested by Epstein and rank the salespeople accordingly.
2. What advice or guidance should Epstein give to each of the salespeople to improve performance?
3. What are the limitations of this evaluation system? What adjustments or additions could Epstein make to more accurately evaluate salesperson performance?

Suggested Readings

Chonko, Lawrence B., Terry W. Loe, James A. Roberts, and John F. Tanner. "Sales Performance: Timing of Measurement and Type of Measurement Make a Difference." *Journal of Personal Selling & Sales Management* 20 (Winter 2000), pp. 23–36.

DeCarlo, Thomas E., Sanjeev Agarwal, and Shyman B. Vyas. "Performance Expectations of Salespeople: The Role of Past Performance and Casual Attributions in Independent and Interdependent Cultures." *Journal of Personal Selling & Sales Management* 27 (Spring 2007), pp. 133–47.

Dixon, Andrea L., Lukas P. Forbes, and Susan M. B. Schertzer. "Early Success: How Attributions for Sales Success Shape Inexperienced Salesperson's Behavioral Intentions." *Journal of Personal Selling & Sales Management* 25 (Winter 2005), pp. 67–77.

Dixon, Andrea L., and Susan M. B. Schertzer. "Bouncing Back: How Salesperson Optimism and Self-Efficacy Influence Attributions and Behaviors Following Failure." *Journal of Personal Selling & Sales Management* 25 (Fall 2005), pp. 361–69.

Dwyer, Sean, John Hill, and Warren Martin. "An Empirical Investigation of Critical Success Factors in the Personal Selling Process for Homogenous Goods." *Journal of Personal Selling & Sales Management* 20 (Summer 2000), pp. 151–59.

Flaherty, Karen E., Todd J. Arnold, and C. Shane Hunt. "The Influence of the Selling Situation on the Effectiveness of Control: Toward a Holistic Perspective." *Journal of Personal Selling & Sales Management* 27 (Summer 2007), pp. 221–33.

Gonzalez, Gabriel R., K. Douglass Hoffman, and Thomas N. Ingram. "Improving Relationship Selling Through Failure Analysis and Recovery Efforts: A Framework and Call to Action." *Journal of Personal Selling & Sales Management* 25 (Winter 2005), pp. 57–65.

Jaramillo, Fernando, François A. Carrillat, and William B. Locander. "Starting to Solve the Method Puzzle in Salesperson Self-Report Evaluations." *Journal of Personal Selling & Sales Management* 23 (Fall 2003), pp. 369–77.

Mallin, Michael L., and Michael Mayo. "Why did I Lose? A Conservation of Resources View of Salesperson Failure Attributions." *Journal of Personal Selling & Sales Management* 26 (Fall 2006), pp. 345–58.

Piercy, Nigel F., David W. Cravens, and Nikala Lane. "Sales Manager Behavior Control Strategy and Its Consequences: The Impact of Manager Gender Differences." *Journal of Personal Selling & Sales Management* 23 (Summer 2003), pp. 221–38.

Piercy, Nigel F., David W. Cravens, and Nikala Lane. "Enhancing Salespeople's Effectiveness: When is More Sales Management Control Better Sales Management Control?" *Marketing Management* (September/October 2007), pp. 18–25.

Ramaswami, Sridhar N. "Influence of Control Systems on Opportunistic Behaviors of Salespeople: A Test of Gender Differences." *Journal of Personal Selling & Sales Management* 22 (Summer 2002), pp. 173–88.

Rouziès, Dominique, and Anne Macquin. "An Exploratory Investigation of the Impact of Culture on Sales Force Management Control Systems in Europe." *Journal of Personal Selling & Sales Management* 23 (Winter 2003), pp. 61–72.

Comprehensive Cases for Part Three

Case 3.1

Wentworth Industrial Cleaning Supplies

Wentworth Industrial Cleaning Supplies (WICS), located in Lincoln, Nebraska, is experiencing a slowdown in growth; sales of all WICS products have leveled off far below the volume expected by management. Although total sales volume has increased for the industry, WICS's share of this growth has not kept pace. J. Randall Griffith, vice president of marketing, has been directed to determine what factors are stunting growth and to institute a program that will facilitate further expansion.

COMPANY AND INDUSTRY BACKGROUND

WICS is a division of Wentworth International, competing in the janitorial maintenance chemical market. According to trade association estimates, the total market is roughly $2.5 billion in 2007. Exhibit 1 shows the nature of this market. Four segments comprise the institutional maintenance chemical market, which consists of approximately 2,000 manufacturers providing both national and private labels.

Total industry sales volume in dollars of janitorial supplies is approximately $1.3 billion. Exhibit 2 shows the breakdown by product type for the janitorial market. WICS addresses 75 percent of the market's product needs with a line of high-quality products. The composition of WICS's product line is as follows:

Special purpose cleaners	46%
Air fresheners	9
General purpose cleaners	16
Disinfectants	15
Other	14

The janitorial maintenance chemical market is highly fragmented; no one firm, including WICS, has more than 10 percent market share. Agate and Marshfield Chemical sell directly to the end-user, while Lynx, Lexington Labs, and WICS utilize a distributor network. Most of

Source: Joan Russler and Jeffrey Forbes, MBAs–Marketing, University of Wisconsin–Madison, assisted in the preparation of this case. Copyright © 2001 Neil M. Ford. Updated 2007.

WICS's competitors utilize only one channel of distribution; only Organic Labs and Swanson sell both ways. Most private-label products move through distributors. Sanitary supply distributors (SSDs) deliver 65 percent of end-user dollars, while direct-to-end-user dollar sales are 35 percent (Exhibit 3).* The following shows the sales breakdown by target market by type of distribution:

Distributor Sales

Retail	20%
Industrial	18
Health care	18
Schools	11
Building supply contractors	10
Restaurants	3
Hotels	3
Other	17

Direct Sales

Retail	47%
Building supply contractors	35
Health care	15
Hotels	2
Restaurants	1

Trade association data plus information from other sources estimate the number of SSDs to be between 5,000 and 6,000. The following shows the sales volume breakdown for the SSDs based on an average of 5,500:

Size in Sales Volume

Less than $100,000	1,210
$100,000–499,999	2,475
$500,000–1,000,000	1,375
More than $1,000,000	400
Total	5,500

According to a recent analysis of end-users, WICS provides cleaning supplies for approximately 20,000 customers. WICS's sales force is expected to call on these accounts as well as prospects for new business. These

*Includes paper supply distributors that carry janitorial supplies.

EXHIBIT 1
Institutional maintenance chemical market

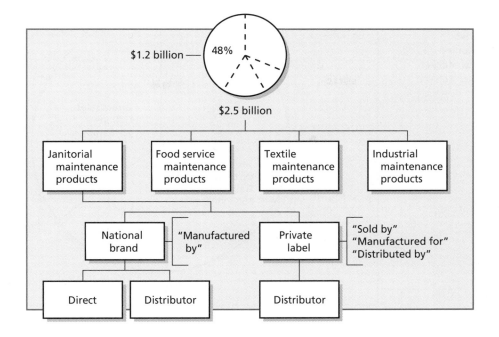

EXHIBIT 2
WICS "served" portion of the janitorial maintenance chemical market

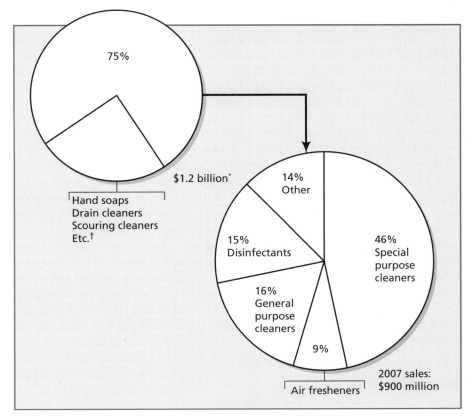

*End-user dollars.
†Includes some general purpose cleaners and air fresheners that WICS does not manufacture.

EXHIBIT 3
Janitorial maintenance chemical market (end-user dollars)

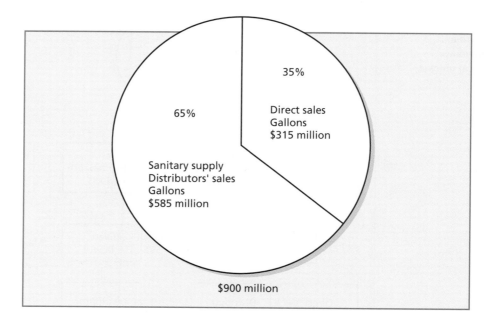

35%

Direct sales
Gallons
$315 million

65%

Sanitary supply
Distributors' sales
Gallons
$585 million

$900 million

20,000 end-users receive product from the SSDs who supply cleaning supplies manufactured by WICS and others as well. About one-third of the average SSD's total sales is accounted for by WICS's products. An exception is the paper supply distributor, where WICS's products account for an average of 10 percent of sales.

The typical SSD carries other related items. In fact, according to a survey conducted by an independent firm, SSDs almost always carry a private-label line of cleaning supplies plus one to two additional branded products besides the WICS line. This survey revealed that 60 percent of the SSDs carry a private-label line along with WICS and a private label. The private label may be a regional label or the SSD's own label.

WICS places almost total reliance on selling through the SSDs, although a small amount of sales (less than 10 percent) are made direct. WICS sells its janitorial maintenance products through roughly 400 distributors, who in turn "see" 65 percent of the end-user dollar market. Thus, 65 percent of sales in the total janitorial maintenance market are made through SSDs (35 percent are direct sales); and the 400 SSDs used by WICS provided 65 percent coverage. The market seen by each distributor, referred to as his or her *window* on the market, is a function of the following:

Product lines carried (paper versus chemical).

Customer base (type and size).

Nature of business (specialization by market versus specialization by sales function).

The combination of these factors produces end-user market coverage of 42 percent (65 percent distributor sales × 65 percent coverage). WICS has very limited direct sales.

To reach its market, WICS uses a sales force of 135 area managers, 21 territory managers, and 4 regional managers (Exhibit 4). Regional managers are located in San Francisco, Denver, Chicago, and Boston. Although WICS is viewed as a giant in the industry, it does not produce a complete line of janitorial chemicals. Janitorial chemicals are rated on the basis of their performance. WICS produces products that have average to premium performance ratings; WICS has no products in the economy class. Moreover, due to various factors, WICS's coverage in the average and premium classes is not complete. The emphasis on premium and average products results in providing only 75 percent of the market's product needs.

To provide high distributor margins and extensive sales support, WICS charges premium prices. Recent estimates reveal that only 40 percent of the served market is willing to pay these premium prices. The impact of WICS's limited product line coupled with its premium prices is evident in Exhibit 5.

An overall description of WICS's marketing program shows that it has focused on market development. Distributors receive high margins (30 to 40 percent) and sales costs are high (10 to 15 percent) due to emphasis on selling technical benefits, demonstrations, and cold calls. Area managers call on prospective end-users

EXHIBIT 4
**WICS's access
to the market**

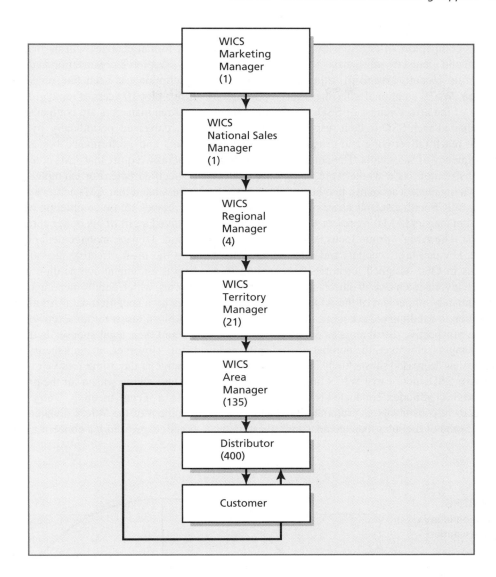

EXHIBIT 5
**End-user product
coverage**

to develop the market for the SSD. By comparison, WICS's competitors offer SSDs low margins (15 to 20 percent) and incur low sales costs (5 to 8 percent).

Griffith recently received a memo from Steve Shenken, WICS's national sales manager, reporting on a study of the effectiveness of SSDs. Territory managers evaluated each SSD in their respective regions on a basis of reach (advertising and promotional programs) and frequency of sales calls. The composite report indicated distributors as a whole were doing an excellent job servicing present accounts. In other words, 400 SSDs provide WICS with a sizable share of the market.

Area managers (AMs) represent WICS in distributor relations. The AMs' "prime focus is to sell and service existing key end-user accounts and selected new target accounts in their assigned territories." According to a recent study, maintenance of current accounts comprises approximately 80 percent of the AMs' time (Exhibit 6). In addition to handling old accounts, the AM makes cold calls on prospective distributors as directed by the territory managers. However, the number of cold calls made monthly has decreased substantially in the past year since the major SSDs now carry WICS products. A study of AM and SSD attitudes, conducted by MGH Associates, management consultants, is presented in Appendixes A and B. Some of the sales management staff question the use of AM time; however, there has been no indication that formal changes will be made in the future regarding sales force organization and directives. The AM job description has seen few revisions, if any, during the firm's past 10 years of rapid growth (Exhibit 7).

Area managers are compensated with a straight salary, enhanced periodically by various incentive programs and performance bonuses. Incentive programs generally require that AMs attain a certain sales level by a specified date. For example, the Christmas Program necessitated that AMs achieve fourth-quarter quotas by November 15; on completion of this objective, the AM received a gift of his or her choice, such as a color television. To date, management considers the Zone Glory Cup the most effective incentive program. The Glory Cup is an annual competition among areas within territories, which entails meeting or exceeding sales objectives by a specified date. An all-expense-paid vacation at a plush resort for area, territory, and regional managers and their legal spouses is the prize for the winning team. However, management at WICS believes that prestige is the prime motivator in this competition and the underlying reason for the program's success.

In a recent meeting, Terry Luther, executive vice president of the WICS division of Wentworth International, expressed his concern to Griffith about WICS's

EXHIBIT 6
Allocation of area manager duties*

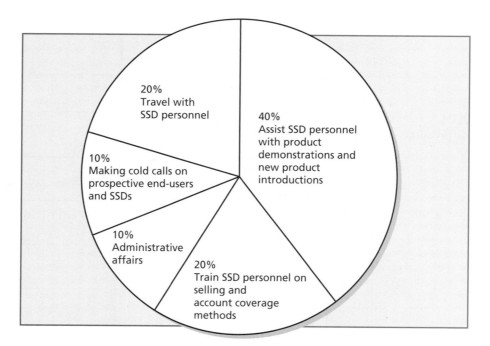

20%
Travel with SSD personnel

10%
Making cold calls on prospective end-users and SSDs

10%
Administrative affairs

20%
Train SSD personnel on selling and account coverage methods

40%
Assist SSD personnel with product demonstrations and new product introductions

*Based on an analysis of call reports.

EXHIBIT 7   Wentworth industrial cleaning supplies position description

Date: January 1, 2007
Approved by: (1) _____
　　　　　(2) _____
　　　　　(3) _____

Position:
Incumbent:

Division:

Area Manager, Maint. Prods.
135 Positions Nationally

Janitorial Maintenance
Products Division
Reports to: Territory Manager
　　　　　　Janitorial Maintenance
　　　　　　Products Division

POSITION PURPOSE:
To sell and service user accounts and authorized distributors in an assigned territory to assure that territory sales objectives are attained or exceeded.

DIMENSIONS:

Annual sales:	$300 M (average)
Number of distributors:	4　　(average)
Number of distributor salesmen:	12　　(average)
Annual expense budget:	$4.2 M (average)
Company assets controlled or affected:	$8 M　(average)

NATURE AND SCOPE
This position reports to a territory manager, janitorial maintenance products. Each district is subdivided into sales territories that are either assigned to an individual member of the district or to a team effort, based on market and/or manpower requirements.

The janitorial maintenance products division is responsible for developing and marketing a broad line of chemical products for building maintenance purposes.

The incumbent's prime focus is to sell and service existing key-user accounts and selected new target accounts in his assigned territory. He multiplies his personal sales results by spending a major portion of his time working with distributor sales personnel, selling WICS maintenance products and systems to key accounts such as commercial, industrial, institutional, governmental accounts, and contract cleaners. When working alone, he sells key-user accounts through an authorized distributor as specified by the user customer.

The incumbent plans, schedules, and manages his selling time for maximum sales productivity. He interviews decision makers and/or people who influence the buying decision. He identifies and evaluates customer needs through careful observation, listening and questioning techniques to assure proper recommendations. He plans sales strategy to include long-term/quick-sell objectives and develops personalized user presentations to meet individual sales situations, utilizing product literature, manuals, spot demonstrations, and sales aids to reinforce presentations. This position sells systems of maintenance to major volume user accounts through the use of surveys and proposals, test programs, and other advanced sales techniques. He develops effective closing techniques for maximum sales effectiveness. This position trains custodial personnel in product usage techniques through the use of product demonstrations and/or audiovisual training to assure customer satisfaction. He follows up promptly on customer leads and inquiries. He services customer and distributor complaints or problems and provides technical support as required. On a predetermined frequency basis, he surveys and sells assigned local accounts currently being sold on national contract. He represents the division in local custodial clinics and trade shows as required. He maintains an adequate current supply of literature, forms, and samples and maintains assigned equipment and sales tools in a businesslike condition.

The incumbent is responsible for training, developing, and motivating distributor sales personnel. This is accomplished by frequent on-the-job training in areas of product knowledge, selling skills, and demonstration techniques. He sells distributor management and assists distributors to maintain an adequate and balanced inventory of the full product line. He introduces marketing plans and sells new products and sales promotions to distributor management. He participates in distributor sales meetings to launch new products or sales promotions, or for training and motivational purposes. He keeps abreast of pertinent competitive activities, product performance, new maintenance techniques, and other problems and opportunities in the territory. Periodically, he communicates Wentworth growth objectives versus distributor progress to distributor management (i.e., sales coverage, volume and product sales, etc.). He assists the distributor to maintain a current and adequate supply of product literature, price lists, and sales aids.

(continued)

EXHIBIT 7   Wentworth industrial cleaning supplies position description *(concluded)*

The incumbent prepares daily sales reports, weekly reports, travel schedules, weekly expense reports, and the like, and maintains territory and customer records. He maintains close communication with his immediate supervisor concerning products, sales, distributor and shipping problems.

He controls travel and business expenses with economy and sound judgment. He handles and maintains assigned company equipment and territory records in a businesslike manner.

Major challenges to this position include maintaining established major users, selling prospective new target accounts, and strengthening distribution and sales coverage to attain or exceed sales objectives.

The incumbent operates within divisional policies, procedures, and objectives. He consults with his immediate supervisor for recommendations and/or approval concerning distributor additions or terminations, exceptions to approved selling procedures, and selling the headquarters level of national or regional accounts.

Internally, he consults with the editing office concerning distributor shipments, credit, and so forth. Externally, he works closely with distributor personnel to increase sales and sales coverage and with user accounts to sell new or additional products.

The effectiveness of this position is measured by the ability of the incumbent to attain or exceed territory sales objectives.

This position requires an incumbent with an in-depth and professional knowledge of user account selling techniques, product line, and janitorial maintenance products distributors, and a minimum of supervision.

PRINCIPAL ACCOUNTABILITIES

1. Sell and service key-user accounts to assure attainment of territory sales objectives.
2. Sell, train, develop, and motivate assigned distributors to assure attainment of product sales, distribution, and sales coverage objectives.
3. Plan, schedule, and manage personal selling efforts to assure maximum sales productivity.
4. Plan and develop professional sales techniques to assure maximum effectiveness.
5. Train custodial personnel in the use of Wentworth products and systems to assure customer satisfaction.
6. Maintain a close awareness of territory and market activities to keep the immediate supervisor abreast of problems and opportunities.
7. Perform administrative responsibilities to conduct an efficient territory operation.
8. Control travel and selling expenses to contribute toward profitable territory operation.

mediocre performance. Luther indicated corporate cash flow expectations from WICS were not being met and that a plan was needed from Griffith concerning how WICS could improve its overall operating performance. Griffith was quite aware that Wentworth International would make personnel changes to meet corporate objectives and that selling off divisions not able to meet corporate expectations was not unlikely. Griffith informed Luther that an action plan would be developed and be on his desk within 30 days.

Griffith's first step was to approve an earlier request made by Mike Toner, sales and distributor relations manager, for a study of sales force and distributor attitudes and opinions (Appendixes A and B). Next, the memo in Exhibit 8 was sent, discussing Griffith's assignment from Luther.

Staff reaction to Griffith's memo (Exhibit 8) was one of frustration and anger. Several managers thought they had already complied with Griffith's request. One person commented, "I've told Randy numerous times what we need to do to turn the division around, and all he does is nod his head. Why go through this 'wheel-spinning' exercise again?" Another said, "The only time old J. R. listens to us is when the top brass leans on him for results." Despite staff reaction, the meeting would be held, and everybody would have suggestions for consideration.

To provide adequate time, Griffith scheduled an all-day meeting to be held at Wentworth's nearby lodge, located on Lake Woebegone. Griffith started the meeting by reviewing past performance. Next, he asked each manager to outline his or her proposal. First to speak was Steve Shenken, who indicated that Mike Toner would present a proposal combining both of their ideas. Shenken also said he would listen to all sales force proposals and try to combine the best parts into an overall plan.

EXHIBIT 8   **Griffith's memo**

Intra-Office Memorandum

To: Steve Shenken, National Sales Manager
    Caitlin Smith, Manager—Sales Analysis
    Ryan Michaels, Manager—Sales Training
    Calla Hart, Manager—Special Sales Program
    Charlotte Webber, Senior Product Manager
    Mike Toner, Sales and Distributor Relations Manager

From: Randall Griffith, Vice President—Marketing

Subject: WICS Performance Review

As you all know, our performance has not met corporate expectations. To rectify this situation, before we all lose our jobs, we need to meet to discuss ways for improving our market performance.

At our next meeting, I want each of you to develop proposals for your areas of responsibility. These proposals need not be detailed at this time. For the moment, I am seeking ideas, not final solutions.

MIKE TONER'S PROPOSAL

Toner's proposal was rather basic. If improving market share was WICS's objective, then more SSDs are needed in all territories. According to Toner,

> Each area manager serves, on the average, four SSDs. Since we can only get so much business out of an SSD, then to increase sales we need more SSDs. I suggest that each area manager add two more distributors. Of course, this move will require that we either add more area managers or that we hire and train a special group to call on new end-users and new distributors. It's difficult to attract new SSDs unless we show them a group of prospective end-users who are ready to buy WICS's products. Now, I have not made any estimates of how many more people are needed, but we do know that present AMs do not have enough time to adequately seek new business.

After Toner presented this proposal, Griffith asked if the existing AMs could not be motivated to apply more effort toward securing new business. Calla Hart thought the AMs could do more and that her proposal, if adopted, would alleviate the need for expansion of the AMs and SSDs.

CALLA HART'S PROPOSAL

As expected, Hart's proposal revolved around her extensive experience with WICS's incentive programs. This satisfactory experience led Calla to suggest the following:

> If I thought that the AMs and the SSDs were working at full capacity, I would not propose more incentive programs. But they are not! We can motivate the AMs to secure more new business, and we can get more new business from our distributors. We all know that the SSDs are content to sit back and wait for the AMs to hand them new business. Well, let's make it worthwhile to the SSDs by including them in our incentive programs. For the AMs I suggest that we provide quarterly incentives much like our Christmas Program. AMs who achieve their quotas by the 15th of the second month of the quarter would receive a gift.
>
> In addition, we need to develop a program for recognizing new end-user sales. Paying bonuses for obtaining new end-user accounts would be one approach. For example, let's reward the AM from each territory who secures the highest percentage increase in new end-user accounts. At the same time, we need to reward the distributor from each territory who achieves the highest percentage increase in new end-user sales dollars. And let's recognize these top producers each quarter and at year end as well. Our incentive programs work. We know that, so let's expand their application to new sales.
>
> Finally, on a different note, I support establishing quotas for our distributors. We have quotas for our sales force, and we enforce them. AMs who do not make quotas do not stay around very long. Why not the same procedures for some of our SSDs? We all know that there are some distributors who need to be replaced. Likewise, I have not made any cost estimates but feel that we are just searching for new ideas.

Griffith thanked Hart for her comments. He wondered whether applying more pressure to the distributors was the most suitable approach. He agreed with Hart that WICS's incentive programs seemed to be very popular but questioned if other techniques might not work. Griffith then asked Ryan Michaels for his comments.

RYAN MICHAELS'S PROPOSAL

During his short time with WICS, Michaels has gained respect as being very thorough and analytical. He is not willing to accept as evidence such comments as "We know it works" as a reason for doing something. Determining the value of sales training, Michaels's area of assignment, has caused him considerable concern. He knows it is useful, but how useful is the question he is trying to answer. According to Michaels, WICS needs to examine the basic selling duties of the area managers:

> Before we recruit more AMs and SSDs, or try to motivate them to obtain more new business with incentive programs, we need to examine their job activities. I favor doing a job analysis of the area manager. Some evidence that I have seen indicates that job descriptions are outmoded. AMs do not perform the activities detailed in the job descriptions. For example, most AMs spend very little time calling on prospective end-users. Accompanying distributor sales reps on daily calls does not lead to new end-user business. Possibly the AMs could better spend their time doing new account development work. But before we make any decisions concerning time allocation, we need to conduct a job analysis. And, while we are collecting data, let's ask the AMs what rewards are important to them. How do they value promotions, pay increases, recognition, and so forth? Maybe the AMs do not want more contests.

Griffith agreed that the job descriptions were out of date. He also contended this is typical and nothing to be concerned about in the short run. The idea of finding out what rewards AMs value intrigued Griffith. Next, Griffith asked Charlotte Webber for her reactions to WICS's market share problem.

CHARLOTTE WEBBER'S PROPOSAL

Webber's proposal was more strategic in nature than the previous suggestions. Her experience as a product manager led her to consider product-oriented solutions and to suggest the following:

> I think we can increase market share and sales volume through the expansion of current lines and the addition of a full line of economy-based products. We can expand our present premium and average lines to cover 100 percent of the product class by adding air fresheners and general purpose cleaners. In addition

we must introduce the economy-based products to counter competition.

> The proposed plan would not be costly because we could use our existing distributor network. If additional SSDs are necessary, we can select those in the $500,000 to $1,000,000 sales volume range. I feel that through these extensions and an increased number of SSDs we can address 75 percent of the SSD end-user dollars.

Griffith agreed that line extensions were a viable means of achieving some corporate goals. He expressed concern over entry into the low-quality segment of the market due to WICS's present customer perceptions of the company as a high-quality producer. Griffith turned to Caitlin Smith for additional suggestions on how to increase market share.

CAITLIN SMITH'S PROPOSAL

Smith's proposal came as no surprise to those attending the meeting. Her position in sales analysis made her critically aware of WICS's high cost of sales. It was only recently, however, that she developed a plan incorporating market share and cost of sales. Her views were accurate, but often given little weight due to her inexperience. According to Smith,

> Our costs of sales are currently running at 10 to 15 percent, while our competitors' costs average 5 to 8 percent. As many of you know I am in favor of changing the job description of the area manager and the sales presentation. These changes are necessary due to our products' stage in the life cycle and customer service level preferences. Recently I have become convinced that there is another means of reducing sales costs. By reducing prices we could increase sales volume and reduce the cost of sales. This strategy would also increase penetration and market share.

Griffith conceded that price reductions were a possibility but expressed concern over the possibility of weakening consumer perceptions of WICS as a high-quality manufacturer. He also questioned Smith's assumption that the industrial cleaning supplies industry was presently in the mature stage of the product life cycle.

Following these comments, Griffith thanked the participants for their input and adjourned the meeting. On retiring to his room, he reflected on the suggestions presented during the meeting and his own beliefs. He knew he must begin to formulate an action plan immediately since the 30-day deadline was drawing near.

Appendix A
Conclusions of Study of Area Manager Attitudes

MGH Associates, management consultants, was retained by WICS to investigate attitudes and opinions of field personnel and sanitary supply distributors. Initially, MGH conducted lengthy interviews with selected individuals, followed by the administration of a comprehensive questionnaire. The results below identify role expectations and attitudes toward their reasonableness.

TERRITORY MANAGER'S ROLE EXPECTATIONS

MGH Associates's interviews included territory managers because the territory manager is really the only management level contact the distributor has.

The territory manager interprets his or her role to be that of an overseer, to assure that WICS objectives are achieved and that quotas are met.

The territory manager interprets his or her role to include,

- Training the area managers to sell WICS products.
- Training and motivating the distributor sales force.
- Coordinating area manager activities with headquarters in Lincoln.
- Hiring and firing area managers.
- Striving for new product commitments from the distributors.
- Acting as referee for competition between distributors.
- "Building the book" for the adding or deleting of distributors.
- Submitting the study to the regional manager, who writes a proposal based on the territory manager's study. It is submitted to corporate management, where the final decision is made.

AREA MANAGER'S ROLE EXPECTATIONS

The following is the area manager's view of the role he or she believes WICS management expects to be performed:

- Multiply sales effort through distributor's sales force (listed first because it was consistently mentioned first).
- Teach and motivate the distributor's sales force to sell WICS products.
- Introduce new products to the market through:
  - Direct calls on end-users.
  - Distributors.
- Keep margins high to keep distributors happy. If they are happy, they will push WICS.
- Follow through on direct sales responsibilities.
- Collect information for management.
- Fulfill responsibilities relating to incentives:
  - New gallon sales.
  - Repeat gallon sales.
  - Demonstrations.
  - 30, 35, 40? calls/week.
  - Major account calls.
  - Cold calls—"to develop business the distributor is reluctant to go after."

AREA MANAGER'S ROLE PROBLEMS

The area manager's perception of what management expects does not imply that the area manager feels that management's approach is working. In general, the sales force appears frustrated by a sales role they see as ineffective:

- A sales role that stresses:
  - New gallon sales.
  - Cold calls on end-users.
  - Product demonstrations.
  - New product introduction.

- "Checking the boxes" rather than being "creatively productive":

  - 15 demos.

  - 10 cold calls.

  - 5 distributor training sessions.

- Incentives stress selling techniques that may not be the most productive ways to sell.

  - Emphasis is on new gallon sales over repeat gallon sales. Incentives weight new gallons over repeat gallons (two to one).

  - Emphasis to "demonstrate as often as possible" for the points. Demonstrate to show you are a "regular guy" who gets his or her hands dirty, not necessarily to show product benefits.

- Bonus incentives appear to be a "carrot" only for those who don't regularly make bonus, that is, "hit 106 for maximum bonus and minimum quota increase."

- The sales role gives the area manager little ability to impact his or her own success to:

  - Change distribution.

  - Move distributor outside his or her window.

- The area manager describes his or her role as:

  - A "lackey."

  - A "chauffeur."

  - A "caretaker of old business."

AREA MANAGER'S ROLE: MAKING COLD CALLS

One of the causes of area manager frustration is the general ineffectiveness of their cold calls sales role:

- The area manager makes cold calls on end-users not presently sold by the WICS distributor, with the difficult objective of moving these accounts to the WICS distributor.

- If the area manager succeeds in moving this account over to WICS products, chances are small that the distributor will keep the business:

  - Without a major portion of the account's total purchases, the distributor cannot afford to continue to call on the account.

  - Distributor sales rep is on commission.

  - After five calls, will stop calling if purchases have not begun to increase.

- The distributor that lost the account will try extremely hard to get back the business. This may mean giving the product away to keep control of the account—maintain majority of the account's purchases. Past experience indicates it is very difficult to move distributors outside their window.

Appendix B

Conclusions of Study of WICS Sanitary Supply Distributor Attitudes

WICS DISTRIBUTOR'S ROLE EXPECTATIONS

The following is the WICS distributor's role as outlined by WICS management and sales force:

- Act as an extension of the WICS sales force.

- Push and promote WICS product line in a specified area:

  - Sell WICS over other brands.

  - Always sell the premium benefits of WICS products to the end-user, instead of distributor's private label.

- Be aware that the WICS line could be lost if private label sales grow too large.

- Actively market new WICS products.

DISTRIBUTOR'S ROLE PROBLEMS

Distributors have been angered by WICS's attempt to run their businesses ("WICS is trying to tell me what to do").

- WICS makes demands—"uses pressure tactics":

  - Distributors say they are told "our way or no way."

  - Distributors feel they are forced to carry products they don't want:

    - High minimum buy-ins.

    - "Won't see area manager if we don't carry the new product."

  - Distributors say WICS management doesn't "realize we make our living selling all our products—not just WICS."

- Communication is poor with WICS management.

  - One way—"Our opinions never reach Lincoln."

- "WICS uses the distributor as a testing ground for new products":

  - Distributor is not told what to expect.

  - After 14-week blitz, "You never hear about the product again."

  - The distributor sales force is not trained to sell to, and cannot afford to call on, certain segments of the market.

- Growth takes the distributor into new geographical market areas, and WICS may elect not to go/grow with the distributor:

  - New branch in different city.

- Growth may take distributor sales personnel out of area manager's district:

  - Receives no support from WICS.

- Worst case—distributor sales rep's territory is completely outside district:

  - No WICS representative at any accounts.

  - Prefer to sell other than WICS.

- WICS does not realize that a distributor's total business extends beyond "its own backyard" in many markets.

DISTRIBUTOR'S ROLE SELLING COSTS

Distributors have shown concern over the high cost of selling WICS products. Sales costs are approximately 45 percent of the total operating costs.

- "WICS products are basically no better than anyone else's."

- Yet WICS asks distributors to switch competitor's accounts over to WICS products:

  - Price advantage is very rare.

  - A problem must exist.

  - A demonstration is required.

- All these make the "problem-solving" sale time-consuming and costly.

- Result: When a WICS product is sold, it is easy for competitive WICS distributors to cut price to try to get the business:

  - They have very low sales costs.

- Required action: Original distributor must cut margin to keep the business:

  - This frustrates distributor salespeople.

  - Causes them to sell private label.

Case 3.2
Hanover–Bates Chemical Corporation

James Sprague, newly appointed northeast district sales manager for the Hanover–Bates Chemical Corporation, leaned back in his chair as the door to his office slammed shut. "Great beginnings," he thought. "Three days in my new job and the district's most experienced sales representative is threatening to quit."

On the previous night, Sprague, Hank Carver (the district's most experienced sales representative), and John Follet, another senior member of the district sales staff, had met for dinner at Sprague's suggestion. During dinner he had mentioned that one of his top priorities would be to conduct a sales and profit analysis of the district's business in order to identify opportunities to improve the district's profit performance. He had stated that he was confident that the analysis would indicate opportunities to reallocate district sales efforts in a manner that would increase profits. As Sprague had indicated during the conversation, "My experience in analyzing district sales performance data for the national sales manager has convinced me that any district's allocation of sales effort to products and customer categories can be improved." Both Carver and Follet had nodded as Sprague discussed his plans.

Carver was waiting when Sprague arrived at the district sales office this morning. It soon became apparent that Carver was very upset by what he perceived as Sprague's criticism of how he and the other district sales representatives were doing their jobs—and, more particularly, of how they were allocating their time in terms of customers and products. As he concluded his heated comments, Carver said,

> This company has made it darned clear that 34 years of experience don't count for anything . . . and now someone with not much more than two years of selling experience and two years of pushing paper for the national sales manager at corporate headquarters tells me I'm not doing my job. . . . Maybe it's time for me to look for a new job. . . . and since Trumbull Chemical [Hanover–Bates's major competitor] is hiring, maybe that's where I should start looking . . . and I'm not the only one who feels this way.

Source: This case was prepared by Professor Robert E. Witt, of the University of Texas–Arlington, as a basis for class discussion and is not designed to illustrate effective or ineffective handling of an administrative situation.

As Sprague reflected on the scene that had just occurred, he wondered what he should do. It had been made clear to him when he had been promoted to manager of the northeast sales district that one of his top priorities should be improvement of the district's profit performance. As the national sales manager had said, "The northeast sales district may rank third in dollar sales, but it's our worst district in terms of profit performance."

Prior to assuming his new position, Sprague had assembled the data presented in Exhibits 1 through 6 to assist him in analyzing the district sales and profits. The data had been compiled from records maintained in the national sales manager's office. Although he believed the data would provide a sound basis for a preliminary analysis of district sales and profit performance, Sprague had recognized that additional data would probably have to be collected when he arrived in the northeast district (District 3).

In response to the national sales manager's comment about the northeast district's poor performance, Sprague had been particularly interested in how the district had performed on its gross profit quota. He knew that district gross profit quotas were assigned in a manner that took into account variation in price competition. Thus, he felt that poor performance in the gross profit quota area reflected misallocated sales efforts either in terms of customers or in terms of the mix of product line items sold. To provide himself with a frame of reference, he had also requested data on the north-central sales district (District 7). This district is generally considered to be one of the best, if not the best, in the company. Furthermore, the north-central district sales manager, who is only three years older than Sprague, is highly regarded by the national sales manager.

THE COMPANY AND THE INDUSTRY

The Hanover–Bates Chemical Corporation is a leading producer of processing chemicals for the chemical plating industry. The company's products are produced in four plants, located in Los Angeles, Houston, Chicago, and Newark, New Jersey. The company's production

EXHIBIT 1 Hanover–Bates Chemical Corporation: summary income statements, 2003–2007

	2003	2004	2005	2006	2007
Sales	$29,835,000	$32,565,000	$28,590,000	$32,970,000	$35,835,000
Production expenses	17,901,000	20,245,500	18,297,000	20,418,000	21,844,500
Gross profit	11,934,000	12,319,500	10,293,000	12,552,000	13,990,500
Administrative expenses	3,909,000	4,330,500	4,188,000	4,387,500	4,659,000
Selling expenses	3,036,000	3,361,500	3,201,000	3,411,000	3,598,500
Pretax profit	4,989,000	4,627,500	2,904,000	4,753,500	5,733,000
Taxes	2,268,000	2,082,000	1,185,000	2,139,000	2,577,000
Net profit	$ 2,721,000	$ 2,545,500	$ 1,719,000	$ 2,614,500	$ 3,156,000

EXHIBIT 2 District sales quota and gross profit quota performance, 2007

District	Number of Sales Reps	Sales Quota	Sales—Actual	Gross Profit Quota*	Gross Profit—Actual
1	7	$ 5,820,000	$ 5,859,000	$ 2,328,000	$ 2,383,500
2	6	5,625,000	5,610,000	2,250,000	2,293,500
3	6	5,475,000	5,109,000	2,190,000	1,858,500
4	6	5,055,000	4,977,000	2,022,000	1,942,500
5	5	4,950,000	4,815,000	1,980,000	1,779,000
6	5	4,695,000	4,807,500	1,878,000	1,768,500
7	5	4,080,000	4,657,500	1,632,000	1,965,000
		$35,700,000	$35,835,000	$14,280,000	$13,990,500

*District gross profit quotas were developed by the national sales manager in consultation with the district.

EXHIBIT 3 District selling expenses, 2007

District	Sales Rep. Salaries*	Sales Commission	Sales Rep. Expenses	District Office	District Manager Salary	District Manager Expenses	Sales Support	Total Selling Expenses
1	$265,650	$29,139	$84,420	$31,725	$50,250	$17,190	$104,205	$ 582,624
2	214,830	28,050	76,140	31,968	51,000	18,051	106,980	527,019
3	236,070	25,545	81,654	33,184	52,500†	18,573	105,015	552,541
4	225,720	24,885	73,656	33,006	48,750	16,507	99,705	522,229
5	188,925	24,075	64,080	31,673	49,500	16,684	114,900	489,837
6	187,275	24,397	62,280	31,488	50,250	17,142	100,650	473,482
7	172,275	26,295	67,050	33,728	47,250	17,464	88,125	452,187
								$3,599,919

*Includes cost of fringe benefit program, which was 15 percent of base salary.
†Salary of James Sprague's predecessor.

process is, in essence, a mixing operation. Chemicals purchased from a broad range of suppliers are mixed according to a variety of user-based formulas. Company sales in 2007 had reached a new high of $35.83 million, up from $32.97 million in 2006. Net pretax profit in 2007 had been $5.73 million, up from $4.75 million in 2006. Hanover–Bates has a strong balance sheet, and the company enjoys a favorable price–earnings ratio on its stock, which trades on the OTC (over-the-counter) market.

EXHIBIT 4   District contribution to corporate administrative expenses and profit, 2007

District	Sales	Gross Profit	Selling Expenses	Contribution to Administrative Expense and Profit
1	$ 5,859,000	$ 2,383,500	$ 582,624	$ 1,800,876
2	5,610,000	2,293,500	527,019	1,766,481
3	5,109,000	1,858,500	552,541	1,305,958
4	4,977,000	1,942,500	522,229	1,420,270
5	4,815,000	1,779,000	489,837	1,289,163
6	4,807,500	1,768,500	473,482	1,295,017
7	4,657,500	1,965,000	452,187	1,512,813
	$35,835,000	$13,990,500	$3,599,919	$10,390,579

EXHIBIT 5   Northeast (#3) and north-central (#7) district sales and gross profit performance by account category, 2007

District	(A)	(B)	(C)	Total
Sales by Account Category				
Northeast	$1,372,500	$2,521,500	$1,215,000	$5,109,000
North-central	1,126,500	2,553,000	978,000	4,657,500
Gross Profit by Account Category				
Northeast	$ 534,000	$ 934,500	$ 390,000	$1,858,500
North-central	495,000	1,087,500	382,500	1,965,000

EXHIBIT 6   Potential accounts, active accounts and account call coverage: northeast and north-central districts, 2007

District	Potential Accounts (A)	Potential Accounts (B)	Potential Accounts (C)	Active Accounts (A)	Active Accounts (B)	Active Accounts (C)	Account Coverage (Total Calls) (A)	Account Coverage (Total Calls) (B)	Account Coverage (Total Calls) (C)
Northeast	90	381	635	53	210	313	1,297	3,051	2,118
North-central	60	286	499	42	182	218	1,030	2,618	1,299

Although Hanover–Bates does not produce commodity-type chemicals (such as sulfuric acid), industry customers tend to perceive minimal quality differences among the products produced by Hanover–Bates and its competitors. Given the customers' perception of a lack of variation in product quality and the industry wide practice of limiting advertising expenditures, field sales efforts are of major importance in the marketing programs of all firms in the industry.

Hanover–Bates's market consists of several thousand job-shop and captive (in-house) plating operations. Chemical platers process a wide variety of materials including industrial fasteners (e.g., screws, rivets, bolts, and washers), industrial components (e.g., clamps, casings, and couplings), and miscellaneous items (e.g., umbrella frames, eyelets, and decorative items). The chemical plating process involves the electrolytic application of metallic coatings such as zinc, cadmium, nickel, and brass. The degree of plating precision required varies substantially, with some work being primarily decorative, some involving relatively loose standards (e.g., 0.0002 zinc, which means that anything over two ten-thousandths of an inch of plate is acceptable), and some involving relatively precise standards (e.g., 0.0003–0.0004 zinc).

Regardless of the degree of plating precision involved, quality control is of critical concern to all chemical platers. Extensive variation in the condition of materials received for plating requires a high level of service from the firms supplying chemicals to platers. This service is normally provided by the sales representatives of the firm(s) supplying the plater with processing chemicals.

Hanover–Bates and the majority of the firms in its industry produce the same line of basic processing chemicals for the chemical plating industry. The line consists of a trisodium phosphate cleaner (SPX); anesic aldahyde brightening agents for zinc plating (ZBX), cadmium plating (CBX), and nickel plating (NBX); a protective post-plating chromate dip (CHX); and a protective burnishing compound (BUX). The company's product line is detailed as follows:

Product	Container Size	List Price	Gross Margin
SPX	400-lb. drum	$120	$ 42
ZBX	50-lb. drum	114	51
CBX	50-lb. drum	114	51
NBX	50-lb. drum	120	52.50
CHX	100-lb. drum	330	135
BUX	400-lb. drum	180	66

COMPANY SALES ORGANIZATION

Hanover–Bates's sales organization consists of 40 sales representatives operating in seven sales districts. Most sales representatives had formerly worked for a Hanover–Bates customer, and none were college-educated. Sales representatives' salaries range from $33,000 to $45,000, with fringe benefit costs amounting to an additional 15 percent of salary. In addition to their salaries, Hanover–Bates's sales representatives receive commissions of 0.5 percent of their dollar sales volume on all sales up to their sales quotas. The commission on sales in excess of quota is 1 percent. District sales manager salaries range from $47,250 to $52,500.

Sales managers are also eligible for a bonus based on district sales performance.

In 2005, the national sales manager of Hanover–Bates had developed a sales program based on selling the full line of the company's products. He believed that if the sales representatives could successfully carry out his program, the following benefits would accrue to Hanover–Bates and its customers:

1. Sales volume per account would be greater, and selling costs as a percentage of sales would decrease.

2. A Hanover–Bates sales representative could justify spending more time with an account, thus becoming more knowledgeable about the account's business and becoming better able to provide technical assistance and identify selling opportunities.

3. Full-line sales would strengthen Hanover–Bates's competitive position by reducing the likelihood of account loss to other chemical-plating suppliers (a problem that existed in multiple-supplier situations).

The national sales manager's 2005 sales program had also included the following account call–frequency guidelines:

A accounts (major accounts generating $20,000 or more in yearly sales)—two calls per month.

B accounts (medium-sized accounts generating $11,000–19,999 in yearly sales)—one call per month.

C accounts (small accounts generating less than $11,000 yearly in sales)—one call every two months.

The account call–frequency guidelines were developed by the national sales manager after discussions with the district managers. The national sales manager had been concerned about the optimal allocation of sales effort to accounts and felt that the guidelines would increase the efficiency of the company's sales force, although not all of the district sales managers agreed with this conclusion. It was common knowledge in Hanover–Bates's corporate sales office that Sprague's predecessor as northeast district sales manager had not been one of the company's better district sales managers. His attitude toward the sales plans and programs of the national sales manager had been one of reluctant compliance rather than acceptance and support. However, when the national sales manager succeeded in persuading Sprague's predecessor to take early retirement, no replacement was readily available.

Carver, who most of the sales representatives had assumed would get the district manager job, had been passed over in part because he would be 65 in three years. The national sales manager had not wanted to face the same replacement problem again in three years and also had wanted someone in the position who would be more likely to be responsive to the company's sales plans and policies. The appointment of Sprague as district manager had caused considerable talk, not only in the district but also at corporate headquarters. In fact, the national sales manager had warned Sprague that "a lot of people are expecting you to fall on your face. . . . They don't think you have the experience to handle the job, in particular, and to manage and motivate a group of sales representatives, most of whom are considerably older and more experienced than you." The general sales manager had concluded by saying, "I think you can handle the job, Jim. . . . I think you can manage those sales reps and improve the district's profit performance . . . and I'm depending on you to do both."

Case 3.3

Biomed Co., Ltd.: Designing a New Sales Compensation Plan

Richard Ivey School of Business
The University of Western Ontario

Ponlerd Chiemchanya had just completed his MBA at the Ivey Business School in May 2006. On the one hand, he was excited about rejoining Biomed Co., Ltd. (Biomed), the family business in Thailand. On the other hand, as the new general manager of Biomed, he had some concerns about the first major decisions he was about to make and implement upon his return. Biomed's parent company, Thai Drugs Co., Ltd. (Thai Drugs), had just revised Biomed's market strategy, a change that created the need to realign the sales compensation system to fit with the new strategy. Chiemchanya was charged with this responsibility. Since Biomed was fundamentally a sales organization working on behalf of Thai Drugs, he knew that getting this right could be the making of Biomed. Of course the opposite also held true. Chiemchanya saw high company risk and high personal risk in this situation.

THE CURRENT SITUATION AT BIOMED

Thai Drugs, a family-owned business, was one of the 170 small-to-medium sized local Thai pharmaceutical manufacturers. It was overshadowed by the five large firms that accounted for over 50 percent of local manufacturers' sales, and also by foreign manufacturers that accounted for 65 percent of the Thai pharmaceutical market. Thai Drugs' main strength was in the over-the-counter market, selling to drugstores. In 1990, Thai Drugs started to use existing manufacturing capacity to expand into the generic pharmaceutical market. Overall, it provided more than 100 items of prescription and non-prescription drugs to hospitals, drugstores and clinics.

Biomed was set up as a subsidiary of Thai Drugs and acted as Thai Drugs' sole agent to sell generic pharmaceuticals to the market. Biomed was basically a sales organization, comprising a sales manager, 11 sales representatives and several sales administration clerks. Despite the total market size of THB14 billion[1] for locally manufactured generics, Biomed sales had been hovering around THB10 million (.07 percent market share). When compared to the over-the-counter arm of Thai Drugs, Biomed sales were minimal. Due to the unsophisticated information systems at Thai Drugs, it was not possible to determine whether these sales were even profitable. This had been of concern to Thai Drugs' management for the past few years.

This concern was exacerbated when changes in GMP (Good Manufacturing Practice)[2] requirements were expected to be effective in 2008, leading to a massive investment to upgrade manufacturing facilities. Most of this investment was to be tied to the manufacturing of Biomed products. Biomed's cost of capital, at 10 percent, had to be considered here. Biomed also knew that it had to cover THB4 million annually in fixed overhead. Given the small market share and small margins in the generics market and the upcoming investment required, management was starting to question the viability of Biomed.

Would it be worth investing in the manufacturing facilities when Biomed may not sell the products? Was Biomed's sales volume actually generating profits? Could Biomed do better, given the market size? Would it be better to close Biomed altogether? These were the questions that management was asking while Chiemchanya was away completing his MBA.

[1]The exchange rate was $1 US = 38.25 Thai Baht (THB) in mid-2006.
[2]GMP is a set of regulations, codes and guidelines for the manufacture of drugs, medical devices, etc.

Management did decide to make an effort to increase Biomed's sales and profitability. To accomplish this, management evaluated the situation and changed Biomed's market strategy. If this was not successful over the next one to two years, Thai Drugs might close down Biomed and abandon the generic pharmaceutical market altogether. Chiemchanya needed to understand what was behind this management decision. He needed to examine the industry, the old market strategy and the existing sales compensation plan, and the new market strategy before he could design an appropriate sales compensation plan.

THE THAI GENERIC PHARMACEUTICAL MARKET

MARKET SIZE

With a population of 65 million people in Thailand, the total domestic market for pharmaceuticals (local and foreign companies combined), in 2002 figures, was around US$900 million or THB40 billion at wholesale prices. Foreign companies and their original products accounted for 65 percent of the market. Local Thai companies accounted for the remaining 35 percent of the market. Since all of the Thai manufacturers were formulating drugs but were not involved in the research and development (R&D) of new drugs, 35 percent was a representative figure for the local generic market. This resulted in a THB14 billion market for generics.

MANUFACTURERS

Beyond the top five generics manufacturers, the market was fragmented. There were 175 Thai manufacturers, providing drugs to the THB14 billion market. Five companies accounted for more than 50 percent of the market (see Exhibit 1). The remaining 50 percent of the market was shared among 170 manufacturers, which were small private or family-owned businesses.

MARKET SEGMENTS

Hospitals

According to 2002 figures, hospitals accounted for 70 percent of the market for domestically manufactured pharmaceuticals. In April 2001, the government implemented the "30-baht universal health care" scheme whereby everyone received universal health care at hospitals by paying THB30 per visit. This new scheme put pressure on public hospitals. Under this scheme, hospitals received funding on a per-capita basis, as opposed to having 100 percent funding of a hospital's annual expenditures. Public hospitals were forced to find ways to cut costs in order to manage and service patients within budget. This led to a dramatic increase in generic substitution. Most hospitals automatically substituted all original products with generics whenever there was a generic version available.

There were two major implications for generic manufacturers resulting from the 30-baht scheme. First, the new government scheme favored generic manufacturers due to the substitution of branded products by generics. However, the second implication worked against these manufacturers. Hospitals in the same province and region collectively formed buying groups to bargain for the lowest generic prices. The process started with sellers proposing their price in a bidding process. The provider with the lowest price would win the bid and then became the primary provider of the drug throughout the province or region. The second and third runners-up would be back-up providers. The result was that only those few providers with the lowest costs could sell to public hospitals and make a profit. Manufacturers that did not have low-cost structures, or who were not interested in pursuing low-cost strategies, could sell only those low-volume products that did not end up in a bidding process. They could also decide to simply abandon this market.

EXHIBIT 1
Top 5 Thai drug manufacturers

Source: epsicom business intelligence, World pharmaceutical markets: Thailand, March 2004.

Manufacturer	Sales (million THB)	Market Share
Siam Bhaesaj	1,975	14%
GPO	1,702	12%
Biolab	1,468	10%
Berlin Pharm	1,261	9%
Thai Nakorn Patana	963	7%
Total of top 5	7,369	53%
Total generics market	14,000	100%

Drugstores

From 2002 figures, drugstores accounted for most of the remaining 30 percent of the market for domestically manufactured pharmaceuticals. There were an estimated 11,000 drugstores in Thailand, most of which were privately owned by pharmacists or were "mom and pop" style pharmacies. Although there were foreign drugstore chains (e.g. Boots, Watson's), these chains were geared more towards selling beauty products and food. When drugs were prescribed in chains, most of the time, the original-version drug would be used. Most generics were prescribed through privately owned drugstores.

Patients viewed drugstores as a cheap and convenient alternative compared to a visit to the hospital or a doctor's clinic. Pharmacists in drugstores had the autonomy to prescribe prescription drugs without a prescription from a physician. This latitude made drugstores a good choice for people with lower incomes, since they could receive an immediate diagnosis and prescription while avoiding waiting times and doctors' fees. Generics were widely prescribed in drugstores due to their lower cost. Drugstores purchased generics either through distributors or directly from a manufacturer such as Biomed.

Doctor Clinics

The market for drugs in clinics was relatively small when compared to hospitals and drugstores. Doctor clinics held drug inventory to service their patients. Patients were diagnosed and given medicine at the clinic. Most clinics were privately owned by the attending doctor. Generics were also widely used in clinics due to their lower cost. Generics were purchased through either distributors or directly from the manufacturer.

BIOMED'S MARKET STRATEGY

Management looked at Biomed's existing market strategy and found a disconnect between the strategy and the changing market environment.

EXISTING MARKET STRATEGY FOR GENERICS

Biomed's overall value proposition to customers was to provide high quality drugs backed by excellent service.

Market Focus

Biomed targeted all three markets (hospitals, drugstores and clinics) throughout Thailand. There was no specific strategy to emphasize one market segment over another.

Products

Biomed offered more than 100 items of generic products covering almost all types of drugs, e.g., analgesics, antibiotics, vitamins, allergy and respiratory drugs, electrolytes and supplements, gastrointestinal drugs, topical agents, and pediatric drugs. Most Biomed products were undifferentiated, commodity-type products. A typical example was Amoxycillin 500 mg $\times$ 1,000 capsules packaged in a plain plastic container. However, a small percentage of Biomed's product line was geared more towards drugstores and clinics. These products had some degree of differentiation, mostly in the unique color and shape of tablets or capsules. Due to the low education level of the general population, drugstores and clinics that prescribed drugs with unique appearances could have a competitive advantage in the community, since the patient would come back to the drugstore/clinic asking for "the drug," which he or she could not find anywhere else.

Price

Biomed products were priced in the medium-high to high range of the generics market. Volume discounts were offered on a case-by-case basis. Biomed seldom used aggressive price promotions with its customers. It could not afford price discounts because of its lack of economies of scale in production, which led to a high unit cost, based on full cost accounting.

Distribution

Biomed utilized third-party transportation companies to deliver products directly to customers. Biomed was not in a position to incur additional costs by using distributors.

Communications

The Biomed sales force was the single contact and means of communication with the customer. No other means of advertising (journal ads, television ads, radio ads) were employed.

EXISTING SALES STRATEGY

Sales Role

Given that the sales representative was the only person who touched the customer, the role of the salesperson was complex. The current role and goals could be described as:

- Generate sales according to quota.

- Find new accounts.

- Build and maintain relationships between customers and Biomed.

- Negotiate prices with customers within a given range.

- Decide whether customers should receive 30-day credit or 60-day credit.

- Take orders.

- Listen to customer complaints and provide feedback to management.

- Gain and share market intelligence.

Existing Compensation Plan

The existing compensation plan had three components:

Salary: The current salary was THB5,000 per month (THB60,000 annually).

Commission: Sales reps received 1.5 percent of sales volume with a progressive ramp. Sales above 100 per cent of targeted annual sales were compensated at three per cent. Targeted annual sales per rep were THB2 million, on average.

Quarterly bonus: A bonus was paid at the end of each quarter if the year-to-date sales quota was achieved for the quarter. This bonus was retroactively paid whenever year-to-date sales reached quotas.

Overall, the compensation package was on par with the rest of the industry (see Exhibit 2).

Expenses

Each sales representative received a basic allowance of THB380 per day. This was to cover all costs, e.g., fuel, hotel costs, entertainment expenses and cell phone. This level of allowance typically covered a basic hotel room and daily meals. No additional expenses were reimbursed. The expense allowance had an incentive portion. Regardless of territory, if year-to-date sales reached a certain level, the daily allowance would increase as follows:

Sales Volume YTD (THB)	Allowance/day
0–500,000	THB380
500,000–1,000,000	THB420
1,000,000–2,000,000	THB460
2,000,000 and above	THB500

Other Benefits

Sales reps were entitled to the same basic benefits as other Thai Drugs employees. This included a medical insurance plan and a company contribution of 7 percent of salary to the provident (retirement) fund.

STRATEGY REVIEW

In assessing the existing strategy against the current environment, management found two major flaws. The first concerned a lack of direction in terms of product/market focus, and the second concerned price.

There was no discipline in approaching the three different market segments (hospitals, drugstores, doctor clinics). Sales representatives called on any customer where they thought they could generate sales. Management came to believe that Biomed's products were not

---

EXHIBIT 2   Existing compensation plan

Component	Base Salary with Commission and Bonus		
Base Salary	THB60,000		
Commission on sales volume*	Performance To Goal		Commission rate
	To 100%		1.5%
	Beyond 100%		3%
Quarterly bonus		Performance	Bonus
	Q1	Achieve 100% of Q1 YTD Goal	THB3,000
	Q2	Achieve 100% of Q1-2 YTD Goal	THB4,000
	Q3	Achieve 100% of Q1-3 YTD Goal	THB5,000
	Q4	Achieve 100% of Q1-4 YTD Goal	THB6,000

*Bonus for previous quarters are retro-backed when YTD goal is achieved. *Sales were credited when money was collected.*

suitable for hospitals. Since most hospitals used a bidding process to purchase drugs, only the lowest cost providers could win in this segment. Given Thai Drugs' limitation in terms of increasing manufacturing efficiency, and given management's preference not to compete solely on price, it was felt that the hospital segment should not be a target.

Complementing this view was that Biomed actually had strength in the drugstore segment. Since Biomed sales representatives could also sell Thai Drugs' leading over-the-counter products, which were in demand in drugstores, Biomed sales representatives could leverage this to get in the door and start a conversation with the owner. Moreover, some of Biomed's products were already designed for drugstores. Thus, it would be sensible, both from a product standpoint and a sales standpoint, to focus more on drugstores and clinics.

As to the second observation, Biomed's existing strategy was to price at a medium-high to high price point. This was based on the belief that customers would pay a premium price in exchange for good service and a rewarding relationship with Biomed. Management was becoming concerned that this was no longer a compelling argument. In selling commodity-type products, having a competitive price is the No. 1 key success factor. This did not mean that Biomed would have to have the lowest price, since some customers were willing to pay more as long as the price was not too high, the seller had a good relationship, and good service was provided. However, if the price was out of the acceptable range, no matter how good the relationship or service level were, the value to the customer would not justify the higher price.

NEW MARKET STRATEGY

Although management decided on changes in market focus, products and price, the overall value proposition would remain the same, i.e., high quality products backed by excellent service. The key changes inherent in the new market strategy were:

Product Market Focus

From the strategy review, management decided that Biomed's products could not compete in the low-price hospital market. The new product market focus was to be on drugstores and doctor clinics.

Product

Instead of selling more than 100 items, the new strategy was to focus on only 10 to 15 items and to reduce the

prices on these select items. The rationale was that by focusing on the right items at the right price, it would be possible to gain larger orders with two subsequent benefits. First, Biomed would lose fewer orders because of price. Second, combining large orders of fewer items would make it possible to have longer production runs. This would yield economies of scale and lower the unit cost of these selected products. This would lead to more contribution and provide more room if further price cuts were required.

The items selected would have three main characteristics. From a cost perspective, there must be enough room to be able to lower the price to the same range as competitors. Since Thai Drugs had strength in manufacturing sugar coated tablets and formulating multivitamins, which were skills that not all manufacturers had, these drugs would be preferred over other basic tablets and capsules. Finally, products that had sold well in the past were also good candidates, since it meant that customers valued these products as high-quality products.

Price

Selling prices would be reduced to the low-medium to medium price range. However, not all prices would be reduced. Price reductions would tie into the reduced set of products upon which Biomed decided to focus.

THE NEW MARKET STRATEGY AND BIOMED'S SALES STRATEGY

After digesting the new strategy, Chiemchanya was in a position to think about the implications for Biomed's sales strategy. Before jumping into redesigning the compensation system, he knew that it made sense to review the overall implications for the sales strategy, and then to revisit the role of the sales rep under the new strategy. (See Exhibit 3 for a visualization of the new market strategy.)

IMPLICATIONS FOR THE SALES STRATEGY

In the new market strategy, the biggest changes included reducing market scope, lowering selected prices, focusing on 10 to 15 items, and the resulting challenge of generating both volume and THB contribution from this sharper product/market focus. Chiemchanya thought that instead of focusing on sales volume, looking at each sale on a contribution basis might make sense. This would mean that reps would have to consider the

EXHIBIT 3
New market strategy

cost of the products, transportation costs and ordering costs before deciding to accept an order. This would require training.

In addition, each sales representative would have to promote the same selected 10 to 15 products so that, collectively, the sales volume for each item from all territories would increase dramatically. This would lead to economies of scale in production and lower unit costs. Sales representatives would have to learn how to convince customers to purchase the items upon which Biomed wanted to focus. This would change the conversation when visiting customers. Sales reps would have to sell versus simply taking orders for any products that the customer wanted.

Finally, hospitals would not be targeted. This change would have minimal impact on sales reps, whose volume came from drugstores. However, there were some sales reps who had a lot of sales activity within the hospital segment. How could Chiemchanya encourage these reps to change their planning and working style to focus away from hospitals?

THE NEW SALES ROLE AND GOALS

The sales force would remain as the single point of contact with the customer. Sales reps would still have a complex set of tasks, and many of the tasks in the old strategy would transfer to the new. As Chiemchanya reflected, he thought the new sales role would have as its overarching purposes: being the single point of contact with the customer, and being the THB contribution

generator for the company. He thought the following tasks would make up the sales role.

- Generate THB contribution, which included the tasks of:

  - Price negotiation—sales representatives would have autonomy to negotiate prices with customers within a range.

  - Credit evaluation/provision—sales representatives would have autonomy to decide whether a customer should receive a 30-day or 60-day credit.

  - Taking orders.

Focusing on contribution margin would fit perfectly with the new strategy. Biomed's new market strategy had prices going down, so reps need to combine these decreases in unit contribution with increased volumes on an order-by-order basis to ensure company profitability. Reps would be informed of the "loaded" cost of goods, including the variable cost of the product, the transportation cost for each order, and the ordering costs. They would be responsible to negotiate with the customer to reach the price and order quantity that maximized THB contribution.

- Focus selling efforts in drugstores and doctor clinics.

- Find new accounts.

- Build and maintain relationships between the customer and Biomed.

- Focus selling efforts on 10 to 15 items selected by management.

- Listen to customer complaints and provide feedback to management.

- Gain and share market intelligence.

Chiemchanya was still not comfortable jumping to a compensation system that would encourage the accomplishment of the tasks inherent in the new sales role. He thought it was important to set explicit goals against each of these tasks. In the past, only one goal had been set: a sales volume goal. He wanted to be much clearer under the new sales strategy and came up with a specific list of tasks and their associated goals (see Exhibit 4).

DESIGNING THE COMPENSATION SYSTEM AND NEXT STEPS

Chiemchanya believed that he was now set to revamp the sales compensation system at Biomed to reflect the new market strategy. He knew that he was following a logical path since he had translated the market strategy into a new sales strategy with a revised sales role and associated goals. He wondered how he would judge the new system as he designed it. Although Chiemchanya was confident that he had developed a logical approach to redesigning the compensation system, he knew that his task did not end with the compensation system documented on a piece of paper. Two other issues still dogged him.

The first was the implementation of the new plan. Anytime a manager makes decisions that potentially have an impact on someone's wallet, careful thought needs to be given to the communication of the proposed changes. There also has to be consideration of any protection that might be given to reps as they move from one system to the next. In addition, if the new plan required the use of territory-specific targets or quotas, deriving these would have to be done in a manner deemed to be fair and equitable by the sales reps. The first person to get on board would be the sales manager. He could act in concert with Chiemchanya to sell the new approach, although Chiemchanya surmised that the initial reaction of the sales reps would be negative. The new plan required changes in behavior, and the sales reps may feel that their income would be at risk as a result.

The second issue that kept Chiemchanya awake at night was the sense that, although important in supporting the new strategy, there were many other things required from the sales program in order to ensure the success of the new market strategy. Chiemchanya needed to think through any training interventions that would be required. He also had to think through whether or not all the sales reps were suited to the new sales role. It is different selling on volume than selling on contribution to a focused market segment with a focused set of products. What if some reps could not make the switch? He also needed to determine whether or not there was a place for recognition, in addition to rewards, to encourage the desired behaviors under the new strategy.

The fun was about to begin.

EXHIBIT 4
Sales tasks and goals

Task	Goal
Generate THB contribution	THB contribution against a quota which might vary by territory
Focus selling efforts on drugstores and clinics	At least 60% of contribution derived from drugstores and clinics (with allowances for reps who currently have a large number of hospital accounts)
Find new accounts	Number of new accounts/year, which might vary by territory
Build and maintain relationships between customer and company	Volume of repeat sales
Focus selling efforts on 10 to 15 items selected by management	75% of contribution derived from the focused items (derived from management's estimate of what is required to achieve economies of scale)
Listen to customer complaints and provide feedback to management	Monthly report of customer complaints, feedback
Gain and share market intelligence	Monthly market intelligence report

Endnotes

Chapter 1

1. Rolph R. Anderson, "Sales Management in the New Millennium," *Journal of Personal Selling & Sales Management* 16 (Fall 1996), pp. 17–32.

2. David W. Cravens, "The Changing Role of the Sales Force," *Marketing Management* 4 (Fall 1995), pp. 49–57.

3. Neil Rackham and John DeVincintis, *Rethinking the Sales Force* (New York: McGraw-Hill, 1999).

4. Ellen Bolman Pullins and Leslie M. Fine, "How the Performance of Mentoring Activities Affects the Mentor's Job Outcomes," *Journal of Personal Selling & Sales Management* 22 (Fall 2002), pp. 259–71.

5. Sean Valentine and Tim Barnett, "Ethics Code Awareness, Perceived Ethical Values, and Organizational Commitment," *Journal of Personal Selling & Sales Management* 23 (Fall 2003), pp. 359–67.

6. Lawrence B. Chonko, John F. Tanner, Jr., and Ellen Reid Smith, "The Sales Force's Role in International Marketing Research and Marketing Information Systems," *Journal of Personal Selling & Sales Management* 11 (Winter 1991), pp. 69–79.

7. O.C. Ferrell, John Fraedrich, and Linda Ferrell, *Business Ethics* 7th ed. (New York: Houghton Mifflin, 2006).

8. Cravens, "The Changing Role of the Sales Force."

9. Catherine Holahan, "Journal Blazes Newspapers' New Trail," *BusinessWeek* (January 3, 2007), www.businessweek.com; Gene Marcial, "Can Zell and Murdoch Rescue Newspapers?," *BusinessWeek* (May 18, 2007), www.businessweek.com.

10. HR Chally Group, *The Chally World Class Excellence Report: The Route to the Summit* (Dayton, OH: HR Chally Group, 2007).

11. Leonard L. Berry, *On Great Service: A Framework for Action* (New York: The Free Press, 1995).

Chapter 2

1. David W. Cravens, "The Changing Role of the Sales Force," *Marketing Management* 4 (Fall 1995), pp. 49–57.

2. This classic line of research on job satisfaction of salespeople was initiated by Gilbert A. Churchill, Jr., Neil M. Ford, and Orville C. Walker, Jr. in the article "Organizational Climate and Job Satisfaction of the Sales Force," *Journal of Marketing Research* (November 1976), pp. 323–32. Measurement approaches and study results within this domain have remained relatively stable for over 30 years.

3. Thayer C. Taylor, "Going Mobile," *Sales & Marketing Management* (May 1994), pp. 94–101.

4. Greg W. Marshall, Daniel J. Goebel, and William C. Moncrief "Hiring for Success at the Buyer-Seller Interface," *Journal of Business Research* 56 (April 2003), pp. 247–55.

5. Stephen B. Castelberry and C. David Shepherd, "Effective Interpersonal Listening and Personal Selling," *Journal of Personal Selling & Sales Management* (Winter 1993), pp. 35–49. See also Rosemary P. Ramsey and Ravi S. Sohi, "Listening to Your Customers: The Impact of Perceived Salesperson Listening Behavior on Relationship Outcomes," *Journal of the Academy of Marketing Science* 25 (Spring 1997), pp. 127–37.

6. Barton A. Weitz, Harish Sujan, and Mita Sujan, "Knowledge, Motivation, and Adaptive Behavior: A Framework for Improving Selling Effectiveness," *Journal of Marketing* 50 (October 1986), pp. 174–91.

7. William C. Moncrief III, "Selling Activity and Sales Position Taxonomies for Industrial Sales Forces," *Journal of Marketing Research* 23 (August 1986), pp. 261–70.

8. Greg W. Marshall, William C. Moncrief, and Felicia G. Lassk, "The Current State of Sales Force Activities," *Industrial Marketing Management,* 28 (January 1999), pp. 87–98.

9. Derek A. Newton, *Sales Force Performance and Turnover* (Cambridge, MA: Marketing Science Institute, 1973), p. 3.

10. David A. Andelman, "Betting on the 'Net," *Sales & Marketing Management* (June 1995), pp. 47–59.

11. Benson P. Shapiro, *Sales Program Management: Formulation and Implementation* (New York: McGraw-Hill, 1977), p. 160.

12. Milt Grassell, "What Purchasing Managers Like in a Salesperson . . . and What Drives Them up the Wall," *Business Marketing* (June 1986), pp. 72–77. See also Edith Cohen, "The View from the Other Side," *Sales & Marketing Management* (June 1990), pp. 108–10; and "Ten Ways to Lose a Sale," *Sales & Marketing Management* (December 1992), p. 35.

13. Frederick F. Reichheld, "Loyalty and the Renaissance of Marketing," *Marketing Management* 2 (1994), pp. 10–21.

14. Donald W. Jackson, Jr., Janet E. Keith, and Richard K. Burdick, "Purchasing Agents' Perceptions of Industrial Buying Center Influence: A Situational Approach," *Journal of Marketing* (Fall 1984), pp. 75–83.

15. Richard G. Jennings and Richard E. Plank, "When the Purchasing Agent is a Committee: Implications for Industrial Marketing," *Industrial Marketing Management* 24 (November 1995), pp. 411–19.

16. Vince-Wayne Mitchell, "Buy-Phase and Buy-Class Effects on Organizational Risk Perceptions and Reductions in Purchasing Professional Services," *Journal of Business and Industrial Marketing* 13, no. 6 (1998), pp. 461–71.

17. Jennings and Plank.

18. Mark A. Moon and Susan Forquer Gupta, "Examining the Formation of Selling Centers: A Conceptual Framework," *Journal of Personal Selling & Sales Management* (Spring 1997), pp. 31–42.

19. Louis V. Gerstner, Jr., *Who Says Elephants Can't Dance?* (New York: Harper Business, 2004).

20. Wesley J. Johnston and Jeffrey E. Lewin, "Organizational Buying Behavior: Toward and Integrative Framework," *Journal of Business Research* 35 (January 1996), pp. 1–15.

Chapter 3

1. Ajay K. Kohli and Bernard J. Jaworski, "Market Orientation: The Construct, Research Propositions, and Managerial Implications," *Journal of Marketing* 54 (April 1990), pp. 1–18; John C. Narver and Stanley F. Slater, "The Effect of a Market Orientation on Business Profitability," *Journal of Marketing* (October 1990), pp. 20–35.

2. HR Chally Group, *The World Class Excellence Report: The Route to the Summit* (Dayton, OH: HR Chally Group, 2007).

3. The Data Warehouse Institute, Industry Study 2000 Survey, p. 1.

4. http://www.PricewaterhouseCoopers.com.

5. Don Peppers and Martha Rogers, *One to One B2B: Customer Development Strategies for the Business-to-Business World* (New York: Doubleday, 2001).

6. Ronald S. Swift, *Accelerating Customer Relationships: Using CRM and Relationship Technologies* (Upper Saddle River, NJ: Prentice Hall PTR, 2000), p. 42.

7. Stanley A. Brown, ed., *Customer Relationship Management: A Strategic Imperative in the World of E-Business* (Toronto: John Wiley & Sons Canada, 2000), pp. 8–9.

8. Frederick F. Reichheld, *Loyalty Rules! How Leaders Build Lasting Relationships in the Digital Age* (Cambridge, MA: Harvard Business School Press, 2001).

9. Ronald S. Swift, pp. 39–42.

10. Ray McKenzie, *The Relationship-Based Enterprise: Powering Business Success through Customer Relationship Management* (New York: McGraw-Hill, 2001), pp. 7–8.

11. Ray McKenzie, p. 8.

12. Daniel G. Simpson, "Why Most Strategic Planning Is a Waste of Time and What You Can Do about It," *Long Range Planning* 31, no. 3 (1998), pp. 476–80.

13. *www.dell.com.*

14. Leonard Goodstein, Timothy Nolan, and J. William Pfeiffer, *Applied Strategic Planning: How to Develop a Plan That Really Works* (New York: McGraw-Hill, 1993), p. 181.

15. Michael E. Porter, *Competitive Strategy* (New York: The Free Press, 1998), Chapter 2.

16. Raymond E. Miles and Charles C. Snow, *Organizational Strategy, Structure and Process* (New York: McGraw-Hill, 1978). Miles and Snow also identified a fourth category of businesses, which they called "reactors." However, because reactors are businesses with no clearly defined or consistent competitive strategy, we do not discuss them further here.

17. For a more detailed discussion of how a business's competitive strategy influences its marketing and sales strategies and programs, see Orville C. Walker, Jr., and Robert W. Ruekert, "Marketing's Role in the Implementation of Business Strategies: A Critical Review and Conceptual Framework," *Journal of Marketing* (July 1987), pp. 15–33.

18. Neil Rackham and John DeVincintis, *Rethinking the Sales Force* (New York: McGraw-Hill, 1999).

19. John F. Tanner, Jr., "Users' Role in the Purchase: Their Influence, Satisfaction, and Desire to Participate in the Next Purchase," *Journal of Business & Industrial Marketing* 13, no. 6 (1998), pp. 479–91.

20. James P. Morgan and Shirley Cayer, "Working with World-Class Suppliers: True Believers," *Purchasing* (August 13, 1992), pp. 50–52.

21. For example, see David A. Aaker, *Managing Brand Equity* (New York: The Free Press, 1991); Linda M. Keefe, "Corporate Voice in Relation to Product Brands," *Design Management Journal* 6 (1995), pp. 45–49.

22. For a more detailed discussion of the role of personal selling and other promotional tools in building long-term relationships with channel members, see James A. Narus and James C. Anderson, "Turn Your Industrial Distributors into Partners," *Harvard Business Review* (March–April 1986), pp. 66–71; F. Robert Dwyer, Paul H. Schurr, and Sejo Oh, "Developing Buyer–Seller Relationships," *Journal of Marketing* (April 1987), pp. 11–27; and Jan Heide and George John, "Do Norms Matter in Marketing Relationships?" *Journal of Marketing* (April 1992), pp. 32–44.

23. Bill Saporito, "Behind the Tumult at P&G," *Fortune* (March 7, 1994), pp. 74–82. For other examples involving B2B goods, see Joseph B. Fuller, James O'Conor, and Richard Rawlinson, "Tailored Logistics: The Next Advantage," *Harvard Business Review* (May–June 1993), pp. 87–98; and W. David Gibson, "Holy Alliances," *Sales & Marketing Management* (July 1993), pp. 85–87.

24. Frederick F. Reichheld, "Loyalty and the Renaissance of Marketing," *Marketing Management* 2 (1994), pp. 10–21.

25. Reichheld, "Loyalty and the Renaissance of Marketing."

26. Louis V. Gerstner, *Who Says Elephants Can't Dance?* (New York: Harper Business, 2004).

Chapter 4

1. Patricia Sellers, "How to Remake Your Sales Force," *Fortune* (May 4, 1992), pp. 96–102.

2. Charles Shaw, "The Rep and the Future—Which Is Now," *Agency Sales Magazine* (January 2001), pp. 28–30.

3. Dan Hanover, "Independents Day," *Sales & Marketing Management* (April 2000), pp. 65–68.

4. Jayashree Mahajan, G. A. Churchill, Jr., N.M. Ford, and O.C. Walker, Jr., "A Comparison of the Impact of Organizational Climate on the Job Satisfaction of Manufacturers' Agents and Company Salespeople: An Exploratory Study," *Journal of Personal Selling & Sales Management* (May 1984), pp. 1–10.

5. Allen M. Weiss and Erin Anderson, "Converting from Independent to Employee Salesforces: The Role of Perceived Switching Costs," *Journal of Marketing Research* (February 1992), pp. 101–15.

6. Bernard J. Jaworski, "Toward a Theory of Marketing Control: Environmental Context, Control Types, and Consequences," *Journal of Marketing* (July 1988), pp. 23–39.

7. Erin Anderson, "The Salesperson as Outside Agent or Employee: A Transaction Cost Analysis," *Marketing Science* 4 (1985), pp. 234–54.

8. Erin Anderson and Barton Weitz, "The Use of Pledges to Build and Sustain Commitment in Distribution Channels," *Journal of Marketing Research* (February 1992), pp. 18–34.

9. Robert W. Ruekert, Orville C. Walker, Jr., and Kenneth J. Roering, "The Organization of Marketing Activities: A Contingency Theory of Structure and Performance," *Journal of Marketing* (Winter 1985), pp. 13–25.

10. Francy Blackwood, "Did You Sell $5 Million Last Year?" *Selling* (October 1995), pp. 44–53.

11. David A. Andelman, "Betting on the 'Net,'" *Sales & Marketing Management* (June 1995), pp. 47–59.

12. William C. Moncrief, Charles W. Lamb, Jr., and Terry Dielman, "Developing Telemarketing Support Systems," *Journal of Personal Selling & Sales Management* (August 1986), pp. 43–49.

13. Robert J. Hershock, "Notes from the Revolution," in *Reinventing the Sales Organization* (New York: The Conference Board, 1995), pp. 10–13.

14. Michelle Marchetti, "IBM's Marketing Visionary," *Sales & Marketing Management* (September 2001), pp. 52–62.

15. Arun Sharma, "Who Prefers Key Account Management Programs? An Investigation of Business Buying Behavior and Buying Firm Characteristics," *Journal of Personal Selling & Sales Management* (Fall 1997), pp. 27–39. See also Catherine Pardo, "Key Account Management in the Business to Business Field: The Key Account's Point of View," *Journal of Personal Selling & Sales Management* (Fall 1997), pp. 17–26.

16. Frederick F. Reichheld, "Loyalty and the Renaissance of Marketing," *Marketing Management* 2 (1994), pp. 10–21; Rahul Jacob, "Why Some Customers Are

More Equal than Others," *Fortune* (September 19, 1994), pp. 215–24; and Sangit Sungupta, Robert E. Krapfel, and Michael Pusateri, "Switching Costs in Key Account Relationships," *Journal of Personal Selling & Sales Management* (Fall 1997), pp. 9–16.

17. Benson P. Shapiro and Rowland T. Moriarity, *Organizing the National Account Force* (Cambridge, MA: Marketing Science Institute, 1984), pp. 1–37; and Jerome A. Colletti and Gary S. Tubridy, "Effective Major Account Sales Management," *Journal of Personal Selling & Sales Management* (August 1987), pp. 1–10.

18. Mark A. Moon and Susan Forquer Gupta, "Examining the Formation of Selling Centers: A Conceptual Framework," *Journal of Personal Selling & Sales Management* (Spring 1997), pp. 31–42.

19. Andy Cohen, "Top of the Charts—Lear Corporation," *Sales & Marketing Management* (July 1998), p. 40.

20. Geoffrey Brewer, "Lou Gerstner Has His Hands Full," *Sales & Marketing Management* (May 1998), pp. 36–41.

21. Dan T. Dunne, Jr., and Claude A. Thomas, "Strategy for Systems Sellers: A Team Approach," *Journal of Personal Selling & Sales Management* (August 1986), pp. 1–10. See also Cynthia R. Cauthern, "Moving Technical Support into the Sales Loop," *Sales & Marketing Management* (August 1990), pp. 58–61.

22. Andy Cohen, "Top of the Charts—Pfizer," *Sales & Marketing Management* (July 1998), p. 41.

23. Tom Murray, "Just-in-Time Isn't Just for Show—It Sells," *Sales & Marketing Management* (May 1990), pp. 62–67. See also Joseph B. Fuller, James O'Conor, and Richard Rawlinson, "Tailored Logistics: The Next Advantage," *Harvard Business Review* (May–June 1993), pp. 87–98.

24. Sang-Lin Han, David T. Wilson, and Shirish P. Dant, "Buyer–Supplier Relationships Today," *Industrial Marketing Management* 22 (1993), pp. 331–38.

25. Barry Farber and Joyce Wycoff, "Customer Service: Evolution and Revolution," *Sales & Marketing Management* (May 1991), pp. 44–51.

26. For a discussion of advantages and disadvantages of outsourced selling, see Andris A. Zoltners, Prabhakant Sinha, and Greggor A. Zoltners, *The Complete Guide to Accelerating Sales Force Performance* (New York: AMACOM, 2001), p. 34.

27. Michele Marchetti, "Can You Build a Sales Force?" *Sales & Marketing Management* (January 2000), pp. 56–61.

Chapter 5

1. For a discussion of some other, less common forecasting techniques, see Spyros Makridakis, Steven C. Wheelwright, and Rob J. Hyndman, *Forecasting: Methods and Applications* (New York: John Wiley & Sons, 1997).

2. See also David M. Georgoff and Robert Murdick, "Manager's Guide to Forecasting," *Harvard Business Review* 64 (January–February 1986), pp. 110–20, which contains a chart that rates 20 forecasting techniques on 16 evaluative dimensions.

3. C. L. Jain, "Delphi-Forecast with Experts' Opinion," *Journal of Business Forecasting* 4 (Winter 1985–86), pp. 22–23.

4. Peter J. Brockwell and Richard A. Davis, *Introduction to Time Series and Forecasting* (New York: Springer-Verlag, 1996).

5. Spyros Makridakis et al., "The Accuracy of Extrapolation (Times-Series) Methods: Results of a Forecasting Competition," *Journal of Forecasting* 1 (April–June 1982), pp. 111–53.

6. Spyros Makridakis and Michele Hibon, "Accuracy of Forecasting: An Empirical Investigation," *Journal of the Royal Statistical Society* 142, pt. 2 (1979), pp. 97–145. See also Robin M. Hogarth and Spyros Makridakis, "Forecasting and Planning: An Evaluation," *Management Science* 27 (February 1981), pp. 115–38.

7. Mark M. Moriarity and Arthur J. Adams, "Management Judgment Forecasts, Composite Forecasting Models, and Conditional Efficiency," *Journal of Marketing Research* 21 (August 1984), pp. 239–50.

8. Pierre Wack, "Scenarios: Shooting the Rapids," *Harvard Business Review* 63 (November–December 1985), p. 146. See also Peter W. Beck, "Debate over Alternate Scenarios Replaces Forecasts at Shell U.K.," *Journal of Business Forecasting* 3 (Spring 1984), pp. 2–6.

9. The reader is referred to "2005 Survey of Buying Power and Media Markets," *Sales & Marketing Management* (September 2005).

10. Wack, "Scenarios: Shooting the Rapids."

11. Alan J. Dubinsky and Thomas E. Barry, "A Survey of Sales Management Practices," *Industrial Marketing Management* 11 (April 1982), pp. 133–41.

12. Raymond W. LaForge, David W. Cravens, and Clifford E. Young, "Using Contingency Analysis to Select Selling Effort Allocation Methods," *Journal of Personal Selling & Sales Management* 6 (August 1986), pp. 19–28.

13. Walter J. Talley, Jr., "How to Design Sales Territories," *Journal of Marketing* 25 (January 1961), pp. 7–13.

14. Donald L. Brady, "Determining the Value of an Industrial Prospect: A Prospect Preference Index Model," *Journal of Personal Selling & Sales Management* 7 (August 1987), pp. 27–32.

15. Walter J. Semlow, "How Many Salesmen Do You Need?" *Harvard Business Review* 37 (May–June 1959), pp. 126–32. See also Charles B. Weinberg and Henry C. Lucas, Jr., "Semlow's Results Are Based on a Spurious Relationship," *Journal of Marketing* 41 (April 1977), pp. 146–47.

16. Zarrell Lambert and Fred W. Kniffen, "Response Functions and Their Applications in Sales Force Management," *Southern Journal of Business* 5 (January 1970), pp. 1–9.

17. A. Parasuraman, "An Approach for Allocating Sales Call Effort," *Industrial Marketing Management* 11 (1982), pp. 75–79; Renato Fiocca, "Account Portfolio Analysis for Strategy Development," *Industrial Marketing Management* 11 (1982), pp. 53–62; and Rosann L. Spiro and William D. Perreault, Jr., "Factors Influencing Sales Call Frequency of Industrial Salespersons," *Journal of Business Research* 6 (January 1978), pp. 1–15.

18. Fiocca, "Account Portfolio Analysis for Strategy Development"; Raymond W. LaForge and David W. Cravens, "Steps in Selling Effort Deployment," *Industrial Marketing Management* 11 (1982), pp. 183–94; David W. Cravens and Raymond W. LaForge, "Salesforce Deployment Analysis," *Industrial Marketing Management* 12 (July 1983), pp. 179–92; and Alan J. Dubinsky and Thomas N. Ingram, "A Portfolio Approach to Account Profitability," *Industrial Marketing Management* 13 (February 1984), pp. 33–41.

19. Raymond W. La Forge and David W. Cravens, "Empirical and Judgment-Based Sales-Force Decision Models: A Comparative Assessment," *Decision Sciences* 16 (Spring 1985), pp. 177–95.

20. Adrian B. Ryans and Charles B. Weinberg, "Territory Sales Response Models: Stability over Time," *Journal of Marketing Research* 24 (May 1987), pp. 229–33.

21. "Sales Analysis," *Studies in Business Policy,* no. 13 (New York: National Industrial Conference Board, 1965), p. 3.

Chapter 6

1. This chapter borrows heavily from the following: Orville C. Walker, Jr., Gilbert A. Churchill, Jr., and Neil M. Ford, "Motivation and Performance in Industrial Selling: Present Knowledge and Needed Research," *Journal of Marketing Research* 14 (May 1977), pp. 156–68; and Orville C. Walker, Jr., Gilbert A. Churchill, Jr., and Neil M. Ford, "Where Do We Go from Here? Selected Conceptual and Empirical Issues Concerning the Motivation and Performance of the Industrial Salesforce," in *Critical Issues in Sales Management: State of the Art and Future Research Needs,* eds. Gerald Albaum and Gilbert A. Churchill, Jr. (Eugene: University of Oregon, 1979), pp. 10–75. See also Richard E. Plank and David A. Reid, "The Mediating Role of Sales Behaviors: An Alternative Perspective of Sales Performance and Effectiveness," *Journal of Personal Selling & Sales Management* 14 (Summer 1994), pp. 43–56; Steven P. Brown, William Cron, and John W. Slocum, Jr., "Effects of Goal-Directed Emotions on Salesperson Volitions, Behavior, and Performance: A Longitudinal Study," *Journal of Marketing* (January 1997), pp. 39–50; C. Fred Miao and Kenneth R. Evans, "The Impact of Salesperson Motivation on Role Perceptions and Job Performance—A Cognitive and Affective Perspective," *Journal of Personal Selling & Sales Management* 27 (Winter 2007), pp. 89–101.

2. For studies of how role perceptions can affect salespeople's job satisfaction and performance, see Douglas N. Behrman and William D. Perreault, Jr., "A Role Stress Model of the Performance and Satisfaction of Industrial Salespeople," *Journal of Marketing* 48 (Fall 1984), pp. 9–21; Alan J. Dubinsky and Steven W. Hartley, "A Path-Analytic Study of a Model of Salesperson Performance," *Journal of the Academy of Marketing Science* 14 (Spring 1986), pp. 36–46; Linda S. Hartenian, Farrand J. Hadaway, and Gordon J. Badovick, "Antecedents and Consequences of Role Perceptions: A Path Analytic Approach," *Journal of Applied Business Research* 10 (Spring 1994), pp. 40–50; George J. Avlonitis and Nikolaos G. Panagopoulos, "Role Stress, Attitudes, and Job Outcomes in Business-to-Business Selling: Does the Type of Selling Situation Matter?." *Journal of Personal Selling & Sales Management* 26 (Winter 2006), pp. 68–77.

3. R. Kenneth Teas, "Supervisory Behavior, Role Stress, and the Job Satisfaction of Industrial Salespeople," *Journal of Marketing Research* 20 (February 1983), pp. 84–91; Ajay K. Kohli, "Some Unexplored Supervisory Behaviors and Their Influence on Salespeople's Role Clarity, Specific Job Esteem, Job Satisfaction, and Motivation," *Journal of Marketing Research* 22 (November 1985), pp. 424–33; See also Goutam N. Challagalla and Tasadduq A. Servani, "Dimensions and Types of Supervisory Control Effects of Salesperson Performance and Satisfaction," *Journal of Marketing* (January 1996), pp. 89–105; Thomas E. DeCarlo, R.

Kenneth Teas, and James C. McElroy, "Salesperson Performance Attributions Process and the Formulation of Expectancy Estimates," *Journal of Personal Selling & Sales Management* (Summer 1997), pp. 1–17; Douglas Amyx and Bruce L. Alford, "The Effects of Salesperson Need for Achievement and Sales Manager Leader Reward Behavior," *Journal of Personal Selling & Sales Management* 25 (Fall 2005), pp. 346–359.

4. Barton A. Weitz, "A Critical Review of Personal Selling Research: The Need for Contingency Approaches," in *Critical Issues in Sales Management,* eds. Albaum and Churchill, Jr., pp. 76–126; Neil M. Ford et al., "Selecting Successful Salespeople: A Meta-Analysis of Biographical and Psychological Selection Criteria," in *Review of Marketing 1987,* ed. Michael J. Houston (Chicago: American Marketing Association, 1987), pp. 90–131; John Andy Wood, "NLP Revisited: Nonverbal Communications and Signals of Trustworthiness," Journal of Personal Selling & Sales Management 26 (Spring 2006), pp. 198–204.

5. Siew Meng Leong, Paul S. Busch, and Deborah Roedder John, "Knowledge Bases and Salesperson Effectiveness: A Script-Theoretic Analysis," *Journal of Marketing Research* 26 (May 1990), pp. 164–78; Richard G. McFarland and Blair Kidwell, "An Examination of Instrumental and Expressive Traits on Performance: The Mediating Role of Learning, Prove, and Avoid Goal Orientations," *Journal of Personal Selling & Sales Management* 26 (Spring 2006), pp. 143–159.

6. R. Kenneth Teas, "An Empirical Test of Models of Salespersons' Job Expectancy and Instrumentality Perceptions," *Journal of Marketing Research* 18 (May 1981), pp. 209–26; Thomas L. Quick, "The Best-Kept Secret for Increasing Productivity," *Sales & Marketing Management* 141 (July 1989), pp. 34–38; and Audrey Bottjen, "Incentives Gone Awry," *Sales & Marketing Management* (May 2001), p. 72. For empirical evidence regarding the things that motivate salespeople in the United States versus salespeople in other countries, see Alan J. Dubinsky, Masaaki Kotabe, Chae Un Lim, and Ronald E. Michaels, "Differences in Motivational Perceptions among U.S., Japanese, and Korean Sales Personnel," *Journal of Business Research* 30 (June 1994), pp. 175–85.

7. Arthur Baldauf, David W. Cravens, and Nigel F. Piercy, "Examining Business Strategy, Sales Management, and Salesperson Antecedents of Sales Organization Effectiveness," *Journal of Personal Selling & Sales Management* (Spring 2001), pp. 109–22; Ken Grant, David W. Cravens, George S. Low, and William C. Moncrief, "The Role of Satisfaction with Territory

Design on Motivation, Attitudes, and Work Outcomes of Salespeople," *Journal of the Academy of Marketing Science* (Spring 2001), pp. 165–78; John W. Barnes, Donald W. Jackson, Jr., Michael D. Hutt, and Ajith Kumar, "The Role of Culture Strength in Shaping Sales Force Outcomes," *Journal of Personal Selling & Sales Management* 26 (Summer 2006), pp. 255–270.

8. "Take a Right and . . ." *Sales & Marketing Management* (September 1997), pp. 91–96.

9. Gilbert A. Churchill, Jr., Neil M. Ford, and Orville C. Walker, Jr., "Motivating the Industrial Salesforce: The Attractiveness of Alternative Rewards," *Journal of Business Research* 7 (1979), pp. 25–50; William L. Cron and John W. Slocum, Jr., "The Influence of Career Stages on Salespeople's Job Attitudes, Work Perceptions, and Performance," *Journal of Marketing Research* 23 (May 1986), pp. 119–29; Lawrence B. Chonko, John F. Tanner, and William A. Weeks, "Selling and Sales Management in Action: Reward Preferences of Salespeople," *Journal of Personal Selling & Sales Management* 12 (Summer 1992), pp. 67–75; William A. Weeks, Terry W. Loe, Lawrence B. Chonko, Carlos Ruy Martinez, and Kirk Wakefield, "Cognitive Moral Development and the Impact of Perceived Organizational Ethical Climate on the Search for Sales Force Excellence: A Cross-Cultural Study," *Journal of Personal Selling & Sales Management* 26 (Spring 2006), pp. 206–217.

10. See Gilbert A. Churchill, Jr., Neil M. Ford, and Orville C. Walker, Jr., "Measuring the Job Satisfaction of Industrial Salesmen," *Journal of Marketing Research* 11 (August 1974), pp. 254–60, for a description of the procedures used to construct the scale. See also Rosemary R. Lagace, Jerry R. Goolsby, and Jule B. Gassenheimer, "Scaling and Measurement: A Quasi-Replicative Assessment of a Revised Version of Indsales," *Journal of Personal Selling & Sales Management* 13 (Winter 1993), pp. 65–72.

11. Steven P. Brown and Robert A. Peterson, "Antecedents and Consequences of Salesperson Job Satisfaction: Meta-Analysis and Assessment of Causal Effects," *Journal of Marketing Research* 30 (February 1993), pp. 63–77.

12. See Alan J. Dubinsky et al., "Salesforce Socialization," *Journal of Marketing* 50 (October 1986), pp. 192–207, for discussion of the socialization process.

13. Robert L. Kahn et al., *Organizational Stress* (New York: John Wiley & Sons, 1964), pp. 57–71. For reviews of this literature, see Mary Van Sell, Arthur P. Brief, and Randall S. Schuler, "Role Conflict and Role Ambiguity: Integration of the Literature and Directions

for Future Research," *Human Relations* 34 (January 1981), pp. 43–71; and Cynthia D. Fisher and Richard Gitelson, "A Meta-Analysis of the Correlates of Role Conflict and Ambiguity," *Journal of Applied Psychology* 68 (May 1983), pp. 320–33. See also Rosemary Ramsey Lagace, "Role Stress Differences between Salesmen and Saleswomen: Effect on Job Satisfaction and Performance," *Psychological Reports* 62 (June 1988), pp. 815–25; and Jagdip Singh, "Boundary Role Ambiguity: Facets, Determinants, and Impacts," *Journal of Marketing* 57 (April 1993), pp. 11–31.

14. Mark McMaster, "Selling for a Failing Team," *Sales & Marketing Management* 153 (March 2001), p. 11.

15. This discussion was based on the following articles: Goutam Challagalla, Tasaddug Shervani, and George Huber, "Supervisory Orientations and Salesperson Work Outcomes: The Moderating Effect of Salesperson Location," *Journal of Personal Selling & Sales Management* 20, no. 3 (Summer 2000), pp. 161–71; Michele Pepe, "Going Mobile Opens Doors," *Computer Reseller News* 27 (February 1999), pp. 45–48.

16. Neil M. Ford, Orville C. Walker, Jr., and Gilbert A. Churchill, Jr., "Expectation-Specific Measures of the Intersender Conflict and Role Ambiguity Experienced by Industrial Salesmen," *Journal of Business Research* 3 (April 1975), pp. 95–112; Raghu Tadepalli, "Perceptions of Role Stress by Boundary Role Persons: An Empirical Investigation," *Journal of Applied Behavioral Science* 27 (December 1991), pp. 490–514; and Kris Maher, "Stressed Out: Can Workplace Stress Get Worse?" *The Wall Street Journal* (January 16, 2001), p. B-6.

17. Neil M. Ford, Orville C. Walker, Jr., and Gilbert A. Churchill, Jr., "The Psychological Consequences of Role Conflict and Ambiguity in the Industrial Salesforce," in *Marketing: 1776–1976 and Beyond,* ed. Kenneth L. Bernhardt (Chicago: American Marketing Association, 1976), pp. 403–8; Douglas N. Behrman and William D. Perrault, Jr., "A Role Stress Model of the Performance and Satisfaction of Industrial Salespeople," *Journal of Marketing* 48 (Fall 1984), pp. 9–21.

18. Kahn et al., *Organizational Stress,* pp. 72–95; Ajay K. Kohli, "Some Unexplored Supervisory Behaviors and Their Influence on Salespeople's Role Clarity, Specific Self-Esteem, Job Satisfaction and Motivation," *Journal of Marketing Research* 22 (November 1985), pp. 424–33; Louis W. Fry, Charles M. Futrell, A. Parasuraman, and Margaret Chmielewski, "An Analysis of Alternate Causal Models of Salesperson Role Perceptions and Work-Related Attitudes," *Journal of Marketing Research* 23 (May 1986), pp. 153–63; and Jeffrey

Sager, "A Structural Model Depicting Salespeople's Job Stress," *Journal of the Academy of Marketing Science* 22 (Winter 1994), pp. 74–84.

19. James H. Donnelly, Jr., and John M. Ivancevich, "Role Clarity and the Salesman," *Journal of Marketing* 39 (January 1975), pp. 71–74; R. Kenneth Teas, John G. Wacker, and R. Eugene Hughes, "A Path Analysis of Causes and Consequences of Salespeople's Perceptions of Role Clarity," *Journal of Marketing Research* 16 (August 1979), pp. 355–69; Richard P. Bagozzi, "The Nature and Causes of Self-Esteem, Performance, and Satisfaction in the Sales Force: A Structural Equation Approach," *Journal of Business* 53 (1980), pp. 315–31; and Gary K. Rhoads, Jagdip Singh, and Phillips W. Goodell, "The Multiple Dimensions of Role Ambiguity and Their Impact upon Psychological and Behavioral Outcomes of Industrial Salespeople," *Journal of Personal Selling & Sales Management* 14 (Summer 1994), pp. 1–24.

20. Charles M. Futrell and A. Parasuraman, "The Relationship of Satisfaction and Performance to Salesforce Turnover," *Journal of Marketing* 48 (Fall 1984), pp. 33–40; and George H. Lucas, Jr., et al., "An Empirical Study of Salesforce Turnover," *Journal of Marketing* 51 (July 1987), pp. 34–59.

21. Richard P. Bagozzi, "Salesforce Performance and Satisfaction as a Function of Individual Difference, Interpersonal, and Situational Factors," *Journal of Marketing Research* 15 (November 1978), pp. 517–31; Behrman, Bigoness, and Perreault, "Sources of Job-Related Ambiguity and Their Consequences."

22. Lawrence B. Chonko, Roy D. Howell, and Danny N. Bellenger, "Consequence in Sales Force Evaluation: Relation to Sales Force Perceptions of Conflict and Ambiguity," *Journal of Personal Selling & Sales Management* 6 (May 1986), pp. 35–48.

23. Orville C. Walker, Jr., Gilbert A. Churchill, Jr., and Neil M. Ford, "Organizational Determinants of the Role Conflict and Ambiguity Experienced by Industrial Salesmen," *Journal of Marketing* 39 (January 1975), pp. 32–39.

24. Ibid.

25. Lawrence B. Chonko, "The Relationship of Span of Control to Sales Representatives, Experienced Role Conflict and Role Ambiguity," *Academy of Management Journal* 25 (June 1982), pp. 452–56; and Linda S. Hartenian, Farrand J. Hadaway, and Gordon J. Badovick, "Antecedents and Consequences of Role Perceptions: A Path Analytic Approach," *Journal of Applied Business Research* 10 (Spring 1994), pp. 40–50.

26. Paul Busch, "The Sales Manager's Bases of Social Power and Influence upon the Sales Force," *Journal of Marketing* 44 (Summer 1980), pp. 91–101; and Ronald E. Michaels, William L. Cron, Alan J. Dubinsky, and Erich A. Joachimsthaler, "Influence of Formalization on the Organizational Commitment and Work Alienation of Salespeople and Industrial Buyers," *Journal of Marketing Research* 25 (November 1988), pp. 376–83.

27. Pradeep K. Tyagi, "The Effects of Stressful Organizational Conditions on Salesperson Work Motivation," *Journal of the Academy of Marketing Science* 13 (Winter–Spring 1985), pp. 290–309; and Susan M. Keaveney and James E. Nelson, "Coping with Organizational Role Stress: Intrinsic Motivational Orientation, Perceived Role Benefits and Psychological Withdrawal," *Journal of the Academy of Marketing Science* 21 (Spring 1993), pp. 113–24.

28. Greg W. Marshall, William C. Moncrief, and Felicia G. Lassk, "The Current State of Sales Force Activities," *Industrial Marketing Management* 28 (1999), pp. 87–98; William C. Moncrief, "Selling Activity and Sales Position Taxonomies for Industrial Salesforces," *Journal of Marketing Research* 23 (August 1986), pp. 261–70; William C. Moncrief, "Ten Key Activities of Industrial Salespeople," *Industrial Marketing Management* 15 (November 1986), pp. 309–17; and Robert E. Hite and Joseph A. Bellizzi, "Differences in the Importance of Selling Techniques between Consumer and Industrial Salespeople," *Journal of Personal Selling & Sales Management* 5 (November 1985), pp. 19–30.

Chapter 7

1. Suzy Ramlal, "Review of Employee Motivation Theories and Their Implications for Employee Retention within Organizations," Journal of American Academy of Business 5 (September 2004), pp. 52–64.

2. For a discussion of motivational theories and their interrelationships, see James L. Gibson, John M. Ivancevich, and James H. Donnelly, Jr., *Organizations: Behavior, Structure, Processes,* 7th ed. (Homewood, IL: Richard D. Irwin, 1991); and ibid.

3. Barton A. Weitz, Harish Sujan, and Mita Sujan, "Knowledge, Motivation, and Adaptive Behavior: A Framework for Improving Selling Effectiveness," *Journal of Marketing* (October 1986), pp. 174–91. See also Harish Sujan, "Smarter versus Harder: An Exploratory Attributional Analysis of Salespeople's Motivation," *Journal of Marketing Research* (February 1986), pp. 41–49; and Dana James, "Web Conferencing, Talk

Eases Salespeople's Fears," *Marketing News* (November 19, 2001), pp. 4–5.

4. The argument is often advanced, for example, that salespeople should be given pricing flexibility in that they are closest to the customers and have the best perspective on the price that will be needed to make the sales. Interestingly, one study found that among a sample of 108 firms, those firms that gave salespeople the highest degree of pricing authority generated the lowest sales and profit performance. See P. Ronald Stephenson, William L. Cron, and Gary L. Frazier, "Delegating Pricing Authority in the Sales Force: The Effects on Sales and Profit Performance," *Journal of Marketing* (Spring 1979), pp. 21–28. See also Richard Kern, "Letting Your Salespeople Set Prices (Sort Of)," *Sales & Marketing Management* (August 1989), pp. 44–49.

5. Abraham K. Korma, "Expectancies as Determinants of Performance," *Journal of Applied Psychology* 55 (1971), pp. 218–22; Edward E. Lawler III, "Job Attitudes and Employee Motivation: Theory, Research and Practice," *Personnel Psychology* 23 (1970), pp. 223–37; and Roy D. Howell, Danny N. Bellenger, and James B. Wilcox, "Self-Esteem, Role Stress, and Job Satisfaction among Marketing Managers," *Journal of Business Research* (February 1987), pp. 71–84. See also Jeffrey Sager, Junsub Yi, and Charles M. Futrell, "A Model of Depicting Salesperson's Perceptions," *Journal of Personal Selling & Sales Management* (Summer 1998), pp. 1–22.

6. Rosemary Lagace, Stephen B. Castleberry, and Rick Ridnour, "An Exploratory Salesforce Study of the Relationship between Lead–Member Exchange and Motivation, Role Stress, and Manager Evaluation," *Journal of Applied Business Research* (Fall 1993), pp. 110–19.

7. Edward E. Lawler III, *Pay and Organizational Effectiveness: A Psychological View* (New York: McGraw-Hill, 1971); Malcolm Fleschner, "Manager as Motivator," *SellingPower.com* (June 13, 2001); and *Sales & Marketing Management* (August 2001), p. 62.

8. Alfie Kohn, *Punished by Rewards* (New York: Houghton-Mifflin, 1993). Also see William Keenan, Jr., "Breaking with Tradition," *Sales & Marketing Management* (June 1994), pp. 94–99.

9. For example, see Thomas N. Ingram and Danny N. Bellenger, "Personal and Organizational Variables: Their Relative Effect on Reward Valences of Industrial Salespeople," *Journal of Marketing Research* (May 1983), pp. 198–205; Neil M. Ford, Orville C. Walker,

Jr., and Gilbert A. Churchill, Jr., "Differences in the Attractiveness of Alternative Rewards among Industrial Salespeople: Additional Evidence," *Journal of Business Research* (April 1985), pp. 123–38; Lawrence B. Chonko, John F. Tanner, Jr., and William A. Weeks, "Reward Preferences of Salespeople," *Journal of Personal Selling & Sales Management* (Summer 1992), pp. 67–76; Thomas E. DeCarlo, R. Kenneth Teas, and James C. McElroy, "Salesperson Performance Attribution and Processes and Formation of Expectancy Estimates," *Journal of Personal Selling & Sales Management* (Summer 1997), pp. 1–17; and Alexander D. Stajkovic and Fred Luthans, "Differential Effects of Incentive Motivators on Work Experience," *Academy of Management Journal* 4, no. 3 (2001), pp. 580–90. For an interesting cross-cultural comparison of reward valences—as well as expectancy and instrumentality perceptions—across salespeople in the United States, Korea, and Japan, see Alan J. Dubinsky, Masaaki Kotabe, Chae Un Lim, and Ronald E. Michaels, "Differences in Motivational Perceptions among U.S., Japanese, and Korean Sales Personnel," *Journal of Business Research* 30 (1994), pp. 175–85.

10. *Sales & Marketing Management,* March 2001, p. 14

11. Gilbert A. Churchill, Jr., Neil M. Ford, and Orville C. Walker, Jr., "Predicting a Salesperson's Job Effort and Performance: Theoretical, Empirical, and Methodological Considerations," in *Sales Management: New Developments from Behavioral and Decision Model Research,* ed. Richard P. Bagozzi (Cambridge, MA: Marketing Science Institute, 1979), pp. 3–39.

12. Ramlal, "Review of Employee Motivation Theories and their Implications for Employee Retention within Organizations." For a study focused on industrial salespeople, see Richard L. Oliver, "Expectancy Theory Predictions of Salesmen's Performance," *Journal of Marketing Research* (August 1974), pp. 243–53.

13. Abraham H. Maslow, *Motivation and Personality,* 2d ed. (New York: Harper & Row, 1970).

14. Frederick Herzberg, Bernard Mauser, and Barbara Snyderman, *The Motivation to Work,* 2d ed. (New York: John Wiley & Sons, 1959). See also Robert Berl, Terry Powell, and Nicholas C. Williamson, "Industrial Salesforce Satisfaction and Performance with Herzberg's Theory," *Industrial Marketing Management* (February 1984), pp. 11–19; David D. Shipley and Julia A. Kiely, "Industrial Salesforce Motivation and Herzberg's Dual Factor Theory: A U.K. Perspective," *Journal of Personal Selling & Sales Management* (May 1986), pp. 9–16; and David Hackett, "Bespoke Bonus," *Marketing Week* 24, no. 12 (2001), p. 45.

15. Clayton P. Alderfer, "An Empirical Test of a New Theory of Human Needs," *Organizational Behavior and Human Performance* 4 (1969), pp. 142–75.

16. Gilbert A. Churchill, Jr., Neil M. Ford, and Orville C. Walker, Jr., "Personal Characteristics of Salespeople and the Attractiveness of Alternative Rewards," *Journal of Business Research* 7 (1979), pp. 25–50; and Robert L. Berl, Nicholas C. Williamson, and Terry Powell, "Industrial Salesforce Motivation: A Critique and Test of Maslow's Hierarchy of Needs," *Journal of Personal Selling & Sales Management* (May 1984), pp. 33–39.

17. See Lawler, *Pay and Organizational Effectiveness,* especially, pp. 46–59; and Maslow, *Motivation and Personality,* 2nd ed. (New York: Harper & Row, 1970).

18. Wesley J. Johnston and Keysuk Kim, "Performance, Attribution, and Expectancy Linkages in Personal Selling," *Journal of Marketing* (October 1994), pp. 68–81.

19. David C. McClelland, John W. Atkinson, Russell A. Clark, and Edgar L. Lowell, *The Achievement Motive* (New York: Appleton-Century-Crofts, 1953); and John W. Atkinson, *An Introduction to Motivation* (Princeton, NJ: Van Nostrand, 1964).

20. See, for example, E.E. Lawler III, "Job Attitudes and Employee Motivation: Theory, Research, and Practice," *Personnel Psychology* 23 (1970), pp. 223–37; and Julian B. Rotter, "Generalized Expectancies for Internal versus External Control of Reinforcement," *Psychological Monographs: General and Applied* (1966), p. 80.

21. Ibid.

22. Abraham K. Korman, "Expectancies as Determinants of Performance," *Journal of Applied Psychology* 55 (1971), pp. 218–22; and Lawler, "Job Attitudes," pp. 223–37.

23. Ingram and Bellenger, "Personal and Organizational Variables," pp. 203–4.

24. R. Kenneth Teas and James C. McElroy, "Causal Attributions and Expectancy Estimates: A Framework for Understanding the Dynamics of Salesforce Motivation," *Journal of Marketing* (January 1986), pp. 75–86; DeCarlo, Teas, and McElroy, "Salesperson Performance Attribution Processes"; Johnston and Kim, "Performance, Attribution, and Expectancy Linkages"; and Andrea L. Dixon, Rosann L. Spiro, and Maqbul Jamil, "Successful and Unsuccessful Sales Calls: Measuring Salesperson Attributions and Behavioral Intentions," *Journal of Marketing* 65, no. 3, (2001), pp. 64–78.

25. See also Sujan, "Smarter versus Harder."

26. William L. Cron, "Industrial Salesperson Development: A Career Stages Perspective," *Journal of Marketing* (Fall 1984), pp. 41–52; William L. Cron and John W. Slocum, Jr., "The Influence of Career Stages on Salespeople's Job Attitudes, Work Perceptions, and Performance," *Journal of Marketing Research* (May 1986), pp. 119–29; William L. Cron, Alan J. Dubinsky, and Ronald E. Michaels, "The Influence of Career Stages on Components of Salesperson Motivation," *Journal of Marketing* (January 1988), pp. 78–92; and William L. Cron, Ellen F. Jackofsky, and John W. Slocum, Jr., "Job Performance and Attitudes of Disengagement Stage Salespeople Who Are about to Retire," *Journal of Personal Selling & Sales Management* (Spring 1993), pp. 1–13.

27. Robin T. Peterson, "Beyond the Plateau," *Sales & Marketing Management* (July 1993), pp. 78–82. See also William Keenan, Jr., "The Nagging Problem of the Plateaued Salesperson," *Sales & Marketing Management* (March 1989), pp. 36–41.

28. Robert House, "A Path–Goal Theory of Leadership Effectiveness," *Administrative Science Quarterly* 16, (1971), pp. 321–39; and Marshall Goldsmith, "What Drives our Greatest Leaders", *BusinessWeek.* July 17, 2007, BusinessWeek Online.

29. Bill Kelley, "How Much Help Does a Salesperson Need?" *Sales & Marketing Management* (May 1989), pp. 32–34.

30. Gilbert A. Churchill, Jr., Neil M. Ford, and Orville C. Walker, Jr., "Organizational Climate and Job Satisfaction in the Sales Force," *Journal of Marketing Research* (November 1976), pp. 323–32; and Pradeep K. Tyagi, "Relative Importance of Key Job Dimensions and Leadership Behaviors in Motivating Salesperson Work Performance," *Journal of Marketing* (Summer 1985), pp. 76–86. See also Susan K. DelVecchio, "The Quality of Salesperson–Manager Relationship: The Effect of Latitude, Loyalty and Competence," *Journal of Personal Selling & Sales Management* (Winter 1998), pp. 31–48; and Vincent Alonzo, "Perks for Jerks," *Sales & Marketing Management* (February 2001), pp. 38–40.

Chapter 8

1. Julia Chang, "Born to Sell?" *Sales & Marketing Management* (July, 2003), pp. 34–38. For a more complete discussion of current research on Sales person performance criteria. see William I. Cron, Greg W. Marshall, Jagdip Singh, Rosann L. Spiro, and Harish Sujan. "Salesperson Selection, Training, and Development: Trends, Implications, and Research Opportunities." *Journal of Personal Selling & Sales Management* 25 (Spring 2005) pp. 123–36; Thomas E. DeCarlo, Sanjeev Agarwal, and Shyman B. Vyas. "Performance Expectations of Salespeople: The Role of Past Performance and Casual Attributions in Independent and Interdependent Cultures." *Journal of Personal Selling & Sales Management* 27 (Spring 2007) pp. 133–47; Ronald Jelinek and Michael Ahearne. "The Enemy Within: Examining Salesperson Deviance and its Determinants." *Journal of Personal Selling & Sales Management* 26 (Fall 2006) pp. 327–44; and Blair Kidwell, Richard G. McFarland, and Ramon A. Avila. "Perceiving Emotion in the Buyer-Seller Interchange: The Moderated Impact on Performance." *Journal of Personal Selling & Sales Management* 27 (Spring 2007) pp. 119–32.

2. Arthur Bragg, "Are Good Salespeople Born or Made?" *Sales & Marketing Management* (September 1988), p. 74.

3. Gilbert A. Churchill, Jr., Neil M. Ford, Steven W. Hartley, and Orville C. Walker, Jr., "The Determinants of Salesperson Performance: A Meta-Analysis," *Journal of Marketing Research* (May 1985), pp. 103–18. See also Neil M. Ford, Orville C. Walker, Jr., and Gilbert A. Churchill, Jr., "Selecting Successful Salespeople: A Meta-Analysis of Biographical and Psychological Selection Criteria," in *Review of Marketing,* ed. Michael J. Houston (Chicago: American Marketing Association, 1988), pp. 90–131; and Goutam Challagalla and Tasaddug A. Shervani, "Dimensions and Types of Supervisory Control: Effects on Sales Performance and Satisfaction," *Journal of Marketing* (January 1996), pp. 47–60.

4. Christen P. Heide, *Dartnell's 30th Sales Force Compensation Survey* (Chicago: Dartnell Corporation, 1999), p. 187. See also H.R. Chally, "Applying Total Quality Management to Managing Talent," (2006), p. 5.

5. Jeffrey K. Sager, "Recruiting and Retaining Committed Salespeople," *Industrial Marketing Management* (May 1991), pp. 99–103.

6. Heide, *Dartnell's 30th Sales Force Compensation Survey,* p. 143.

7. Ibid.

8. Stan Moss, "What Sales Executives Look for in New Salespeople," *Sales & Marketing Management* (March 1978), pp. 43–48; Thomas Rollins, "How to Tell Competent Salespeople from the Other Kind," *Sales & Marketing Management* (September 1990), pp. 116–17, 145–46; and Bristol Voss, "Six Steps to Better Hires," *Sales & Marketing Management* (June 1993), pp. 44–48.

9. Ford et al., "Selecting Successful Salespeople," pp. 90–131.

10. Ford et al., Selecting Successful Salespeople." Also see Seymour Adler, "Personality Tests for Salesforce Selection: Worth a Fresh Look," *Review of Business* (Summer 1994), pp. 27–31.

11. Heide, *Dartnell's 30th Sales Force Compensation Survey,* p. 170.

12. C. David Shepherd and James C. Heartfield, "Discrimination Issues in the Selection of Salespeople: A Review and Managerial Suggestions," *Journal of Personal Selling & Sales Management* (Fall 1991), pp. 67–75.

13. Bobbi Linkemer, "Women in Sales: What Do They Really Want?" *Sales & Marketing Management* (January 1989), pp. 61–65; and Heide, *Dartnell's 30th Sales Force Compensation Survey,* p. 169.

14. John E. Swan, David R. Rink, G.E. Kiser, and Warren S. Martin, "Industrial Buyer Image of the Saleswomen," *Journal of Marketing* (Winter, 1984), pp. 110–16. See also Myron Gable and B.J. Reed, "The Current Status of Women in Professional Selling," *Journal of Personal Selling & Sales Management* (May 1987), pp. 33–39; Bill Kelley, "Selling in a Man's World," *Sales & Marketing Management* (January 1991), pp. 28–35; Nancy Arnott, "It's a Woman's World," *Sales & Marketing Management* (March 1995), pp. 54–59; and Lucette B. Comer, J. A. F. Nicholls, and Leslie J. Vermillion, "Diversity in the Sales Force: Problems and Challenges," *Journal of Personal Selling & Sales Management* (Fall 1998), pp. 1–20.

15. Lucette B. Comer and Marvin A. Jolson, "Perceptions of Gender Stereotypic Behavior: An Exploratory Study of Women in Selling," *Journal of Personal Selling & Sales Management* (Winter 1991), pp. 43–59. See also Judy A. Siguaw and Earl D. Honeycutt, Jr., "An Examination of Gender Differences in Selling Behaviors and Job Attitudes," *Industrial Marketing Management* 24 (1995), pp. 45–52.

16. Franklin Evans, "Selling as a Dyadic Relationship—A New Approach," *American Behavioral Scientist* (May 1963), pp. 76–79.

17. Gilbert A. Churchill, Jr., Robert H. Collins, and William A. Strang, "Should Retail Salespersons Be Similar to Their Customers?" *Journal of Retailing* (Fall 1975), pp. 29–42. See also Barton A. Weitz, "Effectiveness in Sales Interactions: A Contingency Framework," *Journal of Marketing* (Winter 1981), pp. 85–103.

18. Rene Y. Darmon, "Where Do the Best Sales Force Profit Producers Come From?" *Journal of Personal Selling & Sales Management* (Summer 1993), pp. 17–29; Heide, *Dartnell's 30th Sales Force Compensation Survey,* Anthony Zurcher, "Slump Complicates Job Searches," *Washington Post* (April 1, 2001), p. L2; and Judy Rose, "English Isn't Enough in Real Estate Sales: Agents need Foreign Language Skills," *Washington Post* (April 21, 2001), p. H22.

19. Adler, "Personality Tests for Salesforce Selection"; and Cengiz Yilmaz and Shelby D. Hunt, "Salesperson Cooperation: the Influence of Relational, Task, Organizational, and Personal Factors," *Journal of the Academy of Marketing Science* 29, no. 4 (2001), pp. 335–57.

20. While another study examines job-specific abilities, it focuses on only one type of sales job—missionary selling. See Dan C. Weilbaker, "The Identification of Selling Abilities Needed for Missionary Type Sales," *Journal of Personal Selling & Sales Management* (Summer 1990), pp. 45–58.

21. Derek A. Newton, "Get the Most out of Your Salesforce," *Harvard Business Review* (September–October 1969), pp. 130–43. See also Weilbaker, "The Identification of Selling Abilities."

Chapter 9

1. Thomas Rollins, "How to Tell Competent Salespeople from the Other Kind," *Sales & Marketing Management* (September 1990), pp. 116–18, 145–46.

2. Ibid. See also Timothy J. Trow, "The Secret of a Good Hire: Profiling," *Sales & Marketing Management* (May 1990), pp. 44–55.

3. For a detailed discussion of critical job dimensions, see Phil Faris, "No More Winging It," *Sales & Marketing Management* (August 1986), pp. 88–91.

4. Rene Y. Darmon and S.J. Shapiro, "Sales Recruiting—A Major Area of Underinvestment," *Industrial Marketing Management* 9 (1980), pp. 47–51; Julia Lawlor, "Highly Classified," *Sales & Marketing Management* (March 1995), pp. 75–85; Barry Farber, "Start at the Beginning," *Sales & Marketing Management* (March 1996), pp. 24–25; and Carole Ann King, "Frustration Mounts as Recruiting Gets Harder," *National Underwriter* (March 19, 2001), pp. 6–7.

5. George J. Avlonitis, Kevin A. Boyle, and A.G. Kouremenos, "Matching Salesmen to the Selling Job," *Industrial Marketing Management* 15 (1986), pp. 45–54. See also Lawlor, "Highly Classified," p. 84.

6. Marianne Matthews, "If Your Ads Aren't Pulling Top Sales Talent . . .," *Sales & Marketing Management* (February 1990), pp. 73–79.

7. Ibid.

8. Arthur Bragg, "Shell-Shocked on the Battlefield of Selling," *Sales & Marketing Management* (July 1990), pp. 52–58; "Postcards from the Class of 95," *Sales & Marketing Management* (June 1995), pp. 73–77; and Audrey Bottjen, "The Benefits of College Recruiting," *Sales & Marketing Management* (April 2001), p. 20. For a more in-depth discussion of university sales programs refer to "Top University Sales Education Programs", *SellingPower.com.* June 2007.

9. For a detailed review of these, as well as some less commonly used, selection tools, see E. James Randall and Cindy H. Randall, "Review of Salesperson Selection Techniques and Criteria: A Managerial Approach," *International Journal of Research in Marketing* 7 (1990), pp. 81–95. For a detailed discussion of salesperson selection, training, and development, reference William L. Cron, Greg W. Marshall, Jagdip Singh, Rosann L. Spiro, and Harish Sujan. "Salesperson Selection, Training, and Development: Trends, Implications, and Research Opportunities," *Journal of Personal Selling & Sales Management* 25 (Spring 2005) pp. 123–36.

10. John E. Hunter and R.F. Hunter, "Validity and Utility of Alternative Predictors of Job Performance," *Psychological Bulletin* 96 (1984), pp. 72–98. For a discussion of the validity of different selection procedures as applied to the evaluation of salespeople, see Neil M. Ford, Orville C. Walker, Jr., and Gilbert A. Churchill, Jr., "Selecting Successful Salespeople: A Meta-Analysis of Biographical and Psychological Selection Criteria," in *Review of Marketing,* ed. Michael J. Houston (Chicago: American Marketing Association, 1988), pp. 90–131.

11. Myron Gable, Charles Hollon, and Frank Dangello, "Increasing the Utility of the Application Blank: Relationship between Job Application Information and Subsequent Performance and Turnover of Salespeople," *Journal of Personal Selling and Sales Management* (Summer 1992), pp. 39–55.

12. John H. Rose, *How to Recruit, Interview, and Select Prospective Sales Representatives* (Orlando, FL: National Society of Sales Training Executives, 1981); and Lawlor, "Highly Classified."

13 William Keenan, Jr., "Who Has the Right Stuff?" *Sales & Marketing Management* (August 1993), pp. 28–29.

14. Arthur Bragg, "Checking References," *Sales & Marketing Management* (November 1990), pp. 68–71.

15. C. David Shepherd and James C. Heartfield, "Discrimination Issues in the Selection of Salespeople: A Review and Managerial Suggestions," *Journal of Personal*

Selling & Sales Management (Fall 1991), p. 71. See also Allison Lucas, "Race Matters," *Sales & Marketing Management* (September 1996), pp. 50–62.

16. Seymour Adler, "Personality Tests for Salesforce Selection: Worth a Fresh Look," *Review of Business* (Summer 1994), pp. 27–31.

17. Richard Kern, "IQ Tests for Salesmen Make a Comeback," *Sales & Marketing Management* (April 1988), pp. 42–46; and Richard Nelson, "Maybe It's Time to Take Another Look at Tests as a Selection Tool," *Journal of Personal Selling & Sales Management* (August 1987), pp. 33–38; and J. Denrell, "Selection Bias and the Perils of Benchmarking," *Harvard Business Review,* April 2005, pp. 114–119.

18. *www.eeoc.gov,* February 2005.

19. For a detailed discussion of the procedures required to validate employment tests, visit the Equal Employment Opportunity Commission, *www.eeoc.gov.*

Chapter 10

1. Frank Cespedes, *Organizing and Implementing the Marketing Effort: Text and Cases* (Reading, MA: Addison-Wesley, 1991), pp. 87–88. and Ashraf M. Attia, Earl D. Honeycutt Jr., and Mark P. Leach "A Three-Stage Model for Assessing and Improving Sales Force Training and Development" *Journal of Personal Selling & Sales Management* 25 (Summer 2005) pp. 253–68.

2. Annual Report for Lucent Technologies, 2006, *www. lucent.com.* For A more complete discussion on the use of Self-Directed traing and its effect on performance. see Andrew B. Artis, and Eric G. Harris. "Self-Directed Learning and Sales Force Performance. An Integrated Framework." *Journal of Personal Selling & Sales Management* 27 (Winter 2007) pp. 9–24; and Mark P. Leach, Annie H. Liu, and Wesley J. Johnston, "The Role of Self-Regulation Training in Developing the Motivation Management Capabilities of Salespeoole," *Journal of Persons Selling & Sales Management,* 25 (Summer 2005), pp. 269–281.

3. Mark McMaster, "A Tough Sell: Training the Salesperson," *Sales & Marketing Management* (January 2001), p. 42.

4. Garry O'Grady, "Every Rep a Star," *Pharmaceutical Executive* (May 2003), pp. 76–80.

5. Judy A. Wagner, Noreen M Klein, and Janet E. Keith, "Selling Strategies: The Effects of Suggesting a Decision Structure to Novice and Expert Buyers,"

Journal of the Academy of Marketing Science 29, no. 3 (2001), pp. 289–306.

6. "Top Training Priorities?" *Training* (February 2004), pp. 26–32.

7. James F. Evered, "Measuring Sales Training Effectiveness," *Sales & Marketing Management* (February 1988), pp. 9–12, 16–18. See also Alan J. Dubinsky "Sales Training and Education: Some Assumptions about the Effectiveness of Sales Training," *Journal of Personal Selling & Sales Management* (Summer 1996), pp. 67–76.

8. The following discussion is based to a large extent on "Top Training Priorities?" *Training* (February 2004), pp. 26–32; and Gene Hahne, "Creating Credibility for Your Sales Training," *Training and Development Journal* (November 1981), pp. 34–38.

9. Ibid., p. 38; Christen P. Heide, *Dartnell's 30th Sales Force Compensation Survey* (Chicago: Dartnell Corp., 1999), p. 142.

10. Heide, *Dartnell's,* p. 144.

11. Kathleen McLaughlin, "Training's Top 50 Edward Jones," *Training* (March 2001), p. 20.

12. H. Robert Dodge, *Field Sales Management* (Dallas: Business Publications, Inc., 1973), p. 226.

13. Erika Rasmusson, "Training Goes Virtual," *Sales & Marketing Management* (September 2000), p. 48; and "Study Reveals Sales Training Needs of Business Markets," *Marketing News* (March 13, 1989), p. 6.

14. Greg Burns, "Life Insurance: Bogus Bait to Make You Switch," *BusinessWeek* (November 27, 1995), p. 136.

15. Minda Zetlin, "Kicking the Discount Habit: Teach Your Salespeople to Stop Leaving Money on the Table," *Sales & Marketing Management* (May 1994), pp. 102–6.

16. Edward Roberts, "Training Trade Show Salespeople How Caterpillar Does It," *Business Marketing* (June 1988), pp. 70, 72–73; and *www. caterpillar.com,* February 2005.

17. Priscilla Donovan, "Selling Right and Left," *Sales & Marketing Management* (June 3, 1985), pp. 62–63.

18. Willem Verbeke and Richard Bagozzi, "Sales Call Anxiety: Exploring What It Means When Fear Rules the Sales Encounter," *Journal of Marketing* 64 (2000), pp. 88–101.

19. *Dartnell's,* p. 140.

20. Jack Falvey, "Forget the Sharks: Swim with Your Salespeople," *Sales & Marketing Management* (November 1990), p. 8.

21. Ibid.

22. Elana Harris, "Keeping Customers Happy," *Sales & Marketing Management* (April 2001), p. 69.

23. Kevin Dobbs, "When Learning Really Happens," *Sales & Marketing Management* (November 2000), p. 98.

24. Elana Harris, "Stars in the Making," *Sales & Marketing Management* (March 2001), p. 61.

25. Ibid., p. 60.

26. Kevin Dobbs, "Training on the Fly," *Sales & Marketing Management* (November 2000), pp. 92–98.

27. Ibid. p. 96.

28. "Industry Report 2001," *Training,* October 2001, *www. trainingmag.com.*

29. Ibid.

30. Ibid.

31. Robert C. Erffmeyer, K. Randall Russ, and Joseph F. Hair, Jr., "Needs Assessment and Evaluation in Sales-Training Programs," *Journal of Personal Selling & Sales Management* 11 (Winter 1991), pp. 17–31.

32. Earl D. Honeycutt and Thomas H. Stevenson, "Evaluating Sales Training Programs," *Industrial Marketing Management* (August 1989), pp. 215–22. See also Fernando Jaramillo, Francois A. Carrillat, and William B. Locander, "A Meta-Analytic Comparison of Managerial Ratings and Self-Evaluations" *Journal of Personal Selling & Sales Management* 25 (Fall 2005) pp. 315–28.

33. Beverly Geber, "Does Training Make a Difference? Prove It!" *Training* (March 1995), pp. 27–34.

34. Rick Mendoza, "There's a Payoff?" *Sales & Marketing Management* (June 1995), pp. 64–71.

35. Ibid., p. 69.

Chapter 11

1. Bruce Talgan, "Real Pay for Performance," *Journal of Business Strategy* (May–June 2001), pp. 19–22.

2. Leslie M. Fine and Janice R. Franke, "Legal Aspects of Salesperson Commission Payments: Implications for the Implementation of Commission Sales Programs," *Journal of Personal Selling & Sales Management* (Winter 1995), pp. 53–68.

3. James W. Walker, "Perspectives on Compensation," *Human Resource Planning* 24 (June 2001), pp. 6–8.

4. Arun Sharma, "Customer Satisfaction-Based Incentive Systems: Some Managerial and Salesperson Considerations," *Journal of Personal Selling & Sales Management* (Spring 1997), pp. 61–70.

5. Joel Silver, "Building an Effective Sales Incentive Program," *www.saleslobby.com,* January 2002.

6. Ibid.; and Audrey Bottjen, "Incentives Gone Awry," *Sales & Marketing Management* (May 2001), p. 72.

7. Karen Renk, "The Age-Old Question: Cash vs. Merchandise?" *Occupational Health and Safety* (September 2002), pp. 60–62.

8. Ibid.

9. Mark McMaster, "Personalized Motivation," *Sales & Marketing Management* (May 2002), p. 16.

10. Cengiz Yilmaz and Shelby D. Hunt, "Salesperson Cooperation: The Influence of Relational, Task, Organizational, and Personal Factors," *Journal of the Academy of Marketing Science* (Fall 2001), pp. 335–57.

11. Arun Sharma and Dan Sarel, "The Impact of Customer Satisfaction Based Incentive Systems on Salespeople's Customer Service Response: An Empirical Study," *Journal of Personal Selling & Sales Management* (Summer 1995), pp. 17–29.

12. HR Chally Group, *The Great Business Challenges of the New Millennium* (Dayton, OH: HR Chally Group, 2007).

13. S. Scott Sands, "Ineffective Quotas: The Hidden Threat to Sales Compensation Plans," *Compensation and Benefits Review* 32 (March–April 2000), pp. 35–42.

14. Kemba J. Dunham, "Back to Reality: To Lure Workers, Dot-Coms Are Having to Focus on Something Besides Options, Such as Salaries," *The Wall Street Journal* (April 12, 2001), p. R5.

Chapter 12

1. Robert Dwyer and John F. Tanner, Jr., *Business Marketing: Connecting Strategy, Relationships, and Learning* (New York: McGraw-Hill, 2002); and H.R. Chally, "The Great Business Challenges of the New Millenium," (2007), p. 7.

2. Kissan Joseph, "On the Optimality of Delegating Pricing Authority to the Sales Force," *Journal of Marketing* (January 2001), pp. 62–70; also see David Jobber, Graham J. Hooley, and David Shipley,

"Organizational Size and Salesforce Evaluation Practices," *Journal of Personal Selling & Sales Management* 13 (Spring 1993), pp. 37–48.

3. For a review of the controversy, as well as a historical perspective on why it exists, see John J. Wheatley, "The Allocation Controversy in Marketing Cost Analysis," *University of Washington Business Review* (Summer 1971), pp. 61–70.

4. Sanford R. Simon, *Managing Marketing Profitability* (New York: American Management Association, 1969), p. 37. All serious students of marketing cost analysis are urged to read this classic book on marketing profitability analysis. It illustrates the process that should be followed in carrying out a marketing cost analysis and the insights gained from doing so with detailed examples. Much of this and the following section rely heavily on this excellent book. See also Robin Cooper and Robert S. Kaplan, "Profit Priorities from Activity-Based Costing," *Harvard Business Review* 69 (May–June 1991), pp. 130–35.

5. Simon, *Managing Marketing Profitability,* pp. 37–38.

6. Gayle Rayburn, "Accounting Tools in the Analysis and Control of Marketing Performance," *Industrial Marketing Management* 6 (1977), pp. 175–82.

7. See, for example, Simon, *Managing Marketing Profitability;* Charles H. Sevin, *Marketing Productivity Analysis* (New York: McGraw-Hill, 1965); L. Gayle Rayburn, *Financial Tools for Effective Marketing Administration* (New York: American Management Association, 1976); and Robin Cooper and Robert S. Kaplan, "Measure Costs Right: Make the Right Decision," *Harvard Business Review* 66 (September–October 1988), pp. 96–103.

8. Daniel, J. Goebel, Greg W. Marshall, and William B. Locander, "Activity Based Costing: Accounting for a Market Orientation," *Industrial Marketing Management* 27 (November 1998), pp. 497–510.

9. See Donald W. Jackson and Lonnie L. Ostrom, "Grouping Segments for Profitability Analysis," *MSU Business Topics* 28 (1980), pp. 39–44, for a discussion of the segments that are typically used in a marketing cost analysis. See also Robin Cooper and Robert S. Kaplan, "Activity-Based Systems: Measuring the Cost of Resource Usage," *Accounting Horizons* 6 (September 1992), pp. 1–13. For another method of dividing revenue (customers) into segments, see the discussion on decile analysis in Dwyer and Tanner, *Business Marketing,* chap. 5.

10. Edmund D. McCarry, "Some Functions of Marketing Reconsidered," in *Theory in Marketing,* eds. Reavis Cox

and Wroc Anderson (Homewood, IL: Richard D. Irwin, 1950), p. 267.

11. It is, in fact, the most frequently used basis. See Douglas M. Lambert and Jay U. Sterling, "What Types of Profitability Reports Do Marketing Managers Receive?" *Industrial Marketing Management* 16 (November 1987), pp. 295–304.

12. Charles R. Horngren, *Cost Accounting: A Managerial Emphasis,* 2nd ed. (Englewood Cliffs, NJ: Prentice Hall, 1967), p. 381. See also Fred Selnes, "Analyzing Marketing Profitability: Sales Are a Dangerous Cost-Driver," *European Journal of Marketing* 26, no. 2 (1992), pp. 15–26.

13. The example is purposely hypothetical to throw the basic process into more bold relief, while at the same time illustrating some common features of such situations. For actual examples, which at times can get quite complex, see Simon, *Managing Marketing Profitability;* Sevin, *Marketing Productivity Analysis;* J.S. Schiff and M. Schiff, *Strategic Management of the Sales Territory* (New York: New York Sales Marketing Executives, 1980); and Robert A. Howell and Stephen R. Soucy, "Customer Profitability—As Critical as Product Profitability," *Management Accounting* 72 (October 1990), pp. 43–47.

14. In addition to the references previously cited, see Dana Smith Morgan and Fred W. Morgan, "Marketing Cost Controls: A Survey of Industry Practices," *Industrial Marketing Management* 9 (July 1980), pp. 217–21; and Thomas M. Petro, "Profitability: The Fifth 'P' of Marketing," *Basic Marketing* 22 (September 1990), pp. 48–52.

15. For a thorough discussion of specialized training topics see H.R. Chally, total Quality Management (2006) p. 1. Also see, for example, Shawn Tully, "The Real Key to Creating Wealth," *Fortune* (September 20, 1993), pp. 38–50; and Shawn Tully, "Raiding a Company's Hidden Cash," *Fortune* (August 22, 1994), pp. 82–87.

16. J.S. Schiff and Michael Schiff, "New Sales Management Tool: ROAM," *Harvard Business Review* 45 (July–August 1967), pp. 59–66. For the application of ROAM to evaluating sales territories, see J.S. Schiff, "Evaluating the Sales Force as a Business," *Industrial Marketing Management* 12 (April 1983), pp. 131–37. One problem with the return on assets managed measure for evaluating segment performance is that it neglects the firm's opportunity costs for the capital invested in the assets. Residual income analysis is a preferred alternative on these grounds for evaluating the profitability of the personal selling effort. See William L. Cron and Michael Levy, "Sales Management

Performance Evaluation: A Residual Income Perspective," *Journal of Personal Selling & Sales Management* 7 (August 1987), pp. 57–66.

Chapter 13

1. Nigel F. Piercy, David W. Cravens, and Nikala Lane, "Enhancing Salespeople's Effectiveness: When is More Sales Management Control Better Sales Management Control?," *Marketing Management* 16 (September/October 2007), pp. 18–25.

2. David W. Cravens, Felicia G. Lassk, George S. Low, Greg W. Marshall, and William C. Moncrief, "Formal and Informal Management Control Combinations in Sales Organizations: The Impact on Salesperson Consequences," *Journal of Business Research* 57 (March 2004), pp. 241–48.

3. David W. Cravens, Thomas N. Ingram, Raymond W. LaForge, and Clifford E. Young, "Behavior-Based and Outcome-Based Salesforce Control Systems," *Journal of Marketing* 57 (October 1993), pp. 47–59.

4. Benton Cocanougher and John M. Ivancevich, "'BARS' Performance Rating for Sales Force Personnel," *Journal of Marketing* 42 (July 1978), pp. 87–95.

5. Lyndon E. Dawson, Jr., Barlow Soper, and Charles E. Pettijohn, "The Effects of Empathy on Salesperson Effectiveness," *Psychology and Marketing* 9 (July–August 1992), pp. 297–310. See also Neil M. Ford, Orville C. Walker, Jr., Gilbert A. Churchill, Jr., and Steven W. Hartley, "Selecting Successful Salespeople: A Meta-Analysis of Biographical and Psychological Selection Criteria," in *Annual Review of Marketing,* ed. Michael J. Houston (Chicago: American Marketing Association, 1987), pp. 90–131.

6. Cocanougher and Ivancevich, "'BARS' Performance Rating for Sales Force Personnel," p. 89

7. Greg W. Marshall, John C. Mowen, and Keith J. Fabes, "The Impact of Territory Difficulty and Self versus Other Ratings on Managerial Evaluations of Sales Personnel," *Journal of Personal Selling & Sales Management* 12 (Fall 1992), pp. 35–47.

8. Aharon Tziner, Christine Joanis, and Kevin R. Murphy, "A Comparison of Three Methods of Performance Appraisal with Regard to Goal Properties, Goal Perception, and Ratee Satisfaction," *Group and Organization Management* 25 (June 2000), pp. 175–90.

9. Cocanougher and Ivancevich, "'BARS' Performance Rating for Sales Force Personnel," pp. 90–99.

10. Mary Jo Bitner, Bernard H. Booms, and Mary Stanfield Tetreault, "The Service Encounter: Diagnosing Favorable and Unfavorable Incidents," *Journal of Marketing* 54 (January 1990), pp. 71–84.

11. Roger J. Placky, "Appraisal Scales That Measure Performance Outcomes and Job Results," *Personnel* 60 (May–June 1983), pp. 57–65.

12. Scott Wimer and Kenneth M. Nowack, "13 Common Mistakes Using 360-Degree Feedback," *Training & Development* 52 (May 1998), pp. 69–78.

13. "Give Yourself a Job Review," *American Salesman* (May 2001), pp. 26–27.

14. Charles E. Pettijohn, Linda S. Pettijohn, and Michael d'Amico, "Characteristics of Performance Appraisals and Their Impact on Sales Force Satisfaction," *Human Resource Development Quarterly* 12 (Summer 2001), pp. 127–39.

15. William Fitzgerald, "Forget the Form in Performance Appraisals," *HR Magazine* 40 (December 1995), p. 134.

16. Helen Rheem, "Performance Management: A Progress Report," *Harvard Business Review* (March–April 1995), p. 11.

Case Index

Name Index

Powell, Terry, 501
Pullins, Ellen Bolman, 257, 375, 493
Pusateri, Michael A., 134, 496

Q

Quick, Thomas L., 498

R

Rackham, Neil, 88, 493, 494
Raman, Pushkala, 104
Ramaswami, Sridhar, 257, 283, 465
Ramlal, Suzy, 500, 501
Ramsey, Rosemary P., 493
Randall, Cindy H., 504
Randall, E. James, 504
Rasmusson, Erika, 505
Rauseo, Nancy A., 104
Rawlinson, Richard, 495, 496
Rayburn, L. Gayle, 506
Raymond, Mary Anne, 375
Reed, B. J., 503
Reeve, James M., 415n
Reichheld, Frederick F., 73, 494, 495
Reid, David A., 497
Renk, Karen, 506
Rheem, Helen, 508
Rhoads, Gary K., 499
Riberiro, Aurea Helena Puga, 28
Rich, Gregory, 342
Ridnour, Rick, 500
Rink, David R., 503
Rivera, Juan, 273
Roberts, Edward, 505
Roberts, James, 134, 225, 464
Robertson, Bruce, 28
Rodriguez Cano, Cynthia, 67
Rodriquez, Alex, 251
Roering, Kenneth J., 495
Rogers, Martha, 73, 494
Rollins, Thomas, 502, 503
Rose, John H., 504
Rose, Judy, 503
Rotter, Julian B., 501
Rouziès, Dominique, 104, 257, 465
Rudzinsky, David, 366–367
Ruekert, Robert W., 494, 495
Ruettgers, Mike, 45
Russ, K. Randall, 505
Russler, Joan, 468n
Rutherford, Brian N., 67
Ruyter, Ko de, 226
Ryans, Adrian B., 497

S

Sager, Jeffrey K., 226, 256, 282, 499, 500, 502
Sakai, Kelly, 215n
Sands, S. Scott, 375, 506
Sang-Lin Han, 496
Saporito, Bill, 495
Sarel, Dan, 506
Sarin, Shikhar, 375
Schenk, Joseph A., 134

Schertzer, Susan M. B., 257, 442n, 465
Schiff, J. S., 507
Schiff, Michael, 507
Schnake, Mel E., 206n
Schrage, Michael, 364n
Schroeck, Michael J., 438
Schuler, Randall S., 498
Schulz, Roberta J., 134
Schurr, Paul H., 495
Schwepker, Charles H., Jr., 282
Scruton, Steve, 119
Sell, Mary Van, 498
Sellers, Patricia, 495
Selnes, Fred, 507
Semlow, Walter J., 497
Sengupta, Sangit, 134
Servani, Tasaddug A., 497
Sevin, Charles H., 506, 507
Shapiro, Benson P., 493, 496
Shapiro, S. J., 503
Sharma, Arun, 495, 506
Shaw, Charles, 495
Shepherd, C. David, 493, 503, 504
Shervani, Tasadduq A., 438, 499, 502
Shipley, David D., 501, 506
Siguaw, Judy A., 503
Silver, Joel, 506
Silver, Lawrence S., 256
Simon, Sanford R., 506, 507
Simpson, Daniel G., 494
Singh, Jagdip, 282, 312, 499, 502, 504
Sinha, Prabhakant, 376, 496
Sivadas, Eugene, 282, 312
Skinner, Lauren, 67
Slack, Jeffrey, 273
Slater, Stanley F., 494
Slocum, John W., Jr., 497, 498, 502
Smith, A.E., 353n
Smith, Burt, 271
Smith, Ellen Reid, 493
Smith, Michelle, 369
Snow, Charles C., 82, 83, 87, 494
Snyderman, Barbara, 501
Sohi, Ravi S., 493
Solomon, Paul, 226
Soper, Barlow, 507
Soucy, Stephen R., 507
Sowers, Rob, 356
Sparks, John R., 134
Spector, Paul E., 256
Spiro, Rosann L., 226, 256, 282, 312, 497, 501, 502, 504
Spralling, Ken, 119n
Stahl, Michael J., 415n
Stajkovic, Alexander D., 501
Stanton, Anne, 76
Stephenson, P. Ronald, 500
Sterling, Jay U., 507
Stevens, Charles D., 283
Stevenson, Thomas H., 505
Stock, Ruth M., 226
Stone, Robert W., 181
Stone, Thomas H., 312
Strang, William A., 503
Strong, James, 341
Strout, Erin, 35n, 268n

Strutton, David, 342
Sujan, Harish, 282, 312, 493, 500, 502, 504
Sujan, Mita, 493, 500, 501
Sullivan, John, 98
Sungupta, Sangit, 496
Swan, John E., 503
Swift, Ronald S., 74n, 494
Sydow Campbell, Kim, 67

T

Tadepalli, Raghu, 499
Talgan, Bruce, 505
Talley, Walter J., Jr., 497
Tanner, John F., Jr., 51n, 87n, 104, 416n, 464, 493, 495, 498, 501, 506
Taylor, A. J., 226
Taylor, Thayer C., 493
Teas, R. Kenneth, 497, 498, 499, 501
Test, Alan, 248n
Tetreault, Mary Stanfield, 508
Thomas, Claude A., 496
Thompson, Bob, 75
Thull, Jeff, 98n
Trisko, Karen, 19n
Trow, Timothy J., 503
Tubridy, Gary S., 408, 496
Tully, Shawn, 507
Tyagi, Pradeep K., 500, 502
Tziner, Abtron, 507

V

Valentine, Sean, 493
Van Dyke, Melissa, 353
Velarde, Jennifer, 5
Verbeke, Willem, 505
Vermillion, Leslie J., 503
Voss, Bristol, 502
Vyas, Shyman B., 282, 442n, 464, 502

W

Wack, Pierre, 496
Wacker, John G., 499
Wagner, Judy A., 67, 504
Wakefield, Kirk, 498
Waldrop, Dawn, 271
Walker, James W., 506
Walker, Orville C., Jr., 493, 494, 495, 497, 498, 499, 500, 501, 502, 504, 507
Waters, Rollie, 460
Weeks, William A., 134, 498, 501
Weilbaker, Dan C., 503
Weinberg, Charles B., 497
Weiss, Allen M., 495
Weitz, Barton A., 28, 87n, 493, 495, 498, 500, 503
Welch, Jack, 40
Wheatley, John J., 506
Wheelwright, Steven C., 496
Widmier, Scott, 376
Wilcox, James B., 133, 500
Wiles, Michael A., 312
Williamson, Nicholas C., 501

Subject Index

discovery through personal selling, 93, 98
impact of changes on salespeople, 1–2
Customer orientation, 70, 116–117
Customer perspectives, 32–33, 105–106
Customer records, sales analysis data from, 167
Customer relations training, 317–318
Customer relationship management (CRM); *see also* Information technology
alternatives to, 17
competitive information from, 14
elements of, 70–77
failed attempts at, 75, 78
growing importance of, 6, 7
linking performance evaluation to, 458–459
linking sales compensation to, 364, 366–367
personal sales versus, 89
Customer retention, 73, 97–99
Customer satisfaction
Chally report findings, 408–409
linking sales incentives to, 363–364
loyalty versus, 97
Customer service; *see* Servicing accounts
Customer value, 73, 410
Customers
complaints from, 90
internal, 458
organizing sales forces by type, 116–117
recruiting from, 297
CustomerThink.com, 75
Cyclical factors, 145

D

Data mining, 74
Data quality, 169, 427, 460
Data warehouses, 74
Database software, 119
Death of a Salesman, 35
Deciders, 56
Decomposition method, 144–145
Decreasing returns with additional reps, 155–156
Dedicated sales service support, 408–409
Deeper meaning, 204
Defecting customers, studying, 97
Defender strategy, 82, 83
Deliveries, 61, 90
Dell Computer
business-to-business sales, 49
distinctive competencies, 82
distribution advantages, 86
as HP competitor, 23, 84
importance of online sales, 6
mission statement, 81
sales recruiting, 290, 291–292, 299
Deloitte Consulting, 120
Delphi technique, 141, 142
Demarketing, 19
Demographic variables, sales success and, 265, 266, 270
Demonstrations, 54
Derived demand, 58
Desired service levels, 92–93
Detailers, 50
Developmental salespeople, 117
Differentiation strategy, 82, 83

DigitalHatch Inc., 362
Dillard's Department Store, 58
Direct costs
allocating to functional groups, 419, 423
defined, 411
identifying, 412, 417
Direct reimbursement plans, 358–359
Direct selling costs, 423
DirecTV, 366, 367
Disabilities, 303, 307
Discontinuous changes, 23
Discrimination, 15, 16, 269, 305–307
Disengagement stage, 245–246, 247
Distinctive competencies, 82
Distribution
elements in economic environment, 14
sales role in, 47, 95–96
Distributors, 22
Diversity (cultural), 269–270
Division and specialization of labor, 107–108
Door-to-door sales, 15, 54
Dr Pepper/Seven Up, 330
Draws, 350
Dress, 271
Drivers of change, 34
Duplication of efforts, 116
DuPont, 8, 14
Durable goods marketing communications, 95
Dyadic approach, 270
Dysfunctional behavior, 217

E

E-Business Suite, 366
E-mail systems, 17
Earnings; *see* Compensation
Earnings opportunity ratio, 251
eChoice Points, 356
Economic criteria for choosing agents, 111
Economic environment, 13–14
EDS, 7
Education; *see also* Training
effects on motivation, 239
influence on sales success, 266, 272, 273
in personal selling, 299
Education Development Center, 331
Educational institutions, recruiting from, 298–299
Edwards Personal Preference Schedule, 304
Effectiveness, performance versus, 441–443
Efficient consumer response systems, 6, 96
Effort and performance, 231–234; *see also* Motivation; Salespeople's performance
80:20 principle, 163, 174, 326–327
Electronic data interchange systems, 6
Electronic training methods, 325, 326, 328, 332–333
1154 Lill, 5
Ellis Associates, 460
EMC Corporation, 45
eMobility Centers, 41
Emotional factors in vendor selection, 60; *see also* Relationship selling
Employee benefits, 346–347
Employee Turnover Cost Calculator, 258–259

Employment agencies, 298
Encyclopaedia Britannica, 20
End-user consumers, 49
Engineering expertise, 22–23, 126
Enriching jobs, 248
Enron, 10
Enterprise resource planning (ERP) software, 166, 168–169; *see also* Customer relationship management (CRM)
Entertaining, 5, 47
Enthusiasm, 263
Enthusiasts, motivating, 243
Environmental effects
external influences on sales programs, 11, 12–20
internal influences on sales programs, 11, 12, 20–23
on motivation, 233–234, 248–249
Equal employment opportunity laws, 16, 269, 305–307
Eras of professional selling, 98
Ernst & Young, 120, 315
Establishment stage, 245, 247
Estée Lauder, 297
Ethics
importance to sales, 8–10, 17–18
sales training in, 327
Ethnic core values, 9
Ettenberg and Company, 5
European Economic Community, 20
Evaluation; *see also* Measurement; Performance evaluation; Testing
of performance evaluation effectiveness, 460
in sales analysis, 164–165
of sales programs, 11
of sales quotas, 362
of sales training programs, 321–322, 333–337
of suppliers by customers, 61
Evaluation forms, 450, 451–454
Evaluation options matrix, 335
Exceptional performance, isolating, 175; *see also* High performers
Exchange rates, 14
Excuses, 38
Executives
key account sales by, 120–121, 123
salaries of, 39
Expansion stage of relationship selling, 90–91
Expectancies
career stages and, 244, 245, 247
defined, 203
environmental factors, 249
major considerations for, 231–234
organizational effects on, 250, 251
personal traits affecting, 238, 240, 241–242
Expectancy theory, 230, 237
Expectations
conflicting or ambiguous, 214–216
setting, 90, 209
Expeditor Systems, 75, 76
Expense accounts
abuses of, 421
sales analysis data from, 167
types, 358–359
Expense ratios, 446, 447